05:14:18

To Gladys

With love and warmest best wishes. Hope than you ever wanted to know about UW.

David

Front and back cover photos by
Patrick A. Burns / The New York Times / Redux

Library of Congress Control Number: 2016917319

PREFACE TO THE FUTURE:

A HISTORY OF

LONG ISLAND UNIVERSITY

THROUGH THE TURBULENT SIXTIES

by

DAVID JOEL STEINBERG

President Emeritus

Long Island University

To
The Women and Men of LIU
Past, Present, and Future
May The Force Be With You

Table of Contents

An institution is the lengthened shadow of one man.

Ralph Waldo Emerson

Foreward

This book chronicles how one American university (LIU) lost its momentum, and almost its capacity to survive, in the tumultuous decade of the sixties. It is a tale of many talented and caring people who found themselves pledging allegiance not to a single *alma mater* but to several increasingly distinct entities, even though each was legally, financially, and historically an integral part of Long Island University. It remains a complex and disputed tale to understand how and why LIU fractured, and it remains a fascinating story to read how trustees, administrators and faculty searched, often in vain, to find sufficient elements of communality to hold the place together. The multiple campuses of LIU had different priorities and distinct visions of their mission.

Was there ever one university with multiple campuses or was LIU always a loose confederation of campuses with a common dislike of a central administration? Was this fracturing a function of geography or a consequence of human error? Was it *hubris* to conceive of a single but multi-campus institution sharing a passionate dream to build a great, populist university on Long Island, a private institution which existed to welcome, to acculturate, and to educate men and women whose parents and grandparents first migrated either from abroad or elsewhere in America to Brooklyn. After World War II many from the caucasian communities sought to find the American dream in the nation's suburban future in Nassau and Suffolk.

"Starting from Paumanok," LIU embraced a mission worthy of the poets Walt Whitman or Emma Lazarus. It was one that paralleled many of America's great urban public sector universities, traditionally committed to providing upward mobility. The City University of New York (CUNY) was known until the mid-seventies as the "Free University of the City of New York." But LIU's pedagogical model, unlike CUNY's, was to give its students a chance to learn in small classes, to provide individual attention to student needs, and to admit students whose grades in high school excluded them from enrolling in CUNY's four year, senior colleges. The Cooper Union in Manhattan's East Village had a similar mission, but it had private fortune from Peter Cooper to endow its efforts by offering a tuition-free environment. The Cooper Union educated an intellectually superior but financially strapped student body. LIU's mission has always been the educational equivalent to Aaron Copeland's *Fanfare for the Common Man*.

Missions are not accomplished nor dreams fulfilled in the abstract; flesh and blood men and women must deliver on the promise. *Preface to the Future* tells the tale of some memorable people, Admiral Richard L. Conolly, R. Gordon Hoxie, William Zeckendorf, Sr. and Robert Spector. The Admiral was a genuine war hero, a decorated man of action, who dreamed what may have been "the impossible dream" for his university. Hoxie, insecure but passionately committed to the Admiral's vision, tried and tried yet again, to make it happen. He was roundly vilified and then fired in an era when other college presidents and chancellors were cashiered by the score, because of student protests and Vietnam, student militancy and generational rebellion. Like virtually every other college and university in America, LIU was fully engaged in these culture wars, but, as the book chronicles, LIU had a discrete set of problems that were unique to it and that led to his firing.

Hoxie was thoroughly loathed in Brooklyn by many students, faculty, alumni, and local politicians. He was dismissed as pompous, out-of-date, a figure of ridicule. The counterpart groups at the other campuses, at Southampton and C.W. Post College, however, judged him much more gently, seeing qualities in him that Brooklyn rejected. Chronic tuition dependency and that Brooklyn loathing doomed his efforts, but he never gave up trying. Each reader of this book will have to determine his or her own assessment of Hoxie and all the other individuals who populate these pages.

The decade from 1962 to 1972 was a terrible one in American history. Virtually every higher educational institution in the land was badly bruised. And, by 1972, Long Island University found itself on a lower trajectory than the one so optimistically prophesized by Admiral Conolly and articulated by Colonel Hoxie in his ten year plan, *Preface to the Future*. Understanding this institution's historical experience is a prerequisite to understanding what has followed over the decades. The deep antipathy between the Brooklyn campus and C.W. Post; the evolution of multiple faculty labor unions and the militancy of those unions, including dozens of strikes and job actions against the administration; the collapse of comity and a shared sense of community across the multiple campuses; and the near feudal insularity of Southampton, Brooklyn and C.W. Post, which symbolically flooded moats and took up arms against each other, are all part of that historical mosaic.

I served as President of Long Island University for over a quarter of a century. As much as anyone else, I have lived in the shadow of that legacy. I have asked myself since retirement whether it would be foolish to revisit those increasingly ancient fights and ossified angers. Now that the book is written, however, I do not believe undertaking this project was a mistake. The men and women I now chronicle in this book defined my job as they shaped the University. The institution, that emerged by 1973, was in most ways the institution that still exists today.

Every time I entered the Board of Trustees room when I was President, the portraits of prior Chancellors and Presidents looked down upon me, occasionally winking at my follies or nodding in agreement at a decision I took. In a very real sense they became my historical buddies, and I believe that they need to be given the courtesy of explaining in the twenty-first century their own assessment of those battles of fifty years ago. Each deserves the chance to tell his side of the story or to share anew his unique vision for the University. If I have been too hard on one or given a pass to another, I apologize to those whom I have judged too harshly or misinterpreted. It is difficult not to take sides even in those long forgotten battles, but my goal must be to let them speak for themselves with the hope that you can make your own assessment.

My portrait now hangs on those same walls and I too am "wall cover," someone appropriately hung up there in silence. Hopefully, my empathy for their dilemmas, their constraints, can suffuse this book with some charity. That is, of course, what historians should always seek to achieve. Before I went to the dark side to become a university president, I was a working member of the professorate, a tenured University of Michigan historian. It is incumbent on me to be true to the sources and to opine judiciously. I hope I still remember how to do that.

I am fascinated by the history of this wonderful institution I was lucky enough to serve. This book is a labor of love. Those chancellors and trustees, students, faculty and thousands of others deserve to be heard anew through this volume. It is for this reason that I have included so many quotes in the book. And if I have got it wrong, I expect some future historian to put it right. I am fully responsible for the contents of this book. I do not speak for the University and this is not an "official" history. Rather the University kindly allowed me to explore the files, both written and photographic. I was granted the freedom to roam, to draw my own conclusions, to organize the material as I saw fit, and to pose the questions I thought important. In sum, I have taken off the regalia of the University President and donned the ancient, if less gaudy, robes of a working scholar. But, if my portrait mysteriously falls off the walls of the Boardroom late one night, you, the reader, can speculate if one or all of my predecessors have taken offense at some conclusion I have expressed, or acted in anger because I have broken an unwritten code of silence.

This book does not pretend to be a full history of the University, even for that one ten year period. Many thousands of students enrolled annually and a goodly percentage graduated from one or another campus, earning degrees that equipped many of them to become professionals-teachers, pharmacists, librarians, nurses, accountants, marine scientists, businessmen and women, physical therapists, et cetera. Many more simply became educated, thoughtful, and, hopefully, self-aware citizens. Hundreds and hundreds of faculty taught those students, and most did so with sensitivity and passion. Those who earned tenure often became "lifers," teaching thousands of students across many decades. Deans, student life professionals, coaches, and many others nurtured those students and helped them grow up. New programs opened and others disappeared. Whole campuses and graduate programs streaked across the sky like shooting stars before disappearing. A campus devoted to science and technology, a campus to educate military personnel on active service, a law school, a medical school, a dozen or more doctoral programs dot the historical landscape as failed efforts, too expensive to sustain or too difficult to win approval from the State of New York. This volume, already too long, can only summon back some of these people and programs. An all-inclusive compendium would paralyze the reader and bury the story line in thick jungle foliage.

Certain issues, structural tensions, anomalies and inter-generational stresses do recur in the text, however, because there was insufficient collective will or consensus to resolve such matters, including the relationship between the campuses, the definition of what authority was properly ceded to each campus and what were the prerogatives of central administration and how authority was or was not shared amongst the major stakeholders. Dreams and reality often collided. There was never enough money. Perspective shaped perception. Ambition and ego, fate and dumb good luck all impacted the narrative. History is always messy. It is also usually opaque.

This story took place during one of the most explosive decades in American history. National and global events-the Vietnam War; the incapacity of the federal government to sustain the "Great Society" while fighting in Southeast Asia; the assassination of two Kennedys and Martin Luther King Jr.; student challenges to traditional authority and the rejection of hierarchies; free speech; foul speech; racial unrest; the radicalization of protest and student militancy, including "black power," protest against the draft, and violent pushback from other institutions and groups; Watergate, Nixon's resignation; "open enrollment," et cetera-created a climate of distrust and anger that impacted upon virtually every institution of higher education, certainly Long Island University.

Changes in metropolitan New York and its nearby communities also impacted dramatically on Long Island University's definition of itself. The Borough of Brooklyn slowly, and then rapidly, declined, ceasing to be a wealthy, resilient, cultural, commercial, and manufacturing rival to Manhattan. Abraham & Straus was bought by Bloomingdales The departure of the Brooklyn Dodgers for Los Angeles in 1957 presaged decades of painful self-loathing. That abandonment was a body blow to the 2.5 million proud Brooklynites. An influx of new migrants, a transformation of stable ethnic neighborhoods, and "white flight" to Nassau and Suffolk, shifted the center of power and wealth eastward to the new suburbs or westward to Manhattan. The term "Long Island" came to mean only the two eastern counties, Nassau and Suffolk, not the four that share geographically that very beautiful long island, so celebrated by the Island's greatest booster and poet, Walt Whitman. The Brooklyn establishment took the lead in creating the merger at the end of the nineteenth century of those five Boroughs into the modern City of New York. The first Mayor had been the Mayor of Brooklyn, when it was still a self-governing body. But the merger was ultimately a disaster for Brooklyn, sucking Brooklyn's human talent and corporate muscle across the East River to Manhattan.

The State of New York and the City, both but independently, came to believe that CUNY and SUNY had a mission to educate all who sought higher education, provided the individual had the intelligence and skill set to seek a degree. Just as the G.I. Bill had made education accessible to every returning soldier who sought education as a vehicle for expanded opportunities, the Great Society promised higher education for the entire population. The costs would prove to be staggering, but the gravitational pull of these two university systems transformed the reality for private institutions of learning which had suddenly to compete with SUNY and CUNY on price. All but the wealthiest colleges and universities faced ruin if they were tuition dependent.

For nine decades, LIU has been one of Long Island's most important institutions, its first chartered university. This very long island stretches over one-hundred miles from Montauk to Coney Island with 6.7 million people who call it home. It has a population that equals the tenth largest state in the Union, has long been identified as New York City's bedroom and is in fact, a fascinating mix of urban, suburban and ex-urban. The Island has struggled to find its identity as something other than a colonial dependency of Manhattan. For more than a century, it has lacked cohesion with the two inner counties yoked to New York City and the two more remote counties fractured into myriad townships, villages, school districts and now, seemingly endless suburban sprawl. The interrelationships between the University and the Island's more general development dynamically shaped LIU's history, in part because the University grew from West to East just as the Island's population did.

It is axiomatic that the institutional history of Long Island University can only be understood as part of the regional and national tableaux on which it naturally belongs. Modern universities long ago ceased to be monastic enclaves, isolated from the world around them. LIU, especially in the decade from 1962-1972, was on the cutting edge, not always happily, of many of these changes. The University found itself on the front page of *The New York Times* multiple times during this decade. The stories were never good ones. With permission from that newspaper, one is reproduced on the cover of this volume. From an enrollment and public relations standpoint, such marches, strikes and teach-ins damaged the institutional image in a deleterious way. So, the point of this book has never been to relive some bitter struggle, but rather to connect the present with the past in order to inform both. Such a resurrection is one of the glories of writing and reading history.

A Note on Sources

Virtually all of the material for this book comes directly from the raw files of the principals, stored until now in unmarked, disorganized file cabinets in the basement of the University's main administration building, Bush-Brown Hall. There are literally hundreds upon hundreds of these file cabinets. That very large basement holds a *pot-pourri* of financial records, legal documents and files, union negotiation transcripts, tenure applications and denials, and official correspondence all jumbled together. Virtually nothing is identified, and, in some cases, different drawers of the same file cabinet may hold several sets of papers of different people. Researching there was truly a treasure hunt through material dating back to 1926. Archival files are interspersed with legal, corporate, academic or financial records. There have been several floods over the years and this vast basement treasure trove lacks any coherent organization. As officers retired or died over the decades, their files were simply pushed in front of prior sets of files. I myself bear much responsibility for the shabby way the University's past has been stored, but substantial funding would be required to create a proper, dry archive. Whenever such funds have been found in the past, they have instead been used for scholarship relief, a higher priority for me and my predecessors. But, in that, and many other ways, I have been hoisted on my own *petard*, since I will never be sure that I did not miss a key drawer or file cabinet in researching the material for this book.

There are also Archive rooms at both major libraries in Brooklyn and at C.W. Post. These maintain complete runs of school newspapers, *Seawanhaka* and *The Pioneer*, as well as complete runs of the yearbooks. They hold, as well, documents, papers, newspaper clippings, files, and other material, both printed and typed. Up to now, however, they lacked much material that would be seen as sensitive. As a result of this project, many of those central files of the key officers I uncovered have been transferred to the C.W. Post library for safekeeping and eventual classification and indexing. Ms. Jarron Jewel and her Brooklyn counterpart, Ms. Janet Marks, lack staff, space and time to create a single, fully organized, and functional University Archive. Hopefully, in time, these records will get the organizational support necessary to scan the documents and to make them more readily available in both locations. In the meantime, the papers are finally in a dry and caring space. I greatly admire both these women who have struggled to preserve the University's past virtually unnoticed or thanked. I am also grateful to the archivists at the New York State Board of Regents; at the University of Michigan, which holds both the Marjorie Merriweather Post and the Albert Jacobs papers, and to the dynamic Mary M. Lai who has the scrapbooks and other material collected by her late husband, William (Buck) Lai.

After months of internal debate and uncertainty, I made a decision, hopefully correct, to use only that which came from the written record. There are still many people who were present and active during some or all of the events related in the book. These men and women have vivid memories and strong opinions. For decades, for example, Gordon Hoxie has been vilified in Brooklyn. Some of the fights of the past were so bitter that memories may have been distorted by hearsay or false assumptions. Interviews and oral histories are historically a two-edged sword, and I decided to allow the written record to speak for itself. Like the great Japanese film, *Rashomon*, there are always multiple interpretations of the same event. What someone swears to be gospel, someone else may repudiate as slander or misinformation. The historian is always at risk of interpreting documents incorrectly, but it is more important that the historian own those failures than to place his trust in memory when it could be suffused with misremembered events, or cited on hearsay, or just plain wrong. Most of the photographs and copied documents are from the University's holdings. Many of these photos, which come from the University Archives, have been used often before; others, for example, several taken by Alan Tepper when a student, have never been published. Those I used from other sources are identified. I am very grateful to all who assisted this project by loaning pictures and ephemera.

A Note on Citations

Proper footnoting has proven to be impossible, because the documents are not organized chronologically, or by author, or by topic, or even in one location. Over the years secretaries or principals even stuffed some of the most sensitive, and therefore, most interesting material in the back of file drawers. To do this project, I xeroxed material, organized it by chancellor and then tried to fuse chronology with topical organization. There are ten of my file boxes which have been transferred to the Archive room at C.W. Post. Any future researcher who wants to find a document or letter I have cited can go to these boxes, and, following the organizational structure of this book, hopefully locate the document. It is for that reason that I have tried to put into the text dates on virtually every quote so that every piece of data or opinion has an internal reference point.

A Note on People

Many folks have helped me resurrect my atrophied ability to write history after so many years on "the dark side." This book is a testament to the possibility of blowing on those cold embers until they re-ignited. I am particularly grateful to Alexander Gailing, a fabulous, former LIU Masters student in history and an undergraduate from Adelphi, who worked with me primarily in the research phase and who, *mirabile dictu*, became so interested in the LIU story that he could remember details about the cast of characters, what documents or letters were found and copied, and how the University experience jibed with events in the region or nationally. He prepared the concordance detailing the chronology of the LIU story set against a backdrop of events across the nation and at other universities, especially in New York. Hopefully, this will help embed the LIU story within the larger tale. Alex is now pursuing a Ph.D at CUNY, and he will be a superb scholar.

When I announced my retirement in the fall of 2012, a very generous group of trustees and other friends of the University organized a "Legacy Fund" appeal to permit me to have the joy of applying those specially donated funds where I thought they would be best used. In all, just over $175,000 was donated, most went into scholarship endowment. With Chairman Travaglianti's approval, $25,000 was put into a suspense account to help underwrite the production costs of this book whether it was printed by Long Island University Press or, as it turned out, commercially. For their generosity to the University, their belief in the importance of remembering an institution's historical legacy and their confidence in me, I will be eternally grateful.

I am truly in debt to Janet Marks and Jarron Jewel, the archivists at Brooklyn and C.W. Post, for all their help and best wishes. I am also grateful to Heather Gibbs, who served as my Assistant Vice President when I was President and who helped me make sense of those files, once I gained access to the file rooms in the basement. I will always miss my late and much loved secretary, Kathleen Campo, who typed the first portion of this book and tried to teach me how to use *Microsoft Word* and to Eileen Cheek, an endlessly cheerful and very smart successor, who finished transcribing the manuscript and kept trying to teach me how to use *Word*.

I am deeply indebted to Professor Stuart Fishelson of the Brooklyn campus who visually captured the tumult of the sixties at Long Island University by creatively using images found in the photo morgue of the New York Times to capture the iconic Brooklyn Bridge as backdrop to the raucous but passionate LIU students marching to City Hall in protest. He also transformed my text, *mirabile dictu*, out of *Word* into *In Design*, the format required by the printer, thus freeing me (and, more important, you) from the accursed idiosyncrasies of *Word*.

The indomitable Mary Maneri Lai read the entire manuscript. Without her passion for Long Island University, her fortitude, and her faith in LIU's mission, it is doubtful that the University would have survived these many decades. She has loyally worked for all ten of the chancellors/presidents, including your obedient servant, and holds a place unique in the history of American higher education. She appropriately has been named, *Mater Universitatis*, of Long Island University.

My good friend and attorney, Lynette Phillips, read the manuscript to check for factual errors and to ensure that no one was inadvertently defamed. She proved to be a brilliant copy editor as well, changing my semicolons into commas, and providing a level of consistency and good grammar to my prose that otherwise would be lacking. Thanks to Professor Susan Shenker who bravely also edited this book. I am solely responsible my choice of language and apologize in advance whenever my text turns turgid.

My brother, Dr. Jonathan Steinberg, the Walter Annenberg Professor of History *emeritus* at the University of Pennsylvania, read this manuscript with the same love and care he has always bestowed upon his kid brother, as I tried to learn how to think critically and then to write history. Since he first taught me how to conjugate Latin verbs and to decline the nouns, back in the dark ages in the middle of the last century, I have been trying to emulate his gifts. Still am.

And, finally, I owe to Joan, my wife, my everlasting gratitude. While I was President, she served as First Lady with boundless good cheer. She came to endless functions and University events 24/7 for more than a quarter of a century with only the random complaint. She supported and consoled me when things were bad and celebrated with me when things went well. Somehow she continued to love me throughout that marathon. She even has continued to love me, despite my hogging our one computer, as I tried to control my left margin on *Word*. What more could a guy ever hope to find?

Prologue

At 10:07 a.m. on a beautiful early spring day, March 1, 1962, American Airlines Flight 1 roared down the runway at Idlewild Airport on its way to Los Angeles. Three miles beyond the airport and at about 1600 feet the plane suddenly rolled over and crashed fifty feet from the shore in Pumpkin Patch Channel of Jamaica Bay. Debris littered the marsh.

There was no mayday distress call or any prior indication that something was wrong. All 95 passengers and crew were killed, including four-star Admiral Richard Lansing Conolly and his wife, Helen. Admiral Conolly was 69 years old. W. Alton Jones, a close friend and golf partner of President Eisenhower, and the CEO of Cities Service Company, was among the other notables killed.

The takeoff seemed normal. The sky was clear. The pilot, Captain James T. S. Heist, was a seasoned, senior pilot. It was finally over nine months later that the Civil Aeronautics Board concluded that the accident was caused by a short-circuit in faulty wiring affecting rudder control. That report blamed an improper use of tweezers in binding up generator wires - a part of the automatic pilot system - in this still relatively new type of aircraft, the Boeing 707. According to *The New York Times* report of January 16, 1963, this clue turned up only after a painstaking examination of every fragment of the plane.

That same March morning New York City hosted a triumphal ticker-tape parade in honor of John Glenn and his six fellow astronauts. *The New York Times* reported that four million people watched the motorcade. The young President, John F. Kennedy, had pledged that American astronauts would reach the moon by the end of the decade and Glenn's flight was a vital milestone. *The Times* went on to observe that the "loss of 95 lives did not appear to quell the enthusiasm of the public reception," but for Long Island University the death of Admiral Conolly, its President, was a cataclysmic loss, even though the Admiral had already announced his plans to retire from the University by the following October 1st.

Conolly was a true war hero. Born in Waukegan, Illinois on April 26, 1892, he went to Lake Forest Academy prior to the United States Naval Academy. Immediately after earning his commission, he served on the battleship, *USS Virginia*, off Mexico. He was then transferred to the destroyer, *USS Smith* during World War I. While on convoy duty, one of the transport ships, the *USS West Bridge*, was torpedoed twice by the German U-boat 107 while still four hundred miles from Brest, France. Conolly received the Navy Cross for leading a party of sailors who boarded the abandoned and sinking ship and for managing the towlines as the freighter was slowly pulled to port. Over five long nights and days the *WestBridge* increasingly lost buoyancy. When she reached port only 1% of that buoyancy remained.

After the Great War, Conolly taught electrical engineering and physics at Annapolis and then at the Naval War College. He also served as a deck officer on the battleship, *USS Tennessee*. In May 1939 he took command of Destroyer Squadron 6 and on January 30, 1941, of Destroyer Squadron 7. He was at sea when Pearl Harbor was attacked. Reporting directly to Admiral William Halsey Jr., Conolly was at the battle of Midway escorting the aircraft carrier, *USS Hornet*. Of the sixteen ships in that battle group, the Japanese sank six. He was also escorting the *USS Hornet* when Colonel James Doolittle launched the first air attack on Tokyo.

Admiral Richard L. Conolly seated before a photo of the destroyer, U.S.S. Richard L. Conolly.

Conolly saw action at Salerno. He was at Guam. He participated in the battle for Leyte Gulf, one of the most monumental battles of World War II. His sailors gave him the nickname, "close-in Conolly," because he brought his destroyers as close to the landing beach as was possible so that their guns could be most effective. In 1947 the Navy named a new "Spruance-class" destroyer in the Admiral's honor. He was awarded fifteen combat medals and decorations from some thirteen foreign countries. He was on active service in the Navy longer than any of his Annapolis classmates, ending his career in the Navy as President of the Naval War College in Newport, Rhode Island.

There were funeral services for the Admiral at St. Thomas Protestant Episcopal Church on March 5th in New York and at the National Cathedral on March 6th. In attendance in Washington were Allan Dulles; General James A. van Fleet and a dozen Admirals; and among the honorary pallbearers at those two services were ex-Treasury Secretary, Robert Anderson; General van Fleet, himself a Trustee of Long Island University; the President of Hofstra, John Cranford Adams; the founding Dean of C.W. Post, R. Gordon Hoxie; and a cluster of University Trustees led by Chairman, William Zeckendorf Sr., Spyros Skouras Jr., the son of the Hollywood movie mogul, and Arthur T. Roth, the CEO of Franklin National Bank. Zeckendorf was quoted by *The New York Times* as saying that Long Island University had suffered an "irreplaceable loss." Most fittingly, the Admiral was buried with full military honors at Arlington National Cemetery.

Conolly was not supposed to be on that plane. Originally, he planned to fly to his home in La Jolla, California the day before. But at Zeckendorf's request he had delayed his departure to meet and interview Albert C. Jacobs, then the President of Trinity College in Hartford, as his potential successor. Jacobs was born in 1900 and lived to 1976. A professor of law, he had served for two years from 1947-1949 as Provost of Columbia under Dwight Eisenhower. Hoxie and Jacobs knew each other at Columbia. Subsequently, Hoxie had served as Executive Secretary to Jacobs when Jacobs had been President of the University of Denver and had worked briefly for him at Trinity. It is fairly clear that Hoxie had introduced Jacobs to Zeckendorf, and thus, was indirectly a contributor to that fateful delay.

On March 1, 1962, President Jacobs penned Hoxie a hand-written note thanking him for calling immediately with the tragic news. Jacobs wrote, "What a loss! I still cannot believe it." There is no record about how Conolly and Jacobs got along, although at an emergency Board meeting on March 5th, the Minutes quoted Zeckendorf as stating, "that Dr. Jacobs was Admiral Conolly's first choice for the office of the President and that he was awaiting word from Dr. Jacobs as to his availability." Did the Admiral consider him as the right candidate? Did he speak to Zeckendorf by telephone that night? All we know for sure is that after Jacobs declined the offer, the Board decided to appoint one of its own, a patrician Trustee with no higher education experience other than his own college years, John H. G. Pell, as interim Chancellor -an appointment that unexpectedly lasted over two years.

How this war hero died is both tragic and ironic; the Admiral had a deep-seated bias against jets. He had been scheduled to fly that morning on a propeller-driven flight, probably a TWA Constellation, but mechanical problems forced him on the spot, reluctantly, to board that ill-fated American Airlines Boeing 707. Back in 1934 W. Somerset Maugham had written a play, "Sheppey," telling the fable about a servant who inadvertently meets Death in the market in Baghdad. He begged his Master to give him his horse in order that he might flee to Samarra where "Death will not find me." The fable continued that the Master later saw Death and asked him why he had made "a threatening gesture" to his servant that morning. Death responded that it was not a threatening gesture but a "start of surprise." And then Death said, "I was astonished to see him in Baghdad, for I had an appointment with him tonight in Samarra." That story was used with permission by John O'Hara, the well-known novelist, in a bestseller entitled, *Appointment in Samarra.*

Admiral Conolly

Richard Conolly was a strong, charismatic and powerful executive. Assuming a university presidency in an era of rapid national growth and opportunity, he transformed Long Island University from an impoverished, small institution into a dynamic regional university with limitless ambitions to become a major player on the national scene. In his last week as president he informed his Board that the Middle States Commission had communicated to him the good news that accreditation was finally forthcoming. In 1960-1961 the Conolly administration had prepared ten self-study reports and a site team of peers had visited the University in October 1961.

Over the previous seven years Conolly and Zeckendorf had jointly built a prominent Board of Trustees. Among others were Carter L. Burgess, the President of American Machine and Foundry and former Assistant Secretary of Defense in the Eisenhower administration; Carleton H. Palmer, Chairman of the Board of E. R. Squibb and Sons; Ogden R. Reid, the former editor and the President of the *New York Herald Tribune*, Ambassador to Israel, and soon to be elected to the United States Congress; and Roger L. Stevens, the real estate developer, financier and theatrical producer whose plays included *Tea and Sympathy, Bus Stop, Cat on a Hot Tin Roof*, and *The Bad Seed*.

It was during that final week that Conolly wrote to Edward Neimuth, also a Trustee, and the President of National Magnesia. Neimuth was simultaneously the Board Chair of the Brooklyn College of Pharmacy, originally established in 1886, and Conolly was, separately, President of that quasi-affiliated professional school. Thanking Neimuth "for the great honor that was done to me by the Brooklyn College of Pharmacy at its 75th Anniversary Dinner…," he joked that Neimuth's remarks were a "very fine eulogy of my regime as President here." He went on, "I can't thank you enough for the very nice things you said about me and the very warm, sincere and graceful manner in which you delivered your talk." Conolly, contemplating his approaching retirement and, perhaps, his mortality, clearly had pangs of separation.

During that final week, on February 26th, the Admiral approved for submission to the Board of Trustees at its April meeting a series of Bylaw amendments altering the University Statutes by creating a single graduate council with the goal of joining at the graduate level the existing campus in Brooklyn with the newly opened one in Brookville. Middle States had warned Conolly that he and LIU would have to be vigilant to bind the several campuses tightly together or risk a bloody internecine struggle in the years ahead. Emending the Statutes became one of the major battlefields in this struggle.

The night before Conolly's death, Hoxie, in his capacity as the Provost at Post, drafted a message for the up-coming campus yearbook, *The Opticon*, which was published annually after each commencement. In it he celebrated Conolly's legacy. "There were those in 1954 who said that this new college would not long survive," wrote Hoxie, "but there was no doubt in the minds of the first entering class of 102 men and 19 women who began their instruction on September 22, 1955." Along with the eight faculty members gathered around the flagpole for the simple opening ceremony, this community "gained a sense of mission and objective." At that opening ceremony Conolly had predicted that these men and women would "take their places as leaders and useful citizens…. Self proclaimed Pioneers, these faculty and students had the courage and the will, even though there was no endowment and no appropriate campus." Hoxie, in his rotund prose, wrote that Conolly's spirit would always "be in the classrooms, on the playing fields and at commencement itself…. And so we salute you, Admiral Conolly and bid you Godspeed."

By 1962, the Post campus was growing rapidly and had become well established. Conolly had given his approval to the creation of a third campus in Southampton. Signing the legal documents to launch that Southampton Campus was very much on his mind during his last days. In innumerable ways, both for better and for worse, Long Island University had become "the lengthened shadow of one man," to cite Ralph Waldo Emerson.

Ten years later, in 1972, the University found itself broadside in very heavy seas and the lighthouse at safe harbor was obscured by squalls. Many of the earlier dreams had to be abandoned, even as the sibling rivalry between the three campuses grew acute. Moreover, America had changed profoundly. Would the University have evolved in a very different way if Jacobs had become Conolly's successor? Were the Admiral's dreams within his reach but not within the reach of those who followed? Could a tough leader like Conolly have navigated the University toward a sweet spot between the centrifugal and centripetal forces that created such havoc?

The core of this book explores these questions. What actually happened is a complex tale, to be sure, but also a fascinating one. Certainly, the ten years that stretched from the Admiral's sudden death to the Middle States Report of 1972-73 reflect a changed America, a new reality for all universities, and a confused, fractured Long Island University.

On August 25, 1970, the then Chairman of the Board, John P. McGrath, wrote to John C. Baiardi, a professor of biology and senior administrator for most of the decade, in praise and thanks for his decade of service as he returned to faculty teaching. McGrath wrote, "I know that the last several years have been most difficult for you. The passing of Admiral Conolly ushered in several periods of suspended leadership, erratic leadership and, at times, no leadership at all." McGrath further observed that, "In these years the student body found its voice which seemed, at times, strident, harsh and unreasoning. Dissent, unrest and disorder came to our campuses." In saluting Baiardi for his commitment to holding the University together, McGrath expressed empathetic thanks. "You must know that I have a real awareness of the difficulties through which you lived in this trying period and I have the greatest admiration for your fortitude and dedication."

1962-1972 was a decade of chaos, a time of false starts and smashed dreams. Five chancellors succeeded Conolly in ten years. The center failed to hold. Just as America endured war, inflation and defeat, domestic strife, a collapse of respect for authority and a fracturing of consensus, so was the University cracked along many different fault lines, even while it managed to succeed in its core mission of educating and graduating tens of thousands of students.

Part I - Realities and Dreams

Injected, inspected, detected, infested, neglected, and selected.

Arlo Guthrie, "Alice's Restaurant"

Chapter One

American Higher Education in Turmoil

By 1972, America had changed dramatically from the nation which gave John Glenn a joyful Wall Street ticker tape parade on March 1, 1962. The era of the 60s was beyond chaotic, deeply divisive and profoundly transformative. Traditional institutions and mores were jettisoned; an older and a younger generation failed utterly to communicate with each other. Women's "lib," black power, free speech, foul speech, the assassinations of two Kennedys and of Martin Luther King, Vietnam and a wildly unpopular draft all lurched into each other like bumper cars at a carnival. The staid security of the Eisenhower era and the youthful optimism of John F. Kennedy's A Thousand Days morphed into the Chicago riots at the 1968 Democratic convention and Watergate. What had been for an earlier generation a willing buy-in of the existing social order was transformed for the next generation into cynical distrust, leaving jagged scar tissue all across the society's body politic. Confidence in established political, economic, religious and educational institutions eroded. A President declined to run; his successor resigned in disgrace.

The interstate highway system of the Eisenhower era and the suburbanization of America created a new society. Families increasingly were scattered and grandparents lived far away rather than upstairs. Malls and big box chain stores altered how people shopped. The Sears Roebuck mail order catalogue became a quaint memory of the past. Families still gathered together in the evenings but now sat silent in front of a television screen rather than around a kitchen or dining room table talking. As the baby boomer generation came of age and went to college, the number of cars in a driveway went up exponentially. Getting a driver's license was a coming of age ritual, and parents increasingly "did not understand their kids" or know what they were thinking or doing. Generational alienation came into many households silently and perniciously. There were assumptions of common values and shared attitudes that had ceased to exist. It was easier for parents to blame colleges for radicalizing their children in the 60s than addressing the loss of candor and intimacy in the household when the kids were still home.

The Vietnam War shaped the decade, even though much was happening that had other causes and only tangential connectivity. American hubris and a dose of domestic anti-communist pathology drove policy makers to pivot from Great Society programs designed to seek a fairer and more inclusive nation into a literal and figurative quagmire. The War on Poverty announced by Lyndon Johnson in his first State of the Union Address on January 8, 1964, stated that "this administration today, here and now, declares unconditional war on poverty in America." The newly created governmental agencies by which this war would be waged included Head Start, Vista, Job Corps, Neighborhood Youth Corps, College Work Study as well as Kennedy era programs like the Peace Corps. But within a few years most were smothered by Johnson's decision to escalate the struggle against communism in Vietnam, one in which he and his administration misinterpreted indigenous nationalism as metastasizing ideology.

Johnson initially had a national approval rate of 70%. The American economy was growing at 5%. By late 1965-1966 the nation was already struggling with an inflationary surge, prompting the distinguished economist, Eliot Janeway, to comment that "Uncontrolled, the American economy staggered under the burden of a wartime buildup that for the first time in American history, cramped and pinched the economy instead of spurring its expansion."

From his first supplemental budgetary request of $700 million in May 1965, until Johnson declared on March 31, 1968, that he would not run for re-election "with America's son in the fields far away [and] with America's future under challenge right here at home," the nation stumbled from crisis to crisis. Vietnam left bloody markers across the decade: January 31,1968, the Tet Offensive; the My-Lai massacre also in 1968; and the anti-war marches on Washington of the autumn of 1969, et cetera. The Civil Rights transformation caused turmoil and transformed the society externally and internally. The nation was bent to the breaking point.

No sector of society was immune from the resultant turmoil, but America's colleges and universities were among the most exposed and damaged. The war sucked the oxygen out of the nation's commitment to higher education, abandoning a compact that dated from World War II when Truman signed the G.I. Bill into law. College Presidents were forced out of office by the hundreds and student militancy challenged both the administrative hierarchy and the lay Boards of Trustees, which jointly had totally dominated the University world for many decades.

The role of faculty and their place in society, both individually and collectively, also abruptly changed. There had been a time-honored regard for these professionals as wise professors who were given appropriate deference as "master teachers," just as their students accepted their subordinate role as "disciples." Such an acceptance of hierarchy was derisively discarded by the "hippie" generation of newly militant students. The organizational structure of the American university itself was threatened. American universities had long been an admixture of a monastic, communal guild and a unique form of a modern, capitalist corporation. Counter-culture students disliked all elements of the amalgam. Who was entitled to exercise authority within the university and by what right did faculty award grades was debated endlessly at teach-ins, rallies, and in dormitory rooms. The sexual revolution ended monasticism, archaic hierarchy was defined as a root cause of the "troubles" according to the young.

In World War II, and to a lesser extent in the Korean War, it was the height of patriotism for researchers and scholars to assist in the war effort through government funded research, designed to shorten the war and save lives. Vietnam was different. The government insisted on cashing in on its multi-decades investment in engineering and science and the decades of suckling had created a dependency, an obligation that tied the University as a client to Federal patronage. All those buildings, labs and grants had entered the American universities in new and unhappy ways. Now faculty were asked to develop explosives or apply psychological or anthropological skills to advance a war objective many, but not, all faculty opposed. The tension ran deep because "pure" research that was increasingly "applied," confused both individuals and institutions. If a scholar helped develop napalm, was that a violation of the implicit code by which the university saw itself in society? And could a university take taxpayer grants from the government without a reciprocal obligation to give back when the government asked? Different units of the same university often answered those questions differently. Arts and Sciences, the Liberal Arts units, often found themselves at sharp odds with the Schools of Engineering. So, the chasm was not simply between the university and the "larger society," as it was so often phrased, but within the institution itself. In both the legal and moral sense the professorate was "conflicted." Most faculty members found that contradiction very stressful.

Traditional student-run governance was suddenly deemed irrelevant as "student radicals" seized the microphone, often discovering that the sound system was broadcasting their voices quite literally around the world. The Port Huron Statement of 1962, establishing Students for a Democratic Society (SDS) announced the new reality of the "counter-culture." The spectrum of American universities - large and small, research, parochial, liberal arts and giant state run institutions - these were the nearest and most accessible set of established institutions to "liberate." Non-radicalized students were the most obvious group to enlist. The logic was clear; if change was to force America to embrace a new set of priorities, then the reformed, freed university had to be in the vanguard.

Student rebellion generated complex tensions between those who were untenured and those older faculty who gained their lifetime contracts under the *ancien régime*. Faculty meetings became combat zones where a generational struggle erupted between the senior, tenured faculty, and those closer to the student body in age. Traditional verities, including grading itself, were successfully overturned. Many students, often with the tacit or open support of some junior faculty, claimed as a matter of right the power to structure their own curricula, to abolish or trivialize grades, and to define the goals of higher education determined on personal choice. This rebellion, which was often violent verbally and occasionally led to blows, attacked what seemed an ossified undergraduate curriculum. It declared an end to centuries of an established corpus of knowledge that had been taught to the next generation. It sought to sever a continuum that linked what was taught to students at a modern American university with the curricula of Oxford, Cambridge, the Sorbonne and Heidelberg. One distinguished cluster of disciplines at Oxford had long been called, "the Greats." These ancient institutions themselves had led a rebellion against the monastic orders out of which they grew during the Renaissance and the centuries that followed.

Universities were also at the center of the bulls-eye because the young rebelled against the values and expectations of their parents and grandparents and the institutions of higher learning they attended and supported. The gates of universities stood wide open to them, whereas banks, factories and government offices had impenetrable fences that could be, and often were, locked. Universities became the surrogates for all that this new generation of radical students thought was wrong in society. If Dow Chemical, the maker of napalm, was too well guarded to be stormed, the University of Michigan was a convenient stand-in for protest. "Sit-ins" and "non-negotiable demands" became the lingo by which radical students sought "to free" themselves and their fellow students from the dated and rigid formalities of the past.

Moreover, by "liberating" a campus, militant students could gain national attention in order to attack other organs of society. The "counter-culture," the Bohemian instinct, that led to a drug culture and a sexual revolution, were shaped by the post-adolescent young, who used the relative permissiveness of the university to explore activities and counter-culture lifestyles not allowed at home. To bring this kind of protest into one's parent's house was far more complicated than trying on an alternate life style in a dormitory or off-campus housing. The music said it all; bringing the Beatles home was a perilous task.

The realities of how Washington structured and managed the national draft cruelly divided America's 18-25 year-old cohort into those who could escape serving in "Nam" and those who could not. Arlo Guthrie's famed lyrics in *Alice's Restaurant* described the Selective Service experience: "injected, inspected, detected, infested, neglected, and selected." Americans have been traditionally uncomfortable when class distinctions are crudely exposed. Deep anger followed, as those with only a high school diploma saw how college admission was an escape hatch for the wealthier and better educated in society. Not everyone who went to college was wealthy but everyone who went was certainly privileged. By promising to become a teacher, for example, one was spared having to survive in the Mekong Delta.

To be sure, there was a lottery and many college students did serve either out of patriotism or "force majeure" compliance. Coercion must always exist when any government mobilizes its young for war. But this generation made virtually every decision under the specter of being drafted.

In sharp contrast, many fathers had enlisted willingly in World War II, producing deep inter-generational friction at home. Nonetheless, the students, and not only the more militant ones, kept chanting, "Hell no, we won't go." Such massive disobedience, like the Selma marchers, threatened the existing fabric of the American Compact. The anger in such protests drove Johnson out of politics. There remains even today a deep rift between those who grew to maturity in Southeast Asia and those who fled to Canada or used college to escape being called to service. And all of this turmoil existed on virtually every college campus in the land-in its dining halls, dormitories, and student newspapers.

Equally transformative and even more explosive, was the emergence of "black power," challenging how both whites and blacks perceived America. Until this era, college was primarily for whites. As late as 1969, only 10% of CUNY's students were black or Puerto Rican. One of the central "demands" of militant blacks was a chance to climb the ladder of upward mobility to success by establishing "Open Enrollment" at institutions like CUNY (then comprising nine four year colleges, five community and three professional colleges). Black activists and subsequently Hispanic, Asian and other minority groups, also challenged the admissions process, the existing curriculum, the preeminence of "the writings of dead white men," and a grading system that was biased against men and women of color. In the spring of 1969, minority students blockaded and shut down not only CCNY but also Brooklyn and Queens Colleges, among others. "Open Admissions" swelled the freshmen population from 20,000 to 35,000 in one semester. Since there was no tuition charged, the cost to the city for higher education jumped in seven years from $35 million in 1966 to $200 million in 1973. Remediation became a major pre-requisite to academic success and a high cost to bear as the percentage of "under-prepared" black and Hispanic students increased to 40%.

While there was often tension and distrust between students of different races, especially since militant blacks had a somewhat different agenda from white youngsters, there were tactical reasons for those groups to seek a united front. There were many caucasian students, many quite moderate on Vietnam, who saw the injustices of unaddressed racism in American society as a national disgrace. Martin Luther King's emphasis on non-violent protest resonated with many white college students. They became aware how the American Dream was tarnished and how their own universities violated the social compact, perpetuating white hegemony. Students of all races banded together to demand change in the existing order, insisting that their university or college take a lead in addressing this gross injustice.

PART I - REALITIES AND DREAMS

Commencements were cancelled, exam periods were delayed or skipped, buildings "liberated," and senior administrators forced to huddle behind barricaded doors as student militancy reached a crescendo. Many college Presidents became tongue-tied or paralyzed in the face of these and other "demands." Many alumni were outraged and demanded that their President "do something." As buildings were seized, as property was trashed, the police were summoned. Faulted both because of inaction and/or brutality, collectively these Presidents lost their most precious asset; the *gravitas* of their office. And once a President had lost that moral authority, he (and, occasionally, she) became an easy target for one set of stakeholders or another, and, often, all.

Many students concluded, with substantial evidence, that both Lyndon Johnson and Richard Nixon, and their key aides, were serial liars, individuals who lacked a moral compass and who exercised their power arbitrarily. Even Robert McNamara subsequently wrote of Johnson's "frequent efforts to dissemble." For many students of all races, Lyndon Johnson's landmark civil rights activities came to be seen less as measures of national leadership than as pinched responses to the "freedom riders," Martin Luther King, and black militancy. The political trade-offs and compromises required to effect change in a democracy were obscured, as idealistic young men and women saw protest as the best way to change society. Good and evil were defined as absolutes. Right and wrong seemed more obvious to them than it did to others. White students of the 60s, somewhat naively, concluded that student protest and militancy had to change society for the better.

The Black Panther Movement started in Alabama as an outgrowth of the Student Non-Violent Coordinating Committee, but it quickly evolved into a northern, violent and urban protest organization. Bobby Seale, Huey Newton and Stokely Carmichael preached black pride, self-defense, and revolutionary violence, reflexively prompting J. Edgar Hoover to call the Panthers, "the greatest threat to the internal security of the country." Eldridge Cleaver, the author of *Soul on Ice*, became Minister of Information; black leather and pseudo-military berets, the garb of protest. Dr. King's non-violence was increasingly challenged and dismissed as ineffective by a sub-set of younger, inner-city leaders who rejected the gradualism of the black ministerial elite, primarily southern. Martin Luther King's assassination in 1968 confirmed to radical urban blacks, especially those in their twenties and/or at college, the futility of embracing Dr. King's evolutionary non-violence. This schism, which scrambled both black and other loyalties, helped to shape the tumult of the decade.

As many students of color moved to this new phase, they lost many white fellow students who became fearful of the anger and violence they saw unleashed in Watts, Newark, Detroit and many other cities. The rage was legitimate but scary to college age, middle class whites. As black students spoke of toppling a racist society and redistributing power, they broke their alliance with the anti-war white students who quickly realized that it was their present and future privilege that was under assault.

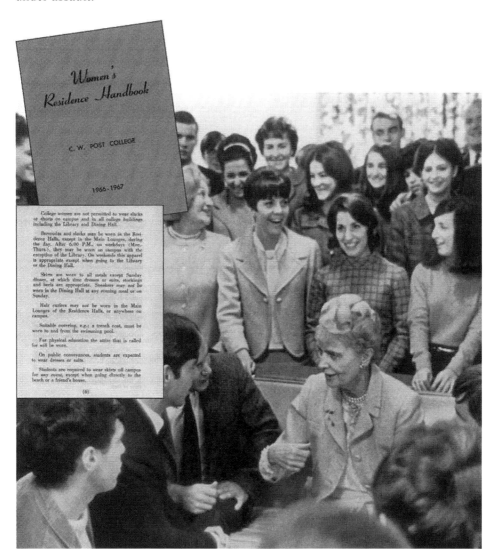

Undated photo of Mrs. Marjorie Merriweather Post seated with C. W. Post undergraduates. The 1966-1967 Parietal Rules are superimposed.

The daily realities of college life were also totally altered in this decade. When Admiral Conolly died there was still a dress code at Long Island University. Female students wore heels and skirts; men came to class dressed in coats and ties. Young women were expected (and did) wear white gloves if they were going to a tea or some more formal event. And virtually every college in America had enforced parietal rules. University administrators never questioned that they were *in loco parentis.* Women's dorms had housemothers to protect and enforce codes of decorum. When men could enter a female dorm was carefully monitored. In a pre-pill era, pre-marital sex was strictly *verboten*. First approved for use in the United States in 1960, the pill transformed how college age student population handled sex. But, by the end of the 60s there was a totally different environment virtually everywhere. Casual sex and a drug culture had transformed college life, certainly ending monasticism. Sexual relations had become permissive, not proscribed. Alcohol was shared freely by men and women and a jeans culture replaced the cardigan sweater as the norm. As a result of this college revolution, it was no longer possible to tell students of affluence from students on scholarship by what they wore or how they cut (or failed to cut) their hair. A new, universal dress code was unisex and classless. The "preppy" look was relegated like white buck shoes to a distant past, even at Ivy League institutions.

The emergence of feminism during these same years had a dramatic impact at every university. Who taught the next generation and what they taught became skirmishes in a major culture war on every campus. Tenured faculty had been dominated by white males, who chose the curriculum as a matter of right. The administrators were even more the domain of the white establishment. As women increasingly got advanced degrees, they pushed hard to be recognized as legitimate scholars and able administrators, exacerbating the notion that the university was appropriately a direct, descendent of the all-male monastery of medieval times. The women's role was being redesigned so rapidly that the moorings of the past no longer recognized male superiority.

Added to this was an admissions revolution in which Jews first, and then Asians, flooded into programs and colleges that previously had rigid quotas to keep them out. As they succeeded, they threatened traditional sinecures of employment, including faculty jobs as well as Wall Street, advertising, medicine, and law. Many of these newcomers were urban, democratic and anti-Vietnam. There were no Jewish college Presidents and then there were many. The same was true for women. They shared a more tolerant and expansive world-view with their students. At Columbia, Grayson Kirk was ultimately succeeded by Michael Sovern; William Birenbaum was a Jew from Waterloo Iowa; R. Gordon Hoxie a high Episcopalian from the same town. They never met growing up, even though they were less than four years apart.

These shifts in taste and culture not only created tension between those who served in Southeast Asia and those who went to college, but also exposed a generational gap that turned many older Americans against what seemed to be the arrogant world of higher education. On April 23, 1968, 1,000 Columbia students seized five buildings. A year later, 400 police made 197 arrests at Harvard. Cambridge police, after waiting generations for the opportunity, entered this elite bastion in full riot gear. The permissiveness found traditionally around any college campus was, during this decade, blamed on weak administrators, and a licentious, undisciplined environment. Many older Americans turned against their own alma maters. Free speech and foul speech were conflated. A blurry but real line appeared, prompting a conservative backlash that was both political and socio-cultural. Alumni donations plummeted as many grads felt alienated from their own university and their memory of that youthful experience. America's love affair with its colleges had certainly ended. And high-powered commissions sought answers in order to reestablish the luster American universities once had.

For example, The National Commission on the Causes and Prevention of Violence, chaired by Milton Eisenhower, the former President of The Johns Hopkins University, linked campus violence to issues within the larger society. Many of its findings were, in reality, warnings to the American public not to be punitive, rash, or biased against these college students or, by inference, their universities. So worried was this very prominent commission of national worthies that it rushed out an edited statement of its findings on June 10,1969, publishing them in *The New York Times*, rather than waiting until the full report could be released in the following autumn. Pundits lamented what was happening and warned the country of the price it would pay, that the students would pay, that the institutions would pay, or all of the above.

Students of the 60s, both those who considered themselves radicals and those not participating in the student protest movement, came to question their parents' generation as too accepting of the existing order, despite its obvious flaws. A contented and comfortable older generation, one that was willing to stand on the sidelines, appeared to their children as "milquetoast," non-engaged sissies in the face of injustice or governmental abuses or racism, sexism and other ancient blind spots. As these students gained a voice on their campuses, they assumed that they had achieved a level of "liberation" that the rest of society was not interested in bestowing upon them. Newspapers became critical and hostile. Editorials became increasingly vitriolic. Parents and students argued at Thanksgiving or over Christmas vacation. And the government, both locally and in Washington, came to see both the students and their seemingly ineffectual administrators, as "the enemy." Legislators asked why they should funnel federal dollars to institutions that encouraged sexual license, a drug culture, and an open rebellion against the national priority of the Vietnam War? When on May 4, 1972, the Ohio National Guard fired on a student demonstration on campus and killed four students, Kent State revealed the ugly tension between the young men in the Ohio National Guard and the protesting students of Kent State University. It became one of a series of symbolic markers delineating the different universes in which the university, especially her students and faculty, and the rest of society inhabited.

In sum, many in adult, traditional society, both Democrats and Republicans, concluded that most, perhaps all, American universities were bastions of anarchy. How dare dirty students in jeans with greasy hair and immature beards feel free to lecture their seniors? And because of the fragmentation of these student movements on each college campus, the younger generation seemed to speak in a babble of voices. To be sure, a few like Mark Rudd or Mario Savio of SNCC found that they possessed a national, even global, microphone. But most campuses, both large and small, seemed to create a cacophony, a societal static that had parents and their college age children talking past each other. Pundits debated the young in endless argument. The armed forces, an organized, powerful force in society, came to view the university as a dangerous, even seditious, threat to America's future.

A report drafted by New York State entitled "The Academy in Turmoil" quoted Socrates who asked, "What is happening to our young people? They disrespect their elders. They disobey their parents. They ignore the laws. They riot in the streets, inflamed with wild notions. Their morals are decaying. What is to become of them?" The point was clear: students had consistently rebelled from time immemorial. This appeal for tolerance, this effort to get others to cut some slack for these young men and women, under estimated the lasting damage wreaked on the university. Pride and support turned into anger and distain. Faculty eggheads were seen as fellow travelers or communists, at least radical thinkers alienating the next generation. As Adlai Stevenson quipped, mocking Karl Marx, "Egg heads of the world unite; you have nothing to lose but your yolks."

Moreover, the fat years had ended and the financial famine was catching many institutions, certainly Long Island University, in a terrible squeeze. Federal and state funding had precipitously dried up. Johnson's expectation that America could provide both "guns and butter" while over one half million soldiers were on active duty in Southeast Asia proved impossible, especially with no increase in taxes. The prior national consensus, which had identified low interest construction loans and funding for higher education as a national priority, was fractured. Support for student scholarships and capital construction dwindled. The war became so expensive that even a prosperous America could not afford to build that "great society." It became easy to reduce the share of federal tax dollars flowing to colleges and universities and, more important, their ungrateful students. Moreover, philanthropic organizations like the Ford Foundation also turned away from supporting higher education in order to help address some of the pressing social concerns that the student movement had done so much to highlight. McGeorge Bundy, then President of the Ford Foundation, turned the Foundation's vast resources to projects like voter registration in Cleveland, slum clearance in Detroit, or black business ventures in Los Angeles. Many foundations followed his lead.

And the private universities in New York encountered two additional challenges for both enrollment and financial support. The governor, Nelson Rockefeller, was committed to the democratization of higher education in his state. During this difficult decade, he lavished state support to build an enormous public university, SUNY. Governor Rockefeller wanted New York to have a higher education system that rivaled the University of California with its three tiers of junior colleges, state colleges and multiple flagship research universities. Rockefeller dreamed big. His privileged birth and place in society freed him to have such an expansive vision.

Across the 1960s, the State University of New York grew from a few scattered campuses into a massive system with at least one SUNY campus in every county of the state. Billions of state taxpayer dollars flowed into the construction mandated by that dream. Thousands of faculty and staff had to be recruited and paid for as well. Rockefeller's vision threatened virtually every private and religiously identified college and university in New York State. Only a tiny few had the reputation and endowment to withstand this tsunami.

The private sector institutions of New York were so anxious about the growth of the SUNY system that they lobbied hard for some redress. Rockefeller appointed McGeorge Bundy to head a commission to explore options. Serving with him were four distinguished college Presidents: James B. Conant, emeritus President of Harvard; Father Theodore M. Hesburgh of Notre Dame; Abram L. Sachar of Brandeis; and John A. Hannah of Michigan State. On January 31, 1968, the Commission proposed a scheme through which private colleges and universities would get a state stipend for each student graduated. Known as Bundy Aid, thereafter, the amount would vary based on the academic degree conferred: advanced degrees fetching a larger sum and entry-level degrees less.

This revenue partially offset the enormous tuition advantage the SUNY colleges and universities had because of their state subsidy. Originally the program was supposed to distribute about $33 million to the 143 independent and religiously affiliated institutions, but the amount granted annually was subject to the governor's negotiations with the legislature. For endowment poor universities like LIU, this annual amount partially softened the enrollment surge at SUNY and CUNY. Both these systems saw their revenues reduced by this sharing of state funds, and there was a bitter inter-sector fight that lasted many years.

From 1961 to 1966, the panel found that enrollment at SUNY and CUNY rose 87% from 83,274 students to 156,008. The Bundy Commission saw "the need as critical," if independent sector higher education would survive. Such support would provide, it claimed, "the margin of difference between gradual decline and continuing improvement" in the private sector. Bundy Aid mattered, but not nearly as much as the Commission claimed it would. To cite a Long Island example, in 1957, the State moved to establish a teacher training institute, the forerunner of Stony Brook. It was initially to become a public sector Normal School, in Oyster Bay, New York. Its category was listed as a State University College. By 1960, a planning committee chaired by Henry Heald, identified Stony Brook as a SUNY Center. From 1964 to 1970, each year the SUNY budget had the largest increase in history. Very rapidly Stony Brook became a flagship campus, a major center for research, an institution with a medical school and a University hospital, and a juggernaut that threatened every private institution on Long Island. And Stony Brook was but one of sixty SUNY campuses in 1968.

The Carnegie Commission on Higher Education, the Ford Foundation, and the Association of American Universities collectively funded yet another report under the supervision of Clark Kerr, the former Chancellor the University of California system. That document, drafted in 1970, by Earl F. Cheit, a Professor of Business at Berkeley, warned the higher education community that the boom years were over. The cost per student was rising at an average increase of 8%. 71% of the colleges or universities in his sample were "at risk" or "in trouble." When he extrapolated those numbers onto the national scene (and LIU was not in his sample), he warned that there were 1,000 universities with 4,000,000 students headed for financial trouble. Cheit wrote, "Growth had not protected the schools but may well have made them more vulnerable to a downturn. Many were undercapitalized or over extended, moving into enlarged areas of responsibility without permanent financing or still raising quality standards." Annual tuition increases of 7.5% risked denying access and "cost cutting alone can not be expected to solve the cost-income problem." He saw tenure as a bar to flexibility and noted "college Presidents have a harder time effecting a reduction in force than do executives in private industry or government officials."

The experience of New York University in the same era is instructive. New York University then had two campuses, one downtown in the East Village and the other, its flagship, was situated on the Heights in the Bronx. For many decades that campus was the home of the College of Arts and Sciences along with the Engineering College as well as NYU's Phi Beta Kappa chapter. Like LIU, NYU was besieged from every direction. In 1970-1971, it projected a deficit of $6.7 million. President Hester spoke of its financial squeeze as a "critical situation." Meeting payroll was dicey. NYU effectively was bankrupt.

NYU had functioned in the Bronx for 76 years. There were 2,145 arts and science students uptown. But the engineering school had lost 700 students over four years. Hester turned to the State, seeking $75 million. The deal finally struck paid NYU $40 million, provided it transferred that uptown campus to Bronx Community College, transferred its School of Engineering to The Polytechnic Institute in Brooklyn, and moved all of its activities onto its downtown campus. NYU Law School also had to liquidate its ownership of the C. F. Mueller Company in New Jersey fetching $115 million. That area of Manhattan was decaying, industrial, and grim; New York's equivalent of Haight-Ashbury in San Francisco. The East Village was a mecca for hippies, eager to live a counter-culture life. NYU's triumph, despite long odds, is another story for another book. Suffice it to note here that NYU and LIU were then very similar institutions. Both were tuition dependent, urban universities for the upwardly mobile. Both were particularly vulnerable to external forces over which neither had control. Both lacked adequate endowment.

And another external force that created havoc for both was the ambitious dream of the liberal, Republican mayor of New York, John Lindsay. He was worried about SUNY overwhelming the City University of New York and he believed passionately in the transformational opportunities that "Open Enrollment" offered the poor, the newly arrived immigrants, and those of color in his City. In 1961, Rockefeller signed a bill that combined the several urban campuses into a single structure, the City University of New York. CUNY moved aggressively toward open admissions, creating among other changes, the SEEK Program (Search for Education, Enlightenment and Knowledge) to provide remediation. The goal was to avoid "ghettoization" in which there would still be elite campuses that would skim the best and brightest and leave those with lower scores and grades to go to second and third tier campuses.

Since the "free university" still did not charge tuition, this explosive growth of students came close to bankrupting the City itself. By 1972-1973, the CUNY budget had risen to $381 million, (by then the State of New York paying 50% of operating costs). But in the meantime, the competition for students with NYU, LIU, Pace, Fordham and similar independent universities had created a crisis for each of these independent universities. Why would an individual student or his or her family pay to enroll in a private university when he or she could get, virtually for free, an accounting degree at Baruch College or a teaching degree at Hunter College or a criminal justice degree at John Jay?

Long Island University was buffeted by all of these national and regional pressures. It was very interesting that there is relatively little mention of these external factors in the correspondence, memos and speeches of its leaders. Certainly they were acutely aware of what was happening, as were the faculty and the students. Much as LIU might wish it be otherwise, it could not exist in a bubble of its own making. Avoiding the draft, on the positive side, brought many high school graduates to enroll at all three LIU campuses. It gave Southampton, for example, an early enrollment boost that helped it get started with almost enough students to balance its early budgets. In retrospect, students came who otherwise might never have chosen to enroll in any four-year college. To cite another example, the emergence of racial politics, especially after Martin Luther King's assassination, transformed the Brooklyn campus and its pool of potential students. Expansion at C.W. Post College and its concomitant building boom now mandated that it increase its debt load through mortgages from banks or through the New York State Dormitory Authority rather than from federal agencies. And LIU women abandoned their heels and the men their coats and ties, virtually all embracing a new lifestyle. They challenged the leadership of the University as avidly as did students at Columbia or Harvard or the University of California.

The student protests of the 60s were a global phenomenon. Even though many of the issues of rebellion, of sexual liberation, of inter-generational anomie, or the permissive drug culture were constant across cultures, there were distinct and specific regional or national grievances that alienated one generation from the preceding ones. Danny Cohn-Bendit in Paris, the students of the Prague spring, German and Italian students raging against their parents' generation for joining the fascists or the Nazis, all participated in their own explosive protests. Television created the twenty-four hour news cycle, and these young men and women, "radicals," as they fashioned themselves, seized their moment with gusto. Few of the American students knew of or had ever heard *La Boheme*, but they knew that European students were in solidarity with their protest over the Vietnam War, were equally against racism, and shared in what became the "culture wars," the rebellion against a reactionary adult culture. It was an extraordinary moment in history.

We are planning the University for Long Island.

Tristram Walker Metcalfe

Chapter Two

Early Hardscrabble Years

Brooklyn in the 1920s was a fascinating, vibrant but downwardly mobile borough of two and a half million people. Manhattan was successfully sucking the marrow out of Brooklyn's body politic, attracting émigrés from that borough, and taking over Brooklyn's hitherto autonomous banking and commercial sectors to dominate the commercial, financial, cultural and artistic life of the city. The extraordinary McKim, Mead and White Brooklyn Museum, initially designed to rival in size and scope of the Metropolitan Museum in Manhattan, ran out of money after building only one façade of four. It stands as a tangible reminder of the over-ambitious dreams of the late 19th century Brooklyn elite. Brooklyn became a major exporter of people, talent and capital for most of the twentieth century, lapsing into a colonial dependency with Manhattan.

Brooklyn was a mosaic of "middle class" communities. Churches and synagogues defined neighborhoods, and the ethnicity and stability of these communities offered security both to immigrant families and to the second generation. But within those residential enclaves, families and individuals craved upward mobility and Americanization, often defined as moving to Manhattan or, in later years, to "the Island." In complex ways, these neighborhoods were both isles of stability and intermediate transit stops as whole families or at least the younger generation plotted how best to move up and out. Luck and grit were both pre-requisites to achieving material success and the American Dream. It concomitantly became clear that the best way to achieve success in America was to graduate from a modern college with a practical degree that opened access to a professional career ladder.

Irish, Italian and Jewish families in Brooklyn could taste the delights of upward mobility. Their American-born children became Brooklyn's most important export crop. Everybody in Manhattan and many in other cities across the country seemed to come from Brooklyn, irrespective of whether they sought their destiny in Hollywood, on Wall Street or as Park Avenue professionals. And while these émigrés from Brooklyn were often defensive about their origins and perhaps insecure about their pedigree, they rarely lacked self-confidence or ambition. This was the era in which many chose to change or shorten their last names in order to pass more easily in a gentile-dominated world and to obscure their origins. And this was an era when Brooklyn became famous for its pugnacious pride. David Daniel Kaminsky, Brooklyn born and educated, became Danny Kaye. When, years later, he was asked for his autograph by a member of the English royal family at a "Command" Performance, he could not resist signing the program David Daniel Kaminsky. Brooklyn's identity was tied closely to its unique major league baseball team, appropriately named the "Dodgers," (and the team's departure to Los Angeles in 1957 was a body blow that has yet to be forgotten.) There was always identification, fierce pride and borough defensiveness in calling these sports heroes, "d' Bums."

A political cartoon from The Brooklyn Eagle.

It was in the context of this dynamic, bubbling culture that a Brooklyn Jewish banker named Ralph Jonas led a group of Brooklyn corporate and civic leaders in creating the first University for the borough in 1926. Jonas was a founder and senior executive of a Brooklyn bank (substantially capitalized by Jews), Manufacturers Trust Company. Jonas was also a key civic leader in the establishment of Brooklyn College. He was a director of the Brooklyn Chamber of Commerce, was involved with Brooklyn Jewish Hospital and helped to organize the Brooklyn Federation of Jewish Charities. He was, in sum, an avid booster of civic society in Brooklyn, an exemplar of Brooklyn autonomy and local pride. He himself would lose his fortune during the Great Depression, as did many in his social stratum.

Founding Chairman, Ralph Jonas.

The idea of a college in Brooklyn for Brooklyn residents did not originate with Jonas. Earlier in the twentieth century there had been several failed efforts to establish just such an institution. The motivation was consistently a combination of local pride, easy access and a pernicious quota system then widely prevalent in American higher education, designed to keep out the very Brooklynites that so craved admission. In the 1920's, when Jonas successfully helped to found Long Island University, elite colleges like Columbia severely restricted the admission of Jews, Catholics and other newly arrived Americans. Jonas dreamed of a place that could and would educate Brooklyn youth, whatever the student's religion or ethnic background. Retaining those students at home in Brooklyn and minimizing any outward migration away from the Borough was an obvious goal.

In the late nineteenth century, Walt Whitman, arguably America's greatest poet, celebrated the urban pulse of Brooklyn and the bucolic beauty of Nassau and the East End without apology or ambivalence. For Whitman, Long Island, his birthplace, his beloved Paumanok (the Indian name for Long Island), captured his idealized dream of America perfectly. Just after he died in 1896, the decision to merge the two densely populous areas of Long Island - Queens and Brooklyn - into the City of New York bifurcated this 110-mile long island, even though there has never been a river separating the Borough of Queens from the County of Nassau.

The lay leadership of this institution debated what should be the name for their new university. Should it be "Brooklyn University" or "Long Island University?"

PART I - REALITIES AND DREAMS

Just as Long Island City is actually on the banks of the East River in Queens, these industrialists and community leaders selected Long Island University as their name of choice, especially since the Free University of the City of New York wanted the name "Brooklyn College" for its new campus on the other side of Prospect Park. They debated but rejected another alternative: "The University of Long Island," probably because Brooklyn and Queens were dense urban areas full of potential students, whereas the rest of the Island in the 1920's was either used as farmland or developed into baronial estates, particularly on the "Gold Coast" of northern Nassau.

The founding Trustees included James H. Post, the President of the National Sugar Refinery, located on the East River in Brooklyn and Matthew S. Sloan, the President of Brooklyn Edison. That company, in turn, became Consolidated Edison, which chose to move to Manhattan from Brooklyn in the post-war era. Its downtown Brooklyn office became the home for the University for some years, until Zeckendorf provided the funds to allow the University to purchase the Brooklyn Paramount Theater and the adjacent office building, still the physical core of the downtown campus off Flatbush Extension. Frederick E. Crain, the chief judge of the New York State Court of Appeals, was also a founding Trustee. But it was Jonas who was the driving force in establishing the new University. He was the one individual prepared to make a major capital gift of a half million dollars to fund the launching of the college.

Provisional Charter of Long Island University granted by the
New York State Board of Regents.

On September 21, 1927, 312 students began their college careers in rented quarters on Court, Remsen and Montague Streets in downtown Brooklyn. The Board retained George Robert Hardie, a classicist from Alfred College in upstate New York, as the founding Dean. It was probably Hardie who selected the Latin motto for the college. He chose *Urbi et Orbi*. That phrase, *Urbi et Orbi*, is the time-honored greeting of the Pope as he begins addressing the throngs at the Vatican. He has always used these three words to salute the parishioners of his own diocese, Rome (*Urbi*), and the worldwide Catholic communion (*Orbi*). It was presumptuous for Long Island University, a brand new and tiny college seeking to attract a large percentage of Jews to its student body, to select such a well-known, papal greeting as its motto. But it also speaks both to the "chutzpah" so characteristic of the culture of Brooklyn and to the passionate belief this fledgling University would serve the polyglot Brooklyn community and the world beyond.

Official Seal of the University.

Prior to the opening of LIU, most Brooklyn high school students had few colleges from which to choose, even if they had the grades and the will to seek a collegiate degree. The cheapest quality choice was City College, the flagship campus of the Free University of the City of New York. But the competition was severe. A student had to have at least an 85% average in high school. If that student did not speak English as a first language or if the family came to America when the child was older, it was very difficult to make the grade. Most high school students in Brooklyn had to work as well as go to school and few had the time to take the long subway ride, usually requiring transfers, from Brooklyn to Harlem and back. Yes, there were other options, including NYU, but its Arts and Sciences campus was in the Bronx, even farther away, and its quality was problematic.

There were other specialized ways to earn a college degree and to gain entry into the middle class. There were church-related institutions. There were professional schools that offered admission without first requiring a bachelor's degree. Among these was the option to become a pharmacist. The Brooklyn College of Pharmacy was founded in 1886. In the nineteenth century, it took a year to graduate as a pharmacist. But, as the 20th century unfolded, pharmacy education became ever more demanding. Medical and surgical advances were paralleled by a cornucopia of new drugs and an ever-increasing demand to regulate and professionalize the men and, increasingly, the women who could dispense those drugs. The pharmacist was an important professional in the community and the local drug store an important institution in society. In 1925, the curriculum nationally became a three-year program. In 1932, it became a four-year degree (in New York State that change was required in 1937). In 1960, it was expanded to five years. Basic sciences were increasingly mandated and established general education requirements added, especially in the first two years, to the requirements decided upon by the professional societies that regulated the corpus. Teaching those arts and science courses was expensive, and an alliance between BCP and LIU a natural fit for both institutions. (It is now a six-year program leading to a doctorate.)

In the early 1930s, the most important recruiter and publicist for the fledgling college turned out to be the basketball coach, Clair Bee. Basketball was a popular street game in any city, but New York was its center. It was still an emerging sport when Bee joined the LIU faculty. He proved to be a brilliant coach and recruiter for the team, attracting to this young institution city kids who could "shoot hoops." The team's successes generated publicity and drew other students. Bee built extraordinary teams, and LIU had a superlative record year after year.

Clair Bee. His 1931 letter of acceptance of his appointment addressed to Dean George Hardie.

After three spectacular seasons in the mid '30s, the LIU squad was invited by the U.S. Olympic Committee to represent the United States at the Berlin Olympics in 1936. It was the first time that basketball had become an Olympic sport. For very poor kids from the inner city during the Great Depression the opportunity to sail across the Atlantic on a great liner, the *Manhattan*, to wear an Olympic blazer, and to represent the United States was a powerfully seductive prospect. The players were primarily Jewish and Italian. Bee told his players that the team would go to the Olympics only if every player agreed to participate. There was a secret vote and three of the players refused to participate in Hitler's propaganda extravaganza by competing in Berlin. LIU never went.

By placing moral principle over glory and excitement, the students traded their fifteen minutes of fame for a sense of ethical well being. The University collectively also lost a unique opportunity to develop a national reputation. Basketball was then overwhelmingly an American sport. LIU was well positioned to win a gold medal. Jesse Owens is still remembered by millions because he was a remarkable black athlete who confronted Hitler's racial views and, by winning, made a mockery of his prejudices. The LIU team might equally have had the same opportunity, challenging through sport Hitler's anti-Semitism. But, instead, the opportunity was lost and the story all but forgotten. Would such celebrity have altered LIU's institutional trajectory? It is impossible to determine, even though the University of Washington oarsmen went to Berlin. They were celebrated then and since in *The Boys in the Boat*. Their cox was jewish.

Sadly, basketball proved to be a terrible curse on LIU. Under Clair Bee the University continued to be a basketball powerhouse until 1951, when a multi-college "point shaving" scandal ended Bee's string of record seasons, concluded his career under a cloud, and destroyed the lives of several of the players, in particular, a superb black athlete, Sherman White, who was perhaps the best basketball player in the country. He went to jail instead of turning professional. That scandal, which involved other city schools, including NYU and CCNY, ended New York 's dominance of college basketball and altered the athletic programs of several universities. The legacy of that scandal remains the thing many people remember first when LIU is mentioned to them. While LIU has remained a Division I team in the NCAA and participates actively in many sports, that scandal, which happened during the first year of the Korean

A newspaper report of the decision not to send the basketball team to the 1936 Berlin Olympics.

War, has haunted the University well into the 21st century. Beyond its terrible human toll, that debacle ended LIU's opportunity to ride big-time sports as a vehicle to student recruitment success. LIU's potential Olympic gold became, instead, a lead weight.

Returning chronologically to the narrative, the 1929 stock market crash and the decade of the Great Depression nearly ended LIU's then brief history. Like many other tuition-driven colleges nationally, especially those with few wealthy alumni, there was no place for the college to turn. Ralph Jonas was wiped out financially, and many of the other Trustees defaulted on their pledges. Students and their families could not and did not pay their tuition, and creditors and suppliers demanded payment from an empty institutional treasury.

But with stubborn doggedness, Long Island University continued to plan for a glorious future. Three times during the '30s it sought accreditation from the Middle States Association of Colleges and Secondary Schools. And thrice it was denied because its finances were deemed too fragile. In 1936, the New York State Board of Regents did agree to amend LIU's Charter so that the University could offer certain master's degrees and find new revenue streams, while training teachers and other professionals in needed professional fields. In 1939, the Charter was again expanded to permit it to offer its first Doctorate: in Podiatry. For mutual survival, the Manhattan-based College of Podiatry chose to affiliate with LIU, seeking initially to share facilities as a cost-saving move and to test a merger option. This quasi-affiliation was more a marriage of joint poverty than a carefully planned strategic partnership. By far, the most important consequence was that William Zeckendorf Sr., already a Trustee of the College of Podiatry, became a Trustee of Long Island University. He served on the LIU Board for thirty-four years, twenty-five as Chairman.

Dean and then President, Tristram Walker Metcalfe.

In 1931 Tristram Walker Metcalfe, a former education editor of the *New York Evening World*, joined the University as its comptroller. He subsequently became the Dean, replacing Hardie, and in 1941, was named the first President of Long Island University. Meanwhile, the military draft, instituted some months before Pearl Harbor, decimated enrollment. After the Japanese attack of Hawaii, virtually all able-bodied men were called to service, while many of the women dropped out to take jobs in the Brooklyn Navy Yard or in other war-related positions. As a result, enrollment dropped from a pre-war high of over 1,000 to a 1943 low of 307. Few faculty were left to teach. Many taught subjects outside their areas of specialization, and one faculty member, in particular, taught history, mathematics, physics, chemistry and German. The University was habitually in arrears in paying its faculty and staff. Survival was tenuous.

Metcalfe and his decimated Board weighed the options: to close the University or to enter into a court-controlled bankruptcy. It opted for court protection as the better choice. The bankruptcy judge appointed two receivers, John P. McGrath and Joseph A. O'Connor, and they, in turn, decided to retain Metcalfe as the chief operating officer. The shrunken University moved into rented quarters at the Brooklyn Law School in downtown Brooklyn. This court receivership continued until May 1, 1947.

The University's prospects dramatically improved when President Roosevelt and the Congress enacted a remarkable piece of social legislation, The Servicemen's Readjustment Act of 1944, better known as the GI Bill, transformed career and life opportunities for millions of discharged soldiers and sailors. It provided access to middle class jobs and career ladder opportunities. It revolutionized the social compact of the nation by declaring that those who fought for their country were entitled to the advantages of a college education, including the non-material advantages of learning how to think critically, to gain respect for other times and cultures and to develop an appreciation of art and literature. Essentially, it also provided a way to master skill-based learning that was directly tied to middle class, professional career prospects.

Of the 14 million returning veterans, over 2.2 million went to college on the GI Bill. Over 5.5 billion dollars became available for tuition. All of this made it possible for those returning servicemen (and some women) to find a path out of wartime fears. The despair of the Depression was replaced with new hope and opportunity, and higher education in America was democratized. It became a right of passage, not just a privilege of wealth. Yeomen were transformed into "salary men." Soldiers whose families had been blue collar had the chance to enter white-collar careers. And America's colleges and universities were suddenly flush with cash. Normal schools (to train teachers) became full service universities. Newly founded universities sprung up all across the nation.

LIU, like many other universities, suddenly had a renewed lease on life, a defined mission and the funds to provide effective higher education. Between 1945 and 1946 LIU's enrollment quadrupled. By 1948 it had expanded by 200 percent more. In other words, the student population went from 382 students in 1944 to 610 in 1945, to 2660 in 1946, and to 6700 in 1947. In 1947 the University had a one million dollar surplus. It had become an entrepreneurial bastion of higher education in downtown Brooklyn, offering accelerated programs to returning servicemen who were eager to get this deeply subsidized education.

This rapid increase in enrollment soon created concomitant space issues. The University was functioning at multiple sites and in temporarily converted space in downtown Brooklyn, including the YMCA, the Edison Building, and the former *Brooklyn Eagle* newspaper building. These were the years when William Zeckendorf, who was arguably the greatest real estate developer of mid-century America, came into his own. His corporate power gave legitimacy to the University. He became a beacon attracting others to join the Board of Trustees. His contact list and leverage made it possible for the University to borrow money, to gain visibility, and to win respectability. He took enormous pride in meeting the challenges of this rapid expansion. In sum, he made LIU a "hot" philanthropy in a way that never happened before or since.

Zeckendorf, America's master builder, changed the post-war urban landscape profoundly, especially in New York City. Writing in 1970 in his autobiography, *Zeckendorf* (a book that deals almost exclusively with his career as a real estate developer), he noted that his firm, Webb & Knapp, "had learned how to create projects that mesh with the surrounding city. In our UN deal, at 1407 Broadway, at 112 West Thirty-Fourth Street, in Denver and in Montreal we had foreseen what would happen when…key parts of a city would act upon each other in new ways." In Cincinnati, Cleveland, Washington, Hartford, Los Angeles, St. Louis, Montreal, New Orleans and a host of other metropolises, Webb & Knapp, with I.M. Pei as its in-house architect, created the modern urban reality of America. A difficult and demanding developer, he was a genius at getting projects begun and finished.

Kips Bay, Lincoln Towers, the United Nations, Sixth Avenue, and Roosevelt Field -the first covered Mall in America- were either projects that Webb & Knapp assembled or built. He assembled the land where the Time-Life building was erected. Webb & Knapp became the largest owner of hotel properties, including in New York alone, the Astor, Commodore, Manhattan, Taft, Drake and Chatham. Along the way it also owned the St. Regis and the Gotham (now the Peninsula). In Chicago it was the Ambassador East and West plus the Sherman. And so the list goes on and on.

A brilliant negotiator with the capacity to dream bigger than anyone else, Zeckendorf moved in a rarified environment with the very highest echelons of bankers and corporate executives. He knew the titans and was their equal in wealth and influence. He borrowed vast sums, wheeled and dealt on every project, leveraged his holdings to the hilt and had a larger-than-life personality. And he bestowed upon Long Island University the glow of his own success. He reached the zenith of his influence in the early sixties, before Webb & Knapp - always over extended - crashed in a shattering bankruptcy. But, during the mid 50s to the late 60s, Zeckendorf made the University his philanthropic alter ego; both were brash upstarts, ambitious newcomers whose over-sized dreams seemed to be coming true. He started with Metcalfe and hired Conolly when Metcalfe died. And he shared with both the conviction that together they would move Long Island University into the top tier of American higher education by demonstrating that in post-war America the common man and woman would end an elite stranglehold on higher education. Everything seemed possible during those seven "fat years" of the Conolly presidency. Like Icarus, to Zeckendorf the sun seemed truly to be the limit.

During those boom years, Zeckendorf assembled, purchased or deeded what became the Brooklyn campus, called University Center for much of this period; the C.W. Post campus, purchased from Marjorie Merriweather Post; the Southampton Campus; and 100 acres for the Zeckendorf College of Science in Brookhaven, a gift technically made by his Roosevelt Field Associates. Zeckendorf was a no nonsense doer. When he was flush, he gave very generously. He advised the Administration (and often his team at Webb & Knapp took the lead) in negotiating and securing construction and development loans for each campus. His leverage and power with the construction trades won favorable contracts from general contractors and their subs, and he used his extraordinary rolodex to curry favor and secure approvals from government agencies at all levels.

William Zeckendorf Sr. speaking at the annual Charter Day dinner.

Well before Conolly was hired, Zeckendorf led the University in the acquisition of the Brooklyn campus at 385 Flatbush Avenue Extension, including the iconic Brooklyn Paramount, one of the great movie palaces of the 1920's. For the next twelve years the Paramount remained as a commercial theater, first as a movie emporium and subsequently as New York's great rock 'n' roll venue. Unlike St.

PART I - REALITIES AND DREAMS

Johns and Adelphi Universities, both of which were founded in Brooklyn but moved further east, Zeckendorf's decisions anchored Long Island University in the heart of downtown Brooklyn.

As Chairman of the Board, Zeckendorf led the University through a complex labyrinth created by the Federal Housing Act of 1949 which under Title I, offered municipalities the opportunity to acquire slum land and then allowing not-for-profit institutions to purchase some of that land for institutional growth. A close friend of Robert Moses, Zeckendorf wrote that "Robert Moses was possibly the only man in America who, when Title I came, was ready." The University was given the chance to buy seven and a half acres out of a twenty-acre parcel condemned for slum clearance. In his autobiography he wrote, "As soon as the new law was passed, he [Moses] and I put it to work rehabilitating one of the worst parts of Brooklyn. I was Chairman of the Board of Trustees of Long Island University, then a diminutive and unaccredited school temporarily settled in a loft building in Brooklyn. Our University, then catering largely to ex-GIs, desperately needed an in-town campus plus more buildings. I donated the necessary extra funds to sponsor a Title I redevelopment project… With Moses' help and guidance, we cleaned out acres of asphalt jungle to put up…the beginnings of a Brooklyn campus for the University. He went on to note that "My 'donation' to LIU was a further means of inducing recently retired Admiral Connally [sic] to take over the school and begin the task of making it into a great University."

Zeckendorf personally gave a half million dollars so that this prime land could become LIU's urban campus. Within a few years the University owned an additional cluster of mid-rise, adjacent buildings, originally constructed for all manner of commerce and manufacturing -- bowling alleys, car dealerships, knitting and needle manufacturing plants to cite just a few. And out of this hodge-podge of ill suited property, a gritty oasis of learning was established, one that captured the love and allegiance of alumni and alumnae to their alma mater.

Metcalfe and Zeckendorf clearly also understood that returning veterans, including those that came to LIU for a degree, increasingly had the capacity through low cost mortgages to move out of the city eastward into Levittown and other planned communities rapidly replacing the open fields of Nassau. Moreover, they had the urge to follow the suburban dream into a new life style, one that would profoundly change the politics, the educational patterns, and the life style of a postwar America.

Metcalfe spent many weekends driving around Nassau in order to find the right estate for Long Island University's dream of educating the children of these new suburbanites. There were many pre-war estates then on the market. The depression and war had ended the Gatsby era of "Gold Coast" lavishness. Real estate taxes and escalating costs of household and estate labor made sustaining these mansions prohibitive even for the nation's wealthiest families. The Gilded Age was but a memory. Suburban living became central to the American Dream, a tangible marker of middle class economic upward mobility. Wealthy families either sold their estates to real estate developers or searched for not-for-profit organizations that could operate such properties without a tax burden. And Metcalfe realized that ideal campus sites were to be found somewhere on "the Gold Coast."

President Metcalfe and Dean Mildred Laxtin Barrit de Barrit
accepting a check following a student fundraising event.

As it turned out, finding an ideal property proved to be the easy task; winning village approval to put a University on that site proved to be a far more complex burden. In 1947, the University signed a contract to purchase the 123-acre estate of Marjorie Merriweather Post (the property was also known as the Davies Estate because she had remarried, for the third time, Roosevelt's wartime Ambassador to Russia). Mrs. Post was one of the richest women of her day. She was the sole heir to a vast cereal fortune, and, as Chairwoman of the Board, built her business brilliantly, gambling successfully on Clarence Birdseye's new technique of quick freezing food and on marketing a range of dry food products such as Jello. All this was in addition to the established line of packaged breakfast cereals and its coffee alternative, Postum.

Her first marriage took her to an estate in Greenwich. When she married E. F. Hutton, the son of the famous Wall Street broker, the two of them built a Tudor style estate in Brookville. This was but one of her several estates, including a 53 room mansion on 92nd Street and Fifth Avenue, a Palm Beach home named Mar-A-Lago, because it commanded spectacular views from the living room of both the Atlantic Ocean and the Intracoastal Waterway, an Adirondack lodge named Top Ridge, the biggest sailing yacht in the world, the *Sea Cloud,* as well as this Nassau property. The Brookville estate actually had two principal residences forming an architectur- ally integrated cluster-the bigger property had 59 rooms and the smaller, 37. One was for her daughter from her first marriage (who also had a daughter) and the bigger house was for herself, E. F. Hutton and their one child together, the actress, Dina Merrill. There were approximately sixty in help to attend to these two small nuclear families. There were magnificent formal gardens, stables, and a racetrack on site.

After Post and Hutton got divorced, the grand estate stood virtually unused. Marjo- rie Post remarried, moved to Washington and served with her husband in Moscow. When Metcalfe first saw this property, he realized that a new, smallish liberal arts college could move in without initially being required to undertake a great deal of construction. Zeckendorf concurred. But the "Burghers of Brookville" were neither impressed by Zeckendorf's wealth and influence in Manhattan real estate circles, nor Metcalfe's dream of a bucolic, small liberal arts college. The home- owners feared the arrival of Long Island University would be disruptive, noisy and a direct challenge to the privacy of their existing world. They were worried that a working-class University would damage property values and put too many cars on the roads. Most of those youngsters did not pay taxes and most inevitably, would use village services without paying for them. And, if resident students ever gained the right to vote, they would transform the village and its power structure completely.

The Post estate was technically situated in the Township of Oyster Bay. Town ordinance permitted the establishment of "schools" but was silent about "colleges or universities." Operating on the tried and true strategy of "deny and delay," an activist group of local residents fought vigorously against the University's effort to win a variance from Oyster Bay. When the University did gain that variance, a local group of homeowners challenged successfully in court that the variance to the University had been improperly awarded. The University appealed that deci- sion only to encounter a second obstacle: the citizen's group managed to get the Post estate moved on the Nassau County property map out of Oyster Bay and into the jurisdiction of the Village of Brookville. In that circumscribed venue, the very wealthy existing homeowners could more easily control local zoning ordinances.

The litigation went on for five years. The strategy of the homeowners was to make the purchase so costly in time and money that the University would seek another property elsewhere. In part to establish an educational foothold in Nassau and in part to make its commitment to this project tangible, the University countered by renting high school classrooms in both Oyster Bay and Hicksville, two working class communities, in order to open both daytime and evening extension programs. And when the Post estate property was formally annexed into the Village of Brookville in 1952, the University hurriedly moved its Hicksville students onto the Post property in order to establish its right to offer instruction there. In October 1953, an appellate court ruled that the University did have a right to develop the Brookville property for educational purposes. It further ruled that the annexation of the estate into the Village of Brookville could not be interpreted as a device to prevent the college from opening its doors on Northern Boulevard. By this time the existing student body from its two initiatives in Hicksville and Oyster Bay had declined from 22-day students in 1952 to none by 1953, and from 307 evening students to 55.

An ill President Metcalfe had written an open letter to the community just prior to the October 16,1952, zoning variance meeting in front of the Village Board. He wrote "We do not want to come into any community where the majority of the residents do not want a University. We seek neither to invade nor intrude." But Metcalfe went on, "Nor do we intend to be thwarted by a vocal minority who do not represent the prevailing view of the community." In this appeal for support from the village community, Metcalfe further wrote, "It is not true that the student body now under instruction in Brooklyn will be moved 'en masse' to Oyster Bay." It would be impossible to know if any students from Brooklyn would choose to come to the Oyster Bay campus. Conceding that a few might, he went on that "we do not expect that any substantial number would come out here. We are planning the University for Long Island."

He asserted that the student body would come chiefly from Nassau, Suffolk and perhaps Queens. Asking rhetorically if the University would hurt property values, he answered himself that "We see no reason why we cannot operate a University on the former Davies Estate without hurting any of our neighbors. We do not see how we can impair the value of any large estate in the area." And he maintained that the owners of those large estates "are well protected in the quiet enjoyment of their properties by their own acreage." Although the point may have been self evidently true, it rankled the neighbors.

The hidden issues were both the encroachment of the inner city upon the bucolic splendor of Nassau and the ethnicity, social class and religion of the prospective students....The preponderance of the enrolled students came from Hicksville and Oyster Bay, the children of working-class families who, socio-economically and ethnically, were from modestly educated parents interchangeable with these students from Brooklyn and Queens. If LIU had been like Dartmouth, the response would probably have been very different. But these potential students were the children of the domestics and the gardeners who once tended the estates or were the recent transplants who settled in communities like Levittown. They were pioneers in a democratizing transformation of American higher education. As late as the mid-60s, the issue for Long Island was not linked to race as much as ethnicity and religion. The student body at Brooklyn was then overwhelmingly white - Jews, Italians, and Irish - as was Brooklyn itself.

The long, convoluted, very ugly legal fight between the University and the home-owners soured Mrs. Post on her decision to sell to a University. She was suddenly seen as a traitor by her former neighbors and country club friends, as someone who "sold out," even though she was among the richest of the rich. Metcalfe had first written to her on February 26, 1947, seeking to discuss the sale of her Long Island Estate. In that letter, he noted that "Long Island University is the only University on Long Island and as the University has been planning to move outside the borough of Brooklyn, it is the logical educational institution to utilize the property and at the same time mutually agree, if desired, that the farm and greenhouses be reserved for their present uses."

Key aides and lawyers to Mrs. Post negotiated this sale over the next months, but no one on her side had anticipated the long delays that actually ensued or the antipathy toward her personally, that such a sale engendered. Her real estate broker, De Beaumont Mott, tried to resell her estate and Marjorie Post wrote him on March 23, 1949, "I have been carrying along with the University and understand that the last court decision will be handed down in May. If it should go against the University, I would be glad to sell the Roslyn [Brookville] property. Frankly, I am sorry I did not close the deal you had lined up before. The other business has been such a long drawn out and confused affair."

To help counter the risk that the property would be sold out from under LIU, the University Board violated a fundamental tenet of fundraising. At the strong urging of one of the University's Trustees, Grover A. Whalen, the famed unofficial protocol official of the City of New York dating back to Jimmy Walker, whose wife was a close friend of Marjorie Post, the University embraced Whalen's recommendation that the future campus be named for Mrs. Post's father, Charles W. Post. This appears to have been done in order to keep her from relisting the property. It worked. There was also a hope that, in the future, the University would receive a major donation in exchange for granting flattering immortality to the family. But a monumental benefaction was probably always nothing but wishful thinking.

Marjorie Post clearly saw this real estate sale as a business transaction. To be sure, Whalen was a shrewd observer of people. The naming of that new campus in her dad's name had to be impactful on her, but it is highly unlikely that she ever contemplated donating a transformative gift. That house and the grounds were a shared, joyful project of Hutton and Post; it was a tangible link to an earlier and happier time in her life, but one that ended in divorce. Moreover, she had already moved to Washington, and her commitment in later years to transforming her Washington estate, Hillwood, into a museum for her art collection became of prime importance

54

to her. When the University decided to fire her most ardent courtier, Chancellor R. Gordon Hoxie, in 1968, she was given the golden opportunity to turn her back on a campus that carried her parents' names. By 1972, it had become clear that she had no ambivalence in doing just that.

It is standard fundraising practice always to get the gift secured legally before a designation is awarded. Trinity College in Durham, North Carolina, changed its name to Duke University, but with a clear and binding commitment from the Duke family that it would support this new venture through endowment, annual support, and leadership. Long Island University, on the other hand, was so hungry for the property as a campus site in Nassau that it traded away up front its most precious philanthropic chip. But the on-going Quixotic pursuit for a benefaction had more to do with the internal politics of the University than the relationship with Mrs. Post. She did over the years eventually donate about one million dollars, still a very generous sum, but a tiny fraction of what it would have taken elsewhere to secure a naming gift for a campus.

The University bought the adjacent land in subsequent tranches from the E. F. Hutton estate, from his brother's neighboring property and from others. It paid cash for each, ultimately assembling 307 acres. The entire assemblage was financed through student tuitions paying down New York State Dormitory Authority bonds or bank mortgages. For many years the campus flourished, but never had the financial underpinning required to be free of tuition dependency. In a letter of January 10, 1947, to Mrs. Davies (Mrs. Post), her lawyer, negotiating with President Metcalfe wrote, "Mr. Metcalf(sic) seems to feel that, for sentimental reasons, you would prefer to make a more reasonable price to the University than you would to an ordinary purchaser. The University, Mr. Metcalf(sic) informs me, has plenty of money as they have been helped by New York State and also have a surplus of property in Brooklyn which they expect to dispose of." There is a handwritten note on this particular letter indicating that Mrs. Post placed the "Roslyn" (Brookville) properties on the market at $400,000. Whatevet the business deal, both campuses had dynamic students to teach.

The returning veterans were mature men who had experienced the horrors of combat. Many had seen death up close and witnessed the suffering that total war wreaks. For them the return to the University with its opportunity to study was a golden opportunity. They had the maturity to value what they were learning. They also had the wisdom to see that their college degree could be used as a passport to a new and higher trajectory in their lives. Their quality as students was even more important than their sheer numbers. For faculty, their curiosity and life experience made them a delight in class. These mature students lifted morale and gave a seriousness of purpose to faculty, suffusing LIU and thousands of other universities with a sense of mission. Administrators and staff took pride in their tasks and those years were pedagogically golden, creating a learning community of a very special sort.

But by 1949-50, the flow of returning GIs was down to a trickle. LIU's fortunes, like the tides, rose and fell with enrollment and its concomitant tuition revenue. Early on, the University had been nimble and entrepreneurial. It marketed itself skillfully to those ex GIs, delivering to them a valuable, usually professional degree, in two-and-a-half or three years. But, as the size of the military contracted dramatically and the World War II vets graduated, enrollment plummeted. Applications from recent high school graduates held constant and the number of women applying increased. The war had altered the self-image of women and in many families both mothers and daughters felt empowered by war work experiences. Going to college was a logical next step toward gender equity, although such a term was still decades away. But these shifts in the social fabric of the nation were not rapid enough to replace the vanishing GIs. The University was overstaffed and once again at risk.

President Metcalfe became seriously ill with cancer in May, 1951. He passed away nine months later, on February 22, 1952. He was a beloved figure who had taken the institution through depression and war. And he cared about the students as individual men and women, often giving hard-pressed students tuition money from his own pocket. He was well respected and experienced, and his illness and death created a leadership vacuum at a very bad time. Under Metcalfe, the University still operated virtually without an administrative cadre. There was a Dean of Women, a director of students, a bursar, a registrar and a tiny staff, including Clair Bee, reporting to a President who served as his own academic Dean.

Acting President, William M. Hudson.

William M. Hudson was for years the Chairman of Economics Department. When Robert Witford, the then director of student life, retired, Metcalfe had promoted Hudson to that position. Upon Metcalfe's death, the still very small LIU Board appointed Hudson to be the Acting President. Hudson was a Yale alumnus and a graduate of Brooklyn Law School. While he was apparently a popular figure and a good lecturer, he lacked real experience in academic administration. Over the immediate post-war years, the University had become a big enough institution to attract the attention of the Department of Education of the State of New York. Through site visits and a careful examination of LIU's own published material, the department concluded that LIU was sloppily managed and lacked an appropriate infrastructure. It demanded the University sharply improve quality control.

The Board of Regents had long held regulatory and statutory authority to ensure that every college and university would meet its obligations both to its own enrolled students and to the general standards set by the Board of Regents. Higher education, especially in New York, where a Hamiltonian vision of centralized state oversight has long existed, was a highly regulated industry. There are, in fact, two external agencies both empowered to enforce compliance: The Board of Regents overseeing the large, bureaucratic, Department of Education and the Middle States Commission of Colleges and Schools, a regional, peer-driven accrediting body. In very different ways both have always had the authority to demand that institutions meet a threshold of excellence; both could penalize any institution that failed to meet the norms established.

Long Island University had "grow'd like Topsy" during the immediate post-war years. Its location was close to virtually every subway line, and it offered unique opportunity for veterans of the GI Bill. LIU, intuitively understanding the institutional benefit of such federal dollars, rushed forward. But, since it had operated for decades bankrupt or virtually so, the University underestimated both the need and the mandated obligation to develop adequate administrative controls. It remained understaffed and insensitive to establishing a bureaucratic culture. In a very Brooklyn way, it did not embrace the obligation of adherence to rules and regulations in order to manage its educational enterprise. From the state's vantage point, LIU was grossly failing to meet its obligations to its students and to professional standards.

On April 14, 1952, Hudson received a letter from the Associate Commissioner of Higher Education, Ewald B. Nyquist, informing him that LIU was being granted only a one-year provisional registration award. Nyquist wrote that he could not "find it in my conscience to grant a longer one in view of the deficiencies found and discussed with you." LIU had to make substantial progress by the following January to stay in business. He noted that "much needs to be done and can only be done with ample support from all who are concerned with the college." He sent a copy of this letter to the Chairman of the Board of Trustees, William Zeckendorf, Sr., "pointing out the seriousness of these matters." He then listed some sixteen weak spots that had to be addressed and soon.

Nyquist noted, *inter alia,* that "The sooner all practicable and appropriate democratic forms of faculty self-government and faculty participation in the affairs of the institution have been implemented, the better." He continued, the University "catalog [Bulletin] is subject to a great deal of criticism." Bulletins are legally binding publications; they serve as a contract between a student and the institution, committing the college to deliver to the student what is stated within. Nyquist wrote that LIU's catalog was "largely inadequate; for instance, it contains a good deal of padding."

PART I - REALITIES AND DREAMS

A faculty handbook and Statutes for the regulation of the University were needed "without question." Nyquist thought that the University was teaching too many graduate courses and observed, in passing, that "many of the programs in education are not formally approved by us." With irritation he noted that there were two references in the current Bulletin to the fact that the University "is fully approved by the State Education Department and that courses in teaching are accredited by the Department." His observation was that "The first is not true and the second is only partially true."

The litany of shortcomings continued with an observation that, "The faculty salary scale is too low. What is more, I cannot find that you have a clear policy in this regard." He made the obvious point that a "clear policy on tenure and promotion must be developed." Nyquist lamented that there was no retirement system in effect for faculty or administration. "Certainly you are unselective in admissions" was point 9. There was "no formalized testing program in effect before you admit students": point 10. "Your grading practice is generous and not at all realistic," given the virtual open enrollment and lack of selectivity: point 12. Further teaching loads were excessive and the library was inadequate. Funding for such essential needs was far too low. And in a postscript, Nyquist indicated that he would have to reschedule a visit to "The Oyster Bay and the Hicksville centers." Those programs would need separate registrations.

In a letter to William Zeckendorf on the same date, Nyquist began: "I regret to say that the deficiencies noted during this visit, the number and seriousness of them, leave me no alternative but to write to you as Chairman of the Board of Trustees..." With candor rarely found in bureaucratic letters, he went on, "Frankly, I am shocked at some of the observations I made....It is incomprehensible to me, if my figures are correct, why for a period of two years or more a total of two and a half million dollars in cash was deposited in banks uninvested; why, for at least the past year and at the present time, one million dollars in cash is uninvested."

Nyquist then turned his attention to LIU's efforts to open a campus in Nassau County. He wrote, "There is no reason why Long Island University, at this state of its development, should be operating branches on Long Island. These branches constitute a drain on the present resources and will for some time to come." He commented that neither programming nor standards could be maintained at the present time or for the foreseeable future. "Again, students in Brooklyn are not receiving in benefit a fair share of their tuition payments, since disproportionately, it costs more to educate a student on Long Island than one in Brooklyn." Finally, sale of Long Island University property on Long Island "should net the institution a not inconsiderable profit, (which you should know better than I)...which will do much to add to needed resources for expansion in Brooklyn...."

This litany told Zeckendorf in no uncertain terms that the future of LIU was in serious jeopardy. There was little bureaucratic obfuscation in this or the subsequent letters. Metcalfe's dream of expanding into Nassau was seen as highly risky and beyond the capacity of Long Island University to accomplish. Nyquist made it clear that the Board of Trustees was failing to provide appropriate supervision. The Board, in his view, needed to be doubled in order "to discharge its responsibilities fully and with facility." He noted "ironically" that a newly drawn organizational chart had more Trustee committees than it had members," and he referred to a good deal of evidence indicating that "the Board has not always assumed its obligations to the institution in the past." Nyquist told Zeckendorf that it would be his "hope" that the University "appoints a permanent President with full power as soon as possible, in view of the circumstances...."

The entire strategy, so dear to Metcalfe's heart, of expanding out into Nassau, was repudiated by the state's top higher education officers. The Nassau campus was seen as a drain of scant resources that had to limit reinvestment in Brooklyn. The Board was excoriated for its failure to manage the institution prudently. Zeckendorf was clearly held responsible, and he could not have taken such a barrage of criticism happily. As the letters of June 16th, June 17th, and January 30th, 1953, make clear, the State of New York was placing Long Island University on the shortest of leashes. A new President was a *sine qua non*.

Judged against virtually every measure of quality control, the Department of Education in Albany had found LIU deficient. These letters were scathing and clearly demanded that Zeckendorf focus intensively if LIU were to survive. On June 16, 1952, Nyquist again wrote to Hudson, as promised, about the educational efforts in Nassau. While accepting that credits earned by students at the Hicksville and Oyster Bay branches would be accepted, he noted "such an arrangement on our part does not mean that the courses of study conducted at the Hicksville and Oyster Bay branches have gained complete recognition from this department." He also made clear that "The Hicksville branch will be abandoned entirely and that future registrations will be confined to the Oyster Bay branch," although students could not be enrolled in Hicksville or Oyster Bay after June 10, 1952, unless the pending litigation between the University and the Village of Brookville had been completed favorably for the University and formal accreditation had been granted by the Middle States Association. On the following day, he again wrote Hudson concerning grading practices at the Brooklyn site. It turned out that grading practices at the new campuses in Nassau were more generous than in Brooklyn.

Nyquist met with members of the Board of Trustees to underscore the seriousness of the situation and, in particular, Zeckendorf and John McGrath. On November 3, 1952, Zeckendorf, as President of the Board of Trustees, formally wrote back to Nyquist confirming that LIU would not expand its Nassau operations following Nyquist's demand, and, on January 30, 1953, Nyquist again wrote to Hudson telling him that registration would continue to be restricted "during this time when

Long Island University is in a constant state of flux." Those restrictions were applied both to Brookville and other extension sites as well as Brooklyn. Nyquist returned to his assertion that "serious consideration must be given to the closing down of your operation in Brookville in view of the great cost to the institution." He also urged that LIU "give serious consideration to the abolition of the graduate school program," with the proviso that if the Board not deem it "in the best interests of the institution to abolish the graduate programs at this time, then I have no alternative but to suggest that a full-time director of the graduate school program be employed at once." He urged the University to draft statutes that would define work responsibility.

To Zeckendorf, Nyquist continued to argue for "some change in your position about Brookville. Financially the Institution is unable to continue the program there as it is conducted at the present time," observing that sharp reductions were mandated. "Drastic measures must be taken to preserve as much as possible of the present funds" Nyquist demanded. On the search for a new President, Nyquist observed, "I am not sure since I saw you last what developments have taken place with the selection of a President of Long Island University, but I can assure you that as each day passes the matter becomes more acute in seriousness." As if his import was not already clear enough, he directed limitation of "the registration of your courses of instruction with the State Education Department for a period of one year and I have, in addition, limited the approval of your courses under public law 550 [concerning GI benefits] for a period expiring October 1st of this year...."

.... the problem of administering at one time two educational operations with such differing objectives and student bodies will not be an easy one.

Claude E. Puffer, Chair of the 1955 Middle States Visiting Committee

Chapter Three

Admiral Richard Lansing Conolly

Long Island University was obviously at dire risk. The State rarely closes any university. Bureaucrats in Albany traditionally would seek any alternative if at all possible. But, it is impossible to read the Nyquist's litany without understanding how exposed the University was at the end of Hudson's brief tenure as Acting President. The reader already knows that the University managed to survive and to flourish. The real question, therefore, is why did Richard Lansing Conolly choose to take this job when, according to his daughter, Ann Conolly Hughes, he had been offered the Presidency of a steel company as an alternate career option when he had retired from the Navy. Conolly was obviously fully aware of the damage to LIU's reputation resulting from the basketball scandal of 1951. Clair Bee had put LIU on the map through the sports pages; in 1951 the dream became a nightmare. He also had to know about the Nyquist letters and the severe restrictions placed upon the University by the Board of Regents. Why did he take the job?

Conolly became a war hero because he was willing to take big risks. He was a man of action who was at his best when his adrenaline was flowing. He was not ready to retreat to the country club comfort of a corporate presidency and eighteen holes of golf on the weekend. His final tour of duty had been as President of the Naval War College. He had on several previous tours taught physics and naval architecture at Annapolis or at the War College. He was truly interested in education and in molding the lives of the young, both as a professor and as a line officer at sea. And, not surprisingly, he was a cold warrior, someone who was convinced that American higher education was critical to defeating global communism by producing a skilled work force that could out-produce and out-innovate those within the Russian bloc.

William Zeckendorf's charisma and the power of his personality must have played an important role in attracting Conolly. He was one of the great salesmen of his day, a dynamic, imaginative mogul who could be a true partner, ally and friend. James Hester, who became Conolly's heir apparent in the late 1950's, wrote in

61

his unpublished memoir that "William Zeckendorf [was] a large bear of a man, famous, handsome, affable, exuding energy and an aura of wealth and power.... Many LIU board meetings and fund-raising events were held at those [Webb & Knapp's] offices. One board meeting was held while the Chairman was having a haircut and manicure in the center of the room. He was covered in a white sheet, with his hands stretched out before him to the manicure table. The room was rather dark, but was brightly lighted by down-lights on the ceiling. The rest of us were seated around the perimeter of the room in a series of alcoves, each illuminated by a down light. It was like a scene in an opera of a gathering of knights or priests around their leader. Zeckendorf conducted the business of the meeting without batting an eye."

Conolly had a chest full of medals for bravery dating back to World War I. Thus, the presidency of LIU seemed to be a new type of opportunity, one that redefined the meaning of risk. The excitement and vibrancy of New York must have appealed to both the Admiral and Helen, his wife. New York was asserting itself as the capital of the world, and the Conollys would have the status and wealth to enjoy this metropolis. And finally, there was this challenge of achieving a turn-around, a chance for a different kind of victory than one at sea. Together with Zeckendorf, he could accomplish something truly important.

Whatever the reason or reasons, Conolly's decision changed the University's trajectory dramatically, at least for the years he held the job and as long as his glow and America's fortunes continued to project an optimistic future. The role of an individual in history provides a fascinating focus for historiography. What would have happened if his health had held up and he had chosen to hold the job longer? Would he have been more adept at changing with the times than those who followed him? Could anyone have insulated LIU from the turmoil that rocked America and changed virtually every other university so profoundly? How important are those external dynamics to this story of one University struggling to find its way?

Such questions are, of course, teasers. The only thing that really matters is the story that actually happened. Between the censuring letters from Nyquist to the tragic death of Admiral Conolly off Idlewild's runway, LIU had nearly a decade to remember, a triumph of growth and success. But eventually many of the warnings contained in Nyquist's letters came to pass. Scold though Nyquist was, he clearly saw the weak points in the University's structure, revealing problems that Conolly's successes obscured but did not resolve. Indeed, as the reader will see, Conolly was well aware of some of the most troubling contradictions that ultimately created internecine warfare within the University and hobbled it in its dream to achieve national status.

In an early, open letter to the alumni of Long Island University, Conolly wrote: "It is extremely gratifying for me now to occupy a position that affords such a stimulating challenge and I want you to know I am in this 'for keeps.'" He noted: "During the years since the close of World War II the University had first a period of great and rapid expansion accompanied by relative financial prosperity, followed by a period of contraction in size, depletion of reserves and current financial insecurity." Speaking directly to the six thousand living alums of the University at the time, he asserted that "We face the need to marshal all forces and to budget our efforts and resources so that we can again 'make ends meet.'" He felt that the New Year, 1954, would be especially significant because it marked his jumping off point as President. He asked the alums to join him in what he called "Operation Shirt Sleeves", commenting that his decision to serve as President was "no idle whim." He went on to speak of the importance of higher education and of the University in American society. In view of the "pressure of our times," Conolly felt that Long Island University's enrollment of students must be stepped up "both in quantity and in quality." He ended this early document by inviting alums to write to him their ideas concerning "the development of Long Island University."

On January 6, 1954, he got a response from one alumna, Harriett Schlussler Starr, urging him to bring back basketball. She wrote "now I know the subject has been 'hush-hush' and a lot of faces turn deep purple when the word is even mentioned." But she went on to note that, "there comes a time when the hurt is a little bit less and when faces just become pale pink." She urged the restoration of big time basketball because it "brought in the money and brought in the students back in the old days" so she proposed to Conolly that "when we remember the boys that 'sold out' we should also remember the boys who brought honor to their school." She urged Conolly to "Bring Back Basketball" saying, "you will have taken the first step towards a victorious Operation Shirtsleeves."

Half a year later, on August 5, 1954, Conolly received a letter from Mildred Loxtin Barritt de Barritt, the Dean of Women, who, in accepting a renewal of her contract, celebrated the Admiral, offering a paean of praise for his ability to restore pride and loyalty. She said, "Wonders have been accomplished since you assumed the presidency last November." Citing the past low morale of a confused organization, she commented that the University "has become a whole different place." This beloved, long time employee asserted that "there has come to it [LIU] a leadership that is indomitable, and optimism and courage that is vitalizing the whole structure."

This very disciplined and formal woman recounted a recent meeting she had had with an LIU student, who came to her to make arrangements for a fraternity dance the following year. The young man had just come from a student meeting at NYU where, apparently, they had been "riding him - an old habit over there." He looked up with "fire in his eye, thumped the desk: 'I told 'em off! I told 'em things were different now...we got a man with guts (thump)...we got a fighter...we're going places!' (Thump, thump)." Dean de Barritt observed, "It had all the quality of a football cheer!" She wrote that "the students are proud -- and it's a good thing to be able to be proud." She concluded: "I am proud, myself, Admiral Conolly, and glad to be serving under and with you - for that's the way you make people feel." James Hester described her as " a refined and amusing English woman who had a very civilizing influence on generations of students."

Richard Conolly was not a big man physically, but he was extraordinarily charismatic, someone who proved again and again that he could lead his sailors into "harm's way" with courage and humanity. At LIU he had that rare gift to radiate confidence and a sense of excitement. Mildred Loxtin Barritt de Barritt was not the gushing type but in this letter she sounded more like a teenage bobby-soxer than a Dean of Women. Conolly exuded confidence - in himself, in the people around him, and in the mission of the University. It had an electrifying impact on the institution.

He was equally a product of the military. He had spent his entire career honoring the chain of command. The license of the academy where faculty felt free to speak on any subject to anybody at any time was antithetical to his hierarchical universe as a career officer in the United States Navy. The notion of issuing and following an order meant something self-evidently different to Conolly than to the administrators and faculty of the University. Every document he signed had under his name first "Admiral, U.S.N.(Ret.)" and then, on the next line, "President, Long Island University." On August 1,1955, his office issued a "Precedence of Officers of the University," a protocol ranking that placed senior administrators in a hierarchy that defined who was superior in authority and who was not.

He was obviously first. The Dean of the Brooklyn College of Pharmacy was second (as its Operating Chief Executive); the Dean of C.W. Post College was third; the Vice President for University Development and Provost of the Brooklyn Center was fourth; followed by the several Deans, including the Dean of University Women, the Director of the University Library, the Marshal of the University and so on down the line. It is interesting that he co-mingled academic positions and administrative ones. In his era, everyone seemed to accept his or her ranking, but after his death, there was a running battle for status in the institutional hierarchy, especially between those with University-wide responsibility and those on a campus. In later years every seeming slight was seen as intentional, and Conolly's reliance on strict protocol was remembered fondly.

He was also staunchly anti-communist, a cold warrior. He rigorously enforced a "loyalty oath" from every employee, including Dean de Barritt, and involved many of his military friends either on the Board or on staff. He would have been appalled by the anti-war movement of the students thet erupted a few years after his death and he would have been a hawk on intervention in Vietnam.

After the chaos of the Hudson interregnum, the Board, especially Zeckendorf, embraced Conolly's leadership style. He brought a military approach to a chaotic civilian institution. He demanded and got willing compliance. And he forged consensus on the mission of the University by taking charge. For the first time the University had a no-nonsense leader, and he was truly embraced as Savior, especially since his charisma softened his autocratic instincts.

Zeckendorf, in his own way equally charismatic, became an enthusiastic partner. These two men saw something in each other, and their friendship, respect and admiration for the other unleashed an extraordinary growth spurt for the University. When he chose to be, Zeckendorf, too, could be charming. While he was often a bully in business, using his power, smarts, and wealth to achieve Webb & Knapp's success, he reveled in his status as Chairman of the Board and the contacts that this philanthropic organization offered. A bon vivant, a great expert and lover of Burgundy wines, Zeckendorf enjoyed the men and women he got to know through his Chairmanship, especially when Conolly was moving the institution rapidly forward. Some partners and friends loved him, especially when he was making them money; others simply feared him. But as long as he and his firm were wildly successful, he commanded everyone's attention.

These two remarkable men became an extraordinary team; in new and exciting ways making Long Island University a college with a seemingly brilliant, dynamic future. In those same years Abram Sachar, the founding President of Brandeis University in 1948, formed a similar partnership with Larry Wien, his Chairman and a real estate mogul, a professional rival but good friend of Zeckendorf's. Wien and his business partner, Harry Helmsley, bought the Empire State building among many other properties. Zeckendorf was, during the same years, wheeling and dealing across the country and the world. Just as Sachar and Wien transformed Brandeis, Conolly and Zeckendorf saw their partnership as an opportunity to create a new Long Island University.

Zeckendorf clearly understood Trustees had an obligation to give generously. Like so many other real estate developers of that generation, he gave to gain influence, to establish ranking with his competitors and for status reasons. But he gave significantly and, by doing so, hoped to set an example for others. He donated five hundred thousand dollars so that Long Island University could leverage his gift through the federal Title I slum clearance program to assemble the Brooklyn campus. He also donated that money to encourage Conolly to take the job because he was an instinctively generous man.

Zeckendorf was very close to the remarkable Robert Moses, an American version of a Roman pro-consul who built massive infrastructural bridges, tunnels and housing in New York.

The Brooklyn Paramount in early 1949.

Zeckendorf convinced Moses that the first parcel to be cleared in downtown Brooklyn should be behind the movie palace, The Brooklyn Paramount, stretching back to the Raymond Street jail. That eight-acre parcel became the permanent home for Long Island University. Without this governmental authority, the University would probably still be haggling many decades later with the small land owners who held property on the site. In a letter from Conolly to Zeckendorf's son, William Jr., also a long-serving Trustee of the University, he wrote, "This will be our first construction project. We will need either Federal or State aid. Legislative provision is made by both to provide loans (100%) at favorable interest rates for dormitory and student union purposes." Through Webb & Knapp's in-house architect, I.M. Pei, the University retained its own architects for only $4,000. A deal like this simply could not happen without Zeckendorf reaching out to Moses and similar help all along the way.

Several years later, *The New York Times* wrote a muckraking series on the way Moses managed the Title I projects, including the Mitchell-Lama projects, the clearance for Lincoln Center and Fordham and, of course, the creation of the Brooklyn campus. Moses was both so enraged and so powerful that his rebuttal letter, three columns long, ran as its own news story on July 1, 1959. Moses mounted a rebuttal campaign that had friends threaten the newspaper with the loss of advertising revenue, including A&S in Brooklyn. Moses was very angry that the Admiral, among others, seemed to remain silent, writing to Robert Blum at A&S: "Incidentally I broke my neck to help Pratt and Long Island University in Brooklyn by way of Title One, and no one highly connected with them has raised a voice of protest or said a word of commendation. That goes also for New York University. I should be happy to return my honorary degrees to all three…"

Not surprisingly, a day later the Admiral wrote to the Editor in longhand a ringing defense that "the Fort Greene project in Brooklyn [was] the first instance of such participation by an educational institution….Without him [Moses] Title I in this city would have been a mockery." And, several days later, he wrote to Moses privately that he had no idea that you felt the lack of support from your Title I beneficiaries." Moses was still raging six months later when he wrote Sam Rosenman, the powerful lawyer in Manhattan: "Is it a fact that L.I.University [sic] made an award yesterday to Haddad of the Post for outstanding services in 'disclosing' Title One 'scandals?'" Moses, the autocrat, believed that the Board and the Admiral had the authority to make the selection of awardees by a faculty-dominated Polk Awards committee. He went on, "What the hell is in Bill Zeckendorf's mind? Who makes these insane decisions for a University whose entire future rests on what we were able to do for them under Title One?" And he frothed, "where does Zeckendorf get off as Chancellor and as the man who came to me begging for help?"

Three days later, Zeckendorf sent to Conolly Moses' screed, noting that, "In my opinion Bob is justified in making this complaint…." On March 1, 1960, Conolly wrote to Moses "with chagrin" that the journalism faculty had, indeed given, as Moses claimed, this Polk Award. He went on to "disclaim any influence or control over" the faculty, but the damage was done. Even a four star Admiral, like thousands of college Presidents before and since, now understood that universities are not like other organizations in society, especially hierarchical ones like the navy. Faculty autonomy rarely can be muzzled, even to please a proconsul like Moses. Both the press and all universities operate appropriately under a different set of rules, however embarrassing it might be for the University President or Chair of the Board.

The University had clearly established itself as an important institution in the City. It had important people on the Board already when Conolly arrived. Board membership in 1956 included John McGrath and Joseph O'Connor, who worked for Aetna Life Insurance and was, with McGrath, the second of the two court-appointed Trustees from the bankruptcy era. It was led by Zeckendorf and Conolly, and now also included: Benjamin Abrams, the President of Emerson Radio; Rear Admiral John Bergen, the CEO of Graham Paige and Conolly's wartime buddy; Franklin B. Lord of the law firm, Lord, Day & Lord; John (Tex) McCrary, the public relations guru; Franklin D. Roosevelt Jr.; Arthur T. Roth, the founding President of Franklin National Bank; George M. Shapiro, a Brooklyn alumnus and young partner in Proskauer, Rose, Goetz, William T. Van Atten, Vice President of Dun & Bradstreet and Grover A. Whalen, who was then Chairman of the Board of the cosmetics firm, Coty.

Governor Averill Harriman and Admiral Conolly attempting to manage a buffet plate on the stairs of Paramount in the late 1950s.

By the time of the contretemps with Moses, the Board had been further strengthened by Zeckendorf, the Admiral, or both. The new members included: David Baird, a very wealthy Wall Street investor; Clinton Blume, an important New York real estate broker; Carter Burgess, the President of American Machine and Foundry; Edward Neimuth, the President of National Magnesia and the Chairman of the Board of the Brooklyn College of Pharmacy; John H.G. Pell, a private investor on Wall Street and a scion of the great Rhode Island family; Sidney Solomon, President of Abraham & Straus, the premier Brooklyn Department store; General James A. Van Fleet, another war hero and the retired Commander of the United Nations forces in Korea; Carleton Palmer, the retired CEO of E. R.Squibb, another long-established Brooklyn pharmaceutical firm; Congressman Ogden Reid, the publisher of *The Herald Tribune* who had become a congressman from Westchester; Roger Stevens; a major force in the New York real estate world but best known as a producer of many of the great musicals on Broadway and Joshua Logan, the Broadway titan.

By then there were also Boards of Governors for both the Brooklyn campus and C.W. Post. The list of members in Brooklyn included a Vice President of Manufacturer's Trust; Max Kriendler of "21" Brands, the famed restaurateur; the President of the Bush Terminal on the Brooklyn waterfront; the Presidents of Piel Brothers (the beer producer), Mays Department Store, the East New York Savings Bank, the director of the Brooklyn Academy and the Executive Vice President of the Downtown Brooklyn Association. Only five of this group of 15 still lived in Brooklyn; the rest were either living in Manhattan or elsewhere on Long Island, a harbinger of the socio-economic changes overtaking the Borough.

At Post, this group was called the Executive Council of C.W. Post College. It embraced a Who's Who of the North Shore. The addresses were very local and very upscale; most were top executives who commuted to New York, especially the financial district. Many were old-line "blue bloods" whose clubs and homes were celebrated by F. Scott Fitzgerald in the pre-war era. Included as well were a few politicians or judges - A. Holly Patterson, the Nassau County Executive, for example. Such a body existed to recruit new Trustees, to use the old-boy network to enhance the reputation of the new campus and to loan a patina of value, even *gravitas*, to this new educational enterprise and the young men and women who enrolled.

For example, Emilio G. Collado was a Director and Vice President of Standard Oil, who graduated from MIT and Harvard with a Ph.D. He was a senior official in the State Department during the war and a Trustee of the Export-Import Bank then Executive Director of the International Bank for Reconstruction and Development. He was on the Board of Visitors at the Fletcher School of Law and Diplomacy at Tufts, a director of the Salzburg Seminar, and active at Harvard on several key committees. Carleton H Palmer, after retiring from E.R. Squibb, became a Director of the Long Island Railroad and Olin Mathieson Chemical Corp. Franz Schneider was a Director of Colonial Energy Shares and Canadian Export Gas.

On November 17, 1961, Conolly wrote to Benjamin Abrams, thanking him for his pledge at the last Board of Trustees meeting. He noted that "At last we are building up a fine Board of Trustees and increasingly, they make a very impressive group." He concluded this letter, "perhaps we are now becoming worthy of respect and attention on a wider base." The individuals listed above, and scores of others, should have provided Conolly and Zeckendorf with a critical mass of individuals who would become donors as well as loyal supporters. But they did not. Again and again in the decades that followed Trustees and alumni and alumnae of means failed to donate as generously as they could.

The contrast to Brandeis was striking. Both Universities were effectively start-ups. Brandeis was first founded in 1948. No two institutions are the same, and there were many obvious differences, including Abram Sachar's brilliant articulation of an American Jewish debt of gratitude to the secular society for permitting Jews to succeed in America by gaining access to higher education. The title of Sachar's autobiography was *A Host At Last.* He built a striking modern campus from scratch. He raised critically needed endowment and generated annually operating funds to hire a glittering faculty. He solicited scholarship money for students-in-need both locally and from around the world. He pushed Brandeis into the top tier of American universities.

PART I - REALITIES AND DREAMS

Letter from Trustee Benjamin Abrams to Admiral Conolly.

The point is not to raise invidious comparisons but rather to highlight the consequences of LIU's failure to achieve something similar, especially in the context of *Preface to the Future*, the very well articulated ten-year fundraising plan originally conceived by Conolly and actually executed by his successors, John H.G. Pell and R. Gordon Hoxie. It was imperative that the University cultivate and engage a new, generous lay leadership. That it never happened requires the closest scrutiny. It was self-evident that a tuition-driven school in Brooklyn, attracting a lower middle class student body, needed substantial external funding. But Conolly and his Development Vice Chancellor, Admiral Chester Wood, had spent their entire careers in the United States Navy where public funding paid for everything. Until the Vietnam War, there was also a flow of federal and state funds for new construction, especially via the Department of Housing and the New York State Dormitory Authority. This public funding initially masked the paucity of private giving.

Long Island University was an anomaly. It was a private institution that had many of the characteristics of a public one. It was an institution for upward mobility, for second chances, for newly arrived Americans and those born in the safety net to climb up and out. In its mission and student body, it was closer to CCNY than to Fordham. It obviously lacked a wealthy donor base of alumni. It wasn't easy to foster pride, especially since the basketball scandals of 1951. In short, to paraphrase Groucho Marx, most alumni would not support a school that would have had them as students.

Ironically, fundraising was also hobbled by the imputed wealth both of William Zeckendorf and Marjorie Merriweather Post. Others happily assumed that both these individuals were so wealthy that there was no need for them to donate. Zeckendorf lived like a pasha but he was massively over-leveraged and by the 60s, in chronic trouble financially. And Mrs. Post, flattered especially by R. Gordon Hoxie, still saw the sale of her house as a business transaction rather than as a great benefaction to memorialize her father.

The files reveal a series of awkward letters between Conolly and Mrs. Davies (Mrs. Post). In 1956, for example, she transferred 40 shares of Chrysler for the annual fund. The shares somehow were not acknowledged promptly, so Conolly wrote an awkward apology. In stilted language, he hoped "that you have enjoyed the winter in the South and that your new home in Washington has reached completion according to your desires." That house, Hillwood, became the central focus of her personal and Foundation's philanthropy, as she planned for it to become a museum holding her art collection after her death.

There is a flurry of correspondence over a check for $1,075, sent to fulfill a $20,000 pledge. A sloppy back office asked the Admiral to write for collection even though the check had been sent months earlier. Conolly had to write an embarrassed letter of apology, explaining that check had indeed arrived and been deposited. In August 1956, another $1,200 came in. There are a series of modest gifts, always to C. W. Post College, including a $700 gift one year and $1,000 of General Foods stock the next. The correspondence is pedestrian and the gifts small. In this ebb and flow there does not seem to be any passion. In later years, Hoxie, ever the courtier, did increase her engagement and philanthropy. But Conolly was either too reserved an individual to charm her into opening her checkbook or too convinced that such an effort would be futile.

There were still some important and wealthy merchants in Brooklyn, in particular those in leadership at A&S who had a strong interest in the campus, because its customers were the parental pool for LIU and because downtown Brooklyn institutions needed to be strengthened. On November 3, 1960, for example, Conolly wrote to Sidney Solomon, the President of A&S, seeking a leadership gift to name the proposed new library for the campus in memory of Walter Rothschild, the late CEO. He wrote, "I think you know how I felt about Walter. He was a good friend of the University, and a respected honorary alumnus." But by then A&S had its own substantial problems reflecting the decline of downtown Brooklyn as a major retail hub, and the corporation could not entertain seriously such a large capital gift.

PART I - REALITIES AND DREAMS

To cite an earlier example, November 15, 1955, Conolly wrote his Board, "You are aware, I know, that the primary aim of Long Island University is to cut across all social and economic divisions, so that all deserving students in our community may take advantage of what the University offers. This can only be maintained if generous financial assistance is available." He sent it with "The earnest hope that before this tax year ends, you may find it convenient to include Long Island University in your philanthropic contributions." This and later ones like it failed.

Development is a hard business anywhere and anytime. Failure is a constant. There are many noble causes and most people don't want to part with their money. The chorus of needy and deserving institutions has always been large, but it is striking how difficult it was for Conolly to get enthusiastic private donations, even from those who had the wherewithal and who were Trustees. One Trustee, David Baird, who had his own firm on Wall Street, made a pledge in the form of a note with a face value of $500,000. Baird had said that within a few years "this note should have a very real negotiable value." But Conolly was obliged to write to Baird, when Zeckendorf informed the Board that he did not believe the note to be prospectively of realizable value. In fact, the University never actually gained possession of the note or of a gift of $500,000 from Baird. Conolly sounded almost pleading when he wrote Baird that the University "so badly needs to further its development as a growing and important institution of higher education."

It is not surprising that Conolly turned to outside development counsel for help. At the Board meeting on April 19, 1961, Conolly brought in the legendary fund raising consultant, George A. Brakeley, to present a detailed plan costing the University $10,000 a month but with a private gift goal of $24,000,000 over a ten year period. Brakeley, according to Board Minutes, indicated that half of the first phase $8,800,000 would have to come from ten major gifts. A campaign organization was proposed with John P. McGrath as General Chairman and three honorary Co-Chairs, Judge Miles McDonald, General James Van Fleet and Mr. Sidney Solomon of A&S. Brakeley in his presentation wrote: "the Trustees of Long Island University, in accepting this bold plan, have lifted the sights of the University far beyond anything it has ever undertaken prior to this decision." The actual contract was signed on April 24th. Then something so totally derailed the campaign that it was terminated three weeks later, on May 15th. The record is silent, but the message was clear. The Board was not prepared individually or collectively to make the campaign a success.

Was the failure an administrative one? Did Brakeley offend or insult the Board somehow? Had Zeckendorf not over leveraged his real estate empire, and avoided taking Webb & Knapp into bankruptcy, would the outcome have been different? If Mrs. Post had made the University a major philanthropic priority with a transformative gift, would that have altered how other donors saw this philanthropy? Was the identification with Brooklyn a plus or a minus? To what degree did social class play a role? Or race? Or religion? Was the University's mission too close to that of a social service agency in attempting to uplift the disadvantaged and poor in society? Why did the University's ardent message to the community fall on such ungenerous ears? Many decades later, these questions remain unanswered.

But none of this was obvious in 1962, or even 1967, the year the University formally launched *Preface To The Future*, a fully articulated development campaign. There were multiple campuses to be built simultaneously. As long as there seemed to be an ample amount of low interest funding from both the Federal and State governments to accomplish this task, the contradiction between the dream and the reality could be obscured by both administration and lay leadership.

LIU was built on anticipated enrollments, not on the generosity of donors. The campuses were constructed on future student tuition revenue, which had to be used to service bond debt, stretching payment out over the decades. With great budgetary strain, this approach more or less worked, but the University could not afford to grant too great a tuition discount in the form of scholarship aid, nor could it escape the specter of deficits, if the parents of its students lacked the savings or cash flow required to fund their children when they went to college. The jerry-rigged reality of this structure was obvious to a state regulator like Ewald Nyquist or to Middle States site visitors, but the aura of Conolly's "can-do" optimism was too widely embraced to be blunted by external naysayers.

An attractive and permanent campus in downtown Brooklyn had been central to Ralph Jonas' initial dream. It was also an important statement to the Brooklyn campus constituencies that they were no longer to be wanderers, itinerants and gypsies trying to find a home. A real campus with dorms was critical to recruit and retain ever larger classes of tuition paying students. All the outside visitors had stressed these self-evident truths. Both Conolly and Zeckendorf fully understood that a modern physical plant was a precondition to winning accreditation. The Board Minutes of the era reflect this major focus on construction. The wish list was long, and in a undated memo from Conolly, written in the wake of a successful Title I grant and entitled, "Draft Plan For Building Fund Drive For The Brooklyn Center," he described the Fund as financing"the clearance and development of the Zeckendorf Campus at Brooklyn (sic) Center…" His memo identified a complex that would house and educate "approximately three thousand students in the three major educational divisions" of Liberal Arts and Sciences, Business Administration and the Graduate School. Among the projects were a refitting of the existing Metcalfe Hall, a 100,000 book library with a cafeteria, a gymnasium, a dormitory, playing fields, an "Air Reserve training center," et cetera. The memo laid out a fund-raising campaign including a lay leadership structure.

Brooklyn Borough President John Cashmore, Admiral Conolly and
William Zeckendorf Sr. burning a mortgage(?) in the late 50s.

In a briefing sheet, "Facts About Long Island University," prepared in February 1958, and written to accompany a fund raising letter, Conolly described the
"Brooklyn Center" as having an enrollment of 2100 students. The C.W. Post College enrolled 950 and was growing at the rate of 400 students per year; and The
Mitchel College facility was educating 300 airmen and officers. He noted, "there
is adequate physical space owned by the University and already available...," including the 7.5 acres acquired through Title I and "126 acres of lovely rural property" on the campus of C. W. Post. There were two other statements worth noting:
"All of these parts of the University are being operated entirely or largely on current income from tuition." And second, "The President of the University, who is
also President of each of its institutional branches, would welcome an opportunity
to present to you or your educational foundation the essential facts." Conolly was
an entrepreneurial salesman hawking "private, free-enterprise in education" and
was seeking "support from free-enterprise business and industry."

As a result of these unsuccessful, fund-raising efforts in the private sector, Long
Island University, in contradistinction to institutions like Brandeis, was compelled
to seek its support in the public sector. In addition to the Title I program, there were
low cost loans available from the Federal Government and the New York State
Dormitory Authority, originally created in 1944 as a "public benefit corporation."
Originally limited to funding dormitories at state teachers colleges, the law was
amended in 1948, 1954, 1955 and 1959 to provide tax-exempt debt for private institutions for educational, classroom and laboratory facilities as well as residential
dormitories. Not surprisingly, Long Island University was in the first bond issue
and in as many subsequent ones as the Dormitory Authority would allow.

In a long report to the Board delivered at a Board Meeting on September 30, 1957, Conolly laid out his aggressive plan for expansion. He unequivocally asserted that "The University, as it is presently composed, needs to be supplemented and augmented.... Particularly, it requires more professional schools and a closer association with the one now affiliated with us." He continued, "To be specific, the University should have incorporated in its structure a law school, an engineering school and, perhaps, a school of "minor professions," which would combine "journalism, nursing administration, teaching, radio and television and such. Some of these," he speculated, "could be acquired as an existing corporate entity. Others, established and built up from small beginnings." As early as June 1956, the Admiral wrote to John McGrath telling him that he "sounded out" several members of the Board of the Brooklyn Law School to explore an affiliation. In 1958, he was entertaining absorbing the two-year, proprietary Academy of Aeronautics near La-Guardia Airport, a flirtation that continued until at least August, 1963.

Conolly saw ultimately an urban division of inter-related schools and a suburban one. He saw each unit as having its own governing body under the umbrella of the Board and, in particular, he wanted an early affiliation with the Brooklyn Law School and the Polytechnic Institute of Brooklyn. He also wanted to alter the existing relationship with the Brooklyn College of Pharmacy from its "affiliated status" to a full merger into LIU. He anticipated that Brooklyn could double its student body in three years and laid out a development plan to achieve this, declaring that 8,000 students would be the maximum Brooklyn could accommodate.

At the C.W. Post campus, he argued for "a moderate-sized and proportioned college that makes fewer concessions to quantity and places continuing emphasis on quality - of faculty, campus facilities and student body." In order not to compromise "the very real advantages of a beautiful 126-acre campus," he would have a student body of a maximum of 1,600 residential students. And he argued for a dominant liberal arts bias rather than a devotion to "specialization in the professional subjects."

Conolly simply did not let the constricting details of inadequate sources of funding, or the Department of Education's or the Middle States Commission's antipathy, alter his plans. It becomes easy to understand why his officers and crew in the Navy called him "Close-In" Conolly. As a man of action, he was trained to be bold, to outfox his enemy, to attack suddenly. In battle he believed that there was often greater risk by holding back than in forging ahead, leap-frogging over his opponents as he had in the Pacific. He knew well Admiral David Farragut's famed quote, "damn the torpedoes" and he insisted that LIU move forward at flank speed. In a typical Brooklyn campus public relations piece of January, 1960, the banner headline read, "Next to Rise: Library, Gym and Theatre." He was confident that the educational bureaucrats in Albany or at Middle States would fall into line and accept the *fait accompli* because an ensuing fight would be out of character for them. In fact, the Brooklyn library did not get built for another decade; the gym and theater had to wait more than a generation. That library project will be a recurring part of the future narrative, because it became the symbol of the survival of the Brooklyn campus itself.

But he did read the educational bureaucracy correctly. As the child's rhyme states it: "sticks and stones might break my bones, but names will never hurt me." As early as 1953, when Nyquist was attempting to block the University from expanding into Nassau, the Department of Education shifted the burden from its own back to that of Middle States. Win that approval, Nyquist was saying, and we will not object to your developing a program in Nassau. In a letter to Zeckendorf of December 10,1953, Nyquist had informed Zeckendorf that, "Should you attain this further recognition of Long Island University at Brooklyn [from Middle States] you would have the encouragement of this department in developing Brookville." Not surprisingly, no effort was spared either in preparation of the Middle States required self study or the site visit, which always follows the self-study.

As early as February, 1954, at a Charter Day dinner in honor of the Admiral and as part of his formal installation, Conolly heard Mayor Robert F. Wagner compare the University and the City of New York: "you dream of a bigger and better University; we dream of a better and perhaps even bigger city." The dinner signaled the opening of a fundraising campaign for two and a half million dollars, which, in fact, was the first organized drive the University had ever undertaken. Zeckendorf had just announced publically his pledge of one half million dollars to purchase "eight acres for new and attractive facilities as part of the Fort Greene slum clearance project of Title I." Conolly, in turn, spoke about the University's will to prosper. This four-star Admiral noted that he had cast his lot with LIU and "had dedicated whatever useful years I have left to the welfare and leadership of this University." Attending that dinner were a bevy of Admirals, Conolly's friends from his service years, as well as General James A. Van Fleet, McArthur's successor in Korea and soon to become a Trustee of Long Island University.

In his inaugural address delivered prior to that Charter Day dinner, Conolly declared his commitment "to strengthen the institution in every possible way: financial, academic and material. What impresses me most about this University," he opined, "is its durability and its vitality, its stubborn, even truculent, and defiant spirit, almost exactly like that which I have found in the citizens of that great metropolis, Brooklyn." He spoke not only of improving the urban plant but also of the desire "to develop property we already own as a suburban educational operation within the University. This development would be first as a branch or branches of colleges and schools of the Brooklyn group with later organization as colleges and schools associated together in a suburban group." With enthusiasm the Admiral embraced Metcalfe's dream of following the returned veterans from the inner city to communities like Levittown. Noting that the University has had "its triumphs,

76

its successes and its vicissitudes," he noted with appropriate modesty, "to add to the latter, it has me."

Several months later on June 16,1954, Grover Whelan telegraphed Mrs. Joseph E. Davies (Marjorie Merriweather Post) at the Hassler Hotel in Rome: "The Board of Trustees met last night in your charming former home and passed a resolution that the Brookville center be named the C.W. Post Campus of Liberal Arts and Sciences, Long Island University...." Following that Board meeting, the Trustees petitioned the Board of Regents of the State of New York to change the name of the new campus from "the Brookville branch to Post College of Long Island University." And four days later, on June 20th, Marjorie Post responded in a telegram to Grover Whelan saying, "delighted your message Board action great pride and satisfaction in decision." In a letter to Mrs. Post from Whelan of July 27th, he indicated that "Admiral Conolly, President of the University, has already discussed the matter with the Board of Regents and he has no doubt they will approve the attached request."

Charles W. Post holding his only child, Marjorie.

On August 11th, Whelan again wrote, now informing her that, "The Long Island University Brookville Center will be known as the C.W. Post College of Arts and Science." He indicated that the University was looking for "important personalities in the area of Brookville" who would serve on a Board of Overseers. Whelan was particularly interested in suggesting Mrs. Stanley Rumbough Jr. an heir to the Colgate family fortune, "if her name met Marjorie's and her daughter's approval." In time, she would become the mother-in-law of Marjorie Post's daughter with E.F. Hutton, Dina. There is a handwritten note in the margin of Conolly's copy with the scribble, "no," probably indicating that she declined to serve. But the goal was clear: to enlist the engagement of the North Shore elite to embed this new college with the very people who were so against allowing it to open.

That romance continued, usually focused towards Mrs. Post and her family. In a letter to Whelan signed by Conolly but obviously drafted by Gordon Hoxie, Whelan is informed that "our Mrs. May [Marjorie Merriweather Post] with her husband, will attend the Convocation" to celebrate the fifth anniversary of the college. He went on to inform Whelan that honorary degrees would be given to Leonard Hall, Herbert A. May and Dr. Albert Jacobs of Trinity College. Speaking of the need to have a large auditorium, Hoxie wrote in Conolly's voice that "the gracious lady, our benefactress, will soon make the big gift essential for such a project.... The gifts from the lady and from General Foods Fund while not even in the aggregate very large, have been a critical factor in permitting our growth. Without your help I very much doubt that we could have had any of that." Implicit, of course was the suggestion that Whelan intervene to get her to give more.

In a widely disseminated first President's Report written in 1955, Conolly summarized his first fifteen months. He bluntly described the period between Metcalfe's death and his appointment: "the University had declined sharply in enrollment, its academic standing was unsatisfactory and its finances shaky." He assured the University community that "the task of rehabilitating the University was undertaken with the assurance of the President of the Board of Trustees that he and the existing members of the Board would give all possible support and assistance."

"The University did not have a good reputation academically," Conolly observed. The last time it sought an "accreditation inspection in 1939" it "had been advised to withdraw the application because of disabling deficiencies, both academic and financial." Middle States declined again to grant accreditation in October 1954, soon after Conolly became President, but a year later, in 1955, the Commission did respond positively, although imposing key caveats. Conolly suggested in his Open Letter that central to the change of opinion by the Middle States Commission was the strengthening of the faculty and a rationalization of program activities. Old time faculty were retired, as was the Dean of the College of Arts and Sciences. The average age of this group was seventy. The eight new faculty appointments averaged thirty-nine.

"The outstanding criticism by the inspecting party from Middle States Association with regard to administration was that the President of the University had too largely centralized authority and the determination of policy into his own office," Conolly wrote publicly. Responding indirectly, he insisted that, "Centralization of authority was necessary in taking over a situation that required drastic rescue operations. Now that a Provost of the Brooklyn Center and a Dean of Post College have been appointed, this criticism is met." Conolly, the four star Admiral, was used to giving orders and to having them obeyed, and was clearly irked by the Middle States team, whom he referred to as "these ultraconservative educational critics." But he conceded that Long Island University had to be restructured administratively to conform more closely to the conventional organization of other educational institutions.

The Middle States Report prepared by LIU focused intensively on institutional finances, also cited in Conolly's memo. "The University, when the present incumbent assumed the presidency, had exhausted its reserve capital and its cash position was already showing a deficit." Speaking of himself in the third person, he described how the cuts were made and other economies achieved. The substantial operating deficit for '53 - '54 of about $220,000 was to be eliminated by the fiscal year 1955 - 1956. He expected that "the cost of operations of the Brooklyn Center will be brought into balance with its income."

"Recruitment of students to the number necessary to reach a break even point and ultimately to saturate the plant is the goal of the Brooklyn Center," the Report stated. Conolly had hired the firm Marts & Lundy to do necessary statistical analysis. At that time 91.4 % came from New York City and 97 % from New York State. Conolly confidently expected that Brooklyn would achieve this enrollment target even as "the scholastic standing and quality of entering students went up. It is a process of pulling itself up by its boot-straps but this is being done." He noted that in the spring semester of this year, for the first time in five years, registration increased. This achievement was the more remarkable because it occurred in the spring semester; almost universally, fall enrollment is about 5% higher than spring. Brooklyn registration was about one hundred thirty five students ahead of its previous year.

Conolly's assessment also hyped fundraising successes led by William Zeckendorf. In addition to Zeckendorf's own half million dollar gift, there was a gift of fifty thousand dollars from Marjorie Merriweather Post for the Nassau campus, a major pledge from Dime Savings for the Brooklyn campus, a firm commitment from Walter Rothschild, the CEO of Abraham & Straus, and solid increases in Charter Day fundraising. In conclusion, Conolly wrote, "This University has a lot of vitality, great potential and unlimited opportunity." Shifting into the first person plural, he enumerated "our tasks for the coming year: (1) achieve accreditation, (2) stabilize current financial position, (3) balance operating budget, (4) prosecute a hard hitting recruitment program, (5) develop physical plans for the Brooklyn Center, (6) raise money for new buildings, (7) develop the Post campus (8) improve all educational activities and (9) be prepared to affiliate more closely with the Brooklyn College of Pharmacy and to incorporate other Brooklyn and Long Island institutions which might conceivably desire this when we have achieved accreditation." Conolly was confident that a corner had been turned and that in relatively short order his optimistic dream would be achieved.

There was good news in this Middle States Report, and the Admiral focused on the positive almost exclusively. A fair reading of the detailed Middle States fifty page text, however, would reveal that the sixteen site visitors, including several representatives from the New York State Department of Education's Board of Examiners for both Pharmacy and Podiatry, were far more cautious about the health of LIU than the Admiral suggested in his memo to the community. The Report was divided into thirteen separate categories; the Chair of the entire team was Claude E. Puffer, the Treasurer of the University of Buffalo.

In his general summation, Puffer celebrated that Brooklyn "is to provide opportunity for higher education for that portion of the young people of the Brooklyn area who (a) come from lower middle income groups and/or (b) whose standing in high school was in the lower range of achievement." This mission, although not "expressly set forth in print… is well known to the faculty; it is subscribed to by the President and the Board of Trustees; it pervades much of the activity of the University." He commended the University for its awareness of the need and its devotion to the fulfillment of it in the inner city, dating back to 1926.

Puffer went on to observe that "the administrative officers of Long Island University tend to set different aims" for its Brookville branch, seeking "to admit superior students from higher income groups at the Brookville site…." Puffer concluded with a brief but critically important section by warning that, "the problem of administering at one time two educational operations with such differing objectives and student bodies will not be an easy one." The next section of the report, drafted by Frank H. Bowles, then a director of the College Entrance Examination Board, picked up the challenge of a discrete, "parallel institution in Brookville." To him it represented "a very serious problem. Far more serious than appears to be recognized within the University."

Bowles, in his next two sections, celebrated the partnership of Zeckendorf and Conolly. He wrote that Zeckendorf "combines to an unusual degree enthusiasm, vision, resourcefulness and competence." And he observed, "His dream of a strong independent institution which will serve the lower middle classes in Long Island and Brooklyn is an essential one…." Listing other key contributions, he lauded Zeckendorf because he secured "Admiral Conolly as the President of the University."

Bowles was obviously very impressed by his time with Conolly during the site visit. He noted that, "Admiral Conolly brings to the presidency of the University skill and competence developed through a long series of important commands in the United States Navy…." He spoke glowingly of Conolly's "remarkable judgment" in managing the University and he observed, "In such a situation as the University when he took it over, it is impossible to see how he could have done anything other than "keep most of the reins of authority in his own hands." He further noted: "The new administrative staff is his creation, both as to personnel and organization."

The Treasurer of Howard University, James B. Clarke, observed in his section: "The question of stable income of Long Island University is a serious one. Present hope of the administration, for relief on this score, seems to be tied chiefly to the interests and activities of a few individuals who apparently have not yet made a firm commitment for financial support." While individuals are not mentioned, the implication was clear - Conolly was prepared to take entrepreneurial risks without securing adequate funding from Trustees and others in advance.

The section of the report dealing with the College of Liberal Arts and Sciences and written jointly by the Dean of St. Lawrence University and a professor of English at the University of Rochester, Katherine Koller, focused on the fact that 86% of admitted students over the prior three years had high school averages of less than 80% and 66% had high school averages of less than 76%. It was noted that "a considerable percent of the freshmen were in the bottom quarter of their high school graduating class." In sum, the uplifting mission of educating underprepared and underfunded students carried the concomitant reality that many were at risk both financially and academically. To bring these men and women through the curriculum to their degrees would require support, both financial and pedagogical, and require resources that, transparently, the University did not have.

When on November 29, 1955, Conolly received the formal letter from the Chairman of the Middle States Association (after Puffer's Report had been submitted by the site visiting team to the Commission for formal approval), the University was granted limited accreditation with a tight schedule of future follow-up visits. That letter of transmission came from none other than Ewald B. Nyquist who had become Chairman of the Middle States Commission. Nyquist limited this accreditation to two years rather than the maximum of ten. The Commission listed six points requiring clear evidence of improvement. It wanted to know that the financial resources of the University had been strengthened. It wanted to see improvement in admissions practices. It wanted to see how the guidance and counseling programs of the University would be enhanced so that marginal "students in satisfactory numbers are successful in completing the programs to which they are admitted." And it wanted to see improvement in scholarship practices, the awarding of tenure and in the progress of the Nassau campus, now renamed C.W. Post College. In addition, the Commission planned to send another team by 1960 to ensure continued progress.

Nyquist summarized, "Finally I must warn you that the Commission is gravely concerned about any intention the University may have to expand unduly the present programs of Long Island University." Expressly, Nyquist underscored that "new departures involving additional outlays of additional funds places in jeopardy the original accreditation granted, to the extent that either resources needed to support the ongoing programs are reduced or in the event that adequate resources are not available to support those contemplated." Implying he did not fully trust the University to keep the Commission informed in a timely way, he wrote that the Commission "does want to make clear that it desires to give continuing close scrutiny to the future development of Long Island University." The Commission's letter was far more constricting and circumscribed than Conolly's overly enthusiastic open letter to the community.

"Close-in" Conolly was clearly moving forward far more aggressively than Nyquist thought prudent. Entrepreneurial guns blazing, he was building a University of his dreams, leaving issues of consolidation and capacity to an undefined future. In his Interim Report transmission letter of September 30, 1957, addressed simply to the Chairman of the Middle States Association of Colleges and Secondary Schools, (probably in order not to have to address Nyquist by name), Conolly reported on the progress of the now several institutional branches of LIU, as mandated.

Clearly irked by what he saw as Nyquist's bureaucratic intervention, Conolly chose never to mention the University's plan, already well underway, to establish a third residential campus located in Southampton. To protect accreditation, however, he did hire Vice Provost and Dean of the University of Rutgers, Albert E. Meder, as a consultant. His charge was to review the burgeoning of graduate programs as well as the structural tensions, already evident, between an emerging C.W. Post campus and Brooklyn.

Conolly was imperious, but still prudent. He understood boundaries and bureaucracies, whether in the academy or in the Navy. There were rules and egos and old boys' ways of doing things. It was apparent that he needed a smart staff of experienced, senior administrators who had management skills, leadership capacity and loyalty, both to him and to the University. And among the most talented was James E. Hester, who subsequently became President of New York University in the late spring of 1960.

What is particularly interesting was that Hester was such a young man, just turning thirty-three, when Conolly "rushed" him to come to LIU. Writing Hester, then working for Gallup & Robinson in Princeton, sometime in early March 1957, Conolly quickly anointed him as his heir presumptive. "What I propose is that you try us for one year. At that time you might choose to return to the business world, or you might want to continue in education." He went on, "You would be employed the first year as the Provost of the Brooklyn Center. The next two years you would add the title and duties of Executive Vice President of the University. It might develop that we would want to employ a separate and new provost by the end of the second year, but that would have to await the confirmation of events and the tempo of expansion." After laying out his salary offer and revealing his own salary to set a context, Conolly wrote that, "by the end of that three year period, you would be ready to succeed me." "I can assure you," he went on, "that if you should take the job, I will back you to the limit."

Vice President James E. Hester ca.1958.

In a second letter dated March 13, 1957, the Admiral urged Hester to come into higher education for a career, describing the field as "wide open." Having shared his vision for the future of LIU with Hester, he wrote, "I need the help of a younger man with the capacity first to assume the executive direction of the Brooklyn Center, be ready to assume the Executive Vice Presidency of the University at an early date, and to be in a position to relieve me of the Presidency of the University in between three to five years time."

Hester was clearly a star on the rise; Conolly had spotted the talent. He had graduated from Princeton with honors, went to Oxford for his doctorate and had served in the Marine Corps during the Occupation of Japan. As he put it in his still unpublished memoirs, he learned from key associates and "a core of hard working faculty" that he came to respect a great deal, "the nuts and bolts of running an underfinanced private urban University in competition with tax-supported free higher education." Hester wrote," From the day I began at the Brooklyn Center, I realized I had chosen the right field, and for that reason we [Janet and James] never noticed the financial pinch of a 50-percent salary cut."

In a third, remarkable letter of November 7, 1958, sent after Hester had joined the University, Conolly wrote of "added inducements [to secure] your indefinite continuation with Long Island University," which he considered "minimum tokens of our esteem for you and your work. Our admiration and confidence is unbounded." Hester had become Vice President of the University and the University voluntarily advanced his salary, by the then considerable sum of $25,000, for each of the upcoming years, 1959-60 and 1960-61. On July 16,1959, Conolly informed Hester formally that the Board of Trustees had elected him to Board membership at its May 28th meeting.

Hester seemed to be doing an excellent job, was well liked and appeared very happy working for Conolly. Yet, almost out of the blue, Hester suddenly accepted an offer from rival NYU to become Executive Dean of Arts and Sciences and Dean of the Graduate School of Arts and Sciences at New York University. Perhaps, he was promised the Presidency, as his colleagues at LIU thought. Did something happen internally to cool the relationship between Conolly and Hester? Did the existence of NYU's many graduate and professional schools seduce him? All he revealed in his unpublished memoir was that, "I realized that if I was to have a successful career as an academic administrator, I needed more and broader experience." Whatever the reason or reasons, Long Island University and the Admiral lost someone who would become an extraordinary college President, to a rival across the East River. Unfortunately, LIU's 36-year-old heir presumptive was gone.

Conolly and Hester looking at architectural renderings of the Brooklyn campus.

Soon after Hester's departure, Conolly asked the LIU Board to redefine the title and alter the job description of Hester's successor, emphasizing the new appointee's responsibilities more specifically to Brooklyn, while establishing the title of Provost and Executive Dean of C.W. Post College. This move would allow R. Gordon Hoxie to move into the top circle of leadership. It also allowed Conolly to appoint a three star Admiral, an old navy buddy, Vice Admiral Chester Wood as Vice President for University Relations and Controller as well as Provost of Mitchel College, LIU's resident college located at the military airbase, Mitchel Field in Hempstead, Long Island.

Bureaucratic intensification and centralized management were what Nyquist so insistently had demanded, and increasingly there was a skilled leadership cadre, capable of running this growing institution. But it raised both professional tensions and interpersonal jealousies. Thus, when Albert E. Meder submitted his consultant's Report on September 16, 1959, he wrote of "certain organizational changes for the Brooklyn Center...." over the delegation of responsibilities and the delineation of authority. "Although the problem facing Long Island University has been posed in the form of whether the University should establish a School of Education as one of the three colleges of the Brooklyn Center," he noted, "this formulation

84

is an oversimplification." Meder stressed that, "The real question has to do with the appropriate academic organization of graduate work." The role of the Dean of Graduate Studies, in contradistinction to undergraduate Deans of liberal arts or business, was critical to avoid "conflict, confusion, and difficulty." In his letter of transmission, Meder wrote,"it is not invidious to mention particularly Dr. James M. Hester, Provost, whose assistance was invaluable" and whose role was central.

Before he left, Hester had sought clarification from Meder on what he meant when he spoke of a Dean who was a line officer in contrast to a Dean who was a staff officer. The issue, which was to remain contentious for years, went to the heart of how the several parts of Long Island University organizationally related to each other; and how authority to hire or to structure degree programs could develop rationally. Hester had written Meder. "Inasmuch as this distinction has not existed here before and habits have grown up which will have to be changed, it will be most useful if you can elaborate your conception of the Dean of the graduate school as a staff officer." It was Conolly's and Hester's design, unsuccessfully embraced in the subsequent Pell years, that there be a centralized command structure at the graduate level, with the undergraduate units having far more autonomy, one from the other. This became a critically important question of academic organization, debated in the fight over the University Statutes as well as in the interpersonal tensions within the officer cadre.

On September 25,1959, Conolly wrote to Meder that he had decided to follow the organizational structure Meder had proposed. He noted, "During the past several years we have given the problem a lot of attention. We are now in the process of implementing your recommendations." He went on to speak of the upheaval and furor that they unleashed within the administration, but concluded that "drastic action is required and I intend to go through with it in order to create a sounder and more workable organization." Conolly had decided that there had to be a single university officer delegated to oversee the academic enterprise, especially at the graduate level, irrespective of the campus on which the degree program existed. But in making this decision, he also was splitting away a portion of Hester's job, which had him serving simultaneously as Vice President of the University and Chief Academic Officer. On September 29, 1959 Meder wrote back to Conolly, "Only drastic action can produce lasting results." Unaware of Hester's imminent departure, Meder indicated how pleased he was that "Dr. Hester is to be in a position to give more attention to educational development and to turn over to another officer of administration some of the less exciting (but nevertheless important) aspects of his position."

Some years later, in his fourth annual report to the Board for 1967-1968 and near the end of his own tumultuous Chancellorship, Hoxie would write that John Pell and he had inherited a loose confederation of campus units. Their successive efforts to make LIU one University was in direct response to both State of New York and Middle States demands. Hoxie cited a letter Meder had written to Conolly some years before, on February 8, 1962, when Meder had become the Chairman of Middle States Commission. Meder, emphasizing "the commission's continued concern regarding the 'integration' reports of the University into a meaningful whole…," had directed Conolly to submit by February 1, 1964, a comprehensive State of the University report, detailing "particularly that it cover in some detail the progress that has been made in the integration of the University structure…." Hoxie cited a conversation that he had with the Admiral just before his tragic accident. He reported that Conolly told him that he realized the need to create a unified structure, explaining "that he purposely kept their development separate." Hoxie then cited a plaque that Conolly had years earlier put up at the entrance to the President's home in Old Westbury, which identified this house as "the residence of the President of Long Island University and the President of C.W. Post College."

If Hoxie's observations were correct they suggest that by the end of his Presidency, Conolly was acknowledging his own role in creating a schism that vested too much autonomy at the campus level. While this issue will be revisited again and again in the next sections of this book, the key point was that Conolly encouraged, or at least acquiesced, as C.W. Post College increasingly went on its own. Was Long Island University to be a confederation like the University of California or the SUNY system, or should it have a unitary structure modeled after the federal government? Where was the balance between the centripetal and the centrifugal? In the 1954 Middle States evaluation, the site visitors wrote that, "Although there seems to have been at one time a good deal of talk of moving the entire University out there [Brookville], that talk has now been abandoned and the discussion is on establishing a new four year college for the local area." Both St John's University and Adelphi left their original moorings in Brooklyn to settle in Queens and Nassau. Long Island University decided differently, despite warnings from both the State of New York and Middle States that it risked Balkanization by allowing the University to become a two campus institution.

Despite these possible misgivings, it should come as no surprise that in Conolly's last years, he enthusiastically entered into successful negotiations to open a third major campus on the eastern end of Long Island in Suffolk County. The townships of the East End were keen to have a local college in their area to serve the needs of their communities. Suffolk County was growing rapidly and it needed institutions to help meet the expectations of these new emigrants from Nassau, the City or elsewhere, especially as there was a spike for high tech, skilled employees to work at Grumman and other cutting edge aerospace and engineering corporations. Teachers, not surprisingly, were in great demand at all grade levels as a farming region became a home for the space race. And rising prosperity made higher education available to women of all ages, both to traditional high school graduates and those who had delayed college earlier to work and to raise families.

There was a new market and there were competitors. Adelphi was actively look-ing east to open a campus and the State of New York was investing heavily in its new flagship campus at Stony Brook. Conolly saw this market as an important one that Long Island University had to enter. In addition, Long Island University looked to protect its moniker, actively challenging the State University over its initial decision to call the Stony Brook campus, "The State University of New York-Long Island Center." With a mail ballot, Conolly got the Board to sign a peti-tion and raise "strong objection" because this "name will cause serious confusion as to the identity of Long Island University and its character as a private, non-tax supported institution." Noting that it "takes no stretch of the imagination to envi-sion that common usage may become the State University on Long Island or the State University of Long Island," Conolly urged that this first choice of name be rescinded. It was. Thomas Hamilton, then President of SUNY, wrote Frank Kille, the Associate Commissioner, on July 20,1960, that he sympathized with Conolly's "desire to avoid confusion." Kille, on August 23rd, used his letter of transmission to celebrate Conolly's Presidency. He wrote, "You have done an extraordinary job, and I would like to say again that higher education in general, and Long Island University in particular, are fortunate in having a person of your commitment and insight in their service."

After several years of false starts and failed projects, Long Island University found a local group of year-round East End citizens committed to help it open on the South Fork. Conolly wrote, on May 10,1961 to Edward Fearon of the Southampton Chamber of Commerce and a school superintendent, committing the University "to establish a cocducational four-year liberal arts college for commuting students in the fall of 1962 in Southampton, provided suitable physical facilities are pro-vided by the local community, and subject to the approval of the Board of Regents of the State of New York of the establishment of such a college by the University." The University and a local group of which Fearon was an active leader, reviewed several suitable properties, including one on Whites Lane as well as the Tucker Mill Inn property, the site finally selected. The leadership of the local community promised to raise enough money to secure the property plus $30,000 to convert it for college use. The name would be the Southampton College of Long Island Uni-versity. On June 13, 1961, Conolly wrote to Frank R. Kille to inform him of the University's intention to move into Suffolk, even though it was clear by then that local fundraising from the year-round local business community would fall short of those fundraising goals.

In this letter, Conolly apologized because for two and a half months he was had been on sick leave "following a surprise major operation at the end of January." Conolly did not return to the University until April 5th. This is the only written re-cord indicating that he had been diagnosed with cancer and undergone surgery for it. But once back to work, he wasted little time fulfilling his agenda. In his June 13, 1961 letter, he wrote to the Department of Education about "our extension program at Hauppauge," yet another extension site where the University could offer degree programs. He reminded Kille that, "at present we are operating the Hauppauge Extension under the approval contained in the letter to me from Mr. Kenneth T. Duran of your office, dated December 2, 1959."

In that same letter, he also noted: "While we had been considering, from the first, the possibility of expanding our operation in central Suffolk County into an institutional branch, when it came to the moment of decision, we were faced with the overwhelming specter of the ever mushrooming plans for the State University's branch at Stony Brook, just a few miles to the northward." In other words, the Admiral realized that locating a private college in an area so close to "tax supported education on the colossal scale that has been announced at Stony Brook" mandated a tactical shift eastward to Southampton. He also noted that Adelphi had determined to open a branch at Sayville rather than pursue a similar East End option. Returning his attention to LIU's rapid expansion at the Hauppauge site, Conolly also commented that "I have exerted a restraining influence in order to control the planning of those operating this enterprise, who are more directly under the pressure of demands from eager and highly motivated adult students and who could easily become overzealous on their behalf."

The Agenda for the Board meeting of December 13, 1960, listed under Organizational Development three items: "(a) Incorporation of the Brooklyn College of Pharmacy; (b) Incorporation or Affiliation of Brooklyn Law School; (c) Establishment of a new College as an institutional branch of the University in Suffolk County to replace extension program now conducted at Hauppauge by C. W. Post College."

The agenda for the Board of Trustees meeting held at Post on July 10, 1961, had five formal items on its agenda. They included: (1) the establishment of an independent branch at Hauppauge - on a two year "resident" basis - to encompass the extension programs then offered; (2) establishing appropriate governing bodies at institutional branches of the University with a special focus on the responsibilities and the controls required; (3) the physical construction of the Zeckendorf Campus in Brookhaven to provide the facilities needed to meet an expected increase of enrollment and a consideration of long-term financing required. (Zeckendorf, as mentioned earlier, through his Roosevelt Field partnership, had donated 200 acres near Brookhaven National Labs to build a science and technology campus); (4) a review of a detailed committee report on the creation of a law school in metropolitan New York and (5) a consideration of architectural plans for new construction at C .W. Post.

More than one-half century later, it is stunning to revisit this era of seemingly limitless growth and unsubstantiated dreams. How confident both the Administration and the Board were in plotting the future! Like the mythical Icarus, they somehow saw only opportunity. Was it hubris? Was it Conolly's excess portion of Tinker-bell's fairy dust? It is almost as if the Admiral's encounter with mortality, his brush with cancer, accelerated his need to push forward with abandon. He was intent on creating a University that would operate on multiple sites from the East River to the tip of Long Island, even as he also moved aggressively to develop MBA programs and, at the minimum, a Ph.D in biology.

On August 9, 1961, Frank Kille wrote to the Admiral: "Frankly, to date I have not been able to marshal any favorable staff opinion in the matter" of approving advanced degrees at Long Island University. Conolly answered on August 24, 1961 with a strong defense of those applications, citing the existence a long-standing masters in accounting, taxation and business administration offered since 1950, and arguing that many other colleges in the metropolitan area were offering an MBA. LIU wanted to join that sorority. Equally, he defended the desire to open a limited number of doctoral programs, citing other schools and arguing, "the quality of the faculty, the adequacy of the facilities and the availability of the substantial corps of qualified graduate students are the important considerations."

These exchanges document the recurring *leitmotiv* in which the Department of Education in Albany and Middle States were constantly pushing a strategy of "containment" for LIU. Long Island University, its leadership, its Board, and faculty kept pursuing a strategy of expansion and growth that seemed so very possible, until it was not. This was the era of aerospace on the Island and the Kennedy years seemed to promise ongoing growth, endless prosperity, substantial public funding for higher education, and a maturation of Long Island into one of the high tech centers of the world. LIU was the educational equivalent of the "Nifty Fifty" on Wall Street. It saw itself as a "high flyer."

And so on September 22, 1961, Conolly wrote Kille, "The Board of Trustees of Long Island University has approved the establishment of an institutional branch of the University at Southampton Long Island which would develop into a traditional four-year liberal arts college." Conolly sought authorization to admit a freshman class. He celebrated the "locale of the site" and noted yet again "the desire of year-round citizens of Southampton to have a college in their village," They had manifested that desire by providing "every possible support to such a venture. They are engaged at present in buying a site for the college." He anticipated a freshman class in 1962 of approximately 150 with a strong academic emphasis on English, History, Mathematics and Business Administration. And he noted again that Adelphi University, which also had been considering an invitation of the local community on the East End, had formally broken off those talks, opting for their campus in Sayville (subsequently spun off as Dowling College).

On the following day, September 23, 1961, Conolly wrote his friend and fellow Trustee at the University, Rear Admiral John J. Bergen, who was serving at the time as Chairman of the Graham-Paige Corporation, asking him to send to his prominent friends with houses on the East End a letter that Conolly or Wood had drafted. The letter was a full throated appeal to the wealthy summer residents to join the year-round business and commerce leaders in raising not only the "approximately $300,000 which, it is estimated will be required to (1) purchase the former Merrill Estate - currently the "Merrill Center for Economics" owned by Amherst College and (2) to make such other purchases and perform such alterations as are essential for the purposes." The letter stated that, "Admiral Richard L. Conolly has done a superb job in the establishment of C.W. Post College at Brookville, New York." And "the same general academic atmosphere on a somewhat smaller scale" is promised for Southampton.

Among the most lasting actions Conolly took in those final years of his Presidency was his decision to seek to incorporate fully the Brooklyn College of Pharmacy (BCP) into LIU. The Kings County Pharmaceutical Society had established a College of Pharmacy in 1886. Back on November 23,1928, the Trustees of BCP petitioned the New York Board of Regents to grant approval for a formal merger which had been signed on April 5, 1929, for "the purpose of securing reciprocal advantages to the University and to the Society's College and especially for the purpose of including the College as a professional school for pharmacists and pharmaceutical chemists in the educational system of the University...."

But this had not been a complete merger. The Kings County Pharmaceutical Society had to maintain financially the building and to meet the expenses of the budget through an autonomous Board of Trustees. The University President was *ex officio* the President of the College, but the Dean of the College was its operational CEO. The financial relationships were complicated with the Society contributing on a pro rata basis to the University, and there were fourteen substantive articles defining the terms and conditions of the Agreement. Organizationally it was an unwieldy agreement, but the BCP was too small to maintain its building and program comfortably.

The then Dean of BCP, Arthur Zupko, and Conolly worked together to complete the merger. Zupko's draft planning document proposed that the College of Pharmacy "serve as the nucleus for the training of students" not only in pharmacy but also in other health sciences. Zupko also sought a "Research Institute" encouraging faculty scholarship and grant-funded programs.

Conolly embraced the entire scheme and on January 23,1962, appointed a working group of senior administrators to work out the details. Eager to have the deal done by the time of his retirement, he insisted that the Committee not dawdle. It met on February 9th and again on February 21st, a week before his plane crash. Central to the planning was the construction of a 40,000 square foot building on the Brooklyn campus, and rapid progress was made defining what services and functions needed to be merged and what kept autonomous. This merger had its bumps and tensions, but it was obviously a viable model to be emulated with other professional programs and advanced degree work.

In his 1960 Report to the Board of Trustees,Conolly had assessed his tenure as President. He saw "substantial improvement in the University's physical facilities, strengthening of its academic programs, and enlargement of its vital role in the growth of Long Island." The five-page document summarized "the cumulative momentum generated since 1955, when the University became fully accredited." Conolly pointed out that the operating budget "had grown from $1 million in 1954 to $5.5 million today" with capital assets at $10 million, writing: "We move into the decade of the 1960s with a clear dedication to the University's mission, and with resources and experience that will contribute materially to the achievement of that mission."

He celebrated the growth of the faculty and student body. "In 1954," he noted, "The student body totaled 2,400 and the faculty 241. Today we have at our eight centers of learning a student body of 6,500 and a faculty of 500." He further noted, "For more than three years the freshman class has grown successively by more than 20 per cent." And he celebrated the construction, achieved or planned, the progress on incorporating BCP, and the developments across Suffolk and Nassau counties.

Conolly's self evaluation, passionately embraced by key administrators, faculty, students and the Board, must be again compared and contrasted to a later site report from a different Middle States team that came in the autumn of 1961. While reaccreditation was forthcoming after Conolly's death, there was an alternate reality portrayed, or, at least, a very different way of interpreting the same facts.

The site visitors must have arrived irked, since they received documentation on some eight items, many significant, only four days before they arrived on campus. The most important addenda was a new set of Statutes adopted by the Board on October 3, 1961. Under the category of "Some Current Developments" there were key personnel and structural changes chronicled. Some of these supplements were to be expected, particularly since the site visit occurred at the onset of a new academic year. But the overall impression was of a University in flux, breathlessly chasing to catch up with itself.

The Statute revision was the most significant item, because the President was seeking "to regularize and centralize the transaction of certain of the educational business of the University and its several institutional branches," as Conolly called campuses, to minimize the risk of fragmentation. The new Statutes also redefined the position of Vice President, particularly in the wake of Hester's departure to NYU. The University now needed a Chief Academic Officer who would oversee program and degree development, faculty hiring, and tenure and promotion.

The site visitors took 75 pages to capture all they had observed when they reported back to the Middle States Commission. As usual, they had spent three days on site and got in advance the detailed self-studies mandated by Commission rules. The document's opening sentence described the University as "A federation of colleges each supported by its own income from tuition, fees, gifts, grants and bequests." Noting that "The Centers differ greatly amongst themselves," because they were trying to meet the diverse needs of students from "varying community backgrounds and interests," the report went on, "There is a single administration supported by pro-rated assessment against each of the federation members and their several extension centers." It was an accurate description of the University structure, although it was challenged aggressively in the following decade.

The site visitors warned that, "as the component colleges become stronger, it will be necessary to strengthen the central university organization further." The President was urged to find "persons of unusual experience and ability who can give leadership to all four centers and whose services will be beyond the financial reach of any of the centers acting separately." The warning was spot-on. There was a clear and present risk that one campus (C.W. Post) would have so much more revenue than the others that it would demand separatist privileges, autonomy or independence.

Echoing the 1955 document, Middle States warned that "Further expansion either geographically or in program should be deferred until the ground already gained has been further consolidated. Too few are attempting to do too much." While Conolly and his team had little patience for such hectoring, hindsight suggests that the University was in deep trouble, especially because private fundraising had lagged so badly.

The site visitors were explicitly also concerned by "the problematic relationship of C. W. Post to the University." The report stressed, "There is a noticeable lack of coordination of relationships, sometimes even of simple concern with other units of the University." Recognizing that "loyalty to the college is commendable within bounds," it still lambasted the Post administration and faculty, because "to be alienated from their Brooklyn peers is regrettable." The Report drew the obvious historical comparison to the long struggle in America pitting states' rights against a strong federal system. It commented that "unity and a common purpose seems to demand greater attention than C.W. Post has ostensibly given to it, witness a different faculty manual, different format and content of bulletins."

In the seven years since Middle States had visited LIU, Post had evolved from "embryo at the time" to "flourishing youthfulness." The Middle States team was worried that the LIU train was coming off the tracks. And the warning came collectively from a very impressive group of peers. The visiting team was large, some twenty-four members, including representatives of the Department of Education in Albany, the National League for Nursing, the American Council for Pharmaceutical Education and the American Association of Collegiate Schools of Business. Key sections were drafted by the Vice President for Academic Affairs at Villanova, the Vice President and Treasurer of Rutgers, the Vice President of Academic Affairs at the University of Maryland, College Park and the entire team was chaired by Stanton C. Crawford, the Secretary of the University and Dean of Faculties at the University of Pittsburgh.

These were serious academic administrators looking closely at a peer institution. Yet their warning did not seem to penetrate the collective bubble in which Long Island University was still moving forward. Conolly was, of course, seriously ill with cancer and anticipating retirement. Zeckendorf was struggling to keep Webb & Knapp from bankruptcy. Nonetheless, this "firebell in the night," to quote Thomas Jefferson, needed to be heard. But it wasn't heeded.

On February 8, 1962, Albert Meder wrote to Conolly telling him that the Commission had reaccredited Long Island University but also required a follow-up visit two years hence. Middle States demanded a "comprehensive summary of the State of the University as of 1963-1964." He told the University that this report must "cover in some detail the progress that has been made in the integration of the University structure, including the role of the faculty in the formation of educational policy."

It is very hard to lose accreditation. Such action virtually will doom any institution's future both because federal and state funds are withdrawn by law and because parents and students would flee in large numbers. Meder, like Nyquist, intended to keep LIU on a very short leash. Reaccreditation was again bestowed only as a two-year probationary grant. The series of mandated internal reports and obligations were designed to push the University away from its expansionist bias toward a far more conservative, incremental approach to growth. The contradictions and structural flaws of LIU were painted in stark colors and the challenges clearly enumerated. Like ghosts of the night, these issues would haunt the next decade in multiple ways, both great and small.

Jim Hester noted in his unpublished Memoir, "the team [from Middle States] reportedly said that in granting accreditation they were accrediting him, "the 'Admiral.'" Conolly was seriously ill. He was now a lame duck President. He left no paper trail that disclosed his reactions. The Commission insisted that the follow-up report "should also cover fully any further expansion or new enterprises that may have been undertaken." In public, Conolly barely heard the warnings. Would he have used the time at his home on the West Coast to alter course? Had John Kennedy lived, would he have handled Vietnam differently? No one knows.

93

Part II - Ralph Gordon Hoxie

Relatively few people who know about Post College are aware that it is part of Long Island University. Nor does its name suggest where it may be located.

John H. G. Pell

Chapter Four

John Howland Gibbs Pell: An Accidental Chancellor

Conolly's succession planning seemingly ended when James Hester chose to leave LIU for NYU, in turn becoming NYU's Provost and then its President. Conolly's bout with cancer in the winter of 1961 must have accelerated Helen's and his decision to retire. By November 17, 1961 he wrote to John McGrath, "What we need is somebody, not necessarily a great scholar but a person, who would be recognized by the educational world and who would be acceptable." On November 21st, he wrote to a new search-committee he was appointing informing them that he was announcing his resignation on October 1st. There were three faculty: Hall Bartlett, the University Secretary; a key alumnus, Dr. Alan Livingston; two Deans and Leonard Karlen. Arthur Zupko was to be Chair.

In the months prior to the air crash, Gordon Hoxie had been maneuvering to have his former boss and good friend, Albert Jacobs, then President of Trinity College, succeed Conolly. Through his intercession, Zeckendorf met with Jacobs, then, asked the Admiral to delay his vacation trip that spring by a day so he also could meet Jacobs. Hoxie had served under Jacobs, as a junior administrator, when Jacobs was Provost and Dwight Eisenhower was President of Columbia. Hoxie followed him to the University of Denver when Jacobs became President there. He remained in close touch after Jacobs was established in Connecticut and Hoxie was hired by Conolly to be the founding Dean for the new campus, C.W. Post. Hoxie, a bureaucratic strategist, was actively promoting Jacobs to be the Board's choice for the next President of LIU. He had already got him an Honorary Degree.

At a special meeting of the Board called by Zeckendorf on March 5, 1962, with virtually the entire Board present, Zeckendorf laid out "the immediate and long-term problems arising because of the untimely death of Admiral Richard L. Conolly." Zeckendorf went on to advise the Board that he and Conolly had met with Jacobs, "looking toward Dr. Jacobs' acceptance of the Presidency of the University as successor to Admiral Conolly." Zeckendorf also stated that Jacobs "was Admiral Conolly's first choice for the Office of President and that he was awaiting word from Dr. Jacobs as to his availability." Zeckendorf obviously understood that even if Jacobs would accept the position, he could not possibly come until the beginning of the following academic year. There was a gap that had to be filled immediately.

The Minutes reported that "The Board determined that pending the election of a new President, an Acting President be selected from the membership of the Board." The Board decided to invite fellow Trustee Carleton Palmer, then travelling abroad, to assume the Acting Presidency. Palmer had recently retired from the Chairmanship of E.R. Squibb, the giant Brooklyn based pharmaceutical company founded in 1858.

The Board Minutes further reported that if he was not available, Mr. John H. G. Pell, himself elected a Trustee only on January 11, 1960, had indicated that he would accept the interim designation. The Board took one other critically important personnel action at that time, determining that "Dean R. Gordon Hoxie of C.W. Post College be elected a Vice President." These decisions were all taken just prior to the revolution in governance that radically transformed how American universities made selections of top administrators, among myriad other changes defining how any university was organized and power shared.

There was no search committee, no advertisements, no consultation with faculty barons and no effort to reach the alumni to sample opinion or solicit names. Even the Committee Conolly had recently established was ignored. The Board felt a pressing need to maintain momentum, despite the death of the Admiral. At the end of that same Board meeting, a memorial resolution of appreciation for Admiral and Mrs. Conolly was unanimously passed. One section stated that, "under his forceful and brilliant leadership the University emerged from a condition of academic and financial frailty to become a sound and respected member of the academic community…" Expressing its shock and grief, it clearly embraced the Admiral's optimistic assessment of the University's progress rather than the far more ambivalent vision of outsiders like the Middle States Commission.

On March 12th, Hoxie wrote to Arthur Roth, his close friend and trustee, laying out his organizational ideas for re-structuring "our Nassau-Suffolk operations of Long Island University." Hoxie was lobbying actively for a regional structure in which C.W. Post College would be elevated to a parallel status with Brooklyn. "I know that it will be applauded by the Middle States Accrediting Association as a further step of unity within the University, since it has been informally discussed as an effective means for further unity within the University." He pushed hard for Roth "to call Bill Zeckendorf on this since I told him that you and I had discussed these concepts of regional operations."

Trustee Arthur T. Roth

Roth, the founder and Chairman of Franklin National Bank and a transformative leader in regional commercial banking (he was the first to introduce a bank-issued credit card), was a strong proponent for a free standing separate economic development zone in Nassau and Suffolk, as a distinct region not tethered to New York City. For him and the others who had migrated East, "Island" meant Nassau and Suffolk which required their own institutions to gain true autonomy and become a self-sufficient region, not simply a bedroom suburb of New York City. Long Island University at C. W. Post fit in perfectly with this vision. It was one of the main reasons he was so active on the Board of Trustees. He was, therefore, Hoxie's natural ally in promoting the Post and Southampton Campuses to an equal status with Brooklyn, still then called University Center.

On March 16, 1962, Hoxie wrote to Zeckendorf, expressing his delight that "You think favorably of the inception of the Operational Vice-Presidency of the Nassau-Suffolk Division of Long Island University." He then took the opportunity to promote for President another friend of his, Dr. John A. Krout, who was a Vice President of Columbia University at the time. He indicated that he thought Dr. Krout should have been Al Jacobs' successor as Chancellor at the University of Denver in 1953, but his wife's terminal illness kept him from applying. Hoxie was moving up and interested in getting the University to hire top executives whom Hoxie knew, and he knew liked him. On May 21, 1962, Pell, now acting President, wrote to Hoxie formally appointing him Vice President of Long Island University and Provost of C.W. Post College with a salary of $20,000 per annum.

That same day, Pell wrote to John Baiardi, who had come to LIU as Chairman of the Biology Department in 1954, appointing him the Provost of the Brooklyn Center. This arrangement shifted Frederic W. Ness into the University Vice Presidency, a position previously held by Hester. Conolly had approved of this promotion before he died. Baiardi, in sharp contrast to the aristocratic Pell, was an archetypical Brooklynite. While he had earned his Ph.D across the river at NYU, his career was in his native borough, having taught at Brooklyn College, St. Francis College and St. Johns College prior to coming to LIU.

Chancellor John H. G. Pell

On March 21, 1962, three weeks after Conolly's death and Jacobs' decision to decline the Presidency, Pell's appointments were publicly announced. Hoxie then wrote to faculty and staff at C.W. Post describing Pell without much enthusiasm as a "financier and historian, a member of the Board for the past two years." In fact, Pell was American aristocracy, a patrician who was a descendant of one of the great Rhode Island Brahmin families. He managed his own and his family's investments in a tightly held firm bearing his name. According to his official biography, he had been born in Southampton on Long Island on August 9, 1904. He went to St. Paul's School and Harvard. He held numerous corporate directorships and was Trustee of the estate and property of the Diocesan Convention (Episcopal) of New York. His true passion was as an amateur historian interested in the restoration and history of Fort Ticonderoga in the Adirondacks. With houses on Centre Island ("Pelican Cove") and at 870 Fifth Avenue, he belonged to the Knickerbocker Club, the Down Town Association, the Century Association, Seawanhaka Corinthian Yacht Club, Piping Rock Club, The Montauk Club (in Brooklyn), The Creek Club, the Metropolitan Club (in Washington), the Colonial Lords of the Manor and the Society of Colonial Wars.

Fort Ticonderoga was unique among America's landmark sites from the Revolution, because it was a Pell family property since 1820. On August 13, 1965, *The New York Herald Tribune* ran a big story in the Food/Fashions/Family/Furniture Section describing the Pell home at Fort Ticonderoga. "The Pavillion" was a Doric-columned house built in 1826 by John Pell's great-great-grandfather, William Ferris Pell. The house was full of Napoleonic furniture, "heirlooms" of William Gibbs, "a former Governor of Rhode Island" who had bought these items in France after the Battle of Waterloo. The property had its own airstrip. In sum, there was little in President Pell's prior experience to prepare him for the turbulent sixties.

On May 29, 1962, Pell wrote to Rear Admiral Chester Wood, Conolly's very close confidant and a University Vice President, "I would appreciate having my name added to the University payroll effective as of April 1, 1962. As Acting-President of Long Island University I understand that I will receive remuneration at the rate of $25,000 per year payable monthly...." He asked that his monthly salary check be mailed to his checking account at the Irving Trust Company at One Wall Street.

100

He wanted the same annual expense account of $7500 that Conolly had received. And a few months later, on September 7th, he again wrote Wood, this time about "the possibility of getting a limousine." As a thrifty New Englander, he wondered "what becomes of Carey cars when they are a year old." Pell clearly enjoyed the perks, titles and status of this interim job.

General of the Army Douglas MacArthur receiving an Honorary degree from John H. G. Pell

That same September, the Board changed his title to Chancellor of Long Island University, probably on a recommendation from Gordon Hoxie. No search was launched. What had initially been seen as a short-term solution was either intentionally or inadvertently extended into a much longer appointment. Perhaps it was out of sensitivity to Pell, a fellow Trustee, who certainly was enjoying his new identity as a college President. Perhaps it was inertia, even laziness. It may have been that there was an informal search by Zeckendorf, which had not yielded any viable candidates. But it is clear that Pell, as a novice, was forced to leave the management of the University to a cluster of administrators who did not share a common vision.

In a letter of thanks for his promotion, Hoxie wrote to Pell on September 19th, that, "this is something which, as you know, I have long hoped for. The wisdom of the members of the Board...is laudatory. You will have my wholehearted support as you assume the duties of Chancellor just as you do in your present duties as

President." He went on to thank Pell and Zeckendorf for conceiving of an Office of President at C.W. Post College and "you're nominating me to fill that office." Celebrating the unanimous action of the Board in electing him, he was nonetheless concerned about his own position. "You will recall in our conversation regarding the presidency at C.W. Post College you assured me that this did not mean my losing my University office." Hoxie wanted to become a Vice Chancellor. He reminded Pell that "you emphasized the point that the action as regards the presidency was an addition rather than a taking away." Then he asked to have his "position as Vice President...." re-designated as Vice Chancellor in keeping with the other re-designations." Hoxie's concern was that he retain his "present position as the senior academic officer of the University," even though, disingenuously, he noted he would "cheerfully accept Pell's decision in the matter."

Pell and Zeckendorf had also elevated Admiral Chester Wood to a Vice Chancellorship when Pell's title was changed (effectively making Wood the most powerful administrator and chief operating officer). Conolly had held the title of President of each campus concurrently with the title of President of the University. The issue going forward was how power was to be shared on each campus and centrally. Pell would continue to serve as President of the Brooklyn Center, while John Baiardi would remain Vice President of the Brooklyn Center in addition to his position as Provost of Brooklyn. To calm Hoxie's worry that he had not been granted the title of Vice Chancellor, on October 30th, Pell wrote a handwritten note to Hoxie describing Post as the University's "shining star" and telling Hoxie that "the opportunity is limitless."

If Al Jacobs had agreed to become LIU's President the following fall, John Pell's interim role would have simply been to manage the flow of business and to officiate at the commencements that spring. But Jacobs had turned Zeckendorf down at some point in those first days after Conolly's funeral. Suddenly John H.G. Pell had to address a range of issues, most significant, a strategic response to Middle States. He had been a relatively new trustee, with, at best, only a hazy notion of how LIU or any university functioned. He may or may not even have understood what the Middle States Commission existed to do, what peer review meant, and why it was so important. He lived for part of the year on Center Island, to be sure, but he also had homes in Florida, upstate New York and Manhattan. His friends barely noticed the "old Post estate" as they drove on Fridays from Manhattan down Piping Rock Road to their homes in Locust Valley. He took the job partially on a whim and partially to help a college whose Board he had joined just several years earlier.

The learning curve had to begin with Conolly's unfinished business. Responding to the Middle States Report was an immediate task. Pell thus asked the then Secretary of the University, Robert A. Christie, to analyze and reorder the Middle States Report so it was not so discursive and so that he could understand the underlying priorities in its text. Like a black herring, the prospectus issued before a stock or bond issue on Wall Street, Middle States Reports have always had their own arcane ways to communicate meaning. Christie did a superb job of translating this document candidly. His was a detailed, hard-hitting and honest analysis. Christie wrote, "Rapid expansion and lack of sufficient reflective planning has generated centrifugal forces inimical to the University." To cite another quote, "Such an upgraded, central staff would tighten up a structural looseness which allows branches too much isolation from each other." Or, "Whereas at Brooklyn Center the Report commended the goals and criticized the execution, at Post they commended the execution but criticized the goals, or more properly their absence." Christie's summation makes sobering reading more than a half century later.

Pell asked each of the officers to respond to Christie's memo. On May 3rd, Admiral Wood wrote about what he believed to be the two outstanding questions raised in the Middle States report: "first what is the basic organization of the University, and second, how can the Faculty be brought into greater participation in formulation of Policy?" He further observed, "I feel that the report is unduly cautious in its approach to 'expansion,' for this is surely a time for intelligent boldness in the educational world. This has served the University well, and it will in the future." During the war, Wood was a direct report to Conolly and they were cut out of the same cloth. It was he who took the lead in completing the Southampton purchase. It was he who spoke as heir presumptive for the Admiral.

Hoxie maintained that Christie has misinterpreted the Middle States Report in several key ways: he overstated its call for central administrative authority; he failed to recognize that the Middle States team "has no quarrel with the principle of federation," he overemphasized the separation between the Brooklyn Center and C.W. Post College, while "failing to recognize the inherent differences," and he sent to Pell an earlier draft of the Middle States Report which Ness on behalf of the Brooklyn campus had returned "for revision."

Hoxie ended his three page memo by turning Pell's focus toward the topics of the admission of poorly trained students, toward faculty who, while professing interest in graduate education, did not complain about the poor library facilities, and, finally, toward admissions standards that would have to be raised, because "Long Island University was established for the training of the average student." Mapping out a cautious approach of soliciting faculty review through campus-based committees, he warned Pell: "To act in haste prior to the completion of this process would be unwise. To act thereafter would be judicious."

Ness, Hester's successor, responded a week later. He wrote Pell, "that certain basic decisions have to be reached at the Board level before any of us can, with profit, accomplish the principal objectives laid down by Middle States." The lack of consensus was obvious and Pell hesitated, because he might be gone soon and, as an accidental Chancellor in the strange world of higher education, he did not know how best to get the job done. Business was done differently on Wall Street, that was for sure.

In the ensuing months this pattern repeated itself with painful regularity. The existing officers, unleashed from Conolly's taut control, disagreed on virtually everything. As will be documented, the Pell administration fell into a kind of administrative paralysis in which each campus rushed out on its own, fracturing whatever communality may still have existed. Fractiousness was the order of the day, issues both large and small triggered, almost always, parochial responses.

Pell certainly tried to summon all hands on deck, but either he lacked the natural charisma to command discipline or he was from the beginning such a lame duck that he was deemed a spectator, not a CEO. A patrician gentleman, he lacked the personal *gravitas* to knock heads together, to fire people easily or to impose his will. Probably he should have appealed to Zeckendorf requesting him to intervene to help him restore order, but he seemingly never asked. Was he embarrassed to do so? Did he misread his own strengths and weaknesses? Was he afraid of what might happen if Zeckendorf also crossed the membrane from Trustee to senior administrator?

The Middle States site visitors, acutely aware of the divisions within the University even before Conolly's death, insisted that the University fill two critically important but open positions: an Academic Vice Presidency and a Deanship overseeing all graduate programs across the University. Pell rapidly discovered how tough that task was going to be. He sought Albert Meder's advice about which one to seek first, visiting Meder with John Baiardi. On October 1st, Meder responded bureaucratically, making the case for both equally. There was no consensus from the key officers about the skills required for either position, much less a list of candidates around whom there was consensus. But it was clear that filling these positions was a *sine qua non* that had to be completed by the time the next Middle States site visit was scheduled for February 1, 1964.

The guerilla warfare that erupted was fought on many fronts over the next two years. To cite one academic example, on May 14, 1963, the Academic Standards Committee of the Brooklyn faculty altered the classic grading grid to clarify the distinction between a "D" and an "F." The Brooklyn grid eliminated minuses. Grades dropped from "A" to "B+" to "B" to "C+" to "C" to "D" to "F." There are no universal norms, and different faculties at different institutions each do whatever that faculty thinks would be the best way to assess student performance. But the Post faculty didn't follow Brooklyn's lead and retained the "minus" grade. Automatically then, Brooklyn and Post/Southampton had different grading grids, which meant that there was no GPA equivalency between a student with a Brooklyn transcript and one issued by the Post or Southampton registrars, even though all transcripts came from Long Island University.

Campus registrars stood mute (or privately supported the local faculty) as faculty committees on one or another campus pulled that campus further and further away from its sisters. It took many decades before a common grading grid was re-established by the faculties at both C.W.Post and Brooklyn. As a result, it was probably easier to transfer from anywhere in the world to either Brooklyn or Post than to transfer internally. Whatever the motivation, the outcome was deleterious and clear evidence that neither Brooklyn nor Post was particularly concerned about symmetry or student mobility from one campus to another. Each faculty on each campus did its own thing and operated as if academically it was sovereign.

In February 1963, Hoxie reported to the Board that C.W.Post College was establishing an extension site at Longwood High School in Yaphank as the first step in creating an institutional branch on the Roosevelt Field land in Brookhaven. According to the Minutes, at the Board meeting Carleton Palmer wondered "whether this would be a branch of C.W. Post College or whether it was to be a University enterprise." Palmer "had a particular interest in the development and strengthening of C.W. Post College and might oppose any new undertaking which could impair or hinder its development." University Counsel, Frank McGrath, responded "that under its Charter from the Board of Regents only the University could establish an institutional branch and that Post College could not itself do so." That response seemingly satisfied Palmer who moved the vote at the Board table. It also suggested that Hoxie and the faculty of C.W.Post were testing the boundaries of autonomy.

To cite yet another example, on May 23, 1963, Hoxie staunchly resisted Pell's wish to alter the colors and the seal of C.W. Post. Pell was learning what the chancellor of a university was called upon to do. He had become aware of the fracturing of the image of the University and he wanted as a public relations matter to present Long Island University with a single logo. Hoxie responded, "It would indeed be an extreme divorcement to change the colors and the seal of C.W. Post College now, eight years after they have been proudly displayed. It would be the more so since the college's principal benefactress had given permission to Admiral Conolly and myself for the use of the Post family heraldic symbols in the College's seal."

Hoxie had invented most of this. Mrs. Post was not "the college's principal benefactress" and the Post family itself had invented its own heraldic coat of arms, then had them placed in stained glass windows in the Great Hall of their Brookville mansion once Mrs. Post and E.F. Hutton were married. They were very rich but they were not noble. Hoxie, at his most histrionic, was alarmed that the loss of these heraldic symbols would be a "great blow to the alumni and the students of the college to be deprived of their colors." Having built up a head of steam, he hectored Pell: "As a student of history, you fully appreciate that it is out of faith and freedom that unity is built." Invoking the English Commonwealth and "allegiance to the Crown" he opined that "the greatness and strength of Long Island University will, to my mind, be borne out of the achievements and service of the University and of its colleges and not out of stereotyped "seals and emblems…stationery…. and letterheads." Hoxie sent blind copies of this response to Mrs. Post and Arthur Roth, two of the staunchest champions of autonomy for the Nassau campus.

On the following day he wrote in his cover note to Arthur T. Roth, "It would be a tremendous mistake for Long Island University to deprive C.W. Post College of its "individual identification." And, that same day Hoxie complained to Pell that he had "not received a formal invitation to the Long Island University [Brooklyn's] commencement this year…." As a result he had, therefore, accepted an invitation to bestow a distinguished service award at the Sands Point Country Day School." He then wrote Pell that he had "always looked forward to this event." In translation, he was informing Pell that he was very irked not to be invited. Then Hoxie continued, "Anticipating that there might be a late invitation, I am asking to be excused on Friday morning June 14th."His temper tantrum was exacerbated by his mock flowery language: "Can Chancellor Pell kindly excuse me from the graduation exercises and convey my warmest well wishes to the participants?"

Beneath the theatrics were fissures, which would increasingly polarize the University and hasten Pell's departure. The symbolism of logos or mascots or the images used in marketing was clearly understood and fought over by the different factions. Arthur Zupko, the Provost/Dean of the Brooklyn College of Pharmacy, had responded to Pell's same request for comments by proposing a shared image in marketing very differently articulated from Hoxie's. Zupko argued for a unified campaign in *The New York Times*, and elsewhere celebrating the image of Long Island University as a federation of colleges. "I have made mention on many previous occasions of my being disturbed at seeing the Brooklyn Center advertised on one page, the Brooklyn College of Pharmacy on the next page and four pages later a large insertion from C.W. Post." He wrote to Pell and his fellow officers that "there are many things that can be done to reinforce the identification of the University's various units with the University itself."

But first comity and trust had to be established within that peer group. At the commencement exercises at C.W. Post College in June 1963, Chester Wood the Vice Chancellor for Administration for the University, John Baiardi, Vice President of the University Center and Edwin C. Broome, then serving as Provost of Mitchel College were the three university officers who took offense at where they were seated. Wood wrote to Pell a stinging memo on June 10, dealing with protocol. "I thought that an inadvertent error must have been made and I so stated to the Marshal of our portion of the procession - Dean DeMarr. I was informed by him that no error had been made - that three of us were in the proper position as assigned by higher authority." He complained to Pell that he and the other two were at the ceremony in their official capacity as Officers of the University, maintaining, "strict adherence to the recognized forms of protocol is essential in the creation and maintenance of constructive relations among individuals and among groups of people. This is of abundant significance in academic life." In high dungeon, he warned that he would decline any "invitation to ceremonial events in the future, *unless* I can be assured that the office within the University organization, which I am honored and privileged to hold, will be paid the respect to which it is entitled."

This contretemps was not going to end easily. Four days later, Hoxie wrote Pell a response, expressing his irritation that Admiral Wood had blown this matter out of proportion. He argued bureaucratically that the Order of March and seating plan dated back to 1958, the first Post commencement; an Order which he added was originally set by the late Admiral Conolly who "was something of a student of protocol." Hoxie continued, "I protest the inference that he, Dr. Baiardi and Dr. Broome were purposely seated in lesser positions than other persons in the same row." This catfight got so intense that in July Pell drafted "ceremonial protocol-precedence lists" to govern what happened at "all formal ceremonies." The rank order established in the document lists first, Vice Chancellors; second, Presidents; third, Vice Presidents and Provosts, fourth.

When a Blue Ribbon Panel, created by Hoxie in October 1962, issued its report on the "Future State of the College," meaning C.W. Post, the document came near to a Declaration of Independence. It was a very long and detailed report. Its charge had been to "inquire into the present state of the College and prepare a ten-year academic and fiscal blueprint for C.W. Post College for the period 1963-1972." It was authorized by Hoxie, and Chaired by two Trustees - Carleton Palmer and Franz Schneider. There were numerous sub-committees reporting on everything from evening extension programs to extra and co-curricular student life. Among the active, Post-centric lay leaders were William J. Casey, Emilio Collado, and J. Burchenal Ault. As Hoxie phrased it, its purpose would be to plot the College's "future character, development and growth."

In granular detail, the report analyzed the wisdom of opening one graduate program or another, the desired mix of resident and commuter students, an optimal admissions process, both the math and verbal SAT scores of current Post students, the intermediate targets to improve the class profile, and the additional steps needed to win a Phi Beta Kappa chapter by 1960 for the Post campus only. The document spoke at length about faculty excellence and the steps needed to improve faculty teaching and research, including steady increases in pay for the professorate. It presented a campus master plan which focused on bricks and mortar. Among its many photos, it included pictures of the R. Gordon Hoxie Hall for Social Sciences and the Arthur T. Roth School of Business Administration.

Hoxie had urged one of the subcommittees to request that the "Post College finances be set up independently, within the overall purview of Long Island University." Current income and expenditures would be under the supervision of the finance department at Post and capital and other donor contributions would be solicited by Post's development officers as well as by friends, alumni, and parents under the general supervision of a lay Executive Committee and senior administrators at Post. Emilio Collado and Franz Schneider were Co-Chairs of this subcommittee and, as Trustees, both must have understood the challenge being presented to the central administration in Brooklyn.

Once the eight sub-committees had completed their work, the document was elegantly, elaborately printed with maps and photographs. It was both a development piece and a public relations document which claimed that "Admiral Conolly recognized the need for a totally new approach" to the effort to build a Nassau campus. "Rather than simply [be] a branch of the Brooklyn operation, a college with considerable local autonomy and identification must be created if it were to succeed." There was a section entitled "The Federation," drawing a distinction between a unified or federated organizational structure. The document by analogy described the structure of Columbia and Harvard, where each division is deemed a "tub on its own bottom," as the models to emulate. At one point the document stated that the committee would view with alarm "tendencies towards centralism and towards financial assessments other than for University services." In sum, "the federated system gives the University and its parts great freedom of opportunity."

Hoxie understood that there was a power vacuum at the center. He also understood that Pell's tenure was finite and that a new President might quickly clip his or Post's wings. Pell, on the other hand, lived on Centre Island on the North Shore, belonged to the top local golf clubs and probably tacitly agreed with Carleton Palmer, Emilio Collado and many others that the future of the University was in Brookville.

Toward that goal, Hoxie wrote Wood on November 11, 1963, requesting that the Board consider three capital Resolutions involving the purchase of the 70 acre Hickox Estate for $400,000 with a 15 year mortgage held by the Franklin National Bank; the purchase of the estate of E. F. Hutton, including twenty-five acres and buildings in Old Westbury and an adjacent 35 undeveloped acres for $500,000 with a $350,000 mortgage again held by Franklin National, and a third parcel of nearly 50 acres reaching as far east as Cedar Swamp Road some two miles away. (That parcel of excess Federal land was referred to the Board but never purchased.) He also submitted the "Future State of the College," for Board review; he made a recommendation that Douglas MacArthur be granted an Honorary Degree, and he submitted revised Statutes governing C.W. Post. Hoxie pointedly reminded Admiral Wood that, "The Chancellor [Pell] has indicated his approval of these Statutes."

Pyrma and John Pell together with Louise and R. Gordon Hoxie greeting students in the Great Hall, C.W. Post.

At the beginning of January 1964, the C.W. Post Office of Public Relations is-sued a press release announcing a "$20 million capital expansion program to be implemented during the next ten years" based on the "Report on the Future State of the College." Separately, the college also acquired from the Tenney family 15 1/2 acres and a beautiful Georgian style home that first became the Fine Arts Center and soon thereafter the administrative seat, renamed "University Center," once Hoxie himself became Chancellor of the University in 1964. That shift of moving the center of the University from Brooklyn to Brookville was a flash point in the relationship between the two campuses.

Hoxie, quite appropriately, was always promoting the growth of C.W. Post. In a letter from Hoxie to Pell dated February 5, 1964, he urged Pell "to recommend that Trustee action be taken to establish the Graduate Library School here at C.W. Post College." Arguing that it was a necessary step for programmatic accreditation by the American Library Association, he celebrated the success of this endeavor, not-ing that it "now has a larger graduate enrollment than most of the graduate schools [of Library Sciences] in the United States."

Hoxie originally tried to get Pell to agree to have the school named after him. "Your own good self clearly comes to mind and I would like to secure your con-sideration for naming it the John H. G. Pell Library School." Hoxie wrote that "In your modesty you will protest this but there are sound grounds for it in your own good deeds." A naming proposition of this sort was seemingly not connected to a solicitation, even though Pell could easily have made a major gift. Rather, it was a tangible form of flattery designed to ingratiate Hoxie in Pell's good graces and simultaneously to get what Hoxie wanted. (The Graduate Library Program became instead the Winthrop and Carleton Palmer School of Library Science, long located in the C.W.Post library.)

Were Pell to have agreed to have his name placed on this graduate school, al-most for sure it would have ended any discussion about whether this new graduate school could be established at Post without first being vetted by a faculty group, the All University Graduate Council. It needs to be recalled that Conolly saw grad-uate education as a common enterprise, one overseen by a powerful Dean and a single faculty council, which would determine where and why professional and, ultimately, doctoral programs would be established. That Dean was supposed to be strong glue unifying the University, provided he or she had the authority to make decisions, subject only to the approval of the Chancellor and the Board.

Conolly believed that LIU needed a full spectrum of graduate programs to become a major force in American education. He believed that those graduate programs would raise the quality of all instruction; that doctoral training would be profitable eventually, and would boost the quality of both faculty and students, both gradu-ate and undergraduate, through increased enrollment and government grants. With typical bravado and some arrogance, he thought LIU was ready to move into the big leagues. He pushed very hard to accomplish this. The authorities in Albany and the site visitors from Middle States sharply disagreed. They looked at library holdings, faculty publications and physical facilities and found both Brooklyn and Post woefully inadequate. The Admiral did not accept the criticism and discounted the shortcomings identified.

On June 4, 1962, Pell got a letter from Elbert K. Fretwell Jr., the Assistant Com-missioner For Higher Education. He wrote, "The University originally petitioned the Regents in June 1961 for an amendment to the charter to secure the authority necessary to award the Ph.D for the completion of programs in the fields of psy-chology and biology. Admiral Conolly, Vice President Ness, Associate Commis-sioner Kille and I discussed the matter here in Albany last summer." He chronicled the several visits to campus that followed and concluded that, "Since we would have to file a negative recommendation if your petition for a charter amendment for [the] Ph.D is presented to the Regents, it would save embarrassment all around if you could see your way clear to withdrawing your petition at this time."

On June 14th, Fretwell sent a second letter, as promised. It included a very negative report on the quality of graduate education, focusing it on the high attrition rate associated with a "liberal admissions policy." The State asked Pell to impose "minimum admissions standards that would be applied uniformly in all departments." The State hoped, "this process would result in admissions only of candidates who have demonstrated capacity in their undergraduate programs to pursue study of the field selected." The letter then had sections dealing with budget, space allocation, library collections and supervision of graduate programs, arguing for "university-wide arrangements for the supervision of programs and for the sharing of resources, including faculty, library and laboratories."

The State raised questions about the quality of the Master's programs. It commended the University "for recently taking the courageous step of discontinuing Master's degree programs in economics and sociology, English history, and public administration at the Brooklyn Center" but was unwilling to accredit Master's "programs in mathematics and political science at C.W. Post" at that time. Conolly would have been furious, raising a ruckus; Pell was disappointed, obviously, but also may have agreed with the State.

Why was graduate education so contentious an issue? Because there was a clear demand across the City of New York and Long Island for people with advanced degrees. Conolly and others believed that there was money to be made in servicing this need. Moreover, doctoral-trained faculty wanted to teach their fields at an advanced level. There was increased status, recognition from peers nationally, and reduced workloads for those lucky enough to hold appointments in either graduate or professional schools, especially in a Ph.D program in Arts & Sciences. Professional accreditation organizations demanded improved library resources, reduced faculty-student ratios and other goodies that made the anointed faculty natural allies of any administrator who could deliver such a program, provided, of course, that the State of New York and Middle States agreed.

John Baiardi wrote to Pell, on June 3, 1963, complaining about the unilateral establishment of another major graduate program, "the establishment of the Arthur T. Roth Graduate School of Business Administration" at Post. He expressed his deep concern that "the principle of "the All University Graduate Council had been violated; that is, that no changes would be made without the advice and counsel" of that body. Baiardi was suggesting that, henceforth, a precedent was being established that allowed each campus and its relevant faculty to do as it pleased, subject only to its capacity to fund autonomously new hires, labs, library resources and graduate scholarships mandated by the accreditors as a *sine qua non* to any new graduate program gaining approval on any campus.

To a novice administrator like Pell, the registration of graduate programs must have been an arcane ritual, a rite of passage hard to fathom. On the other hand, Pell was galvanized by the symbolic but potent impact of logos, icons, typeface, and copy. He recognized the deleterious impact on Long Island University when its presentation through marketing and public relations was disjointed. Pell made marketing and institutional image a flash point during the next six months. In an early but undated version (drafted by Mary Lai) of what he ultimately presented to the Board prior to University wide distribution, he sought a "formula" that would "require each center of the University [to] be named by its location." He cited the University of California at Berkeley, Davis, Los Angeles et al., observing that, "Relatively few people who know about Post College are aware that it is part of Long Island University. Nor does its name suggest just where it may be located."

Irked by the arrogance of many at C.W. Post College, Pell also bemoaned how the senior Post librarian had been appointed without even courtesy consultation with the Brooklyn librarians, even though they had played a key roll in the establishment of Post's library. He observed, "all liaison was abruptly curtailed." Using strong language he subsequently edited out his text, he commented that "C.W. Post personnel appear almost resentful of the 'Brooklyn office' and carry an attitude which seems to suggest that everything that goes 'wrong happens in Brooklyn.'"

At the Board meeting on July 11, 1963, hosted by Trustee C. Russell Feldmann on his yacht, the "*Savitar,* lying in waters adjacent to the City of New York" as the Minutes romantically described the setting, Pell informed the Board in a final document that "there was a failure on the part of the general public to identify constituent elements of the University with Long Island University as an integrated whole." Because Zeckendorf was away during that meeting, as Chancellor, he presided. He was alarmed that "the University's expansion over a wide geographic area" had created "increasing confusion in the public mind with respect to the relationship, which the University's constituent colleges gave to the University."

Pell said, "In view of the current activities leading to the establishment of still another branch campus [Southampton], this one yet farther from the University's home base, it is particularly urgent that this problem be dealt with forthwith." He asked his fellow Trustees to adopt "A Directive" addressed formally to the Chancellor, one which he had drafted, "to make clear its [LIU's] over-all mission in serving the area from which it takes its name, its role as the creator or incorporator of branch colleges, and its identity as a single, large, educational organization with a single governing body responsible to the State for its total operation."

Pell expressed his irritation that the name of the University did not have a prominence equal or greater than that of C.W. Post College on Post letterheads. He was still smarting at a C.W.Post press release in which the type size for "C.W. Post College" was four times larger than that printed for Long Island University and the logo used was the ersatz Post shield, not the University's equally ersatz coat of arms. "In illustration," he wrote, "this can be done by giving the University a prominence equal to that of the college in letterheads, programs, signposts, newspaper advertising and in publications of all types and designed for all audiences; ... and above all, by fostering pride of association with the University family."

EXHIBIT-+

LONG ISLAND UNIVERSITY
ZECKENDORF CAMPUS
BROOKLYN 1, N. Y.

June 27, 1963

Memorandum to the Board:

I have felt for some time that a greater identity of each of our various branches with the University, insofar as its public image is concerned, was highly desirable, and am now prepared to take positive action to this end.

However, in studying the matter, it has become evident that this matter of public image is closely interwoven with basic policy as to the desired relationship between the University and its component units. Inasmuch as such basic policy is under the direct purview of the Board, it appears proper that I should present this matter to the Board for its consideration at this time.

Accordingly, I herewith present a proposed directive (Attachment A) which, in my opinion, does reflect the desired relationship.

I strongly recommend its approval.

Respectfully,

John H. G. Pell
Chancellor

Attachment A - Proposed Directive

Cover memo from Chancellor Pell to the LIU Board about its "Directive."

Following the unanimous Board's affirmative vote on Pell's "Directive," the Minutes report that John Baiardi next asked the Board to approve a change in the University Bylaws "relating to the Graduate School and [the powers granted to] the All University Graduate Council... made at the suggestion of the State Education Department and the Middle States Association." The Board dutifully then voted this change, making "The Provost of the University Center [John Baiardi] the Dean of the Graduate School and, "in this capacity, will be responsible for the educational administration of the Graduate School...."

A few minutes later during that very same meeting, it was Hoxie who informed the Board of "a convocation that would be held at C.W. Post College of Long Island University in September on the occasion of the dedication of the Genevieve Roth Hall of the Arthur T. Roth Graduate School of Business Administration and the dedication of the women's dormitory to be known at Marjorie Post May Hall." Hoxie also spoke of "the establishment of a non-commercial educational FM radio station at C. W. Post College...through the generosity of the Trustee, Ben Abrams". It should have been obvious that the Agenda of the Board meeting had on it diametrically conflicting items, but no one seemed to notice or to care.

As if there was not already a surfeit of conflicting issues on that particular Board Agenda, the Trustees then listened avidly to a consultant, a law professor from the Catholic University, Arthur J. Keeffe, who shared his preliminary but optimistic survey on the feasibility of establishing an LIU law school in the Mineola area. Unanimously, the Board asked him to convert that survey into " a report to the Chancellor for presentation to the Board."

Later that month, on July 24, 1963, Chester Wood wrote to the University attorney Frank McGrath (with a visible copy to Hoxie) asking for a legal opinion on how the University should report out such matters as endowment, library holdings and enrollment for the Ninth Edition of the American Universities and Colleges Compendium prepared by the American Council on Education. Wood indicated that, "President Hoxie of C.W. Post College has requested that a breakdown of these figures be made and that those pertaining to C.W. Post College be published as such."

The next day Hoxie responded to McGrath defiantly noting that there was "no implication that the gifts and properties listed in the financial question belong to any corporation other than to Long Island University." He continued, "as you know, the University receives substantial gifts earmarked C.W. Post College, and this volume is our principal publication for acquainting persons on this aspect of the College's activity." He once again invoked Conolly by noting that in 1960 it was handled in this same way "under Admiral Conolly's direction." He sent a copy of his letter to Pell but did not send a courtesy copy to Wood. Trying to shape Frank McGrath's response, he ended his letter, "Chancellor Pell has concurred in the view that the full statement is of value to C.W. Post College, and he may call you in this regard."

Given Pell's interim status, the uncontrolled infighting of his senior team on matters both important and petty, and the larger inter-campus struggle seeking to define the University, it should not be surprising that the search for an Academic Vice Chancellor was consistently a major issue of dispute.

Pell was constantly trying to bring some heightened consensus to the management of the University. Early on he established a "Cabinet" to meet the first Monday of each month. It included Baiardi, Hoxie, Wood and Zupko as well as Edwin Broome, then in charge of the much smaller Mitchel College. The first agenda item that Pell brought forward at the first meeting was a draft of new Statutes. He announced even then, that "a Vice Chancellor for Academic Affairs is being sought and will be appointed," he hoped, "in the not too distant future." There then followed a disagreement over whether' this should be "a staff position versus a line position…" Pell spoke "of hoping to first find the man and then write the statute."

At that first meeting, there ensued a heated discussion about what the University needed to seek in a Vice Chancellor for Academic Affairs. What would be his or her job description? Wood felt that "we should not give anyone 'carte blanche' because it would be 'weakening to the Chancellor.'" (And also himself!) It was agreed by all, however, "that the man must come from outside the University." The group also collectively agreed that there should be a search committee formed to review candidates and the Minutes report that, "Mr. Pell asked Dr. Hoxie to call a meeting of the Senate of the University at Post College for the earliest convenient date so that this matter could be brought before the group and a committee appointed. It was then suggested and agreed that the notice go out over Mr. Pell's signature even if the meeting was to be held at Post College." This would not have been a debatable issue were the Admiral still in charge.

When the issue was revisited later on, Chester Wood's first choice of some nine finalists was William Birenbaum. He was trained as a lawyer at the University of Chicago, and, at 39, served as a charismatic Dean at The New School in Manhattan. Birenbaum had entered the LIU orbit as a part time, confidential consultant to the Chancellor. Pell, the patrician banker, had sought an outsider whom he could trust, even while translating for him the arcane traditions of the academy. Birenbaum was filled with imaginative ideas. He was a man of the '60s. He was cocky and brash. He and Hoxie both came from Waterloo, Iowa, but had never previously known each other until then.

Hoxie sent his priority-ranking list to Pell on April 16, 1963. He listed as his top choices three individuals who were not on Wood's list. Hoxie's top choice was, Stanton C. Crawford, then 66, who had a long career as a biology professor and administrator at the University of Pittsburgh. He had served as Chairman of a

Middle States site visiting team to LIU. "His background and extensive knowledge of Long Island University would make him first choice in spite of the age factor," wrote Hoxie. Pell, unable to find a consensus, postponed making any appointment. The position remained vacant until the spring of 1964, after Pell himself resigned and the Board had chosen Hoxie to be his successor.

Another running battle was over the redrafting of the Statutes of the University. There was no set of Statutes that could win broad acceptance. The Board would vote in favor of a draft, only to have another one placed before it. Because no one knew the limits of his or her authority, no codification was possible. The weeds and thickets of arcane legalisms obscured the struggle to define the institution.

Both the Middle States site visitors and the bureaucrats in Albany watched with alarm as the University drifted broadside in the heavy seas of Bylaw revision. With every revision, the Bylaws became increasingly baroque, as if greater specificity in codification would resolve the underlying structural tension of the centripetal vs. the centrifugal. All Bylaws in all institutions are always struggling to catch up with the realities of any organizational design. But from 1962 to 1972, the LIU Bylaw paralysis reflected a disintegration of comity and increased alienation from a common mission.

The failure to agree on Bylaws made the fluidity of title change within the senior cadre of administrators much worse. Nomenclature meant little except as a way to follow who was winning and who was falling behind. The handicappers studied these shifts as a fortune teller studied tea leaves. Those less attentive were simply befuddled. The confusion was compounded, since different campuses used different titles for the same job. And there was comparable confusion with University-wide titles. The appointment, "Dean of Graduate Studies" was a University-wide official, in contradistinction to the Deans on the campuses. And even the CEO was at one point, President and at another, Chancellor, and then back again to President. The Board appointed Hoxie, President of Post, but Pell kept that same title at Brooklyn. John Baiardi, therefore, became Vice President of the Brooklyn Center, even though he and Hoxie held comparable positions. It was dizzying.

On September 19, 1962, six months after Pell took office, both Baiardi and Hoxie wrote to Pell requesting that neither of them report to him through Chester Wood, the Vice Chancellor. Their goal was to limit Wood's role to Development and Business and to ensure that each of them had direct access to Pell. They sought a title change for Wood that constricted his authority to those two specific spheres. They wrote that "It is further imperative that the Vice President and Provost [Baiardi] reports directly to you in your capacity as President of the Brooklyn Center and Chancellor of the University and that the President of C.W. Post College [Hoxie] reports directly to you in your capacity as Chancellor."

116

On November 8, 1962, Hoxie sent to Pell a memo seeking "Revision of the University Statutes as Related to C.W. Post College." It defined Hoxie, the President of Post, as the "Chief Administrative and Executive Officer of the College...responsible...for the administration of the internal business, development programs, the discipline of the faculty, staff and students, the educational services and activities, the planning construction and maintenance of property and facilities, including assignments of space and the allocation of funds to the various departments and divisions together with formulation of the budget...." In Hoxie's proposed revision, the Provost "could be appointed by the Board of Trustees upon nomination of the President of the College, to serve as the President's executive in all matters pertaining to the College."

What was the role of a President of one of the Institutional Branches (Conolly's earlier term for campuses)? What powers were the Chancellor's alone? While Dr. Zupko said he felt this had all been gone over before, there was a discussion focusing on the powers reserved for the Chancellor. At the first Cabinet Meeting, John Pell likened the Chancellor's role to that of the President of the United States, saying, "that while he was, in effect, Commander-in-Chief of the Army and the Navy, he really did not exercise this power in practice." Dr. Baiardi countered, "that a University is an educational institution and should not be run like a military organization, a business or industry...."

In those first same months, John Baiardi submitted a critique of the proposed By-law descriptions of the responsibilities and powers of each of the Officers. He believed "that the primary functions of the President of an institutional branch are to supervise, organize and develop the academic programs and should be so indicated." And in a memo from Hoxie to Pell dated December 3, 1962, Hoxie argued that the Academic Vice President must be a staff rather than line position. While many eyes may glaze over when revisiting these disputes, the central debate always centered on where decisions got made, especially in the academy: which issues were best decided at the campus level and which were properly the purview of University Center? The distinction between staff officers serving the Chancellor and those who had executive authority was not a trivial issue. And thus it mattered when the position of the Academic Vice Chancellor was posted on February 1, 1963, describing this position as a "staff position with no intrinsic executive authority or responsibility except that which is delegated by the Chancellor." An ill-prepared Chancellor had allowed power to flow to the campuses, and neither Baiardi nor Hoxie, whatever their sharp differences on other matters, wanted any arrogation of their authority especially to a powerful, centrally located Vice Chancellor for Academic Affairs.

The search was an exercise in futility. There was no agreement on the top candidates, no agreement on the powers to be vested, if any, in that office and little willingness by the existing executives to see it filled. On May 22, 1963, Pell wrote the obvious: "We have had some difficulty in locating acceptable candidates for the proposed Chancellor for Academic Affairs." He therefore asked for "a rewrite (of) 'our job description' in the light of our experience which has been gained to date." With either alarming obtuseness or poor clerical proof reading, he concluded that,"this matter was of no great urgency." Each member of the group was to respond with further suggestions in two weeks.

The officers rushed their responses back to Pell. Hoxie was first out of the starting gate, writing to Pell on May 24th. It was Hoxie's view that the "job description is quite admirable." For him the difficulty in locating acceptable candidates did not stem from the description, but from the description of the University itself. He argued that, "Instead of stating that 'at present it is essentially a federation of colleges,' I would suggest stating that Long Island University is organized with a federated type structure." "I am not at all certain," he wrote, "that the University needs an additional Vice Chancellor."

On May 28th, Edwin Broome of Mitchel College, a bit player but seemingly an intelligent administrator, proposed "a line position with 'command' authority over the respective branches of the University." The "need for strong control over the academic programs is paramount as is also the need for communication among the branches in the area of academic matters," he wrote. Concerned about duplication, he argued for specialization at one branch or another. And he concurred with their earlier decision that "no one from the main branches of the University should be considered." He sent a copy to Admiral Wood; Hoxie had not.

Baiardi sent his memo on May 29, 1963. He wrote, "If we wish to unify the academic programs throughout the University, the position of Vice Chancellor for Academic Affairs should be established." He recognized that this would be at variance with "the concept of a federation of colleges, each member developing according to its own geographical resources and community demands." But Baiardi clearly sought a line position directly beneath the Chancellor with the stipulation that this individual serve as the Acting Chancellor during temporary absence or disability of the Chancellor. He concluded his memo with what was historically self-evident: "Therefore, before we truly set out on a campaign to seek qualified applicants, we must define clearly in our own minds what we want the University to be. Is it to be a federation or should it be an academic organization?"

Seeking wisdom from other institutions, Wood wrote to a cluster of outside organizations, including the Council of Higher Education, inquiring how other institutions linked their various branches to the parent. He indicated Long Island University was "particularly interested in the relationship when the branch is located in another place other than the principal place of the parent institution, and is authorized to offer courses for residence credit and has its own administration and supervisory organization."

Pell also was adamant that his "Directive" on marketing be distributed. But to whom? How widely ought it be disseminated? The document kept going through multiple drafts. Pell still hoped that the section on the "unity of the University" would be placed at the beginning or the end of the piece. It had been months earlier, on June 27, 1963, that Pell had got from the Board its approval to promulgate his "Directive." The question ever since was how to implement it in order to find common ground. In early November, Pell sent out another draft to the senior officers for their thoughts. This was, in effect, a continuation of the same running fight. He invited them to opine yet again. Unfortunately for Pell, the disagreements had not dissipated. Pell hoped that somehow his message could still win their collective approval. It was a naïve dream.

Maintaining that "there exists a simple formula for clarifying these ambiguities" of commonality, Pell embraced an idea long espoused by the University Treasurer, Mary Lai, that "each center of the University be named by its location." Thus, "The Brookville unit should be called 'Long Island University in Brookville.'" He finessed the issue of the use of C.W. Post's name by proposing that it be transferred to the name of the Liberal Arts College, the first academic unit on the campus. His draft document specifically said that the "University should have one school of graduate studies for each set of disciplines even if it spanned several campuses. His revised and edited "Directive" concluded, "If we intend to build a University which will span one-hundred miles of space, we need an organization structured to transcend distance."

The first to speak out against it was again Gordon Hoxie. He hinted in a letter to Chester Wood that he suspected it had been Wood who had drafted this "Declaration" for Pell. Wood's files retained his first draft of a response to Hoxie. It was abrupt and angry. That first draft was in memo form from Vice Chancellor Wood to President Hoxie. It lacked any salutation. The sent version was in letter form. It started "My dear Gordon". But the substance remained more or less the same. His first point addressed "the Question of Unity." Wood, referring to Pell, noted that "He is deeply concerned, as you know, about the confusion -internal and external- created by the swift development of the diverse and far-flung operation, and he feels that an expression of concern is pertinent…."

The following day Hoxie with a collegial salutation wrote back, also in a memo: "Thank you for your memo of November 4th, subject as above…." And then Hoxie revised his memo with a more civil letter opening, "My dear Chet." Hoxie disputed that Pell was as concerned as Wood suggested. He noted that "your reference to the 'confusion - internal and external -' to my mind overstates the case and arouses unnecessarily a sense of misunderstanding which otherwise does not exist." Hoxie then asserted that the Post Deans were far more outraged by Pell's draft document than anything he, Hoxie, felt or wrote. "It had not been my desire to place these views before you because, quite candidly, they are far stronger in their opposition to include in this portion of the report than I felt necessary to express, yet, even here, with respect to personal feelings, I shall leave out the strongest of these comments and I will not here quote them."

Hoxie then excerpted a series of decanal responses, none identified, but all clearly protesting Pell's or, perhaps, Wood's assessment. One Dean declared that, "The report itself dismayed me. No other word will do. For thirteen pages it describes an enviable record of growth, a constant strengthening of academic and financial resources, and a bright hope for the future. And then, as if a completely different mood had suddenly taken hold, the final pages contradict and reverse everything that went before. How could a University with a fuzzy sense of mission have achieved so much so quickly? Success is not inevitable; nor is it a matter of luck."

The anonymous Dean went on to raise the specter of private universities being overtaken by tax-supported ones. "Maybe we should proudly announce a formula that others will follow, for we can truly say the LIU formula works! The balance between central authority and local autonomy is delicate in education as well as in government." Arguing for a period of consolidation, if necessary, he urged the University "not lose the autonomy that made us strong enough to do what seemed impossible a mere decade ago." Similar comments from five other Deans followed.

Hoxie's "major contention" was when "the harmony of an institution is seriously affected," the institution does not flourish as this one has....."Now, you may say that the section of the report on the 'question of unity' does not mean the above quoted things. Yet dedicated senior educators, reading this report, have said this - and more." Arguing for a truce, he exhorted Wood "to delete that portion of the report which can only render a disservice."

Toward the end of this long letter Hoxie wrote, "we would recommend such a brief statement as: 'in the years ahead we must strive for the ever-strengthening of the University and of its parts. Working whole-heartedly together, the units strengthen one another and the University as a whole."

John Baiardi also wrote to Chester Wood urging, "that these matters should be recognized internally but not aired publicly. The solution is not to simply omit these comments from the Report nor just to change them but rather to recognize their existence and do something about them immediately." He urged that the Cabinet meet "as soon as possible and continue to hold such meetings as frequently as necessary until the matter is resolved." It is interesting that all this correspondence went to Wood, not Pell, since it was fairly or unfairly believed that the words if not the impetus were probably coming from Wood rather than the Chancellor.

On November 8, 1963, the newly appointed Provost of Southampton, Edward C. Glanz, jumped into this round-robin debate, after indicating that as the new boy

120

on the block he was still feeling his way. He wrote, "There are serious questions of unity within Long Island University at the present time according to my experience." Glanz commented on "the confusion of names of individual units, varying college colors and varying college policies and procedures…." He indicated that "Faculty members are frequently uncertain about the question of College and University loyalty." He thought that there was confusion in the mind of the public because of the many extension centers, some of which were extensions of individual college operations while others were connected to the University. In trying to prepare the new catalog for Southampton College, "It was immediately apparent that there are needless differences of course numbering, titles, degree offerings and educational philosophy statements."

Arthur Zupko, the Provost-Dean of the Brooklyn College of Pharmacy finally felt compelled to offer his own judgment. He wrote to Wood that "I have endeavored to stay out of the controversy…. However, the time has come, perhaps not too late, to voice an opinion." As far as he was concerned making this a public statement would generate negative public relations, but he did not dispute the ill will that clearly was manifest between those who lived and studied in Brooklyn and those further east.

On November 18th Hoxie again wrote Wood, triggered by Glanz's comments, faulting Southampton for a curriculum "which is most different from the other liberal arts and science programs…." Hoxie was particularly irked by Glanz's comments: "those who can remember the trying days of 1954 when Long Island University was deemed by many to be a sinking ship, and who stood valiantly by, simply cannot appreciate Dr. Glanz's reference to 'the question of College and University loyalty."

At the meeting of the University Cabinet on November 22, 1963, the first agenda item was "the question of unity" section of Pell's message. The prepared Agenda posed several questions: "Is the revised statement valid? If so, is it of sufficient significance to be reported to the Board by the Chancellor?" And should it be circulated to the faculties given the probability of a leak? Those questions were followed by a "Note: There is *not*, nor has there ever been any intention of including this section of the report in any material printed for public or general distribution."

The contretemps died down and the matter was tabled. Pell's intent was deflected, and his wishes were ignored. Did he see this as a defeat, a personal rebuke? It is impossible to tell. What is certain is that there was no change in policy, no centralization of marketing services, no restructuring of how the campuses related to the parent institution, Long Island University. The status quo meant that each campus would continue to market itself as if it were a free standing, autonomous institution with some ill-defined connection to an abstraction, Long Island University.

The senior officers, however, were sensitive to the ill will which had been expressed too openly. The University Cabinet tacitly agreed to disagree. Comity, shared sacrifice, and a common sense of purpose still received nominal lip service, but increasingly a *laissez-faire* mindset, "each campus for itself," became the prevailing attitude. The shift was gradual, but each of these fights further confirmed that the destiny of each campus had to be determined on that campus and by the local faculty and administrators. To be sure, the central administration could and did provide useful services - auditing, payroll, benefits, budget - but enrolling students, shaping curricula and fundraising increasingly became local tasks, managed locally. By the end of the decade, the center could not hold, to paraphrase William Butler Yeats' famed line.

The contradictions, the organizational tensions, and "dry rot" that was papered over were easily minimized because growth still seemed so easy. The national political scene was shaken by Kennedy's assassination, but Johnson was introducing his "Great Society" initiatives and higher education nationally was seemingly thriving. Government money kept flowing in and enrollment was strong. For that period, the guiding philosophy was a mercantilist free-for-all in which each campus sought to achieve as much support as possible to build out the plant and expand into new academic fields and disciplines. There was a gold rush mentality as buildings, programs and teams proliferated. It had been Conolly's dream that LIU would, like the Sherwin Williams paint ad, cover Long Island from one end to the other. To use contemporary parlance, there was nationally a higher educational "bubble," allowing too many colleges and universities to overbuild too easily. Long Island University was caught up in the euphoria. It all seemed so easy, almost preordained.

There were to be two tiers to this expansion. The first was to build out all three campuses so that they were fully formed and competitive with other colleges and universities in labs, classrooms, libraries, gyms and dormitories. The second tier was to expand into new areas of professional education, especially a law school, a medical school, a school of engineering and science, and a robust set of doctoral programs. Even if the funding was already secured (and it was not), there was always a cycle for construction and faculty recruitment that would take years. What was started by Conolly would be finished under Pell; what was started by Pell would be completed under Hoxie; and so on.

The new campus in Southampton was the most immediate matter. It needed to be built as quickly as possible and it had opened, even though the year-round community had failed to raise even the purchase price for this property. As the development brochure, "Quest for a College in Eastern Long Island" had stated, "Residents of Eastern Long Island are planning to get a college for their area in a way never before attempted in New York State. They intend to buy a campus site, alter existing buildings for classroom use, [and] turn the property over to a private University." The improved property cost $325,000 and naïvely it was asserted that an additional $50,000 was required for conversion. But even those fund-raising goals proved far too ambitious, and the costs of conversion woefully under-estimated.

The town of Southampton had a year-round population of approximately 26,000 in 1962. There were an additional 10,000 in residence in the summer. These tended to be the wealthy people who owned the great estates, but they were disinterested in supporting a new college, except possibly to educate the children of their domestic help. They were graduates of the Ivy League and had loyalties to institutions scattered near and far. As became clear over the next decades, there was no natural constituency of supporters except those who themselves had graduated from Southampton. The shortfall in the initial promises put the campus into debt from its very inception and insured, like the other units of the University, that Southampton would be tuition driven.

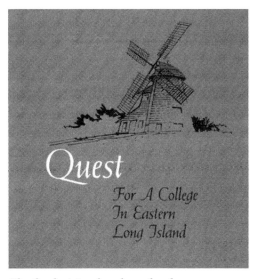

The fundraising brochure for the new campus at Southampton.

After Conolly died, Admiral Chester Wood became the moving force behind Southampton College. He shared Conolly's love of this seaside campus, and his energy, skill and persistence carried Pell and the Board forward, even though prudence might have dictated otherwise. Conolly had written on September 22, 1961, asking for the "department's [Albany's] approval in principle" to opening a campus in Southampton, but there was no answer in the University files, according to the University Secretary, Robert A. Christie, who wrote a memo to Admiral Wood. The files do contain an undated, draft letter from Pell to Frank Kille, then the Associate Commissioner of the State Education Department, asking again for approval in principle for what Pell characterized as the "Southampton Project." Pell had corrected his draft letter by listing himself in ink as "Acting President."

On September 12, 1962, Wood sent a fundraising report to Pell for inclusion in the upcoming Board book, indicating that "about $100,000 has been received in cash and pledges to date. The members of the committee [the local citizen's donor committee] feel that a total of about $200,000 in cash and pledges will have been received by the end of the option period, December 31, 1962." The question for the University, he asked, was whether to go forward even though there was a substantial fundraising shortfall, or to abandon the project as the agreement permitted. Admiral Wood noted to Pell that "the present owner is hopeful that our project will fall through in order that she may sell the property for a sum in excess of her contract price to us - $325,000." Again and again, Post had been held up as a model, indicating the Nassau success was likely to be duplicated on the East End. On November 12,1962, the Executive Committee of the Board examined the Southampton project in detail, while tabling the motion to move forward until the full Board had a chance to consider the matter. On December 11, 1962, Pell formally submitted his recommendation to move forward as well as a formal Resolution to that effect. It was approved.

By November 5, 1963, the newly appointed Provost, Edward C. Glanz, wrote to Pell submitting an outline of "a ten year development plan for Southampton College of Long Island University." Glanz called for "an ultimate size of 1200 to 1600 students (full-time, day). This size can permit the college to operate as an economically sound, self sufficient unit." He submitted a formal resolution authorizing Long Island University to borrow from Chemical Bank $325,000 to acquire the property and an additional $175,000 for renovation and rehabilitation. These debts would be partially offset with the approximately $150,000 actually raised from the community. On that financial basis, the formal resolution empowering the Chancellor of the University was "to establish a four year college of liberal arts and sciences on the property mentioned above, such College to be known as Southampton College of Long Island University...."

Edwin C. Glanz, then 38 years old, was born in South Carolina. He had been Chair of the Department of Psychology and Guidance at the College of Basic Studies at Boston University and prior to that was Assistant Dean and director of Student Personnel at Quinnipiac College. A World War II pilot who commanded B-24 and B-25 planes, he went to Bates College and received an EdD from Teacher's College at Columbia. He had no known fundraising experience.

In an early document, unsigned and undated, "The Proposed Curriculum of Southampton College" was to be "best suited to the needs of the areas served by the college." Written by Conolly himself or by Wood, the goal was to allow "comparably autonomous branches, each of which has freedom to develop in the way best suited for the needs of the locality. The hard core curriculum will be of the traditional variety for the first two years with nursing, education, a business program and a very limited set of graduate offerings projected for the years to come." At this point a future emphasis on marine science was not even mentioned.

By the end of November 1963, Wood wrote Pell that it was becoming increasingly clear "that our capital expenditures at Southampton have been far beyond our planned expenditures and expectations. The full extent is not yet known but it will probably be in the order of $500,000 - over twice as much as had been contemplated." Optimistically, he projected that the budget would "be in good shape and need give us no concern, either for this year or next." Wood believed that the College would break even in the foreseeable future, "but its ability to pay off capital investment made by the University within a five year period - as had been contemplated - can no longer be expected."

Wood detailed the causes of over expenditure, including underestimating construction costs, termite troubles in the main building, overtime delays and inefficiencies of the general contractor, et cetera. "As the project manager, I [Chester Wood] bear full responsibility to the Chancellor for this over expenditure in the planned budget." He offered his mea culpa. "I deeply regret the concern and embarrassment to you which this situation may well entail, particularly so in the light of the full support and trust which you have placed in me." But he assured Pell that in the absence of "some cataclysmic event" the College "will be able to pay off this outlay in due course of time."

Classes for full time freshmen began on September 23, 1963, with 251 day students and about 100 enrolled in the evening. In a progress report to the Board, the administration stated, "In summary, we feel the College is off to a good start and fully warrants our confidence as regards to capital outlays recommended herein." That same report noted that "the cost of renovation work on the existing buildings was more than twice what the architect had given us as his budget estimate, although there was no significant change in the work accomplished." The final figures indicated that there was an $865,000 deficit for Southampton's first year. Nevertheless, on November 18, 1963, the Board passed a resolution to construct three dormitories for 154 students at a cost of $572,880, payable in twenty-four equal semi-annual installments for twelve years.

Southampton was set on a course of constantly scrambling to meet its bond debt in order to pay for a physical plant that was under built from the beginning. There was no founding endowment or major capital gift. The campus was chronically in the red in its operating budget (with one short period of surplus), with the academic quality of the instruction consistently better than the resources available to pay for it. Almost from the beginning the student body was bi-modal: there were some very smart and interesting students attracted to this new facility, and there were also young men and women enrolled to avoid the draft, or unable to gain admission anywhere else. Without adequate financial assistance or quality facilities, it was difficult to recruit and retain its students, despite some extraordinarily interesting and talented faculty attracted by the area, by the adventure of a new school, by the chance to evade the draft, and by the exciting opportunity to create a new curriculum from scratch. (Southampton finally was forced to shut its doors with a cumulative operating deficit of $44 million many decades later.)

A much more successful part of Admiral Conolly's grand design was the merger of the Brooklyn College of Pharmacy into Long Island University. Detailed planning had been started while Conolly was still alive and continued in the months that followed. John Baiardi wrote to Pell on July 11, 1962, "As per your instruction, I have met with Dean Zupko and we critically discussed principles which would be involved in the relocation of the Brooklyn College of Pharmacy on the campus of the Brooklyn Center." It had been agreed, even before Conolly died, that Pharmacy would need 50,000 square feet of classroom and library space on the Brooklyn campus. The Welfare Department of the State of New York was interested in buying the existing Pharmacy Building and at a meeting, Admiral Wood suggested that the University and the City "exchange the existing plant for city-owned ground adjacent to the University."

But, on April 2, 1963, the Department of Social Welfare in Albany informed Wood that the legislature had struck from the Governor's executive budget the money required to purchase the Pharmacy Building, which meant that the necessary funds for construction would have to be found elsewhere. It would take close to a decade to find the donors, Arnold and Marie Schwartz, who would make the enabling gift for this merger to be effected. Before that happened, there was a serious plan to move the entire College of Pharmacy from Brooklyn to Brookville, further exacerbating the tensions between those in Brooklyn and those at C.W. Post. The federal government refused to provide a grant of $2.8 million unless Pharmacy remained in the inner city. The relocation scheme collapsed and the Brooklyn College of Pharmacy became the Arnold & Marie Schwartz College of Pharmacy and Health Sciences after Arnold Schwartz committed $1 million over ten years to name the school.

Another project, dear to Admiral Conolly's heart, was establishing a college at Mitchel Field to offer degrees to officers and enlisted men and women on active service. On May 22, 1962, the Board of Trustees passed a resolution authorizing the University to apply to the federal government "for acquisition of the land the buildings occupied by Mitchel College at Mitchel Field in Hempstead, Long Island." There were three two-story wooden barrack buildings, which had been modified for classrooms, as well as two other barracks buildings then unused that were part of this transfer. During the Korean War, this scheme might have gained traction, but it had far less viability in the 60s. Once the air force concluded that Mitchel Field was no longer necessary for military use, the entire rationale fell away. The five and a half acres located at Merrick Avenue and Hempstead Turnpike, which the University had bought for $170,000, ultimately was sold as excess University real estate. The purchase agreement had stipulated that if the University did sell the land in the future, it would put any surplus profit above $212,500 toward repayment of the construction loan from the Department of Health Education and Welfare to build the main library at C.W. Post. That is what happened.

At a meeting of the Executive Committee of the Board of Trustees on January 24,

1963, Pell requested that the Board accept with gratitude the tendered gift of 100 acres in Yaphank by Roosevelt Field Inc., as mentioned earlier, one of Zeckendorf's real estate partnerships. The dream for this site was the proposed Zeckendorf College of Science and Technology, another of the plans that failed by the end of in the decade.

Judge Miles S. McDonald, a University Trustee and sitting member of the State Supreme Court, submitted to a Board committee "a full and complete report on the feasibility of the establishment of an operation by the University of a law school in Nassau County." A week later, on January 30, 1963, William Casey, Leonard Hall's partner and a future Director of the CIA, wrote to Hoxie sharing his views on the need for a law school on Long Island. Casey, who had played such an important role in the University's winning the case against the Village of Brookville more than a decade earlier, presented a cogent argument for why LIU should be the institution developing such a school.

On July 2, 1963, Howard Hogan, a Mineola based Supreme Court Justice, presented to Pell a detailed brief analyzing the viability of such a school, the existing competition in the New York area and the interest evinced by both Hofstra and Adelphi. Hogan concluded his long and detailed presentation by writing "The need is evident, the time is now. If one or all three of the local institutions do not take the leadership, it is safe to predict others will. All that is required is a little courage and a little get-up-and-go!"

All of these efforts to expand were fed by demography and by economic intensification on "the Island." But to read the Post "Ten Year Report on the College," for example, is to enter a dreamland of wishful thinking, based an economic security blanket of limitless future students. Long Island was growing rapidly; the demand for skilled labor was extraordinarily high. The risks of SUNY, Vietnam, inflation and the draft had not yet clouded the picture. America was going to the moon and Grumman was making that lunar landing craft. Thus, the sub-committee that was examining full-time undergraduate student enrollment projections wrote, "By 1970 the enrollment and full-time undergraduate programs on the college level is expected to reach 100,000. The new state supported institutions in the region proposed modestly to provide for only 26,000 students through 1970. This figure leaves 70,000 to do their work elsewhere. The plans of our neighboring private institutions are for tremendous expansion." This sub-committee recognized that consolidation is essential, that buildings take time to erect, that the recruitment of faculty is a slow and costly business. But underlying all of these caveats was the optimistic belief that demography and the demands of a trained workforce would carry the day. The numbers seemingly spoke for themselves, and there was bullishness, even hubris, suggesting an open-ended growth spurt that would solve virtually all future problems.

PART II - RALPH GORDON HOXIE

The 1963-1964 LIU budget estimated that total current income at Post, in its tenth year of existence, was $6,106,730, whereas at Brooklyn it was only $6,032,000. The instructional costs at both campuses were virtually the same. While there were a few Jeremiahs at the University, their warnings were ignored by the seductive lure of the seeming inevitably of open-ended growth. In a letter from Emilio Collado, the Standard Oil executive and Trustee, to Gordon Hoxie with visible copies to Franz Schneider and Carleton Palmer, and a blind copy to John Pell, Collado asked about Post's future plans. He was trying to get Hoxie to prioritize which desiderata were more important than others. He wrote, "In other words, what must you do and what must you undertake only if additional gifts fill up the picture? If the additional gifts are not forthcoming, do you have to scale down size of student body, faculty, subject coverage, and does the plan make possible an integrated proportionality?" Collado's worries seemed excessive.

Despite the increasingly visible decline of the Borough of Brooklyn, optimism encouraged plant construction there as well. On October 15, 1963, the Executive Committee of the Board discussed "the desirability and feasibility of acquisition of the land and buildings known as "University Towers" which were on the other side of Willoughby Street from the campus. The Executive Committee after discussion, agreed that paying the price of $1,150,000 above the existing FHA mortgages of $6,482,000 was a prudent and wise thing for the University to do. Zeckendorf and the others saw these apartment towers immediately adjacent to the campus as a natural further extension of that campus so that faculty and staff could afford to live very near. Creating a tight-knit campus community would counter the urban rot spreading across downtown Brooklyn. It would also permit Brooklyn to be competitive with other urban schools by offering subsidized faculty and staff housing. And it would strengthen the concept of *in loco parentis* as students and their professors shared a common space.

While the available land around Brooklyn was far more restricted than the open spaces at Post where hundreds of acres were available for purchase and/or development, Brooklyn also remained a campus under construction. At substantial expense, the Brooklyn Paramount, the second largest movie palace in New York City with over 4,600 seats, was converted into four lecture halls, a bookstore, a reception hall and a gymnasium built where the main seating area of the movie theatre once existed. There were few gyms in the world with a Mighty Wurlitzer able to rise through the parquet floor to fill the space with extraordinary sound. Student lounges, a game room, locker rooms for men and women all were shoehorned into this ornate fantasy building that once presented Bing Crosby and Rudy Vallee doing vaudeville acts on main stage.

Owners of local gas stations vied to get the University to buy them out. The University was negotiating with the Parks Department over the Raymond Street Jail site, attempting to create an agreement with the City similar to what Columbia proposed for the Morningside Park site. The Brooklyn-Cumberland Hospital Complex, directly across the street from Long Island University was also struggling to find the necessary funds to buy the Raymond Jail site. The University was eager to expand and actively exploring its options, especially along its Ashland Street perimeter.

On February 6, 1963, John Pell spoke at the Charter Day Dinner. He noted that his first year had been one "of substantial progress for Long Island University." Admissions requirements had been raised at both major centers. Faculty salaries had been increased and plans called for further increases. Noting that the book value of its real property was for the first time in seven figures, he indicated that the University's management and administrative structure had been greatly strengthened. Post College had come of age "with the appointment of Dr. R. Gordon Hoxie as President of the college." And "John Baiardi's leadership has given renewed momentum" at University Center, the Brooklyn campus. The University has acquired "a large industrial building on site to house an expanded library." His report was upbeat, as one would expect to hear at a fundraising dinner for any institution. But Pell seemed genuinely delighted by what had happened at LIU, ending his remarks: "Admiral Conolly would be proud of us tonight."

The internal divisions and discord of the senior team were papered over in his final draft of the Report to the Board dated November 14th. Gone were references of a lack of unity and internal conflict. The University he showcased to the Board exuded confidence about its future growth. He celebrated the "further improvement this year in the overall caliber of the incoming class. This was achieved along with a 20% increase in the size of the freshman class. With a continuing rise in admission applications, the University will be able to become increasingly selective in the years immediately ahead…."

Pell also detailed the signing of the "sister agreement" with Chung-Ang University in Korea. He expressed his pleasure at receiving an honorary degree there himself, and spoke about the opportunities that this affiliation could bring. Trustee James van Fleet, William Zeckendorf Sr., Admiral Wood and others had close personal and professional ties to the post-war Korean establishment and they collectively pushed this connection, especially after Professor Leon Sinder, the Chair of the Brooklyn Department of Sociology, spent a Fulbright year at Chung-Ang.

As Pell reviewed the past twenty months of his Chancellorship, he celebrated increased student enrollment, the growth of the budget, expanded ownership of real property, and an increased scope of services. In his words, "The University today stands as the sixth largest private University in New York State." More specifically, enrollment of full-time undergraduates went from 5,530 to 7,536. The total number of students served had gone from 9,100 to 12,361.The teaching staff stood at 354 full-time members and 184 part-timers, while in 1961 there were only 256 full-time faculty. The budget had grown from $10 million to $13.5 million. The value of the physical assets went from $15 million to nearly $21 million. Pell singled out "the establishment of the new four-year liberal arts college in Southampton," noting that it was "one of the most important undertakings of this administration.

The Pells arriving in South Korea to receive an Honorary Degree from President Louise Kim of Chung-Ang University. Also in the photo are Professor and Mrs. Leon Sinder.

He concluded this longish report by raising in a very subdued way that nagging issue, "the question of unity." Pell repeated several of the themes that had already been debated endlessly, including problems such as "a multi-campus operation extending over a distance of 100 miles." He noted that this lack of clarity about how individual parts of the University related to the whole "is a matter of concern to outside agencies whose respect and good will is essential to our well being -- organizations such as the U.S. Department of Health, Education and Welfare, the State Education Department, the Middle States Association, the various professional associations and councils in higher education, the federal and state lending agencies and private financial organizations." All these needed to know the relationship of the various campuses with the central administration and with each other. He then added, almost as a footnote, that "Perhaps saddest of all is that the members of the University family itself - faculty, students and alumni - are not at all certain what relationship their College bears to the University or to the other Colleges in the University."

As already mentioned, he offered as a partial solution, the creation of the University Senate and, "for the first time, a University-wide Graduate Council to guide the development of graduate studies at the various centers in a more cohesive manner." Pell ended his sixteen-page report with a summary that could have been recited by Pollyanna. "In the years ahead we must strive for the ever-strengthening of the University and of its parts.... each performs a unique role of service.... as each of the units is strengthened so is the University as a whole is strengthened. Each gives freely of its resources for the development of the other parts and of the whole. We have here an opportunity to make an unusual and splendid contribution to the academic world."

Then, as a postscript, he took "a look to the future," indicating that he was "satisfied that the University has maintained its progress and at a pace consistent with the Conolly years." He reported that he had initiated work on a ten year prospectus, one which would tell the University, for instance, "how large we should aspire to grow, and where, and in what manner." And as part of articulating future tasks in order to continue to grow the University, he wanted "a thorough investigation...to determine the possibility of an affiliation with an existing law school or the establishment of a new law school." Pell concluded, "If we *can* grow - and we can - we should. Indeed, it is our obligation."

Some months earlier, on September 9, 1963, he had issued that "directive for long range planning." He established November 15, 1964 as the date when this had to be completed - the day after his summary report to the Board. What he wanted was a specific plan in broad outline to cover the development of the University for the next ten years. "Because Middle States demanded it and other agencies wanted it," he submitted that "it now seems necessary to have an overall University plan of development," based on *"what we expect to be able to do, rather than what we would like to do."* He wanted this document "in such a form that it could readily be kept up to date and meaningful," in sum, a multi- dimensional blueprint for the future.

That passing reference to the accreditors glossed over a much more complex relationship between Long Island University under John Pell and separately both the State Education Department and the Middle States Commission. On September 19, 1963, almost exactly a year before, Robert H. McCambridge, the then Associate Director of the office of Administrative Services in Higher Education for the State, sent Pell multiple copies of a preliminary report on Faculty-Administrative Relationships for general discussion and very limited, more candid distribution of five additional copies for the University officers. In the final report, dated April 9, 1964, The State Department of Education continued to find serious flaws with how Long Island University was structured.

After a brief paragraph of fluff, the Report noted, "It is particularly important in any university for the man at the top and those with whom he surrounds himself to develop and share a clear philosophy and objective as to what they mean by a university-type program." McCambridge and his boss, Irwin K. French, who co-signed the document, reiterated a long held goal from Albany "that the total university has a strength that is greater than the sum of its parts." The co-authors further required "that formal organizational patterns be effectively developed; that there be an adequate staff of university as well as college administrative officers to carry it out." The Report focused on four areas: the structure of the Board; the role of the Chancellor; the appointment of an Academic Vice Chancellor; and the chief administrative officers on each campus.

The Report proposed structural reforms for membership and operations of the Board, as if the authors were a management consultancy hired by the Board to improve operating efficiency. They observed that, "One college, C. W. Post, is apparently considering a twenty million dollar program which should be related to other university objectives." And they questioned why "The report by C. W. Post entitled, 'The Future of the State of the College,' for example, is not clearly worded as a recommendation to the Chancellor and the Board, although steps are apparently underway to give it such consideration."

Among many other recommendations: "In the long run, the Chancellor of the University should not also act as President of any campus unit. To have a close relationship to any part of the University diminishes his ability to coordinate the program of the entire University. No Provost or President should report and recommend action directly to the Board." R. Gordon Hoxie was clearly their target, and when they turned their attention to the Academic Vice Chancellor, the Department of Education insisted that, "The administrative heads must recognize the legitimate function of such an officer." They addressed openly the long-running, internal dispute of the Pell years: "If that requires a line rather than staff relationship, then the appointment should be made in those terms." They suggested that the Statutes of the colleges be modified to give adequate recognition to important University officers. They urged that each chief administrator on each campus hold the same title as their peers throughout the system.

The language was atypically blunt, not bureaucratically opaque. There were many "musts" and "should" sentences throughout the document, and the tone was proscriptive. Albany seemingly suggested that Hoxie and his team at C.W.Post were on the wrong side of virtually every disagreement that had surfaced during the two Pell years. There is nothing in the several files of the University principals to establish whether this document was ever submitted to or discussed by the Board.

As had been promised two years earlier, Middle States was also sending a follow-up site visit on March 8, 1964. The University's written document was due by February 1, 1964. This time Middle States sent a site visiting team of six, joined by Elbert K. Fretwell Jr., then Assistant Commissioner of Education for the State.

Claude E. Puffer, the Chair of the 1954 visiting team was Chair of this visiting team, and there were three members of the 1961 team. All of this was unusual. It indicated that Middle States, as interpreted by Pell in an internal memo to the LIU board, remained exceedingly nervous about whether LIU was making progress in hiring a Vice Chancellorship of Academic Affairs; in ending the practice since Conolly of the Chancellor holding campus Presidencies as well as a University position, and in the names of each of the campuses.

The Board of Trustees met while the Middle States visiting team was in New York. It heard briefly from Fretwell and another member, a Vice President of Howard University, James Clark, but the Minutes moved quickly to the next agenda item, the renaming of the Paramount Theatre, as Founders Hall. There was apparently little Board interest in the Middle States visit, and most of the Board meeting focused upon routine matters or funding resolutions for new construction. This was the meeting where Hoxie proposed successfully that the Graduate Library Program be named for Carleton and Winthrop Palmer. It was also the meeting where Judge McDonald reported that neither Brooklyn Law School nor New York Law School was prepared to affiliate with LIU. The Board treated Middle States site visits like honorary degree selections or faculty promotions-they were routine matters.

On March 24, 1964, Pell got another letter from Fretwell, informing him that the State was sending three quite large delegations "to complement the Middle States visit." The State teams were to "evaluate programs for purpose of registration." Staff from both the Division of Higher Education and the Division of Teacher Education were involved. Brooklyn, C. W. Post and Mitchel College were the campuses to be visited, each for two or three days. Such visits were extremely unusual and storm flags should have been flying. If the Board missed the signals, it was clear that Pell was no longer so enchanted with his job as Chancellor. The internecine struggles were exhausting, the external regulators were circling like a pack of wolves, and the novelty and status of his job no longer seemed so seductive.

The received report on Mitchel College was, in particular, curdling. "The criticisms included in this report reflect upon the central University administration ultimately responsible for Mitchel College's development over the past seven years." History, social science, mathematics, science, and industrial management had departmental Chairs who neither had a Ph.D. nor were full time. Education, engineering, modern languages and philosophy were headed by part-time faculty. The site visitors then chronicled a list of regulatory and pedagogical failures, including a major offered in Russian studies when there was only one faculty member who earned a Ph.D; a Math major without anyone to teach in it who was full time or held a terminal degree; a Science major where everyone was adjunct and without a Ph.D; and an overall faculty of 82 of whom only six were full time. The Chair of the Science Division taught at Mitchel courses in biology, chemistry, earth science, physics and principles of retailing while the Chair of the Humanities Division taught western literature, Shakespeare, creative writing, history of the language, the novel, modern drama, Chaucer and medieval and Renaissance drama.

Of the 82 students admitted in 1964, only 17 met the announced standards for matriculation. Record keeping was poorly organized. Academic credit for military service allowed one Lt. Colonel to be granted 37 college credits for his basic training, officer candidate school, and Command and General Staff College. Many courses used only one textbook. The library had 8,200 volumes, although in LIU's Middle States report the library holdings claimed by LIU met the requirements set by the American Library Association - a minimum of "50,000 carefully chosen volumes." There was one multi-purpose science lab to service 18 different science classes in four disciplines. This six page, single spaced report found nothing of quality at the Mitchel Field campus.

The eight site visitors the State sent to Brooklyn were much more positive about what they discovered. They applauded the redeployment of resources from weaker programs to centers of excellence, but noted the anomaly that Post was building graduate programs "across the board," while Brooklyn was emphasizing "retrenchment and cautious growth." The site visitors speculated that "the time is coming, if it has not in fact arrived, for the University to set up these two graduate centers on a completely separate basis." Such a "decentralization might lead to 'inconsistencies and anomalies' as well as a further fragmentation of the University." But, "if a University-wide approach and philosophy regarding graduate education is not forthcoming, such a separation may evolve because of a lack of administrative action." The State regulators were clear: "there is a real urgency to have a Vice Chancellor for Academic Affairs with line power to administer all-University graduate programs among his other duties."

The separate C. W. Post team also focused on LIU's failure to establish the concept of a unified university-wide set of graduate degrees and programs. But it came out with a different recommendation. "It might be best if the idea of all-University graduate departments and programs be abandoned until such time that there is a clearer definition of leadership on a University-wide basis." The team also faulted the Post administration for allowing too many full-time faculty to teach "overloads," for inadequate science facilities, a weak advisement system, and inadequate office space. It particularly worried that with 600 students on probation, and many more close to failing, it was essential that student services and academic counseling be expanded.

And, it observed that growth for its own sake eroded the pursuit of excellence. "At all levels and in all divisions, academic quality control and elimination of the proliferation of courses and program should be a matter of self-discipline within the college. A quality higher [education] institution should not need a State Education Department to exercise this control. If such control can not come from within

Post then it must be exerted by the central administration of the University." The Brooklyn report was dated May 6th; the one on Post was dated May 7th. Neither Pell nor Hoxie emerged from this barrage unscathed.

Four days later, on May 11, 1964, John H.G. Pell informed the Board in a "Personal and Confidential" memo that he was resigning as Chancellor. This announcement was followed in the next sentence with a recommendation that "President R. Gordon Hoxie of C. W. Post College, as the next senior line officer of the University, deserves to be considered as a candidate for the chief executive officer of the University." After writing a tepid recommendation about Hoxie, he next acknowledged that the University "has been reviewed, checked and evaluated by several independent agencies and authorities."

But he failed to chronicle accurately the depth of their critical judgments, minimizing, for example, the State's stinging criticism of Mitchel College. By sloughing off how the critique was delivered in "an informal, oral discussion with the Chancellor," he avoided sharing the criticism fully. He did mention that some of the academic programs at Post had come in for criticism. But there was no detailed sharing of the tone and severity of what was said, nor the implicit criticism of Hoxie or himself. Key thoughts went unsaid, perhaps because he was tired and no longer felt responsible. And, perhaps, there was a coup in which Hoxie told Zeckendorf how near to disaster LIU was coming. But without any written records, such speculation is but gossip.

What is clear was that the decision had been made days, maybe weeks, before Pell wrote his memo to the Board. On May 11, 1964, four days prior, Zeckendorf had written a "thank you" response to a letter from Hoxie dated May 7th. Zeckendorf celebrated the close partnership he and Hoxie would enjoy. Whatever informal deliberations there might have been at the Board level, there was no search process, no review of other candidates, and no quasi-public debate as to whether Hoxie was the man to lead the University forward. The "Composite Committee" established by Conolly in late 1961 was never reconstituted or summoned. Did Pell even have any real say about his successor? Was it decided just by John McGrath and Zeckendorf? By Zeckendorf alone? Again, there is no written record, no paper trail. Certainly Pell's memo to the Board about Hoxie was tepid. Running out of things he wanted to include in his endorsement, he observed that "Mrs. Hoxie is devoted to the University." She was.

In the very brief lame-duck period before the Hoxies moved into the Chancellor's home, Pell still had to deal with the State Department of Education and Middle States. On May 18, 1964, he got a letter from Fretwell, confirming a prior meeting he and his deputy, Allan Kuusisto, had had with Pell, when they had entered into an oral agreement on Mitchel College, the Vice Chancellorship of Academic Affairs and the "role and authority of the all-University Graduate Council." In polite language it mandated "a proposal…" by early June. Referring to Mitchel College, Fretwell wrote, "we do not feel justified at this point in continuing any curriculum registration at Mitchel beyond July, 1964." The two options for LIU were to close it that summer or convert it into an extension of Post. Fretwell was resigning, taking a job in California, but he was resolving this bit of outstanding business first.

A few days later, Pell wrote to Hoxie, asking him how he wanted to handle these three issues. On June 1, 1964 he got back a formal letter from Hoxie with a tone that suggested he no longer needed to flatter Pell. He was in charge and wanted Pell to understand that.

"May I further acknowledge your report of May 11, 1964, addressed to President [Chairman] Zeckendorf and Members of the Board of Trustees of Long Island University. There is one point within your report of May 11th to the Board which the written report from the State Education Department does not, I am happy to say, bear out; that is your reference that 'The State Education Department visiting team, in an informal, oral discussion with the Chancellor, spoke with considerable criticism of the Mitchel College operation as well as of certain of the academic programs of C.W. Post College.' In the oral report they did indeed offer criticism particularly of our accounting program. I am happy to note that this written report contains no such criticism."

Hoxie wanted agreement that Mitchel be transferred to Post, not closed, and he wanted it done on the date of his formal accession to authority but only after the Board actually elected him. He pushed Pell hard for an early Board meeting, a point he returned to in a second letter of the same date, now referring to a letter Pell had also received from Al Meder at Middle States, who noted that the site visit of March 8th would be reviewed by the Commission later in that June. Meder wrote of "the need to [make] the prompt appointment of an exceedingly capable Vice Chancellor for Academic Affairs," noting that this urgent bit of business "runs like a refrain throughout the entire Puffer report." Meder asked Pell if such an appointment would be made within three weeks, since LIU would stand a much better chance of keeping its accreditation if that appointment was announced in time. In case Pell and Hoxie missed the point, he wanted to "know about it by letter, telephone or telegram as soon as possible." That threat, Meder was saying, is the difference between loss or accreditation and survival. Hoxie's second letter is a clear acknowledgement of that risk.

It is impossible to know whether the State and Middle States coordinated their efforts or not. But both insisted that re-registration and reaccreditation depended on hiring an Academic Vice President. On June 2, 1964, Allan Kuusisto, Fretwell's successor, reinforced this pressure while technically clarifying the Brooklyn site visit report.

In fact, the University already had an offer out to Henry C. Mills, the Vice President of Educational Administration at The University of Rochester. He had met Pell and Hoxie at the end of May and was eager to take the job after minor perks and an entertainment allowance were agreed upon. As a result, Pell wrote Kuusisto telling him that the Board had met on June 10th and that he was resigning, Hoxie was taking over, Mills was coming, Wood was marginalized by becoming Vice Chancellor of Development, and Mitchel college was becoming "an extension of C. W. Post College in accordance with the recommendation of the State Education Department...." Kuusisto responded that these changes "flow directly, I am completely confident, from your [Pell's] own desire to set things in order."

On June 25th, Pell got a formal letter from Meder indicating that re-accreditation was forthcoming. The Commission "complimented Long Island University on progress in a) deciding what kind of university structure it wants; b) establishing procedures to facilitate faculty participation in the formation of educational policy; c) the first year of Southampton College." The Commission then requested "the following future reports: 1 April, 1965 - on Mitchel College; 1 October, 1965 - on Southampton College; 1 March, 1966 - on the Library School; 1 March, 1966 - on the MBA program at C.W. Post College; 1 October, 1966 - a general report on the University which will be followed by a visit."

The twenty-eight months since the Admiral died must have seemed like an eternity to Pell. Swept into hand-to-hand combat, unprepared for the savagery of academic politics, never certain exactly what the academy expected of him, he must have longed for more time at Fort Ticonderoga. Always the patrician gentleman, he understood that the University he took over when the Admiral had tragically died was coming off the rails, but he was not sure how to stop the train wreck or how to manage as a Chief Executive Officer. He had never run a large, impoverished, bureaucratic, insecure institution. He probably never had to fire anyone in his life but a maid or a secretary before assuming this interim job.

Out of a sense of loyalty, Pell stayed on the Board for much of the ensuing decade but rarely spoke or intervened, even when he had been central to one issue or another. Or, if he did speak, it was always behind closed doors and in executive session. The written record does not suggest that he was given special deference by his fellow Trustees, even though he was so well informed.

Why he stayed as Chancellor those twenty-eight months is a mystery. The Conolly era already seemed very distant. Was it that he didn't know what to do? Was he fully aware of what was actually going on, or did he float above the fray, managing his own portfolio of stocks and focusing on his beloved Ticonderoga? John H.G. Pell was an accidental Chancellor. He had volunteered to do a job for a few months because of a dreadful accident and a lack of other candidates. He was a decent, well-meaning man who took the job because there was a need and the job sounded like fun. He ended up in charge of a fractious and increasingly dysfunctional institutional family for several years. Neither he nor the University were much the better for his sacrifice.

This is the story of one University, its aspirations and hopes. Founded in Brooklyn... [it is] today one of the ten largest private Universities in the nation.... Presumptuous? Perhaps. But it also a study in courage of a unique bootstrap operation carrying forward from the brink of bankruptcy and no accreditation a dozen years ago.

R. Gordon Hoxie

Chapter Five

Preface to the Future

Chancellor Ralph Gordon Hoxie

On June 16, 1964, a University press release announced that, "R. Gordon Hoxie, head of C.W. Post, was appointed Chancellor of Long Island University." In a draft of a "suggested message from Mr. Zeckendorf to the faculty and the staff of the University," the text informed the community that on June 10th, the Board of Trustees elected Hoxie to be the new chief executive officer effective July 15th. In the typescript version it read, "Dr. Hoxie will have the title of President of the University. The title of Chancellor, which was held by Dr. Pell during his interim term of office, will be retired." That second sentence was crossed out in ink and Hoxie in his own hand reasserted the word Chancellor instead of President. The message continued, "The Board is especially pleased that it has been able to select for the permanent office of President a member of the University family. Dr. Hoxie's brilliant and forceful leadership has been conspicuously demonstrated during his 10 years of service with the University by the extraordinary development of C.W. Post College, which he has headed, and by his extremely productive role in advancing the University's overall development." Hoxie continued to hold the title of President of C.W. Post. At the age of 45 he had skillfully climbed around and over others to achieve his most ambitious goal. There was no search. He was elected unanimously. There was also no review or exploration of other possible candidates.

Hoxie had proven himself to be a skilled infighter. From his first appointment by Admiral Conolly, dated July 28, 1954, when he was appointed Dean of the Faculty of the newly opened C.W. Post College and simultaneously Dean of the College of General Studies at Mitchel Air Force Base, to his election as Chancellor a decade later, the files revealed a consuming ambition. There was also a constant effort to improve the odds of his own promotion by encouraging others to burnish his reputation.

Facsimile of original appointment letter from Conolly to Hoxie as edited by Conolly.

In 1954, he had signed the obligatory anti-communist "loyalty oath" in his contract, a commitment he readily accepted. He was paid $10,000 a year plus housing with an expectation that he would teach three hours in the fall and three in the spring. While accepting the Admiral's appointment, he also bargained for interim pay, "bearing in mind the value of service to Long Island University at this important juncture and my loss of income from Columbia University and Trinity College." (It is unclear what he was doing at Trinity while working at Columbia. This is the only acknowledgement of that brief Trinity College employment.) In response, Conolly began his pay a month early.

Hoxie also maneuvered to get his wife, Louise, a position in the Department of Modern Languages at Post with the rank of Assistant Professor. The following year, he requested a separate letter appointing him as Professor of History, backdated to August 1, 1954: "In view of our mutual interest in the development of political science, I would respectfully recommend that the appointment be professor of history and political science." By 1961, he was offered the titles of "Provost and Executive Dean of C.W. Post College performing also the duties of Dean of the Faculty."

The day after Conolly died, as mentioned in the Prologue, Hoxie sent both Arthur Roth and Bill Zeckendorf a message he had just written for the following year's C.W. Post Yearbook noting, "In these days of sharing a very real sense of mutual loss, I though you might be interested reading the attached message which I wrote the evening before Admiral and Mrs. Conolly died." He wrote both Trustees, "I only wish that the Conollys might have read it; yet, I believe they somehow know."

In the following week he wrote Zeckendorf again: "I enclose a letter just received from our friend Al Jacobs. When I telephoned him, I did not discuss the nature of my call and my desire to see him. However, having known him these many years, it would appear that he is so wrestling with a problem at hand, my visit should be deferred." It is impossible to know exactly when Jacobs turned down the LIU Presidency (the Jacobs Archive at the University of Michigan shed no light on Jacobs' flirtation with LIU), but it is far more likely that he did not want to see Hoxie because he did not want to tell Hoxie something he had not already told Zeckendorf. A month later, on April 9, 1962, Hoxie again wrote Arthur Roth as noted in Chapter Four, defining his own upcoming promotion to a Vice Presidency. "I strongly recommend that it be defined either as Vice President for the Nassau Suffolk region or as Executive Vice President with my principal responsibilities being in the Nassau Suffolk area."

On May 21st, Pell had obliged with a letter appointing him as Vice President of Long Island University and Provost of C.W. Post College effective June 1, 1962. And within a month of that Hoxie wrote to Pell, "It is recommended that you, as Acting President of Long Island University, and I, as Vice President, confer with the appropriate officers of the New York State Education Department...." Hoxie's memo did not begin with a phrase such as "may I suggest" or some other deferential phrase, but rather with that slightly condescending, "it is recommended that you...." Consciously or otherwise, Hoxie was subtly reversing the power relationship with Pell, trying to gain the upper hand from the very first weeks of Pell's Chancellorship. There was a vacuum and, psychologically, Hoxie was making himself indispensable by telling Pell what to do next.

His use of the imperative with Pell was quite distinct from his obsequiousness with Zeckendorf or Mrs. Post or others he was trying to flatter. On July 19, 1962, he began a letter to Zeckendorf, "Having just returned from active duty with the Air Force, I hasten to write this expression to you. The action taken by the Board of Trustees at its last meeting in naming the new social science building here on the campus, Hoxie Hall, came as a tremendous and quite overwhelming surprise!" Few things actually surprised Hoxie and he usually manipulated virtually all of these "overwhelming surprises." He was in campaign mode all the time. He wrote in that same letter to Zeckendorf, "There are daily evidences of the increase of a sense of 'family' within the university. Certainly you have contributed mightily towards this. At the suggestion of our friend, George Shapiro, Louise and I are inviting all the senior faculty of all the colleges of the University here for a little party...." Pell was an accidental Chancellor and Hoxie was looking for every way possible to establish himself as "heir presumptive."

He chronically enlisted friends and supporters to write to Zeckendorf on his behalf. Thus, he convinced his friends, Gladys Rockefeller Underhill and Dudley Field Underhill, to write Zeckendorf in July 1962: "During the past several months we have given much thought to C.W. Post College. Be assured this letter is written only in our desire to be helpful to you, to Mr. Pell, and to the University's Trustees." The Underhills then went on to speak about how "Gordon Hoxie certainly has made a most important contribution to the phenomenal success achieved by C.W. Post College." The Underhills in this jointly signed letter lobbied Zeckendorf, commenting, "there seems to be an intangible yet quite persistent undercurrent of local opinion which maintains that C.W. Post should have autonomy, as do Hofstra and Adelphi." The Underhills requested "that you receive this letter as a private, privileged communication between yourself and ourselves," but the letter, its phraseology, and its timing had Hoxie's fingerprints all over it.

This was a technique he used again and again, but most frequently, with Marjorie Merriweather Post, then married to Herbert A. May. For example, on August 2 1962, she was encouraged by Hoxie to write to Zeckendorf: "I am hoping so much that when the regents meet in September they will look favorably upon Dean R. Gordon Hoxie for the President of C.W. Post College." The old-fashioned use of "so much" was a favorite construction of Hoxie's who, almost for sure, drafted the letter for Mrs. Post. And this campaign worked. Zeckendorf wrote Pell on August 7, 1962, enclosing both the May and Underhill letters. This correspondence prompted Zeckendorf and Pell to meet to review this additional promotion for Hoxie. Hoxie also lobbied John McGrath on October 11, 1962: "your assurance that the Trustees desire that I retain a University office comparable to my present vice presidency is, indeed, gratifying. Your wise counsel that the President of C.W. Post College should also be a Vice Chancellor of the University will assuredly pay rich dividends." Hoxie had the instincts of a ward boss in a municipal election. And he cultivated those people whose voices would sway how Trustees would view him or support the things he wanted to get from the Board.

Hoxie's goal was not only to influence the Board, but also to use the Board to strengthen his hand when dealing with his peers in the administration. In a letter to McGrath of October 11, 1962, he wrote, "With regard to the question of an Academic Vice Chancellor, the wisdom of your judgment is likewise sound. Perhaps a strong academician can be named as assistant to the Chancellor and Secretary of the University." In a letter to Zeckendorf on the same day, he urged that the University move with caution in appointing any Vice Chancellor of Academic Affairs. "It may well be that a strong academician can be appointed as assistant to the Chancellor and Secretary of the University, rather than Vice Chancellor for Academic Affairs." And he concluded by promising to discuss this matter with John Pell "who has my wholehearted support."

Hoxie was a congenial self-promoter. He loved dedications and convocations; always had. On September 21, 1962, he organized a dedication ceremony for the R. Gordon Hoxie Hall as well as one for the Everett C. Jessup Health Centre. Marjorie Post clearly loved the attention she received at these ceremonies. And with mock modesty after this dedication event, Hoxie insisted that the reception was in honor of Mrs. Post and Dr. Jessup. Hoxie, a worthy descendent of Polonius, declined to be in the limelight. Later that autumn, however, he did organize an inaugural ceremony for himself, sending to Zeckendorf, who was away at the time, and to Arthur Roth, his remarks. "Under separate cover I am having sent to you 20 copies of my inaugural address with your forward statement. You might desire to send these to business associates and friends." And to Zeckendorf he observed, "There have been a great many requests for my inaugural address which, with some modesty, I can report, was received with real enthusiasm."

Beneath this veneer of self-confidence and rotund flattery, Hoxie was always a vulnerable and insecure man. He was without physical stature - short, plump, with a double chin, even as a young man, in a body that gave him a pear-like physique. As a child, he must have been acutely aware of his physical shortcomings, and serving under Conolly, a true charismatic individual, must have been stressful to him. He used language to compensate. His stilted English was 19th century pompous. He delighted in using an old-fashioned Victorian style, one clearly anachronistic in the counter culture world of the '60s. And when he either spoke or wrote while under stress, his language became ever more convoluted and ornate. He had a habit of starting sentences with a participle phrase, as if he had translated his speech out of Latin, and his efforts to strive linguistically for the grand and the hyperbolic made him a figure of ridicule, especially to students, who were rejecting nationally and at Long Island University the old order of academic hierarchy and automatic respect for authority.

Born on March 18, 1919 in Waterloo, Iowa, Hoxie was the son of a doctor who practiced in this small Midwestern city. He graduated with high honors from Iowa State Teachers College in 1940. This was not an alma mater he often boasted about. He then won a scholarship to the University of Wisconsin for his masters in 1941. After the war, he earned his Ph.D from Columbia in 1950, having received a doctoral fellowship and landing a job with Al Jacobs, then the Provost of Columbia. His doctoral dissertation was on John W. Burgess, a 19th century Columbia professor. Hoxie was a principal author of *A History of the Faculty of Political Science at Columbia University*. When Jacobs became President of the University of Denver, he took Hoxie with him as his administrative assistant.

In 1953, Hoxie came back to New York and Columbia as a project associate to assist in planning Columbia's bicentennial celebration. Jacobs also returned east to assume the Presidency of Trinity College (Hartford). He seems to have been willing to hire Hoxie at Trinity once the Columbia bicentennial was over. It is unclear how Conolly learned of Hoxie, but thereafter Hoxie moved rapidly up an administrative ladder at LIU. Hoxie proved to be skilled at management and was in the great courtier tradition of Polonius. He could be charming or ruthless. He knew when to flatter and when to attack. When Conolly first appointed him to be the founding Dean at the new Nassau campus, few would have guessed that he would become President of any large university. And yet, through his ambition, skill and doggedness, he clambered to the top. Those who underestimated him soon discovered that they had badly misread him, often at their own peril.

Within two weeks of becoming Chancellor, Hoxie was ready to announce his new management team. He wrote to Zeckendorf requesting Trustee votes and their sequence at the upcoming Board meeting on June 10, 1964. He wanted a clear hierarchy established within this group. He obviously came first, still to be designated President. In his letter to Zeckendorf he wrote, "John Pell and I agree that the title of the chief executive officer of the University should revert to that of President, with the chief administrative officers of each of the units with the title of Provost." But quickly thereafter he reversed himself. The title of Chancellor had a certain ring to it that flattered his ego and established his position as equal to that of the SUNY and CUNY chief administrators.

Hoxie had in mind a new first choice for Academic Vice President. Arthur Jensen, who was a good friend from Dartmouth. C. W. Post College had already given Jensen an honorary degree. Hoxie wrote to Zeckendorf on April 16, 1964, that Jensen "is to my mind one of America's most inspiring, sound and vigorous educators." Jensen was then Dean of Faculty and Professor of English at Dartmouth. There he founded and directed the Great Issues Program. Hoxie, in his letter to Zeckendorf again used the Conolly card, "Admiral Conolly joined with me in the sense of the highest regard for Dr. Jensen. He is the man we are looking for as Academic Vice Chancellor of Long Island University."

But Jensen turned Hoxie down. "This is one of the hardest letters I have ever written…. The fact that you are to be Chancellor is perhaps the most attractive feature of the post of Vice Chancellor. To work closely with you and to have a close social relationship with you and Louise [Hoxie's wife] is enormously attractive, but that feature must not weigh against my conviction that the job needs a man who has a different grouping of strengths than I have." Jensen concluded, "I am not really your man." In a parallel letter to Zeckendorf, he wrote, "I know myself fairly well, and I have come reluctantly to the conclusion that the job really required a man of slightly different temperament from mine. Moreover my roots in Dartmouth are deep and strong and not easily broken."

Two days, later Hoxie wrote to Jensen, "It was very good talking with you this morning. Bill Zeckendorf and I are heartened by your further consideration of the invitation to serve as Vice Chancellor of Long Island University." Did Jensen waiver in his decision on the phone? Did Hoxie simply confuse his politeness for opportunity? Or was Hoxie simply unable to take a polite "no" for an answer?

In any case, Jensen declined this critically important job for Hoxie and LIU, since both the State of New York and the Middle States Commission had made the early appointment of an Academic Vice President a *sine qua non* for continuing accreditation. Hoxie moved rapidly to appoint his second choice, Dr. Henry (Harry) C. Mills from the University of Rochester.

Third in the new hierarchy would be a Vice Presidency for Development, a new position for the experienced colleague of Conolly's, Admiral Chester C. Wood. He had been *aide de camp* to Conolly, *de facto* chief operating officer under Pell, and Hoxie was demoting him by limiting him to a circumscribed sphere of authority. Next, in sequence, came a new Provost for Brooklyn, William Birenbaum, someone urged upon Hoxie by Pell, among others. And finally, John Baiardi was also given a contracted sphere of responsibility, marginalized as "project officer for the proposed Zeckendorf College of Long Island University." The letter ended with Hoxie proposing a series of dates in order to secure a quorum early enough so that "the public announcement should be aimed for the newspapers of Sunday, June 14th," a date just after the last of the University's commencements. The letter ended, "May I leave this in your good hands," a typical Hoxie use of language deployed to shift the power relationship between himself and the Chairman of the

Board.

Almost immediately after sending this letter, Hoxie changed his mind on his own title. When the Board met on the 10th of June, Board Minutes reported that "after full consideration it was determined that the title of 'Chancellor' for the chief executive officer of the University be retained." And the Board reiterated that Hoxie was to remain simultaneously "President of C.W. Post College." A week before, on June 3rd, Hoxie confirmed his offer to Mills with a salary of $22,000 and a university-owned house on Norgate Road near to the C.W. Post campus. There was a post-script in that letter to Mills. "The Board acted in accordance with your desire and conferred the title, Vice Chancellor for academic affairs."

At that same Board meeting, Hoxie requested and the Board approved moving the legal address of the University "from Kings County to Nassau County" - in other words, from the Brooklyn campus to the recently purchased Tenney estate, a quarter of a mile west of the C.W. Post campus. The Board Minutes noted "the view was expressed that since the University was now operating institutional branches on all of Long Island, from Brooklyn to Southampton, and since the newly elected Chancellor resided in Nassau County in close proximity to C.W. Post College, it was desirable that the principal office of the University be established in Nassau County as of July 15, 1964."

John McGrath, William Zeckendorf, Sr. and R. Gordon Hoxie on Charter Day.

One of the Trustees, Judge McDonald, proposed that the name "The University Center" be assigned to this new location and the Brooklyn campus, which had previously been known as University Center because it housed the administrative and executive offices, "be re-designated as the 'Richard L. Conolly College of Long Island University.'" If further proof was needed that the Hoxie era had begun, the Board also "voted unanimously to change the status of Mitchel College to an extension of C.W. Post College of Long Island University." Immediately after this Board meeting, Hoxie proposed that the Brooklyn campus be named in honor of William Zeckendorf Sr.

This prompted a letter back to Hoxie from Zeckendorf, dated June 12th, expressing his delight at the high honor. He noted that this was "the most heartening news that the Zeckendorf family has received in a long, long time. It would be insincere and hypocritical for me to say other than how pleased I am. Whether the honor is deserving is a matter for others to judge." Webb & Knapp was struggling to survive bankruptcy. The Zeckendorfs, both father and son, had built their empire by pyramiding debt. In his autobiography, Zeckendorf Sr. had commented that he had never "been afraid of debt, because debt is what gives you leverage...." But in this crunch the Zeckendorfs were scrambling to salvage what they could by renegotiating their ownership share of a particular property and/or by selling that interest outright. Trapped in this real estate squeeze, Zeckendorf was truly flattered by the University's recognition.

And in a further letter of July 6, 1964, Hoxie wrote that, "At the Board of Trustees meeting this week it is my desire to secure firm action on the naming of the Zeckendorf College, also on the naming of the Dr. Peter K. Ewald as the Provost of C.W. Post College, Dr. Andrew Spiegel as the Dean of Faculty of C.W. Post College and Dean Eugene Arden as Dean of the Graduate Faculties of Long Island University." By filling in these three key positions prior to Mills' arrival, he hand-selected his choices, and, in particular, filled the critically important Deanship of Graduate Faculties, with his own choice. He linked these promotions to his own formal appointment date of July 15, 1964.

Emilio Collado, Franz Schneider, and the President of the Alumni Association at the Brooklyn Center, Dr. Alan Livingston, were elected Trustees of the University. All three would play very important roles in the years ahead. Hoxie requested, "that Mrs. Marjorie Merriweather Post be elected an honorary member of the Board of Trustees of Long Island University." It was Hoxie's long-held hope that she could be brought ever closer into the orbit of the University, both as philanthropist and as protector of her most ardent admirer, R. Gordon Hoxie. And in a related vein, he asked and got a further Board resolution, to "let residence hall number 6 on the C.W. Post Campus be named Adelaide Riggs Hall in honor of Mrs. Augustus Riggs IV, member of the Executive Council of C.W. Post College, major benefactress of the College, and oldest child of Marjorie Merriweather Post." Designating buildings without a donor was a skillful way to flatter individuals he sought to engage in the University.

Mary Lai, who retained her position as the chief financial officer, reported to the Board on University operations, including a comparison with the two prior years under Chancellor Pell. She reported that current income over expenditures had been steadily rising. It had been $2.5 million two years before, but in fiscal year 1964-65 she projected a $4 million surplus. She warned, however, that because capital costs were funded by the general fund surplus, there was a serious risk that the expenses of construction would come in higher than budgeted and the bills would have to be paid out of the general fund. She noted, for example, that in the 1963-64 fiscal year, the operational surplus was almost $3 million, but servicing the capital debt required $3.5 million, including "$700,000 at Southampton College." The Hoxie era, therefore, started with optimistic but fragile budgetary numbers. Mrs. Lai commented almost as an afterthought, "we can anticipate a surplus next year - only on the condition that you approve item six on the agenda [the tuition increase plan]."

Hoxie called this new team together on the day he formally assumed office, July 15, 1964, and briefed them on the changes that had been voted by the Board. He designated this group, in size approximately a baker's dozen, "the Chancellor's Cabinet." At that first meeting he circulated a letter from Albert Meder, the Chair of the Middle States Commission, listing the various reports which Middle States mandated be submitted over the next several years. The task of managing that process was delegated to Harry Mills. And Hoxie reacted to the scathing report about Mitchel College by the State of New York very blandly, reporting, "The New York State Department of Education stated that Mitchel College should either become a branch of C.W. Post College or close by June 30, 1964. There was no wish to close the college so the option was taken to make Mitchel College the Mitchel Extension Center of C.W. Post College." Hoxie took charge firmly and was off to a fast start. The budget was growing, albeit highly vulnerable to cost overruns and inflation. The University was in the black, provided it raised tuition substantially.

With the new team in place, Hoxie asked Mills to help augment academic excellence by recruiting superstars as faculty. For example, could Mills approach his Rochester friend, the distinguished musicologist Howard Hanson? Hanson had long been the Chair as well as serving as the famed conductor of the School of Music at Rochester, funded by Eastman Kodak. All of this was part of Hoxie's larger organizational effort to draft his own ten year plan, which would outline how LIU would enter into the first rank of large American universities. Both Conolly and Pell had sought to draft similar ten year plans, and each of the campuses had already prepared its own, especially on the C.W. Post and Southampton campuses. Hoxie was adamant that this development plan be accomplished early on his watch. The effort would become the central focus of his first two years of his Chancellorship. The title of this book, *Preface to the Future* was that report. It was also the apogee of his dream for the institution.

Hoxie designated Chester Wood to organize the staffing, design and scope of this university-wide effort, and he authorized the hiring of Muriel Greenhill to serve as chief of staff to Wood in this process. The document, which ultimately consumed an enormous amount of time by a great many people, was something that had Hoxie's fingerprints all over it. Far more carefully crafted than anything submitted to Middle States, this was truly to be a consensus document that engaged all the key stakeholders. It still exists as a subtly constructed development piece, which also enthusiastically engaged the key players. It proved to be a flight of fancy.

In a long memo to the University community in early September 1964, as the new school year was opening, Hoxie wrote with great optimism about the future. He described the new staff members who were assuming leadership positions. He chronicled the creation of the all-University Graduate School of Education, the designation of the Arthur T. Roth Graduate School of Business as an all-University school as well as the Carleton and Winthrop Palmer Graduate Library School. He announced the appointment of Professor Howard K. Rice as Dean of the Arthur T. Roth School and detailed how graduate education would move forward. He detailed as well the creation of Richard L. Conolly College, defining the five instructional divisions, which would be central to Brooklyn's future. He spoke of the appointment of Dr. William (Buck) T. Lai, Mary Lai's husband, as the University-wide director of athletics, and the appointment of Percy Rinde-Thorsen as the University's director of buildings and grounds.

The sun seemed to shine on Long Island University as Hoxie took charge in the summer of 1964. There was a profound contradiction surrounding Hoxie's elevation, not evident at first. How could a man so identified with C.W. Post suddenly win the loyalty of those on the other campuses when he had attempted in myriad ways to distance C.W. Post from them but a few months earlier? How could he create sufficient centripetal mass, when he had so openly argued for centrifugal fragmentation? How could the leading spokesman for a loose confederation of campuses create a federal system through both compliance and coercion? How could someone who seemed so hostile to Brooklyn, become its protector, especially as the turbulence of the '60s upended that campus most of all?

Did Hoxie's drive for power and his ambition to be the University's Chancellor overwhelm his own instinct for self-preservation? Like his mentor and idol, Conolly, he was vicar of a large and diverse congregation, but unlike Conolly, he carried very heavy baggage into the position. His engagement with and positive bias toward C.W. Post made it almost impossible for him to start anew. He could not cleanse himself as a "born again" administrator. The Board had chosen him without a search. To be sure, he had successfully demoted or banished those with whom he fought most vigorously during the Pell's two-year interregnum. But in the academy, memories and grudges do linger for a long time. Brooklyn remembered and worried. Ancient and current grievances festered.

On October 9, 1964, Hoxie was inducted as Chancellor of Long Island University. He held a very elaborate ceremony on the C.W. Post campus, a point not lost in Brooklyn. His prepared remarks, entitled "The University and the Pioneer Spirit," was a speech that in typescript ran 21 pages, double-spaced. It is still recalled as an extraordinarily long address. Filled with quotations from Shakespeare, John Keats, and Alfred Lord Tennyson among others, it was inflated, old fashioned, pompous and obsequious. It stroked Marjorie Post and her daughter, Mrs. Augustus Riggs IV, John Pell and others. Hoxie announced the name of the physical sciences and engineering building, almost complete, as the John H.G. Pell Hall. He talked expansively of higher education in the United States and the role that Long Island would play in the future, emphasizing that LIU would help articulate the nation's direction, "that we may help define the good society and our role in its building."

In all that verbiage, there is one paragraph that deserves closer attention. "Multi-campus institutions such as our own have especial challenges in the realm of organization. Local operational autonomy, proven highly successful in industry, has with such large multi-campus educational systems as the University of California been found indispensible. Whereas the principal offices of Long Island University are in the process of removal from Brooklyn to Brookville to make them more central to the University as a whole, and whereas I am increasing the all-University educational staff, I pledge myself to preserve local autonomy at the several centers." Hoxie went on to articulate a theme that he would repeat often in the years to follow: "our Brooklyn Center for example, provides a great urban laboratory where such programs as city planning and urban renewal can flourish, our Southampton environment lends itself to a marine biology station, and our C.W. Post campus to a major fine arts center." In other words, diversity in programs would allow each campus to find its niche and its student population. This mantra, he was asserting, would allow the University to find unity in multiplicity. Could Hoxie have thought he could jettison years and years of trying to take Post toward independence? Very possibly, if he could deliver what Brooklyn faculty and administrators wanted. But, if he could not, unlike a molting snake, his prior skin would be stuck to his back.

America was now descending into the chaos of Vietnam. Universities everywhere were domestic battlefields. Hoxie was a true conservative at a time when radicalism was the rage on campuses from one coast to the other. To students and many faculty at Brooklyn, in particular, Hoxie seemed on the wrong side of history; Bill Birenbaum, his new appointee, intuitively grasped what was happening and that each campus would have to adjust. From Hoxie's early decision to move the University's central administration from downtown Brooklyn to a quarter of a mile from the Post campus until the failed University effort to sell the Brooklyn campus, Hoxie's actions, if not his words, would make him Brooklyn's hated enemy. His honeymoon would be brief, his battles, long and ugly. The concomitant damage to the University, would be crippling.

But during these early years, speaking at a 1965 scholarship fund dinner, Hoxie declared, "In my estimation no other private University has such a hopeful future for growth to greatness." With a passion that was heartfelt if naïve, he declared, "This University, whose enrollment has multiplied six times, and whose budget twenty times, in a decade, will, I predict, in the final third of the twentieth century take its place among America's greatest centers of learning."

Hoxie was a dreamer who graduated from a state teachers college with limitless ambitions. At LIU he so fused his own destiny with that of the University that achieving those ten year goals became his life's calling. He truly believed that the prior success of the University from the mid - 50s to the mid - 60s would be a harbinger for the next decade, provided there was enough hard work and passion for the mission. Reversal after reversal over the next several years simply would not knock him down for the count. Fifty years on, his is still a poignant story.

On September 8, 1964, Bill Zeckendorf sent Gordon Hoxie a note indicating that he had signed and duly notarized two depositions "for the purpose of changing the name of Long Island University to 'The University of Long Island.'" But how would the colossus fit together? The gears had to mesh. The existing units, plus the potential multiple new campuses and units, had to collaborate in greater harmony. As Mills and others soon discovered, drafting those pesky Bylaws was like a low-grade infection that stubbornly lingered. But with typical optimism Hoxie wrote to the Dean of the Graduate Faculties, Eugene Arden, on September 15, 1964, that "In the light of the many recent changes in University structure, it is important that the University Statutes be thoroughly revised to note these changes, and I am asking you to prepare a draft of changes of the Statutes…. this is a major task. I should be happy to consult with you and work closely with you on it, and I would hope to have a first draft completed within the first four weeks, if possible."

Arden reached out to Francis A. McGrath, the University's counsel (and brother of John McGrath), for help and got back instead, a well meaning letter that did not tell him much. Instead, Hoxie and Arden exchanged general ideas and by November, the files hold a revised draft of those University Statutes. In reality most of the text was actually drafted by Vice Chancellor Mills. It was subsequently sent out to members of the cabinet. Arthur Zupko, the Provost-Dean of Pharmacy, responded, "I believe the greatest loophole in the present rough draft is the lack of definition particularly of the duties and academic responsibilities in the chain of command to insure the autonomy of branches, which you have indicated repeatedly to be your desire." And the following day, Edward Glanz sent a three-page memo complaining, "The provosts, however, who are actually the administrative and academic chief officers on the branches and, as such are University officers, are not mentioned in the section [on officers of the University]." It would not be until 1965 that a revised document finally got back to Hoxie's desk which could be sent on to the Board for approval.

The arrival of Henry Mills had at last filled the position of Chief Academic Officer with someone competent. One of his first acts was to report to the Department of Education in Albany on the status of Southampton College as it began the second year of operation, on the transfer of Mitchel College into an extension site of Post and on the establishment of an "all-University graduate school." In Hoxie's response to Mills' draft, he told Mills that the Arthur T. Roth Graduate School, the Graduate School of Education and the Palmer Graduate Library School were all already functioning on a University-wide basis. Hoxie also underscored that "the appointment of Dr. [Eugene] Arden as Dean of the Long Island University graduate faculties" had been made. The University was seemingly addressing the consistent demands from both from the Middle States Commission and the Department of Education in Albany for an academic chain of command.

Quite appropriately, Mills began to meet with the Provosts. He reported back to Hoxie that collectively they addressed curricular matters and course offerings. Mills noted, "it was a frank and interesting discussion which helped immensely to give me a better understanding of the university." Two of the key items they discussed dealt with the transfer of credits, what he called the "full faith and credit," from one campus to another. The second was the development of a unified sabbatical leave policy for faculty from every campus. Of the four Provosts who attended, two were brand new, William Birenbaum at Brooklyn and Ken Ewald at Post. Edward Glanz was still a relative newcomer to his Provostship at Southampton and the only veteran was John Baiardi who had been sent into the wilderness by Hoxie as the new Provost of the proposed Zeckendorf School of Science and Technology. Hoxie clearly understood that he needed to integrate educational services at the graduate level, and this initial effort seemed to "yield good results."

During that first year, Mills had become a stabilizing force, helping to resolve many of the academic tensions so evident during of the Pell years. He insisted that, "Long Island University students count all graduate credits even if some were taken at Post and others in Brooklyn, towards a masters degree." He defined a membership on the graduate faculty as including those who "regularly teach one or more courses which are designed primarily for graduate students." He drafted rules governing the administration and the administrative procedures of the several branches, insisting that "all planning for future development of a given campus" must be done in consultation with appropriate officers of the University. In the same way, he mandated that "any substantive change in the curriculum, such as the introduction of a new major at the undergraduate level or a new method of instruction or the establishment of an institute or center or other type of academic program at the graduate level be subject to review and approval" by his office.

He moved to standardize titles both of administrative officers and faculty, noting "the goal of relatively uniform titles and uniform groupings of duties and responsibilities under these titles should be sought." At the same time he began to equalize salaries for those who had the same duties and responsibilities "irrespective of the campus on which they serve." And he started a process by which there would be "a single salary range covering the salaries of faculty members of the same rank on all campuses." He insisted all promotions to the ranks of associate and full professor be subject to his review. Academic budgets were his responsibility, as well as the construction of academic buildings. None of these procedures were atypical or radical; virtually every university in the country had rules just like these. But, for the first time at LIU, they were being codified under a single administrator.

He did not have total success, however. He asked innocuously, for example, about basic structural matters and encountered silence or hostility in response. On September 10, 1964, for example, Mills wrote Hoxie, "It occurs to me that it might be worthwhile at the next meeting of the Cabinet to discuss briefly why it is that the calendars of the Brooklyn Center and C.W. Post College differ. As I mentioned to you yesterday, one minor way in which the concept of the total University can be strengthened would be by having a uniform calendar." He also wondered about "the pros and cons of establishing an Office of University Registrars."

Routinely the Provosts would meet with Mills prior to a larger meeting of Vice Chancellors, Provosts, Deans and other officers. The Provosts debated whether it was feasible or not "to have one commencement for the whole University." Admiral Wood "thought the parents of the graduates would prefer to participate in a commencement on the campus where the student has attended," while Southampton Provost Ed Glanz, sought a "way it would be possible to have something of an all University nature at the time of commencement." Unlike NYU, which annually rented Yankee Stadium for a vast, single commencement, LIU debated but rejected a common graduation for more than a half a century.

Mills had come from a large institution, the University of Rochester, and was sensitive to issues of turf. What authority was delegated to the Provosts or the Deans, and what was reserved to the central administration? Who could sign contracts? How was decision making clarified so that an individual knew the decision was his or hers to make? Interpenetration of authority easily threatened to become bureaucratic paralysis. He wanted, for example, the position of "Dean of Faculty, which is now found on the Post and Southampton Campuses" to disappear. Hoxie responded the following day, seemingly concurring with Mills' reasoning, but wondering whether "the Dean of the college additionally" might be named "as the Associate Provost of the campus...."

Not surprisingly there was pushback, especially from C.W. Post. The centralization of authority circumscribed power that had been freely exercised on that campus. Mills wrote to Ken Ewald, Hoxie's successor as Post Provost, for example, when he heard that Ewald intended to eliminate all classes with less than 12 students. Ewald saw himself as the official in charge. He was focused on the budgetary bottom line at Post. Mills who spent years at the wealthy University of Rochester challenged the automatic notion of closing sections with fewer than 12 when "a responsible, realistic program... for advanced students must be offered." This was for Mills an academic decision and could only be taken by an academic administrator. No budget could trump the integrity of a student's experience; in his view it would be better to close the program.

One of the C.W. Post Deans, John Lahr, complained to Mills that he was "reluctantly reaching the conclusion that the title of 'Dean, University Graduate School of....' is nothing but an empty gesture." If a Provost could appoint an Associate Dean of a graduate school without consultation, (as happened) that Graduate Associate Dean would be responsible to the Provost not to the Dean of the University graduate school. The matrix was fraught with tensions of this sort. Lahr wrote, "Of course, cooperation is the answer but it takes two to cooperate." He was angry with Birenbaum, in this particular instance, but the issues were systemic to the University and embedded in the matrix.

These tensions were exacerbated because Eugene Arden, as Dean of the Graduate Faculty, was also attempting to deliver all graduate level education from a common platform. He wrote Mills: "Specifically, the following relationships need clarification: 1. That between the Graduate Dean and the Provost of the campus; 2. That between the Dean and the Associate Dean, whose office is on a different campus; 3. That between the Associate Dean and the Provost of the campus at which he has his office; 4. That between the Dean and the Associate Dean; 5. That between each of the above with this office." It has long been easy to make jokes about academic politics. The old saw went: the reason why academic politics were so savage was that the stakes were so small. But management within this matrix was a complex matter, demanding a sense of shared ownership by the faculty and academic administrators in order to deliver quality programs for the students.

On January 26, 1965, Arden commented to Mills, "A thorough review of administrative relationships and flow charts is really premature." To Arden, "Any university is complex; one which is spread over a hundred miles in several branches is fantastically complex." He asked rhetorically, "what is most striking about the administrive plan of Long Island University?" And he answered himself, "Clearly it is the way graduate work has been organized horizontally across the University with undergraduate work organized as vertically at each center." Arden observed, quite correctly, that the interests of a Graduate Dean and a Provost only partially overlap. And so he asked Mills about different alternatives.

154

One option was to put graduate programs on each campus directly under the control of a campus Dean who would be responsible to the Provost. "But that will put us right back to 1961, when the State Education Department and the Middle States Association both cautioned against fragmentation...."

A second alternative was "to make each graduate school more autonomous by establishing separate budgets for graduate instruction." He noted that he did not think the University was ready for such autonomy, even though other Graduate Deans sought it.

A third option he proposed was to heighten "the authority of the University graduate council over graduate programs," even while providing the Provosts with ample opportunity to have their voices heard.

Finally, his fourth option was to "assume that there is no answer which is simple, foolproof, and immediately available; be grateful for the many evidences of achievement throughout the University in the half year since the University was reorganized; have faith for at least another half year!"

These were the nitty-gritty operational issues plaguing Mills and Arden. Mills did not respond to John Lahr until March 23, 1965 "with respect to the relationships among and between Graduate Deans, Associate Graduate Deans, Provosts and this office. I have delayed on this deliberately because I wanted to see what stresses and strains would emerge as a result of the somewhat undefined relationships under which we are present operating...." That same day Mills wrote Hoxie, "A question which was asked of me today raised a problem which we had not yet answered. The question was, 'who issues contracts for next year to the associate Dean of a graduate school or a graduate faculty?'"

Another academic initiative that revealed the structural tensions across campuses was the creation of a marine science institute for the University. The senior faculty member at C.W. Post, already teaching in this field, was Professor Hugo Freudenthal. At Hoxie's recommendation Freudenthal travelled out to Southampton to meet with Dr. James D. Barton who was the first Chair of the Natural Sciences Division at Southampton. Freudenthal reported to Hoxie "that there appears to be no conflict of interest between our campus and Southampton." He gave credit to the success that Southampton had had in the natural sciences in its first few years of operation, but went on to note "Southampton is a long way from any sort of graduate institute in terms of facilities, enrollment and faculty."

Freudenthal assumed that his graduate program at Post would be the lead agency, while Southampton would function "as a [marine] station of the LIU Institute." The research vessel and headquarters "should be based in the Post area." Freudenthal saw Southampton as at "the other end of the world." He did not think, "we can attract researchers or graduate students to such an isolated spot." Freudenthal then drew a comparison with Woods Hole which was founded a century before. He observed that "the science of today is not the same as in Agassiz' day." This was to be a University-wide institute, part of the graduate faculty, and a research unit with a limited academic commitment to "supervising graduate students or offering courses in their specialties."

Freudenthal's imperial assumption rankled those at Southampton. Glanz indicated to Hoxie that the Southampton science faculty's "support for the developing program is not completely in accord with Dr. Freudenthal's current statements. We are especially concerned that Southampton College is not viewed as 'the other end of the world!' Most importantly, however, we are anxious to insure that any program be a total University effort and not an isolated or non-connected effort." In fact, the two campuses developed separate programs with ever less connectivity as the years passed. The institute at Post survived even after Southampton developed multiple graduate programs in marine science. Marine sciences became the academic flagship of excellence for Southampton in the decades that followed.

Arden wrote the Chancellor's Cabinet informing them that a subcommittee on marine science, including Mills, Birenbaum, Glanz, Ewald, and Arden had met twice and agreed unanimously to recommend the establishment of a Graduate Department of Marine Science at Post. Arden stated, "there is no precedent intended here as a solution to future problems of organization. The Marine Science Department itself might be altered in structure after a review of its early work. At this juncture, however, the graduate department on one campus, with courses offered as needed on the other campuses, appears to be the best way to accommodate the new program of advanced instruction and research in Marine Science."

Who controlled the development officers for this or any other academic project? On March 4, 1965, Arden wrote Admiral Wood, then Vice Chancellor for Development, asking that Colonel John Tyler, Wood's fundraising professional on the Post campus, be permitted to work with Professor Hugo Freudenthal to seek gifts and grants for this new program. Wood, who had not received the first memo, responded very positively: "I, personally, want to do everything I can to assist Professor Freudenthal in seeking gifts and grants.... I am very much interested in this program." But the Post Provost, Ken Ewald, abruptly challenged Arden on March 11th, 1965, writing, "Your memorandum of March 4th to Admiral Wood regarding the new Graduate Department of Marine Science is somewhat premature. Since the program is being mounted on the C.W. Post campus, any fundraising should be cleared through the campus administration in order that these may fit into the campus plans." Ewald, a hawk in defense of his own authority, continued, "as you know we have a Director of Development and we have a campus plan. The request for the services of Col. Tyler should have been put through the Provost's office before being sent directly to Vice Chancellor Wood." In other words, Ewald was clearly telling Arden not to try to poach Tyler's time or energy without Ewald blessing this as a campus priority.

On March 15th, Arden wrote Ewald a very irate response. He noted that Hoxie had encouraged him to move forward in seeking federal support for graduate programs through the Higher Education Facilities Act. Hoxie specifically stated, "you are encouraged to go full steam ahead." He detailed how Col. Tyler was extremely knowledgeable in seeking federal support for research in oceanography. Arden had written first to Wood "asking for permission to use Col. Tyler," because Tyler reported to Wood. He transparently sent a copy to Ewald. "I fail to see why on March 11th you would characterize my memorandum as 'premature.'" He readily acknowledged that Ewald had his own development plan with Col. Tyler as his senior development officer, "But I could not sensibly ask your permission to use Col. Tyler's services, since Col. Tyler has multi-campus responsibility and reports to Admiral Wood." Arden's memo continued, "as long as we are here reviewing the question of administrative flow, I believe I should emphasize that the [Post] program of Marine Science is a segment of the total graduate offerings of the University. The Chairman of that department reports in regular fashion to the dean of graduate faculties [Eugene Arden]." This bureaucratic infighting would normally be forgotten after a half century, but is here resurrected as a tangible example of how difficult it was to make the far flung matrix work without a shared sense of mission, good will, and trust.

Sustaining consensus was always fragile. It was sorely tested when on March 31st, Vice Admiral Chester Wood suddenly resigned his position as Vice Chancellor. A "direct report" during World War II to Admiral Conolly, Wood was an important link not only to the Admiral personally but to an era when chain of command was honored without challenge. Wood had spent 39 years in the Navy before LIU. At the time of his retirement, he indicated he wanted to spend more time painting and sailing. In fact, he was already seriously ill with cancer and within a few months, on July 24th, passed away.

With Wood's retirement and death, Southampton lost its most fervent supporter. Like Conolly himself, he had had an extraordinary naval career during the years after graduating Annapolis in 1924. He had been assigned to a flotilla of gunboats on the Yangtze River in the late '20s and had served with distinction in the Pacific, taking command of a destroyer commissioned at the Brooklyn Navy Yard in October 1941. He was Chief of Staff to the Admiral commanding the North Atlantic fleet. He became Assistant Naval Adjutant to President Roosevelt in the White House in 1943. He was with Roosevelt on several of his secret wartime trips, which Roosevelt took at sea, usually on cruisers. The winner of the Legion of Merit with a Yangtze Campaign ribbon, he won the Navy Cross at Okinawa as commander of Squadron 64. His immediate superior was, of course, Admiral Conolly. For a period he commanded the cruisers _Fargo_ and _Albany_ and was in charge of the Cruiser-Destroyer Flotilla in the Pacific. When he died, the Brooklyn edition of the *World Telegram* published an editorial and *The New York Times* an extensive obituary. Wood, like his friend and mentor Richard Conolly, was not only a decorated war hero, but also a seasoned and experienced judge of people. He was used to taking command and accepting responsibility for his decisions. LIU could ill afford to lose men of his ability and experience.

Hoxie had already eased Wood aside when he became Chancellor. In the long Pell interregnum, Wood had, de facto, become the chief operating officer of the University. By personality and years of service he had a close and direct relationship with key Trustees, and was never shy or retiring. After Conolly died, it was Wood who negotiated the purchase of Southampton and its opening. That campus was his baby, his legacy. His major memorial at the University was fittingly to have the Southampton student-dining hall named for him.

As Chancellor, Hoxie had the savvy to encourage both Mills and Arden to assume leadership positions. He invited Arden to sit regularly with the Provosts at the Provost Council, because "he felt the all University Deans should be represented." In the Minutes of a Provost meeting that summer, for example, Hoxie said, "We hear about the integrity of the campuses; while this is important, we should also bear in mind the integrity of the University and not limit it to the campus." In those same Minutes he discussed the necessary reorganization of Development at the University because of Wood's illness and retirement, but rejected the suggestion that Development "should be put at the campus level," noting that "it is possible that this may defeat the proposed integration of the University."

It was a chronic struggle to determine whether power rested in the centralized hierarchy or on the campuses. And during 1965 and 1966, that fight was waged not by Hoxie but by Mills, who struggled with the C.W. Post Provost, Ken Ewald, and his Brooklyn counterpart, Bill Birenbaum. The issues were certainly not new, even though the participants were. Hoxie, who had for years been on the other side of this fight when he was at Post, now retreated to the sidelines while Mills asserted that the central administration was sovereign. To be sure, new leadership injected different egos and ambitions into the dynamic, but that tension seemed to be embedded in LIU's institutional DNA.

Since the question was how to bring the University toward academic stability, Mills was the obvious person to achieve this stasis. Hoxie himself had drafted a memo on February 18, 1965, titled "Appointive Officers for the Several Campuses," and the following week, Mills was proposing "certain ground rules or principles which should be observed in formulating a policy." He listed five general categories. Mills sought to define the powers of the campus Provost and particularly wanted to eliminate the "position of Dean of Faculty," which would, in his opinion, get in between the regular campus Deans and both the Provost and Mills himself. By early June that document had matured into "Administrative and Other Relationships Among and Between Graduate Deans, Associate Graduate Deans, and Other Principal Administrative Officers of the University."

A few weeks later, on July 7th, Mills wrote Hoxie, "In the interest of furthering the concept of the University as opposed to the individual campuses, it seems to me it would be wise for us to make every effort to publish a single bulletin for the graduate schools and the graduate faculties." This had been a recurring argument in previous years, but had been postponed because the tasks of scheduling, course numbering and developing a single set of admissions criteria seemed overwhelming, especially to campus-based administrators who did not like the concept. Mills noted that the Deans were still "strongly committed to the principle that a single graduate bulletin will be a most effective instrument in contributing to the integration of the University which we are trying to achieve." It failed to happen because the registrars had their loyalty to their own campus, not the abstraction of a multi-campus University.

It turned ugly and personal at the beginning of the 1965-1966 academic year. As so often is the case in fights of this sort, the details do not really matter, but the power dynamics do. In this case it had to do with who was in charge of administering the Graduate Record Exam and who got to make that choice. The Graduate Council got a stinging memo from the Post Provost, Ken Ewald. The Council in turn, wrote collectively to Mills: "even more serious than any factual error is the aggressive and unfriendly spirit of Dr. Ewald's message." At its core was Ewald's assertion that he was the "proper authority." The Graduate Council responded, "The principal line of responsibility for such academic matters goes from the Deans to the University Graduate Council and then to the Chancellor. And so it shall be, unless the Chancellor, not the Provost, changes it."

Ewald, certainly not pleased, responded to Mills that the Statutes gave campus authority to the Provost. He wrote, "On a number of occasions which are too numerous to recount, there has been confusion as to the line of authority regarding graduate programs." He continued, "Everybody seems to have thin skins around here, except those who are in charge of an operation…. As you know, Harry, I have always been willing to cooperate, but I will not be coerced…." About the same time, Ewald was also resisting hiring any faculty who taught solely at the graduate level. "Any employment at Post College should mean undergraduate as well as graduate teaching."

Graduate education was supposed to be the glue that held the University together. This thinking dated back to the Admiral. But balancing the centripetal and the centrifugal forces was the task that LIU administrators were still unable to master. If campus Deans controlled graduate education at the campus level, then the system was fractured and the campuses were autonomous. A few days later, October 22,

1965, Arden, the Graduate Dean, wrote to both Ewald and to Mills: "The fact of the matter is that the Deans do claim the right to maintain active management of the academic affairs in the graduate programs." It surfaced as well in November when Ewald and Mills argued over the position of Director of Libraries. Was that a University-wide job and, if so, was it not Mills rather than Ewald who should be in charge of the search?

So much ill will surfaced that Hoxie on January 18, 1966, informed the Vice Chancellor and the Provosts that they were requested to prepare comments on a document drafted by Mills, which would be circulated for discussion. The next day, Mills circulated a five-page, single-spaced report he had originally written in October 1965. It embraced planning, educational policy, faculty and staff appointment and promotion, building plans and relationships with governmental agencies, foundations and other sources of financial support. Included was the following statement: "The Dean is the academic leader of a graduate school. The Provost is the chief administrative and academic officer of a center and an officer of the university. They are jointly responsible to the Vice Chancellor of Academic Affairs for the graduate educational programs of the University." This clearly described the status quo, but it offered no way out of the structural box that Hoxie had created at C.W. Post with the Admiral's tacit approval.

Mills wrote Ewald on May 4, 1966 that he was "somewhat confused as to what to do next." He acknowledged that endless discussions "were certainly inconclusive." "You and Bill Birenbaum," he wrote, "as far as I can tell, simply will not accept the statement, despite such key sentences...." which were added over the months in the search for middle ground. He concluded, "that no useful purpose would be served by further discussion at this time...." He then listed alternatives: to keep talking in the remote chance that common ground could be found "to do nothing and hope the problem will go away," or "to write the Chancellor, admit failure, and say that it has not been possible to get sufficient agreement...." Parenthetically, he threatened almost for sure incorrectly, "if nothing is done, the Chancellor will act."

The following day, Ewald responded, indicating he was open to further meetings, although with no promise to seek a negotiated agreement. He also suggested that the issue could be kicked upstairs to the lay committees of those drafting the C.W. Post Ten Year Report or to the Board itself, or put before the faculties for their comment. All of these options, would have likely resolved any dispute on the side of the Provosts. The confederate structure was victorious over a federal construct.

By the end of May, the battle was over. On May 20, 1966, the Provosts and Mills had a special Provosts' Meeting. The key, first proposal stated: "The Provosts should be responsible for all programs [including graduate] on their campuses, including the academic, physical and financial aspects of each program. Should differences occur between a University program and the campus administration," only then would the Vice Chancellor have a chance to intervene, subject to being overruled by the Chancellor.

On June 6, 1966, Mills sent Hoxie a detailed memo recapping this six month fight. He clearly knew he had lost. It is not clear how Hoxie read the exchange of memos. His heart was always at Post, and Ewald's reaction was very similar to what one would have expected from Hoxie several years earlier. Alas, there does not seem to be a Hoxie response to Mills' memo in the files, although he probably wrote one-he usually did. The triumph of the Provosts was a key victory for the campuses, as each sought as much autonomy as possible within the framework of a single charter. Admiral Conolly's construct either could not work or had been allowed to wither. Over the next five years the devolution would accelerate as the University abandoned even a pretense of trying to be an integrated institution. A very strong Chancellor might have altered this reality, but Hoxie had been a supporter of devolution for many years, and his fights with Brooklyn over the next several years guaranteed an ugly cleavage. Brooklyn and Post increasingly lost a common loyalty and communality with the other. Virtually no one maintained any faith that the two campuses shared a mission or destiny. Southampton bobbed behind like a rowboat towed from the stern. By 1972, chaos reigned.

Hoxie understood that his new job required him to focus almost exclusively on external issues. He left to Mills the struggle to build a viable rationale for the academic enterprise and focused on how to position the University as a dynamic new player in American higher education. He understood that he needed to mobilize lay leadership at campus and University levels, and increasingly devoted his energy toward building a donor base. There was an interesting exchange between Glanz and Hoxie, for example, over the powers and responsibilities of the Southampton Executive Council, the advisory group of local business and civic leaders from the East End. This group was uncertain about the limits of its authority and was groping to find its place in a network of lay leaders involved with the University. It understood that it had a fundraising task to meet, especially since the year round community had failed to raise the relatively modest funds promised prior to Southampton's opening. However, collectively it also wanted to ensure that Southampton in the future would be granted a voice at the LIU Board table.

The Council members wanted to change its name from "The Executive Council" to "The Board of Governors of Southampton College." The members felt they should have first say in the naming of buildings and facilities on the Campus, subject to the approval of the Board of Trustees. Glanz had sent their Minutes on to Hoxie, who was clearly miffed not only that Glanz had not insisted that they invite Hoxie to the meeting, but also that these individuals were self-defining their Council's future role in the University. On several occasions Hoxie also bristled at being called a transmitting agent. He was particularly upset that Glanz saw himself as the appropriate University officer who should speak on behalf of Southampton, its academic and physical developments, and its strategic mission. He had wanted that same authority when he was Provost and President of Post, but now, as Chancellor, he felt the need to slap Glanz down.

Hoxie also moved very quickly to change the composition of the Board to ensure that he had a very solid, loyal cadre of Trustee support. He wanted to get rid of people who either were inactive or recruited by Conolly, or both. On October 15, 1964, he wrote to Zeckendorf noting that certain Board members, "for example… Joshua Logan has never attended a Board meeting." As new trustees he recommended Emilio Collado, a member of the Board of Standard Oil of New Jersey, Franz Schneider who had served as Vice Chairman of the Health Council at Post, and Judge Howard T. Hogan, a Nassau Supreme Court judge, who was one of the great proponents of creating a Long Island University law school at Post as part of the campus ten year plan. They were Hoxie loyalists.

Of far greater significance for the future of both the Board and the University, however, was the bankruptcy in the spring of 1965 of Webb & Knapp. There were also ugly press allegations that Zeckendorf had moved money inappropriately. On May 10, 1965, Zeckendorf contacted John McGrath, resigning both from his Chairmanship and as a Trustee. He wrote of protecting "the best interests of the University's image and for the purpose of relieving my fellow Trustees of any possible embarrassment."

This first bankruptcy, followed by a second personal bankruptcy a few years later in 1968, severely damaged not only Zeckendorf's business career, but also his capacity to mobilize others to support LIU. His fall had a profoundly deleterious impact on the University's future. Like the shorn Samson, Zeckendorf's outreach and his influence over other Trustees was dramatically diminished thereafter.

It is hard to overstate how important a figure Zeckendorf was in the years from 1943, when he first joined the Board until then. Le Corbusier, the extraordinary architect, said that Zeckendorf had "done more than anybody else for architecture in America." The United Nations buildings, Kips Bay, Roosevelt Field, America's first covered mall, Mile High Center in Denver, Place Ville-Marie in Montreal, Century City in Los Angeles, and Co-op City in New York were among his many projects. At one point he was the biggest hotel operator of high-end hotels in the United States, including, in New York City, the Astor, Commodore, Manhattan, Taft, Drake and Chatham. At another time, he controlled the St Regis and the Gotham. Even after the bankruptcy, he was involved in the sale of the Queen Mary to the City of Long Beach in California and the acquisition of the London Bridge. Chronicling these projects is a reminder of his sway as a real estate baron and his wealth and power in the metropolitan area. He was Mr. Long Island University, a foundation stone on which the institution had been built. William Zeckendorf cared passionately about Long Island University and communicated that passion to others, whether they chose to share his enthusiasm or not.

The Board was an extension of him, and its response to his travails was based on love and gratitude. With sensitivity Hoxie wrote on May 13th, "that the entire membership of the Board holds you in the highest regard with a sense of needing you now and always." It was decided to name the Brooklyn campus in Zeckendorf's honor. Deeply touched, Zeckendorf described his involvement with the University since 1943 "as, by far, the most important non-business interest in my lifetime." And at a Board meeting on June 14th, the Board unanimously rejected his offer to resign, despite the adverse publicity in the press because of the reorganization of Webb & Knapp. This unanimous vote of confidence truly touched both Zeckendorfs, father and son. In a letter the next day he wrote to Hoxie of his "effort at eloquence through brevity." He ended his letter by thanking Hoxie for his friendship "that has grown between us over the years. I pray it shall continue for a long time."

Hoxie, although formal in manner, had a rare gift of empathy with others. He was gracious not only to someone like Zeckendorf, his Chairman, but also to many others. Insecure himself and sensitive to insults and slights, he was good at thanking people, especially when he was relaxed and in his comfort zone. This human dimension helped him cement loyalty. There is a letter, for example, from Mary Lai to him of April 29, 1965 expressing her loyalty and gratitude. She wrote by hand, "I have previously expressed my high regard for you as Chancellor of Long Island University. I have told you how much I think you are doing for the University. Now I want to thank you for what you have done for me personally…. I have always worked hard, but your regard for me has made me more determined than ever 'to put on a good show.'" 1964-65 had been a good year for the University. Mrs. Lai was proud of that performance. She wrote, "that this year has been one of the happiest years I have spent and I do think you are responsible for making it so."

Hoxie was a prodigious worker. He was passionate about the University. He was irrepressible. He picked himself up whenever he was knocked down. Whatever internal hurt he felt, he rode out into battle day after day with confidence and good cheer. He certainly would have liked to have been remembered as a happy warrior.

In his own mind, he was fulfilling Conolly's dream, after idling for two years in neutral under John Pell. John F. Kennedy had been assassinated, but Lyndon Johnson was addressing issues of race and poverty, and Congress was passing into law Great Society programs. Higher education was still seen as a key vehicle for social change and proof that America was "the last best hope of mankind." To Hoxie, Long Island University was poised for greatness and it was his mission to lead it to a new plateau.

In its miniscule way, LIU mirrored the national dynamic. Things were already going terribly wrong, but the shattering of the bubble was not yet evident. On

PART II - RALPH GORDON HOXIE

February 1, 1964, the University submitted its interim report to Middle States, as required in reaccreditation in 1961. The subsequent site visit went as well as could possibly be hoped. "Since 1961," the visitors said, "The University is ready to renew and increase its efforts 'to do the right thing' academically." They reported to the Commission "the desire to become a better institution has been more powerful than the desire to meet all the demands for increased quantity of education on Long Island."

Southampton, one of the three topics mandated for review by the visiting team, was given a positive endorsement. That campus had "a relatively young, enthusiastic and apparently well-qualified administrative staff." The campus opened with 250 freshmen. And, "what impressed itself most on the visitors is that this new unit, located a hundred miles from the University Center [in Brooklyn], has from the start been fully integrated into the University structure." Moreover, "Faculty participation in the formation of the college's educational policies and programs has been wholehearted, detailed, and complete. Members of the faculty express a deep sense of belonging to both the college and Long Island University."

Hoxie's decision to place Mitchel College under the umbrella of C.W. Post satisfied the site visitors, and the third area of concern, the "Role of the Faculty in the formation of Educational Policy" was judged to be the area of "greatest progress." The All-University Senate was "discussing significant questions," and was deemed to be contributing "toward the achievement of more integration of the University structure." In addition, "the All-University Graduate Council" appeared "to be especially helpful in pulling together all the units of the University."

The site visitors were aware that there was "still some ambivalence with respect to the merits of a unified structure versus a federated structure," but it noted the "progress that had been made since…1961. The progress has been both tangible in terms of institutional structures and intangible in terms of faculty and administrative attitudes." And much of this was even before Mills was on the job as the chief academic officer. In anticipation, the site visitors reiterated that the staffing of this position "can scarcely be over stated."

Over the four years he was Chancellor, Gordon Hoxie submitted a State of the University Report presented at the opening Board meeting each autumn. In his first one, he had reason to boast, both then and in the months to follow. His prose was florid, his message confident. The opening paragraphs were full of words like "esteemed," "revered," and "beloved." Verbal treacle was spread generously. For example, he observed the ease of transition was "made possible by the soundness of his [Pell's] administration." Beyond such hyperbole, however, Hoxie was laying out his claim to success: "What had been a confederation of colleges is emerging as a university, with the integrity of the separate campuses preserved but with their purposeful identifications with and working toward the greater whole established."

He celebrated that the Statutes had been rewritten, that the position of Vice Chancellor of Academic Affairs filled, the graduate faculties integrated and that there now existed several new University-wide positions, including Athletics, Buildings and Grounds, and Institutional Research. Happily, he reported he had a "most able and dedicated cabinet and staff." And he clearly demonstrated his belief, much appreciated by the Trustees, that a University had to be run with firmness like a business. "In brief, democracy in government is splendid; democracy in administration is chaos."

The finances, he asserted, were "phenomenally successful." The newly established "Ten Year Development Committee," Chaired by Arthur Roth, was well launched. The President emeritus of Cornell, Dr. Deane Malott, had been retained as the University's consultant. Grants and enrollment were both up, and Hoxie predicted "conservatively" that total enrollment in a decade would reach 25,000 students. There would be ten doctoral programs and $30 million in new construction. Among the major projects would be a complete consolidation of Pharmacy, a new Law School and a Zeckendorf College of Science and Engineering. And this was possible, despite the "lessons" of Buffalo, Kansas City, Houston, and Pittsburgh-all universities that were forced to sell themselves to the public sector because they went broke. Lapsing into secular prayer, Hoxie concluded "we may well be thankful for the opportunity and the trust which is ours, the building of one of the Nation's great private Universities, dedicated to public service. Few have ever had such a splendid opportunity in such a noble purpose." These were the talking points fully incorporated into his 'stump' speech.

After Cornell, Deane W. Malott had become a consultant with the Association of American Colleges. He first entered into the Long Island University orbit when hired by Hoxie some months after he became Chancellor. His Report, dated December 7-8, 1964, endeared him to Hoxie. He therefore was chosen to be the external consultant for a very high-powered committee of key Trustees, administrators and faculty charged with drafting the working document for the ten year plan, *Preface to the Future*.

Malott also became the outside expert who was called on to defend Hoxie and his administration when the University went to war with itself. Like Hoxie, he was a staunch defender of the traditional university, its ways of decision-making, and its priorities. He became a lightning rod when Hoxie needed to have his "expert" respond to other experts, in particular, Henry Heald, a critically important consultant brought in by Zeckendorf after Hoxie's fight with William Birenbaum.

At Cornell, Malott had managed a hybrid institution. Cornell was partially an independent sector, Ivy League university and partially a unit of SUNY. Its bifurcation gave him a sensitivity to what he found at LIU. His initial consultant's report stressed institutional structure. He urged that there be Provosts in charge of each campus reporting to Hoxie as Chancellor. "A congeries of Presidents would be a factor of psychological isolation for the Chancellor, and tend to weaken a bit his leadership. Because of the local tradition, however, a President for C.W. Post College may be a continuing necessity. However, I strongly urge you [Hoxie] to relinquish that title yourself, at the earliest possible moment.... In the eyes of many of your constituency this dual role must appear to be a special favoring in your own eyes of the Post campus." Malott urged Hoxie to exercise strong leadership in academic affairs himself, and thus, he should carefully shift the Vice President for Academic Affairs "into a staff rather than a line position."

On the topic of expansion, Malott noted, "You have lots of hay down; you are moving as rapidly as possible on many fronts. You are in a hurry." But instead of warning Hoxie about rushing headlong into new programs, campuses and commitments, he encouraged Hoxie to keep up this pace, because "He who waits can never overcome the lost momentum." In 1964 he incorrectly predicted that the Federal Government would continue to loom "larger and larger as sponsor for higher education in the years ahead." And he argued that the State University would fill any void, for example, on founding a law school, "If the private institutions do not fill the vacuum...." He ended his report: "Long Island University, under your leadership, is capable of creating, and attaining, great objectives." Malott was a conservative, he had a prestigious pedigree, and he was flattering to Hoxie and the University. He was the perfect consultant to support Hoxie's own proclivities.

Hoxie had created a Blue Ribbon panel to address the future of Mitchel College, a serious embarrassment to Hoxie and to Long Island University. That committee was initially chaired by Hoxie's Columbia friend, Harry Carman, but following his death, was led by Deane Malott. There were several high-ranking military officers on active duty as well as other Hoxie friends serving on it. Its purpose was to give Hoxie cover as he discontinued the Mitchel programs. On February 17, 1965, Hoxie wrote a "Dear Colleague" letter, which thanked everyone profusely, never addressed the realities of academic rot uncovered by the New York State report, and closed an embarrassing chapter in the life of the institution with a quick burial. Malott officiated.

Gordon Hoxie was fixated most of all on the ten year development plan that was conceived by Conolly, sustained by Pell, and left to him to try to achieve. It was all laid out beautifully in *Preface to the Future*, published elegantly in 1967 with a grant from the United States Steel Foundation. With charts, pictures, plans, and lists of participants, it captured Hoxie's dream, ending, as he put it, "on a note of optimism." Available in the Libraries of the University and elsewhere, it is a document that should be read and studied as a cautionary tale. By the time it was printed, it was already dismissed as a gigantic fantasy; an embarrassing monument to his ambition. Virtually no part of it came to pass. To read it now, decades after publication, is an elegiac journey into a lost world. Hoxie never could fully under-

166

stand why that was so. He never saw the amber lights warning him that there is a difference between a carefully crafted plan and something that can be made real.

Preface to the Future was a cornucopia of expansionist projects. The ambitious dream of developing a medical school dated back as early as May 26, 1960, when the Board Minutes identified the possibility of a two year medical program in close conjunction with Glen Cove Hospital or some other institution, for example, the Meadowbrook Hospital (now Nassau University Medical Center) in East Meadow. Conolly was interested in an affiliation or merger with the Brooklyn-Caledonian Hospital. Chester Wood wrote a detailed memorandum for Hoxie dated April 12, 1965. The University looked at its students' performance at other medical schools and sought support for its existing allied health units, especially nursing. It corresponded with Nassau County Medical Society only to discover it was the community hospitals which were in need of subvention from the University, not the other way around.

On March 16, 1968, Hoxie corresponded with Clifford Lord, the President of Hofstra, to explore the possibility that one institution would take the lead in creating a law school while the other would focus on medicine. Hofstra proved a disinterested partner. Hoxie then wrote to Dr. Mark Kenyon, the executive director of the Nassau Academy of Medicine, indicating, "Dr. Lord's approach smacks of a regular gas station war at a time when higher education should be working together comparatively." The University explored a "contract" type of College of Medicine similar to that which existed in other disciplines at Cornell or Alfred. However seductive the idea might have seemed, without lead gifts or State support, it was more talk than action.

In a similar fashion, there had been many exhaustive studies about opening a law school either in Brooklyn or Nassau over the past decade. Judges and lawyers had opined. Studies, commissioned. Consultants, paid. Plans drafted and redrafted. A Dean hired. The University was a mendicant, attempting to peddle its sheltering accreditation in exchange for sufficient funding for public sector or philanthropic start up costs, facility needs and faculty payroll. Again, Conolly's dream collided with the reality of a changing America in the mid-1960s. One of the LIU Trustees, Judge McDonald, explored whether either Brooklyn Law School or New York Law School would seek an affiliation. When that failed, Zeckendorf as Chair appointed Pell, Hoxie, Roth and Palmer to speak to the leadership of the Nassau and Suffolk bars and, "if favorable to initiate the formation of a local committee to raise the necessary funds for the establishment of a law school." An earlier President of Hofstra, John Cranford Adams, tentatively proposed that Adelphi, Hofstra, and C.W. Post College share the burden. The University retained a law professor from the Catholic University, Arthur John Keefe, to study the possibility of LIU acquiring some other law school or founding one from scratch. A second study was undertaken by Howard T. Hogan, a justice of the New York Supreme Court from

Nassau. There was a running discussion about whether a law center would be a better approach than a law school. Even Hoxie understood the University could not move forward without first acquiring a gift of at least $2-3 million. All the while, LIU was looking over its shoulder at Hofstra.

On November 17, 1965, "Dr. Hoxie opened the meeting of his [Chancellor's Cabinet] and announced that a statement had been made by Hofstra University that they were preparing to open a law school. The charter of Long Island University authorizes the granting law degrees. Extensive study has been made regarding the establishment of a school of law. This was incorporated in the 10 year plan of the University." On December 21, 1965, *Newsday* ran an editorial, which suggested that Hofstra University and Long Island University, instead of operating competing law schools within a mile of one another at Mitchel Field, should pool their resources and open one jointly-operated law school.

On February 3, 1966, Edward Mearns Jr. submitted a 43-page memo proposing a law center. Mearns, an Associate Dean at the University of Virginia Law School, prompted Carleton Palmer to note, "It was his feeling that while he was in favor of the University's sponsorship of a law school, he did not believe the timing was propitious or the expense involved was now justified." On July 6, 1966, Hoxie submitted to the law committee of the Board, Mearns' report, despite Hofstra University's rejection of a joint collaborative effort. Hoxie asked the committee to recommend, "that we endorse Dean Mearns' recommendations and continue to act as expeditiously as possible in this matter."

Hoxie asked his friend and prominent attorney, Milton Seaman, to view the report to the law committee written by Mearns. Seaman waxed poetic: "the plot is thrilling, the narration fascinating, the characters credible, the scenery breath-taking, the ending…. a glorious beginning." Everything about the law school was perfect except that there were no donors to step forward to provide seed money. On March 13, 1967, Hoxie nonetheless still appointed Edward A. Mearns, Dean of Long Island University's future law school effective June 15, 1967. William J. Casey, a long-time supporter of opening a law school in Nassau, became Chair of the development council for that law school. He agreed to lead an effort to raise $3 million. There even exists correspondence between Arthur T. Roth and the then Chancellor of the Board of Regents to limit competition by prohibiting Hofstra from opening its law school as planned. At the end of the month, an LIU law school opening was announced in *The New York Times* and *Newsday*. In that same *Times* story, Bill Birenbaum was quoted as opposing this move because he was afraid of "overexpansion."

Two months later, Zeckendorf wrote to Hoxie, citing a letter of May 15th from Carleton Palmer. Palmer had seen in the *Times* a report that the law school project was going forward. He reminded Zeckendorf "that no Law School will go forward until we have $3 million in hand and not on the cuff." Zeckendorf continued, "I do not think that $3 million will even scratch the surface and I hope that we will not embark on an enterprise which will result in a deficit for the next five years. This is a time to consolidate what we have and then go forward with the Law School, if needed, when we're able to swing it. I will not appear before the student body with a deficit and ask them to make up the difference with added tuition nor do I wish to curtail the advancement of faculty salaries."

Zeckendorf continued his letter to Hoxie noting, "There are other Trustees who have the same apprehension with particular reference to the Law School." Zeckendorf made reference to Henry Heald's consultant's report to the Trustees (a Report treated in detail in subsequent chapters). "In view of the fact that Dr. Heald has expressed some concern over the future expansion of our programs, including the Law School and graduate study endeavors and, in light of the foregoing, I think perhaps it is appropriate to pause in the pursuance of the Law School until we receive the Heald Report." Zeckendorf copied all members of the Board on this letter.

Hoxie answered Zeckendorf's letter the following day, acidly noting, "The above-mentioned Trustees should further be apprised of the fact that we have established a development council...." for a law school and that fundraising has already commenced. In his letter Hoxie reminded Zeckendorf that Mearns had accepted the appointment as Dean and signed a contract to purchase a home. Fundraising has already yielded one gift in six digits. This was an angry Hoxie writing back, "you may recall that, at a meeting of the Board of Trustees on March 13, 1967, you directed that we proceed with the public announcement of the Law School establishment which we did on March 29, 1967 as reported in *The New York Times*. Further, the law school after a two year study was given high priority in the ten year development plan of the future of the University and was strongly recommended by our consultant on the ten year plans." He made it clear to Zeckendorf that Mearns understood that there was some risk in his accepting a Deanship to a school that did not yet exist. Hoxie ended this letter, "since you have sent copies of your letter of May 16, 1967 to which I am hereby responding, I am sending copies of my reply to all the members of the Board of Trustees, and I am confident that you join me and our fellow Board members in carrying forward the commitment to Dean Mearns which we have entered upon and which we have accepted." On July 6, 1967, Mearns joined his fellow Deans at the Chancellor's Cabinet meeting. George Stoddard sat in as an observer and Hoxie announced he would be "a general consultant."

By the beginning of Hoxie's third year as Chancellor, any honeymoon that might have existed was over. The open display of friction between Zeckendorf and Hoxie over the issue of the law school chronicled the growing gap between Hoxie and his Board over expansion into new areas of professional, post-baccalaureate training.

The head to head competition with Hofstra only made the issue more charged. One LIU Trustee, Sol Atlas, agreed to pay for a building for the law school, provided the race against Hofstra ended. He added several additional conditions, most importantly, that LIU reach out in compromise so that the two universities could collaborate. Atlas was clear that the Island could only support one law school, which would "ensure a successful appeal to the public, whereas if two entities, separate and apart, would continue operations in their own behalf, I feel it would be a failure for both."

There was a summit convened at a dinner on January 18, 1968, at the Island Inn with the then Chairman of Hofstra, Eben Breed. Soon after, Breed wrote to John P. McGrath, indicating that Hofstra was moving forward whatever objections came forward from LIU, because any joint project would be "an administrative monstrosity." Hofstra indicated that it was ready to proceed at once. "We have the ideal site, conservatively valued at some $300,000." The Hofstra Board had committed "$500,000 to this project several years earlier, "which is banked in escrow and available tomorrow. Moreover, the Charles Hayden Foundation had donated $200,000 and the university had in hand over $1.2 million of the $5.5 million target already committed to the school."

The ill-will was evident on both sides and McGrath concluded his response to Breed, "however, after four decades in the law courts I have learned how futile it is to argue with a judge who has already made up his mind." It was a rancorous end to a long held dream. Hofstra had more money and was prepared to commit it; LIU simply could not match.

As the national economic climate grew stormy across the '60s, higher education across the country suddenly started to face serious cash flow issues, inflation, a sharp reduction of federal support, decreases in alumni support and tuition shortfalls. The draft raised havoc with new student enrollment and retention. Long Island University had all of these headaches plus the enormous costs associated with accomplishing the ten year development plan that Hoxie was committed to achieve. Hoxie rapidly had to address where to find major additional resources, or be forced to watch *Preface to the Future* fail.

There were lots of ways to achieve this - and he tried them all - but each proved impossible to accomplish. One way was to increase net tuition revenue. New programs, both at the masters and at the doctoral level, could attract more students who would pay more, in part because financial aid was severely limited for graduate students virtually everywhere. It was also possible to create new professional schools and undergraduate academic programs to bring in new students, and therefore, tuition revenue. But enrollment growth is inevitably slow and budgeting anticipated revenue profits, an inherently risky proposition. Moreover, prudence would mandate test marketing and a careful hiring of additional faculty and staff, which would limit net income.

Doctoral education in particular is expensive to deliver and very expensive to deliver well. Accrediting bodies insist that there be a separate graduate faculty. Each faculty member usually has a reduced teaching load to advise and direct doctoral candidates, especially thesis supervision. Labs for graduate education and faculty research are expensive to build and run, and graduate students usually do not gamble their careers unless such programs have received approval from the New York State Department of Education. The State uses its statutory authority to regulate curriculum as a means to assure quality control. Specialized fields are reviewed by special accrediting bodies (for example, the American Library Association, the ALA). Middle States decennial revues always focus, in particular, on the standards maintained in all doctoral programs. Higher education was and is a regulated industry, and no part of it was more regulated than advanced and professional training.

There was a more subtle problem that had first to be adjudicated internally if the development of new doctoral, masters and advanced professional degrees were to help LIU find the marginal dollars necessary to break into a higher tier of national rankings. Graduate education ever since the Conolly era had been seen as both a means of generating those necessary extra funds and as a marker of quality, announcing to the world that Long Island University had emerged as a research university. But who would own those doctoral programs? Were they part and parcel of one or another campus or were they new units of an integrated, multi-campus LIU? Who hired the faculty? Who had to prepare the budgets? Who decided what new labs or buildings were needed and on which campus they would be? Where was the risk located? Who was in charge? In a closely related way, this was the running battle of the previous years. During the Pell years, these same issues had been fought to a draw. The dispute had mutated slightly, but still existed as the unsolved tension at the core of LIU's identity. Although the lofty rhetoric in *Preface to the Future* glossed over this dispute, the argument was likely to scuttle any hope that a University-wide graduate set of programs could generate the excess net tuition revenues needed to help make the ten year campaign a success.

Mills summarized the conundrum of relying on net tuition from all sources to generate key surpluses. In a memo to Ewald dated July 26, 1965, he addressed both undergraduate growth and graduate degree expansion. "The C.W. Post campus has substantially no endowment. Annual giving cannot produce substantial sums for some years yet, in part because the alumni are young and there are not many of them and in part because annual giving from other sources needs long, intensive and intelligent cultivation. This leaves tuition receipts as almost the exclusive source of income." He went on, "increased tuition can only come from more students. Moreover, increased tuition receipts can only be effective if the size of the faculty remains constant or increased at a much slower rate than the number of students. This in turn means a larger average class size."

This long-festering dispute about graduate, and, in particular, doctoral education, was not some arcane argument between one cluster of administrators and another, but rather an unresolved defect in the way Long Island University had evolved after the C.W. Post campus started on an autonomous course. The core issue was articulated by Hoxie himself when he wrote to William Zeckendorf Jr. on March 15, 1966, "At the meeting of The Committee on Educational Policy you appropriately inquired as to why the graduate work was organized on a university basis, rather than on a center by center basis, and at both meetings you expressed interest in the progress of the Ph.D programs. As I indicated on both occasions, it is my firm conviction that Long Island University cannot fulfill its destiny as a truly great university unless it has strength in its graduate programs. If we are to be, not just a loosely knit federation of colleges, but rather, indeed, a great university, the direction of that greatness and the strength and unity of that greatness were in large measure to be established by strong all-university graduate schools and faculties."

Hoxie stopped before answering the question that needed to be posed (but was not raised) in all the discussions of how the University would grow as a unitary organization rather than a hybrid. Was Conolly's construct fatally flawed? If not, what could be done to create a sense of allegiance to the larger whole from faculty, students, staff, and trustees? The campuses were tangible to the various stakeholders, but creating a transcendent loyalty to Long Island University remained a hazy abstraction. Each campus had it own teams, colors, college anthems and traditions. How could new doctoral programs be overlaid without exacerbating the friction that already existed?

In an exchange of correspondence between Allan A. Kuusisto, the Assistant Commissioner for Higher Education for the State, and Henry Mills, this tension was candidly exposed. The State had voiced several central concerns, including issues of quality control and the allocation of resources to ensure that the teaching and research expected of faculty remained paramount. The State engaged the famous sociologist, Kenneth Clark, as its consultant, and Kuusisto's comments had a familiar ring to them. "We don't have to tell you that the decision to move into Ph.D programs has implications in terms of money. Even though the present proposal involves only one program, there will be others to follow. We understand that Chancellor Hoxie has publicly indicated that there would be ten or a dozen Ph.D programs by 1970."

Mills responded on March 10, 1966, answering as best he could specific questions about space, library resources and commitments to new faculty, student graduate fellowships and a host of other details. "Of greater import is what seems to me to be its total import. It may well be that have I misread the letter, but it seems to be that you are making two points: (a) we do not at Long Island University have the money necessary to support a Ph.D program in clinical psychology, and (b) Long Island University should devote all of its energies to consolidating what it is now doing and forget any new developments."

On page eight of that detailed letter, Mills closed, "To be frank, your letter really puzzles me. What must we do to convince you and the department that we will only offer the program in question or any program if it is a good one? Or can we convince you?" Months later, Hoxie reported to the Board, "It is clear that these programs, far from being a drain on the resources of Long Island University and its undergraduate colleges, contribute an income to the University." He then noted that in the fall semester 1966-1967, the excess of income over instructional cost was $390,000." But that seeming revenue surplus did not factor in the overhead cost of plant, fringe benefits, and general expenses that must be shared by every revenue-generating (or money losing) program in any university. Such details were breezily left out by Hoxie who continued to speak often about the rosy opportunities to expand doctoral work, for example, a Ph.D program in history and political science at C.W. Post.

The files are replete with plans for the development for this or that doctoral program. Hoxie simply chose not to hear what he seems to have viewed as static from outsiders. For example, there is a blueprint for the Arthur T. Roth Graduate School of Business Administration on the Merriweather (Post) Campus. It assumed that by 1973 it would have a student body the equivalent of 500 full time students, "about half of whom would be enrolled in the night program and half in the day program." It further assumed after the MBA program won accreditation, the University would move to offer a DBA, a doctorate in business administration. The future of advanced business education at Brooklyn remained opaque in the haze.

The organizational struggle between University Center and the campuses over who had control of graduate education was, not surprisingly, directly linked to how the budget was constructed annually. Which unit got to account for those revenues and expenses within the larger budget? Who was charged to pay for faculty or to build the buildings and facilities? In effect, who owned that program? If, for example, the Graduate Dean at C.W. Post reported to the Post Provost, then that graduate program would be part of the Post budget. But, if on the other hand, that Dean owed allegiance to a University Dean for Graduate Education, the revenue stream and concomitant expenses would never come near the Post campus budget. This issue had been simmering for years; any plan to expand graduate education had to have it answered first.

Were there other revenue sources from tuition that could be tapped without having to resolve that core structural tension first? One alternate potential source for revenue was to develop programs at the low end of the higher education spectrum. There were options to expand programs for entry-level students needing remediation, because they had learning disabilities, because they were not prepared for college level work or wanted to avoid the draft, or because they needed to work or raise a family and could only come part-time. The University Charter allowed Long Island University to confer two-year degrees, and junior colleges were thriving across the country in the public sector. In California, the junior colleges had become a very big and profitable business, but junior colleges and remedial programs lacked the academic elegance and high status which LIU had long sought. The University boasted often about how the student profile was improving both as measured by SAT scores and high school grade point averages. To market programs in remediation or two year degree options would impact negatively on a university seeking doctoral programs and professional schools. To be sure Columbia had a unit called Columbia School of General Studies, and NYU had several very successful similar programs, but both already had the full panoply of high-end doctoral and professional programs that LIU so coveted.

One effort given close attention by Mills and Hoxie was to create an "All-University College". This was to be a new unit of the University "designed primarily, if not exclusively, for part time students studying in the evening and perhaps on Saturday mornings." What was particularly attractive to Mills was that it would reach across every campus and "would offer programs on all campuses of the University and within which there would be complete interchangeability of credits, just as is true in the case of graduate faculties and the graduate professional schools." Mills called a meeting with the several Provosts in attendance to explore the concept.

Mills reported to Hoxie, "After fairly lengthy discussion, a general and preliminary conclusion was that it would be premature to move towards the establishment of such a new unit of the University at this time." Birenbaum was against it because it would divert Brooklyn resources toward entering students for a period. Ewald took a very similar position and saw such a new effort as dissipating focus. "What the provosts are saying in sum is that we should use next year for further study of the possibility you presented." There is reason to suspect that it was the "all-University dimension" that left all of them deeply ambivalent about making common cause.

On June 28, 1965, Hoxie responded oddly passively to Mills' memo. He agreed "that we continue to analyze and discuss the matter during the next academic year. I am confident that there is merit in the proposal." Had the Chancellor really wanted such a program to happen, he certainly had the capacity to insist that his colleagues make more of a good faith effort. For whatever reason, the idea was stillborn a year hence.

It was also possible to expand and increase net revenue, by absorption or merger, although winning approval from the State and from Middle States was always slow and, in the case of LIU, very slow. If the other program or school was profitable,

174

it would be expensive to buy and move, depending on its location and existing facilities. There was a high risk that any acquisitions or mergers would hurt the bottom line rather than help it. To be risk adverse was to surrender the dream of rapid growth; to be overly ambitious was dangerous, especially in an environment of contraction and scarcity.

Beyond tuition revenue were the traditional modalities of fundraising for higher education-alumni contributions and an annual fund, fundraising events, major gift solicitations and Trustee giving. According to the Board Minutes of November 14, 1966, when *Preface to the Future* was ratified, Zeckendorf reminded his colleagues, that their "yes vote carried a financial commitment on the part of each Trustee." Apologizing for his bluntness Zeckendorf observed that "the financial support of the University had been assumed by only a few" while others did not carry their weight. This was certainly painfully true.

The LIU Board members remained philanthropically mute. They authorized but they did not give. Campaigns of this sort at other colleges and universities, especially when the stakes were so high, have usually had a "quiet" phase when those closest to the institution step forward to pledge a very substantial percentage of the campaign goal in advance. This did not happen. The LIU Trustees remained by-standers. If Hoxie was soliciting them systematically, as he surely should have been, he remained silent as they violated one of the essential fiduciary obligations a Trustee has to a university. This was a campaign that planted its feet firmly in mid-air. Unlike the patriarch Abraham, there was no one who stepped forward to declare, "*Hineini*, here am I."

Marjorie Merriweather Post was the one potential donor who could truly have made a difference. Hoxie believed she was a real prospect. He may have been sold by his own flattery. After all the tributes, designations and events, he believed he could get Marjorie Post to act like the Dukes. But tapping into her fortune proved a chimera. He tried in every possible way to transform her interest in C.W. Post College and beyond that, in the University. And he marginally succeeded. What had originally been solely a real estate deal at the end of a broken marriage became one of her active philanthropies. But despite being treated like American royalty, Margorie Merriweather Post was only interested in the campus bearing her father's and mother's names, and, even on that campus, her giving was always well below what professional fundraisers would call her philanthropic capacity.

PART II - RALPH GORDON HOXIE

PRINCIPAL DONORS (Since 1955)

Marjorie Post	over $1,000,000	
(Zeckendorf	886,275	Mostly Brooklyn)
Schwartz (Brookdale)	550,000	
General Foods Fund	173,450	
Abrams	153,480	
A. T. Roth	121,500	
Palmer	121,200	(plus)
Esso Foundation	117,935	
Hickox	117,474	
Mrs. William Woodward, Jr.	117,420	
Lilco	82,000	
Pope Foundation	75,000	
Republic Aviation	63,000	
Robert Winthrop	52,000	
Mrs. Augustus Riggs IV	51,150	
Merrill (Kathleen & father)	44,000	
J. H. G. Pell	40,700	
Grumman	34,000	
Jakob Isbrandtsen	31,072	
Ingram Merrill Foundation	29,000	
Spectral Data	23,875	
Schneider	23,600	(plus)
Francis & Townsend Burden Fdn.	22,100	
Skouras	21,300	
Smithers	18,438	
Franklin National Bank	16,058	
Airborn Instruments	15,300	
Sol Atlas	14,375	
Sidney L. Solomon	13,745	
John McGrath	13,600	
Barnes & Noble	13,186	
E. W. Howell (Ralph)	11,898	
Roosevelt Raceway	11,000	(pledged 20,000)
Alan Finder (parent)	10,002	
Guttman Foundation	10,000	
Jack Skodnek	9,386	
Capt. Paul Hammond	9,035	
Mr. & Mrs. Rosenberg	8,600	
Texaco	8,500	
George Morton Levy	8,000	(pledged 10,000)
Time, Inc.	7,452	
Bergen	6,000	
Collado	5,000	

$4,039,906

(Less Zeckendorf = $3,153,631)

Undated facsimile of leadership gifts received from major donors.

176

January 31, 1968

MRS. MARJORIE M. POST

GIFTS TO C. W. POST COLLEGE (CASH & SECURITIES)

1962 - 1967

1967 - For the first of the graduate lodges for the Graduate Resident Center Miscellaneous	$182,197. 2,645.	$184,842.
1966 - Chapel Fund Miscellaneous	$101,022. 6,488.	107,510.
1965 - Chapel Fund (to complete pledge) Chapel Fund (additional pledge) Adelaide Close Riggs Hall Miscellaneous	$ 76,787. 49,025. 25,175. 425.	151,412.
1964 - For President's House For Special Purpose Chapel Fund (Payment on account $100,000 1964 pledge) Miscellaneous	$ 25,040. 10,000. 25,742. 1,180.	61,962.
1963 - Building Fund (to complete 1962 pledge) Building Fund (additional pledge) Miscellaneous	$ 49,592. 25,337. 3,372.	78,301.
1962 - Building Fund (Payment on account $100,000 pledge)		

Facsimile of gift report, annotated in Mrs. Post's own hand.
Courtesy of the Bentley Historical Collections, University of Michigan.

Hoxie was always sure she was about to make a large gift. He wrote Zeckendorf on April 10, 1962, "We are further made happy by the letters of congratulations received from so many members of the University family including from those from Marjorie Post May and Herbert May who were especially pleased by the news." Hoxie was reporting to Zeckendorf that Marjorie "will make possible 'in a year or two' a 2,000 seat auditorium here at the C.W. Post College." In a letter of September 12, 1962, to Trustee and alumnus George M. Shapiro, Hoxie wrote, "Mrs. Marjorie Post May is indicating a wonderful, increasing interest in C.W. Post College and we may anticipate a substantial gift from her in the very near future." And indeed, a $100,000 gift was forthcoming for the C.W. Post College building fund.

Air Force General Curtis LeMay after receiving an Honorary Degree from Chancellor Hoxie.

Hoxie dedicated the Marjorie Post May Hall of C.W. Post College on September 7, 1963, and made it into an academic convocation awarding Gen. Curtis LeMay an honorary degree. LeMay, who became infamous by proposing to bomb the Vietnamese Communists back to the "stone age," was window dressing to flatter Mrs. Post. In Hoxie's formal remarks he said, "Now we come to a deeply significant event of this day, that which permanently joins here on this beautiful campus, which was her homesite, the name of Marjorie Post May with that of her father. My memory goes back to that day, now nearly nine years ago, when she and her daughter, Deenie, whose childhood dollhouse is behind you, unveiled the portrait of C.W Post marking the commencement of the College." Speaking with stunning hyperbole, he noted, "All we had to start with was that portrait,…but what a priceless ingredient there is in that portrait, in the heritage of the man for whom the college was named on the one hundredth anniversary of his birth! There was a sense of a dedication, of quiet determination to build for the future"

"Through all this time, always giving aid and, when asked for it, giving quiet counsel for whom this handsome building now is named." His formal rhetoric reached

178

a crescendo: "Proudly is our college named C.W. Post. Warmly is the name now joined with that of his only daughter, his only child, who when he passed on-now nearly sixty years ago-carried on so magnificently both his business and his responsible sense of service." The family was clearly flattered. On August 17, 1964, Hoxie received a hand written note from Marjorie's daughter, Adelaide, pledging $50,000 of her money for the chapel. Adelaide was Mrs. Augustus Riggs IV. And Marjorie sent $300 anonymously in order to buy raffles for a sable coat being auctioned.

Provost Peter (Ken) Ewald, the Hoxies and
Mrs. Post at a C.W. Post football game.

In a letter to Adelaide of July 13, 1966, Hoxie wrote, "Through the years it had been my hope, which it still remains, that the much needed auditorium for this campus might be the exclusive gift of your family, principally your mother, that it be named the Merriweather Auditorium." As an alternate he made a second proposal. "There is one other means by which your grandmother's name might be memorialized, and that is by naming the total campus the Merriweather Campus. In brief then, C.W. Post College named for your grandfather would be on the campus named for your grandmother. This would be a magnificent memorial and would make a great deal of sense." On July 22, 1966, Hoxie wrote to Adelaide quoting from Marjorie Post's letter to him. She concluded that naming the Merriweather Campus would be the most appropriate. "As you pointed out, the College was named for my grandfather and naming the campus for my mother would be appropriate and I would like it very much." Hoxie ended his letter to Adelaide by inviting her to come to C.W. Post when Leonard Bernstein and the Philharmonic would open the Long Island Arts Festival.

179

Hoxie wrote to Zeckendorf on November 9, 1966, about that just-passed Convocation, an event that came at a peak point in the struggle in Brooklyn. He had the audacity to say the Post family and friends "were thrilled by my convocation address." He enclosed a copy of the program and his address. "You may note that I identified Mrs. Post as a member of our Board of Trustees, in her capacity as an honorary member, which she is proud, indeed, to have, and she sends her well wishes." Hoxie said out loud what others would be embarrassed to utter. The printed program celebrated the dedication of the Merriweather Campus. Included with it was supposed to be a memento, commissioned to please Mrs. Post and her daughters. It was a medallion, struck without concern for expense. On one was side was a likeness of Marjorie's mother, crafted by Alfred Loen, a modernist European sculptor on the Post faculty. But Marjorie Post loathed it so intensely that she demanded Hoxie destroy the entire lot and have a new medal by a different artist struck. A very few of the old ones were hoarded and have survived. The incident demonstrated how imperious Mrs. Post was and how soft the sand on which Hoxie stood.

At that ceremony, Hoxie awarded honorary degrees to Army General Omar Nelson Bradley; Chauncey W. Cook, Chairman of the Board of General Foods Corporation, and Senator Joseph Tydings of Maryland. Printed messages had been secured from Vice President Hubert Humphrey, President and Mrs. Truman, President and Mrs. Eisenhower and others. As a tableau in academic theatre, it was a smashing success, even though the medal fiasco left a bad taste. But no major gift followed and no transforming announcement was made. Moreover, events were moving very rapidly in Brooklyn. Hoxie was out of time. Mrs. Post had pledged never to give more money if Hoxie was fired. When later he was, she never did.

Hoxie understood that a precondition to any successful fundraising campaign was a marketing strategy that would make the institution "hot." Somehow LIU needed to get good press, to be seen on the move, and identified as a winner by other universities, the donor pool and students. Hoxie sought to raise the university's reputation by associating it with the great and mighty in society. Free with honorary degrees and flattery, he loved convocations, special events and commencements. He used them to flatter the super rich and the politically powerful. Most people who were awarded honorary degrees accepted the degrees but not the implicit obligation to send a check. A few did come into the orbit, and one or two accepted a Trusteeship after receiving his or her degree. But even then, LIU failed to establish an annual financial expectation for each Board member. Trustee giving was, at best sporadic both from old timers and those newly elected. Nonetheless, the Board Minutes were filled with long lists of the famous or powerful, and three spring Commencement gave ample scope for flattering wealthy donors.

Hoxie was very skilled at what could be called academic triangulation, bringing powerful Washington worthies or other rich and famous individuals to mingle with the elites of Long Island, New York City, or Washington. Marjorie Post or others in her family were often the bait to entice guests to come. Since she loved the attention (and Hoxie showered her with adulation), she allowed her wealth and fame to be used by the University.

To cite a another example, Hoxie got an LIU Trustee, General James A. Van Fleet, to write to former President Dwight Eisenhower urging him to come to receive an honorary degree. While that invitation was turned down because Eisenhower's health was failing, other attempts succeeded. Arthur Ochs Sulzberger, who did received an honorary degree in June 1967, in a letter of thanks, quoted his father, also the publisher of *The New York Times*, as saying, "flatter me - I can stand a lot of it!"

A variant strategy used several times over during his Chancellorship was to hitch the University's reputation to a famous academic, usually someone near or at retirement age, in order to establish excellence through osmosis. There were several Columbia faculty members who would fit that bill. Thus, in addition to corporate CEOs - the President of American Airlines, for example - Hoxie romanced academic superstars, hoping to parley their distinction into support at foundations and internally with the LIU faculty. Burnishing the University's reputation was a constant goal, achieved by getting photos and stories in the press.

But storm flags were flying on every college flagpole across the nation and the sky darkening for all of higher education. This was not a time to raise sail, but to seek safe harbor. Yet Hoxie moved aggressively to transform LIU by launching *Preface to the Future*. His introduction in the printed book began, "This is the story of one University, its aspirations and hopes. Founded in Brooklyn 41 years ago, still a struggling little institution in that borough a dozen years ago, it is today one of the ten largest private Universities in the nation.... Presumptuous? Perhaps. But it is also a study in courage of a unique bootstrap operation carrying forward from the brink of bankruptcy and no accreditation a dozen years ago." Hoxie noted that many private universities, were forced to go "public" to survive. He then acknowledged the help of Cornell President Emeritus Deane Malott, as well as Dean Margaret Kelly, the Academic Vice President of St. John's University, and a new name, George D. Stoddard who in the next several years would become of critical importance to the survival of the University. On August 2, 1966, Hoxie invited Stoddard to consult "in the richness of your experience on long range educational planning in *Preface to the Future.*"

Still, how to fund the investments promised in *Preface to the Future* remained an unanswered question. There seemed to be one other seductive but very dangerous partial solution: raise tuition. There were profound marketing risks, of course. Students could vote with their feet and go elsewhere. The State and City Universities were already much cheaper because of governmental subsidies. Both were expanding exponentially. Returning students could transfer elsewhere, especially

if they had good grades. New students could opt to postpone, go to a public institution, go to a junior college, or be drafted. Student militancy could and did turn
violent about much less serious issues than the price of tuition, room and board.

At any tuition-driven university, certainly at LIU, raising tuition was particularly
sensitive. Most campus construction is financed through debt, which means that
the bonds are repaid with interest out of tuition revenue. Bond debt must always
be paid first. This results in less money for merit scholarships, familial need, for
faculty, than a better-endowed institution. Parents expect their tuition dollars to be
used to house, feed and educate their own children. The arcane dynamics of NYS
Dormitory Authority financing violated what parents thought they were buying
with their tuition dollars. LIU financed seventeen construction projects between
1965-1967.

Books have been written on the challenges of raising tuition, even to an annual inflation level. Within the executive suites of universities everywhere, it has always
been a wise rule of thumb to raise tuition as little as possible while still balancing
the budget. It was far more complicated at LIU because each campus had a different debt structure, enrollment outlook and expense base. If LIU was truly one
institution, tuition should be the same on each campus. When all the expenses and
income were tallied, the University, the legal corporation, either ended that fiscal
year with an excess of revenue over expenses or was in deficit. Those numbers
were the bottom line, which were sent to the Board, the financial rating agencies
like Moody's, to foundations, the federal and state government, and to Middle
States.

Almost inevitably, some units made more money than others, or were in the black
when other units were in the red. Over the decades it had been an annual debate
about whether it was fair to the students at a profitable center or in a successful program to see their tuitions on that campus go up disproportionally in order to cover
the shortfalls that might exist because another campus or program was paying for
an expensive building or trapped in a cycle of under-enrollment. If everyone in
the institution shared a common vision and sense of purpose, there could be the
necessary camaraderie and bonding to share the pain, especially if circumstances
balanced out over the years. But if not, there was likely internecine conflict.

Few students or their families were prepared to pay more to underwrite new construction, campuses or graduate programs so that LIU would thrive a decade hence.
Hoxie argued that a transformed LIU would retrospectively make the worth of all
LIU diplomas greater, even to students who had acquired their degrees at an earlier
moment in time. Indeed, this argument was and is valid. The value of all NYU
degrees, including those conferred in the 60s, have been enhanced because of what
transpired over the last half century. As that university's reputation grew it cast a
halo around those who graduated in earlier years. Every alumnus and alumna must

182

want his or her degree to grow in value over the decades.

But tinkering with tuition at the height of the student movement of the 60s was still fraught with danger, as Gordon Hoxie was about to discover. Students at every university enter into a compact: a contract to exchange money for education. On one side of the equation is something very concrete, precious money. On the other is something that is hard to quantify. There is the expectation of a good job, one which will allow the graduate to achieve better income, greater security and the chance to improve his or her family's standard of living. The American Dream is predicated on climbing that ladder. But there are also non-monetary gains from higher education, including the capacity to think critically and clearly, the capacity to appreciate beauty, a sensitivity to others and other cultures, an awareness of mortality and the capacity to live with that awareness. It has always been hard, therefore, to value the worth of that educational contract. If a car on a dealer's lot is too expensive, a buyer just walks away. But what happens when students protest the price of their education? Hoxie would discover student power.

The main reason I am going to LIU is that it is clear to me that the future of our great universities is urban.

William M. Birenbaum

Chapter Six

William Marvin Birenbaum

President William Marvin Birenbaum

William Marvin Birenbaum and Ralph Gordon Hoxie were as different as two men could possibly be, even though both were born and bred in the same small Midwestern city at roughly the same time. Hoxie was High Anglican, Bill Birenbaum, Jewish. Hoxie was a Conservative Republican, Birenbaum a Hubert Humphrey Liberal. Hoxie, a traditionalist, sought to preserve both institutions and ideas from the past; Birenbaum, a reformer, believed passionately in social change. He saw higher education as an essential vehicle to perfect democracy; Hoxie believed in the power of education as well, but as a way to conserve the best of the American past. Birenbaum was rumpled but charismatic, Hoxie was elegant but pompous. Birenbaum was against American intervention in Vietnam; Hoxie was a staunch supporter of American engagement in Southeast Asia. He was thrilled to get an honorary degree in Korea, saluting the Korean Rainbow division's engagement in the Vietnam conflict. At the same college in Waterloo, Birenbaum majored in sociology as an undergraduate, Hoxie in American history. Hoxie adored proximity to the great and the wealthy; Birenbaum saw himself as a provocateur for change with the Brooklyn campus as his potential field station. Birenbaum sought radical transformation, Hoxie conserving the old order.

Between 1959 and 1961, Birenbaum was the founding director of the *Detroit Adventure*, an association in Michigan that brought together 25 cultural and educational institutions in the greater Detroit area. Before coming to the New School as Dean, Birenbaum was the first Chair of the Michigan Cultural Commission appointed by Governor G. Mennon Williams. Among his publications were *Freedom in Authority in United States Higher Education*, published by the Indiana University Press in 1960 and an article, "Challenges of the '60s." He had come to New York in 1961 to be the Dean at the New School of Social Research. According to Birenbaum's own CV, he and his wife had three children and lived in the Riverdale section of the Bronx, "where he was a member of the local school board and an active citizen." He also had become a board member of the Little Red School House on Bleeker Street, very near the New School, which was one of the most progressive private day schools in New York and was widely believed to have been on the Attorney General's list of subversive schools in the 50s.

In March 1963, Birenbaum called John Pell's office, seeking an appointment. Pell asked his secretary, Elinor Dickey, to find out why Birenbaum had sought to see him. In her memo back to Pell, she said, "He sounded like a very 'touchy' type." Birenbaum had indicated on the phone that that it was "purely a social and personal call…there was no other motivation," but she subsequently learned that the Faculty Senate had forwarded his name to Admiral Wood's office as a candidate for Vice Chancellor for Academic Affairs.

On April 1, 1963, Birenbaum wrote to Pell, "A week or so ago I called your office for an appointment. Quite informal purposes motivated my desire to see you, and when your secretary called last Tuesday for an elaboration of the reasons for the appointment, I could not in all honesty say any more." He continued that when he had worked at Wayne State and, more recently at the New School, "I had heard much about the unusual recent growth of Long Island University, for Wayne was deeply concerned about comparable problems of its own." "It seemed to me," he continued, "that yours is one of the more youthful and exciting educational enterprises in New York about which we ought to know more."

Although Pell and Birenbaum were unlikely soul mates, they clearly hit it off. The following autumn, on September 13, 1963, Birenbaum again wrote to Pell, "After our session I roamed about the campus. What I saw was impressive. All of you there have every reason to be proud and excited about the future of Long Island University." In response, Pell thanked him for his article, "Challenges of the '60s." Birenbaum had interested Pell in his approach to higher education in the inner city. On December 2, 1963, Pell appointed Birenbaum "as Special Consultant to the Chancellor," initially for the following three months. He announced this appointment in a memo "to University Officers and Heads of all Units," indicating that Birenbaum would advise him on "precisely where we are going."

On March 4, 1964, Chester Wood wrote to Birenbaum, "Mr. Pell is anxious to have you continue in your present role as Special Consultant to the Chancellor and has asked me to carry out the negotiations." When one of the faculty leaders, Professor H. R. Gillis, the Chairman of the University Senate Health and Welfare Commit-tee, wrote via Senate Chair, Lionel Reis, to Pell to seek information on University salary and benefit issues, sick leave, and retirement practices, Pell wrote Biren-baum, "I would appreciate having an opportunity to discuss these three commu-nications from Professor Gillis with you and having your views and suggestions."

On March 16th, Birenbaum responded to Pell, addressing "the relationship of the faculty governments of various units to the overall governmental unit for the Uni-versity." Birenbaum advised Pell how to "make clear here the boundary drawn between what is properly administrative and what is properly a faculty govern-mental concern, and [how to] throw the initiative back to the Senate to be precise, aborting, therefore, any general fishing expedition Dr. Reis and his friends may be contemplating."

On March 18th, Birenbaum visited C.W. Post as Hoxie's guest. In his thank you, Birenbaum asked, "to return for an afternoon to chat informally with a few faculty persons and academic administrators." How Hoxie responded is not clear, but it was obvious that Birenbaum was supplying important academic advice to Pell, for example, in drafting a memo on sabbatical policy. Birenbaum had the Chancellor's confidence and ear.

Pell wrote on June 3rd what for him was an effusive letter to Birenbaum, following the visitation of both the New York State and Middle States' site visiting teams. He told Birenbaum, "it was absolutely imperative to seek outside, independent, edu-cational advice: being able to consult with you and ask you to analyze the various reports as they came along has been invaluable to me and I want to thank you for your patient understanding during this period. I feel that we have paved the way for working together in the future." Since this was but a few days before he announced his resignation, it suggested either that Pell did not know his tenure was about to end, or, and far more likely, that Hoxie and the Board had plans for Birenbaum in a post Pell era. On June 11th, Hoxie wrote to Zeckendorf, "We should in the imme-diate future take action on the appointment of the Provost-Vice President of [the] Brooklyn Center, the title currently held by John Baiardi…. To replace Dr. Baiardi as Vice President and Provost of the Brooklyn Center, it is my desire to name Dr. William Birenbaum." Whether Hoxie was so intent on exiling Baiardi that he did not think carefully enough about what kind of Provost Birenbaum would be, or whether this was simply a way to placate Pell on his way out, is uncertain. The fol-lowing day, Zeckendorf signed off on these two appointments.

There is in the files a handwritten note of June 17th to Birenbaum from somebody senior at the New School, whose initials are impossible to read. The author cel-ebrated Birenbaum's achievement in developing the adult education program at the New School, calling it "the most distinguished program of adult education ever known in America." That individual continued, "We are shopping for a President. Have we anyone in sight up to you? No, I don't see him. But we have many Jews on the Board who say we must have a gentile. Stay with us, Bill. Cultivate the Graduate faculty a bit. You could so easily be it [despite being Jewish]."

Birenbaum, nonetheless, wrote Hoxie on June 18, 1964, giving his enthusiastic affirmation to becoming Provost and Vice President of the University. "I have great faith in the future of Long Island University under your leadership. I am eager to serve you and to be part of the adventure which will enfold there." The Brooklyn edition of the *New York World-Telegram*, in covering this story on July 9th, quoted Birenbaum, "The main reason I am going to LIU," he said, "is that it is clear to me that the future of our great universities is urban."

By October 30, 1964, however, Hoxie and Birenbaum were exchanging pointed correspondence on "the powers and responsibilities of the Provost, the Powers and responsibilities of the Chancellor." In November, an angry Birenbaum wrote Eugene Arden on the topic of the proposed Ph.D in Psychology: "It seems incredible to me that this matter could proceed as far as it has (1) without any official notification to the Vice President and Provost of the Center concerned and (2) without any consultation whatsoever between that officer and the Dean of the Graduate Faculties." Two days later, on November 5th, Arden pushed back testily, "There is nothing 'incredible' about the matter at hand having proceeded this far without official notification to the provost." The details of the fight were less important than how quickly Birenbaum was caught up in the structural tensions of the matrix.

On November 6th, an excited Birenbaum sent his fellow officers a statistical breakdown of the Brooklyn freshman class. He stressed that "43% of these youngsters come from families with an annual income of $8,000 or less," that "58% percent of those students received 75% or more of their educational support from their parents;" and that 63% of the student population were first generation collegians, "the first members of their families ever to go to college." 86% of the students sampled, came from the minority religious or ethnic groups of New York City. 65% of the students were Jewish, 21%, Catholic, and 8%, Protestant. One third spoke a foreign language at home with Yiddish first, Italian, second and German, third, followed by Polish and Spanish. "These facts, which have long been suspected here, but never really compiled before, explain a great deal about our spirit and tone and indicate several unusual educational obligations and possibilities.... I could go on and on about the spirit and tone; but in brief, I find this profile downright inspiring. Never before have I been so enthusiastic about an educational challenge. Long Island University has an extraordinary story to tell through its Brooklyn Center...."

And then, on November 18th, Birenbaum wrote Hoxie about a much more explosive topic-how to handle another tuition increase. "My predecessor had created a very delicate situation here in December of 1963 with the last tuition raise announced. At that time students were in revolt. It was implied then that no further raises would be undertaken here for two years. This 'commitment' would have carried us through 1965-1966."

The profile of the current students prepared by Birenbaum's staff documented how many of the Brooklyn students and their families were lower middle class or in the governmental safety net of working poor. Student growth, as projected by *The Preface,* had anticipated substantial enrollment growth but assumed that the socio-economic status of those future students would be level or improve slightly. The hypothetical students of 1972-1973 were projected to come from wealthier families than the actual Brooklyn cohort did; it would be a student body that was more suburban, more middle class, more like C.W. Post. The ten-year document ignored the consequences of the collapse of the Borough of Brooklyn with large swathes of the community living in ghettoized slums. Raising tuition levels would thus jeopardize the financial viability of the campus. A second statistical study, examining 500 seniors at the Brooklyn Center, empirically established that there was very little elasticity surrounding any tuition increase. This issue was about to explode like a roman candle in Hoxie's hands.

But even before that issue detonated, Hoxie was unhappy that Birenbaum had created four Brooklyn-based faculty and administrative working groups in planning the Brooklyn section of *Preface.* Hoxie wanted ten, certainly covering summer school, graduate studies, community service, and several others. With sarcasm he wrote, "I trust you will invite the Chancellor of the University to present his conceptual views on the work of the Ten Year Planning Committee." Birenbaum was doing to Hoxie what Hoxie had done to Pell, claiming local management authority to present and manage the campus.

The two men also sparked over the wisdom of establishing a university-wide salary structure and job classification scheme. Birenbaum maintained the individuals although "bearing similar titles at the various Centers, in fact possess very different bundles of responsibilities." He also argued that the "The cost-of-living...varies sharply" from Brooklyn to Brookville to Southampton. Hoxie argued, on the other hand, for a common list of jobs and equal pay for each. He wrote, "Your apprehensions as regarding persons of merit at the Brooklyn Center suffering in regard to the salary scale must surely be a figment of your imagination. Before continuing this tilting at windmills let us arrive at a fair scale and salary range."

On April 6, 1965, Birenbaum wrote a long memo to Mills dealing with "Procedures for Relating to the Administration, Etc...." It is unclear why the memo was written and whether Hoxie and or others beside Mills received it, but it was an outspoken challenge to the organizational structure Hoxie had put in place the previous year. Arguing, "'campus autonomy' is presently a central issue in the reorganization of the University," Birenbaum maintained that this issue distracted

189

attention from "the more difficult organizational problems of the institution." The fundamental thrust of the Provost's eight-page, closely argued memo was his rejection of "top down" management. Birenbaum was concerned about "an eroding and stifling initiative at the basic operational levels and discouraging the kind of diversity" which makes a University most interesting.

He posed a question to Mills, "Why must prior revue and approval be secured from the Vice Chancellor for Academic Affairs?" He asserted, "the Provosts are the chief *academic* officers at their Centers. The Deans are the chief *academic* officers of their schools and colleges -Center or University-wide." Birenbaum asserted "a normal process for academic deliberation naturally would result in an upward flow of educational policy matters to the Academic Vice President for his action, where such action is required." And he rejected "the necessity for the Vice Chancellor and the Chancellor to approve in advance the hiring of associate professors from the outside or the necessity of permission of the Chancellor to *make an offer of employment* to a perspective candidate at the professorial rank." Birenbaum was challenging a structure that dated back to Conolly - a military style chain of command. "There must be at some point an element of trust here. Experience already indicates that complexities of our existing approval mechanisms work to our disadvantage in the hectic marketplaces of talent in which we operate."

Hoxie and Birenbaum disagreed profoundly about where authority was vested and why. Nonetheless, at least through 1965, the two men superficially celebrated the other's achievements. Thus, on April 22, 1965, Birenbaum wrote Hoxie that, "the convocation at Post on the 21st was one of the finest academic occasions I have been privileged to attend anywhere, anytime." That event "made me very proud of this University." And Hoxie celebrated that Birenbaum had been invited to lecture at the Salzburg summer program run annually during these years. The file copy had typed across the top, "'Personal' by Dr. Hoxie [and placed in a sealed envelope]", even though the sentiments expressed were pleasantries without anything confidential about them. A few days later, on May 25th, there was a handwritten note from Birenbaum to Hoxie, "I look back on this year with deep warmth for this University under your leadership…. I think next year will be our greatest. As I look ahead I'm really eager to work with you as we build." And Hoxie responded, "May I say that I join with you in the sentiment that this has been a good year in the life of Long Island University. Your leadership here at the Brooklyn Center has been inspiring and strong. I only hope that we may have many years of working together in building the University." On the surface, it seemed to be a mutual admiration society, even as they warily circled each other like fencers.

On June 7th, just as Birenbaum was leaving for Austria, he wrote a printed letter to alumni, including an editorial from the student newspaper, *Seawanhaka*. The editorial celebrated, "student morale at the Brooklyn Center." With mock diffidence, Birenbaum's letter commented, "Their confidence in the provost is frankly a little bit embarrassing and frightening to me, but our students everywhere - at Berkeley and St. John's, at Yale and Cornell - are not blind to serious debilitating influences, which have overcome many of our academic corporations." The next day he wrote a letter to the faculty telling them he was going to Salzburg, thanking them for their service, and noting that they had shared a common endeavor during a "difficult year just ended." Birenbaum's letter was philosophical and opaque. It spoke of working "to keep the peace," and in a different section, "A tenuous line separates peace-keeping from administrative tyranny." It is hard to tell exactly what Birenbaum was saying or why he wrote it.

There were different drafts of at least one of these letters, perhaps both. The materials got deep under Hoxie's skin. On June 15, 1965, he wrote to Zeckendorf, sending him copies of both letters, including the alumni letter, which had gone to 12,000 people. What really angered Hoxie were two key sentences containing a set of assertions: "this should be a faculty-oriented University in which independent faculty government throughout is strong." And second, "This should be a University based on the assumption that students are adults, capable of adult responsibility and conduct."

The files at University Center only hold the benign language of what was probably an early draft. At some later point Birenbaum decided to share his vision of a progressive university in which faculty and students would be autonomous centers of decision-making. This was vintage Birenbaum, and it set Hoxie off. In his angry letter to Zeckendorf, with copies shared with Admiral Bergen, John McGrath, John H.G. Pell and Arthur T. Roth, Hoxie challenged Birenbaum's vision for the future of LIU. What could have been easily dismissed as trivial if both men had been less ideological, became a flash point, igniting an open conflict between those two sons of Waterloo, Iowa. The die was cast for a struggle that would change the University's future.

Hoxie, clearly furious, turned openly against Birenbaum. In an early draft of a letter he never sent, he wrote, "Frankly, there is a whole history of events this year which places in question Dr. Birenbaum's loyalty not only to me, but more important, to the integrity of the University." He then laid out four areas of "specific concern," including Hoxie's profound disagreement with "Certain ideologies which he furthers;" his "failure to cooperate with other principal officers of the University...." and "his persecution of valued staff employees whose mistake has been perhaps one of enthusiasm for the Chancellor." His rant included enclosing a draft of a letter "inviting Dr. Birenbaum to take a leave of absence from the University for one year with his services to be terminated at the end of that period."

A few days later, on June 19th, he sent Zeckendorf and the same group of Trustees a letter he actually delivered to Birenbaum. Zeckendorf, Roth, and McGrath must have individually or collectively tried to calm Hoxie down. They failed. In his letter to the key Board members of the 19th, the Chancellor explained, "There is less amusement in Dr. Birenbaum's statement of principles for the University in which he would place the University's governance in the hands of a 'strong independent faculty' with no reference to the Board of Trustees, and would accord the students, whose anger he applauds, full responsibility as adults. This may be a means towards popularity with some faculty and students, but it also an invitation to chaos which I can not countenance."

The letter sent to Birenbaum at this same date marked "personal and in confidence," was syrupy with the anger hidden in a gush of prose. It welcomed him back from Austria. It celebrated his achievements. Hoxie then defined his own mission, "to bring the parts of Long Island University into greater unity and a more meaningful whole, and to build the foundation for future greatness." He went on, "The leadership at the Brooklyn Center is crucial in this noble design, and I regret to advise you that, despite your brilliance and your energy, I do not believe you have advanced this objective." After quoting the Sermon on the Mount, he "took the blame" for failing to get Birenbaum on his team. "To be on the team does not make one a 'yes man.' So long as I am Chancellor of Long Island University, there will always be room for honest differences of opinion. But there must be a larger sense of purpose. Rather than a divisive force, there must be a sense of integrity, of unity in this University."

And then he translated what he meant. "Before you move into #10 Pineapple Street [originally bought by the University for James Hester], before we settle down for the long haul, the air must be cleared. I shall strive valiantly towards that end both for the good of the University and for the good of a young man who could grow tall - and I want him to do so." These two men were nearly the same age. The condescending tone toward Birenbaum was Hoxie's way of telling him who was boss. And then he ended with treacle, as he often did, "My best wishes always go to you and Helen and your family, believe me."

It is impossible to know if the two men ever did sit down to have that heart to heart discussion. If so, it made little difference. Birenbaum's strategy with Hoxie was superficially to flatter and to stroke him. On September 22, 1965, Birenbaum wrote a letter of abject apology because at a plenum meeting of the drafting committee for *Preface to the Future*, Hoxie had taken umbrage, finding fault with Birenbaum's efforts to draft "underlying principles" for the document. He wrote to Hoxie, "As you must know I tried very hard to compose a chapter which would be a source of satisfaction to you." And he went on to express his sadness at Hoxie's response. "Nothing that happened to the report at the committee meeting had at all upset me - except your own critique. That crushed me. My purpose in this drill was to produce a result in which you might take some pride. I had carefully consulted you in advance. I had chosen words and expressed ideas with some precision and care and the failure of my effort was complete when I realized that in spite of all this an impression of exactly the opposite of what was intended was created."

Three days later, Hoxie got a handwritten note from an anonymous Brooklyn alumna and member of the faculty who felt "doubly concerned by the widely-known policy of Provost Birenbaum to denigrate the Chancellor and to sabotage his efforts whenever possible." Was Birenbaum consciously duplicitous? Hoxie certainly thought so, especially when the anonymous letter spoke about one group as being "pro-Chancellor and the other pro-Provost." This individual indicated that Birenbaum boasted that, "this year [1965] he will succeed in leading the Chancellor voluntarily to his grave through flattery." Superficially both Birenbaum and Hoxie remained overly polite toward each other. On October 1ˢᵗ, for example, Hoxie wrote Birenbaum celebrating the subsequent draft of the Brooklyn section of *Preface*, which Hoxie thought was "splendid." His note went on, "This is brilliantly conceived and written."

Were they playing cat and mouse? Battle lines were being drawn, faculty and staff were taking sides, and the Provost actively was courting the loyalty of the student body. In the Brooklyn section of *Preface,* Birenbaum was thoughtfully trying to articulate the role of the Brooklyn campus in a changing and downwardly mobile Borough. He wrote of concentric circles. The newly renamed Zeckendorf Campus was at the core, the immediate environment around the campus was the second circle, the Bridge (The Brooklyn Bridge) to the Plaza (the gateway to Prospect Park), the cultural and economic heart of Brooklyn, was third concentric circle. The fourth was the world beyond-the rest of New York City, Long Island, and the World. It was a document of the 60s, an era when Brooklyn was in decline, and the despair of the community ever more apparent. Birenbaum sought to define the changing mission of the Brooklyn campus. He wrote in his Preface to the Brooklyn section, dated February, 1966, "What follows, therefore, is not the recitation of a dream; it is a conscious effort to think." And he concluded this introduction, "And the academic center we have thought about is neither in a quiet meadow nor in an orbiting capsule. We are excited about a center of learning in Brooklyn, a borough of New York City." Mary Lai wrote Birenbaum, "It is a different approach which I found stimulating and exciting. I think you have captured the spirit of the Brooklyn Center which has been and is so much a part of my life."

Key officials in Albany also responded to Birenbaum's planning document for Brooklyn. On July 15,1966, Assistant Commissioner For Higher Education, Allan Kuusisto, wrote to Birenbaum quoting one of his colleagues (perhaps Kuusisto himself). He wrote, "This is an excellent document. This look-ahead is commendably well done. A reasonably honest look at self, it is a valuable self-study. The language at least reflects the proper appreciation for conditions congenial to quality education. There is reflected here an openness of mind, an alertness to current movements in higher education and quality control, and a sensitive awareness of the university's role in the community and in relation to other educational institutions." This paean of praise continued, "this report casts an image much more favorable than the Division's impression of L.I.U. and may stem from excellence of the writer rather than the institution."

Kuusisto talked about physical facilities being planned with "vigor and drive," the development of programs such as urban studies, film, and international affairs, "though not entirely fresh, displays a responsiveness to community needs...." It concluded, "in my opinion, the 'Ways of Thinking about its Future' does it credit." In effect, the State told Birenbaum that he was on target, suggesting indirectly the rest of the *Preface* was far more problematic.

Hoxie's anxiety over Birenbaum became more complicated when the Brooklyn Center opened the 1966-67 academic year with a freshmen enrollment in Brooklyn up 25%. Birenbaum was doing something that drew students. The University's press release indicated that 1,950 students had enrolled, "by far the largest in its 40 year history," and Birenbaum was quoted as indicating that over 7,000 applicants had applied by June 30th. Another press release four days later announced that the stage directors Alan Schneider and Dory Schary, as well as the city's Superintendent of Schools and Professor E. Sculley Bradley, the former head of undergraduate instruction at the University of Pennsylvania, were all going to teach at the Brooklyn Center in a "Distinguished Seminar Program" established by Birenbaum. All of these were superstars. Schneider, for example, had staged all of Edward Albee's plays in the United States, as well brought to the American stage Harold Pinter and Samuel Beckett.

Birenbaum also organized a 15-part public lecture series on the performing arts in conjunction with the Library and Museum at Lincoln Center. The topic of the first program was "The Role of the University as a Patron of the Arts." The three speakers were Birenbaum, Dore Schary, and Howard Taylor, the President of the American Theater Foundation and the former President of Sarah Lawrence College. An elegant printed invitation was sent out, indicating that the sessions were free. Moreover, Birenbaum had convinced Abraham & Straus to take a full-page ad in *The New York Times* celebrating LIU at Lincoln Center and listing the fifteen separate programs. The list of speakers was diverse and glittering; R. Gordon Hoxie was never mentioned.

Hoxie was jealous. On October 19, 1966, he wrote "Hearty congratulations to you on Long Island University's most recent activity at Lincoln Center...." But he could not avoid showing his pique. "Whereas I was not invited to participate in your Lincoln Center programs, you may be assured of my interest and support, and I encourage the conversations of the Library and the Museum of the Performing Arts on this subject." He then sniffed around for an invitation to one of the scheduled programs, "The May 3 meeting on the Roles of Business and Labor in the Performing Arts is of especial interest to me, since I am addressing a national conference of business leaders on this subject." And then he included a one sentence paragraph, "Although I have not been asked to participate in the Lincoln Center meetings, please be assured of my abiding interest." Greater than a Freudian slip is a Freudian sentence.

Meanwhile, as the academic year wore on, the two men contiuned to circle each other warily but still politely, even while Hoxie was plotting to replace Birenbaum and Birenbaum may have been scheming to replace Hoxie. On December 6, 1966, there was again a full-page ad in *The New York Times* paid for by Abraham & Straus. It read, "A&S joins all of Brooklyn in welcoming nationally prominent educators, teachers, scholars, and practitioners of constitutional law to the Brooklyn Center of Long Island University." The conference, which ran over two days, featured "The Bill of Rights - Today and Tomorrow." The sessions were open; the invited guests, nationally prominent. Norman Thomas addressed the first of the three sessions, followed by Roger Baldwin, the Founder of the American Civil Liberties Union. The third speech was given by Associate Justice William O. Douglas of the United States Supreme Court. The list of panelists was a "Who's Who" from the liberal establishment, including William Kunstler, Sir Dennis Brogan, Morris B. Abram, then American Representative to the UN Commission on Human Rights and soon to become President of Brandeis University. Father Robert F. Drinan was participating in a session on "Race Equality and the Bill of Rights" with James Farmer the director of CORE, William Maslow, the executive director of the American Jewish Congress, and Martin Duberman of Princeton. Hoxie's reaction to this particular program is lost to time, but he must have been even more jealous that A&S was sponsoring it, that it brought so many national figures together, and that it was Birenbaum's brainchild.

On December 27, 1966, Birenbaum got another letter from Allan Kuusisto. Birenbaum had sent him the Minutes of his second faculty meeting of the autumn on November 2nd. Kuusisto was again rhapsodic. He wrote, "I think what all of us applaud is the high regard indicated for faculty prerogative and the active involvement of the staff in academic decisions and campus planning. Your comments defining the academic problems facing the Brooklyn Center are especially challenging, and your identification of pertinent questions regarding your general education program is most discerning."

In the next months were a running series of spats about development officers and alumni staff personnel and their budgets. Under whose authority was someone hired or fired? On February 18th, Birenbaum reported to Hoxie that spring registration rose to 6,313; in 1965 that number was 5,445. On March 4, 1966, Hoxie wrote Zeckendorf complaining that Birenbaum did not seek prior approval of a relatively modest capital expense, which was not in the budget and totaled $27,200.

In a general update to Zeckendorf sent months later, Hoxie wrote, "Bill, my greatest concern remains the Brooklyn Center and the Campus which bears your name and for which you have worked so hard, as you have for the University as a whole." Hoxie articulated his concern about the quality of student life and the tone of student behavior at Brooklyn. He profoundly disagreed with Birenbaum's declaration to the students that "the essence of learning is controversy." To challenge authority was in Birenbaum's DNA, but for Hoxie there was a time-honored tradition to cherish learning and to accept the wisdom of one's elders. Universities existed to preserve that past and to expand knowledge. Students were supposed to be exposed to those riches and to absorb as much as they could. As novices, they were not to challenge their professors or the canon.

The Vietnam War and the fractured American polity also were factors in the internal struggle between Hoxie and Birenbaum. Alan Livingston, a Brooklyn alumnus and Trustee of the University, wrote Zeckendorf in August 1966, alarmed that the campuses were going "leftist." "Last March there was a Teach-in on Vietnam in the Brooklyn Center. Dr. Hoxie was dismayed to discover that Dean Klein was the only one to volunteer to support the government position.... Subsequently, Dean Klein resigned as Dean of Humanities and accepted a position in upstate New York.... These professors [several from Post who travelled to Brooklyn to represent with Klein the American government position] might reasonably ask, 'Has it become dangerous for a professor in Long Island University to support our government in its foreign policy?'"

Back at the beginning of the academic year, on August 31, 1966, University Treasurer, Mary Lai, drafted a note for Hoxie addressed to Clifford Lord, the President of Hofstra, and Arthur Brown of Adelphi. Hoxie rewrote her draft and sent his letter on September 7th. "May I suggest that the three of us sit down together to discuss the matter of tuition and also our fee schedules together with our chief business officers." Such a meeting probably came close to violating the Sherman Anti-Trust Law's provisions on price fixing, but the letter was sent and the meeting, held.

On October 13th, Birenbaum held an open meeting with the Brooklyn students and was questioned by the students about tuition. He wrote Hoxie a memo that same day, "I want you to know exactly and completely what I said to students here when asked about the problem of tuition for 1967-68 at an open meeting on October 13th, during which the students discussed many aspects of University life." Birenbaum claimed that he made it clear that tuition was set by the Board on the recommendation of the Chancellor. If what he said is what he wrote, he made a completely neutral statement, "The problem of future tuition charges and the larger related task of developing the University's future budget, are currently under consideration in the Office of the Chancellor, Dr. R. Gordon Hoxie."

Hoxie believed that Birenbaum either said more than he wrote or privately signaled to Brooklyn student leadership that a big increase was coming. He himself issued an undated memo to the C.W. Post community detailing why costs would increase: "There are two basic causes for these increased costs. We are in an inflationary period. Instructional standards are rising. This means that our faculties must possess higher and higher scholarly and scientific qualifications." While Hoxie was writing specifically to the Post campus, his message applied University-wide. His point was that "the increased requirements of the Merriweather Campus cannot be met on the present tuition fee basis." Without a tuition increase, the Post budget alone would have a $1,681,000 deficit.

This issue had fired up the Post students without Birenbaum's help or involvement. On October 13, 1966, there was an editorial in the Post *Pioneer* stating, "Contrary to the opinion of some, we feel that this College has grown too fast for either its own or the students' good. Quality has been sacrificed for quantity, and this is reflected in the often-voiced boast that 'C.W. Post is the fastest growing small college in the country.'" The editorial continued, "The students of C.W. Post College pay an exorbitant amount of money to attend this College, and we feel that for the amount spent the goods and services received are not enough to merit the expenditure." It spoke about the "Palace down the road," where Hoxie had his office (now Bush-Brown Hall), and lamented that the Post students did not have a Provost whose sole job was to worry about what happened at Post.

The following week, the *Post Pioneer's* editorial page again lambasted Hoxie. Hoxie had delivered an address at Mackinac College in which he said, "In our age, sadly characterized by so-called 'participatory democracy' in academia, ranging from the Berkeley demonstrations to the so-called 'free universities' where existentialists, anarchists, and Communists have denounced traditional higher education...." This prompted the student editorial board to observe that, "Dr. Hoxie seemed to be stating an antiquarian philosophy of education." The editorial board went on, "we are glad that Dr. Hoxie is not teaching classes any longer." Accurately, the students observed that this speech was a major expression of both Hoxie's political and academic philosophies.

On that same day, by chance, Hoxie and John H.G. Pell were at the same dinner. Hoxie subsequently wrote him, "I am glad you and I had an opportunity to have a word regarding the 'mischief' within Long Island University, which I am confident we can resolve." He went on, "The tragic part of it is that it appears that a few persons are trying to exploit the students for their own ends. As a case in point, I am enclosing my letter to Provost Birenbaum on the subject of tuition, which I mentioned to you last evening." It was unlikely that he was making reference to the Post Pioneer's criticism, focusing rather on Brooklyn and on Birenbaum.

Birenbaum sent Hoxie a very moderate and, on the surface, a conciliatory letter on October 27th, denying that he and the Deans meant to, "be unfair, hostile, or malicious" in their opposition to any tuition increase. Hoxie had met with the students ten days before, indicating to them that the budget was not yet fixed, even though it was obvious to Mrs. Lai, Hoxie and others that the University had to raise tuition if it was to balance its books. Birenbaum wrote, "The deans and I felt we had a responsibility to you and to the Center to state our questions and thoughts, about our general situation as clearly as we could. As members of your staff we regarded doing this as our duty.... we meant no veiled threats of demonstrations or anything else by telling you that the decisions being shaped may very well seriously upset the Center. Our Center has 7,000 students, and none of us can control the actions of our student newspaper, Student Council, or agencies of faculty government." Hoxie certainly believed that Birenbaum was behind the student agitation over the proposed tuition increase. Birenbaum vehemently denied this. "I have always assumed that there is a responsibility in the staff to discuss issues freely, to think fully, and even to dissent when necessary, believing that in this process-so much the warp and woof of a University."

Four days later, Mrs. Lai, wrote a detailed message to Hoxie, refuting item by item the fifteen distinct arguments offered by Birenbaum and the Deans who had jointly written opposition to the tuition increase. That campus-based document had warned Hoxie of trouble with students. At its core it argued, "It is our considered judgment that the Brooklyn Center cannot balance its budget in 1967-68, and maintain the present impetus for improvement without substantial new dollars. In view of the fact that in reality there does not exist a corporate surplus to draw upon, and in view of the provost's approval of your philosophy that each Center stand on its own two feet, how then can he justify operating at a loss next year." Later in Mrs. Lai's text: "It is clear that our student newspapers have been editorializing, however mistaken in their conclusions, to the tune and lyrics of the provost. It is also clear that the provosts have been holding themselves up as champions of the students and faculty while casting the shadow of their shortcomings to the Administration Centre." Mrs. Lai, and her key aides, Paul Magali, and Robert Pavese claimed collectively, "that a tuition raise will have no appreciable effect on new student enrollment." Rightly or wrongly they saw Birenbaum's actions as an open challenge to Hoxie's authority. A few days later, on November 3, 1966, Hoxie wrote Birenbaum and the cadre of Brooklyn deans. He rejected categorically a statement in the memo from them to him in which they stated, "We believe we assembled mainly to learn of the decision, not to participate in shaping one."

And on that same day Hoxie wrote to Zeckendorf and six other members of the Board, whom he called "Truth Squad Members," attaching press reports of his speech at Mackinac College. Hoxie was now clearly furious. "It appears that the mischief makers were not satisfied with the story as in the *New York Post - a copy of which I enclose herewith* - and approached *Newsday* to get a more vindictive story." He went on, "aside from the sensationalism of the headline, the story is quite factual. The result is, [in] both papers, we get a view that the Chancellor and administration have expressed faith in liberal learning and refused to be cowed by the extremist, either left or right." This contretemps had convinced him, if he needed additional convincing, that Birenbaum had to be fired.

On November 7, 1966, the Southampton student newspaper, *The Windmill*, printed an Extra edition, indicating the student government Presidents from the three campuses had met to prepare a joint response to the tuition increase, anticipated to be $8 per credit at Southampton and, on other campuses less. It further reported that the Brooklyn SGA and Hoxie had met on November 2nd in an atmosphere of "hostility." The next day, Adelphi announced that it was increasing its tuition by $6 per credit hour. On November 10th, Charles Isaacs, the president of the Brooklyn SGA and clearly someone close to Birenbaum, wrote to Zeckendorf urging that the Board not raise tuition. "Almost 80% of the students at the Brooklyn Center are subsidized by some sort of a loan or grant....Dr. Hoxie insists that a tuition raise is absolutely necessary at this time; the figures he has presented us thus so far do not support his statement."

And that same day, *The New York Times* ran a story about City College President Buell Gallagher who, "refused yesterday to bow before a student threat to hold a sit-in demonstration in the college's administration building." The central issue there had to do with the college computing academic standing for use by draft boards. Each campus had its own flashpoint, but virtually everyone was in crisis. At LIU it started as a rise in student tuition.

Newsday reported on November 10th, that 1,000 students at Southampton met with Hoxie in a very angry environment, protesting the tuition increase. Early that evening the police received a call that Hoxie would be killed at 9:45 at the meeting. It was a hoax, but over 50 Southampton police and plainclothes men had to search the hall first and to be on campus throughout this raucous meeting.

The following day Hoxie wrote Zeckendorf, including a copy of a letter he had received from Charles Isaacs, President of the Brooklyn Student Government. "It is clear," Hoxie wrote, "to the responsible leaders throughout the University, including the Brooklyn Center, that this entire mischief began with the provost of the Brooklyn Center." He then recounted his interaction with the Provosts on the tuition increase and noted that Birenbaum's challenge "was clearly based on the larger issue as to where the center or centers of power reside."

"We must not be coerced or intimidated; we must be on our guard regarding a possible situation not unlike that presently being faced by President Gallagher of City College, as noted in the enclosed copy of an article in *The New York Times*...." Hoxie concluded the letter by observing how ironic he thought it was when Birenbaum, speaking at a Brooklyn alumni fundraiser had "declared that it is his role to make the Brooklyn Center 'the image of the City College of the 30s.'"

That same day, November 11th, Hoxie responded to Charles Isaacs. "It is patently clear that you are either confused, have forgotten, or are, which is understandable, anxious to protect the provost of the Brooklyn Center of Long Island University, to whom you sent a copy of your letter." Isaacs had written Hoxie, indicating that the students did not see "a necessity for a per credit increase now, or in the immediate future, moderate or substantial." Isaacs also indicated that several hundred Brooklyn students would be petitioning that decision in Brookville. The buses would be arriving all morning.

Edward Glanz wrote to Hoxie, thanking him for coming out to Southampton several days earlier to speak to the students. "I congratulate you on your willingness to speak with the students, to discuss the issues, and to overlook the obvious excesses of youth, inexperience, and occasional thoughtlessness." He thought Hoxie's willingness to treat the University as a whole was an important milestone. "I congratulate you on your patience, your ability to clarify complex problems for students and your personal courage and strength." Glanz indicated his active support for the tuition increase, calling it "absolutely essential. The facts of our financial life clearly demand this step." Glanz described what happened to Southampton as "discussion engineering." He lamented the "personal attacks upon you were matters of significant distress to me. Throughout the four year history of this college, this tenor and this attitude has never before existed on our campus."

Five hundred Brooklyn students demonstrated at University Center in Brookville on November 11, 1966. They marched outside Hoxie's office chanting "one, two, three, four, we won't pay anymore." And their signs read "education not exploitation." The increases being challenged had also been reduced by Hoxie so that there was a three dollar per credit increase for Brooklyn students, five for those at Post, and eight for those at Southampton. Forty percent of all Brooklyn students boycotted class, but at Post far fewer appeared at the rally, much to the annoyance of the Brooklyn students. At a meeting on November 15th, despite the student protests, the Board ratified Hoxie's amended proposal and raised tuition unevenly across the three campuses, the Brooklyn Center being charged the smallest increase of three dollars a credit.

That same day Hoxie met with his cabinet. He spoke about "institutional integrity," meaning, "while there is a place within the academic community for differences of opinion, there is a vast difference between that and conduct which may tend to weaken the fabric of the institution. Academic freedom should not be confused with means, which undermine the integrity of the institution."

Hoxie went on to indicate that the Board had approved its ten-year development plan, which would be formally announced on February 16th, in two months, on Charter Day. He indicated that Dean Arden had proposed calling it *Preface To the Future* and invited alternate suggestions, if there were any. Finally he reported that the Board had decided to retain an outside management consultant to help resolve "various internal administrative and organizational problems about which concern had been expressed." He told his team that the Board had just selected Heald, Hobson and Associates, with an understanding that it would report its findings by February 1967. To his query about whether anyone had reservations, "none were expressed."

Hoxie also informed his key administrators about the tuition increase. "Dr. Hoxie also suggested that the Provosts, after meeting with student leaders, faculty and Deans, send out a letter to the students and their parents giving the new rates and flat rates for full time students. Dr. Birenbaum stated that at the time of the announcement of the last two increases letters had not been sent. Dr. Hoxie urged in view of the circumstances this year a letter be sent as a means of notifying parents as soon as possible of the increase."

Glanz reported this tuition decision factually to the Southampton community on November 15th, explaining, "such an increase at Southampton is inescapable to maintain a sound fiscal position and still meet spiraling educational costs, increased costs of campus operations, and the results of many years of inflation in the nation as a whole." *Newsday*, covering this tuition story, also quoted Birenbaum, "we may take pride in the quality of our student leadership, the intensity of its belief in and conviction for their university. But the time for discussion is over. The final decision has been made by those who have the responsibility to make it."

On November 29th, Hoxie wrote a premature memo to the Board. He was "glad to report that the action of the Board of Trustees regarding the tuition increase was greeted favorably throughout Long Island University." He contrasted this to the response at Polytechnic Institute in downtown Brooklyn where there had been demonstrations and the threat of a lawsuit. "Incidentally, the Hofstra tuition increase was not entirely greeted with wholehearted enthusiasm!" Shortly thereafter, he sent another memo citing a story in *The New York Times* about City College entitled, "Student Activists vs. Educators."

On December 1, 1966, *The Leader*, a Locust Valley weekly newspaper, called for Hoxie's removal as President of Post and Chancellor of LIU. It felt that "his handling of the current student protest against a fourth straight tuition increase has been fumbling and undignified." A highly criticized speech of October 1st, made at the dedication ceremonies at Mackinac College in Michigan were "riddled with meaningless clichés of a pedestrian mind." It found fault with the "Educational standards at Post College [which] are so low that the student body through its newspaper, the Post *Pioneer*, has been begging for a tightening of admission requirements and an upgrading of educational requirements." It concluded with the observation that when the student body had lost respect for its President, "he must go. It cannot happen soon enough."

As 1966 ended, NYU also endured sharp protests over a tuition increase. James Hester found himself in the same position of explaining to students why such an increase was necessary. Student militancy was spreading everywhere. On December 7th, *The Times* reported that 800 NYU students protested their tuition increase of $200. In a private letter to Zeckendorf accompanying his memo to the Board, Hoxie first spoke about Jim Hester's problems then took a swipe at Birenbaum, who had organized a Bill of Rights Forum on the Brooklyn campus. "Incidentally, I am not participating in this for the same reason I am not participating in the Lincoln Center programs - both for the simple reason that I was not invited to do so."

What ultimately set Long Island University apart from its sister institutions in the greater New York area was the growing power struggle between Hoxie and Birenbaum. Superficially they continued to be overly polite as if they were best friends. But both clearly loathed each other, based on conflicting views about how universities should function, who should hold authority, and how power should be distributed. On January 9, 1967, Hoxie wrote to Birenbaum forwarding a possible Presidential position at Illinois State University in Normal, Illinois. He concluded that letter, "Whereas it would be a distinct loss to Long Island University, I do believe that you and Helen would make a splendid team as president and President's wife of a major middle Western university...." And Birenbaum responded, "about Illinois State, I am really very pleased by the confidence your letter of the 9th expresses in me."

On February 24th, Birenbaum issued a position paper arguing that Brooklyn needed to maintain authority over the Office of Planning for the Brooklyn Center. Hoxie was looking to centralize the planning process University-wide and Birenbaum was fighting to retain local control. "Brooklyn... is urban. Post and Southampton are not." He urged Hoxie to reconsider his " proposal to abolish the Office of Planning in Brooklyn, [and thus] to tamper at this strategic point with the ongoing planning efforts in this Center. There is no more profoundly disturbing policy decision which might be made at this time." On February 27th, Hoxie responded, "the Chairman of our Board of Trustees believes strongly that long range planning was an appropriate function of the central administration of the University." Hoxie's position was that the University could ill afford full scale planning offices for each of the campuses. His memo was sharp and detailed. He spoke of the success of building the library at Post, whereas the Brooklyn library construction project remained a high priority left in the talk phase. His single spaced three-page letter encapsulated the irritation that Hoxie had with Birenbaum, "I exhort you to learn that cooperation and good faith are a two way street. May I assure you that I do not retreat before the veiled threat with which you end your position paper when you warned me not to 'tamper at this strategic point with the ongoing planning efforts in this Center.'" His letter ended, "Before I painfully document other aspects of your administration, may I invite you to meet with me at my Brooklyn Center office for a conversation and decision. It is my desire, as it has always been, believe me, to be of all possible assistance in your future career which can be character-ized by the brilliance, the integrity, the wisdom which can make you a truly great educational leader."

Copies of this exchange were sent to Bill Zeckendorf, Arthur Roth, Mary Lai, and Henry Heald, the consultant. In Birenbaum's memoirs, *Something For Everybody Is Not Enough: An Educator's Search For His Education*, Birenbaum described that face-to-face meeting as "unusually cordial." "We sat down at his huge empty conference table, the two of us alone, and then he said, as sweet as he ever ad-dressed me, 'Bill, I think you better resign now and start writing that book you've been talking about. Of course, if you don't want to resign, then I'll have to fire you. Now let's discuss the details.'"

Hoxie wrote to Birenbaum on February 28th, confirming their verbal conversation and indicating that it was "with regret that I shall accept your resignation as Vice President and Provost effective June 30th." After the terms were laid out, he asked Birenbaum to co-sign that letter.

On March 8th, Hoxie again wrote Birenbaum, this time dealing with the house on Pineapple Street and a joint press release. This letter, with an accompanying set of terms, was signed by Birenbaum on March 10, 1967. There were handwrit-ten notes, indicating how the document was photocopied, delivered by courier, et cetera. But, as Hoxie soon discovered, Birenbaum was not going gently into that good night. Their mutual distain exploded into a polarizing battle.

On March 13th, a Brooklyn faculty petition signed by many department Chairmen, senior faculty members, and some administrative officers was sent to the Board "to express our deep commitment to and confidence in the administration of William M. Birenbaum. We cannot overstate our high regard for his accomplishments in the office of Provost, our respect for the man and what he has come to represent and symbolize, and our conviction that his continued presence in the office of Vice President and Provost is essential to the continued progress of the whole Long Island University as well as the Brooklyn Center." That petition was signed by fifty-seven individuals.

On the same day the files hold the text of a telegram or a draft of a letter, (which may or may not have been sent) from the Trustees to the petitioners. It was likely authored by Hoxie. The Board asserted: "your petition completely by-passed duly constituted internal and external faculty and administrative bodies; the Board of Trustees has complete confidence in the Chancellor of the University," concluding this issue "has been agreeably settled by the provost and the Chancellor after ap-propriate Board consultation." Also on the 13th, the Brooklyn campus student lead-ership sent its own telegram to the Board: "we feel that Dr. Birenbaum has come to symbolize the spirit of innovation and adventure that is so vital to the growth and development to the Brooklyn Center and Long Island University." The students requested a hearing with the Board.

The following day Zeckendorf himself wrote to Robert Spector, as the member of the faculty designated to serve as the point person. He noted that Birenbaum had signed the Agreement and that the Board agreed to pay Birenbaum at full salary with benefits and allowances at least through the following November and "if desired by him, through May 31, 1968."

Hoxie received letters and appeals from students and faculty. For example, he heard from Mordecai Abromowitz, who was director of teacher education, "I have become more convinced than ever that the Brooklyn Center of Long Island University is becoming and can become a great academic center. (My criteria for a great academic center are: continuous dialogue, intellectual stimulation, and concern for the problems of the community.) Six new faculty members [from the University of Chicago, Columbia University, the University of Victoria in New Zealand, Cambridge and Nottingham University in England-including two Fulbright scholars] who are playing important roles in our effort came to the Brooklyn Center because they were impressed with the administration of Dr. Birenbaum and with the man himself." The letter pushed hard to get Hoxie to reverse himself. "This man is a leader who inspires others to think, to plan, and to act. I have been advised that faculty and student morale has never been higher than it is now under the administration of Dr. Birenbaum."

And on March 16th, *The New York Times* quoted the student newspaper, *Seawanhaka*: "the resignation of Dr. Birenbaum will plunge the University into an abyss from which it may never emerge." It was clear that there was a "deep and philosophical, political and educational conflict between the Provost and the Chancellor." The article suggested that the core issue was "Chancellor Hoxie was a conservative, whereas Dr. Birenbaum was said to be interested in educational experimentation and in developing a relationship with the Brooklyn Community...." *The New York Times* further reported "large numbers of students and members of the Brooklyn Center faculty rallied to his side. Fifteen hundred students held a protest rally.... and authorized Charles Isaacs to call a strike any time he deems fit." The number of faculty and staff who had signed a Spector petition had reached 102 members and the student petition had signed up over 2,000 students. *Newsday* quoted Isaacs as saying that the students were "up in arms." He then threatened that if Birenbaum was not reinstated, "I am sure there will be a student strike."

Meanwhile at C.W. Post the honors program faculty voted 42-1 on March 21st, to express its concern that their Dean, Andrew P. Spiegel, had not been offered a renewal contract. The Open Letter called Hoxie, an "ineffective, unpopular, and reactionary Chancellor," who should be fired. "If Dean Spiegel is forced to resign, will it be long before reactionary educational policy takes our entire College in its grasp and stifles academic freedom and intellectual innovation."

March 21st was one of many days when LIU and its turmoil made the front page of *The New York Times,* because "hundreds of shouting students surrounded Gordon Hoxie yesterday on the Long Island University Brooklyn campus and demanded the reinstatement of Provost William M. Birenbaum." The students were chanting, "We want Bill." They roughed up Hoxie, ripping his coat as he left his "chauffeur-driven car" and started across the campus. Approximately fifteen hundred students were in the crowd. Hoxie, "in a shaking voice lamented, 'This is a day of infamy in the life of the student body.'" *The Times* noted, "students have pointed to many other issues on which they support Dr. Birenbaum… he abolished a dress code that compelled male students to wear ties and he defended a student's right to have a beard."

R. Gordon Hoxie under assault by students on the Brooklyn campus.
Photo by Alan B. Tepper, '68

Meanwhile, upstairs the faculty voted 145 to 38 to demand that Hoxie rescind Birenbaum's termination. The Chair of the Brooklyn Faculty Senate, Edward A. Clark, tried to calm tensions by raising three choices about how to select a new Provost. He wrote Hoxie, also on March 21st, with those options. He recommended that the best option was to have him, as Senate Chair, take charge of the process. For his efforts, he was censured by his own faculty 51 to 29.

As the Birenbaum matter grew in intensity, virtually every member of the faculty took one side or the other. Alvin C. W. Bahnsen, for example, wrote Hoxie, "Your devotion to the cause of C.W. Post College and now Long Island University can never be doubted by those of us who have served with you so long. Your zeal, concept and principle have been an inspiration and guide to those of us who like you have wished only the best for our institution of learning." Hoxie immediately had that letter sent to the entire Board. Arthur B. Coleman, professor of English at Post wrote, "I am not easily impressed and I am notoriously stingy on tribute, but there is no hyperbole (only some awkwardness) when I say that I believe that Long Island University is a very fortunate institution indeed to have as its generating force a man of such good will, such tireless energy and devotion, and such remarkable talent." And Arnold Sklare in the Southampton English Department affirmed his support to Hoxie "for the fundamental rightness of your decision in Brooklyn...."

Hoxie had a deep reservoir of good will at C.W. Post and at Southampton, but in Brooklyn most were negative. The Brooklyn Center chapter of the AAUP voted 70 to 10 to ask the Chancellor "to rescind the resignation of the provost." The University became convulsed by the fight, and the press had a field day covering it. Even Deans and others, caught in the crossfire, took sides. The more conservative someone's political instincts, the more sympathetic Hoxie seemed. The more liberal, the more Birenbaum deserved to be reappointed.

In a further twist to the plot, Birenbaum suddenly asked to withdraw his resignation. He announced this decision at a highly visible meeting with Hoxie organized as a result of Trustee pressure. Was this his calculated plan from the beginning? Did he, instead, test the depth of his political support and make a tactical decision based on it? Did he simply bargain for an exit package too quickly? He was a shrewd political operative, far more politically nimble and public relations savvy than Hoxie. He must have known that if he could force Hoxie to reappoint him, Hoxie would be finished. Birenbaum was no mere supplicant, asking to be taken back into the fold; he was skillfully building support with those stakeholders who were his allies.

Hoxie indicated during a special meeting of five Trustees, including Hoxie, and five committee members of the Brooklyn special faculty committee, he would make a decision at some point the following week. He needed to buy time. Birenbaum and Hoxie met separately with this group. The division of Brooklyn campus opinion was in itself a Rorschach reflection of the worldview and political persuasion of the individual writers of letters. Thus, Florence Miller, who was a professor of business administration as well as the Chair of the Brooklyn chapter AAUP, actively refuted many of the claims of the pro-Birenbaum supporters. Her second-in-command, Michael Siciliano, wrote a long and pro-Hoxie letter to John McGrath with a copy to Hoxie. To read this letter was to gain a nuanced picture in which Hoxie was the gentleman and Birenbaum, the conniver.

Hoxie, in turn, funneled correspondence to the Board to cast himself in a positive light. The files contain a letter from Eugene Ormandy to Hoxie of March 23, 1967 in which Ormandy celebrated Hoxie "for his kindness, his consideration of others, his warmth of heart." There are letters from friends, faculty and administrators urging him to stand fast. The Associate Dean of the Graduate Faculties in Brooklyn, George Weitzman, wrote to the Board on March 23, 1967 "The picture of an academic professor, Dr. Isidore Nicholson, being forcibly escorted by two guards from the student meeting prompts this letter. Dr. Nicholson was denied the right to speak, which was granted to other faculty members with convictions that supported the cause expounded by Mr. Isaacs." Weitzman observed, "In administrative affairs, a provost cannot be in insurgency against the chancellor when a contrary decision has been reached."

Anthony A. Reidlinger, the Chairman of the Brooklyn Department of Chemistry, observed that, "These are indeed troubled times in the life of Long Island University....I, too, believe that the acceptance of the Provost's resignation is an administrative matter....we need firm leadership, such as we had under the late Admiral Conolly." Reidlinger argued that the tactics that were used were similar to those of a union organizer and he attributed this to the influence of Provost Birenbaum. And later in his text he observed, "I would suggest that Dr. Spector's behavior in the current milieu [is] more out of a concern of the survival of the Brooklyn Center as an entity than from any great concern over Dr. Birenbaum." But the "Ad Hoc Committee to Keep William Birenbaum Provost" spoke of "the medieval minded ultra reactionary Chancellor Hoxie (who has been the perpetrator of what amounts to a criminal action enforcing the resignation of Provost Birenbaum)."

All of this publicity prompted Fred M. Hechinger (a three-time Polk Award Winner) of *The Times* to write an op-ed, "In-fighting at LIU," on March 26th. He opined that, "Nothing is murkier than conflicts in higher education resulting from academic infighting."

On March 27, 1967, Hoxie wrote Spector a very formal letter in which he spoke of himself in the third person. He indicated that he was accepting Birenbaum's resignation as of March 27th, that he anticipated a letter from Birenbaum accepting the terms, that he was naming Henry C. Mills as acting Provost in Brooklyn, that he was not changing in any way the structure at the Brooklyn Center, "pending the completion of the current study by Heald, Hobson and Associates, other than those already affected to date." He ended, "Finally, the Chancellor desires to reiterate his support of the principle of the fullest possible degree of local autonomy for the Brooklyn Center consistent with carrying out the orderly administrative processes of the University." After talking about some specific ways by which there could be better communication between several campuses and University Center, he wrote, "It is not the intention of the Chancellor to preside over 'a loose confederation of Indian tribes,' but rather a University which has at its heart a community of scholars, of which you are one of the most respected members."

That same day he wrote to the faculty of the University a three page summary letter confirming the appointment of John Baiardi to be Vice Chancellor for Development to oversee *Preface to the Future*. He announced that he had hired Dr. George Stoddard to work "closely in development and more particularly in the development and community service program at the Brooklyn Center." Stoddard, who was to become Hoxie's interim successor in 1968, was a most distinguished figure in American higher education, having served as Commissioner of Education for the State of New York, President of the University of Illinois, and numerous other senior positions.

Finally, on March 27th Hoxie released a long press statement, sharply critical of Birenbaum and his behavior during the month of March. He framed the decision in terms of Birenbaum's refusal to accept directives from University Center, detailed the terms of his original agreement, referred to the special Board meeting of March 23rd that voted unanimously, "it is the judgment of the Board of Trustees that Chancellor Hoxie has dealt fairly with Provost Birenbaum and his actions as aforestated be approved as in the best interest of the University." He announced the consultancy of Dr. Henry Heald with an initial anticipated report due by June 30, 1967, and described fully his efforts to meet with Birenbaum, Spector and others at several opportunities, all of which had been rejected by Birenbaum.

At a rival press conference on the 27th, Birenbaum leveled charges against Hoxie, claiming among other things that Brooklyn income had been used to finance deficits elsewhere in the University. Birenbaum was obviously now in full battle mode.

As the fight raged, more and more faculty and staff were polarized into taking sides, whereas the students at Brooklyn were overwhelmingly on Birenbaum's side. Robert Ballweg, an assistant professor in biology, for example, wrote to Hoxie on the 28th of March, "I am aware of the pressure because I am on the faculty of the Brooklyn Center and have witnessed the various efforts on the part of both faculty and students in behalf of Birenbaum. The campaign has been awesome, well organized and capably directed, so much so that there can be no doubt that spontaneity was not a factor in the endeavor." Charles Isaacs, the student leader, told the press, "in the interest of the future of the University there is no question that Hoxie must be removed from the Office of Chancellor and that Dr. Birenbaum must be reinstated as the chief academic and administrative officer of an autonomous Brooklyn Center."

Meanwhile, Leo Pfeffer, a Birenbaum loyalist, skilled political scientist and lawyer, proposed mediation. Pfeffer said, "this is not a battle of personalities-what's involved here is, what is a University. Is it the possession of a single individual who can run it like a store? Is the Chancellor the servant of the University or the master of the University?" The Brooklyn faculty voted no confidence in Hoxie 168 to 32.

On March 31st, Mills wrote to the faculty of the Brooklyn Center, "It is my understanding that a student strike has been called for Monday. My best information is that this will consist principally of a break out of classes and not a line of demonstrators with placards. I am informed that this will not be a picket line in the sense that the demonstrators will try to prevent people from entering the building; however, this may not prove to be the case." Mills was indeed, misinformed. Most faculty did not teach on this first day of classes after spring break and the students themselves rated the strike as 80% effective. Approximately 2,000 students and faculty were protesting outside the campus on Flatbush Extension. There is no way to know whether Birenbaum actively incited Isaacs and the students, quietly encouraged them, or simply rode the wave of their conviction that the University could be transformed through student power. LIU had entered the '60s with a roar.

Professor Robert Spector addressing colleagues on the Brooklyn faculty with Professor Hildreth Kritzer, presiding. Chancellor R. Gordon Hoxie can be seen in the third row.
Photo by Alan B. Tepper, '68

In any case, it was obvious that the University itself was at grave risk, not just Birenbaum or Hoxie. That Sunday night, therefore, Zeckendorf called a meeting at George Shapiro's apartment. Shapiro was both an alumnus of Brooklyn and a Trustee. He was also a very shrewd attorney and well wired into the political establishment. The collective purpose was to search for a way out. Present, among others, was Robert Spector, Leo Pfeffer, Mordecai Abromowitz and Charles Isaacs. As Zeckendorf phrased it in a memo to the Board of April 3rd, "The purpose of this meeting was to hear the grievances of these people and those whom they represent." It was stated at the outset by the Chairman that no discussion could be fruitful which dealt with the subject of the reinstatement of Dr. Birenbaum. Notwithstanding this, a lengthy discussion on this issue ensued upon the insistence of Dr. Pfeffer. After approximately one hour on Birenbaum's future at Long Island University, the group discussed structural changes, administrative reorganization and Bylaw modification in order to bring about a more workable *modus operandi*, and a closer rapport between the faculty and students with the Board of Trustees.

209

On the following day, April 3rd, as more than one thousand students continued to strike outside the Brooklyn Center, Zeckendorf called a key group of Trustees, including John McGrath; Hoxie; Alan Livingston, a graduate of Brooklyn; John H.G. Pell; Vincent Macri, a young Post alum; Benjamin Abrams, and William Zeckendorf Jr. There had been an agreement, Zeckendorf wrote, that the "thoughts of the faculty and students would be set forth in writing and delivered in advance" of a Trustee meeting already scheduled for 4:30 in the afternoon. But that document did not arrive and the Trustees called Pfeffer at 5:00 p.m. He thought that the faculty committee was going to be at the meeting with the Trustees. Pfeffer then read the Memorandum to the Trustees over the telephone. Zeckendorf commented, "It was the unanimous judgment of those present, upon hearing the demands of Dr. Pfeffer, et al., that their nature and scope were so outrageous as to have no practical basis for discussion. The committee was mindful that the group which promulgated this memorandum had obviously been directed by Dr. Birenbaum (as witness the last paragraph contained therein)." The text of the faculty document stated, "it is requested the Dr. Birenbaum be restored to his office forthwith and be charged with the implementation of this agreement in the name of the Board for the benefit of the students and faculty of the Center."

On April 4th, Hoxie met with his cabinet. He told the Provosts and officers that the students in Brooklyn "were in violation of the City Ordinance in their blocking the stairways and elevators. Charles Isaacs as their leader must either remove the students or other steps will have to be taken to clear the stairs and the elevators." These Minutes chronicled how the others in the Hoxie administration responded. Baiardi was concerned about what was happening to the image of the University, and Hoxie revealed that he "had proposed that Dr. Henry Heald act as a mediator and he agreed to make a statement about the relationship of the areas within the University." That proposal was voted down by the Board. The Trustees insisted that Birenbaum be removed immediately. Arthur Zupko of Pharmacy stated that, "during the past week 18 applications for admission have been withdrawn." Thus, the debate flowed backwards and forwards as the consequences of this debacle had become obvious.

The elected officers of the C.W. Post Student Government Association also wrote Zeckendorf on April 4th, requesting "a growing recognition of the semi-autonomous campus unit in the life of the University." Eager to distance Post from Brooklyn, the Post students argued that Brooklyn was too large and distinct in terms of both environment and composition of our respective student bodies, for individual units to be run efficiently under present circumstances of centralization." The letter continued in this vein, "We are of the opinion that the present Chancellor-President role is an inefficient and cumbersome one and that each campus should be entitled to its own President who would be responsible for the running of that campus, and would not have the burden of also running the entire University. This campus President, we believe, should also be a member of the Board of Trustees so that the problems and needs of the semi-autonomous campus may be brought directly to the attention of the entire Board." The fragility of the University structure was obvious, and the distance that Post students felt from their Brooklyn counterparts boded ill "in terms of both environment and the composition of their respective student bodies...." Hoxie or Birenbaum or both of them had broken whatever allegiance others had to Conolly's earlier concept of a single University capable of winning and holding the affection and allegiance of each of the campuses.

Both John McGrath and Carleton Palmer received a telegram signed by most of the Executive Council of C.W. Post College and the Merriweather campus, including J.B. Ault, Helen Dartt, Raymond French, A. Hoxton, Waldo Hutchins et al., expressing their "profound distress over the course of events at the Brooklyn and Merriweather Campus." They anticipated "damaging consequences to the University on the Merriweather Campus and within the Long Island Community unless steps are taken now...."

At the end of March, Birenbaum had issued a nine-page statement sent to all the faculty and students at the Brooklyn Center. On April 4th, the Chancellor's Cabinet issued a multi-page rejoinder. Anger was on open display and petty grievances were argued over passionately. On April 5th, Zeckendorf and Hoxie announced that effective the first of June, George D. Stoddard would be become acting Provost and William T. (Buck) Lai would fill that position effective immediately. The adverse publicity was stunning. Not surprisingly, on April 5th, Hoxie received a letter from the State Education Department. "Reports have reached us that very little or no instruction is going on at the Brooklyn Center of your institution since the first of April. Indeed, these reports include the fact that the Vice Chancellor of Academic Affairs has instructed the faculty to respect the picket lines set up by the students. This is merely to remind you that the section of the Commissioner's Regulations under which your courses of study are registered requires a minimum amount of actual work."

The campus was now close to regulatory distress. Somehow the strike needed to be lifted and the required hours fulfilled. On April 6th, Hoxie again wrote to the full faculty, "the imperative matter now is the immediate restoration of the full educational programs at the Brooklyn Center of Long Island University. In this matter there is no choice, as we are so directed by the Commissioner of Education of the State of New York." He then cited the letter and wrote, "This is a tragic situation which can only be remedied by the full restoration of classes Monday morning, April 10, 1967. If this is not done, we are faced with the distinct possibility of the Commissioner's removal of approval of our instructional programs...." He also sent a similar letter to all students reminding them of the risk that they might not graduate or gain credits they had enrolled to earn during the spring of 1967.

Zeckendorf turned, as well, to the new consultant Henry Heald, former President of the Ford Foundation and recently hired to produce a study of the organization of the University, asking him to expand his charge from the Board to ameliorate the ill will that had formed. "Everyone on both sides is desirous of creating a fair and just 'cooling off period' during which time inventory and appraisal of all facts can be reviewed in the absence of emotionalism." He asked that this sub-section of the report come to him by June 30th even as he reminded Heald, "that it is the firm intention of the Board to continue the incumbency of Dr. Hoxie as Chancellor and Chief Executive Officer of the University." It is impossible fifty years later to interview the key Trustees about their decision to protect Hoxie, but it was clear that Birenbaum's challenge went to the heart of the definition of Long Island University. To remove Hoxie at that point would have sent a highly disruptive signal just as the University was struggling to launch its ten-year plan, *Preface to the Future*.

To add insult to injury, ten teams of police raided the Southampton Campus on April 6th, seeking seven students and one ex-student on charges of peddling "more than $200,000 of LSD, marijuana and DMT to their campus colleagues." These raids, the first such narcotic raids on a Long Island campus, were the result of seven months of undercover work. In the *Newsday* article it noted, "The raids came at a time when Long Island University, of which Southampton College is an affiliate, has been wracked with internal dissention. A student strike protesting the ouster of Provost William Birenbaum went into its fourth day today at its University's Brooklyn campus." Francis X. Clines, a top reporter for *The New York Times*, wrote the following day about the operation "Sigma Pot" which relied on the undercover work of the Suffolk Police. Several detectives had enrolled as undercover agents. The use of these undercover agents gave an aroused student body another issue about which to protest, giving the Long Island and City newspapers a field day with the story.

The Southampton student body also mobilized to protest Hoxie's handling of the Birenbaum matter on the Brooklyn campus. Six hundred Southampton students met. Only eighty-two students voted to oppose the sympathy protest, as *Newsday* reported on that meeting on April 10th. "One student, Thomas Miller, Jr., said afterwards: 'we are not a bunch of rebels, not a Berkeley. We are people trying to get a good education. We're trying to build a good University in spite of a dictatorial and archaic administration.'"

The *Long Island Press* of April 14th, reported in its opening paragraph, "after five Southampton College students appeared yesterday in Commack District Court to answer narcotics charges, two were promptly dragged by their angry parents to the Court barber for haircuts. Said the barber: 'that was a lot of hair.'" The student leadership turned on Glanz accusing him of knowingly aiding the police in its undercover investigation; Glanz denied the charges. The local community itself divided between those who rallied to support the campus, Glanz and the Southampton students, and those who used this incident to document their belief that the entire college age generation were ne'er-do- wells, potheads and un-American.

Photo of students protest button.

Meanwhile, the student strike in Brooklyn continued. Picketing students, according to *Newsday*, "sang to the tune of Frère Jacques, 'Gordon Hoxie, Gordon Hoxie, we'll fix you, we'll fix you....'" Even as the students continued to harass Hoxie and go after him, some parents applauded Hoxie for facing the students down. On April 7th, Hoxie received a telegram, which read, "If you quit you will be dealing a blow to all who believe in standards of decency and respect for authority. Let the rabble rousers teach somewhere else and show the misguided kids the principle through which our country once became great." It was signed, "a parent of an LIU student." An undergraduate at Brooklyn, James V. Morelli, wrote Hoxie, "Charles Isaacs and various others must not be given into. If they obtain their demands or any portion thereof the same type of anarchy will be used each time a new excuse can be found.... you must stay on as our Chancellor."

Birenbaum, on the other hand, clearly saw Charles Isaacs as an ideal student leader. A senior in mathematics and honors student, he was headed toward business administration. In his memoir written in 1971, Birenbaum commented that Isaacs's family "could afford to pay his tuition. They were decent professional folk, who like so many residents in Brooklyn and Queens had sought some refuge from the trials and tribulations of the city in a Long Island suburb." Birenbaum observed that Isaacs was always clean-shaven and neatly cropped, wearing a shirt and tie, usually a suit with a vest, and he was no "militant activist." Birenbaum celebrated that Isaacs not only honored his parents, but actively liked them. He participated in the Red Cross blood drive and was a model student, someone that Birenbaum helped get into the University of Chicago Law School in the next year. "In fact, he was a typical child of the Revolution-the American one, that is."

By April 8th, Zeckendorf, at his wit's end, declared that he would close the Brooklyn Center if the student boycott continued into a second week. Maintaining that the students "had agreed to end the walk out, but were now reneging," he openly threatened their graduations, or ability to gain credit for the term, and their capacity to move forward toward their diplomas. The deal Isaacs had wanted was to get from the Trustees a promise that Heald would be given the power to make a binding recommendation on Birenbaum's reinstatement. And even that proposal, which the Trustees would not agree to voluntarily, was challenged by more radical students, who saw Heald as compromised by Zeckendorf's statement to him that "it was the firm intention of the board to continue the incumbency of Dr. Hoxie as Chancellor and Chief Executive Officer of the University."

As the crisis reached a feverish peak, scores upon scores of telegrams and letters came in supporting or opposing virtually every possible option. One friend of Hoxie thought, for example, that Birenbaum "ought to be on the faculty at Berkeley and not at L.I.U." The mail room employees at Post sent Hoxie a very supportive letter. Stakeholders throughout the system and alumni scattered around the world responded positively or negatively. The Southampton faculty voted 40 to 13, with 17 abstentions, to vote no confidence in Hoxie, asserting that he had lost his capacity to function effectively as Chancellor.

Meanwhile, on April 9th, Charles Isaacs and Robert Spector drafted a proposed joint press release with William Zeckendorf. In the document they proposed an elaborate system of selecting arbitrators with the hope that all sides would agree to "arbitration on all outstanding issues." Attached to this draft document, Zeckendorf in his own hand wrote, "Yes, Charles Isaacs recognizes that the students desire to get back to their classes and I believe he is making a genuine effort to achieve this. Further, I believe that the vast majority of faculty desire to return." Zeckendorf went on to wonder whether Birenbaum would demand "the continuation of the strike."

There was a furious effort to shape Zeckendorf's opinion and the other members of the Board. Hoxie kept in his files those letters which supported him. There was less evidence from the other side in the files, but that certainly does not mean such letters and telegrams were not sent. As this battle dragged on across the academic term, the anger expressed increased exponentially. Thus, Arnold B. Sklare, a professor of English at Southampton, wrote, "The Board exercised superb judgment when it elevated Dr. Hoxie to the Office of Chancellor, and it exercised equally sound judgment in holding for the release of the former Brooklyn provost. It deeply grieves me that Dr. Hoxie should be made the target of vilification and lies. He is, in my opinion, a martyr to the cause of truth. Chancellor Hoxie is an extraordinarily gifted educator and administrator, and he is an exceptional human being."

Hoxie drafted and kept in his files a most curious document entitled, "On the Birenbaum Matter." Dated April 10th, it is a long, tendentious bill of particulars chronicling all of the reasons he thought Birenbaum had to be fired. Two copies exist, but there is no evidence that it was ever distributed, even just to Zeckendorf. It excoriated Birenbaum. Was it a document that Hoxie wrote to let off steam; did his wife say after he drafted it, "put it in a drawer," or did events move so fast that he never got to use it? It is impossible to say, but it revealed the depth of Hoxie's anger and frustration. Philosophically, administratively, and personally these two men were oil and water. They both tried at first to put up a façade, but no one believed either of them. The document cited how Birenbaum drove able - and loyal to Hoxie - staff away. It commented on other private universities, which had to be bailed out by their state governments. It rehashed the need for a tuition increase. In sum, it read like a playground spat, which probably is why it never surfaced.

Zeckendorf himself became convinced that Trustee Ogden Reid's mediation plan was the best option. *The New York Times* reported that Reid, Trustee, congressman, and former publisher of the *Herald Tribune,* had taken the lead in arguing for a compromise. However, when the Board put the issue to a vote, a "substantial" number of Trustees voted down any such deal. As a result, a wedge was driven between Zeckendorf and his ally, the Congressman, and many of the others. This intra-Board schism created its own problems, even while Charles Isaacs was talking about a "University-in-exile" with classes held in the streets, in churches and in schools, and Spector was talking about a plea to the State Education Department to intervene. Standing on the steps of The Century Association, next to the Princeton Club in Manhattan, where the Board had met, Zeckendorf indicated that the Board had voted that "under no circumstances would Dr. Birenbaum be provost of any campus in the University." As Hoxie came out of the meeting, he indicated that he had decided against resigning, though it was unlikely that he seriously even entertained that idea.

Governor Nelson Rockefeller with Arthur T. Roth.

On April 12, 1967, Hoxie issued a statement to the faculty and students at Brooklyn in which he described what had happened as "a horrendous experience." Hoxie was conciliatory about meeting the demands of faculty and students, in the construction of a library, a student union, and a health sciences building. He indicated that he was in favor of the Chairman of the Overseers of the Brooklyn campus being named an *ex officio* Trustee of the University. He indicated, as he had to Spector at the end of March, that he supported "the principle of the fullest possible degree of local autonomy for the Brooklyn Center consistent with carrying out the orderly administrative processes of the University." And he closed with a statement of attrition. "All of us are, I hope, wiser after these weeks of stress. I, for one, emerge with a [great] deal of humility. I shall need the help of all of you, and I therefore hope you will, for the sake of this University, which is our common bond, join me in building that better Brooklyn Center, which you deserve and your posterity may enjoy."

The struggle was not over, nor was the schism within the Board healed. On April 12th, Arthur T. Roth sent a telegram addressed to Zeckendorf to each member of the Board. It read, "Board of Trustees disapproved of any negotiation. Consideration of changes is to await Heald report. If this is your understanding, I urge you to immediately contact the Chairman or the Chancellor." Fourteen Trustees plus Zeckendorf had received this cable and it was clear that Zeckendorf saw negotiations as the fastest and best way to regain some semblance of normality within the University. Roth did not. It was also clear that Zeckendorf's financial problems had seriously eroded his authority with his fellow Trustees.

That same day the *New York Post* wrote an editorial headlined as, "Debacle at Long Island University." It began "In their bullying, bungling attempts to deal with the Birenbaum case and the explosive student and faculty protest to which it gave rise, the administration and most of the Trustees of Long Island University have followed a steady, senseless progression. It was clear almost from the outset that they had lost contact with the spirit of the school's Brooklyn Center. As a result of their stubborn effort to suppress it, they rapidly lost respect, now they have lost control." The *Post*, a liberal newspaper in those days owned and published by Dorothy Schiff, spoke of the inability of the leadership, both lay and professional, to see a new approach, especially in urban higher education. The *Post* spoke of these reforms "as a sort of dangerous plague," as the editorial opined. "What amounted to a last chance was developed last weekend by Representative Reid (R-N.Y.), an LIU Trustee. His plan calling for mediation 'of all issues by a prominent educator' was accepted by students and faculty and introduced by Chairman Zeckendorf of the Board of Trustees at the Board's Monday meeting. In an act of panic and desperation, the Board spurned it." With scathing language the editorial warned, "The LIU administration and the Trustee majority have not only lost control; they have forfeited it. They have mistaken authoritarianism for authority; they have rashly resolved to teach students and faculty a lesson. In fact, they have sought to substitute a dismal despotism for academic freedom...."

Then, on April 12th, *The New York Times* reported that the boycott was ending at 3:00 p.m. with the student vote the following day to test whether there was desire to establish "a University in exile." At that student meeting both Birenbaum and Zeckendorf unexpectedly attended. Birenbaum, who had not been expected to attend, was cheered wildly by the 2,500 students gathered. He wore a button produced by student government that said "education not exploitation...the April 3rd movement." When Birenbaum spoke he said, "but no one is telling you to stop this fight for a Center attuned to the last part of the 20th century." Zeckendorf, not surprisingly, received a much more muted response from the students, but he said that, "it was high time for a heart-to-heart discussion. It may well be that your action will in the long run be the greatest thing in the history of the University. You will accelerate by years radical change on the various campuses."

Bill Birenbaum addressing the student rally in the Paramount gymnasium. William Zeckendorf Sr., and "Buck" Lai are standing behind him. Photo by Alan B. Tepper, '68

He also observed he felt fairly sure that Henry Heald's Report would call for greater autonomy on each of the campuses. That evening there was a meeting of some Trustees, administrators, faculty, and students at the Montauk Club in Brooklyn. They agreed to joint committees "which will be charged with the responsibility of exploring and arriving at mutually acceptable recommendations in areas which will involve finance, local autonomy, faculty, and student participation in the decision making process and additional matters of community and non academic concern."

Hoxie declined to meet with the students and faculty, writing Zeckendorf on April 13th, that "It is clear to me that we are getting ourselves involved in negotiations contrary to the wishes of a vast majority of the members of Trustees of the University, and I cannot in conscience, as their chief executive officer of the University, other than carry out the clearly defined policies of the Board. I say this in keeping with my profound respect for you, Bill, as Chairman of the Board. Hoxie then quoted from an Isaacs's speech to the students that day, "CHANCELLOR HOXIE MUST GO. What we have accomplished in the last two weeks is to set up a model for participatory democracy in the educational process. Certainly, this kind of university *cannot* be led by a man who says that participatory democracy cannot work in the University." He noted that Isaacs asked "whether or not the budget will remain an esoteric document which juggles the figures at the pleasure of the Chancellor." Hoxie made clear that he would await the report from Heald, Hobson.

In the C.W. Post student newspaper, *The Pioneer*, published that day, the editors tore into their fellow students for their apathy "We are disgusted with students and faculty of C.W. Post College. Last week we requested to hear from anyone who had something to say concerning the present University Crisis. We have received only two letters concerning this matter. Thank you, the interested members of the C.W. Post College community." Just when Isaacs was optimistically telling his fellow students, "I place great faith in this process [of negotiations]; its results will revolutionize LIU, and perhaps all higher education," the C.W. Post students were barely focused on the turmoil at their sister campus. A suburban campus was a far

217

more conservative environment than one in a metropolis.

April 13th was another complex day. Franz Schneider also wrote to Zeckendorf, urging that nothing be agreed to until the Heald Report was issued. "I suppose what I am saying is that meetings between your committee and any representing students should be described not as negotiations but as discussions to assist the Trustees in their decisions after they have received the Heald Report."

The following day Zeckendorf wrote an extraordinary response to Hoxie. "Your letter of April 13th disturbs and disappoints me very much indeed." Zeckendorf then went on to recount his understanding of what was and was not authorized by the Board, maintaining that the meeting at the Montauk Club was for the "express purpose of obtaining direct discussions with duly constituted representatives of the student of the body and faculty." And he noted, that you, John McGrath, Ogden Reid, Spyros Skouras, James Van Fleet, Vincent Macri, son, Bill, and himself had all been present. He went on that there was a clear agreement from all of the participants that Heald, Hobson would be present at all meetings to render guidance. He urged Hoxie to attend, whatever other commitments he might have, accepting that "no conferences can be successfully conducted in any atmosphere other than one having proper decorum." Zeckendorf was positive that, "A default of our commitment on one campus would be interpreted as our policy *everywhere* and will lead to a lack of confidence and subsequent disruption." He continued, "By far the worst thing we can do, at the time, is to breach the letter or spirit of our agreement with these people who called off their strike in reliance of our word. Speaking personally, I just cannot and will not abide by any such course."

Zeckendorf observed, "It was a matter of good fortune that months ago, in contemplation of exactly the series of events which have subsequently ensued, I urged the Board, over some objections, including your own, to seek outside advice. This culminated in the Heald, Hobson and Associates' agreement. We now have them and are paying for their services. We should make maximum use of their abilities, because as stated above, it will help in the present crisis and will be of immeasurable value in the presentation of their final report." Zeckendorf urged Hoxie to be "present at all meetings." He indicated he would not permit any indignities to Hoxie or his position "at any meeting Chaired by me."

He went on to state the obvious, "The situation at the University is grave. We have finally agreed upon an orderly procedure in an effort to abstract [sic] ourselves from further tumult and anarchy, at this time. We are now in an area of dignified consultation dealing directly with the proponents. Nothing can be more constructive...." And he concluded this letter, "Gordon, we have been friends and colleagues for many years. We have been through a number of crises.... I pray we shall follow this path, together."

On the following day, Friday, April 14, 1967, the Brooklyn students voted by a ratio of five to one to end their boycott and to return to their classes. There were 3,000 students gathered in the Old Paramount gym to take that vote. Birenbaum issued a statement, "I tried to stand for what an urban center of learning should be. If the faculty and students at LIU have achieved conditions for such a center then I am satisfied. The struggle at LIU has not been for a man's job. It has been for the ideas and integrity of the Brooklyn Center, its people, and its communities."

Meanwhile, Henry Mills had been negotiating with the State to work out what would be necessary to permit sufficient contact hours for students to graduate and to earn credits towards their degree. By eliminating the examination period by one day and forgoing Memorial Day as a holiday, combined with extra teaching to make up two and a half days of class time, the revised calendar won New York State approval.

John H. G. Pell wrote to Zeckendorf on the 14th, (one of the very few times he stated his opinion in writing) in agreement "with Arthur Roth's conclusion that at our recent meeting the Board of Trustees disapproved of any negotiation-by an overwhelming majority. The danger of dealing with an unauthorized revolutionary minority is that you will erase the possibility of orderly evolution." He concluded his letter "the danger is that your efforts to save the University will destroy it."

Zeckendorf answered Pell on the 17th, refuting his observations in a strongly worded letter, "The surest way in which I believe the University can be destroyed is by the avoidance of frank, open discussion which will air differences of viewpoints. As a matter of fact, there is a *right* of direct appeal to the Board by persons who feel they cannot have their grievances satisfactorily heard [Article Three of the Bylaws]." Zeckendorf continued,"I heartily agree that we should not deal solely with dissidents whether they be a minority or a majority but rather with proper representatives of all factions." He ended his letter by focusing on Henry Heald's future role. "In view of the justified reliance which the Board places on Dr. Henry Heald, you will be pleased to learn that at luncheon yesterday, he expressed himself as being gratified by the 'route' which we are taking and expressed his desire to be present at all subsequent meetings. For the first time in a long while, I believe we are in an area of growth through understanding."

The next day Hoxie wrote a five page letter to the Trustees which was diplomatically apologetic, optimistic, and saccharine. In particular, he wanted to use this quasi-public letter to heal his rift with Zeckendorf for what he called a "regrettable misunderstanding." He contrasted Birenbaum's exhortation to the students to use "alternate levels of weaponry," with the way, Mr. Zeckendorf announced that the student protest "has clearly demonstrated that there is the need for decentralization and greater autonomy on a campus-by-campus basis...." He ended with a pledge to build "a University of which our posterity may be proud!"

Hoxie's long, single spaced letter prompted Zeckendorf to write on April 19th, "I fear that the amount of mail being foisted on our Trustees,... must by this time be reaching the breaking point in their patience. Let us-in the interest of getting on with our work-cease in our forensic efforts so that we might have more energy and mental resourcefulness available to all of us to solve our problems at Long Island University. Please, please, do not answer this letter so that we may terminate our correspondence with this brief note in the spirit of good will, helpfulness and perhaps even an element of humor." And then he added a P.S. which said, "I am not circulating this letter among the Board as a first step in the plan above outlined."

And so the strike finally ended. A joint student, faculty, Trustee committee was charged with the task of addressing a cluster of central issues that virtually all the stakeholders would agree needed to be resolved. Isaacs, at the last student rally that spring, hailed the formation of this committee, "At last, our Board of Trustees seems to have realized that they must deal with the students and faculty if they are to govern the University."

He also was still demanding that Hoxie had to go. Passions were still running very high, and Isaacs himself was under pressure from more radical students who believed that he, Isaacs, had sold out by agreeing to any compromise. According to *Seawanhaka*, in the April 19, 1967 issue, "One bearded student, a senior, stated 'I have a four year fellowship waiting for me at the University of Pennsylvania-and I am willing to risk that for Bill Birenbaum.'" He then held his April 3rd movement button and, screaming above the din "cried, 'the button I wear has been betrayed. I refuse to wear it anymore.'"

But for all of the hyperbole and adolescent language, the strike, if not the term, was effectively over. In that same issue of the student newspaper there was a wistful note of sadness in the editorial. "The case for a pessimistic future has a very solid basis in fact. We cannot help feeling that any apparent willingness to talk on their part [the Board's] is nothing more than a superficial act, motivated more by the wish to silence the opposition than a sincere desire to rectify any injustices.... Anyone who has had any confrontations with the Board and especially with the Chancellor, almost instinctively approaches future associations with great wariness.... We must, from past experience, view the current efforts to establish a dialogue with the feeling that it is all for naught." At the end of the strike, as in the beginning, many students and virtually all of the Trustees were still talking past each other, with Zeckendorf, his son, and Ogden Reid, the exceptions.

On April 20th, John Pell responded to Zeckendorf's letter, "I continue to believe that it is both improper and inadvisable for any committee or group of Trustees to meet with self appointed committees of faculty and students. I believe such a meeting will constitute a negotiation and, in support of this position, I refer you to the lead article in *Seawanhaka*," (the headline read: "Negotiation Committees Formed

As Students Officially End Strike").

The following day an article appeared in *The New Republic*, entitled "Behind the Scenes at Long Island U." The article focused on two aspects of the story that have not yet been discussed in this narrative. First, was there a Brooklyn surplus that could have been used to hold down the Brooklyn tuition increase? Mrs. Lai was quoted as indicating that it was only "a paper surplus," meaning that the books at the University were integrated and there was a single bottom line for the entire institution, even while each campus's revenues and expenditures were broken out. The second issue dealt with the interlock of business dealings between the University and individual Trustees and between one Trustee and another. The article focused on those Trustees who had real economic leverage, starting with the Zeckendorfs, father and son. It then talked about John McGrath as "an old lion Democrat," who was corporation counsel under Mayor William O'Dwyer in the late 1940s. McGrath was Chairman of the East New York Savings Bank and a real estate developer as well as a lawyer. Mayor Robert Wagner was on the Executive Council of Southampton College, Edward Cavanagh, Wagner's brother-in-law and a former New York City Fire Commissioner, was Chair of the Development Council for C.W. Post. And so it went on chronicling a presumed nepotism, which seemed rampant.

The article accused the LIU Board of borderline corruption. It hinted that such connections were nefarious, an example of how political and business elites could prosper at the expense of a University. The personal ties had an aroma of illegality and, it hinted that individual Trustees benefitted more than the institution. Among others, it focused on Arthur T. Roth who did business with Zeckendorf and was a director of Webb & Knapp. Franklin National Bank and East New York Savings both held many of the University's mortgages. Franklin National was owed $1,382,000 when Webb & Knapp went into bankruptcy in 1965. The article pointed out that General James Van Fleet was also a director of Webb & Knapp. *The New Republic* uncovered no scandals, although it tried, but it was embarrassing to read of the extent of the financial interlock of these individuals. The concept of a "conflict of interest" has been much more sharply defined in the 21st century than it was in mid-twentieth century America, but there was a casualness of business dealings that clearly embarrassed the University and its Board. Even if those University mortgages were below market and the University benefitted from the Trustees' generosity, it was impossible to refute the claims easily which made the whole structure seem dirty. The piece ended, "And they say it is wrong for Trustees to be doing business with a University whose interest they are suppose to represent."

Martin Buskin, then *Newsday's* education editor, further tarnished the good name of the University when he wrote in an editorial, "If the Trustees learned anything from the academic earthquake of the last few weeks, they should realize that there is deep bitterness and resentment against current administrative policies and that the focal point of this resentment has been Hoxie." Hoxie, in turn, outraged by Buskin's tone and approach, wrote to his friend, the owner and publisher of the newspaper, Harry F. Guggenheim. "His [Buskin's] hostility clearly comes through in the editorial in the Monday, April 17th, issue of your otherwise esteemed newspaper.... One thing I believe you and Bill Moyers [the editor-in-chief] will certainly agree with me on, in this recent disturbance is that the proposal of Mr. Buskin for a 'impartial mediator' would be the abandonment by the Board of Trustees of Long Island University of their responsibilities."

The New York Times also wrote an editorial on April 20th. "Long Island University's rapid growth, its inadequate financial resources, its hazy sense of direction, and the clash of personalities have all contributed to the present controversy. Trying to serve simultaneously an underprivileged clientele in urban Brooklyn and a more affluent suburban following, the University has been pulled in opposite directions with such force that its warring administrators seemed to have been unable to control either their institution or themselves." *The Times* felt that many of Birenbaum's educational and civic aims appeared sound and had the support of students, faculty, and the community. The editorial continued, "Blame for the open hostilities must be taken in small part by Dr. Birenbaum for lack of diplomacy, but a large part by Chancellor R. Gordon Hoxie and the Trustees for lack of leadership." And then a further damning sentence, "The central administration and the governing board vacillated between autocracy and indecision, often substituting platitudes for policies."

Even more serious than these blasts from the press, however damaging they might be, was the erosion of comity and cohesion on the Board. The fracturing was, in part, personal. Whether Zeckendorf was right or wrong about the students and their "demands," he often came across to his colleagues as a bully or as arrogant. The Trustees with estates in Nassau and a suburban, conservative world-view, saw the crisis in America as threatening the traditional verities they associated with the Republic. Like college Trustees all across the land, they interpreted what they experienced in Brooklyn as a generational descent into anarchy. It was only two decades earlier when many of them, or their golfing partners, were so hostile to LIU moving from the City onto the "Gold Coast." The world of the Creek Club and Piping Rock Country Club was clearly challenged by the social upheaval of the 1960s. John H.G. Pell, John McGrath, William Casey or Arthur Roth and most other Board members had come face to face with the next generation in Brooklyn. They did not like what they saw. It had been almost exactly five years since Conolly had died in the plane crash, but it could have been one hundred years instead. Both America and Long Island University had changed beyond easy recognition.

And the decade was still not over. Indeed, the spring term was not yet over. Birenbaum increasingly faded as the central issue. But the relationships of the stakeholders to one another was a fight just beginning. In their own unique way, the

Brooklyn students were changing their college and taking part in a movement that was national. The story of LIU in 1966-1967, recounted in such length above, has been told without constant references to student power, militant protest, and challenges to adult authority manifest on virtually every other campus across the country. The presence of William Birenbaum, already a counter-culture hero and administrator in a senior leadership position, certainly made this a special situation. Yet, the demands from Isaacs and his peers resonated with those at Berkeley or Columbia or the City University of New York.

At a Teach-In on April 21st, the President of the LIU chapter of Students for a Democratic Society (SDS) opened the program entitled "Students and the Contemporary University." There were panels on "How LIU is Run," and "Student Power and Where Do We Go From Here." Meanwhile, Hoxie had replaced Mills as Acting Provost with the University Director of Athletics, William T. (Buck) Lai, Mary Lai's husband. He was sent to Brooklyn to regain control of the day-to-day management of the campus and get the students and University through the last weeks of this extraordinarily rocky spring term. The University had to celebrate the ancient rites of Commencement. Then it had to get back to normal, if possible.

Letters, both printed and personal, were written from virtually every possible vantage point. Some supported Hoxie, others attacked him. Faculty complained about colleagues, about the way self-appointed faculty leadership claimed to speak for them. The Board was pilloried by some and praised by others. Egos, grudges, ancient grievances all surfaced. It was a time for catharsis. There was anger that some had seized the symbolic and actual microphones and were heard while others were not. Depending on the campus, there was a Rashomon effect. Hoxie loyalists wrote letters to the editor of the major New York papers, and others wrote to refute what colleagues had asserted as truth. Before the summer doldrums, seemingly everyone had an opinion to share.

Just as the Board turned on itself in anger and disarray, so did the existing leadership of the Brooklyn faculty. Florence Miller, the President of the Brooklyn chapter of the AAUP, was vilified because she was deemed too conservative and too pro-Hoxie. Hoxie, in rising to her defense, only added fuel to the fire. "It is tragic to see a devoted person, such as Professor Florence Miller, unfairly charged by some of her faculty colleagues…. I have complete confidence that Professor Miller will not only be vindicated for her forthright position, but in retrospect in the history of our University, her name will be high on the honor roll for her unswerving devotion to the highest principle to her profession and to the University." Miller wrote a long letter to the Editor of *The Times* on April 17th in defense of her actions, claiming that there was coercion on Brooklyn faculty by the pro-Birenbaum faction.

This fracturing of the faculty exacerbated anger still percolating at the end of the three-month struggle. The Chairman of the Physics Department and of the Campus Faculty Senate, Edward Clark, wrote a long letter on April 27th to Zeckendorf, describing what he perceived had happened within the faculty during the chaotic days of the strike and thereafter. A former marine himself, he wrote, "My present view is that we have been witness to a deliberate, well-executed, power struggle, motivated by less than honorable intentions, using any tactics that would achieve the purpose, coupled with an almost complete failure of the ordinary channels of authority to correctly interpret and rectify the situation." Deeply concerned about the irresponsibility of many of the statements made, some of which he considered libelous, he felt "would be grounds for dismissal of even a tenured member of the faculty." He argued that the pro-Birenbaum faculty sought to destroy "the credibility of anyone who might oppose them; they have done this by rumor, by late night phone calls, by the distribution of unsigned propaganda sheets, by the submission of distorted and libelous press releases, by votes of censure at meetings called in complete disregard of notification or quorum requirements at which neither the requirements of due process nor propriety were accorded the victims of their attacks, and by other means which would suit their purposes." Clark was offended by what his colleagues had done, as he saw the matter, complaining that the Faculty Senate should have been the elected agency to take the lead and noting that strike committees were appointed without due process, or respect for open disagreement. He wrote, "I am fully aware that someone not personally witness to the events would find it difficult to believe what has transpired-it is difficult for me to believe what I have myself seen."

Soon thereafter some twenty-one senior members of the Brooklyn faculty, including twelve full professors, seven department Chairmen and the Chairman-elect of the University Senate sought a meeting with Zeckendorf and the other leaders of the Board on the grounds that they had a different perspective from the committee that had rallied to Birenbaum's defense. In their letter, they spoke of "the present drift of the University academically and administratively believing that irreparable injury to our reputation and to our academic status will ensue."

The young Post alumnus and Trustee, Vincent Macri, wrote a sharp letter to Zeckendorf on June 5th suggesting that Zeckendorf had brushed off this distinguished group of senior faculty, as Macri calculated it with more than 193 years of collective service to the Brooklyn campus.

On June 6th, Zeckendorf exploded in response: "for the life of me I cannot understand your letter of June 5th!" He noted that everyone was sending him complaints and that, "Actually, I hardly have time to attend to anything else! I believe that the Trustees must be getting 'fed up' with all the exchange of correspondence." Macri responded on June 13th arguing, "I believe that Dr. Clark and other faculty members should be heard as per their requests." On June 21st, Macri again wrote Zeckendorf complaining that the faculty representatives to this joint committee "were not formed according to proper procedure at faculty meetings, that the faculty meeting at which Hoxie received a vote of no confidence was described 'by an eminent member of the faculty as a howling mob displaying considerable hysteria,'" that members of the Brooklyn Center administration favor a union which is at the present time recruiting faculty members and which espouses collective bargaining rights on behalf of the faculty and that this dual representation appears to be inconsistent." A few weeks later, Zeckendorf, just back from a trip to Europe, wrote to Macri, "The purpose of this letter is to acknowledge all of your various communications. Apparently, something has gone amiss in your thinking and I wish to put it straight."

On April 24th, a month before this angry exchange with Macri, Zeckendorf hosted the first working meeting of the tri-partite Committee. Present were three students, six faculty, two Brooklyn administrators, eight Trustees, and Henry Heald and his partner, Roger H. Sheldon. That same day, he wrote to John H.G. Pell, reporting to him the membership, including the committee structure that would allow the group to do its work. He again assured Pell that "no commitments will be made which will bind the Board."

Universities go into summer hibernation, in sharp contrast to bears and other animals that shut down for the winter. In a pre-air-conditioned 1967 environment, that summer vacation proved to be a welcome opportunity for everyone to escape LIU's tensions and travails as well as New York's heat and humidity. There was no shared cohesion or trust left among students, faculty, and trustees. The urban Brooklyn campus, in particular, got hot and empty quickly. The optimistic collegiality that had emerged while *Preface to the Future* was drafted, disappeared.Any surviving commitment to a shared mission vanished. At most other colleges and universities then in turmoil, the main impetus for unrest was external: Vietnam, the draft; a changing core of social mores and cultural values. What happened at LIU, in addition to those external dynamics, was intrinsic to its structure, its management, and its identity. This double whammy turned key stakeholders against one another. Consensus and collegiality were fractured among the three residential campuses. In sum, morale hit bottom.

Birenbaum had quietly finished the course he was teaching that spring on the Federalist Papers and left the University without student or faculty send off. Acording to a *New York Times* profile of June 29, 1968, he had become the President of Staten Island Community College.

He had openly advocated the abolition of rigid structures in higher education, including formal exams, credit hours and even some of the broad categories of the organization of knowledge-economics, political science, sociology or psychology. *The Times* in a profile commented, "these ideas, and their fluent expression, make him at once a hero and an enemy. The most visible battlefield was at Long Island University about fifteen months ago." *The Times* noted that, "Although affable, quick of wit and often flippant, he is essentially a serious man." And *The Times* profile also quoted Hoxie who said, "'The real and only issue'" in the LIU dispute was 'whether there is within our University a role for the Board of Trustees or only for Dr. Birenbaum himself.'"

It is perhaps fitting that Birenbaum have the last word in a chapter named for him. In 1971, Random House published his autobiography, *Something for Everybody Is Not Enough: An Educator's Search for his Education*. It was self-serving and surprisingly smug, funny but without charity. Bill Birenbaum clearly understood that the world had changed; universities were different places than they had been even five years earlier. He opined, "I have found that men - and institutions, too - who aren't sure of themselves and of what they are supposed to be often caricature expertly what they are. Ugly ducklings who think they are swans are ludicrous." He mocked Zeckendorf "on Madison Avenue, on the morning after, the God of Choice, bankrupt, reigns supreme."

Birenbaum maintained that it was Zeckendorf who had called him to help John Pell as Chancellor, quoting Zeckendorf, "There were organizational problems involving the multi-campus structure and operation of the institution...." He also remembered Zeckendorf observing, "Decisions had become painful for John Pell because those he had made as Acting Chancellor seemed to please no one, and he was a gentle man, convinced that people should get along together reasonably. He was a man determined not to hurt people at a time and in a place where it seemed to him that everyone was bent on hurting everyone." And once he joined the University as Pell's advisor "almost immediately I had found myself in one of the strangest and most intriguing zoos imaginable.... Each of the three provosts, it seemed, perhaps a few others--in view of Mr. Pell's temporary status-was convinced that he himself ought to be the new leader." He chronicled an environment of fear and "outrageous allegations" where telephones were tapped, offices bugged, and wastebaskets searched. The name of the game, according to Birenbaum, was to make no decisions whenever there was a meeting of the Chancellor's Cabinet. "Each time the Acting Chancellor gently approached a conclusion designed to make reasonable men live together reasonably, a multitude of complications expressed in long, haranguing orations, led the group inevitably into indecisive dissolution."

Birenbaum concluded, "Each part [campus] in pursuit of its own interest, had a version of itself it wished to impose upon the whole. And among these versions, with a few exceptions, the gamut of some of the more depressing options in American higher education was present."

"We were living in the backwash of the Berkeley uprising, and one did not have to be very bright to understand that we were entering a new era of student participation in the conduct of higher education." His memoir, unfortunately, fails to detail his own role during that last tumultuous year. He presents himself as the observer, not the actor. He did comment that, "The job at stake was mine. But the loss of it brought into sharp focus issues that were theirs. It was to be their fight, and fight, they decided they must." To read this chapter entitled "The Battle of Long Island," was to view a drama in which Birenbaum defined himself as but a bit player.

Perhaps it is so that new forces in history --discontinuities, not individuals-- shape events. Certainly, that is how the Birenbaum matter ended, even if he was a critical catalyst in how the struggle began. He ultimately became President of Antioch College in Ohio, shifting his leadership skills to a very different, truly more "progressive" kind of institution. But nowhere in his memoir did he indicate the hand to hand combat he openly waged with Hoxie before Hoxie terminated him. They had behaved like two seven-year olds in a playground spat, kicking the dirt and calling each other names.

What was clear by 1967, a few years later when Birenbaum wrote this memoir, and still a half a century later, was that the University was badly wounded by this immature fight. Conolly's dream already seemed like ancient history. While Hoxie survived this debacle, he was in serious trouble and he should have known it. If 1966-1967 was, to use Queen Elizabeth II's quote, an *annus horribilis* for Long Island University, 1967-1968 proved to be even worse.

Without a very substantial increase in endowment and gift support, it is not possible for a private institution such as Long Island University to offer in Brooklyn at reasonable tuition levels the range and quality of academic programs which are now, and will be increasingly required to serve the largest borough of New York City.

Henry T. Heald

Chapter Seven

The Failed Sale of the Brooklyn Campus

In late 1966, Zeckendorf had written to Henry Heald, the former President of the Ford Foundation, former President of New York University, and before that, the Illinois Institute of Technology, to explore whether he would serve as a consultant to LIU. Heald had formed a consultancy with Jesse E. Hobson at the beginning of 1966, and the firm had rapidly built a national practice dealing primarily with mergers within the higher education sphere. He chaired the Commission which recommended the merger of Case Institute of Technology with Western Reserve University. In the Dallas-Fort Worth area, he was hired to create the so-called TAGER, bringing Southern Methodist University, Texas Christian University, and the Graduate Research Center of the Southwest into a collaborative effort to strengthen graduate education and research in the area. In the Albany-Schenectady region he helped restructure Union College, the Albany Medical School, and the Albany Law School into Union University. In Virginia he and Hobson had a contract to review how the University of Virginia was organized. He also had clients at the University of Louisville, the University of Hawaii, and the University of Pittsburgh. As a firm, Heald, Hobson charged $300 per day for the time of one of the principals; $200 per day for one of the associates.

Heald had spent the first part of his career as a professor of civil engineering at Armour Institute of Technology. He rose through the ranks, became Dean of Engineering in 1934 and finally President in 1938. In 1940, he brought about the consolidation of the Armour Institute of Technology and the Lewis Institute to form Illinois Institute of Technology. Later, he served as Chairman of New York State Commission on Educational Finances and was the principal author in 1956 of a comprehensive report on Financing Public Education in New York State, a foundation document leading to the creation of the SUNY system. He also was Chairman of the Committee on Higher Education for New York, whose report, "Meeting the

Increasing Demand for Higher Education in New York State" was an operational document to make that system a reality. He had been awarded 21 honorary degrees when he became a consultant to Long Island University. He was also a director of the Equitable Life Assurance Society, the American Telephone and Telegraph Company, United States Steel Corporation and Lever Brothers. A commanding figure in the nation, he seemed to be the ideal consultant for Long Island University.

His junior partner, Jesse Hobson, had been a Vice President for planning at Southern Methodist University. An electrical engineer, he had worked under Heald at the Illinois Institute of Technology and served for eight years as Director of Stanford Research Institute. On November 18th, four days after Heald indicated he would be available to serve as a consultant, Hoxie wrote to Zeckendorf, attempting to define narrowly the parameters of Heald's assignment. Cribbing almost verbatim from a memo Hoxie had received from Lester S. VanderWerf, a pro-Hoxie loyalist at C.W. Post, Hoxie sought to define Heald's mandate. Among other things, he wanted to be assured, "that Long Island University is to remain one institution....that the structure of the University reflects the integrity of the University." And his memo went point-by-point, detailing the future structure of undergraduate colleges, the priorities for hiring the faculties, the role of Provosts, et cetera. Hoxie delineated what he considered to be legitimate "areas of study." And then even tried to define the procedures by which Heald was to gather whatever data and interviews he and Hobson might seek.

He sent copies of this memo to the ad hoc committee that Zeckendorf had established, including among others Pell, McGrath, Neimuth, Palmer, Roth, and William Zeckendorf Jr. By January 1967, this group authorized the hiring of Heald, Hobson to undertake a thorough review of the University, including its long range plans, its present and future financial resources, and the structure needed to achieve successfully those goals. In effect, this report was to review the viability of the newly Board-approved ten year plan, *Preface to the Future.*

Heald, Hobson was to deliver an oral report to the Board by July 1967, with a written report to follow. Heald laid out his understanding of the scope of priorities of this study in a letter to Zeckendorf of January 20th. "We would give particular attention to the relationship between the central administration and the various campuses of the University, and the relationships of the Board of Trustees to the administration, the faculty, and the students."

The retention of Heald, Hobson took place as the crisis between Hoxie and Birenbaum was just erupting into public view. It was inevitable that this high level consultancy got sucked into that struggle, as both Hoxie and Birenbaum sought to manipulate Heald, Hobson for their individual advantage. In one letter from Hoxie to Heald of March 2nd, Hoxie focused on the fate of a candidate for Director of the Libraries of the University, Ray R. Suput, who had withdrawn from consideration the previous week because he was not prepared to accept "veto power over the Director's actions in the hands of the four provosts (rather than the University Administration) which could have some undesirable results." Suput, who saw the Directorship as a University-wide position, was not willing to allow either Ewald or Birenbaum define his job. By writing Heald, Hoxie's goal was to shape how Heald addressed the politics of the institution, using the Suput matter to underscore the risks of empowering each of the campuses against the center. "In brief it would appear that such a reasonable proposal of a major university to have a Director of Libraries should not be opposed by the provosts. Perhaps, some or all of them need a bit more education regarding the warp, woof, and spirit of the University."

During the student strike over Birenbaum's dismissal, it was necessary to remember that Zeckendorf had proposed to the students that Heald be asked to play a role in adjudicating the crisis. Initially, Heald had said that he did not want to decide who should be Provost because that was, according to *The New York Times*, "an administrative matter for the University." But, under obvious pressure from Zeckendorf, Heald "agreed to study the reasons for Dr. Birenbaum's removal and recommend to the University's Board of Trustees by June 30th, whether the former provost be reinstated." Virtually all consultants are reluctant to be pulled from their third party perch as objective observers into the proactive task of serving as arbitrators, in this case asked to adjudicate a battle for the soul of the University. As he feared, Heald was abused shamelessly, leveraged into making near-binding decisions, when consultancies traditionally only make recommendations.

During the trance-like sleep of university life, during the summer, students and faculty are gone. There is much routinized work to prepare for the following fall term-registration of students, dormitory assignments, class rosters, et cetera. This historically is the work of staff trained in student life, buildings and grounds, admissions and advising, whose vital labor is rarely recognized by the major institutional stakeholders: faculty, students and Trustees. But the summer of '67 would prove to be profoundly different, even though on the surface it seemed to be "business as usual."

On July 24, 1967, as contractually promised, Heald, Hobson gave a confidential oral report to the Board on the state of the University and on the Birenbaum affair. Hoxie was still in office as Chancellor; Birenbaum was gone. But few doubted that the institution was bruised. And no one knew for sure what would happen when the students came back in September.

In a long, single-spaced memo to the Board on August 15, 1967, Hoxie attempted to combat what he called the consultants' "unduly pessimistic" oral assessment. Much of his long memorandum was an effort to refute the statistical analysis conducted by Heald, Hobson. Hoxie challenged many of their factual assertions, including the number of books in the several libraries of the University, faculty salaries, the profile of the entering freshman classes over the preceding several years, fundraising and research. Maintaining he was trying to set the record straight, Hoxie was attempting to undermine the legitimacy of the Heald, Hobson findings, by suggesting that they had done a sloppy job.

For example, on the category of faculty salaries, Hoxie wrote, "Here Mr. Roger Sheldon [a senior staff member of the consultancy] was confused with the information he supplied to Dr. Jesse E. Hobson, who thus reported the Long Island University average salary rating as" in the C-B category. Hoxie thereupon launched into a detailed critique that no lay Trustee could possibly follow, indicating what Sheldon did wrong. He concluded this section by indicating that LIU's average and minimum salary scale was in the same ranking as Boston College, Boston University, Fordham University, NYU, Purdue, Syracuse, and Trinity.

By the document's conclusion, however, Hoxie had dropped his third party, lawyerly tone, writing a paragraph worthy of a German history text. "More notably the Heald-Hobson Report completely ignored the fact that for the first time in the history of Long Island University the overall accreditation by the Middle States Association *without* reservation was achieved on April 26, 1967 - and this in light of the progress of the University during my administration. Finally, Heald, Hobson concluded that our Ten Year Plan is completely unrealistic. On this count, the professional reputation of so many who labored for two years without compensation is at stake, as is that of our principal consultant for this study, Dr. Deane W. Malott, President Emeritus of Cornell University, who in the volume *Preface to the Future: The Ten Year Plan of Long Island University* has written 'The result is one of the best University Ten Year Plans I have seen emanate from any institution of higher learning....'"

Hoxie, regaining control of his anger, softened his tone: "Perhaps the pessimism of the Heald-Hobson oral report is good for us, especially since so many other professional educators have found so much so praiseworthy. There is much in the view of Heald, Hobson and Associates on the subject of organization - which is what they were hired to study - in which I wholeheartedly concur. They believe strongly in a *university* not just a *loose federation*." And then in a critically important but in an off-hand way, Hoxie continued, "Heald-Hobson advise that they endorse this organization. They further advise that they endorse certain geographic consolidations. May I suggest that their written memorandum on these two counts, that is, the organization chart and the geographic consolidations would be most timely and valuable." Beneath those seemingly innocuous observations, was a redefinition of the very meaning of the University: the sale of the Brooklyn campus to the City University.

Without initially fully appreciating the scope of the seismic shock that this recommendation would have on the institutional body politic, Heald had suggested informally and then in writing that Brooklyn be sold to the City University of New York. Both the idea and its source seemed like a godsend to Hoxie. The records do not indicate when the concept first emerged over that summer, but such a sale would solve Hoxie's two greatest problems: the profound enmity of the Brooklyn campus toward him, and the inability to find big money required to grow the University. A major cash infusion would permit the Southampton and C.W. Post campuses, the two surviving units, to achieve what the *Preface* promised. It may well have been that Hoxie convinced Heald that selling Brooklyn was in the University's best interest, but once Heald proposed the concept, Hoxie spent the next year and a half ensuring that Heald had ownership of the idea.

Some months later, on November 17th, in a letter to Robert McCambridge, the Assistant Commissioner for Higher Education and Planning, Hoxie explained his version of what happened. He had received a call from McCambridge because the University had once again erupted in controversy. McCambridge had asked Hoxie, first on the phone and then in writing, to clarify for the State what had happened.

Hoxie responded, "As I explained to you, there has been no written report [at that date] of Dr. Henry T. Heald to the Trustees of Long Island University in his capacity as a consultant to the University. His report on July 24, 1967…was verbal. Subsequently, for the Board of Governors of the Brooklyn Center of Long Island University, Dr. Heald did prepare a written memorandum, summarizing his recommendations with regard to the sale of the Brooklyn Center, a copy of which I enclose herewith." Hoxie indicated that the July 24th oral presentation confirmed that LIU "was presently fiscally solvent but too dependent on tuition income." Heald had pointed out that the majority of the Brooklyn Center students could ill afford to pay the high tuition, suggesting it was a "fortuitous circumstance that City University desired to expand its services in the Borough of Brooklyn and had an interest in acquiring the Brooklyn Center of Long Island University as a nucleus for a major new campus."

Hoxie continued, "He further indicated that with the sale of the Brooklyn Center, the additional resources would be helpful in the building of a quality medium-sized university centered on the Merriweather Campus." Hoxie quoted Heald as maintaining "that the students on the Merriweather Campus could better sustain necessary tuition increases, but also that the Merriweather Campus had a better opportunity to rally future gift support."

McCambridge had asked Hoxie who had initiated the inquiries with the City University. (There is no extant documentation in the University files in Bush-Brown Hall nor in the Albert Bowker files at the Archive at City University of New York.) Hoxie diplomatically parried McCambridge's query, responding, "may I reiterate that as sometimes in the occasion of a marriage, it is difficult to indicate who was the suitor, so it is in this instance. However, as early as February 1967, at about the time Dr. Heald began his study, both the 'then Provost' of the Brooklyn Center,... Dr. William M. Birenbaum, and myself, expressed concern with regard to the prospective expansion of City University in the Borough of Brooklyn. Our concern then was specifically with regard to the statements in the public press that the then proposed York College might be located in the Long Island Railroad Terminal area in Brooklyn, not far from Long Island University's Brooklyn Center."

Hoxie indicated that he expressed his concern to both his Board of Trustees and to Dr. Heald, and "it was suggested that I seek to ascertain from Chancellor Albert H. Bowker [the Chancellor of the City University] whether he envisioned this potential development as affecting Long Island University's Brooklyn Center." (The mystery remains over who did the "suggesting." It might have been Heald, Zeckendorf, or Hoxie himself).

Bowker said he "was seeking to establish a senior college in Downtown Brooklyn," that would offer much that paralleled what LIU's Brooklyn Center already was teaching. "It was only, however, after the Heald Report on July 24th, followed by the meeting with Dr. Paul Bulger, Associate Commissioner for Higher Education and Professional Education, of the State Education Department, and Chancellor Bowker and myself on July 28th, that intensive conversations were begun with City University in this matter."

On September 26th, Heald had drafted a four page memorandum entitled "The Future of the Brooklyn Center of Long Island University," a briefing document for the Overseers of the Brooklyn campus. It concluded: "Without a very substantial increase in endowment and gift support, it is not possible for a private institution such as Long Island University to offer in Brooklyn at reasonable tuition levels the range and quality of academic programs which are now, and will be increasingly required to serve the largest borough of New York City." Earlier in the memo he had indicated that, "the City University of New York is planning new branches, new community colleges are being established, and the State is developing new universities and colleges." Heald indicated that LIU's plant was inadequate, with its library and equipment minimal, its scholarship funds insufficient, its salaries too low, and a capital debt structure that was overwhelming. Heald raised the option of a consortium of colleges and universities, a recommendation his firm had effectively helped achieve elsewhere in the country. The tone of this presentation from Heald and Hobson, engineers both, articulated the sale of the Brooklyn campus to a burgeoning City University as a win for both institutions. CUNY would get a fast start and "the City University will have sufficient resources to build and to support the enlarged plant and to relate it to the redevelopment of downtown Brooklyn."

The lead paragraph in a *New York Times* report of September 23rd read, "Long Island University's decision to negotiate the sale of its Brooklyn Center to the City University was based on advice from Henry T. Heald, former President of the Ford

Foundation." Hoxie had made public "Heald's recommendations that LIU 'give serious consideration' to selling the Center and consolidating its programs on the Long Island Campuses in Brookville and Southampton." If this deal went through, Hoxie would rescue his own career, free himself from student and faculty hostility so evident in Brooklyn, and bail out LIU from the inflationary squeeze that was increasingly impacting all universities. Indeed, it was that same squeeze that had led Hoxie to raise tuition leading to the student strike the previous fall. *The Times* reported that the City was prepared to pay $30 million for the Brooklyn campus; in fact, the negotiated price was $32 million. *The Times* also reported, "Relations between the students and the teachers and Dr. Hoxie have been somewhat strained since last March...." This was a most charitable statement!

Hoxie successfully got ahead of Bowker, trying to control how the story would appear in Brooklyn. By presenting this sale as Heald's idea, initially he gained important internal political cover. Baruch, a division of CCNY housed at City College, needed far more space than was possible to construct on the Harlem campus. Both the business faculty and the arts and sciences faculty of CCNY saw the value of moving the business division into its own quarters where it would become a separate senior college in the City University system. The Brooklyn campus of LIU could accommodate a greatly expanded Baruch, which would then be able to market itself very quickly as a professional institution rather than an academic unit of City College. When *The Times* broke the story, Hoxie, sensitive to Bowker's internal dynamics, denied that he knew anything "about the validity of the rumor that City University's Bernard M. Baruch School of Business and Public Administration might be transferred from Manhattan to the Center if the City acquires the site." What soon emerged as Bowker's problem was that the Baruch Dean, Emanuel Saxe, was truly ignorant of such a plan. Bowker was forced to declare, "that while the transfer was possible, a decision had not been made."

On September 23, 1967, Hoxie issued a press release based on this key recommendation from Heald. According to that release, "At a meeting yesterday with the LIU Faculty Senate and the students at the Brooklyn Center, Dr. Hoxie advised faculty and students that Dr. Heald's recommendations would be presented to all LIU faculty, staff, students, alumni and others associated with LIU within the next week. He stated that no action had been taken by the University, or would be later, without full exploration and discussion of Dr. Heald's recommendation."

On the 26th, George Stoddard (who became acting Vice Chancellor for Academic Affairs, when Henry Mills had left to take a similar job at St. John's) wrote to Hoxie: "I note in some of the documents prepared by dissident groups at the Brooklyn Center regarding its future status, an alternative to the proposal of total transfer is mentioned, namely, 'the creation of a special contract college for City University students, operated in the same manner as the State University's contract colleges of Home Economics, Agriculture, and Labor Relations at Cornell University and the

Colleges of Ceramics and Forestry at Alfred, and Syracuse Universities.'"

The Brooklyn Center Chapter of the AAUP sent a cable which strongly opposed the dismemberment of the Brooklyn Center and pledged "to use all efforts to continue it as a living, growing, and undivided liberal arts college as it is now constituted, whether as a unit of the City University of New York, the State University of New York, Long Island University, or independently of any of these." In sum, the initial response of faculty, in particular, was to hold the place together whatever its future-be it an institution like Pittsburgh or the University of Buffalo, a private university taken over by a public sector system, or absorption as a campus of CUNY or as a free standing campus of LIU.

The following day, September 27th, the Acting Provost, Dean and Associate Deans of Brooklyn, together with the Chairs of the academic departments, submitted: "no decision be taken which would penalize the current students at the University should City University withdraw from these negotiations." In their collective view, the City University was "morally obliged to complete negotiations and to guarantee the security of all members of the faculties, students and staff." They insisted that "tenured faculty would be retained in present rank and tenure; non-tenured faculty be retained in their present positions and be given consideration for tenure; that all non-academic staff would be retained in their current positions; that all currently matriculated students would be guaranteed fulfillment of their graduation requirements in effect at the time of their original matriculation."

The students, obviously concerned "since it is our educations that are at stake," mobilized by hiring a lawyer, by seeking a delegation visit to the Mayor's office, and by attending a rally at which both Hoxie and the national head of the National Students Association (NSA) spoke. Hoxie told the students that the sale would probably be completed in "much less" than four months, but the takeover would not happen until June 1969. He indicated that the Board was recommending that all juniors and seniors be allowed to graduate from the Brooklyn Center, that lower classmen in good standing would be permitted to transfer to the City University, and that students on probation or who are otherwise judged as not in good academic standing, would be given the opportunity to go to C.W. Post or Southampton instead. He made the sale contingent upon the City University's agreeing to protect both students and faculty.

The campus of Brooklyn College, like the campus in Harlem for CCNY, was too small physically to absorb comfortably the thousands already at Baruch. As the City University planned to ramp up the size of the University, it became clear that new sites were required. The Brooklyn campus of LIU would be the fastest and cheapest way to open a major new facility for Baruch. Virtually every subway line in the City had a station nearby. Many bus routes converged in downtown Brooklyn. Atlantic Terminal, one of the three major terminuses of the Long Island Railroad, was but a few blocks away. Moreover, it would take many years to construct classroom buildings, dormitories, and other requirements for a mature campus, whereas the Brooklyn facility could be converted quickly, especially for a College of Business and Finance. There had been talk for several years of building a major new campus for the City University at Atlantic Terminal just a few blocks away, and Bowker conceded to Hoxie at one of their conversations that the existence of such a facility would seriously impact LIU's enrollment were it to be constructed.

Hoxie appointed George D. Stoddard to be the chief negotiator for LIU. Edward T. Hollander, the Dean of Planning at the City University, was his counterpart. From the very beginning, the issues were less about plant or price than about job security for Brooklyn faculty and staff and transferability of students who initially enrolled at LIU, but would need to graduate either from the City University or LIU. If their GPA scores were below the 3.5 floor mandated for admission to a senior college at the City University, would that GPA determine which campus he or she would attend? And structurally, would LIU function as a unit of the City University, or be renamed and given a new mission?

For decades, the Brooklyn campus of LIU had filled a niche for high school students who lacked a strong high school record but still wanted to go to a four- year college. Admission to the four-year City College system prior to "Open Enroll-ment" mandated that the student pass his or her Regents exams and graduate with an 85 or better average. There was a market for students who had the ability and the interest but not the high school grade point to guarantee a place in "the free University of the City of New York." Long Island University was one of the inde-pendent-sector, urban colleges that filled this need.

There was great anxiety among the full time Brooklyn faculty, both tenured and untenured. Career paths were jeopardized and job security uncertain. Concomi-tantly, there was dismay among the faculty on the other campuses of Long Island University. Would C.W. Post or Southampton have to absorb Brooklyn faculty? Would non-tenured faculty at Southampton or C.W. Post be denied tenure, or have a much tougher time earning it, so that Brooklyn faculty could be absorbed with a guaranteed workload? The deep divisions which had surfaced the previous spring between Hoxie supporters and Brooklyn faculty critics, made the prospect of a merged faculty seem a nightmare not an opportunity. In the non-academic areas, would strict seniority be the rule? Would merit or skill or experience count? If so, who would make that judgment?

Elsewhere in the nation, some of these problems had been addressed successfully by a string of mergers in which private universities across the country joined forces with existing public sector colleges or were absorbed into state-funded systems. Buffalo became a flagship center of the emerging State University of New York, to cite one example. But those models did not necessarily mean that LIU could easily be absorbed into Baruch, which already had its own arts and sciences faculty teaching business and accounting students. Able and productive faculty could always find a welcoming position, but mediocre teachers and non-productive researchers, people who were lucky to have won tenure at LIU in years past or who had gone slack after gaining tenure, might be in dire trouble.

On September 27, 1967, the University Faculty Senate sent two resolutions to Hoxie through Vice Chancellor Stoddard, appointing G.M. Gilbert, who chaired the University Faculty Senate, "to act as representative of the senior faculty of the University in any negotiations that the Board of Trustees may undertake, effecting a change in the structure of the University" and, as well, "a resolution requesting the Board of Trustees not to make a final decision on the sale of the Brooklyn Center until the University Senate had expressed its position on such a move."

Every stakeholder group had a different set of highly individualized concerns. For example, what would happen to the subsidized apartments in University Towers that were occupied by graduate students and young faculty? Those who had such apartment leases could afford to come to New York to teach or to study. What would happen if this deal fell through, but the City University still built a health sciences campus at the Atlantic Terminal? Would LIU students still be able to compete successfully for practicums mandated by the accrediting bodies of nursing, pharmacy, physical therapy and so forth.

Some months earlier, William Zeckendorf had written Nelson Rockefeller. He wanted the Governor to link the development of higher education in Brooklyn to a solution for the rehabilitation of Bedford-Stuyvesant. This document, dated May 15th, offered a way for government to address the rapid erosion of a vital neighborhood into a slum by investing in a consortium of existing higher education institutions. Zeckendorf proposed "working from the perimeter." By harnessing the talents and human capital of five local institutions into an "assemblage and concentration of *existing* higher-educational institutions which require only cohesion," he saw an exciting but inexpensive option. He went on to underscore how LIU, Polytechnic Institute, Pratt, the Brooklyn Hospital and the Brooklyn Academy of Music could form a cohesive super institution, which would transform Bedford-Stuyvesant. He insisted, "the leadership and sponsorship for this *must* come from State and/or Municipal levels."

Zeckendorf was prescient in this scheme as well as so many others. By transforming some portion of the population who lived in the area, decades later, MetroTech became the catalyst that restored downtown Brooklyn to the glory it knew before World War I. The Brooklyn Academy of Music, Long Island University, Pratt Institute, Polytechnic Institute, and The Brooklyn Hospital are in the early 21st century part of a renewal led by developer Bruce Ratner with substantial governmental support. The collective goal has been to create a renaissance in downtown Brooklyn of the sort Zeckendorf envisioned. In the late 1960s, however, both Rockefeller and Mayor Lindsay chose an alternate route to address the decay of the Borough-the rapid expansion of SUNY and CUNY. Governor Rockefeller did send Charles T. Lanigan, his chief planning officer in Albany to talk to Zeckendorf, but this was a pro forma visit. Lanigan ended his bland thank you note with, "I hope our paths will cross again in the future…." Had Zeckendorf not been bankrupt, soon to be twice over, would Rockefeller have listened more carefully?

News of the negotiations to sell the Brooklyn campus spread faster than either Bowker or Hoxie wanted. Both Chancellors were forced to negotiate in the glare of publicity and swirling political pressures. As early as August 2nd, Zeckendorf was joining Hoxie and others at the City University headquarters on 80th Street to discuss the sale. But by mid-August, Spector, the Chair of the Brooklyn Center Faculty Senate, wrote to Acting Provost Buck Lai. He got back a letter from Hoxie which stated, "Whereas I cannot dignify such rumors by even responding to them, my historic position to seek all possible support for the Brooklyn Center, should be clear to you and to your colleagues." In a clear reference to the move of the Brooklyn Dodgers to Los Angeles, Spector had written to Lai "A University is not a baseball franchise to be transferred without interest regarding the players." Only one month after this exchange, Hoxie was publicly talking up the reasons for such a sale.

In fact, Hoxie used that summer to solicit funds aggressively for the Brooklyn Center. He had to test whether Brooklyn could regain its footing and appeal to philanthropic donors, especially large foundations. There were long delayed capital needs in Brooklyn, in particular the construction of a modern library. Moreover, in the wake of the Birenbaum matter, he had to show that Brooklyn still mattered. Finally, *Preface to the Future* had to be restarted with some large visible gifts, if any of its ambitious goals were to be reached.

On August 11th, Hoxie sought a very large grant from the Ford Foundation, in part because it had expressed interest in issues of urban renewal, especially in Bedford-Stuyvesant. On August 28th, he sent a memorandum of some twenty-two pages to Robert Schmid, the program officer for Higher Educational and Research at Ford. The document sought just under $15 million from the Foundation with funding for Southampton, Post, and, almost parenthetically, urban renewal, community rehabilitation and redevelopment for downtown Brooklyn. Included in this smorgasbord of proposals was money for a law school as well as the science and engineering programs in Brookville. He even sought funding for the Korean exchange program.

Schmid responded quickly and negatively. He was startled and "somewhat chagrined to be the recipient of a twenty-two page special memorandum asking us to consider grant support for $15 million for a variety of programs and projects for

LIU." He went on to note, "we are no longer making challenge matching grants to universities for general support," and observing that, "none of these [major capital proposals] is sufficiently close to our current centers of program priority to justify my encouraging you to inform us further about them." Although Hoxie continued to seek funding from the Ford Foundation and other similar agencies, the era of substantial support for colleges and universities was past. The deal with the City University increasingly looked to be the only option available.

In his response to Schmid, Hoxie made the point explicitly. "Unless Long Island University could secure some massive gift support it must regrettably withdraw from its Brooklyn Center." He was so keen to drive the point home to Schmid and the Foundation that he wrote almost the exact same thing, even using many of the phrases in the next paragraph. He suggested that the Board of Trustees was committed to sell the campus unless it was saved by Ford. Several years earlier, McGeorge Bundy and the Ford Foundation had been truly concerned about Bedford-Stuyvesant's future; by 1967, the Foundation's focus was elsewhere.

Zeckendorf wrote fellow Trustee Clinton W. Blume on September 8th. This was a testy letter, complaining that the $32 million sum now the accepted price was grossly too low. He pointed out that rebuilding the Maltz Building, "to be the new Humanities Building" cost $6.5 million, and more than $1 million was being spent to air condition and modernize the Paramount. "Our book value, including our land at the written-down Title 1 price in 1948 of $500,000, is over $32 million, inclusive of the two items above." He cited one of Bowker's colleagues who thought the Brooklyn campus was worth about $75 million. "It is inconceivable to me," wrote Zeckendorf, "that any knowledgeable person could value this entire property, with 850,000 square feet of land in fee together with improvements, for less than our book value." But $32 million had become the operative and public number, and it would be politically impossible for the City University to raise its purchase offer. Moreover, thirty-two million would provide adequate working capital and endowment to protect Post and Southampton.

By the end of September, opposition to the sale had hardened at Brooklyn. The fight over Bill Birenbaum was but a few months earlier, and the residue of that anger exacerbated every facet of this new crisis. On September 28th, the Brooklyn Chapter of the United Federation of College Teachers cabled the members of the Board of Regents that the Brooklyn Chapter of the UFCT was "strongly opposed to this sale because it would involve the dissolution of the Brooklyn Center. The Chapter insists that no change take place that would in any way endanger the integrity of this Center." The following day a cable went out to the Board of Higher Education, then the equivalent of the Board of Trustees of the City University, saying much the same: "The destruction of a viable educational institution by the City University would be an unconscionable and immoral act." The Executive Committee also requested permission to speak before the Board of Higher Education at its next meeting.

On October 2nd, Hoxie chose to write a "Dear Colleague" letter to the University community. "On July 24,1967, the Board authorized me to seek loans and grants for a $7 million library at the Brooklyn Center, a priority project in the ten year plan." In retrospect, that date may be viewed as marking the high tide of fundraising for the Brooklyn Center, for on that same date, the Board received its oral report from Dr. Henry Heald and Dr. Jesse Hobson, the consultants, warning that the University was overextended in its commitments. The Brooklyn Center was heavily mortgaged with an indebtedness of $14 million, and was badly in need of additional facilities costing at least that much, for which it had no monies." Hoxie chronicled his "strenuous efforts …to secure major private support for the Brooklyn Center," indicating that these efforts had failed. These circumstances, he submitted, should prompt the Executive Committee of the Board to agree to "sell the Brooklyn Center to the City University" at its September 19th meeting.

Recognizing that opposition was growing quickly, Hoxie got three members from the Board of Governors of the Brooklyn Center to serve as a fact finding group. Frederick W. Richmond, a wealthy businessman with political aspirations, chaired. Richmond had been a civic leader in the effort to save Carnegie Hall, subsequently becoming its Chair of the Board. Hoxie promised not to commit the University until this group had issued its report. At Hoxie's bidding, the Board guaranteed that all tenured faculty who were not hired by the City University would be given employment at an appropriate rank elsewhere within LIU. The students were assured that they too would be welcome on another campus if they did not transfer to the City University.

But Hoxie's diminished voice after Birenbaum no longer carried the authority to make such assurances ironclad. The academic cabinet of Deans and Directors of divisions of Southampton wrote to Glanz, for example, "Morale of students and faculty of Southampton College of Long Island University is once again this year being undermined. Lack of communications and contradictory information about University plans in regard to the Brooklyn Center, apparent mismanagement of relations between the University and the Brooklyn Center, rumors of decreased instead of increased autonomy for Southampton College, and lack of involvement of faculty and students in the decision making process at Long Island University are some of the many problems causing real concern."

On October 2nd, Zeckendorf released a statement, read on his behalf to a mixed group of 40 students, faculty and alumni. It quoted a letter from Heald, promising security and choice to both students and faculty. In a private side letter to Zeckendorf, Heald was "glad to reaffirm our recommendation that the Trustees of Long Island University sell the Brooklyn Center to the City University of New York if satisfactory arrangements can be made." He went on, "I am convinced such a sale would be in the best interest of Long Island University and of the community.... I see no reasonable future for the Brooklyn Center as it is presently constituted."

However rational Heald's assessment might have been, there were powerful forces lined up against this decision. Scars of the fight with Birenbaum were everywhere, especially among faculty and students. The political, social, cultural and generational tensions of the day made this an easy issue to divide LIU stakeholders once again. Trustees, who represented the wealthy and conservative leadership at the University and elsewhere in society were pitted against a younger generation of students who rejected rational, economic arguments in favor of a new ethic. These students attacked what they believed was a shirking of duty by the Establishment and a parsimoniousness of the Trustees toward their University.

Both Bowker and Hoxie had heard from Albert E. Meder at the Middle States Association, that he had "received both oral and written communications from persons on the staff of the Brooklyn Center of Long Island University expressing apprehension and misgiving concerning the discussions or negotiations that are apparently going on between Long Island University and City University concerning the future of the Brooklyn Center of Long Island University." Meder concluded, "be assured that the Commission has no desire whatsoever to intervene, but I thought you should know that representations obviously intended to promote such intervention had been made to us."

All manner of subordinate complexities surfaced. LIU had received a grant from the Department of Health, Education and Welfare to transform the Maltz Factory into the Humanities Center. That grant of $1.5 million would have to be transferred in its entirety to the City University, and its inclusion in the $32 million asking price was a matter of debate. This was the issue raised by Zeckendorf in his letter to Blume of September 8th.

As the days passed, the negotiation to sell the campus became a political football in the politics of the City as well as both universities. The local Chapter of the United Federation of College Teachers got the AFL-CIO's New York State Convention to pass a resolution claiming that both administrations were showing "a total lack of concern for LIU's students and teachers..." It labeled the proposed transaction "a callous action." Copies were sent to Mayor Lindsay, Governor Rockefeller, the State Education Commissioner James E. Allen, and the Chairs of the two Boards.

Newsday reported on October 4th that 4,000 faculty and students marched across the Brooklyn Bridge to City Hall to protest. The march contained a contingent "of Negro LIU students from a group known as Students Organized for Black Unity." Hoxie's effigy was destroyed at City Hall. Students carried all manner of signs, but one motif kept repeating, "Hoxie must go."

On the next day, Hoxie responded to Albert Meder at Middle States. He justified the possibility of a sale because "Both this Commission and the New York State Education Department have long expressed concern about the possible over-expansion of Long Island University and the importance of consolidating its gains." In other words, he was confounding his external critics by suddenly accepting their recurring concern about over-expansion as valid. He now was offering up Brooklyn, the mother campus, to indicate that the University would retrench. The near-limitless ambitions articulated in *Preface to the Future* had seemingly vanished. Hoxie's inference was that LIU had learned its lesson and would dutifully retreat to a suburban existence. Consolidation had replaced expansion.

That same day, October 5th, Hoxie also responded sharply to a memo from Ken Ewald. "Quite candidly," Hoxie wrote, "I cannot comprehend how you or anyone else would interpret my aforementioned memorandum to Dr. Stoddard as indicating a possible mass exodus of faculty and students from the Brooklyn Center." There were only 85 tenured faculty total in Brooklyn and he estimated that no more than a fourth of them would seek a relocation under any circumstances. "Regrettably, on the basis of rumor and misinformation, the effect on Southampton and Post has been blown all out of proportion, and I do hope that you and Ed Glanz can get it back into perspective on your respective campus."

Tamping down the crisis proved far more difficult than he breezily first thought. The next day Hoxie wrote to every parent, trying to explain the proposed sale "on the grounds that tax-supported higher education in Brooklyn could best provide the high quality, low or free tuition, educational opportunity needed for the City of New York and most especially for the Borough of Brooklyn." In sharp contradistinction to what he had written in the *Preface to the Future*, Hoxie indicated that Brooklyn was heavily mortgaged and that gifts from the 14,000 alumni only averaged a total of about $25,000 per annum. Hoxie indicated that he had organized a major fundraising appeal effort at Post and Southampton as well as at Brooklyn.

But there remained an undercurrent of distrust from the Birenbaum affair, which had focused in part on the validity of budgetary numbers. The intermediate term prognosis was clearly not good, but the severity of the crisis was hard to prove. Heald's recommendation was based on an extrapolation of cumulative deficits projected over the next several years rather than an immediate shortfall. Trend lines are much less definitive than an audited shortfall. Moreover, it was unquantifiable that a City University campus somewhere in downtown Brooklyn, would draw potential LIU students to the "free university of the City of New York." From Heald's perspective, the timing was unfortunately premature but the economic logic, solid. The sale of the Brooklyn campus was a prudent business decision, especially since Bowker's interest was a unique opportunity that would not last.

Bertram Davis, the General Secretary of the American Association of University

Professors (AAUP), made this point explicitly. He cabled Leo Pfeffer on October 7th, when the potential sale became public knowledge. "We greatly regret that vital information regarding pending sale of Brooklyn Center has apparently not been made available to academic community at that Center. In particular, we recommend release of Heald report in time for consideration by Brooklyn Center faculty and others concerned. Information available to us suggests Center is not experiencing immediate and severe budgetary crisis and that haste in disposal of Center is therefore unnecessary and undesirable." The AAUP urged postponement of any action. The inflated, publically optimistic numbers projected in the *Preface to the Future* presented a much more secure and financially successful institution than suddenly appeared to be the case. To make matters more confusing, the University had decided to shift its fiscal year from ending on May 31st to one ending on August 31st "to coincide with the academic year which begins September 1st." That meant that the financial report issued on October 9th spanned 15 months, ending August 31, 1967.

This Treasurer's report, entitled "Financial Review," optimistically indicated that the "University's multi-campus operations continued to establish new records. The gross income for each of the campuses exceeded that of any previous year reaching a total University income of $26,650,396 for the year ending May 31, 1967. This new high was 15% higher than the previous record....The gross income for the fifteen month period amounted to $29,940,964." Over $5 million were appropriated for plant funds including debt service. The Brooklyn campus received $1.781 million and "the excess of income over expenditures, including all appropriations to other funds, on May 31, 1967 was $719,567...."

The University received over $2.6 million in gifts and grants, an increase over $1.27 million of the previous year. "The University's net investment in plant increased 20%, or about $5 million so that its equity in its plant was close to $30 million. The University's total plant funds had increased from $48 million $78 million. And the report went on, "faculty salaries were substantially improved. While scholarship aid was up 30%." These figures, although unaudited at that point, reflected a reality that simply did not conform with Heald's pessimistic assessment.

To be sure, there were very dark clouds overhead. The City of New York, the State and the nation had rapidly entered an inflationary cycle. The war in Vietnam was creating havoc, in particular because Johnson refused to raise taxes to pay for its costs. The economic tax base of Brooklyn had collapsed. The City itself was in a precarious position. White flight to Nassau and Suffolk was rapidly reducing the stable, middle class of Brooklyn and Queens, and the ghettoization of many neighborhoods raised sharply the social service and police costs for the Lindsay Administration. The costs of education from K-12 had spiked because federal mandates and remediation added new burdens. Open Enrollment in the public higher education sector required a rapid build-up of physical facilities and massive increases in faculty and staff. Yet, as Bertram Davis correctly noted, there was no severe budgetary crisis at the Brooklyn campus, nor any immediate need for the Board to move in haste.

It was soon obvious that Hoxie had been severely wounded by the slow motion struggle with Birenbaum. It was a kabuki dance that drained the energy of the entire institution, leaving Hoxie with inadequate moral suasion or sufficient political power. Brooklyn was the epicenter, but even C.W. Post and Southampton felt its effects. And because Hoxie was so distrusted and disliked by the Brooklyn faculty, there was a deep suspicion that Heald, despite his glittering resume, had been taken in and was serving as Hoxie's shill.

At the Board meeting on October 9, 1967, John McGrath, as already mentioned, became the new Chair of the Board, replacing William Zeckendorf, Sr. This transition, the first in a quarter of a century, represented an important passage, especially since the new Executive Committee of Hoxie, George Shapiro, John H. G. Pell, Emilio Collado, and Arthur T. Roth had only Shapiro to represent Brooklyn interests first and foremost.

Chairman of the Board
John McGrath

At that Board meeting, Zeckendorf offered remarks. "The 25 years that I have been privileged to serve as Chairman of the Board of Trustees of Long Island University have been a source of great happiness to me as well as the most rewarding single effort of my career." Referring indirectly to the Board split the previous spring, Zeckendorf urged "any differences which might exist amongst us be henceforth forgotten… and, that we join hands in supporting our newly elected officers, giving to them all of the aid of which we are capable-an essential factor in the execution of their responsibilities."

John McGrath in response focused on "the dramatic change in circumstances since last July. We stand tonight on the brink of a new era in LIU history. We face the prospect of divesting ourselves of the Brooklyn Center and converting the assets there located into additional capital for the fulfillment of our mission in Nassau and Suffolk counties. A new Chairman assuming office last July would have faced the immediate implementation of the ten year plan which was made public last February. This would mean the mounting of a massive fundraising campaign." McGrath then speculated on that new reality, "the Chairman today must give top priority to the sale of the Brooklyn Center which manifestly supersedes all previously formulated plans since it alters so radically the present structure of the University." McGrath wanted to defer the selection of a new Chairman until it was clear that Brooklyn would not remain within the LIU universe. He went on "I could not in good conscience accept election if the operation of the Brooklyn Center is to continue as part of the ten year plan."

But, he acknowledged, deferring the transition was not possible (in large measure because of the financial crisis in Zeckendorf's career), "I am willing to assume the chairman's role in continuing the negotiations and closing the deal [with CUNY]. I recognize that there will be many problems of restructuring and consolidating the University organization in its more limited area of service and in the orderly phasing out of Brooklyn. With what competence I possess, I will address myself to these tasks, thus enabling us to avoid the collision course with disaster which, in Dr. Heald's pessimistic view, and Dr. Malott's optimistic view, confronts the leadership which would tackle the ten year plan, including the Brooklyn operation." McGrath was very forceful: "You are selecting a chairman who will not remain in office if the Brooklyn deal is not closed." Moreover, he felt that his Chairmanship should be limited under any circumstance, because he felt he lacked the qualifications and time necessary to do the job properly.

Included in the Board material was a twenty-five-page report by Gordon Hoxie to the Board covering the period from September 12, 1966 to October 9, 1967 (his third annual report). It is a classic Hoxie document, but he was correct when he said that it "comes at an historic crossroads in the life of the University." In sharp contrast to the *Preface to the Future,* he wrote of building "a strong medium sized private University." But despite that opening declaration, he then celebrated how enrollment had grown such that "Long Island University is now the nation's sixth largest private University ("exempting Pittsburgh and Temple which are now quasi public"). He celebrated the growth of construction giving and endowment, noting a total of $7 million in gifts and grants since he became Chancellor. In his classic style, he indicated all of the ways in which the University has prospered during the preceding three years of his era.

When he got to the Brooklyn Center, Hoxie wrote, "Thus far in this annual report but little reference has been made to the Brooklyn Center, and this because the enormity of its problems requires an 'agonizing reappraisal.'" He briefly acknowledged the "pressing problems of the ...urban environment" as articulated by Birenbaum and his Brooklyn colleagues in the Brooklyn chapter of *Preface,* but moved quickly on to discuss at greater length how Columbia had received a challenge grant of $35 million, $10 million of which was for community service in Harlem from the Ford Foundation. In the context of the Foundation's rejection of his fundraising efforts, he wondered why Fort Greene and Bedford-Stuyvesant were not seen as worthy of Ford's support as was Harlem. He never posed the question that it may have been the Foundation's differing assessment of Long Island University and Columbia University.

He spoke of the delays in implementing the development plan "occasioned by the excesses of internal problems of the Brooklyn Center. For all those faculty, staff, and students who remained unswerving in their support of the University administration during that period of travail, we should be everlastingly appreciative." There was no *mea culpa* in his report.

"Wistfully, we may recall," Hoxie continued instead, "the great hopes and great momentum of February 16, 1967, when in the Grand Ballroom of the Waldorf Astoria, in the presence of 1,500 friends and members of the University's family, the ten year plan had been announced." In his very stilted prose, "Alas, the hopes of that evening, when the volume, *Preface to the Future,* had for the first time been distributed, had been damaged by the March and April demonstrations. Yet, we had not given up, far from it!" In this grandiose way, Hoxie seemed more to be talking to himself than to his Trustees. He then drifted into a description of how his efforts to build a consortium of institutions in downtown Brooklyn had failed and at length quoted himself from the speech he had delivered at the Veterans Administration Hospital in Brooklyn on June 29, 1967, when he indicated he was making a special presentation to the Ford Foundation for support of the Brooklyn Center.

Rhetorically, Hoxie asked "the question…whether a private University with but little financial endowment, can offer the needed higher educational opportunity in an area currently characterized by so much blight,... This is one of the problems, which our Board of Trustees must wrestle with and is seeking the counsel of Heald, Hobson and Associates." Hoxie continued by discussing the physical needs at Brooklyn: a library, which would cost between $7 and $12 million; a health sciences building at $6 million; a student union and gym at $8 million. He maintained that the cumulated surplus at the Brooklyn campus was only $1.3 million, which included "any and all credits for any funds advanced to either C.W. Post or Southampton College through the years." He then noted that this was the approximate outstanding debt on the Humanities Building in Brooklyn. He estimated that there would be a five year $8.8 million deficit, thus asserting that selling to CUNY was the only possible option.

In a section entitled "Organization, Development, and Spirit," Hoxie wrote, "While I believe, in the fullest practicable measure of so-called 'local autonomy,' I do share the concern as to whether we have been building a University, or only a loose federation of varying campuses." The document goes on and on, defending the optimism of the *Preface to the Future* and the wisdom of Deane W. Malott, the opportunities for the Brookhaven Campus and role of John Baiardi, and the law school opportunities and the development of the Arthur T. Roth Graduate School. There is no mention however, of the struggle with Birenbaum or its impact on the

University. It presented an alternate reality, a report of what Hoxie would like to have had happen.

Meanwhile, Robert Spector was writing to parents asking them to write to Mayor Lindsay, to the Chairman and Chancellor of the City University, to the Borough President and others with an appeal to help the students and faculty who were fighting "to save their school." A Save LIU/Brooklyn Committee was established to block the sale. The same techniques used during the Birenbaum issue were re-deployed. In addition, the President of the local Chapter of the United Federation of College Teachers, Israel Kugler, met with Joseph Kottler, who was a Brooklyn Assemblyman who served as the Chairman of the Joint Legislative Committee on Higher Education. Kottler was immediately interested in conducting a joint legislative investigation into the proposed sale.

The students similarly mobilized. 1967-1968 was a peak year of student activism nationally, and these Brooklyn students had substantial experience from the tuition strike and Birenbaum protests. "The Committee for Truth in Education" issued an angry document without date or further attribution. The heading was "LIU Students Want to Know!" The format was "Tell us, Mr. Chancellor," posing a series of questions to Hoxie. A typical set of questions were: "Why not auction off your Cadillacs and chauffeur and your $100,000 palace with its guards and gardeners, and servants? Why not sell the luxury dwellings purchased for University officials with student tuition fees? Why not drop the $100,000 football budget at Post? Why not cut out those expensive horse shows? Or those free luncheons for the administrators in Brookville?" And it went on, "Why have you hired a Law School Dean just now at $40,000? Why do you insist on a Law School when your law dean advises you that the Law School can never pay for itself? When he tells you that it will lose at least three quarters of a million dollars every year?"

The Student Council demanded a "final veto through referendum of all provisions of any such sale." On October 12th, *Seawanhaka* interviewed the University Senate Chairman, Gustave Gilbert. He recounted a conversation that he had just had with Henry Heald. According to Gilbert, "Heald's recommendation was primarily for the University to 'pull in its horns' and that the sale of either C.W. Post or Southampton would have served the same purpose of consolidation as the sale of the Brooklyn Center. But Gilbert noted that 'only the Brooklyn Center had a buyer.... no one wanted Post or Southampton.'"

By October 16th, Hoxie had received a letter from Bertram Davis of the American Association of University Professors, politely criticizing the University for the way it had kept the faculty, in particular, ignorant about the sale. Davis noted, "As you are well aware, there can be no more fundamental decision affecting the academic careers of a faculty than a decision to dispose of the college in which they carry on their professional work. With such a momentous decision at hand, confronting the faculty and students of the Brooklyn Center quite suddenly, at a time when the faculty and students and indeed the administration and Board were fully expecting to expand and improve the educational facilities of the Brooklyn Center, it is understandable that the reaction of the faculty and students would be severe."

On October 10th, Joseph Kottler, the Chair of the Joint Legislative Committee of Higher Education, sent a letter to John McGrath indicating that his committee would hold hearings on the proposed sale. There were three specific agenda items the Joint Committee wanted to pursue. The first was, "What are the specific plans with regard to the present student body at the Brooklyn Center?" The second was, "What plans are being made to accommodate applicants who would normally have been accepted to matriculation at the Brooklyn Center in 1968 and thereafter?" And the third was, "What are the specific plans for the present faculty and staff at the Brooklyn Center?"

These hearings were an obvious godsend to the faculty and students opposing the sale and embarrassing for the University itself, since they created a continuing flow of negative public publicity for the Board, the City University, Hoxie and his team. Kottler, who was a Brooklyn Democratic politician, sought to rally the delegation. While he and his colleagues never made direct mention of the move of the Brooklyn Dodgers from Brooklyn to Los Angeles, they saw the potential demise of the Brooklyn campus as further evidence that the Borough was in deep decline. Although questions were raised as to whether Kottler's Joint Committee had any standing in this matter, Kottler vigorously maintained that the Assembly and State Senate did have a legitimate voice, even though such issue normally fell under the authority of the Board of Regents. Further, as a political matter, this story was too newsworthy to be killed by what Kottler would have described as a technicality.

According to *Newsday*, Kottler did acknowledge that the legislature "has no actual power over such a transaction by City University, but that its committee had worked closely with" the City University and he was sure that the Chancellor, Albert H. Bowker, would listen to what was uncovered.

That announcement prompted Robert Spector and his Ad Hoc Emergency Committee to issue a position paper which was then sent to the academic community of the greater New York area, arguing that the City University Board of Higher Education, would likely vote on this proposed sale at its October 22nd meeting. In his memo, Spector wrote, "It is important to understand that what is not involved in the sale is the absorption of a private university, like Buffalo, into the structure of a public one, like the State University of New York." Spector went on, "What is involved is a bureaucratic, cynical, and callous real estate deal, unworthy of either of its participants. The plant and facilities of the Brooklyn Center are being sold to the City University, which intends to move an expanded Baruch School of Business Administration into the Brooklyn Center facilities while the existing

Brooklyn Center is *dissolved*, its educational program put to an end, and *its* faculty and student body dispersed." Spector argued that the deal was "morally unconscionable." He rejected the notion that the Brooklyn Center was in serious financial difficulties, and he lamented the fact that the Heald-Hobson Report on which this decision was being made, had "not been presented as yet to press, public, or the University family." Moreover, he argued that Brooklyn funds were "siphoned off, having largely made possible the rapid-indeed over-rapid-expansion of the University in Nassau and Suffolk." In sum, the Board "is engaged in lopping off its healthy limb, the urban one, for the benefit of its weaker suburban ones," a claim staunchly denied by Mrs. Lai, speaking as the chief fiscal officer of LIU.

Underclassmen would be absorbed into the City University system only "if their grade-point averages qualify them to enter. It has been suggested-but by no means guaranteed-that those with academic indices below 3.00 *might* be admitted as non-matriculated students." Similarly, faculty rights were being trashed. He asserted, "Outside the negotiating room, the City University has indicated that it considers the problem of faculty a Long Island University problem for which it has no responsibility, although a Board of Education spokesman has admitted the problem is 'sticky.'"

This memorandum went on to argue that the dissolution of the Brooklyn campus "would diminish rather than increase educational opportunities" for the college age population of New York and particularly Brooklyn. "A break down of our student profile, however, indicates that the bulk of our students are drawn from those who cannot meet the rather mechanically determined entrance requirements of the City University, although their averages and their SAT scores are higher than those required by the community colleges. These are students, who, despite the considerable financial sacrifice often required, are determined to pursue a liberal arts and sciences degree, rather than a semi-vocational, technological or terminal two-year education. In 1966, the percentage of the Brooklyn Center's students going on to graduate studies was 19% above the national average."

Turning to the educational niche of the Brooklyn Center, Spector stressed that LIU students did not "meet the City University entrance and transfer requirements because those requirements are geared towards a middle-class, college-oriented population. Our student body," he asserted, "is largely drawn from lower middle-class, self-employed, and wage-earning groups. They are first-generation college-goers and often first-generation Americans. And increasingly they are coming from the poverty belt of downtown Brooklyn itself."

Spector submitted: "the transfer of the Brooklyn Center facilities to the Baruch School will not provide for the continuing education of such students, either those presently enrolled or those who would be following them in the normal course of affairs." He concluded, "If the City University were truly interested in expanding educational facilities and opportunities for downtown Brooklyn population groups, it would make sense for it to integrate the Brooklyn Center of Long Island University into the City University. This Center is an existing institution already playing a vital and unique role in that community. Faculty, student body, and community, we are sure, would welcome all the advantages such an integration would bring. But it would seem to make no sense at all for the City University to participate in the destruction of the integrity of an educational institution which has demonstrated every justification for its continuance merely to make *Lebensraum* for one of its own units."

Spector framed elegantly the fundamental arguments against the sale. After the tumult of the Birenbaum affair, he was not arguing that Brooklyn needed to survive as an independent, private-sector institution. Most members of the faculty appeared to have been willing to have LIU Brooklyn transferred en masse to CUNY, provided their tenure would be protected and provided they were treated as equal to existing regular faculty within the City system. The pay scale would have increased their take-home salaries and benefits as well.

The first day of hearings was on October 14th. Kottler had a long list of individuals who wanted to testify or were summoned to appear. Charles Larsen spoke on behalf of the Secretary General of the American Association of University Professors (AAUP), an organization of over a thousand chapters and eighty five thousand faculty members. He argued that the faculty had not been consulted adequately and urged that the sale be postponed to allow consensus to form, or, at least, a full and fair hearing to take place.

Both Porter Chandler, the Chairman of the City's Board of Higher Education, and Albert Bowker, the Chancellor of CUNY, spoke early in the process. Bowker informed the Joint Legislative Committee that he had not received a formal offer of sale from LIU until a week before, October 9th. Long Island University's formal offer had set the boundaries of the Campus, the money due, and LIU's expectations for dealing with the needs of existing students and faculty.

In his formal testimony, Bowker, felt compelled to respond indirectly to Spector and other critics of the deal, at LIU, at CUNY and in the press. He sounded both defensive and irked. "Today I hope to be able to answer the questions which have been raised, quiet the fears which have developed, and report on the negotiations between City University and Long Island University. I will also undertake to describe our plans and hopes for the use of this property for the development of a great new Center of post high school education for both the academically well prepared and those less well prepared-a new institution with both educational quality and social purpose."

Bowker underscored, "The decision of Long Island University *not* to continue in

Brooklyn-and this is the decision of Long Island University Board of Trustees-creates both an opportunity and a problem for the City University." The Chancellor insisted that, "In moving to this downtown location in Brooklyn, a third major commitment of the City University would be to expand the SEEK program [the CUNY opportunity program] in a very major and dramatic way." He then restated CUNY's commitment to the social fabric of the City, noting that in 1962, the total number of students in the University in all categories was 104,000. "Today it is 154,000." By the beginning of the next decade, after Open Enrollment was fully established, that number would sky-rocket, nearly bankrupting the City of New York.

CUNY estimated that approximately half of the students who would come to its new site in Brooklyn would arrive directly from high schools, while the other half would be transfers from other institutions of higher education, primarily the CUNY junior college network. The CUNY Campus on the Brooklyn site, he maintained, would admit 1,500 freshman, predominantly from Brooklyn, in effect, addressing some of the political issues which had motivated Kottler to call for these hearings in the first place.

Hoxie also testified that same day, October 17th. He detailed the efforts made to raise "the kind of massive support needed by the Brooklyn Center." He spoke relatively briefly (his text was only four single spaced pages) about the pressure to raise tuition, the evolution of the decision to retain Henry Heald, his long-standing commitment to preserve the Brooklyn campus, and his confidence that the City University would meet the mission that LIU was struggling to fund. The University's case was not strengthened when Kottler asked Hoxie to explain what Arthur Roth may have meant when he said "urban rot [that] is spreading to Long Island."

Professor Robert Spector was perhaps the most important witness to testify that day. He made the same general points as he had in his memo to the larger New York academic community, but with even greater emotional force. He submitted that Brooklyn campus was a living thing, "a vital force in its community and a thriving, powerful friend to those whom the City cannot or will not educate." He spoke of the limitless ambitions of *Preface to the Future,* published only six months prior to news of this potential sale. "The Brooklyn Center of Long Island University has been my life-as student, alumnus, and faculty member-for the last twenty two years. We are no second-rate, second-chance institution. Our students, for a variety of reasons-but mainly social and economic-do not meet the arbitrary entrance requirements of City University. We offer them an atmosphere, a dedication, a concern that compensate for the earlier failure to stimulate them. We offer a climate in which scholarship students and international students help to provide additional stimuli.... we need not apologize to anybody. A quality professional staff is achieving quality education.... To kill us is to destroy the heart of our community."

He was followed by others who spoke equally passionately about what Long Island University had meant to them. For example, Edward Hershey, a former senior editor at *Seawanhaka*, and, after graduation, a high school teacher at North Babylon High School, said, "Perhaps I should have realized my academic potential at an earlier stage and attained the grades that would have qualified me for acceptance in the City University. But I didn't." Hershey also spoke about the struggle between Hoxie and Birenbaum, noting that Hoxie had been censured by faculties on two of his campuses and by the student bodies on all three.

Edward Grant, the President of the Student Organization for Black Unity (SOBU), testified before the committee, and SOBU member Irving Davis submitted a position paper "in profound support of the students organization for black unity." A physically challenged and brilliant undergraduate, Judy Heumann, stressed to the legislators the special care and attention she had received at the Brooklyn campus. Individual faculty members spoke out of their personal experiences, including Edward Clark, Israel Kugler, and Nathan Resnick. Kottler and other local Brooklyn politicians had much to say. The New York press corps had a field day.

Several days later at a faculty meeting in Brooklyn, some Board Trustees were accused of misconduct in "their failure to carry into effect the educational purposes of the Brooklyn Center." The faculty voted to "request the Board of Regents of the State of New York to suspend the Board of Trustees pending the outcome of a full review of all the circumstances leading up to the proposed sale of the Brooklyn Center of Long Island University." A day-long teach-in was held on October 19th by among many others, the newly formed Student Organization for Black Unity.

On the 19th, the Executive Council of the Brooklyn Alumni Association retained Howard Rubinstein Associates, a public relations firm long associated with the Zeckendorfs, to help mobilize public opinion against the sale. That same day, Hoxie wrote to Bertram Davis of the AAUP. His involuted and ornate opening sentence was a mark of the stress he felt. He wrote, "Very much I am grateful to you for your splendid letter of October 16, 1967, a copy of which was handed me Tuesday by Mr. Charles Larsen of your staff." The political significance in that letter was his claim that the United Federation of College Teachers had used its political muscle in Brooklyn to have the hearings held. He asserted, "the hearing had convened at the behest of the United Federation of College Teachers, which I believe has taken a most unfair view of the good faith and works of Long Island University. The UFCT, would, if it could, break off the Long Island University negotiations with CUNY even if it meant the very demise of Long Island University."

On October 21st, Bertram Davis wrote to Commissioner of Education James E. Allen in Albany, proposing that the Board of Regents "conduct a new and thorough study of the financial problems confronting Long Island University, a study which would include consideration of alternatives to the sale of the Brooklyn Center."

This study commission needed to include "representatives freely chosen by the academic community of the Brooklyn Center, as well as representatives of the administration and governing board of Long Island University." The net effect of his proposal would be to postpone any real estate deal at least for a year.

Hoxie obviously wanted this dreadful public relations disaster over. *Seawanhaka* quoted him as saying that week that "the Brooklyn Center will be 'phased out' whether or not it is sold to the City University." Any delay jeopardized enrollment revenues and made hiring new faculty almost impossible. It exacerbated tensions from campus to campus. Uncertainty threatened nearly everyone in the University and morale kept sinking. Nothing good could come from delay.

The Brooklyn faculty, on the other hand, clearly saw that in delay could be ultimate victory. The Kottler hearings had already become a circus. CUNY Central, the administrative office for the system, was embarrassed and angry. Politicians, many with their own agendas, were taking control of the process. The Southampton College student newspaper summed up the situation perfectly. It ran a banner headline for its October 23rd issue: "Dissent Racks LIU....Brooklyn Campus Scene....Constant Turmoil." And in a smaller typeface, "Trustees Asked To Resign."

On October 22nd, Kottler again summoned Hoxie to testify. The second round of hearings was to take place on the LIU Brooklyn Campus the following day. To his own fellow legislators he wrote, "It is urgent that you attend." Hoxie cabled Kottler, "Having fulfilled your request 'to respond to "provisions for the Brooklyn Center faculty and students [and] proposed site utilization', neither the Chairman of the Board nor myself deems it appropriate to appear at the October 23rd hearing." Both Hoxie and McGrath were loath to allow Kottler to berate them in public and were afraid that the hearings would be a fishing expedition against the LIU Board and Administration.

A livid Kottler cabled back on the 23rd. "We consider your refusal to appear inappropriate. In the event that you do not appear as requested, we will conduct an executive session to exercise our power of subpoena." Maintaining that the Joint Committee sought "clarification" of Hoxie's prior testimony, Kottler made it clear that he would escalate those hearings until he got his way. The Brooklyn student government put out a bulletin to the entire student body: "Make sure to spend your free hours in attendance at the hearings. Your futures are at stake." The student government further told the student body that there was a petition calling for the Regents "to remove the Board on the grounds of incompetence and misfeasance of office." It ended: "All students are expected to sign the petition."

Hoxie had asked Stoddard, his Vice Chancellor of Academic Affairs, to ask Spector to lead a group of faculty in working out the mechanics of transfering faculty to other campuses of LIU, provided the sale went through. Spector responded on the

23rd that a separate faculty vote was needed to determine who would participate. It was not for Hoxie or his designee, Stoddard, or even Spector, the Chair of the Faculty Senate, to assume that role unless the faculty specifically named Spector or someone else to participate. Moreover, he argued, such a discussion would be premature, since the sale might not happen. But he did concede the faculty would elect a committee if it could "discuss with representatives of the City University the possibility of the Brooklyn Center being maintained as a unit within the City University...." Here was a compromise that Brooklyn faculty would embrace, since it offered the survival of the Brooklyn Center under a different governance structure.

However attractive this might be to the Brooklyn faculty, it was not something that the City University wanted. The City University was looking for a place to move and grow Baruch. If CUNY simply absorbed the Brooklyn campus of LIU, Baruch would still need a new home and would want to maintain its existing curriculum, taught by existing faculty. The CUNY goal was to make Baruch an autonomous, senior college of the system, not a hybrid. That would be a terrible shotgun marriage.

The flurry of letters continued. Hoxie also wrote Allen in responding to Bertram Davis's letter. Hoxie argued, as one might expect, that there was already a joint committee, which included two faculty to represent LIU faculty opinion, Robert Spector and Gustave Gilbert, the Chair of the University Senate. Both he and Bowker had consulted with the State already, and it would be "disastrous to indefinitely postpone these matters and renew admissions processes for the Brooklyn Center of Long Island University, creating a climate of uncertainty."

Against this chaotic and fluid backdrop, Kottler convened the next session of the Joint Legislative Committee. The list of individuals wanting to speak was a long one, thirty or more in all, including faculty, civic members of the community, politicians, alumni and students. And this list did not include Hoxie, McGrath and other administrators from the University mandated to testify by threat of subpoena.

One of those speakers was another Brooklyn Assemblyman, Bertram L. Podell. Podell was a staunch defender of all things Brooklyn, an old-time politician who reveled in the sound of his own voice. In fact, he leaked his own remarks so that they appeared two days before he testified in *Newsday*. Podell wanted Governor Rockefeller, Attorney General Lefkowitz, and the Board of Regents to investigate what he called "the crime of sophicide, the crime of destroying knowledge and education...." Attacking the LIU Board as "allied with the barbarians and the Philistines, who through the ages have sought to destroy civilization and education," Podell wondered, "What manner of meat do these Trustees feed upon, that they dare assert the right to disrupt the lives of thousands upon thousands of youngsters, now and in the future, youngsters born and unborn? By what authority do these Trustees profess the power to convert an institution of higher learning into a marketable piece of real estate?" Podell wanted legislation prohibiting the City University Construction Fund from "the use of its borrowing capacity to buy the properties of an existing institution of higher education." With full-throated indignation and to the delight of the press, he ranted, "Any one who thinks that Long Island University can survive, after severing its heart and soul in Brooklyn, manifests a clear case of catatonic schizophrenia."

Professor Donald Baker, director of social science division at Southampton, offered in thirteen single-spaced pages, a series of schemes all in lieu of the sale. Kottler himself had plans for "a grassroots college," a suggestion he had originally made a few days before to Harry Van Ardsdale, the President of the City Central Labor Council. M.A. Farber of *The New York Times* highlighted this idea with a headline that read, "L.I.U. Asked To Sell Center To Unions." The second day of hearings went on for more than eight hours. A thousand students, teachers and the press attended.

Not everybody from the Brooklyn campus was in opposition. G.M. Gilbert, Chair of the Brooklyn Psychology Department and President of the University Faculty Senate favored the sale. "I must say I regard the takeover of the Brooklyn Center by the City University as both inevitable and desirable. It has long been apparent that the Brooklyn Center could not long survive the competition with the City University and better endowed private universities in its long struggle to balance scholarship with solvency. We have seen how increased class sizes and increased tuition have been necessary to keep pace with increased faculty salaries which are still low by comparison with most other institutions in the metropolitan area." He argued that Chairs could not afford to keep faculty they wanted to retain, because excellent faculty were outbid by the City University and other universities. Quality programs, research support and adequate student services had "constantly been throttled by the budgetary restrictions by the college trying to do the impossible-exist on the students' tuition only." He speculated what would happen when the demand for seats in classrooms declined. "Will we double tuition? - or double or triple class sizes? - or just cut faculty salaries in half-or just go bankrupt again?"

Making Hoxie's argument far more succinctly and directly than the Chancellor himself, Gilbert asserted "a poorly endowed private college charging high tuition *cannot* give adequate opportunity to the culturally deprived and that it should be willing and eager to have its facilities and some of its faculty absorbed into a tax supported system....To be specific: Negro students who suffer more from cultural deprivation than any other group, number at best a few hundred at L.I.U., for the simple reason that they can rarely afford $1,500 a year tuition." He regarded this potential sale "as the best thing that ever happened to L.I.U. and to the college-seeking population of the City. I dread the thought of being confronted in the years ahead by the agonizing choices between lower standards, lower salaries, or bank-

256

ruptcy. I regard the suggestions bruited about of a possible takeover by a private group of academic adventurers as downright immoral." Gilbert closed, "We are witnessing another step in the gradual democratization of higher education in this country, and he who would obstruct it had better be sure of what he is doing."

The New York Times on October 25th, indicated that twenty-nine Brooklyn legislators, headed by Assemblyman Stanley Steingut, planned to block the sale. The intensity of the opposition and its breadth prompted *The Times* to note "that City University officials were having second thoughts about acquiring the unit." On the Tuesday after that long day of hearings, a letter went out to all Brooklyn alums signed by Irwin Fields, B'48, the President of the Brooklyn Center Alumni Association, who began his note, "It's Now-or Never."

At the same time, the Administration found itself defending audited budgetary numbers and the methodology of running a single corporation while accounting for each campus as an autonomous profit and loss center. Professor Philip Wolitzer, the Chair of the Accounting Department in Brooklyn, insisted that Brooklyn was not then in debt and did not have a cumulative deficit built up over the years. His testimony before Kottler was that Brooklyn had substantial assets, a point refuted by Mary Lai and her team, when she and her Comptroller and Budget Officer all testified. Wolitzer was suggesting that the sale was predicated on a claim of financial exigency that did not exist. He suggested that this was a smoke screen because Hoxie was angry at Brooklyn for the Birenbaum affair, and wanted to retreat from the inner city just as Adelphi and St. John's had many years before. He argued that economic realities did not justify a hasty sale, even if trend lines suggested an upcoming maelstrom and a sea of red ink.

Hoxie had done himself no favor when he ignored Kottler's threat of a subpoena. He was asked why he missed the hearing on October 23rd. A *Daily News* story of October 25th quoted him as answering, "I received a telegram Sunday afternoon; so I figured I wasn't really invited because they would have asked me earlier." Kottler was looking to humiliate Hoxie. He would succeed and the press, in the meantime, portrayed Hoxie as arrogant, adding grist to this long-running public relations debacle.

Murray Kempton, the respected and widely read columnist for the *New York Post*, wrote a scathing attack on both Hoxie and the University Board responsible for "tenth largest private college in the U.S. in the year 1967." In Kempton's judgment, "there is nothing wrong with LIU that a new Chancellor and a new Board of Trustees could not cure." Kempton trashed Hoxie as someone who had "long passed beyond the interest of anyone except those zoologists who study the methods by which animals defend their lairs. In the last six months, these Trustees have lied to their students, their teachers, and even to the U.S. Steel Foundation, which they induced to pay for the mendacities in the fund-raising brochure that promised so much to the Brooklyn from which they were proposing to abandon not six months later." Kempton celebrated that Kottler "may have caught and stopped them in the act of abandonment." And he ended his piece, "Brooklyn has a right not just to an LIU but an LIU managed by men of honor."

The next day, the Brooklyn Chapter of the AAUP demanded that student admissions to Brooklyn be reopened and those incoming students, (however many might actually enroll), would be guaranteed the right to graduate from LIU in Brooklyn after four years in 1972. Uncertain about what the future would hold, LIU had frozen all admissions activity for its incoming class for the autumn, 1968. The Admissions operations effectively went dark. Student pranksters nailed wooden planks across the Admission Office, indicating that it was closed for business. This AAUP demand if met would, de facto, delay any sale by a full year. Operationally, it would ensure that Baruch would have to postpone taking over the campus.

All eleven Brooklyn elected representatives to the City Council joined a collective resolution calling on the City's Board of Higher Education to stop its negotiations for the purchase of the Brooklyn Center. The Board of Regents felt compelled to announce that it too would investigate this potential sale. According to *Newsday* on October 28th, a spokesman for the Regents described the "furor surrounding the sale as an unusual situation," with the State Education Commissioner, James E. Allen Jr. commenting that "the Regents were not taking any sides in the issue but that he had been instructed to complete the investigation as soon as possible." By now the Brooklyn congressional delegation entered the fray. The long-serving Emanuel Celler called the potential sale "a sellout of Brooklyn" and indicated he was planning to see if it was possible to cut off federal funds if any were committed for the Brooklyn campus.

A few days later, on November 1st, the three-man special committee drawn from the Board of Governors of the Brooklyn Center issued its report. This was the committee Chaired by Frederick W. Richmond, who was aspiring to a congressional seat. "We have, therefore, taken the position that, unless conclusive evidence to the contrary is available, it is preferable to preserve the diversity provided by our institutions of higher learning, particularly when they fulfill a special need not easily matched by the public sector." Writing some years before the City embraced "Open Enrollment," it saw LIU as playing a key role for students who lacked the GPA scores for admission to a senior campus of the City University.

The committee concluded that approximately $2.5 million revenue annually was needed to build an appropriate college library as well as a student union and a humanities classroom building. It recommended that these funds come from the New York State Department of Education as the cheapest way to hold tuition down. It ignored the probable stampede of other private colleges that would follow such a decision. That solution would allow LIU to meet the capital needs of the Brooklyn campus without alienating the campus, or raising tuition to a point which students and their families could not meet. The City University could build its Baruch campus elsewhere in Brooklyn or in the metropolitan region.

The University files include eight prepared questions for Dr. Heald, when he met the University Faculty Senate also on November 1st. There was a general preamble: "we feel that Dr. Heald owes it not only to the University family and the academic community at large, but to his own professional reputation to provide a far fuller explanation of the precise recommendations of his report and the context in which the particular recommendation to sell the Brooklyn Center plant to City University was made." One key issue the faculty wanted to probe was whether an urban educational center in Brooklyn could somehow function like Home Economics, Agriculture and Labor Relations do at Cornell and the Colleges of Ceramics and Forestry do at Alfred and Syracuse Universities. The structure for "contract colleges" already existed across the State and could serve as a template for the needs of Brooklyn and the inner city.

Following an inconclusive meeting with Heald, the Executive Council of the University-wide Senate and the full Senate membership passed a resolution then sent to each of the Trustees. It read, "The Executive Council of the University Senate is not convinced by any evidence available to us that the sale of the Brooklyn Center of LIU is necessary at the present time or that such a sale would be consummated on terms favorable to the interests of L.I.U. It, therefore, urges that the Brooklyn Center be retained as part of L.I.U. and that a new University administration be empowered to pursue this policy." Although the words "no confidence" never appeared, the message was clear. And by an overwhelming vote of 147 to 9, with 10 abstentions, the Brooklyn faculty passed a separate resolution indicating that negotiations could only be held on the basis of preserving Brooklyn and its educational purposes as a unit.

Kottler held a third session of hearings on neutral territory, the Granada Hotel in downtown Brooklyn, on November 3rd. Most of the testimony came from University officials, including Chancellor Hoxie, who spoke twice. Much of his first statement was lifted verbatim from his third annual Report to the Board. The second statement answered several questions on the University's financial status and served as an introduction to a much more detailed set of remarks from Mary Lai and her comptroller, Paul Magali. Debt structures, cumulative deficits, annual budgets, scholarship percentages, and audited statements were the major topics. The file contains remarks from John McGrath as well. But the "take-away" was perhaps best summarized by an op-ed piece of a student, Stan Gelman, who wrote two days earlier in *Seawanhaka* "John McGrath has said that LIU can not stay in business 'for children who can't pay tuition.' Lacking the Chairman's talent for subtlety, Vice Chairman Arthur Roth said essentially the same in his infamous 'urban rot' declaration."

It did not help in a day devoted to detailed financial disclosures, that Hoxie and Kottler got so angry with each other that they engaged in a shouting match, as the *New York Post* reported on November 3rd. There had been an obscure reference to Douglas MacArthur's return to the Philippines in World War II. It allowed the two men the opportunity to trade barbs in public. It was, in sum, a public relations nightmare. Hoxie was forced to admit publicly that his development efforts had failed as he searched for funds from government, foundations, and individuals. He further acknowledged, "we are faced with some harsh realities. I do not wish to be critical, but with 14,000 alumni the Brooklyn Center has for the past five years averaged in alumni gifts about $25,000 a year." And he concluded, "that the broad public interest as well as future viability of Long Island University would best be served by City University of New York acquiring our Brooklyn Center." The reality he described was light years away from the promises of *Preface To The Future*.

Mary Lai testified in great detail about the financial condition of the University and the Brooklyn campus. She noted, "The present cumulative surplus of the Brooklyn Center is $1.370 million. There has not been any siphoning of Center funds for other campuses. We maintain separate accounts for each campus to which we credit all the income from that campus and to which we charge all the expenditures related to that operation." She refuted the claim that there had been at $10 million surplus and rejected that there was a $3 million surplus projected for Brooklyn for that year, noting that for the present year Brooklyn had a "break even budget" with a small contingency. She observed, "The Brooklyn Center is presently not in financial trouble, but it certainly is not 'flush' as one newspaper indicated."

The financial argument both she and her comptroller, Paul Magali, tried to make was that salary increases presented a serious inflationary pressure. There were major, long overdue facility expenditures necessary, including, most essentially, a major new library. Stable enrollment was problematic, especially as the City University expanded and siphoned off students who might otherwise have gone to LIU. Federal support would increasingly shrink as the war in Vietnam tilted government priorities. And Chairman McGrath, when he spoke, summarized, "It is the belief of LIU's Trustees and the administrative staff that in the next ten years the Brooklyn Center of LIU would find itself in a period of deficit financing as a result of dwindling numbers of qualified students, coming from inevitably higher tuition costs and the competition 'on our door step' of far less expensive tax-supported education."

In the days following the hearings, Hoxie actively lobbied for the sale. He wrote to Abe Stark, the Borough President of Brooklyn, made famous to Dodgers fans by his promise of a free suit of clothes if a batter could hit a pitch against his sign in the outfield of Ebbets Field. In that letter, Hoxie talked about York College being established in Queens not in Brooklyn and the gossip that Baruch College would be established in a new location in Manhattan rather than in Brooklyn. The risk, he warned, was that "no new senior college of City University will be located in Brooklyn."

He also wrote to Edna Kelly, the Congresswoman in whose district the Brooklyn campus was located. "Quite candidly, Edna," he wrote, "the real issue, and the only issue in the matter, is whether City University of New York is prepared to continue the employment of all persons employed at the Brooklyn Center. If City University would so agree, the sale will be welcome by the faculty and staff....I believe that you and other political leaders in the Brooklyn area could best serve in this matter by seeking to persuade City University of New York to such a course of action." He commented that City University, with its access to construction funds could "bring to consummation a great educational center which will do more for the Borough of Brooklyn than Long Island University, in its fondest hopes, could even dream of ever accomplishing." And he again asserted, "But no funds have been siphoned off to any other part of the University, using an old Harvard phrase, 'each tub must rest on its own bottom.'"

Hoxie understood that he was in a squeeze and in trouble. That same night, after the third round of hearings, he wrote the Executive Committee of the Board indicating that December 1st had become an unrealistic date for consummating the sale, whatever the longer-term prospects might be. Therefore, he felt it necessary to reopen 1972 enrollment for the freshman class beginning in September 1968 with an increase in undergraduate tuition to $50 a credit a semester hour (the same as the tuition at Post), and he acknowledged that any use of the $32 million from a sale of Brooklyn "for a gymnasium at the Southampton College, or for a Law School on the Merriweather Campus, can arouse particular bitterness unnecessarily. Accordingly, I should like to have it as a matter of policy of the Board that they concur in our September 19th position with regard to the establishment of an educational endowment fund from the proceeds of the sale."

When Hoxie met with his Chancellor's Cabinet to review the tumultuous events of the prior several weeks, they were concerned that Post would be swamped with students from Brooklyn who would have to be guaranteed admission and full transfer of credits. This was a difficult meeting and there were no easy answers to be had, given the uncertainties and tensions that had surfaced. Since Long Island University had made a formal offer to the City University and since it was still waiting for a formal response, its only option was to resume business as usual, raise tuition on the several campuses based on need and the politics in each situation and carry on with the routinized business of admitting, educating and graduating students.

Unbeknownst to any of them, the ongoing contretemps, prompted *The Chronicle of Higher Education*, the national weekly newspaper of the industry, to publish a multi-column story on the "Furor at Long Island University." It cited Bowker who observed that, "'it would be difficult for a public institution to do something so much at variance' with the views of public leaders and legislators." *The Chronicle* observed, "The fuss and the solid opposition of Brooklyn politicians, appears to have cooled off City University's desire for the deal." From its national perspective, *The Chronicle* article explored "some of the most complex issues in higher education today-the role of urban universities, admissions' policies for lower middle class students, and the fiscal plight of private higher education." That story guaranteed that the entire higher education community from the Atlantic to the Pacific knew of LIU's troubles.

The *Seawanhaka* issue of November 9th featured two surprises in addition to the Douglas MacArthur brouhaha of the third day of hearings. The first was that Hoxie arrived wearing a "save LIU Brooklyn Center" button. The second was the unexpected appearance of Emmanuel Celler, who, at eighty, was the Dean of the House of Representatives. Celler announced, "LIU would be on the agenda" of the next meeting of the New York's Congressional Delegation. He felt sure that Brooklyn's hostility to the deal would cool the City University's interest in the purchase. Celler garbled both the facts and the names. He said NYU when he meant LIU and he confused the Brooklyn Center with Brooklyn College. But there was nothing muddled about Celler's power in the House of Representatives.

That next hearing of the Joint Committee was delayed because Henry Heald could not attend. An editorial in that same November 9th edition of *Seawanhaka* began, "While we're on the subject of maturity, we have to express amazement (for the umpteenth time) at the Chancellor's marked propensity for making a fool of himself." Was Hoxie's decision to wear that button his way of saying that he, too, was in favor of saving the Brooklyn campus by selling it to CUNY? Did he realize he was becoming a figure of ridicule? Probably not.

But for the moment, Hoxie, the University Board and the University continued to push aggressively for the sale. At the next Board meeting on November 13th, John McGrath updated his fellow Trustees on the status of the negotiations. There had been a meeting with McGrath, Hoxie and University counsel on the second of November, just prior to public hearings with Associate Commissioner of Education Paul G. Bulger, and Assistant Commissioner Robert H. McCambridge. Bowker and his senior team were also present. Since the process of evaluating the pros and cons of any deal of this magnitude would take time, it was jointly agreed, albeit reluctantly, to wait until early 1968 to reach any firm decision. Long Island University was left still floating broadside, unable to get under way in any direction.

Edward Neimuth, speaking on behalf of The Brooklyn College of Pharmacy Board, was deeply concerned about the future relationship of the Brooklyn College of Pharmacy with the Brooklyn campus. He requested and got agreement for a working group of LIU Trustees to revisit the wisdom of an association of the Brooklyn College of Pharmacy with Brooklyn. Pharmacy had remained outside of the discussions about the potential sale, but clearly there were important issues that had to be addressed quickly: Should Pharmacy move to Brookville? Should Pharmacy associate itself with City University? Should the College of Pharmacy attempt to function as a freestanding institution once again?

On November 27th, McGrath invited Sidney Solomon, President of A&S Department Stores, Clinton Blume, the real estate mogul and the younger Zeckendorf to be that working group. In his letter to Neimuth that same day, McGrath also urged the Brooklyn College of Pharmacy to remain within the LIU family. "Certainly there is no valid reason why the affiliation should not continue even though the activities become centered mainly in Nassau and Suffolk Counties." That invitation to move to C.W. Post became the operative assumption at Pharmacy until 1972 when the federal government linked continued capital support to Pharmacy remaining within the inner city.

Pharmacy's future and location were among the many unresolved questions in the autumn of 1967. New student enrollment, including pre-pharmacy, was completely out of normal cycle. Formal admissions had been suspended for six weeks, a critical period in the annual process of recruitment. Seemingly endless adverse publicity and the uncertainty about future tuition costs stymied the building of a class both in pharmacy and related subjects. The professional staff was demoralized and uncertain about their own individual futures. By winning a postponement for a year, the Brooklyn faculty and students had scored a tactical victory with the potential of a strategic win. The stakeholders in the Brooklyn College of Pharmacy's had no real choice but to watch and to wait.

Hoxie consistently argued that the mission of providing a more meaningful equality of opportunity would better be delivered by the free University of the City New York than by a private institution, especially if there was no massive private support for the endeavor. When, the year before, the Ford Foundation granted Columbia $35 million, its then President, McGeorge Bundy, spoke of "urgent concern for the future of the City and the future of those in our cities who lack full equality of opportunity." This, Hoxie indicated, was a key reason for embracing the possible sale. The press quoted Kottler as delighted by this new argument from Hoxie. "He [Hoxie] was under the gun for more than an hour on this one point," Kottler had said. And the students, sensing their victory, were, according to the *Daily News* of November 15th, jubilant over the delay. The head of the student government spoke to a rally of 650 students and claimed "student power" was the reason.

Meanwhile, the faculty voted unanimously to keep Acting Provost William T. (Buck) Lai as the Provost rather than interview Wilbert Gustad, a friend of Hoxie, for that position. He was the Provost and Dean of New College and had served as Dean of Liberal Arts and Sciences at Alfred University in a prior appointment. Clearly, the faculty was sending Hoxie an unsubtle message that he could not appoint anyone who did not first win faculty approval. The balance of power had shifted and both students and faculty understood that.

On November 16th, Kottler held the fourth session of the public hearings. Frank A. McGrath, the University's attorney and brother of John McGrath, attended and filed Minutes of what he heard. There were three witnesses: Paul Magali, the comptroller of the University, Julius Hallheimer, an alumnus who had served on the Richmond committee of three and who opposed the sale, and Dr. Heald. Heald and Kottler sparred about the written report, when it had been or would be submitted, who could read it, and whether it sooner or later would be a public document.

Heald asserted that the investigation was continuing, and that ultimately a full report, which was privileged, would be submitted to the Board. But the gist of Heald's testimony was that the Brooklyn campus was trying "to fulfill the function of a public university without the resources with which to do so." Frank McGrath felt the most important disclosure made by Kottler was when he asked Dr. Heald whether he considered any alternative to the sale of the Brooklyn Center to CUNY. Heald then said that he had not. "Kottler then suggested the possibility of a sale of the physical plant not to the City University or the State University but governmental acquisition of the physical plant and a 'contract arrangement' whereby the facilities would be leased 'to insure continued operations in terms of its present thrust.'" McGrath observed, "The emphasis placed by Kottler was that some means should be found to insure the continuance of the Brooklyn Center as it is now set up."

Kottler ended the fourth and final hearing, by indicating that he was planning a second round of hearings, which would focus on the development of plans under which "'the unique function of the Brooklyn Center could be continued' under some auspices other than Long Island University or incorporating it as part of the City or State University."

The press covered the fourth hearing and reported fully. The *Daily News,* on November 17th quoted Heald as saying, "none of LIU's four branches is 'economically viable' but the Brooklyn Center is 'the least viable' because it receives virtually no endowments." In *Newsday* the reporter wrote, "Heald came under sharp questioning from Kottler, who asked if any recommendations had been made regarding the role of LIU Chancellor R. Gordon Hoxie and the school's Board of Trustees. Heald admitted that the recommendations were part of the report but refused to disclose his findings on the grounds that it violated the 'privilege client relationship.'" *Seawanhaka,* reported as well on the testimony of Judge Hallheimer, who served on the Commission that Richmond had chaired. Hallheimer "labeled the proposed sale of the Brooklyn Center 'a direct repercussion of the Birenbaum affair.'" There is no direct evidence of this in the University files, but certain things don't get written down. It was widely believed to be true then and entered into University folklore, where it has festered ever since.

The following Sunday, November 25th, *Newsday* education editor Martin Buskin, wrote a very long piece in *Newsday's* magazine section titled, "The University In Crisis." "While headlines around the country shout of student unrest and dissent, and attention is focused on student opposition to Vietnam and military recruiters, a major Long Island University has been piling up a record of protest, upheaval, and dissent that has been topped only by the 1963 riots at Berkeley. An internal hot war has been wracking the 20,000-student Long Island University, and the issue has not been peace or student power, but one that is much more basic: the survival of private higher education." With care and acuity, Buskin chronicled the prior many months. He quoted Heald: "LIU was 'in a much worse position than most other private institutions…The way they have been able to exist is by constantly growing, having inadequate facilities and being over expanded.'"

Buskin was particularly interested in the inherent contradiction of the post-1945, non-endowed private university. Tuition income alone "cannot support an adequate program and plant," he argued. Public support was rapidly decreasing, and there was inadequate private philanthropy for LIU, especially in Brooklyn. Quoting Heald again, 'I talked to people in Brooklyn. There is no money for LIU, Brooklyn Poly, or Pratt, even for the Brooklyn Museum. You can't raise any money in Brooklyn.' Hoxie was foolishly hoping for a miracle in the form of private support, Buskin suggested. But from July to September, his efforts to raise money from business and foundation sources had failed utterly. Buskin noted that Heald was "harsh in his depiction of LIU Brooklyn's current situation. 'The plant is impossible,'" Heald said. "'The library is totally inadequate. Nothing is designed for the purpose for which it is used. You need to spend millions of dollars on the plant.'"

Buskin had also interviewed Ogden Reid, at length, quoting Reid, "there has been an overexpansion at the expense of faculty salaries and educational excellence. When you get into graduate fields, the first question to be asked is, are the undergraduate courses in good shape?" Reid said there had been too much concern with bricks and mortar and not enough with raising educational standards. Echoing Heald, he added that LIU "has relied far too much on tuition for its operations and growth. It is wrong fiscally and wrong from the point of view of the students." Buskin asked him the question, "How LIU had been able to build campuses for 11,000 students in Brookville, 1,400 students in Southampton, and 7,700 students in Brooklyn with such a small amount of annual total gifts and grants?" Reid replied, it "is by long term federal mortgages and loans of more than $14 million in construction now underway in Post and Brooklyn. The University had to put up only $3 million in cash and financed the balance." Buskin also interviewed Hoxie, "who admits that he does have some internal problems and has committed some public relations blunders in his handling of the Brooklyn situation." Buskin's article was detailed, seemingly accurate, and very damaging to the reputation of the

University. It described in detail an institution in crisis.

At a University Council meeting on November 28th, the major topic, not surprisingly, was the potential sale of Brooklyn. In the room were some of Hoxie's most outspoken critics from Brooklyn. It was a rare moment for full and frank discussion.

Hoxie turned for solace to the opening paragraph of Charles Dickens's, *A Tale of Two Cities*. "The best of times" he felt was the sharp increase in gifts and grants, which over the prior three years had totaled more than $7 million, and the improvement in faculty salaries, which moved all salary ranks of faculty from a "C" category to an "A," except for full Professors who had a "B" ranking. In the "worst of times" category was the Buskin article, and in particular, how Buskin dwelled upon the "credibility gap." The argument he made to the thirty assembled senior faculty and administrators was that until the alumni became generous, institutions like Ford would not open their wallets very wide. He urged everyone to join with him "to raise money for the support of the Brooklyn Center," arguing that an increase of new gifts and grants would allow him to go back to the Ford Foundation. Nate Resnick from Brooklyn submitted that Brooklyn had suffered a "distinct disservice," arguing "that the first step is to stop talking about the Brooklyn Center as defunct or as being in any greater difficulty than any other unit of the University."

Robert Spector then chimed in, saying there was a "credibility gap." He believed that the first thing that needed to be done was to stop the sale of the Center to the City University and spoke about the faculty resolution "that a new administration be appointed to carry out this recommendation." Hoxie responded "that he did not believe there was anything personal in the desire to have the Chancellor fired," but rather that Dr. Spector "wanted this for the good of the University." Hoxie refused to accept that he was so thoroughly loathed in Brooklyn. He argued that on "February 16, 1967 when the ten year plan was distributed it was felt that the University had the greatest sense of unity ever, but within a month there was the start of trouble at the Brooklyn Center." He went on to say, "Nevertheless, in spite of all the bad publicity," he believed, "that the image of the University, including Brooklyn, is better locally and nationally than ever."

Spector rejoined by urging that "the sale of the Brooklyn Center be stopped." Hoxie evaded him by saying "that there had been no negotiation on the part of this central administration as he made manifestly clear in his last conversation with the Chancellor of the City University." He argued, "he could never think of it merely as a real estate matter." One of the Deans then chimed in, "that in the spirit of candor and honor the criticisms were aimed at the Board of Trustees." He suggested that if the Board were truly concerned, they "undertake to launch a gift program from among their own members, thus making their interest known by their own specific actions." Dr. Resnick followed by suggesting that, "we should take another look at

the ten year plan." Dr. Baiardi stated, "that we are already in the process of reap-
praising the plan." And so, this key debate simply slid along with unusual candor
but without any closure.

At the end of the meeting, Hoxie was asked whether the Heald-Hobson report
would be released, and, if so, when. Hoxie answered that the report was made
orally to the Board and that Zeckendorf said, "this should be made to the Board
only." He then went on to indicate that there was not yet any written report. "It is
possible," Hoxie stated, "that there may only be a series of recommendations and
no complete written report." Hoxie was reminded that, "the Board of Trustees
publicly promised the Brooklyn Center that the report would be published and
made public." And Hoxie stated that, "he would convey this recommendation to
the Board."

Two days later, Kottler submitted to the Speaker of the Assembly and the President
pro tem of the Senate a long report of some forty-eight pages. He and his staff had
taken their charge very seriously. The Committee had heard some 50 witnesses.
Kottler established his own point of view early on. "All of the remaining witnesses
bitterly denounced the proposed sale as a callous and inconsiderate sell-out of the
students and faculty of the Brooklyn Center and an abandonment of LIU's responsibility to the urban community of the Borough of Brooklyn." Kottler observed,
"Since CUNY could absorb no more than 3,000 of the 7,000 students who would
normally be enrolled at the Brooklyn Center over a four year period, some 4,000
would face displacement as a result of the sale of the Brooklyn Center."

Until CUNY moved to Open Enrollment, that institution operated on a very restric-
tive admissions formula, based on an 85 grade point average of admission to the
four year, senior campuses. LIU had an enrollment floor of seventy to seventy-five
percent for its admissions. Kottler's report focused on those who were at risk of being denied admissions. There were whole categories of students who could come
to LIU, but would be rejected by CUNY, including Operation Reclaim - specifically designed to train black teachers, Operation Prima-designed to train Puerto
Rican teachers, black students, "many of whom will not qualify for CUNY," handicapped students, students in journalism, and a wide range of others. It is essential
to remember that there was a draft deferment for those who enrolled full time in
college. As one of the black students remarked, "we become draft bait."

In his final report, Kottler was still angry that Hoxie had ignored the summons to
return to testify at the second session of the hearings. He reprinted his own statement issued at the time: "I can't get myself to believe that the Board of Trustees
and the Chancellor are so utterly indifferent as to completely ignore a request of
a Joint Legislative Committee of the New York State Legislature to appear before it." He then quoted Senator Manfred Ohrenstein, the Vice Chairman of this
Committee, who had commented that he "was unaware of any witness who ever

declined an invitation to appear before this Committee since the Committee came into existence."

With extraordinary detail Kottler then went into the financial situation of LIU based upon multiple individuals who testified and materials submitted. He noted, "it is clear that the financial condition of the Brooklyn Center is much healthier than the books of LIU have reflected in 'Exhibit B.'"

Kottler focused a great deal of attention on *Preface to the Future.* "The most startling contradiction of the proponents of the sale, was the attempt by LIU officials to disavow and disassociate themselves from LIU's own publication, dated January 2, 1967, and entitled *Preface to the Future; The Ten-Year Plan for Long Island University.*" Kottler was amazed that, "Suddenly, in July of 1967 and solely as a result of an oral recommendation of consultants Heald, Hobson and Associates, LIU's Board of Trustees rejected the glowing future of the ten year report and instead embraced the projection of financial gloom espoused by Dr. Henry Heald, who since refused to testify before the Joint Legislative Committee concerning details of his recommendation to sell the Brooklyn Center."

Pointing out that Hoxie had "sought to disassociate himself from the Report, claiming it was written by the faculty of the Brooklyn Center," Kottler described how Hoxie was bitterly denounced for his later reversal, after having signed the *Preface* earlier that year. Judge Julius Hallheimer when he testified, berated Hoxie for this about-face. "Gentlemen, I am not so overpowered by his high-sounding phrases. Now, ordinarily a man who signs a preface must have read the book." The contradictions were striking. At the hearings, the University Treasurer, Mary Lai, referred to that ten year report as "promotional." But, later on, in cross-examination, she acknowledged, "she helped draft the 'Ways and Means Chapter' and 'the financial projections' of the ten year report."

Heald himself came in for a full measure of criticism. "Dr. Heald produced no evidence - no figures, no financial statements, no specifics - to spell out for this Committee the basis of his conclusions. On the contrary, when pressed by the Committee for details of his recommendations, he refused to answer, on the grounds of what he called 'professional privilege'". Kottler actively rejected Heald's notion that there was anything privileged in Heald's recommendations. "It would likewise be most naïve for this committee to assume that Dr. Heald was not fully aware that the privilege he asserted had no legal basis." Kottler also quoted from Spector's testimony that Heald had no true sensitivity to the mission of the Brooklyn campus-dating back to 1926, but clearly reinforced by William Birenbaum: to help disadvantaged students make it in America. "Ask Mr. Heald about the profile of our students. Ask him about our relationship to the community we serve. Ask him about what our faculty does inside the classroom and in the academic world. Mr. Heald cannot tell you. He has not been inside our classrooms."

Kottler accused Heald of frustrating his Committee's "lawful efforts to obtain the facts.... He has thus manifested his contempt for the legislative mission of this Committee's public hearing." Kottler next asked rhetorically why Heald did not address the Birenbaum matter. "Was he fearful that, by doing so, he would have to let the public know the truth behind LIU's dismissal of its former provost, Dr. William Birenbaum, after Dr. Birenbaum had recommended reductions in tuition because of what Dr. Birenbaum considered to be the good prospective [sic] of the Brooklyn Center?"

Such excoriation must have been embarrassing and very awkward for Heald. Kottler wondered, "is it possible that Dr. Heald fears that the publication of his findings would contradict his own conclusions?" And he continued, "the shadows and suspicions, which have shrouded the turn-about of LIU's Board of Trustees from the optimism of its Ten Year Growth Report in the spring of 1967, to their pessimism of July 1967, based, allegedly, on an oral report of Dr. Heald, are only lengthened and deepened by Dr. Heald's refusal to divulge the facts upon which conclusions are based." Heald clearly did not get paid enough to see his reputation so openly attacked.

Kottler had a series of general recommendations and some specific ones. He maintained that the Brooklyn Center was a viable institution, economically self-supporting with a substantial surplus. He believed that the financial problems were the result of a siphoning of funds for expenditure elsewhere despite the clear objection of Mrs. Lai and her team. As a Brooklyn Assemblyman, he believed that the LIU Brooklyn campus provided "a unique educational opportunity for students of the City and State of New York," and he went on to argue that it would be greatly enhanced if the Brooklyn Center could be operated as a free-standing institution.

He actively supported what became known as "Bundy Aid" and other state programs to "ease the financial burden for the students at the Brooklyn Center and enable them to pay current or increased tuition." More specifically, he called for the enactment of LIU as a contract college; the acquisition of Brooklyn by SUNY or CUNY on the basic condition that it be operated by its present faculty and with its current standards and educational policies and with a new Board of Trustees manage the campus. And finally, if the LIU Board did not cooperate properly, he wanted to "suspend or revoke" the Charter of Long Island University so that it was granted only a "provisional Charter conditioned upon the compliance by the Board of Trustees of Long Island University with the recommendations of the Board of Regents." Dismissing what he called "the cavalier attitude of the Board," he proposed that, in the following year, all Boards of Trustees of universities and colleges be made "more democratic, to prevent them from being self-perpetuating and to ensure appropriate participation in their functions by faculty, students, and alumni representatives."

The Kottler report was issued on December 12, 1967. That same day Hoxie issued a rejoinder. He began it by lamenting that, "The report is regrettably replete with hostility toward the Board of Trustees of Long Island University and the Board's consultant, Dr. Henry T. Heald." He observed that, "one of Kottler's recommendations was that the State take over the Brooklyn Center as 'a contract college' or that either the City University or the SUNY system acquire the Brooklyn campus." Hoxie repeated his claim that the free University of the City of New York could meet the needs of disadvantaged and minority students better than LIU and that "Currently Long Island University's Brooklyn Center has less than 7% of the student population drawn from minority groups." At his press conference, Kottler called for both the Chairman of the Board and the Chancellor to resign, a specific recommendation not made in the report itself. Hoxie responded that this "appears to bear out the somewhat prejudicial view running throughout the report itself. The greatest service of the Kottler report is in pointing out the financial needs of the Brooklyn Center."

The *Daily News* spoke of the Kottler Report as "a long-fused bombshell." In reporting the story, *Seawanhaka* also noted that a group of alumni had hired Paul O'Dwyer, the brother of the former mayor, both to block the sale and initiate legal action to remove the Board of Trustees. In that same issue the student editorial Board, commenting on the Report, wrote: "it took the legislative committee on higher education two months to discover what we had known at a mere glance. The Board of Trustees of Long Island University has been fighting a losing battle with competency...." And later in the editorial, it called on the students to raise $10,000, "At a $1.50 a head" to underwrite the costs of hiring Paul O'Dwyer.

One of the named litigants was Alan Livingston, who was in the anomalous position of serving as an Alumni Trustee while suing the University and Board over the sale of the campus."The suit charged," according to *The New York Times* of January 12th, "that the Trustees wanted to sell the Center to escape their responsibility for serving the educational needs of young people from minority groups and other Brooklyn youths and to obtain funds for the 'suburban and rural oriented Long Island campuses.'" Both sides were, in fact, pivoting even though the Brooklyn campus was an institution that still had an overwhelmingly white student body. "The complaint accused the LIU Board of Trustees of trying to 'destroy' the Center so that it could turn the University 'into a glorified institution catering to the suburban residents of Nassau and Suffolk County.'" Racial issues and socio-economic tensions were seeping into every aspect of this fight as they were in the society at large.

At the same time, Hoxie, always the tactician, lobbied Robert McCambridge, the New York State Assistant Commissioner for Higher Education Planning, to support his and the Board's position. McCambridge was charged with drafting a background paper for the Regents. It could be an important document, since it would shape how the Regents viewed the merits of this proposed sale. Hoxie wanted, if possible, a counterweight to the highly critical Kottler report, which had received coverage in the press. Approval by the Regents would be a key hurdle in winning Governor Rockefeller's blessing of the sale, and McCambridge would have great influence in shaping how the Regents themselves understood the pros and cons of the deal.

Hoxie began his lobbying efforts by proposing a small but swanky dinner party for a few of the Regents and senior administrators of the Department of Education at Mrs. Preston Davie's home on East 71st Street in Manhattan. On December 8th, he pushed more directly, writing how both Albert Bowker and his Board Chair, Porter Chandler, continued to "wholeheartedly desire" the deal to go through. He then indicated that the "City University of New York does need your personal support and that of the Board of Regents in the matter of the acquisition." Suddenly turning nasty, he chronicled that Kottler and Podell were recently at a Vietnam Day symposium at LIU in a program with Jerry Rubin, Abby Hoffman and a long list of anti-war activists and leaders of militant organizations. The implication was clear: those two Assemblymen were in the pocket of the left-leaning radicals. Their hostility to the sale, Hoxie hinted, was somehow linked to their political hostility to the American intervention in Vietnam.

The dinner party never happened, so Hoxie invited McCambridge and two colleagues to the Metropolitan Club on January 8th to discuss the capital needs of LIU in Brooklyn, first with the Executive Committee of the LIU Board and then with the full Board. He offered to invite Heald to the meeting if McCambridge saw value in such an opportunity. Behind the scenes he mobilized Mary Lai, Rinde-Thorsen, the head of capital planning, and others to meet with McCambridge's staff to convince Albany that the buildings in Brooklyn would cost at least $20 million, and perhaps $26 million if the Brooklyn College of Pharmacy was to build its new facility in Brooklyn rather than in Brookville. The memo to Mrs. Lai was marked "personal and in confidence." The two of them had the task of demonstrating that these new buildings were vital to the campus if it was to remain competitive, even though LIU couldn't afford to build them without external support. He also wrote Baiardi and his assistant James Wilson, a "personal and in confidence" memo alerting them to an upcoming visit by a member of McCambridge's staff. He anticipated that they would want to explore prior fundraising for Brooklyn, the present organizational structure of the Development Department, and future prospects.

On January 4, 1968, Hoxie sent to McCambridge a Position Paper drafted by George Shapiro and Frank McGrath reflecting the Board's attitude on the acquisition of the campus by CUNY. It was a thorough, well-articulated statement of the LIU position.

When he next wrote McCambridge on January 8th, he presented a different rationale, explaining why CUNY had "a strong moral obligation to consummate the transfer… at the earliest practical date." The delays were severely damaging new student enrollment. On a year to year basis, applications to the Brooklyn campus had dropped from 1,896 potential students to only 859, partially because of the adverse publicity and partially because the admissions process had been frozen. Transfer student applications were also far below the previous year. He sent a copy of this letter to Chancellor Bowker, because both LIU and CUNY separately had a strong need to move the sale towards completion without excessive bureaucratic delay. Hoxie seemed indefatigable.

Among many other efforts encouraged by Hoxie over the Christmas period was a long letter written by George Stoddard published on December 19th in *The New York Times*. Stoddard identified himself as a former President of the University of the State of New York and Commissioner of Education. There was no mention that he was then the Academic Vice President of Long Island University. Entitled "Brooklyn's College Needs," Stoddard maintained, "the young people of Brooklyn will call for expenditures of tens of millions of dollars above the present public appropriations" if Brooklyn is to meet the higher education needs of the community. He argued that New York was way behind the Midwestern and West Coast states in delivering quality public-sector higher education. Such education required subvention, and most private-sector colleges could not compete.

"Long Island University will doubtless reach the decision that recent Presidents have put into effect at New York University. I refer to the efforts of Henry T. Heald, Carroll V. Newsom, and James M. Hester to transform NYU from an opportunistic 'pinch hitter' for public education into a selective university with high standards of admission and performance." Stoddard's argument proved to be historically accurate. Highlighting the policy contradiction of asking a poorly-endowed private university to fulfill a job that public sector institutions were established to achieve, he underscored that there was an increasing confusion between the educational and civic purposes of a university. Johnson's Great Society efforts had posited the university as a key institution to help disadvantaged men and women gain upward mobility, social equity and opportunity.

The Vietnam War not only transformed the domestic economy and the nation's priorities, but also blurred the purpose of a university. Private, non-endowed universities could not fulfill that mission without massive subventions. NYU succeeded in transforming itself from a commuter institution into highly competitive, elite university; one that could and would compete with Columbia at every level. That, suggested Stoddard, was what should also happen at LIU in Brooklyn or on the Island. In sum, publicly funded universities and colleges might need to create Open Enrollment if that is what society mandated, but privates like LIU could not support that expense as LIU in Brooklyn was trying to do.

On January 1ˢᵗ, Spector, in a letter to *The New York Times* wrote that readers had "a right to know that he [Stoddard] is not the disinterested educator suggested by your description of him 'as President of the University of the State of New York and Commissioner of Education 1943-1945.'" He went on to point out, among other issues, the plan to house the Baruch School of Business on the site would not create a great increase in entry level seats for underprivileged students. Spector continued, "I do know that our mission at Long Island University has a quite positive purpose: to provide a quality education for those whom the City University has neither the desire nor the understanding to educate." Spector disputed the seven percent figure used by Stoddard for minority students, maintaining instead, that the actual number should be eleven percent.

Baruch would stay in Manhattan. LIU in Brooklyn became overwhelmingly minority. Open Enrollment almost bankrupted the City of New York. It was educationally the final fulfillment of the generous vision of the role of an educated citizenry dating back to the G.I. Bill. But after Vietnam, America could not afford free, universal higher education. Moreover, the country no longer saw the value of such an expense.

Tapping into Stoddard's thoroughbred contacts in the foundation world, Hoxie, also secured a lunch meeting with J.A. Stratton, the Chairman of the Board of the Ford Foundation, and his associate F. Champion Ward, the Vice President of the Education Division. In his confirming letter to Stratton, he wrote that without a miracle "there will pass from our midst the only private non-sectarian university in the largest borough in the City of New York. We believe with McGeorge Bundy, who, at the time of the recent major Columbia gift, declared that 'the great university in a metropolis must have a special and urgent concern for the future of the city and for the future of those in our cities who lack full equality of opportunity.'" Because Ford had committed itself so generously to encouraging educational opportunity and upward mobility, Hoxie could not understand why Columbia was different from LIU and why Harlem was different from Fort Green. But it was.

On January 10ᵗʰ, Hoxie again wrote to McCambridge, chronicling his efforts to solicit the Ford Foundation over the past several months. "As I indicated to you, my one last, best hope with regard to staving off the seemingly inevitable, that is, the loss of our Brooklyn Center, was my appeal to the Ford Foundation." He continued, "That appeal...has been at several levels up to and through the Chairman of the Board, and the final decision is now in, under the date of January 8, 1968." He quoted from a letter from Ward with a copy to Stratton: "I am afraid that we must pass *up* this one, rather than pass it. This is not just a matter of the scale of the financing required to stave off the immediate transfer of the Center, but a matter of subsequent financing, as well as the special minority constituency, which it would be necessary to serve in Brooklyn."

Hoxie used rejection to push McCambridge to support the sale of the Campus to the City University. Hoxie had been doggedly attempting to get Ford to duplicate what it had done by giving $35 million to Columbia in order to make Columbia's relationship to the people of Harlem more collaborative. But the nation and its mood were changing rapidly. The Foundation was moving away from institutional grants, and in particular, from grants to pay for bricks and mortar. And so, Hoxie returned to the standard refrain, "I must conclude that transfer to the City University is the best solution for all parties concerned and will provide the best benefit for future generations."

On January 12, 1968, Robert McCambridge prepared a four-page briefing for commissioner for Allen and the Board of Regents. He noted, "The forces set in motion by Provost Birenbaum have been continued since his leaving...." This document, found in the files of the Board of Regents, indicated that there were "no grounds to find that the Brooklyn Center of the University is currently in difficulty." In a recommendation section, McCambridge proposed a new Board to be "drawn fifty percent from the Borough of Brooklyn, twenty-five percent from other parts of New York city and twenty-five percent from other parts of the State." The Legislature should provide $100,000 for special programs "as are important in the downtown Brooklyn areas and in neighborhoods surrounding the Center." McCambridge supported that the existing Board should transfer the assets, facilities and liabilities to the new corporation, getting in return $500,000 annually for ten years.

In both subtle and violent ways, the discussion was rapidly turning into a debate over race and equity. It paralleled the national debate unfolding over every university's obligation to help remedy centuries of discrimination against those of color, the disadvantaged and community impoverished. Black Power and the rage in downtown Brooklyn transformed the terms of the local debate, especially as Nixon and his Southern Strategy suggested the end of "Great Society" optimism at achieving racial equity. Just a few years earlier, the question was how to address the claim that poor Italian, Jewish, and Irish kids could not afford private education. By the end of the decade, angry and militant students and their families wanted local universities to educate and empower the next generation of urban students of color, most of whom had received a deficient school education at failing inner city schools.

On January 19, 1968, Trustee George Shapiro wrote a "personal letter," to James E. Allen, the State Commissioner of Education, specifically about the background study being undertaken by McCambridge and other staff for the Board of Regents. Shapiro repeated his personal experience of graduating from Brooklyn in 1939 after holding a four-year scholarship.

After the most thorough consideration, Shapiro voted with the other Trustees in favor of the sale to CUNY. He had met with McCambridge and his colleagues twice when they were in New York and had commented to Allen that, while it was always dangerous to infer what a man will recommend on the basis of his questioning, "the line of questioning was most disturbing to me." He felt that Mc-Cambridge had "accepted the propaganda being disseminated by a troublesome faction of the faculty at the Brooklyn Center. If I do him an injustice, let me apologize now, but it is of great importance that you and the Regents have the straight story." He emphasized, "If City University established additional attractive new tuition-free facilities at a nearby site in Brooklyn, we would undoubtedly be faced with the loss of many of our better students to City University and the middle tier of students to the Community College program."

Shapiro was puzzled that McCambridge's team had been so keen to "ascertain whether the Brooklyn Center is now bankrupt or insolvent or losing money. None of us have ever claimed that to be the case. Surely we are justified in taking into account the long-range situation and deciding where we may best concentrate our resources." Shapiro was rational and calm. He wrote passionately, but reasonably. He spoke directly, "The Trustees need the help and support of the Department [of Education]." Even though it was obvious Hoxie had organized a public relations campaign, Shapiro's letter was effective.

John McGrath wrote to Joseph McGovern, a Wall Street Regent who chaired the Committee on Higher and Professional Education, seeking an opportunity to testify before that committee and/or seeking a joint meeting with the Chancellor of City University and Porter Chandler, its Chair. And Hoxie wrote to Deane Malott, enclosing the Shapiro letter, and asking for him to add his support. Malott's letter was sent on the January 22nd.

Henry Heald also reached out to Allen on January 23rd, making several critical points glossed over by the others. He wrote, "Our studies of LIU lead us to believe that it is over-extended managerially and financially to the point where the development and maintenance of a quality program are seriously jeopardized. Sale of the Brooklyn Center would permit the concentration of university resources on the remaining portion with reasonable hope of producing a sound program." Elsewhere in his letter he observed, "In view of all of the emotional and political involvements, brought about to some extent by the previous difficulties between the LIU administration and the Brooklyn Center faculty and students, it is doubtful that the Center can continue to operate effectively as a part of LIU in any event." He urged that the Regents endorse the sale of Brooklyn to CUNY "as being in the public interest, as I am sure it is."

Hoxie also asked George Stoddard to write Allen a "dear Jim letter." Because of Stoddard's future role at LIU, this particular letter deserves close scrutiny. Stoddard said, "My interests in the cultural affairs of the borough of Brooklyn precedes by two years any contact with L.I.U. In 1964, officials of Brooklyn Institute of

Arts and Sciences approached the Carnegie Corporation for aid in the study of problems of policy and finance. In 1965, I agreed to conduct such a study. It was started in 1966 and finished in the spring of 1967." Citing his own assessment of Brooklyn's cultural future, he wrote,"For the Borough of Brooklyn there emerges a choice of heroic proportions-either a grand design, cost what it may, for physical, educational and artistic renewal or a backward step toward a cultural wasteland."

Stoddard wrote of the vast acreage of slum housing, white flight and an unemployment rate of fourteen percent. He saw a pressing need for massive intervention by both the public and private sectors, especially to educate the next generation of Brooklynites. Stoddard understood that "Columbia, Fordham, Rockefeller, and more recently, New York University, have developed magnificently, free from the obligation to do what really must be done at public expense, namely, to offer at low cost *some form of higher education* to the majority of high school graduates in the city...." He concluded, "As you know, in the current negotiations the public image of the City University and Long Island University has been seriously distorted. Doubtless L.I.U. can carry on after a fashion in Brooklyn. Doubtless C.U.N.Y. can find other sites there. But the one cannot prosper and the other cannot fully serve you (as is done in the Middle West and the Far West) without dramatic changes in educational goals."

Allen wrote thank you notes to all of these friends and old associates. Most were pro forma. His letter to Stoddard, however, had a much warmer and responsive tone. "The Regents and I and the staff are giving much time these days to this problem and are planning some special meetings with the groups involved. Your letter has been duplicated for the members of the Board of Regents and will, I am sure, be very helpful to them and to me in reaching a decision as how we might be of maximum help." The lobbying campaign was working.

Meanwhile, the domestic and idiosyncratic issues of Long Island University and, in particular, its Brooklyn campus, were becoming increasingly interwoven with national movements of student protest. For example, on February 5th, Franklin National Bank planned to recruit at the Office of Student Placement on the Brooklyn campus. A protest flyer explained, "This bank is largely controlled by Arthur T. Roth, also Vice President of the LIU Board of Trustees, and very active in the group which is trying to sell the Brooklyn Center. The presence of Franklin National Bank on campus is an insult to the students who have been fighting for local autonomy." This document was signed by SDS, Students for a Democratic Society.

There is also a sad letter in the files from Hoxie to Regent Joseph King, which read, "In connection with the views of certain members of the New York State Education Department regarding academic freedom at the Brooklyn Center, I wonder whether they realize what academic freedom was being extinguished at the Brooklyn Center by Provost Birenbaum, who forced the resignation of so many able administrators before I finally secured his own resignation. It is Dr. Birenbaum who is quoted in Volume II, No. 2, 1965-66 *Graduate Comment* of Wayne State University, on how to seize power in a university. (This well in advance of his separation from Long Island University): 'Our students would be well advised to direct their attack at the weakest points of the going concern. The weakest points are the greatest centers of power - the decision making battle stations.'" Switching from the Birenbaum matter, Hoxie raised the protest of the SDS students at Brooklyn. "Moreover, I wonder whether these members of the State Education Department also believe that academic freedom obtains in the situation as currently exists in the Brooklyn Center wherein threats are made upon the acting provost for permitting recruitment on Campus by the Franklin National Bank."

Hoxie attacked the President of Hofstra in this same letter. "President Clifford Lord of Hofstra, who as you have noted has long been hostile to Long Island University with the New York State Education Department and the Regents, had an observer at all of the Kottler hearings on the Brooklyn Center matter. What President Lord allegedly states in the public press that he shares Kottler's evaluation of the Long Island University Board is certainly conduct unbecoming any college President." And then he sent a copy of an article from *Newsday* of January 25th.

These skirmishes were just that. The whole university awaited the outcome of the Regents' decision on the sale of the Brooklyn campus to City University. Rumor abounded. In early February, *Seawanhaka* ran a story which claimed that McCambridge's report would "recommend that the Center become an independent university with its own Board of Trustees by August 1, 1968," although it was not decided what part of the university would retain the name "Long Island University." Neither McCambridge nor Joseph McGovern, the Chair of the Committee of Higher & Professional Education would comment, but it was presented as solid inside gossip.

Meanwhile, in the Assembly and the Senate, three bills based on Joseph Kottler's findings had been introduced. The first would give the Board of Regents the power to remove a college's Board after public hearings, if the Board was found to have failed in its fiduciary duties. The second would prohibit the sale or disposition of any campus or school without prior review of the Regents. The third would mandate at least one member of the faculty, one student, and one alumni representative to serve on every private college and university board in New York State.

Whatever the ultimate outcome of the three pieces of legislation, the spotlight was on the Board of Regents and, in particular, on its Committee on Higher and Professional Education. The Committee took its time and did its homework.

It met on January 31st with an agenda devoted solely to this topic. On February 15th, it invited Kottler, students and faculty to the State office building in Manhattan to hear first hand their views even though behind the scenes Allen's mind was made up. Everyone understood that the full Board of Regents would defer to its own Committee, especially one that had immersed itself in the details.

Although Zeckendorf was no longer Chairman and was struggling to salvage whatever property he had previously partially or fully owned, he remained intensely interested and active in the University. He urged Hoxie to strengthen the public relations side of this fight, since he saw Hoxie personally and central administration as losing calamitously the public relations battle. Hoxie responded, probably intentionally, by letter on February 19th, to a phone call from Zeckendorf a few days earlier. "I am grateful for your counsel." Translated, that meant, of course, that Hoxie was irked to be told what might be done better at the University. His three-page letter was a defensive celebration of the skills of his staff. He promised that once the Brooklyn issue was resolved he would reorganize the senior administration and strengthen the public relations effort. He indicated that he wanted to bring closer together the public relations function at both the campus and the University levels, something he felt was easily achievable once the dissidents in Brooklyn were silenced. "We are countering this through the instrumentality of an informal faculty relations committee, chosen from among our loyal supporters throughout the University, working closely with our loyal director of public relations and myself." A pompous sentence like this last one must have enraged Zeckendorf.

Zeckendorf had called specifically to urge Hoxie to look closely at the credentials of someone named John Bell, a professional whose expertise Zeckendorf thought could help LIU mount a more effective institutional response. Hoxie's response: "I should be glad to invite John Bell to visit us here. As a matter of fact, I researched him and his organization quite thoroughly, and I was favorably impressed with his record of public relations service with business enterprises. However, I saw nothing in the record related to university public relations." Again, in "Hoxie-speak" he was dismissing Zeckendorf's recommendation. He followed these observations with a ringing endorsement of Jo Chamberlin, his public relations officer, who had "many assets which we simply cannot buy." He listed the many things that Chamberlin had done, including publications such as the *Preface to the Future*, and he sent a box load of these documents, some fourteen in all, to Zeckendorf. He ended his letter, "I would be happy to confer with Mr. Bell. His employment would be followed by Mr. Chamberlin's resignation, which I do not believe in the best interest of the University."

Hoxie was telling Zeckendorf not to meddle, in common parlance, to get lost. He was still in charge. He missed, of course, Zeckendorf's more detached strategic concern for the University's vulnerability whether Brooklyn was ultimately sold or not. Zeckendorf and Hoxie were no longer on the same page, muchless the same book. Hoxie was casual and dismissive of Zeckendorf's residual power, because, like Samson, the several bankruptcies made him seem diminished. Six months later, it became clear how arrogant and foolish this was. But much was still to happen from mid-February until then.

The Executive Committee of the Board met on February 18th with Dr. Heald and Dr. Stoddard to consider among other things "the proposed structural reorganization of the University...." Heald orally had recommended that the University be structured as one organization and not as separate units. "There would be one President with no provision for separate Presidents at the various centers as provided in our Statutes." Heald proposed that "the title of Chancellor be discontinued and that the Chief Executive Officer be designated as President of the University." That individual would have three Vice Presidents, the Executive Vice President whose responsibility would be the academic enterprise, a Vice President for Development, and a Vice President for Business Affairs. He also wanted to consolidate the position of Provost and Dean, ideally called an Executive Dean, of the sort already functioning in the College of Pharmacy.

McGrath also asked Heald and Stoddard, together with Frank McGrath, to "prepare a report for the Executive Committee on the proposed changes in the Statutes which would be required if the structural organization of the University is to conform to the organizational chart considered by the Committee." In the general discussion that followed, Henry Heald agreed with Hoxie's recommendation that the written report from Heald, Hobson would not be transmitted until later that spring, at some point after the Brooklyn question was resolved.

The front page of the *Seawanhaka* on February 21st had three lead stories. One dealt with the Regents' decision, which was expected within a few days. The lead sentence read, "The crisis surrounding the proposed sale of the Brooklyn Center, which has been dragging on for over a term, seems finally to be heading for a resolution." The second dealt with an alleged dope pusher, and it quoted Hoxie in a *Daily News* poll as describing the narcotics problem as "the challenge of our times." The third piece was a survey of seniors about the draft. The lead sentence of that article was, "Even though the U.S. Army plans a romantically disenchanting adventure for seniors graduating this June, many students have different ideas." One student was quoted, "I think the draft is totalitarian. It is involuntary servitude. I don't think I'd serve whether there was a war or not." The reporter noted, "The prospect of spending time in jail is hardly pleasing to anyone. For students, it is usually the point at which resistance activities are dropped and draft laws complied with." But the Student Council President declared, "I will not wear an American Army uniform as long as this war continues." And yet another student said, "I am planning to teach in September, but if I am drafted, I wouldn't resist. We live in an imperfect world where we're always faced with disagreeable choices. Although I am against the war, very little is fair in this world." One more student ended all debate when he said, "so far I am medically deferred."

Meanwhile McCambridge raised, yet again, his unhappiness at allowing LIU to be sold to CUNY. He was bothered about closing a "going concern" enrolling about 6,000 full-time students and constituting an important educational resource in the State. Asking Commisioner Allen if Brooklyn might be purchased by another university, he wrote; "The Brooklyn campus was not distinguished, but it has shown an ability to serve successfully what we have now recognized as a legitimate group of students, specifically those who graduate in the second quarter of their class." On February 7th, Allen wrote by hand a response down the side margin. "Bob - I like your idea, but frankly I think it is unrealistic to think that another private institution could make a go of it in Brooklyn. Even if it could, I doubt that it could maintain much quality." With his initials, he ended further discussion.

On February 23rd, at long last, the Board of Regents approved the request from the Board of Higher Education (the governing body of the City University) "to convert and expand the Bernard M. Baruch School of Business and Public Administration into an autonomous senior college of the University. The school will be located in downtown Brooklyn and will be known as the Bernard M. Baruch College." The Regents noted that they were "charged by law with the responsibility for the orderly and economical development of higher educational opportunities within this state." Therefore, the Regents gave approval along the lines of Bowker's letter. LIU issued a release over John McGrath's signature claiming that, "The public interest will thereby be best served, both for the present and future generations of Brooklyn youth." As the archive reveals, there were multiple drafts of that decision.

The approval of the Board of Regents was not, as so many people had assumed, the last step in this long, bitterly fought and complex project. It was, however, front-page news in *The Times* the following day. And Hoxie, perhaps heeding the criticism from Zeckendorf, wrote to the Education Editor of *The Times*, Fred Hechinger, urging an early lunch with Bowker, himself and Hechinger to share with *The Times* in detail plans that they jointly had evolved so that there could be a "wider public understanding of the whole situation."

The following Monday, February 26th, the student newspaper had a large aerial photo of the Brooklyn campus with a banner headline "Regents Stamp Their Approval" and superimposed on the campus photo was an erstaz stamp, a chop in bold print, "SOLD." On the editorial page, there was a very angry editorial that concluded, "They're still selling us and our principles out. But they haven't sold us yet...."

That issue of the paper had one article with the headline, "What Regents Guarantee You," another indicating that, "Suit Against Board of Trustees Unaffected by Regents' Decision," and another story, ultimately the most important, "Leaders Pledge to Continue Fighting for the Brooklyn Center's Survival." It reported that the "political leadership of Brooklyn was shocked but undaunted," Kottler, Stanley Steingut and newly elected Congressman, Bertram Podell, were vowing to keep up the fight to block the sale. To change the CUNY Master Plan required Governor Nelson Rockefeller's signature, and thus, there was still hope, although even these Brooklyn politicians realized that success would not be easy to achieve. The Regents had voted unanimously in favor of the deal. Condemning this decision, the Brooklyn politicians all said the right things from the campus's perspective, but their statements had a "whistling in the dark" quality that often leads to a rapid loss of political momentum.

On February 27th, the University moved in court "to dismiss the law suit brought by Allen Livingston and others against the University." As Jo Chamberlin reported back to Hoxie, "O'Dywer did not touch much on the legal aspects, but made more of a 'civic talk' on what BC [the Brooklyn Campus] meant to Borough, charged the LIU Trustees not with 'a real estate deal,' but with 'destroying a University' and so on."

To complicate matters, unrest broke out within the Post faculty after the Regents' action. The underlying issue was the likelihood that tenured Brooklyn faculty would "bump" both tenured and non-tenured Post faculty in promotions as they claimed seniority over their Post counterparts. The arrival of Brooklyn students and Brooklyn faculty seemed imminent, and Hoxie suddenly found himself addressing the Post faculty and administrative leadership. The key element of the story, according to *Newsday* on February 27th was "there is no financial crisis at the University." But buried in that news column was that the Post faculty AAUP chapter had mobilized the faculty to protect existing C.W. Post positions.

Meanwhile, Brooklyn students and faculty, resurrecting their honed skills at protest from the previous year, held a rally on February 27th with 2,000 students in attendance. Robert Spector proved to be the spark plug once again. "There is no Long Island University without the Brooklyn Center," he asserted. Firing up the students with a passionate defense of the survival of the campus, he shouted, "it's not all over, it's not begun." His fiery rhetoric and passion energized the students, especially "I will go to hell before I stop fighting him [Hoxie]."

It was agreed that once again there would be another march across the Brooklyn Bridge, this time to appeal publicly and privately to John Lindsay, the Mayor, asking him to intervene as he had the authority to do. The students were also asked to write to the Board of Higher Education, the governing body of CUNY. Each student was given the names and addresses of the CUNY Board members and a sample letter to help expedite the process.

The March 1st *New York Times* reported (exactly six years from the date of Conolly's death) that the day before, February 29th, "eight hundred rain-soaked students

from Long Island University's Brooklyn Center demonstrated near City Hall yesterday to protest the proposed sale of their Campus to City University. Chanting, 'Save L.I.U.,' the students marched up and down Murray Street...while a
six member delegation met for an hour with Deputy Mayor Robert W. Sweet and
David S. Seeley, the Mayor's educational liaison officer." That rally had begun on
the Brooklyn side of the bridge with an address by James Farmer, the former head
of the Congress of Racial Equalities (CORE) from the Bedford-Stuyvesant area.

When the students were unable to meet with Mayor Lindsay, they held an im-
promptu meeting and decided to conduct a vigil-around the clock if necessary-
until Lindsay agreed to see them. The vigil was a bust-the cold rain drove virtually
all the students indoors without ever seeing the Mayor. But the Mayor's office
was listening, not necessarily to the wet, bedraggled students, but to the phalanx
of Brooklyn politicians who had lined up against this sale and whose voices were
critical to the Mayor's future political ambitions.

All of a sudden Hoxie found himself in the cross fire yet again. The Post faculty
became a new political force, highly concerned about the sale and rampant gossip about the lack of adequate cash to maintain the University's momentum. At a
well-attended faculty meeting, Post faculty called for retrenchment, including selling Hoxie's elegant "mansion" and the former Tenney estate, which had become
the Administration Center (now Bush-Brown Hall). Martin Buskin again wrote
a scathing op-ed against Hoxie in *Newsday* on March 4th. "Something has to be
drastically wrong with a university when the C.W. Post College faculty protests
cuts in its budget and calls for the sale of the LIU Chancellor's home and administrative headquarters; when a member of the university board of Trustees sues that
same board to stop the Brooklyn sale; when an LIU law school dean quits his post
before a projected law school is even built; and when a legislator files bills aimed
at curbing the power of a private board of Trustees after investigating the LIU situation." His damning broadside challenged the Regents to "take seriously their role
as guardians of all education in the state-both public and private."

Picket to stop LIU sale

The status of the Brooklyn Center of Long Island University still remains in doubt. Gordon Hoxie, the chancellor of LIU, maintains that the sale of the center to the City University is merely a formality because preliminary negotiations between the two parties have already been completed. The Board of Higher Education of the City University, however, has refused to put the item on its agenda.

Dr. Hildreth Kritzer, chairman of the center's chapter of the United Federation of College Teachers, claims that she is concerned lest the board postpone consideration of the pending sale until the summer when, with professors and students recessed for vacation, it will be extremely difficult to mobilize a campaign to save the campus.

On March 25, approximately 100 faculty and students picketed the Board of Higher Education while another 350 held a rally on the campus in an attempt to pressure the City University to take up the matter now. They urged affirmation of informal statements previously made by board members to the effect that they were not interested in purchasing the center because of the ill will and bad publicity such a move would create.

The sale was not discussed at the board's meeting on March 25, nor has the item, as of this date, been placed on the agenda for its meetings in April or May.

VOTED AGAINST SALE

Sentiment is running against the sale not only at the Brooklyn Center, but also the Brookville (C. W. Post) and Southampton campuses of LIU. Late in March, a university-wide senate voted overwhelmingly against the sale of the Brooklyn Center and, in turn, charged a committee to look into the possibility of affiliating all three campuses with the state university system.

Difficulties at the C. W. Post campus are now building up to crisis proportions. On February 21 the faculty voted at a mass meeting to urge the trustees to sell the chancellor's "opulent" residence and a lavishly appointed administration building as the first step of a university-wide austerity program. The faculty was agitated because the chancellor and trustees had substantially cut departmental budgets.

If the Brooklyn Center should be sold, the Post campus would have to absorb most of the former's 101 tenured faculty. As a result, nontenured faculty at Post are concerned for their jobs. Hence it is becoming easier to mobilize sentiment against the administration on the Brookville campus.

It was almost exactly a year ago that the faculties of the Brooklyn and Southampton campuses voted "no confidence" in the chancellor. In the face of such a vote, Hoxie has not only remained in office, but is evidently more secure in his job than he was a year ago.

Published Monthly by the United Federation of College Teachers

action

VOL. V, NO. 6   APRIL, 1968

Reproduced from the monthly publication, Action,
from the United Federation of Teachers, April, 1968.

The Post faculty also targeted the administration because of the costs. A Post faculty member, Lawrence Ritt, the university Chair of the faculty Finance Committee, sought a meeting with Arthur Roth, maintaining that they should replace the University Senate Finance Committee with his. "The imminent sale of the Brooklyn Center and the necessarily limited extent of the Southampton Campus's contribution to the University's administrative overhead, have the practical effect of making Long Island University's financial problems mainly (and almost exclusively) the concern of the Merriweather Campus. Since the members of the University Senate who sit for the Brooklyn Center represent a vanishing constituency, it would clearly be realistic for Mr. Roth to meet with our committee, rather than the Senate's."

A few days later on April 2nd, Ritt wrote Hoxie a second time: "I think it would make for a franker exchange of views if our discussion could be held with Mr. Roth alone, and am accordingly accepting your offer to arrange a meeting at which *you* and the University treasurer would not be present." In forwarding this message on to Roth, Hoxie wrote Roth on the 4th of April, "you will recall that you received a telegram from him following his proposal to sell the Chancellor's residence, Long Island University's Administration Centre and the W.E. Hutton property." Hoxie lobbied to maintain his own home and the Hutton residence and he noted to Roth, "it would be inappropriate to sell the valuable and strategically located Long Island University's Administration Centre contiguous as it is to New York Institute of Technology's six hundred acres plus campus, particularly with the prospects of New York Institute Technology's close relationship with Long Island University." As a personal aside, he added that, "at least one member of Professor Ritt's committee, Dr. Donald Frank, resigned in protest of the highly vindictive and unprofessional character of Professor Ritt's charges."

When the Board had met on March 11th, it noted formally that on Monday of the previous week, William Zeckendorf Sr.'s wife had died in an airplane crash. Her Air France Boeing 707, flying from Lima, Peru had crashed into a mountain on the Island of Guadalupe. Zeckendorf and his son were both at that Board meeting. For Zeckendorf Sr. this was a further, crushing blow. At that same meeting, Carleton H. Palmer resigned for reasons of health. Palmer was one of most level-headed, savvy members of the Board, and his departure came at a particularly bad time for the University. Hoxie moved that he be authorized to invite Judge Howard Hogan to fill that vacancy, noting "Judge Hogan's singular service to the University in connection with its establishment in Brookville." The Judge had a close and longstanding involvement; he was one of the strongest proponents for a Law School, although that was not mentioned at the Board meeting. Hoxie's motion was unanimously carried.

As might be expected, the Board focused much attention on the sale of the Brooklyn campus, particularly the dynamics of how the City of New York reached a decision that involved the expenditure of funds. The Mayor had four Board of Estimate votes, while eight others were split between the City Council Presidents and the Comptroller. In effect, the funds for the purchase had to be approved out of the capital budget of the City; both Assemblyman Kottler and Assemblywoman Shirley Chisholm, the future Congresswoman, sought to derail the sale either by getting the Board of Higher Education to reverse itself or at the next rung, a vote to deny by Board of Estimate.

Hoxie, meanwhile, remained an endlessly optimistic entrepreneur. At this meeting, he was looking to win approval for an arrangement with the owners of New York Institute of Technology, then a proprietary school located immediately adjacent to University Center and less than a quarter mile from the Post Campus. NYIT was owned by Dr. Alexander Schure. He also owned hundreds of acres adjacent to the

Post campus. Hoxie had written to Roth and McGrath, raising the question whether NYIT would want to keep a distinct corporate identity, even if it entered into an agreement similar to the one negotiated years before with the Brooklyn College of Pharmacy. Such a management agreement would, at the minimum, shift the administrative services and facilities management on a fee for contract basis to LIU. Moreover, Schure was prepared to offer employment "to large numbers of the Long Island University Brooklyn Center faculty and staff." Hoxie concluded his memo, "All of the foregoing offer great promise. President Schure and Executive Vice President Theobald, and two leading members of their board would like to meet with both of you and myself at a mutually convenient time and place at a date as early as possible."

Meanwhile, the All-University Faculty Senate was still attempting to assess the future impact on the University and its campuses of Kottler's efforts. It passed two resolutions worth noting. The first was, "That under whatever aegis, whether State, City, private or Long Island University, the Brooklyn Center should remain intact as a unit dedicated to serve its special role." The second resolution put the University Senate in favor of talks bringing together the University Senate, the Board of Regents and Trustees to seek some form of affiliation between other campuses of Long Island University and SUNY. The Post faculty was worried about competition both from SUNY Stony Brook and, Post's immediate neighbor to the south, SUNY, Old Westbury. Long Island University was dissolving as a corporate entity, and different groups and factions were seeking for themselves the most positive restructuring option.

Hoxie wrote to McGrath on March 25th, suggesting that McGrath and May Davie reach out to Governor Rockefeller. "Both the Governor's office and the Mayor's office should, I believe, be made appreciative of the fact that the transfer of Long Island University's Brooklyn Center to the City University of New York will make possible the critically needed opportunity for education for minority groups, which both the Governor and the Mayor are concerned with."

On April 1st, Edward Clark, reached out to Hoxie privately, but sympathetically. "It has always been evident, to those willing to take an objective view, that your one interest since assuming the Chancellorship has been to make Long Island University into a truly great university." Taking Hoxie's side in the battle with Birenbaum, he continued, "Last year you suffered vilification and indignities because another placed personal ambition above your vision of the university's future." He then presented options, even though the Brooklyn faculty had already voted many of them down.

There was a growing level of fatigue and ill-will bubbling to the surface throughout Brooklyn. The March 28th *Seawanhaka* issue reported that the faculty had passed unanimously a resolution calling upon the City University to break off negotiations. By a vote of sixty-five to fifteen, the faculty also defeated a series of austerity measures proposed by Ed Clark. Elsewhere in that same issue was an article entitled, "Physics Chairman Faces Defecation of Character." "Some people have suggested that Physics Chairman Edward Clark is full of it. Last Friday he got an envelope that was. Clark responded that, he could not imagine who would have done something of that nature but it was 'indicative of the climate prevalent here.'"

That issue also reported on how forty students greeted Hoxie who held a meeting on campus chanting, "Hoxie must go." But, this time the student turnout for Save LIU Day protest demonstrations on Wall Street, at the 42nd Street Library, at Grand Central, at Baruch College, at A&S, and elsewhere across the City, was underwhelming. James Farmer, the former head of CORE, spoke only to a small crowd. Another modestly small group marched to the CUNY Central headquarters on 80th Street. As *Seawanhaka* reported it, "unexpected support arose inside one of the Board offices. Someone apparently inspired by the chants of 'Save LIU,' put a handwritten cardboard sign in an office window facing the demonstrators which read: 'Jesus-Save LIU.'"

On April 11th, Hoxie received a letter from Mayor Lindsay who finally clarified his position in this long-playing tale. The Mayor wrote, "I have carefully considered the educational needs of our City and feel that the Long Island University-Brooklyn Center is an essential resource." Arguing that LIU provided a unique service, he continued, "I have advised Chancellor Bowker that I will strongly support the location of the Baruch School in the Atlantic Terminal urban renewal area. I am hopeful that in the light of this decision you, the Trustees, the students, and the faculty of Long Island University work to develop the strength of the Brooklyn Center."

He ended his letter by offering a politician's promise, "to work with you to maintain it as a growing educational resource in our City." As *The New York Times* correspondent noted, "he did not say how." This story also made page one of *The Times*. The following day, John McGrath issued a statement on behalf of the University suggesting that, "Mayor Lindsay may have been victimized by a lot of misinformation...." Hoxie and McGrath called an emergency meeting of the Executive Committee to review a draft response to the Mayor. That letter would be dated April 24th with a view to release it to the press on April 25th.

Lindsay's decision was a bolt out of the blue. The senior CUNY administration and its Board had not wavered, at least publicly. The Board of Regents had overruled its professional staff and seemed clear in its decision. Rockefeller had been approached and given tacit approval. The opposition of Kottler and the Joint Committee had seemingly been neutralized. But Lindsay did control those four votes on the Board of Estimate and his decision profoundly changed the equation. Moreover, his notion of building a major new CUNY campus a few blocks from the existing Brooklyn site meant that financially strapped but academically solid students would flock to the spanking new facilities, at the expense of Long Island University enrollment. And if, as had been widely rumored, the City University moved to true Open Enrollment, the scales would tilt even more traumatically toward the public sector. Lindsay's vague offer to help LIU was the type of a promise which had very little credibility at the bank window. Increasingly, there was little likelihood with both the State and City University systems absorbing whatever capital funding there might be, especially if the City University was building, cheek to jowl, a major new campus at Atlantic Terminal.

Hoxie reached out to Chancellor McGovern, the newly elected head of the Board of Regents. He reached out to Carl Pforzheimer and to James Allen, seeking, if possible, to find an ally who would talk the Mayor out of his decision. At his Cabinet Meeting on April 23rd, he tried to spin the defeat, noting, "no one was talking of closing the Brooklyn Center, but they were talking about the best means of preserving the Center, whether this would be as a private, public, or quasi-public unit." The seven-page letter drafted by Hoxie, jointly signed by McGrath and himself, tried to convince Lindsay that he had made a mistake. The points had been well developed over the previous months. "The future of the Brooklyn Center is indeed threatened. This threat comes from inexorable forces, inherent in the economics of higher education, which endanger our continued existence within a few short years if we do not move now to counteract these forces." The need for substantial capital investment was again detailed. "It is axiomatic that no institution of higher education can operate successfully on tuition income alone." The advantages of an early sale of an existing campus were paraded in contradistinction to the decade plus building a new campus on an undeveloped site. And finally, there was a plea to meet with Lindsay face to face on this important subject. The letter went through multiple drafts before it was finally sent, but there was little change in its structure or content.

Hoxie appealed to Arthur Ochs Sulzberger, asking him, in particular, to assign one of his education reporters, Myron Farber, to treat this story "in depth, if given the go ahead" by you. And in a letter to his friend Arthur Jensen at Dartmouth, Hoxie wrote, "it would appear that the wisdom of the Board of Regents may be set aside by the intervention of the politicians...." Hoxie had a new slant. In a letter to Farber, Hoxie underscored the need to address the immediate needs of disadvantaged and minority students rather than wait for a new institution slowly to be designed and developed. In a second letter to Sulzberger, he maintained the issue was "still timely and newsworthy and the detailed treatment in *The Times* would be of crucial importance."

But *Seawanhaka*, in its April 24nd issue, had as its lead, "Joy was the word at the Brooklyn Center this week in the wake of Mayor Lindsay's surprise announcement of his opposition to the sale of the school."

On the following day, of greater immediate significance, were the demands suddenly issued by a small group of black students in an organization, called SOBU (Student Organization for Black Unity), with the rallying cry: "when you mess with one black man or woman you are messing with *all* black people." Suddenly, there were non-negotiable demands including an office with telephones and typewriters for militant black student groups, a space "for a liberation school for our people, [and] a permanent meeting room." The group demanded a black curriculum. Mimicking minority student unrest at Columbia, the students seized the Provost's office with the Provost William "Buck" Lai inside, declaring it a black holiday in Brooklyn. There were fifteen students and Lai stayed with them until they finally decided to let him go that evening.

That same day the University was celebrating its Charter Day Ball at the Waldorf Astoria, the 42nd anniversary of the founding of the University. The black students demanded to meet with Hoxie, Lai, and others to review their six demands, including "total amnesty" for their actions. The meeting took place following the Charter Day function at the St. George Hotel at 11:30 in the evening. The students' demands for a black curriculum and more scholarships were approved in the wee hours of the morning, but as *The New York Times* reported on April 26th, most of the 7,000 students had no role in the protest, even as onlookers, and many seemed more preoccupied with the electioneering campaign for campus offices than with the mobilization of black student power. This unrest, however, gained national press coverage and suddenly Long Island University realized that like other universities across the country, it too had to redefine how to enroll, retain and educate minority students.

There were collateral consequences in Brooklyn. The Borough was clearly in economic decline and the decision to try to sell the campus with its iconic Brooklyn Paramount was a further rejection of a once proud place. Admiral Conolly had convinced the leadership of Mays Department store whose flagship store was located just up the street from The Brooklyn Center, to take an active role in the life of the campus. He successfully asked the CEO Max Shulman to join the Board of Governors of the Brooklyn campus. On April 29th, Shulman resigned noting, "it was my understanding that the Board would act as an advisor and consultant body to the then President of the University." He was angered, quite reasonably, because his opinion was never sought on a matter as sensitive as the further erosion of the autonomy of Brooklyn itself. So he found "it necessary to submit my resignation as a member of said Board, effective immediately." Hoxie responded, telling him that his "forthright good letter…is a cause of some considerable distress." Schulman responded back to Hoxie that his "decision to resign…was made only after careful review and earnest consideration…It did not seem prudent then, nor do I deem it advisable now, to delve further into the reasons for my action."

Hoxie must have understood that his own career was in grave jeopardy if Lindsay could not be reached to change his mind. Through Trustees and other surrogates, he attempted to lobby the Mayor. Once again, the most lucid letter was written by George Shapiro. It was direct, candid, and without hyperbole. It began, "This is a personal letter....I do not know who advised you on Long Island University program, but to those of us familiar with the problem the decision is a disaster-for the University, for the City, and the underprivileged young people in the Brooklyn area." Shapiro argued that, "It would enable City University to move quickly in creating major new educational opportunities for the non-white population in Brooklyn. Under the Atlantic Terminal plan, the City University program in Brooklyn will be set back from five to ten years." There followed five succinct points. Shapiro put a P.S. at the end of his letter. "After dictating this letter, I learned from Porter Chandler that City University has set a deadline of *12:00 noon, Friday May 3rd*, for announcing the withdrawal from negotiations for the takeover of the site."

Bowker's office sent an advance copy of the proposed resolution to go before the Board of Higher Education, indicating that CUNY would "decline to consider the purchase of the Brooklyn Center Campus of Long Island University...." That formal offer from Hoxie, which had been before CUNY for so many months, was now firmly to be rejected. A second provision to be voted on by the Trustees of the City University charged its Committee on Planning and Development to "consider the location of the Baruch College in the Atlantic Terminal Urban Renewal area."

Seawanhaka in its May 2nd issue, reported that, the "students had demanded the resignation of Chancellor Hoxie and the Board of Trustees' Chairman, John P. Mc-Grath, by passing out leaflets at the annual Charter Day Dinner last Thursday." The paper called on McGrath to resign because "the sale has failed." Maintaining that McGrath himself had staked his position on a successful sale, the paper quoted him as indicating that he would resign if it were blocked. Steve Fishbein, just elected President of the Student Government Association, had been barred from the dais by George Shapiro after Fishbein wanted to rebut "McGrath's lies." Shapiro is reported to have threatened him, "you better get away from here, kid." He successfully did keep the student from trying to seize the microphone.

Elsewhere in that edition was a story of a teach-in in which "the Vietnam War, racism, and politics-all interrelated issues, were thrashed out" at an all day International Student Strike for Peace. Another story detailed how the sophomore class President at Brooklyn, Shawn Bayer, was jailed during a Columbia University protest. National issues certainly had reached into Brooklyn by 1968.

There is a fascinating letter from Hoxie to Arthur Ochs Sulzberger, dated May 3rd. It is not the letter that was finally sent that is of historical interest, but rather the anger in Hoxie's earlier draft, before his staff, wife or others were able to soften his prose. Consider this paragraph. "The intervention of the Mayor of the City of New York and other politicians into a matter which the Board of Regents of the

State of New York had faithfully studied for so many months, the failure of the City University to wait a few days until a committee of the Long Island University Board of Trustees had an opportunity to see the Mayor and express their position, the subjection of the Board of Higher Education to harassment and political pressures to such an extent as to force that Board's Executive Committee to reverse its position-all point up a little understood part of the higher educational crisis of our time." There is a paragraph in the final letter, for example, in which he indicated to Sulzberger that what he had written was not a "letter to the editor" submitted for publication, "but rather of appreciation for your [Sulzberger's] understanding." Whoever intervened, the actual letter sent was polite and non-inflammatory.

When Hoxie tried to meet the Brooklyn faculty soon after Lindsay's decision became public, students broke the meeting up. During a brief confrontation, according to *The New York Times*, one student "grabbed the microphone away from the Chancellor." That student, Phil Brown, was President of the Students for a Democratic Society. The meeting was supposed to be closed to outsiders, but about 200 students took the meeting over and Hoxie was forced to slip out, according to the *Newsday* reporter. The students were chanting, "Hoxie must go."

To make matters yet more complicated, on Friday, May 3rd, Hoxie and several Trustees felt obliged to meet with Floyd McKissick, the national Chairman of CORE, as well as other Brooklyn leaders and two lawyers, to explore CORE's offer to the LIU Board to buy the Brooklyn campus for the same $32 million CUNY had offered to pay. CORE wanted "to operate the Brooklyn Center as a black university offering courses in black culture, African languages, history, etc." It wanted to provide its own faculty, administration and staff, stating that it was important for black students to see "a black man in a position of authority," as Frank McGrath's Minutes memorialized the discussion.

Both Hoxie and Ed Neimuth asked if CORE would be interested at a much lower price in buying the College of Pharmacy facility at 600 Lafayette Avenue. The cost for that building would be $1,250,000. There was discussion whether CORE could buy any property without first being chartered by the Board of Regents. McKissick was comfortable that the Regents would pose no problem. The University also made clear that the commitments to the faculty, students, and staff made during the discussions with CUNY would have to be honored or, at least, renegotiated. McKissick, at one point, wanted the Brooklyn campus leased to this new university for a dollar a year.

On May 8th, Lindsay finally met with John McGrath, George Shapiro and Hoxie at Gracie Mansion. Lindsay pledged his wholehearted support to helping the University succeed in Brooklyn, according to Hoxie, who had no option but to feel "encouraged." Lindsay specifically agreed to give his "full assistance…to the quest… for private funds… to enable the Brooklyn Center to maintain and expand its programs." He did follow through at least once by writing to McGeorge Bundy for support from the Ford Foundation.

To compound Hoxie's sea of troubles, Acting Provost Buck Lai resigned on May 7th, declining to become the full time Provost in Brooklyn. Lai had been popular. He was a straight arrow, a great student athlete, a leader in the class of 1941, an active alumnus, well respected by the faculty and much liked by the students. He had no personal agenda and was calm, fair and candid. But he was an Athletic Director, not a scholar. He did not pretend to have research credentials, and the baroque quality of faculty politics was not an environment in which he wanted to dwell. For LIU, Lai had been a stabilizing influence during a chaotic period. His decision to return to his prior position as Athletic Director widened the gap between University Center in Brookville and everyone who worked on the Brooklyn campus.

At the Board meeting of May 13th, Hoxie briefed the Board on all that had happened. He stated that the lack of political support from the Mayor and the Brooklyn political establishment had undermined the commitment of the Board of Higher Education, and led Bowker and his Board to decline further consideration of the Brooklyn Center as a future home for Baruch.

There was also a full discussion of the CORE offer, even assuming that it could actually raise the necessary $32,000,000. CORE's mission statement represented a "radical departure from educational policies in the State." McKissick wanted to establish a completely black institution. The University Board maintained that it was against any segregation in education "whether it be black or white and it deemed the Bowker plan for increased enrollment of black students at the Brooklyn Center as preferable to an all Negro college." The Board thus rejected further discussion with CORE. Hoxie turned the Board's attention quickly to a possible affiliation of some sort with the New York Institute of Technology. Hoxie had been exploring expansionist opportunities for C.W. Post, even while Brooklyn was broadside in very heavy seas.

The next day, Buck Lai addressed the last faculty meeting of the year. His formal remarks are very interesting because of his candor. He wrote, "On April 5, 1967, I was appointed the Acting Provost of the Brooklyn Center to serve until June 1, 1967, approximately a period of seven weeks. A year has passed since that time." He continued, "The campus was in a state of turmoil when I arrived and you are as much or more familiar with the reasons for this disturbance as I am….Briefly, from the time I came to the Brooklyn Center things went from bad to worse-from the 'frying pan into the fire.'" Then he spoke of the need to establish-or re-establish-"a system of orderly behavior." He summarized his position, "Frankly, I am tired of fighting academic brush fires while the future plans of our academic world remain obscure and undefined."

President of the Ford Foundation, McGeorge Bundy, with permission of The Rockefeller Archive Center.

On May 15th, Hoxie received a letter from the Mayor who indicated that he would "be in touch with McGeorge Bundy and do everything that I can to assist the Brooklyn Division of Long Island University." Hoxie had asked Lindsay specifically if "he could secure a $10 million grant from the Ford Foundation for Long Island University's Brooklyn Center, particularly in support of its community service programs, including the substantial enlargement of a scholarship aid for minority students."

He wrote back to the Mayor on May 20th about Ford's $35 million gift to Columbia, which had included $10 million specifically for community services. McGeorge Bundy had then pointed out "the urgent need of strengthening the services of private higher education in urban centers." Hoxie had sent Lindsay a copy of *Preface to the Future* with his May 8th letter and a copy of his Commencement Remarks with this second letter.

Whenever Hoxie was profoundly angry or felt he had been dealt a poor hand, his ornate prose revealed his inner turmoil. "So very much I am heartened by your desire to sit down with McGeorge Bundy and seek aid for the Brooklyn Center of Long Island University. So very earnestly, I hope that some good word in this regard might be received by me prior to the commencement of the Brooklyn Center, Tuesday, June 4th. Nothing could be more inspiring on such an occasion than word from you that you had been successful in securing aid for the Center." Of course, it is essential to remember that the Ford Foundation had already rejected a major grant to Long Island University after Hoxie had solicited the Chair of the Foundation Board. The likelihood that the Mayor, could and would deliver a major gift on such short notice and despite the baggage of that prior effort was extremely remote. But Hoxie was trapped; his career was in a death loop.

On May 24th, Governor Rockefeller wrote to Commissioner of the Department of Education James Allen, approving "the amendment to the City University Master Plan in regard to the conversion and expansion of the Baruch School into the Bernard M. Baruch College to be located in downtown Brooklyn." He urged that the Department of Education work closely with the City University and private colleges in downtown Brooklyn "in order to foster cooperative arrangements with regards to academic programs, library collections, computer capacity, specialized technical facilities, educational television, and other areas of potential economies." Rockefeller noted that Brooklyn would be an ideal testing site for such inter-institutional cooperation "because of the many colleges which are or will be located in close proximity to one another." He ended the letter "I withhold commitment on the possible acquisition of the Brooklyn Center of Long Island University by City University."

Jim Allen subsequently sent a copy of Rockefeller's letter to Hoxie, who expressed Long Island University's continuing opposition to locating Baruch at the Atlantic Terminal site. Hoxie said, placing Baruch so near to LIU, "exacerbates rather than removes the critical problems facing the private sector of high education in the Brooklyn area...."

That same day Hoxie wrote to Frank McGrath, including a copy of both Rockefeller's letter and his response. Hoxie seized upon what he interpreted as an ambivalent statement from Rockefeller about the sale of the Brooklyn campus to City University. "It would appear that as far as the governor is concerned that that [sic] yet remains a possibility."

The Brooklyn Commencement was on June 4th. Hoxie entitled his remarks as "Our Destiny at the Brooklyn Center." He used this opportunity to make a defense of his actions in Brooklyn for the previous year, however inappropriate the forum. With a tin ear, he began his remarks by talking about the *Preface to the Future* and by quoting Deane Malott, once again celebrating the quality of the plans. He then talked at some length about the City University's plan to move to Brooklyn, and the role of Henry Heald.

More interior monologue than Commencement address, this was a classic apologia. He talked about his support for a great new library. He quoted McGeorge Bundy's comments about Columbia's commitment to the community around it. He proposed moving to Division I of the NCAA. He told the students and their families that he was working with "national and local leaders of the black community." He even announced, "I cannot lead...from Nassau County and I intend to reoccupy, effective July 1st, my Brooklyn Center office." On page nine of this Commencement address, he shared, "Yes, there have been times when I have been discouraged..." And finally he ended with a two line quote from St. Paul to the Apostle Timothy.

Not surprisingly, he was hissed by hundreds of students wearing "Resign" buttons. Brooklyn graduated a record number of 1,584 students. It was a humiliating experience. The head of Student Council, Jay Dravich, handed Hoxie a "Resign" button as he entered the Albee Theater near the campus. "When Dravich handed me a button, as I walked into the theater, I was taken aback a little," Hoxie later said.

The last issue of the student newspaper for the year reported that Hoxie would be his own Acting Provost in Brooklyn until one was selected in August. Among the candidates was Major General Alden Kingsland Sibley, who had become a very close friend of Hoxie's. The Chancellor was extraordinarily keen to land him one job or another at the University, but sending a career military officer and a close personal friend into Brooklyn at that particular time had to be the height of folly. The school newspaper further reported that the Alumnus of the Year, an award given in the name of Tristram Walker Metcalfe, went to Dr. Alan Livingston, the Trustee who had sued his fellow Trustees over the possible sale of Brooklyn. As Buck Lai had trenchantly observed, "things went from bad to worse." Even Commencement had a pall cast upon it.

The removal of Dr. R. Gordon Hoxie from his present position... will preclude future support from us in any way whatsoever.

Marjorie Merriweather Post, and Adelaide Close Riggs

Chapter Eight

Hoxie's Demise

Gordon Hoxie was an advocate of the "willing suspension of disbelief." His Chancellorship was in tatters and his career in higher education under the gravest threat, yet he carried on as if every thing was going wonderfully. Did he believe the press releases he wrote or approved? He clearly saw himself as a "Christian soldier" marching forward in defense of traditional values and Admiral Conolly's dream. There is no evidence he was plagued by self-doubt or uncertainty about himself or his priorities for the institution. And he took great pride in being a fighter, someone whose optimism and belief in the righteousness of his mission constantly drove him forward.

A few days after the Brooklyn Commencement, he wrote to Henry Heald. He ended his letter, "All of these commencement remarks to date were, I am glad to say, received with enthusiasm, even including those in Brooklyn, and both Chairman McGrath and I were most heartened. On to Southampton tomorrow!" He noted further, "Bishop Edwin B. Broderick delivered an inspiring address, in which, to my amazement, he took as his text a portion of my annual report to the Board of Trustees. Perhaps this is the first time a sermon has been so constructed." His writing to Heald, who had been seriously ill, was more than gossip or good wishes for a speedy recovery. Heald still owed his written report to the Board.

On July 1st, there was a meeting in New York, including Heald himself, Jesse Hobson and Roger Sheldon, together with John McGrath and Trustees Collado, Neimuth, Pell and Skouras. Hoxie and Stoddard also participated. Hoxie wrote to Heald on July 3rd, "It is heartening to note the general agreement regarding the future organization of the University." Once again, one of the central topics was the organizational structure of the University, including, particularly, the graduate deans. Hoxie noted, "There is general agreement that the graduate deans must have greater academic and fiscal responsibility and that they and the undergraduate deans should report directly to the officer now termed the Vice Chancellor for Academic Affairs. There is additionally general agreement with you the office of the Provost would be eliminated under this structure." He observed, "I am glad to say that my return to my office there [Brooklyn] is warmly greeted." "Please be assured," he concluded, "of my wholehearted, continued desire to be of assistance to you, Jesse and Roger, in this significant report which you are preparing on the future organization of the University."

On July 9th he wrote Mayor Lindsay, still prodding him to seek the assistance of McGeorge Bundy on behalf of the Brooklyn Center. "Your letter of May 15, 1968 assured me that you had this very much in mind, and I am hopeful that you have now had an opportunity to do so and may have some encouragement in this regard." And then, in classic Hoxie style, he was suddenly lobbying the Mayor "regarding the possible removal of certain gasoline stations which might be replaced by an attractive vest-pocket park" adjacent to the campus.

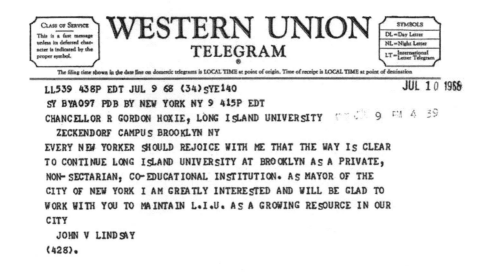

*Facsimile of Mayor John Lindsay's telegram to
Long Island University promising his support.*

Meanwhile, the files contain a series of letters from members of the Board of Governors of the Brooklyn campus who resigned from that council. Walter R. Miller, the President of the East Brooklyn Savings Bank, resigned on July 3rd. On July 9th, the Chairman, Abner Grossman, tendered his resignation, claiming the press of business of kept him from giving the University the time and attention it deserved. Yet despite this erosion of leadership, *Newsday* reported on July 11th that LIU was launching a $17 million fundraising campaign for the Brooklyn campus after a "kick off meeting of 50" Brooklyn businessmen. $9.5 million would be sought from federal and state grants, $5 million would be debt, and $2.5 million would come from private sources. The funds would be used for a new library, four new laboratories and additional scholarships. Hoxie told this group that "there's been a drying up of federal funds lately," according to *Newsday*, but he hoped this would change.

The article quoted Hoxie as having previously said, "the low rate of gifts to the Brooklyn campus meant that, 'barring a miracle,' the campus would have to close if it was not sold." *Newsday* also quoted him as saying that "things are different now," maintaining, "the fight over the sale has increased interest in the campus." Having acknowledged that federal funds were drying-up, Hoxie quoted Lindsay's pledge to help. A University press release listed approximately a dozen corporate leaders, in attendance, including Richard Aldrich, the Vice President of International Basic Economy Corporation, Walter Miller (who had just resigned), Frederick Richmond and Paul Screvane, the long-time politician who was then Vice President of Maclean Service Corporation.

Seawanhaka was publishing every two weeks during the summer. The July 11th issue observed both that Hoxie, who said he would be on the Brooklyn campus two days a week, was very scarce and that his commitment to a search committee for the new Provost had not been met, even though there was an August 15th deadline. The Student Government President, Steve Fischbein, felt that Hoxie was intending to name "Major General Alden Sibley provost. Sibley has already met with the committee in the company of the Chancellor last month." Fischbein was quoted as saying, "I think he [Hoxie] is going to try to ram Sibley down our throats, but we won't stand for that." Two weeks later the paper reported that there were six candidates for Provost, who would meet the following week with the search committee.

Normally, history does not focus on those who are passed over for a position, but Hoxie's relationship with General Alden Kingsland Sibley, "Sib," was remarkable, revealing a different dimension to his personality. Sibley was a career army officer who won a Rhodes scholarship to Oxford after West Point, before World War II. He earned a doctorate in nuclear physics in the fifties. He was a favorite of Marjorie Merriweather Post and either he or his wife was related to her; a Julia Sibley officiating at her Memorial service. The General usually referred to Mrs. Post as Aunt Marjorie. By 1957, he was a brigadier general who had served during war and peace all over the world. He and Hoxie developed a close friendship and corresponded virtually every second or third day with the other. Hoxie tried to hire him at the University for any number of senior jobs and asked him to help get C.W Post College designated an ROTC site. Among many requests, Hoxie asked his friend, then stationed in St. Louis, to secure a large grant from the Danforth Foundation to help fund *Preface to the Future*.

Sibley seemed to be everything Hoxie wanted to be. He was aware of his charm, comfortable with his capacity to move through all strata of society with ease. He was handsome, athletic and charismatic. Sibley was popular, always chosen as "the most likely to succeed" by a senior class; Hoxie was the nerdy manager of the football team. Sibley had lived for years in Grosse Point, inheriting a level of privilege that Hoxie craved. He was on first name basis with the high and the mighty. Their friendship and those letters echoed *The Great Gatsby.*

In St Louis, the general was the commanding officer of the XI Army Corps. It was a retirement job. For whatever reason, he had been passed over for command in Vietnam. He did not know what the next phase of his life would be and was obviously flattered by Hoxie's position and interest. Hoxie offered Sibley something new and different at Long Island University, just as Zeckendorf had for Admiral Conolly. Many of their hundreds of letters were without significant import - almost military exchanges, factual, a chronicle of possible dates to meet. But what set them apart was the frequency of the exchange itself. Both men cultivated the other. They clearly deemed the other a close friend. Sibley was intrigued by the possibility of a significant University appointment after his retirement from active service.

The general attended the dedication of the Merriweather Campus; Hoxie sent his car and driver to fetch him. Sibley tried to get Hoxie to an event in St. Louis with Mrs. Douglas MacArthur, tempting him to ride back to New York on a private plane. Sibley in another letter casually spoke of hoping to see the Hoxies at Top Ridge, Mrs. Post's Adirondack estate. He noted to Hoxie that he and his wife, Ellie, would be driving over from his farm in Maine and would be staying at the Post estate for a week. In September 1967, Hoxie set up a lunch for Sibley to meet his staff. He clearly had spoken to Sibley by that time because on the 16th of October, 1967, Sibley wrote back that the two of them would be delighted to be a part of Hoxie's team "in whatever capacity you feel we could be most useful." He casually ended the letter with an invitation to the Hoxies to dine in Manhattan at Pavillon, at the time the most expensive restaurant in New York.

By the 24th of November, Sibley was gushing about the visit to Hoxie's home in Old Westbury, including the dedication of the chapel at which the Verdi requiem was sung. He wrote to the Hoxies, "We eagerly look forward to the day when we are associated and become part of the splendid University team." They met in Acapulco that year for Christmas break. Favored Post students like Ron Sylvestri got stationed at Fort Dix in New Jersey rather than South Carolina because General Sibley intervened at Hoxie's request.

And so the correspondence went back and forth. There is a long letter dealing with how to position C.W. Post in the best possible light to become an ROTC unit, one of fifteen in a pool of just under thirty. In March 1968, Hoxie set up a meeting for Sibley to meet Arthur Roth, the Chair of the Finance Committee, proposing that he become Vice President for Business. This new position, Hoxie explained on March 11th "was not to supplant or replace our able, dedicated Treasurer Mrs. Mary Lai, but rather to have an officer overall in charge of our business, financial, buildings and grounds, auxiliary enterprises, and other aspects of the thirty five million dollar annual budget and a seventy five million dollar physical plant." Mrs. Lai responded very negatively, as one might expect, indicating that she was fully up to the job. She counter-proposed to Hoxie that Sibley be considered for the job of Vice Chancellor of University Relations. Not wanting to leave Mrs. Lai angry, he concurred and proposed to Arthur Roth and John McGrath that Sibley become Vice Chancellor for University Relations.

Sibley was asked by Hoxie to speak to his friends at Monsanto to secure AstroTurf for the C.W. Post football field. The CEO of Monsanto responded to Sibley that the corporation was unprepared to donate any AstroTurf, because it did not want to encourage solicitation by other colleges, even though the professional teams were all rapidly moving to convert their fields from natural to artificial turf.

Meanwhile, Sibley indicated he would be delighted to accept becoming Vice Chancellor of University Relations, commenting in a letter of March 27th, "Believe me, it's increasingly harder for me to keep on soldiering these last few months with my life-long dream of an academic career about to be realized." By mid-May Hoxie was bringing Sibley into discussions with the Zeckendorfs, father and son, Emilio Collado, Franz Schneider, John H.G. Pell and Mrs. Preston Davie. Sibley was sending Hoxie a long list of individuals who could serve as references, including McGeorge Bundy at the Ford Foundation, Dean Rusk, Edward Teller, and a Who's Who of America's most powerful people, including Henry Ford, Dwight Eisenhower, General Maxwell Taylor, Governors, Senators, and other people prominent both present and past.

During this very long courtship and, perhaps, simultaneously, the former Undersecretary of the Army, Karl Bendetsen, (who was now Chair of the Board of US Plywood-Champion Paper) also offered Sibley a job. Hoxie thought Sibley should take it, perhaps indicating as early as late May 1968, that Hoxie was uncertain that he would survive in office past the early fall. Hoxie had suggested that Bendetsen's offer be accepted. Sibley, unaware of how precarious Hoxie's tenure had become, responded that if "it should not work out in the first couple of years, I could still come to you as we had planned." It was at this juncture that Hoxie suddenly thought that Sibley might be an excellent Provost, if the Joint Faculty Student Alumni Committee liked him. And so, he urged Sibley to come in to the City for another weekend. On June 4th, Sibley wrote Hoxie that Bendetsen was initially offering three times the salary and a corporate senior vice presidency within a few months of employment. He offered to withdraw from the search, if Hoxie felt that would be the better course.

Hoxie responded, merely urging Sibley to come if for no other reason than "to give the Faculty Student Alumni Committee a sense of the higher caliber person we were going after. I believe it would be very good for them." But finally, on June 24th, Sibley stopped wavering, informing Hoxie that he was accepting the position at US Plywood-Champion Paper. He may have realized how impossible it would be at the height of the Vietnam War for a recently retired General to become Provost of Brooklyn over the active opposition of both students and faculty.

After Sibley withdrew from the search, the committee recommended William Kelly, the national director of the Job Corps as its first choice and Dr. William Heston, a Vice President at Case Western Reserve University as its alternate. Neither got the job.

Sibley did agree to serve on a National Development Council for the University, despite his failed efforts to raise substantial money from either Danforth or Monsanto. Their correspondence, at least that is archived in University files, broke off with a letter written just after Hoxie had been terminated on October 18th. Hoxie penned, "For your Friendship I am grateful."

The position of Provost remained the most problematic senior management job across the University. Over the summer, Hoxie abolished the position of Provost at the Merriweather Campus (Post), claiming that the decision was based on the Heald-Hobson study. Peter Ewald was terminated, and granted a one-year administrative leave after which he was appointed as a Special Assistant to the Chancellor. The press release of July 20th did not mandate what responsibilities, if any, would be given to Ewald.

Three days later, Hoxie wrote to Heald, "I have been considerably heartened this summer by the rising state of morale throughout the University and particularly at the Brooklyn Center." In a letter to George Shapiro a few days later, he made the same claim: "I am much heartened by the greatly improved climate which has been achieved throughout Long Island University in recent weeks, and particularly at the Brooklyn Center." He went on to Shapiro, "I have been receiving expressions to put behind us past misunderstandings and to move ahead as a united team. One of the expressions of this is the desire to drop the lawsuit against the Board of Trustees, another, to drop the American Association of University Professors' inquiry. There is also a clear understanding that Dean Samuel Bieber remove himself as a candidate to be the administrative head of the Brooklyn Center, and he, I am glad to report, has done this. For his part, Dean Bieber is actively pursuing positions elsewhere and I am helping him in the regard." Hoxie was attempting to move his opponents out to ensure that by September he could trust the new Brooklyn leadership team.

On the 27th, Hoxie wrote to Harold V. Gleason at the Franklin National Bank, both saluting him at becoming Arthur Roth's successor, after a Franklin Bank Board coup, and soliciting him for an Arthur T. Roth Professorial Chair in Banking for Long Island University. He was looking for a donation of at least $600,000, which would yield $30,000 a year in interest, the goal being to establish this Chair around Roth's sixty-fifth birthday. Not surprisingly, Gleason firmly turned Hoxie down on August 9th, claiming that since Arthur Roth intended to remain active in banking, he thought it inappropriate to create a Chair in his honor at this time.

According to Roth in his autobiography, *The People's Banker*, Gleason was avoiding him prior to the Bank's July Board meeting: "I tried to get in touch with him and he was always unavailable. He has told people to have nothing to do with me; several officers have helped me, and he reprimanded them." Roth was voted off the Board at Franklin while presiding over the meeting as its Chair, in a singularly ugly way. Yet Hoxie still plowed forward in his flattery of Gleason, despite the contretemps. Arthur T. Roth had been his greatest supporter; someone who fought to protect him when most of the Board members agreed with Zeckendorf that Hoxie had to go. Roth gave Hoxie a job after he was terminated. Roth would have been mortified if he had known of Hoxie's efforts, as he saw Hoxie as a dear and close friend.

Dr. Henry Heald, with permission of The Rockefeller Archive Center.

On August 16th, Hoxie received a preliminary draft of Henry Heald's long-awaited report. After twenty-two tumultuous months, this document was the denouement of the Hoxie Chancellorship. For the next six weeks it dominated everything else that was happening on the campuses. When released in late September, it was printed in its entirety by *Seawanhaka* as a Special Supplement. It ran twelve dense pages, each of which was three columns long. It offered a scathing assessment of the University and its leadership. And yet Hoxie's response was remarkably passive. Five days later, seemingly in shock, Hoxie wrote Heald, "Very much I appreciate your invitation to me to present my 'comments and reactions' before putting it…in final form. However, I do not believe that I should suggest any changes in the report itself" beyond some statistical corrections.

On August 20th, Hoxie wrote McGrath an extraordinary letter. He seemed flummoxed. "At a cursory glance, it would appear that the report is overly pessimistic; to the best of my knowledge, the last visit to the University by Heald, Hobson and Associates was in the midst of the controversy last spring over the possible transfer of the Brooklyn Center. If they could visit the University now, I do not believe there would be such emphasis on the 'present state of crisis and controversy….'"

301

After a year of Birenbaum and another of the failed sale, Heald had ample chance to take the measure of the institution. He had seen plenty. In sum, the Heald-Hobson Report was a devastating critique of the University since Conolly's death.

Hoxie further asserted, "Their pessimism on the achievement of our ten year goals simply does not bear with past record of accomplishment of the University." He argued to his Chairman that LIU was on target to double faculty salaries in a decade as promised among the projections of *Preface to the Future*. And he then confessed, "Quite candidly, I would take issue with the picture on page six of the great power of the office of the Chancellor; this Chancellor is not seeking power but only to carry out the policies of the Board." Hoxie was somehow impervious to his impact on others, and this claim after two years of running abuse by students and faculty in Brooklyn was either simply self-serving denial or, much more probable, his psychological inability to see reality as did others.

There were seven key recommendations. The first identified the Trustees as custodians who "must assure themselves that the University is as capably administered as possible." It maintained that the Board had to receive more objective information on which to make its judgments. It summoned the Board to become "more intimately involved with the life of the University, particularly as it is experienced from the point of view of the students, faculty, and surrounding communities."

The second recommendation dealt with governance. It argued that efficiency and economy mandated a more centralized structure, in particular in its professional and graduate schools. The organs of governance "at nearly all levels have not worked well." And the relationship between the University and the several administrations needed "to be rationalized." It made the obvious point that to achieve such changes would require "a revision of the Statutes."

Echoing what both Middle States and the State of New York had been saying for more than a decade, the University needed to achieve quality "within its present commitments." The University, it argued, "should not dissipate its energies and dilute its resources by expanding programs at any level, even though seemingly attractive opportunities may present themselves."

The fourth recommendation was that the goals and objectives of the University "be realistically reformulated." Heald-Hobson argued for honesty in the financial possibilities, student talent and faculty resources. "Only with realistic goals and objectives can the University hope to build relevant programs of distinction which will create its identity and build its reputation." The fifth recommendation: "All operations of the University presently suffer because of the uneven quality of the management of the University. Improvements in the quality of the staff and the organizational structure are basic to the many other changes required." This point dealt primarily with public support and fundraising. The sixth point, the report argued, "The very large amount of public support which the University has received in the past six years and can expect to receive in the future is restricted or categorical support." It made the obvious point that the University would have to have a much greater volume of unrestricted private support, "If it is going to remove present deficiencies and cover necessary or unforeseen operating deficits in the future." It declared, "The present development program of the University is totally inadequate. This critically important area must be professionally staffed at the earliest possible moment."

The seventh and last recommendation observed that the present environment "of controversy and politicking seriously undermines the basic scholarly pursuits of the University. The root causes of this situation are complex and perhaps lie in each area where we recommend a major change. It is crucial, therefore, that these recommendations be studied carefully and fully by all."

On August 29th, Hoxie wrote in a thank you letter to Zeckendorf, how he happily celebrated the speedy recovery of the University from the nightmare of the past two years. "My own faith in the fulfillment of the ten-year goals of the University remains undiminished as does yours, and there are daily increasing evidences of an impressive support in keep with the building sense of unity of the University." In the next paragraph he came back to the identical theme, "As I indicated to you last evening, there is a splendid new sense of unity developing in both instances and the combining of the office of dean and provost on the Merriweather Campus has contributed much to this. It is believed that, in accordance with Heald-Hobson recommendations, it will likewise do so at the Zeckendorf Campus where I am especially heartened by the advent an era of good feeling, exemplified in the enclosed articles from yesterday's issue of *Seawanhaka*."

Was Hoxie dissembling? Not in any simple sense. He appears to have been unable to comprehend how deep were the still-bleeding scars on all of the campuses. Was he insensitive or unaware of the degree of anger he had instilled in many of the stakeholders? Or, did he simply have the capacity to believe what he wished to be true, and thus, by wishing, make it so? It was unlikely that Hoxie was consciously trying to bamboozle Zeckendorf. He so wanted a speedy recovery that he came to believe he heard Gabriel's horn, rather than trucks rumbling down Flatbush Extension.

Hoxie took the Heald-Hobson Report and sent it to the University Officers for comment. Stoddard responded by focusing on specific details, phraseology, and title changes. He stayed clear of any substantive commentary, keeping his remarks solely tactical. He was trying not to be judgmental, choosing instead to be focused on details. Mary Lai focused on her own areas of responsibility, challenging some of their statements, while accepting others. She was moderately defensive about some of the accusations that Heald-Hobson leveled, but also stayed away from any broad condemnation or praise summarized in the Heald-Hobson recommendations.

John Baiardi wrote back to the Chancellor about the development program. "If we should the accept the really negative premise that has been outlined throughout the Heald-Hobson Report, i.e., the difficulty in attracting sizable amounts of funds from private sources, then the conclusion derived in the report regarding the ten year plan might be justified." His memo argued that the plan could be successfully carried out, however, provided the respective Development Councils could be motivated to function well. He accepted some of the development recommendations, rejected others, but throughout focused on specifics of various projects and campaigns rather than an overall strategic assessment. These detailed responses were almost useless, because Hoxie's key officers were unwilling to argue openly with their Chancellor. The last one to have done so was Birenbaum and he did not fare well. Hoxie did collate all of these memos along with his own to compile a massive tome of refutation for the Board, as if bulk and detail would negate structural and leadership deficiencies.

That tome was dated September 12, 1968. Hoxie's memo was eleven pages, single-spaced and contained detailed charts and graphs with appendices. It was a significant document from Hoxie, and a useful sourcebook, clearly worked and re-worked in defense of his Chancellorship and soaring vision for the University.

Hoxie began by acknowledging that Heald-Hobson, "makes a significant contribution" particularly in the section dealing with the organization of the University. He then immediately noted that, "The recommendations contained in Part Three [*Preface to the Future*] are essentially my own," endorsed by his three senior Vice Presidents in their memos.

He next argued that the interviews conducted by Heald and Hobson were held in the spring of 1967, "at a most unusual time in the history of the University, that is, at the time of the removal from office the Provost of the Brooklyn Center." The Report had said, "it was difficult to develop objective information and it is equally difficult, therefore, to make recommendations...." He seized on that conditional quality in Heald's report writing, "I do not concur in the authors' conclusion, however, that 'it is very apparent that the University has suffered in most respects from this controversy.'" He lamented that the interviews could not have been done in September 1968 "when the climate is one hundred percent better and the attitude is one hundred and eighty degrees different from that which obtained in during the Birenbaum episode...."

He referenced his own memo to the Board of fourteen months earlier when writing in his unique, formal English, "'very much I share the concern of Dr. Henry Heald whether we are indeed building a University, or only a loose federation of various campuses.'" He stated that in this earlier report were not only his verbal responses to Heald, but also a new action plan designed to strengthen the University where Heald argued it needed to be strengthened.

Hoxie aligned himself with his other senior staff, "I agree with my senior staff members that the report by Heald, Hobson and Associates is more pessimistic than the facts warrant with regard to the future both with regard to financial stability and with prospective academic excellence of the University."

Hoxie then set out to establish that *Preface to the Future* was, in fact, a realistic, even conservative, document with goals that were achievable. Specifically, he insisted that it would be possible to raise faculty salaries a hundred percent, library expenditures by a hundred and fifty percent, student enrollment by seventy percent, and scholarship aid by three hundred percent in ten years. He cited statistics on each of those topics, indicating that the University was "well ahead of the ten year report in all of these categories, except scholarship assistance, where we are on schedule."

An entirely separate section of his response was entitled, *Preface to the Future: The Ten Year Plan of Long Island University*. Hoxie wrote, "Since there is such a divergent view of the goals and objectives and their obtainability in *Preface to the Future* and the Heald, Hobson and Associates' Report, it might be well for the members of the Board to carefully re-read both documents. Actually *Preface to the Future* is a conservative document, cautioning against overexpansion and advising the establishment of new programs only in the areas of strength where and when funds are attainable."

There were qualifiers in *Preface to the Future* indicating that all of these projected dreams, "a law school, a school of social work, a health sciences center, an institute of public administration, an institute of advanced scientific study, and five additional doctoral programs" would only happen if there were funds, faculty and students, and facilities to make such dreams come true. Hoxie was correct, there were these qualifiers. But what the Heald-Hobson report had focused on was the pursuit of these other dreams, when the University should have instead focused on solidifying and improving the quality of what it already was doing. Hoxie turned to the Heald, Hobson and Associates' term, "steeples of strength," to justify why chemistry and biology were selected in the ten year plan for doctoral programs. He pursued that same premise when discussing the quality of students, the level of faculty research activity, the library holdings and the structure of the administration. He concluded this extended apologia by once again quoting Deane W. Malott, who, in a very optimistic way, also had cautioned the University to ensure that the "first order of business" be in the basic fundamentals, "with well paid teachers and high caliber and students of such stature that in generations ahead, they will form the nucleus of loyal and generous supporters...." Malott had ended his comments,

"You have, I am confident, the inspiring leadership and the sound wisdom to so plot your course...."

Hoxie directly sought out Malott to write reactions to the Heald-Hobson report. Dated September 12, 1968, Malott dismissed "The [consultant's] recommendations [which] at the end seem to me to be rather verbose generalities, most of which have been recognized by you and your associates-therefore, scarcely worth belaboring." In the next section he observed, "The fact that costs are rising faster that income is known to every university throughout the land. This is a fact which makes university administration so exciting: we live always on the verge of bankruptcy...Long Island University has always faced critical problems, seemingly insurmountable tasks-but look at the history of its remarkable development throughout the years." He had no fears on enrollment and he discounted the Heald-Hobson reorganization structure as "entirely too specific."

Moreover, Malott refuted Heald's concerns about relatively low admission standards. "I thought it was agreed that Long Island University was neither competing with Harvard nor seeking an oasis of 'brains,' but was offering a sound collegiate education to the large number of normal young people, particularly in your area, who would become more intelligent useful citizens by virtue of exposure to the University's experience."

Toward the end of his commentary, Malott turned his attention to the level of involvement of the Board, noting "in spite of its complete authority and responsibility, it is not able to enter into every phase of the institution.... Their [the Board's] prime responsibility is to select the Chancellor, to back him wholeheartedly-or to fire him." He thought that "the Trustees, individually or collectively by committees, should not be meeting with Faculty or student groups," arguing instead that the Chancellorship is the sole means of communication between the Board and the University...." Malott firmly believed in a strong central authority of a Chancellor. "I myself would be unwilling to be a Chancellor, removed and immobilized behind a battery of Vice Presidents."

Which consultant was correct? Deane Malott or Henry Heald? Was Long Island University a sinking institution, overly ambitious, and underfunded? Or was it, as Malott argued, an institution which understood its mission and was capable of fulfilling it? Was Hoxie a dynamic leader or a delusional fogey, out of touch with the transformed university of the '60s? Or both? Perspective mattered. Stakeholders at C.W. Post-faculty, overseers, students, administrators-had a very different perspective than those at Brooklyn. These were among the issues that the Board would have to address at its September meeting, one of the most critical in the history of the University.

Seawanhaka Supplement Sept. 26, 1968

Report of
Heald Hobson and Associates
on
Long Island University

Following is the text of Heald, Hobson and Associates controversial report on the status and future of Long Island University's administrative, educational and organizational functions, along with evaluations of each and pertinent recommendations. The charts that accompany the text are reproduced here as they appeared in the formal bound report presented to the Chancellor and the Trustees by the Heald associates. Only those tables deemed particularly relevant by the editors are included in this Supplement; other charts were omitted either because of lack of space or lack of relevancy. None of the original copy has been edited or omitted, either in content or in form.

I. INTRODUCTION

II. GOALS AND OBJECTIVES

III. THE ORGANIZATION AND ADMINISTRATION OF THE UNIVERSITY

Present Organizational Structure and Philosophy

Proposed Organizational Structure

Facsimile of page one of the Heald-Hobson Report reprinted in Seawanhaka, September 26, 1968.

Hoxie, well aware of the importance of that meeting, lobbied his Trustee supporters aggressively in the days before. On September 13th, he wrote to Arthur T. Roth, his stilted writing style demonstrating his own nervousness. "Very much I have

307

appreciated your counsel this week related to the important matters attendant upon the Heald, Hobson and Associates' Report." When he sent John McGrath the material for the Executive Committee meeting on September 17th, he wanted to meet with McGrath, ostensibly to discuss "the possible appointment of Dr. Edward Mill, as Executive Dean of the Brooklyn Center," the first reference in the files of any other candidate to fill that job.

His real purpose, however, was in his last paragraph. "The new academic year is off to a good start auguring well for the future." On September 16th, he sent out a very heavy packet to the entire Board, repeating that mantra: "this I do believe, that there is today a greater unity and a finer *esprit* than has ever previously obtained in the life of our University." He concluded his cover memo by quoting from one of his oldest and closest supporters, Kenneth Colegrove, whom he had made Distinguished Professor of Political Science at C.W. Post after he served as Chair of political science at Northwestern. Colegrove wrote, "returning from a month and a half in Evanston, I am astonished to see your amazing accomplishment in resurrecting a new academic institution from the ruins of the turmoil on the Brooklyn Center Campus. By the wave of some magic wand, you have raised a new Phoenix from the ashes of obstruction and rebellion. These words may sound too classical. But the feat is a classic." Hoxie did not have to write Colegrove's letter for him, but he certainly asked for something similar to what he received.

He also turned to his senior staff, asking each for his or her reaction to the Heald-Hobson recommendations. Gene Arden, Dean of Graduate Faculties, wrote the Chancellor back. He pointed out "that even the recommendations of an accrediting agency are generally taken as guide lines, and the University is expected to respond creatively rather than slavishly. In both cases, [a Middle States Report and a consultant's report] a small group of visitors tries to analyze the innermost functioning of a complex institution; it is not surprising that some of the subtleties could be misunderstood, or that some of the suggestions might prove unworkable or inappropriate." Arden ended his three page assessment by observing, "The record of what we have accomplished in the past decade is visible enough; there must be no failure of nerve as we confront the next decade."

On September 20th, Hoxie convened a meeting of the University Council, some thirty-five faculty, administrators, Deans, and officers. They all had read the Heald Report as well as the many documents written in response by the officers, Deane Malott and others. Hoxie reiterated his view that the report "took a far too pessimistic a view regarding the University as a whole and its parts." When the meeting was open for discussion, there were those who wanted the report rejected outright. Hofstra and Adelphi, it was claimed, had rejected the studies made by Heald-Hobson firm as well. Professor Resnick of Brooklyn referred to the report as "nonsense," arguing that it was contradictory. Dean Spiegel indicated that it seemed to move in two directions at once. "Other comments were that Heald, Hobson and

Associates had presented the whole idea of a single-campus university and tried to superimpose it on Long Island University, a multi-campus institution for which it would not be appropriate." Dean Arden "referred to the study as a thesis without an oral examination," and Dean Wiseman "offered the idea that it be considered a preliminary presentation and used as a spring board for further self-study."

Dean Spiegel "asked how seriously it was being taken by the Board of Trustees since it was a critical report." Hoxie responded that, "there were varying views among members of the Board regarding the report," a non-answer. At the end of the meeting there was a unanimous resolution expressing regrets and reservations about Heald-Hobson. "We believe with considerable enthusiasm in the progress and future of the University and desire to have a Committee of the University Council meet with a Committee of the Board of Trustees to discuss the report and the role of the University Council with regard to it."

Hoxie invited his director of Research Administration, Col. John Tyler, to brief (and, perhaps, influence) the several Boards of Governors of Brooklyn and Counsel of Overseers at Post and Southampton. Tyler's five-page document was mailed by Hoxie to both groups of key lay leaders. Tyler, a retired colonel in the military, was very negative about what Dr. Heald had written. "I find the report full of generalizations, inaccuracies, and opinions, which are frequently subjective rather than objective. The report is not constructive, and provides little reason for optimism for the future of Long Island University." Arguing that "the big challenge in higher education today is in providing suitable programs for the majority of students-the middle fifths," he took exception to the assertion in the Heald report that "The University…cannot realistically aspire to become a high quality private university in the near future."

Hoxie forwarded to all these groups, including the Board, critiques from others, including Dr. Seymour Lowell, the Chair of the Chemistry Department at C.W. Post College. *The Long Island Press* published a three column article on September 21st which summarized the counter-attack organized by Hoxie: "It all boils down to the consultants telling the University to trim its sails, put the ship in better order and delay any major voyage into the high seas of major expansion, conditions not being seen as favorable. And the University telling the consultants, in effect, they were looking through the wrong ends of the telescope-the minimizer when looking at the LIU performance and potential and the magnifier when looking at its growth goals."

By September 20, 1968, Hoxie clearly understood that these efforts might "not supply sufficient counter weight." There is a letter from Leonard Hall, William Casey's partner, to John McGrath reminding McGrath of his role in getting the zoning changed so that Post could open as a college. Clearly primed by Hoxie, he wrote, "looking back through the years, great credit for all this must be given to

Dr. R. Gordon Hoxie and I am saddened to hear that an effort is now being made to remove Dr. Hoxie as Chancellor of Long Island University and President of C.W. Post College...." Along with others who wrote or called, he wanted "to raise my small voice against any such action."

That same day, Hoxie wrote to David Rockefeller, whom he had casually encountered the previous evening at the Guggenheim Museum. Hoxie had lambasted Zeckendorf, whom Hoxie understood to be leading the faction that wanted Hoxie fired. This attack must have puzzled Rockefeller who was completely disengaged from the politics of LIU. Hoxie celebrated the growth of the University over the years, then tried to engage Rockefeller on his behalf. "In candor, however, there is one problem of which I believe I should apprise you, and this relates to the behind the scenes efforts of Bill Zeckendorf to unseat me and replace me by Alexander Aldrich [his and Nelson's cousin]. As you may appreciate, with an earned Ph.D degree and with some knowledge of university affairs, one does not dismiss someone who has weathered the storm and safely brought the ship to port, especially one does not do so on such opportunistic grounds, that the appointment of an Aldrich would bring favor with the Rockefeller family. Whereas I am not personally acquainted with Alexander Aldrich, I cannot believe that he would ever entertain the position if he were aware of the backstage method in which Bill zeckendorf [sic] was planning to pull this off." Hoxie went on to report that both Arthur Roth and May Davie saw this as "a fight for principle." "Moreover, the University's benefactress, Mrs. Marjorie Merriweather Post, is threatening to cut off all her support for the University, if Bill Zeckendorf prevails in this scheme."

Over the next several days, battle was joined openly and savagely. The past six months had been a terrible time for Bill Zeckendorf. His wife had died on March 5th, in an Air France 707 crash trying to land in Guadeloupe. She was on her way to meet her husband for a Caribbean cruise; he had landed two hours prior. Then on August 29th, Zeckendorf was forced to file for personal bankruptcy. He had personally guaranteed over $55 million of Webb & Knapp debt on May 18, 1965, in a desperate attempt to save what was once a vast real estate empire. He and Bill Jr. managed to shelter their Madison Avenue office by creating a new company named General Property Corporation. The legal petition named two hundred and five creditors and ran four and a half pages of court document. Among those many creditors was David Baird, a fellow Trustee, and the estate of his late wife, Marion. Another was the Franklin National Bank. He owed money to a wide assortment of people and institutions, including banks, the Roosevelt Hotel, the Waldorf Astoria, and the FAO Schwartz toy store.

The 1968 court filing was a humiliating experience for a man who built billions of dollars of America's physical infrastructure. The Court required him to remit ten percent of his salary monthly to the County Sheriff of New York. He was granted an annual salary of $37,500. The *Daily News* quoted from his petition, "your petitioner is insolvent." He listed assets of $1,885,000 and liabilities of $79,076,000. At its heyday, Webb & Knapp was a three hundred million dollar corporation, although during its last years, the Zeckendorfs increasingly received only very small percentages of the total investment of a project, deriving most of their income from management and construction fees.

William Zeckendorf died of a stroke when he was seventy-one years old, on September 30, 1976. He had his first stroke six years earlier. During his successful years, he had an extraordinary impact on America's urban landscape. The list of buildings he owned or helped build is enormous. Among the architects who worked for him were Wallace K. Harrison and Le Corbusier; for many years, I.M. Pei was his in-house architect. At his funeral service at Temple Emanuel on October 3, 1976, he was eulogized by John McGrath and Robert Moses, among others. Moses began with the rhetorical question "For what purpose does the gentleman rise? I rise to speak briefly about the end of an extraordinary American pioneer, of immense imagination, courage and nerve. He was a man of fathomless loyalty, generosity, and public spirit. Take him for all in all, we shall not look upon his like again. The roster of those he brought within his immense orbit reads like a list of the greatest builders of our times." A bit later in those same remarks, Moses quoted himself when he spoke at C.W. Post some years before. "I run out of metaphors when I attempt to describe, interpret, and explain Bill Zeckendorf. When you look at 'Z' at the very end of the alphabet recollect that at the final trumpet the last shall be first...." John McGrath had sent these remarks to Albert Bush Brown, then the Chancellor of the University, because "I think these last words about our great Chairman should repose in the files of the University."

Did the bankruptcy in late August influence Zeckendorf's perception of Hoxie or the situation for the University? There is very little evidence to suggest that he allowed his two worlds to cross. Rather, he seems to have concluded that Hoxie could not lead the University after Birenbaum and the failed sale, whatever Hoxie might claim. There was also a badly botched personnel matter one that would have embarrassed the University had it become public. Zeckendorf was livid at the way Hoxie mishandled it.

Zeckendorf was sure enough of his judgment about Hoxie to cross his dear friend and long-time colleague, John McGrath. When McGrath had honored Zeckendorf on his retirement from twenty-five years as Chairman, Zeckendorf had written, "Last evening was, for many reasons, the most memorable occasion of my life." Zeckendorf obviously felt so strongly about the need to make a change in the University's leadership that he was willing to split the Board and to defy not only McGrath but also Arthur T. Roth and other close colleagues.

The LIU Executive Committee had met on the 16th at an emergency meeting without Hoxie present. Either that night or the following morning, Arthur Roth called

Hoxie to inform him that Zeckendorf had sought his termination. There were no Minutes of the meeting and no indication of exactly how the Trustees had voted. But there was clearly a sharp divide and the fight revealed deep fissures.

In a subsequent press release, Hoxie initially termed the Trustee decision as "a baseless rumor." By the 19th, however, he had organized a Citizens' Committee to fight the decision and spread the word to all of his friends and allies. The University files contain a hundred and twenty letters of support for Hoxie. There was also a group letter to McGrath, conceivably drafted by Hoxie himself, which stated, "We, the undersigned, believing strongly and wholeheartedly in the leadership of Dr. R. Gordon Hoxie as Chancellor of Long Island University and of C. W. Post College, desire to hereby go on record to the Board of Trustees of Long Island University, indicating our complete support for his leadership.... We would view with the greatest concern any change with the executive leadership of Long Island University at this time." This letter concluded by speaking of "a great moral wrong to a dedicated educational leader were Hoxie to be fired."

Many of the individual letters were based on some kind of crib sheet prepared by Hoxie, because they speak of errors in the Heald-Hobson conclusions and other specifics that no one who was not close to the story could possibly have known. A very active member of the Post alumni body, John J. Zureck, wrote a letter addressed to other alums with the heading, "What the hell is going on?" Zureck urged his fellow Post alums to cable John McGrath urging postponement of the September 30th Board meeting, noting, "Your response at this time is critical." It ended: "now is the time for all C.W. Post alumni to STAND UP AND BE COUNTED."

More important from the Board's perspective were the signatures of many of Long Island most important leaders, including Bill Casey, Leonard Hall, A. Holly Patterson, Eleanor S. Whitney, and a powerful list of North Shore citizens, most of whom also belonged to one or another of the socially exclusive country clubs.

William Casey was a perfect example of how serious the schism had become. Casey, who in future years would become the Director of the CIA, had been involved with the University since the purchase of the Post campus. He cabled the Board, "I have given time and money to Long Island University because of my respect and admiration for Gordon Hoxie's leadership. I see no evidence for loss of confidence in his leadership. There is growing admiration for his handling of campus difficulties, which seem inevitable these days. I have strong conviction that failure of Trustees to support Hoxie at this time and in these circumstances will severely undermine the confidence of the community in the university and its future." He sent a copy of that cable to Hoxie, who responded to thank him by noting, "Perhaps through your friendship with John McGrath, you can ask the question, 'Why the contemplated action of the Board of Trustees'" against the Chancellor?

Letters came from the local Episcopal Bishop, from local newspaper sources, and from faculty, almost exclusively at C.W. Post. There were a few letters from Brooklyn. For example, LeRoy Greenberg, class of '35, wrote in support of Hoxie; he was a Great Neck resident whose child was at Post. The dispute pitted those from Long Island or connected to the Post campus against those connected to the Brooklyn campus. Much of this was openly orchestrated by Hoxie from his office at University Center in Brookville; a letter signed by the officers and directors of the C.W. Post Associates carried a note from Hoxie's secretary indicating that it was sent to all of the Trustees. In his own handwriting Hoxie wrote, "good." Hoxie even wrote draft statements to the press on behalf of loyal Trustees. He prepared such a statement for Joseph Lindemann, the President of the Nestle-LeMur Company, ghost writing: "since Dr. Hoxie's record is completely beyond challenge, his enemies are resorting to erosion of confidence tactics…. It is also grossly unfair to try to pin on the Chancellor the Board of Trustees' responsibility for the proposal related to the possible transfer of the Brooklyn Center of Long Island University to City University." George Henning wrote to the Board on behalf of the Development Council at C.W. Post College asking, "In the face of this week's publicity-'what do we have to sell?'" He added a handwritten post script, "Good luck, Gordon-you have a lot of friends."

Hoxie directly approached Arthur Ochs Sulzberger at *The Times*, urging that *The Times* write an editorial on "the importance of leadership in higher education in these times." Hoxie sent him a copy of a letter from the Bishop, and implored Sulzberger to print it before September 30th, when the Board would meet, noting with his classic modesty, "Thousands of people will be grateful, myself among them."

And he sent all the Trustees a letter, possibly drafted by him personally, but signed by B. Davis Schwartz and addressed to John McGrath. Schwartz had pledged $500,000 and in exchange, Hoxie had agreed to name the massive new library under construction at Post, first named Brookdale, the family's Foundation name, and later for B.D. Schwartz himself. It was an excellent philanthropic venture for the Schwartz family, since they paid a fraction of the normal percentage of construction costs required for a naming gift at virtually any college or university in the country. In any case, Schwartz (or Hoxie) "was shocked to read the article in *The New York Times*." Schwartz wrote, "Dr. Hoxie's monumental record of service to Long Island University is one of the best, if not the best in the nation, and any action, other than one that rewards him, could be construed as a lack of gratitude for selfless devotion and utmost competence."

The B. Davis Schwartz Library at C.W. Post College.

On another front in his counter-offensive, Hoxie wrote to the entire faculty on September 24th, selectively sending those articles in the press that praised his leadership. He wrote to them, "You appreciate that I inherited a divided institution. After the strenuous storms we have today a university united and moving ahead. Yet, it would appear, if one can read these newspaper clippings correctly, that there is one not content to permit us to move ahead together." Later in the same long letter, he wrote, "It is a pusillanimous course of action for anyone to try and pin on me the sole responsibility for the unpopular course of action of the past year related to the possible transfer of the Brooklyn Center of LIU."

During this hectic period, Hoxie had another North Shore friend, Brinkley Smithers, call Adelaide Riggs, Mrs. Post's daughter, asking the Post family to weigh in. Hoxie then wrote directly to Adelaide: "William Zeckendorf has sought to muster his forces to secure my ouster and has even threatened to seek to change the name of C.W. Post College and the Merriweather Campus." Hoxie asked for a strong telegram to the Board, "indicating that your past and future *financial* support was related to my future role in the University." Hoxie continued, "Mr. Arthur T. Roth, the Vice Chairman of the Board of Trustees of the University and Chairman of the Board of Franklin National Bank, believes that this is the opportunity to create Post University. Such opportunity would especially require your mother's help." He urged that she send a telegram to each member of the Board indicating "her future financial support is related to my position." He urged that, "no mention of Mr. Zeckendorf be made in the telegrams so that we can keep the matter on an impersonal level."

On the 28th, a telegram arrived at Hoxie's home. "We are greatly distressed over the contemplated change at Long Island University and C.W. Post College and want the Board of Trustees to know that the removal of Dr. R. Gordon Hoxie from his present position of Chancellor of Long Island University and President of C.W. Post College will preclude future support from us in any way whatsoever. We are confident that in your wisdom you will review and recognize Dr. Hoxie's good works and great assets and retain his leadership for the benefit of the University." The telegram was signed both by Marjorie Merriweather Post and her daughter, Adelaide Post Riggs IV.

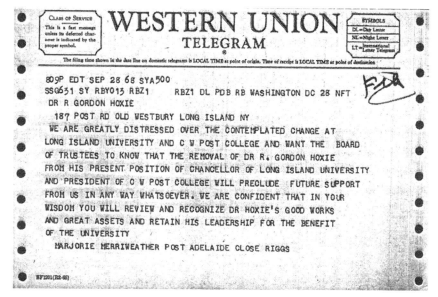

Facsimile of the telegram from Mrs. Post and her daughter to the LIU Board linking their future support to Hoxie's survival as Chancellor.

There is in the file, as well, an unaddressed, undated, and unsigned pledge agreement for ten million dollars, payable over five years. It had four provisions. Hoxie had written by hand "File" across the top of the page, storing this bit of fantasy in case fortune struck.

The Brooklyn Center was described as "non-compatible with Post University (C.W. Post College and Southampton College)." It indicated that these two units needed to become separate and independent universities. It further proposed that the Brooklyn Center and the new Post University each receive five million dollars. This clearly was Hoxie's most cherished dream. Ideally, he would want this "gift is to be divided equally." Hoxie's second provision was that the Trustees who resided on Long Island would become the Trustees of Post University, while the remaining Trustees would become the Trustees of the Brooklyn Center. Third, in

315

his fantasy, there were to be ten new Trustees elected within the next two years at Post, provided he, Hoxie, screened each name. The text actually stated, "with my approval." Fourth and finally, R. Gordon Hoxie was to become the Chancellor of Post University. There is no evidence that he ever sent this to either Mrs. Post or her daughter, or that he shared any of it with Arthur T. Roth. Nor is there any indication whether he or his loyal public relations officer, Jo Chamberlin, had written it. But seventy-two hours before Armageddon, it was clear that Hoxie had no intention of going "gently into that sweet night."

By playing the "nuclear option" and asking Mrs. Post to threaten severing of her relationship with the University, Hoxie was banking that his many years of flattery-naming the campus Merriweather for her mother, calling her the University's chief benefactress, naming buildings for her children, et cetera - would tempt her into donating a transformative gift that would save his Chancellorship.

In January 1968, he had written her a solicitation letter, including an update on the memorial medallion of her mother being recast by a second sculptor, John Terken. He wrote, "as I recall this past fall, you advised me that you hope to make a gift to C.W. Post College and/or the Merriweather Campus in February." He asked her for help in funding the Management Center, seeking $125,000 at that time. He gave her several more expensive philanthropic alternates. That letter included a breakdown of her total giving from 1962 to 1967. It indicated that she had donated just under $635,000 in those five years. Mrs. Post's handwriting was clearly deteriorating during her last years, but she went over each of these items, doing the arithmetic in her own scraggly hand. There was no indication at any point that Mrs. Post was prepared to make a transformative gift; she had been coaxed and flattered by Hoxie into giving substantially more than she had ever anticipated when she sold the Brookville property almost twenty years prior. In the final analysis, there would not be a pot of gold at the end of that rainbow, however much Hoxie dreamed that it might exist.

Much more evident were the scars formed by the ugly fight between Arthur Roth and William Zeckendorf, both of whom were confronting crises in their own professional lives. Zeckendorf was financially a broken man. Roth had been stripped of his Chairman's position at Franklin National Bank in July 1968. These once close friends and business associates pounded away at each other in an exaggerated but mean-spirited fight with R. Gordon Hoxie's head as the prize.

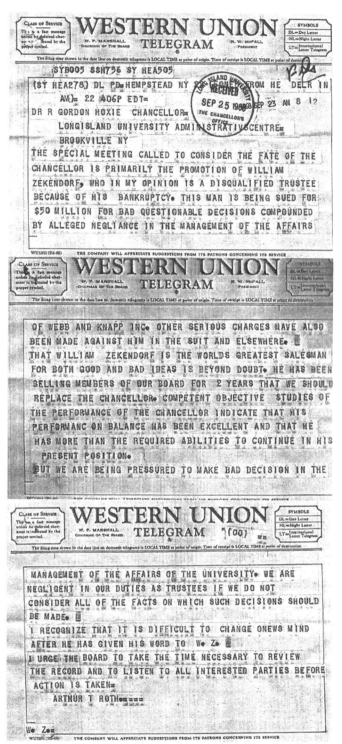

Facsimile of Arthur Roth's long telegram to the Board of Trustees, angrily opposing Zeckendorf's recommendation to terminate Chancellor Hoxie.

PART II - RALPH GORDON HOXIE

Directly after the secret meeting of the Executive Committee of Trustees, Arthur Roth sent a telegram to all of the other Trustees, including Hoxie, making public what Zeckendorf clearly wanted to be held in confidence. That "special meeting," Roth stated, was called to "consider the fate of the Chancellor" It was "primarily the promotion of William Zeckendorf, who in my opinion is a disqualified Trustee because of his bankruptcy. This man is being sued for fifty million dollars for bad questionable decisions compounded by alleged negligence in the management of the affairs of Webb & Knapp, Inc."

Roth, whose bank had outstanding loans both to Webb & Knapp and to Zeckendorf personally, claimed that other serious charges had been made against Zeckendorf, whom he called "the world's greatest salesman for both good and bad ideas...." Roth accused Zeckendorf of trying to replace the Chancellor for two years, arguing that, "Competent objective studies about the performance of the Chancellor indicate that his performance is in balance and has been excellent, and that he has more than the required abilities to continue in his present position...." Roth maintained that the Board was being "pressured to make bad decisions." He recognized that, "it is difficult to change one's mind after he has given his word to W.Z." But, he urged the Board to slow up, to review the record, and "to listen to all interested parties." In fact, Roth had prepared his own grading system to test Hoxie's suitability to remain in office. In his non-professional way, Roth created a simple grid, listing Hoxie's achievements and failures and putting a score against each. His grid included such items as accreditations, faculty quality, graduate programs, increases in faculty compensation, gifts and grants, facilities, student and faculty participation in governance, et cetera. It went on for pages. Roth's personal grading score gave Hoxie a ninety out of a possible one hundred.

Several days later, another Trustee, Clinton W. Blume, also sent a telegram to all of his fellow Board members. A personal friend and colleague of Zeckendorf, he lamented Roth's attack. "It is to be regretted that Mr. Arthur Roth has seen fit to resort to personal vilification of a Trustee, who for more than twenty-five years has at all times dedicated himself with time and money to do what he believed to be in the best interest of Long Island University. The issue is not Mr. William Zeckendorf but the office of the chancellor. Mr. Zeckendorf's record at LIU requires no defense nor do his motives. I shall not indulge in an intemperate response to Mr. Roth's allegations. I urge only that every member of this Board consider problems which stand before it based on their best judgment, and without regard to one Trustee's opinion of another."

The Times' headline, read, "Move to Oust L.I.U. Chancellor Splits Trustees." The article continued; "A source close to the Trustees said yesterday that Dr. Hoxie had lost the confidence of the students and faculty to the point that he could no longer be effective in his post." It then chronicled the exchange of telegrams, quoting Zeckendorf as saying he would "not get down to that level of diatribe." Hoxie,

318

in turn, was quoted, "'I can't quite comprehend what's going on,' he said. The University is going so beautifully this year and then, wow this thing.'" In a follow up article of September 30th, Hoxie said, "the move to oust him had stirred such bitterness that could cause 'irreparable' damage."

Hoxie had now gone public with his interest in splitting the University into two. The friction might be so great, he suggested, that the only answer would be to separate the University's Brooklyn and Long Island branches into two distinct institutions. Hoxie gave *The Times* a ninety-minute interview in one final effort to improve his odds at the meeting the following day. He justified firing "Dr. Birenbaum, who was actively undermining my position and striving for power control...." "If I go tomorrow, he said, unwittingly it will be a Birenbaum triumph." Asked by *The Times* reporter if he would accept "a post as head of a suburban branch of a divided university, Dr. Hoxie hesitated for a moment, then said he "would cross that bridge when he gets to it." *The Times* quoted a source close to the Trustees, probably meaning one of the Trustees, that, "there has been a growing feeling among members that Dr. Hoxie is not attuned to the needs of today-especially in the ghetto."

Seawanhaka, on September 25th, had a feature article entitled, "Hoxie: It Was A Long Year." The article began, "Most college administrators choose to remain in the background and always make certain their public appearances are painted in sunlight. The career of R. Gordon Hoxie, however, has been largely an unwanted foreground and has been tainted in a deep grey." The paper then repeated a tale, which has taken hold as fact, even though there is no written evidence to verify its central assertion. "From the first days of his association with LIU, faculty members say a disagreement developed between Hoxie and then LIU President Admiral Richard L. Conolly. At the age of 35, Hoxie was appointed Dean of Liberal Arts and Sciences in Brooklyn. High sources at the Brooklyn Center claim Admiral Conolly was dissatisfied with Hoxie's work, and subsequently sent him out to C.W. Post with the vague title of Dean. There, the sources say, Conolly repeatedly visited the new campus to 'check or rearrange' Hoxie's work."

The article chronicled in detail what happened in 1966 and 1967, including the long and drawn out Birenbaum affair and the tuition strike. "The tuition battle was viewed not only as a fight over finances, but also as a test of strength between Provost Birenbaum and Chancellor Hoxie." It continued, "On March 22, 1967, the Chancellor was mobbed by over a thousand students as he walked across the Mall to the Main building. Eight police cars were eventually called to the scene with five separate precincts involved." The article explained how the student demonstrations moved into the arena of extreme activism and militancy. "The protest, in which the Chancellor's overcoat was ripped, was a prelude to an eight-day student and faculty strike which severed ties between Hoxie and the Brooklyn Center."

On September 27, 1968, three days before the Board meeting, Hoxie wrote a blunt memo to his fellow Board members, "It is my earnest hope that we may come to our meeting with the right matter in focus: *the future of Long Island University,* and in that light, put behind us the personal misunderstandings which have arisen. First, let me assure you that you will have no problem with Gordon Hoxie if you want to relieve him as Chancellor. It is *not,* however, in the best interest of Long Island University that you do so at Monday's meeting; it will result in irrevocable harm to the University, creating a divisive force and the deepest bitterness among the University's friends and supporters. I shall gladly and quietly go, three, six or nine months from now, or at any future time you may desire, but not under the glare of the present controversy, which was *not* of my making. Make no mistake, editorial opinion and public opinion, as well as thousands of members of our university community would view with deepest despair either my dismissal or my resignation *now.* The largest benefactors of the University would in either instance cut off their support and thousands of our loyal supporters would be deeply hurt...." Hoxie could not have made the threat more explicit.

The following day, on September 28th, he wrote a letter to John McGrath, originally drafted as private correspondence. He liked the letter sufficiently, however, to decide to mail it to all the Board members. It began, "With a bit of sadness and a heavy heart I write you on the eve of our special Board meeting." He had indicated in the text that he was sharing this letter only with Arthur T. Roth "in the interest of understanding," but instead, went quasi-public to complain about how he was being treated.

Hoxie was bruised and angry, he wrote, because he was being treated so cavalierly. He complained about "visits to the principal Campuses of the University by a candidate for the position of Chancellor, his indication of his willingness to accept the position, and an informal meeting of some Board members convened by a person other than the Chairman on September 6th, to discuss his candidacy." The individual in question was Alexander Aldrich, someone, Hoxie maintained, Zeckendorf had met on the plane back from Guadeloupe in the aftermath of his wife's death. Hoxie claimed to being treated shabbily, cloaking himself in the mantle of being a victim of a conspiracy rather than a Chancellor who had lost his mandate, at least with this important University constituency.

He continued, "One Board member [Arthur Roth] who attended that meeting, believing so strongly that irrevocable harm might be done the University, took the responsibility of directing me the following morning, September 17th, to advise the Chancellor's Cabinet of the aforementioned action. I advised the Cabinet to treat the matter in confidence." Hoxie maintained that someone had leaked Aldrich's name and campus visits to the press. How ever Aldrich's name became public, the uproar that followed made it problematic for the Board to appoint Aldrich without the consultative process that had become the norm throughout the country, even assuming he was under consideration for the Chancellorship, rather than the head of the Brooklyn campus.

Hoxie was still angry about Zeckendorf's intervention in his conflict with Biren-baum. "There is one especial matter which I believe I should detail to you since one Board member's position has been that I should be removed for erosion of confidence on the part of the faculty and the students. (If there had been such, he unwittingly, and Bill Birenbaum wittingly, were the prime contributors.)" Hoxie maintained that he never was interested in popularity "but rather to gain their re-spect, making unpopular decisions in the interest of right...."

He then observed that it was unfortunate "that one of the faculties of the Univer-sity, that of Southampton College, whose average length of service at the Univer-sity is only two years, took what I deemed poorly advised action, by voting for my removal. Some sixty members so voted." He then chronicled in detail how other faculty groups had not voted against him, observing that only a total of "75 faculty members out of 1000 in the University" had voted for his ouster, as if this was truly a referendum on the past twenty-two months.

What finally mattered was that Zeckendorf and many other Trustees had agreed that Hoxie had to go. Heald probably advised Zeckendorf and the others about this during one of their face-to-face meetings. Someone had to take over quickly, and Zeckendorf concluded that an outsider would be best if possible. An interim Trustee appointment, someone like John Pell, no longer would be tolerated by the faculty. Zeckendorf, although no longer chair, acted as if he still held office. Roth's anger at Zeckendorf and fondness for Hoxie prompted him to turn tattletale. McGrath had lost control. All in all, despite Hoxie's massive public relations ef-forts, his days were numbered. It was remarkable how much loyalty he still could summon, how many important people he could mobilize, how schizophrenic the University had become. But at some point in the next few hours, Hoxie grudgingly accepted that he was finished.

On the next day, he mailed "The Statement of the Chancellor of Long Island Uni-versity to the Board of Trustees, September 30, 1968." He spoke of how he and McGrath had discussed his stepping down by January 6, 1969 if his effectiveness was sharply diminished. He talked about how he had worked with SDS and SOBU, the Student Organization for Black Unity, to transform the anger of minority stu-dents in Brooklyn. He quoted his old friend, Kenneth Colegrove, about his success in creating a recovery for the University. And then, in his own involuted way, he gave up. "Whereas you have not requested it, may I say that my resignation today would serve no useful purpose. Quite the contrary, it would be of irrevocable dam-age to the unity of the University and its major sources of support. It remains my desire, however, to serve beyond today only at your pleasure.... Thus, I am hereby advising you that, even though you may protest my resignation, I intend to submit it whenever I cannot in conscience serve as your Chancellor. I say this without reservation and recognizing all the efforts of all the years we have worked together." It is almost impossible to parse those sentences into a coherent whole, but Hoxie could count heads as well as the next. It must have become obvious to him that all his efforts notwithstanding, he could not maneuver to remain Chancellor.

After a letter of resignation as opaque as that one, it should come as no surprise that there was no simple separation from Long Island University. At other institutions and other times at L.I.U., when a CEO was terminated, he or she would take a job elsewhere, return to teaching or retire. Hoxie hung around. Thus, the day after that Board meeting, Hoxie wrote Arthur Roth, "Very much I appreciate your services and those of John Pell and George Shapiro in the matter of appropriate financial arrangements in the light of my services to Long Island University. It is my understanding that the University may desire to have me serve as a consultant during the transitional year and I am agreeable so to do. He then asked that his salary for the rest of that academic year be fifty thousand dollars, "which is in keeping with the size and character of the complex which is Long Island University, the sixth largest private University in the nation." And he asked that Louise and he might continue to occupy the University residence and to have the services of the staff related thereto "to be paid by the University during the year of employment." He listed his salary from 1954 to the present, indicating that he was at present receiving thirty-five thousand dollars a year plus a housing allowance of six hundred dollars per month with utilities and two domestics in addition to having access to a car and chauffeur.

Several days later he wrote to Marjorie Post, "It was so very good being with you during those difficult hours, following the shock of my resignation from the University which I have served to the best of my ability now for more than fourteen years, since the time when it was a little unaccredited Brooklyn institution." Even in resignation his stock phrases and boasts rolled off his lips and across his letters with ease. He sent her copies of all the telegrams and letters he had received, sharing with her that, "expressions of friendship and support and editorials of appreciation keep pouring in, from near and far. Enclosed is one copy of each of a number of these."

The resignation was accorded a front page story in *The New York Times* on October 1st, even though McGrath's statement, with Hoxie standing at his side, was very simple: "I wish to announce that Chancellor Hoxie presented his resignation to the board of Trustees and it was accepted by the Board." The article continued, "The resignation was effective immediately."

Hoxie spoke emotionally, with tears welling in his eyes from time to time. Mc-Grath stated that in the absence of a Chancellor, the Bylaws mandated that the Vice Chancellor of Academic Affairs become Acting Chancellor. At the time, George Stoddard was in East Africa advising on the development of local colleges. He would return as quickly as possible to New York. During the question and answer period, McGrath spoke about the Heald-Hobson Report which had called for a stronger centralized structure to bring, per *The New York Times*, "the university's loosely tied units together into an effective whole." The column indicated that the Vice Chair of the Board, Arthur Roth, had come out strongly for splitting the university into two separate institutions, saying "the suburban and city campuses will tear each other apart unless this is done." Another Trustee, Congressman Ogden Reid, noted that further decentralization would be necessary if the Brooklyn Center was to "fulfill its main function of serving the ghetto."

Of the twenty-one members of the Board, only General James A. Van Fleet was absent at that special meeting. He was in Florida. *The Seawanhaka*, reporting on the meeting and the subsequent press conference, claimed that Alexander Aldrich, "first cousin of Governor Nelson Rockefeller and director of the Hudson Valley Commission, reportedly was named as a candidate for the vacated Chancellorship." The student paper quoted Hoxie as hoping that he would be elected to the Board of Trustees, further confusing what the future might hold. Hoxie hoped that he would be elected at the next regularly scheduled Board meeting on October 21st. In a sign of the times, *Seawanhaka* further reported that there had been a multi-campus meeting of student leadership, demanding "a voice in future plans or else." Speaking of this new level of student power, *Seawanhaka* quoted the student document as stating, "Although we will strive for a peaceful resolution of the situation, we accept the responsibility to take any and all actions necessary to insure the full acceptance of our demands."

Hoxie's ego and political calculus sought a continued supportive correspondence; the letters poured in. They came from an executive of General Foods Corporation, the successor corporation of the Post food empire, who called it a "sad day." From Jeannette Rattray, the wife of the publisher of the local newspaper on the East End: "I wouldn't say that the young people I saw on the Southampton Campus came from the affluent, would you? But there is so much jealousy and chips-on-shoulders between races and classes that I doubt if anyone in the world could hold together the combination as it stands." After speaking about the resignation of the President of Dartmouth, she concluded, "College Presidents, politicians, and policemen are in very dangerous occupations today, aren't they?"

Joe Lindemann, a Trustee, wrote to fellow Trustee, David Baird: "Lilyan and I watched the news conference over television at 11 p.m., and I told her how instrumental you were in arranging for the quiet and dignified withdrawal of Gordon Hoxie. I am sure most of us present were quite relieved and thankful to you for your counsel." Hoxie got a hand written letter from his former mentor, Albert Jacobs, who had stayed at Trinity College rather than come to LIU in 1962. Jacobs wrote of his own retirement, noting "My last year was a difficult one for me, having endured first a hernia operation and then an aneurism on the aorta."

Having retired to Chappaquiddick Island, Jacobs spoke of how Hoxie had been "a tower of great strength" when Hoxie worked for him. Not surprisingly, Hoxie responded to Jacobs almost immediately, boasting how successful he had been in fundraising and in other ways, "but alas, I did not enjoy the full confidence of all the Board, particularly that wing of the Board led by the former Chairman William Zeckendorf." Hoxie found himself at age forty-nine "reconsidering my life's work. Perhaps the enclosed copy of my vitae may be suggestive to you."

With endless optimism Hoxie wrote to Arthur Ochs Sulzberger of *The New York Times,* including his curriculum vitae and indicating that he was "a bit disappointed that *The New York Times* did not see fit to print the letter to the editor from my good friend, the Right Reverend Jonathan G. Sherman, bishop of the Episcopal Diocese of Long Island. Whereas *The New York Times* has not editorially spoken to my career, I am nonetheless appreciative of your own personal interest in this regard." To his friend C.R. Smith, the former President of American Airlines and Secretary of Commerce in Washington, he included an editorial that did run in *Newsday* sent to him by Capt. Harry Guggenheim and Bill Moyers. *Newsday* called him a "builder." Hoxie continued, "In the hope that you may be helpful, I am enclosing a half dozen copies of my vitae, and I do hope that you and I can sit down at a further little visit in this regard soon." It was amazing how he could self-promote even in the chaos of those days after his firing.

It was even more amazing how he was able to shape the debate, influencing the perceptions of so many people, grand and little, who accepted his analysis and saw him as a defender of private higher education in a time of assault and change. As the Post student newspaper *The Pioneer* noted in passing, Hoxie still remained at that moment President of C.W. Post College, even though he was no longer the Chancellor.

The co-editor-in-chief of the 1966-1967 *Seawanhaka*, Peter Robin Weiss, wrote a very illuminating op-ed for *Seawanhaka*, attempting to connect the ways in which this internal University struggle related to the societal turmoil between one generation and the next. He wrote that "Chancellor Hoxie's resignation is not a victory for student power, and it is not a victory for the progressive faculty of the Brooklyn Center." He said it was "bad enough that Hoxie had become an object of derision to students and faculty. When this image of incompetence started going outside the University - and not only in the Heald Report - it was time for a change. The volleys of abuse fired at Hoxie were becoming so frequent that the Board felt itself no longer safe from the ricochets. And so they removed the target before they became casualties…. Those things that Hoxie espoused a parental, authoritarian administration, traditional rather than innovative educational policies, downgrading or dumping the Brooklyn Center - he espoused with the approval of the Board of Trustees." Weiss observed that Hoxie's dismissal did not mean that the Board had changed its views; "only that it had decided to change its mouthpiece."

By October 17th, Hoxie had agreed to write a book on Arthur Roth and The Franklin National Bank. He asked if the bank would "be interested in the enclosed copy of my curriculum vitae for internal purposes, publicity or both as you deem appropriate." And he suggested that he should have some formal identification at the bank such as "Special Assistant to the Chairman."

Simultaneously, he aggressively continued to pursue Marjorie Post in Washington. On October 16th, he hoped to discuss with her "his future," trying to finagle dinner and an overnight stay at her Hillwood estate. On the margin of his letter, Mrs. Post, wrote in her own hand to her secretary "no," either because she was already busy or did not want to be importuned.

Her secretary wrote a memo to Mrs. Post on October 21st, indicating that Hoxie had called back. He was told he could spend the night, but that she would have no time to discuss his future prospects. The secretary told Hoxie that "actually there was nothing to discuss at this point," and that it was known he was coming to see Mrs. Post, "which surprised him greatly." The source of the leak was unclear, but the secretary speculated that it was Hugh Behymer, the Dean at The Palmer School at Post and friend of Mrs. Post. According to this same briefing memo, Hoxie told Mrs. Post's secretary "that some of the Board have actually been sounding him out to see if he would reconsider coming back-they are reorganizing and talking about keeping the Chancellorship for Internal Affairs and the President for External Affairs." Hoxie also indicated that he had been approached by Syracuse University, Colgate and Dartmouth. Whether any of this actually happened is impossible to ascertain but the secretary wrote, "I tried to stop him bothering you further about this to indicate that you were still interested as I am sure you must be, but that you could not be involved." And so it went.

Hoxie sent to Marjorie Post a copy of a letter from John McGrath detailing the severance agreement, worked out by a special Board committee chaired by Arthur Roth, with John Pell and Franz Schneider as members. He was to receive thirty five thousand dollars per annum for fifteen months and be available "at the call of the Board Chairman to consult and render assistance, but he had to vacate the Chancellor's home by June 1, 1969 or sixty days after a new Chancellor was hired. The Presidential housing allowance was cut to three hundred dollars per month. He lost the car and chauffeur, retained his health and retirement benefits for the interim, and got nothing else.

But he did get to write for the Board a long, self-serving Fourth Annual Report of the Chancellor dated October 21, 1968, which he had the University distribute on a wide basis. It celebrated real and imagined triumphs, dealing with organizational structure and accreditation, future developments and bureaucratic systems, as if he were still the Chancellor in good standing, with a Board interested and responsive to what he had to say. While Hoxie would never have used the word, this Report was the height of *chutzpah*. It read as if much of the past year had not happened. He did acknowledge that "Long Island University represented in microcosm the spirit of turbulence and unrest sweeping higher education throughout the nation and inspiring a record number of three hundred and sixty five presidential vacancies." But he wrote as if he was but an observer of those events rather than a participant. And he was free with advice (much of it self-serving) about how the University should move forward.

He sent this - thirty-four-page - document, to community leaders like Colonel Harry Guggenheim at *Newsday*. His cover letter actively promoted his own world-view, his successful career, and his leadership at the University. Similarly, he wrote to all members of the C.W. Post College Council enclosing a copy of a recent Post Viewbook. He used the Chancellor stationery, although his secretary "x'ed" it out. Hoxie still was continuing to operate as if he were in charge.

Hoxie attended the October Board meeting to report on the previous year's business. He remained naively hopeful he would be elected as a Trustee-something that did not happen. The University's senior public relations officer, Jo Chamberlin, actually had to announce "Dr. R. Gordon Hoxie is not serving the University in any capacity from now on." The Minutes of the November 18th Board meeting reported, "Dr. Hoxie presented orally the substance of his annual report which was heard by the Board with interest. The written report will be mailed in the near future. Following Dr. Hoxie's remarks he retired from the meeting." One can only wonder what William Zeckendorf said to those sitting at the table after Hoxie left the room.

Page four of those Minutes state, "Mr. Zeckendorf Sr. submitted for consideration of the Board, a resume of Mr. Alexander Aldrich, copy of which is annexed hereto, in support of his nomination of Mr. Aldrich as the Chief Executive Officer of the Brooklyn Center." Chairman McGrath told the Board that he tried to secure student and faculty participation in considering Aldrich at a series of meetings: October 11th with faculty, and October 18th with students and alumni. The Board voted to offer Aldrich the position for a salary of thirty thousand dollars a year, including expenses and the house on Pineapple Street in Brooklyn.

Based on what Heald had recommended, McGrath then suggested that a working group of leaders representing LIU stakeholders be established to address how best to reorganize the University structure. The Board established a Committee on Reorganization of five of its members. This group was to be joined by faculty, students, and alumni leaders to assess the Heald-Hobson Report and report back detailed findings to the full Board. In its resolution, the Board agreed that George Stoddard should continue as Acting Chancellor until the blue ribbon reorganization committee presented its recommendations. The Trustee members of the committee were Emilio Collado as Chair, William Zeckendorf Sr., Arthur T. Roth, John

Jay Bergen and C.W. Post alumnus and trustee Vincent J. Macri.

Unlike Pell before him, Stoddard, a seasoned professional, was vested from the onset. It would be his task to revisit the Statutes yet again, defining more exactly the underlying organizational principles that would inform the University and its several campuses.

Meanwhile, Hoxie remained active on Long Island. At Franklin National Bank, he was writing "the fabulous history... which when Mr. Roth came in 1934 had total resources of about seven hundred thousand dollars and today with resources of nearly three billion dollars is one the major financial institutions in the nation." This was described in a letter to Marjorie Post dated December 10, 1968. In that same letter Hoxie wrote, "There is a strong sentiment growing throughout the C.W. Post College family…that…the schools on the Merriweather Campus can best serve together in the future as POST UNIVERSITY." Hoxie then told her that this proposal was being prepared for submission to the Board of Trustees of the University, with number of persons "prepared to reinforce their position by substantial pledges of financial assistance."

That same day, Mrs. Post received a three-page, hand written letter from a former Post student, Damon Scarano, who wrote about the need to protect that campus from the evil forces that seemingly were overtaking the American society. Scarano was in his third year of law school after graduation. He had an apocalyptic vision of American society and identified "dark little princes of power and evil that are busily maneuvering to destroy all our hopes in the manifestation of a Long Island University in place of C.W. Post College."

A week later Mrs. Post wrote back to Damon: "I have done what I could without avail and I now feel that I cannot intrude further so that there would really be no point in discussing it as you suggest. I have been very distressed over all of this and to my mind it is all a great pity…." And she cut him off by claiming her confidence that "in the end through the prayers and efforts of those who love the school and appreciate what it has stood for, everything will work out for the best." Was this truly a spontaneous letter from a C.W. Post alumnus? That is suspect, for how could this young man have had Mrs. Post's home address in Washington?

For the next several years, Hoxie remained on the North Shore. On January 8, 1969, Douglas R. Smith of the National Savings and Trust Company of Washington, got a letter from Mrs. Post thanking him for gifts to Mount Vernon Seminary Junior College and C.W. Post College. She wrote to thank him for both. She commented on Hoxie's termination the previous autumn. Blaming Zeckendorf, she wrote, "Gordon Hoxie was removed from this position as Chancellor of the University and President of C.W. Post College, despite Gordon's wonderful contributions to the College over the years…Quite frankly, I hold no respect or regard for

PART II - RALPH GORDON HOXIE

Bill Zeckendorf and I am sure you know his history as well as I do. He had been the Chairman of the Board of Long Island University for about twenty-five years so of course the Board members were largely composed of his 'own' men and Gordon never had a chance, nor was his extraordinary record given any consideration. I was thoroughly upset and annoyed about this entire affair and for this reason I am cutting myself off completely from C.W. Post College."

Smith hastened to write Hoxie, "I was so completely caught off guard.... I had no indication at all of this.... In any event please don't let me lose touch with you and if and when you are in town, let me know so I can see you." Hoxie responded to Smith on Franklin National Bank stationery that he would be in Washington for Presidential Inaugural festivities and he looked forward to having "a little visit." Employed or otherwise, Hoxie was always looking for a new or better opportunity.

The Post family archives at the University of Michigan contain a press release from the Human Resources Center in Albertson on Long Island. It announced that Henry Viscardi Jr., its long-serving President, had hired Gordon Hoxie to spearhead a three million dollar campaign to construct a special facility for individuals who were physically challenged. The press release indicated that Hoxie "established C.W. Post College as the major branch of Long Island University on Long Island, and under his leadership, Long Island University developed into one of our nation's leading educational complexes."

Whatever Marjorie Post or Henry Viscardi might have thought, William Zeckendorf remained an implacable foe. On January 21st, he wrote his fellow Board members, "Now that C.W. Post College has been disinherited by the family for whom it was named, I thought it appropriate to circulate a letter written by me to Dr. R. Gordon Hoxie on 15 May 1967, bearing on this subject. It seems to me that we are faced with a 'knotty problem' as how to handle the fundraising situation in light of the foregoing."

Zeckendorf had asked Hoxie for information "bearing on the contribution to the college by Mrs. Post and her family, in light of the extent of honors which have been bestowed upon the Post-Merriweather family and, the consequent preeminence of those worthy names in the College's image. It has been observed by certain Trustees that the family's omnipotence of name through dedication of College, campus and buildings, might somewhat impede solicitation for substantial funds from other wealthy persons, families and foundations because of their possible reluctance to make large grants to an institution where titular domination by a family of such vast means exists-as in this case." Zeckendorf noted "Rockefeller University, Stanford University, Duke University, Vanderbilt University, Fairleigh Dickinson University, Russell Sage University, and many others have been heavily endowed by their founders or namesakes. Mrs. Post, in her wisdom I feel sure, is well aware of this and the consummate responsibility which naturally goes with the foregoing set of facts." If Hoxie ever sent Zeckendorf such a report, it no longer exists in the files.

All manner of people kept writing to Mrs. Post suggesting a break up of the University. It is impossible to tell whether some or all of these letters were written because they were requested by Gordon Hoxie or were written spontaneously. The odds are that he continued to push to see if she would yet be that great benefactress whose gift would permit the family to break the Charter entrapment which tied Brooklyn, Southampton, and C.W. Post College together. A letter of January 27, 1969, sent to Mrs. Post's Florida home, Mar-A-Lago, by one of the leaders of the pre-war Citizens Committee in Nassau, James N. MacLean, submitted that "Long Island University should be decentralized; that C.W. Post College, one of the great educational institutions located on the beautiful Merriweather Campus.... should be given a greater autonomy in the handling of its educational and financial responsibilities; that it should be separated from Long Island Center, known as the Brooklyn Center and the Southampton college." Similar letters came from others arguing the same point.

She, in turn, answered each of these graciously, constantly making the point that she simply could not become involved. Hoxie also asked his friends to solicit her for a gift for the Human Resources Center fund drive, which he had promised to lead to that three million dollar goal.

In early February, *Seawanhaka* ran a story that Hoxie had returned to campus to meet with the editors of the paper. It was intercession. The newspaper maintained that Zeckendorf also attended. The story was a hoax, probably written late at night to see if anybody actually was reading what was published. It claimed that Hoxie denied that any member of the Board had been pressured by Zeckendorf into asking for his resignation. Hoxie was quoted as saying, "My resignation was my own fault. I took full responsibility for it." And so the spoof continued. The student reporter, David Medina, wrote, "Both men looked remarkably well and occasionally complimented each other on their accomplishments as LIU administrators. Hoxie was his jolly self again, apparently recovered from the strenuous ordeal of the last months of his tenure." Perhaps, it was written to fool historians fifty years later. Perhaps, farce was the best way to carry on. Perhaps the student editors wanted to prove that "grass" grew in Brooklyn.

Whatever the February reality, on May 5, 1969, Hoxie complained to Marjorie Post about the ungenerous way the University was handling his move out of the Chancellor's home. Later in the letter he wrote, "I am convinced the day is closer than we realize that POST UNIVERSITY will be born. If it is not, then C.W. Post College and the Merriweather Campus will die as such." Hoxie went on, "Since my departure last fall, the University has been unable to raise any money, four of the Trustees have resigned, and others are threatening to." He spoke about how the

Charter Day Dinner was a flop and claimed, "The faculty and students at Post are in a revolt and a committee has asked me to consider returning. This I cannot and will not do under the corporate structure of Long Island University. If I am wanted perhaps some day I shall return with Post University but not before."

In the same letter, he solicited Mrs. Post for a gift of $12,500 for the Library of Presidential Papers, which was an early name of The Center for the Study of the Presidency, the organization which became his life's work after LIU. The letter mentioned that the Nixon administration was exploring whether he might become Assistant Secretary of State for Educational and Cultural Affairs and solicited a letter of support from her to the Secretary of State, William Rogers. On May 19th, she did just as he asked. She also contributed $10,000 to the Center, making a notation on his letter in her own hand. He later compared the generosity of the Trustees involved with the Board of the Center with those at Long Island University. It was an invidious comparison, speaking of the LIU Trustees as "the little people" on the University Board. He could not resist sending her two of his recent speeches on student unrest nationally.

Marjorie Post got a memo from her secretary indicating that Hoxie had called yet again on May 21, 1969. "He discussed C.W. Post College and raised the point that several prominent people were interested in divorcing it from Long Island University, and again mentioned money…. I reiterated that you could not get into this at this time, that it was up to the people there to make definitive definite and concrete moves first, etc…. Hoxie said that (not too long ago, I take it) he had a meeting with John McGrath and Zeckendorf was there…. McGrath became so furious he was shouting at Hoxie and Hoxie, who did not want to become involved in an argument with him, excused himself saying he had an appointment in Washington…."

One of Mrs. Post's other Long Island University correspondents throughout these years was Hugh Behymer, the C.W. Post librarian, himself an erudite upper class patrician who had his own farm, Birch Brook, in Great Barrington, Massachusetts. He wrote in 1969 to bring her up to date on the Board's new appointment, Glenn W. Ferguson, who later became George Stoddard's permanent replacement. Behymer referred her to *The New York Times* of June 27th, where his CV was printed in a *New York Times* story about his appointment. Behymer wrote: "I have only met him once and talked with him very briefly, but I liked him, and somehow he is just what the University needs-a vigorous, young, personable man who seems to have leadership qualities. I understand nothing has been done yet to resolve some of the problems which have faced Post College for a year and that the Board felt it best to wait until a Chancellor was appointed who would straighten things out." Behymer then commented on Stoddard's Interim Chancellorship. "I feel that Dr. Stoddard handles things as well as he could, that we are better off at having him with us."

He then turned his attention to gossip about the Board. Apparently, the Board of Regents was not releasing its report on what happened at the University during the last stages of Hoxie's Chancellorship. Behymer commented that the Regents would "recommend some strong medicine." The word was that Stoddard had a very low opinion of the Board. So Behymer speculated, "I think it was one reason he simply stood up and walked out." Behymer first briefed her on how the chapel was progressing as this was one of her substantial ongoing philanthropic interests on campus, then indicated that he would step down after the Post library received accreditation from the American Library Association. In a letter of response to Hugh Behymer of August 8th, Mrs. Post indicated that Glenn Ferguson wanted to come down to meet her, and she continued to reject a meeting.

Meanwhile, Hoxie was sharing with her how one of her senior employees, Leonard Genz, had nominated him for the Presidency of Columbia University. Hoxie quoted Genz as saying that Columbia was looking for a second campus outside of Harlem, maintaining, "the Merriweather Campus and C.W. Post College would find a happier home in relationship with Columbia University in the event that you feel unable to bring the birth of Post University." Hoxie immediately sent Genz a list of Columbia Trustees he knew. He pushed him to write to Arthur Ochs Sulzberger, Arthur F. Burns, head of the Federal Reserve, and Allan Nevins, a famed Columbia historian, whom Hoxie had wooed unsuccesfully in his last months as Chancellor.

Hoxie quite clearly was functioning in some alternate sphere as he projected what he considered to be possibilities professionally at Columbia and Long Island University. Through inadvertence, the C.W. Post College Bulletin had a picture and a message of greeting from Hoxie written before he was fired. This was to appear in the 1969-70 course catalog and Stoddard, when he learned of it, had the entire run pulled and a new catalog printed. Eleven thousand copies had been printed, so Stoddard paid $8,000 to have those still in the possession of the University destroyed and a new document printed. This gaffe, a year after Hoxie had left, was deeply embarrassing to the Post administration. The *Daily News* had a field day making fun of the University incompetence and the fact that Hoxie still loomed over Post as if he was still President and Chancellor of the University.

Around Thanksgiving of 1969, Mrs. Post returned to the campus because the national fraternity, Sigma Alpha Epsilon, was establishing a Post Chapter and she had been very interested in this. When Hoxie learned, he wrote Mrs. Post, indicating that he too had been an SAE member at the University of Northern Iowa and hoping, "I can get together soon for a little visit."

On December 19, 1969, Hoxie wrote McGrath attaching a copy of a letter from Francis Wilson, a Hoxie loyalist and member of the Post Political Science Department. Wilson had been recruited to help build the doctoral program and had written Hoxie a few days before on a then current tenure case. "Gradually, I learned it was a battle of no quarter given." Hoxie thought nothing of intervening with the Chairman of the Board to try to reverse what was obviously a faculty matter.

Gordon Hoxie was incapable of separating from the University, whatever else he might be doing; wherever he might be living. But after he asked John McGrath a few weeks later to contribute to the American Friends of Chung-Ang University in Korea, an organization which Hoxie chaired, McGrath really blew his stack. He drafted a pithy letter that said it all. "Dear Gordon," he wrote, "Please go away! Yours, John P. McGrath."

A souvenir of a happier time. Chancellor and Mrs. Hoxie being congratulated by President Lim of Chung-Ang University in Korea just after she conferred an honorary degree on him.

Part III - The Aftermath

[It is important] to restore a measure of influence and authority to the Office of [Vice Chancellor of Academic Affairs] .... I am proposing that the Presidents of the Centers report directly to the Vice Chancellor of Academic Affairs. It is the only place above the office of the Dean where one can be reasonably assured of academic expertise.

George D. Stoddard

Chapter Nine

George Dinsmore Stoddard: Another Accidental Chancellor

1968-1969 was one of the worst periods in the history of higher education in America. Student protests reached a peak as anti-war sentiment swelled. The draft impacted directly on the lives of the student-age population. The national student cohort, wrestling with a near mindless demand for compliance because of a flawed domino theory, chanted "hell no, we won't go." There were two quagmires: the rice paddies of the Mekong delta and the college campuses across America.

In retrospect, it is clear that student and faculty protests helped force the American body politic to end the war, but not before deep and lasting tensions surfaced between the generations as well as between America's higher education institutions and much of the rest of American society. Because of profound anger on both sides, universities and colleges were vilified rather than celebrated for standing against these devastating overseas misadventures. During this two year period, one President announced that he would not run for re-election, the Democratic convention was convulsed by riots and police brutality against student protestors, and America elected Richard M. Nixon, a man later forced to resign as President because of malfeasance and dishonesty.

Meanwhile, the Borough of Brooklyn had become scary to a growing number of families who had previously called it home. It was increasingly filled with broken windows and boarded-up doors. Young angry men and women of color joined gangs. Brooklyn became a potpourri of minorities speaking a babble of tongues, new Americans from elsewhere, and orthodox Jews in 18th century garb-an alien, exotic place. The great 19th century mansions of Fort Green became single room occupancies. The Navy Yard go-downs were dilapidated. The pharmaceutical factories of Pfizer and E.R. Squibb were abandoned as those corporations moved their plants to New London or offshore and their headquarters to high-rise office towers in Manhattan. Increasingly, Brooklyn seemed populated by only the elderly, the poor or new Americans struggling to learn English. To flee the inner city "for the burbs" was to escape a national set of challenges that America was not willing to address at that time.

It was within this maelstrom that a fragile Long Island University attempted to survive. R. Gordon Hoxie was fired one month into the academic year. Relieved of responsibility, he still plotted to regain his Chancellorship even if that effort would split the University asunder. Hoxie's dream was to jettison the Brooklyn campus to allow C.W. Post University to emerge liberated from its roots. Many who taught and worked at Post shared this view. It was commonly believed that the Nassau/Suffolk suburban culture would be triumphant. It followed that the inner city -Brooklyn and Queens- was viewed as the decayed remnant of a city enduring very hard times.

With Hoxie suddenly gone, what would happen next? Who would take charge? While few paid attention to the University Bylaws, they mandated that, absent a Chancellor, the Academic Vice Chancellor would automatically become Acting Chancellor. When Hoxie was terminated, therefore, George Stoddard automatically became his successor until such time as the Board hired someone else. He did not want this position and, once in it, was eager to shed it as soon as possible.

Chancellor George D. Stoddard

George Dinsmore Stoddard was a 19th century administrator called on to address 20th century challenges. He was born in Carbondale, Pennsylvania in 1897. A graduate of Penn State with a Ph.D from the University of Iowa in 1925, he had been awarded 15 honorary degrees, had written or co-authored some ten books and 500 articles. He was a committed internationalist who was a former Chair of the United States National Commission for UNESCO. He had studied in Paris after graduating Penn State, and he had traveled the world over, becoming a leader in the internationalization of American universities and their connections to the world beyond. From 1942 to 1946, he was President of the University of the State of New York and Commissioner of Education. He took an early lead in creating the State University of New York. He was President of the University of Illinois from 1946 to 1953, then held a series of ever more responsible positions at NYU, serving as its Chancellor from 1960 to 1964. Well placed, extraordinarily experienced, cultivated and a global citizen, he represented

336

the best in the education establishment of New York. He played an important role in hiring James Hester, then the NYU Board promoted Hester over him.

On March 11, 1968, six months before Hoxie was fired, Hoxie wrote to Bob Spector in his capacity as Chairman of the Faculty Senate. Spector had challenged how Stoddard had been appointed Vice Chancellor for Academic Affairs without faculty review and input. Hoxie recalled that he "had conversations with Dr. Stoddard regarding his appointment with Long Island University to be engaged in the development program of the University as outlined in the ten year plan." After NYU Stoddard, had become involved with the Brooklyn Institute of Arts and Sciences. Hoxie engaged him to assist in the final stages of preparing *Preface to the Future*.

When Henry Mills suddenly resigned to go to St. John's just before the Fall 1967 semester, the Deans asked Hoxie to name Stoddard as an Acting Vice Chancellor to get through the academic year. Hoxie also wanted him because he needed help in negotiating with CUNY. Thus, when Hoxie was fired, the LIU Chancellorship became filled automatically. This was a job Stoddard did not seek, so he defined his mandate narrowly. His job was to hold the place together until a permanent replacement to R. Gordon Hoxie could be found. Central to his tasks were to draft and get approved a further revision of the Statutes, one which would give his successor a manageable institution. Somehow, those Bylaws needed to provide more autonomy to the several campuses. In addition, Stoddard understood that he needed to heal the raw anger in Brooklyn and restructure governance in the University so that influence was distributed to student and faculty leadership in a way that had previously not been done. The place to begin was in organizing the search for his successor.

Six years earlier, John H. G. Pell had taken the interim Chancellorship on a lark. Stoddard was a battle-tested but tired University administrator. The world was profoundly different in 1968 than in 1962. Stoddard must have wondered how he got entrapped so deeply in the affairs of Long Island University.

Even before he became Acting Chancellor, he wrote "a Modest Proposal Concerning the Future of Long Island University with Special Reference to the Brooklyn Center." Initially drafted on May 14, 1968 and revised on June 24, 1968, it was sent to Sam Aldrich when Zeckendorf first brought him into the University's orbit in August. The file copy carried a note from Glenn Ferguson, Stoddard's successor, asking, "were conclusions of this report ever discussed at Brooklyn Center?" The Proposal was much more politically attuned than the Heald-Hobson report. Its goal was to tease apart the complex nexus of issues that made management of the Brooklyn campus so problematic. There were thirteen discrete points discussed, virtually in bullet form. Each was a pragmatic set of steps to improve Brooklyn's future prospects. The document itself, had been drafted in the immediate aftermath of the collapsed option of selling the Brooklyn campus to the City University.

Among the Proposal's many suggestions was that Dormitory Authority funding be secured so that facility construction would not be dependent on tuition revenue. He also proposed establishing a dual-track student admissions system. He wanted the College of Arts and Sciences (the Conolly College) to set its admissions standards equal to those of NYU, while there would be a lower standard for programs that led to a two year associates degree. He proposed a Basic Studies plan to be folded into all two year, junior college level degree programs. Financial aid would be funded-according to Stoddard's recommendation-from multiple levels of government, federal, state, and municipal. In subsequent years, the Tuition Assistance Program, the Higher Education Opportunity Program (HEOP), Pell Grants and Stafford Loans would all become important alternate sources of funding for the entire University, even though by the end of the decade government support was far less predictable or generous a source of student support than was widely hoped.

Echoing Heald's report, Stoddard, wanted the Conolly College to "concentrate on the undergraduate years, planning only a few additional Master's programs" in the Arts and Sciences. He thought that perhaps two or three Doctoral programs would be the outside limit. He acknowledged the possibility of a few additional Masters and Doctoral programs at C.W. Post, especially if "some of the new programs should be professional or quasi-professional, as in business administration or teaching, or be of an interdepartmental nature." No mention of Southampton was made in this section of his memo.

He also suggested increasing "the credit-hour tuition rate for all students who are not full time. Permit only a modest increase for full time students, the tuition preferably to be paid on a lump sum semester basis." He noted, "those who carry college work while holding a full-time or part-time job already have benefits equal to a scholarship. Students who live at home also have benefits equal to a scholarship. Since students in those categories are likely to be part-time, they will automatically enter into the part-time tuition bracket." There followed a series of recommendations designed to run the institution more efficiently. Net tuition revenue was the one reliable source of income. Stoddard also wanted to increase the number of faculty members who had to carry a twelve-hour teaching load (four courses a term). "Permit only research-minded faculty members or members in departments offering the Ph.D to teach exclusively at the graduate level. Permit no extra payments for thesis supervision or teaching beyond a full load, or teaching on the part of administrators beyond what is called for in their contract." And in a similar fashion he wanted to "reduce the number of classes of small size, retaining only those in certain esoteric fields where classes are traditionally small." The University (and in these many recommendations he was talking not simply about Brooklyn) must "provide more large lecture sections, as long as they can be accompanied by smaller recitation or seminar groups which can be staffed in part by younger faculty members or teaching assistants."

None of these efficiencies were terribly innovative or new; they all represented time-honored ways to manage the instructional function of any university more efficiently.

Stoddard wanted curricular reforms which would "place the LIU plan out in front on a nationwide basis." Here he suggested his own plan, "A New Design for the College of Liberal Arts & Sciences," published in *School and Society*. He proposed the Brooklyn Center work with the City of New York School System to create a junior and senior high school in underprivileged areas "to salvage and encourage more students to prepare for college." As his title for the memo suggested, these were relatively modest ways to reposition the role of the Brooklyn campus in the years ahead.

He also proposed "a two year program modeled on the technical community colleges and institutes of applied arts and sciences of the State of New York." If possible, those were to match the low tuition charges of public institutions "intertwining work and study and, if necessary, requiring registration for three years on the calendar." Cooperative education of the sort developed at Northeastern University, the University of Cincinnati, and other "co-op schools" was an alternate modality to build enrollment while offering students an option to earn while learning and blend theoretical study with on-the-job experience.

His last point was "it must be proclaimed that Long Island University does not carry the responsibility for educating all the youth of college age in Brooklyn or elsewhere. Its resources are, and presumably will always be, limited. It is held that the responsibility to see that somewhere all qualified youth are given a college opportunity is *a public function*." Many of Stoddard's ideas were, of course, already implemented at NYU and familiar to LIU. An early form of cooperative education, for example, was developed before the Depression when students worked at Macy's on the sales floor, while attending classes in Brooklyn.

What the cluster of recommendations clearly suggested was a scaling back of Hoxie's dreams, and replacing them with down to earth, experience-proven ways in which a tuition driven college could survive. Stoddard noted, "If anything is to be done along such lines, a giant step should be taken. At LIU the time is late for gradualism." Finally, he offered the self evident if unexciting option of testing the market. "If, after a three-year or five-year tryout of an original plan based on the above proposals or others, there are no 'takers' - the reference is to the student body, faculty, and external support - then indeed Long Island University could withdraw from the community with the feeling that it had done everything within reason to remain there as a vital educational force. At this impasse presumably public higher education would take over." Even while Hoxie was still Chancellor, Stoddard was lowering the trajectory of the University's dreams, offering mundane but achievable ways to survive, despite direct competition from low tuition public-sector institutions.

Once he became Acting Chancellor in October 1968, he moved rapidly to end the confrontational tone of the Hoxie era. There is a fascinating, hand-written set of notes dated October 11th, laying out what was his agenda for his interim Chancellorship. He wanted the Executive Committee of the Board, seven Trustees in all, to be constituted as the "search committee for the new Chancellor or President." Separately he wanted a Trustee committee of five with John McGrath and himself *ex-officio* to redo the organizational charts and Bylaws. He indicated he wanted Emilio Collado as the Chair with Zeckendorf, Roth, Vincent Macri, and Admiral Owen as the committee, and anticipated approximately a half dozen key staff below the Chancellor to staff these two committees.

He insisted that the search for a new Chancellor and the struggle to revise the Statutes begin at once, literally within days of Hoxie's termination. Brooklyn, he clearly understood, was in a special situation, one which might require a different organizational structure from the other campuses and a President or an Executive Dean appointment. In note form, he jotted down "centralization versus decentralization not the issue." There were those who embraced the Heald Report versus those who were anti-Heald. "Rather sufficient autonomy of each center" was the key issue for the Statute revision, which prompted him to lay out an agenda on a third index card, setting the priorities of his brief administration: "(a) start with Heald-H (b) solve the Brooklyn leadership (c) reorganize the U (d) find the new Chancellor." There was no mention of *Preface to the Future*, but much attention to involving the major stakeholders in sharing in the essential life of the institution. By Friday, October 18th, *The Pioneer* reported that student and faculty leadership had met with Stoddard and participated in the Cabinet discussion. The article noted that, "the Statutes of the University, as they stand now, do not permit such spokesmen at the meetings. Nevertheless, Dr. Stoddard arranged for the presence of these representatives and assured their full participation in the Cabinet's decisions."

The Minutes of the October 21, 1968 Board meeting noted the approval of Alexander ("Sam") Aldrich as the chief executive officer of Brooklyn, after consultation with Brooklyn faculty and students. The Board, in addressing the Heald Report, recognized "that appropriate changes in the University's structure must be made in order adequately to discharge the functions imposed by the massive growth in student enrollment and the multi faceted activities in which the University is engaged...." The Board approved the formation of a Committee on Reorganization, as Stoddard had requested. In a follow-up letter to Stoddard from McGrath, annotated by Stoddard's handwritten notes on the text, it was clear that the Executive Committee and Stoddard were in complete agreement about how to move forward.

The head of Public Affairs, Jo Chamberlin, sent a memo to Stoddard on the 28th, summarizing an important meeting Stoddard had with faculty, students, alumni, and key administrators. Chamberlin included several pages of background notes for Stoddard, detailing what was said at that meeting. Those notes quoted McGrath as saying to the group that "he hoped that it would be possible to give the new Chancellor a restructured University which would work better than in the past...." And at the very end of the meeting Zeckendorf was quoted as saying that, "this was an historic occasion, marking a new era in University relations, with representatives of alumni, faculty, and students meeting with Trustees and administrative officers to discuss University problems and goals." By the end of the year, Stoddard had managed to lower the anger level within the University and get the institution to resume its educational tasks in a manner resembling normality.

There is a frivolous memo from John Baiardi to Stoddard in mid-December 1968, making a similar point. "Although I expect there will be fewer ceremonies involving the Chancellor's presence in full regalia, nevertheless, in anticipation of those ceremonies, such as Charter Day Dinner, I think it would be advisable to request that the former Chancellor return the Chancellor's gown and two sautoirs, i.e., the Chancellor of the University and the President of Post College. The gown was originally designed and prepared during Mr. John Pell's tenure." Baiardi went on to ask Stoddard whether this should be done through the woman in charge of commencement gowns or from "higher authority?" Stoddard, in his own hand, indicated, "it should come from the woman in charge."

Stoddard had a sustaining interest in Africa and had become Chair of a working group, the American Educators, whose goal was to help in the building and strengthening of East African universities. The program office, located in Nairobi, wanted Stoddard to meet Glenn Ferguson, the American Ambassador in Kenya, would become Stoddard's chosen successor at LIU. During that first Christmas vacation, Stoddard was committed to be in Nairobi, so he kept up to date on University activities through a series of personal letters from John Baiardi. They were hand typed and included weekly gossip as well as appointments held or decisions taken at various meetings. Of some significance was his report of an early meeting of the Statute drafting committee Chaired by Emilio Collado. Baiardi reported, "It is the considered opinion of those who were present, faculty and administrators, that the deans of the graduate schools must report to the campus executive officer and that they cannot simply bypass that office and go directly to central administration as was proposed in a white paper presented by Deans Scott and VanderWerf to the committee last night."

This issue of the reporting relationships was a flash point dating back through graduate deans to Hoxie and Pell to Conolly. It was a throw away couple of sentences in Baiardi's January 10,1969 letter, but telegraphed a profound transformation in the way Long Island University was going to function. Stoddard was abroad, and in his absence, the drafting committee determined to arrogate back to the campus-based executive a power which both Hoxie and Pell had kept them from acquiring. That decision empowered the campus CEO, the President, to control graduate as well as undergraduate education. Simultaneously it weakened beyond recognition the notion of a single Long Island University graduate school. A unified and single graduate school had been Conolly's bulwark against fragmentation of the entire University. This restructuring reoriented the axis on which the University turned, and shifted to each campus and to the Pharmacy Dean a level of control which was new to LIU.

The chronic tension between the centripetal and the centrifugal has been one of the continuities in the history of Long Island University. There was rarely a happy medium, never a state of equilibrium. The University lurched back and forth, pushed or pulled between those two force fields. Under the proposed new Bylaws, each campus could decide for itself what it wanted to do, provided it had the funds. That meant that Post rode high in the saddle and the other campuses made do. Brooklyn, the Mother campus, lost enrollment and soon would begin to face painful deficits. Southampton, starved for endowment and capital investment, subsequently graduated generations of trained marine scientists but lacked the resources to become something more. C.W. Post became the dominant revenue engine, angry that it was trapped in a University structure that carried the familial burden of helping two weak sisters, each needy of support.

Another long and folksy letter from Baiardi to Stoddard in Africa, touched on several significant topics for the future. The first dealt with the Brooklyn College of Pharmacy, which had been immobilized during the long struggle over the Birenbaum affair and while the possible sale of the Brooklyn campus to CUNY was under negotiation. The Trustees of the Brooklyn College of Pharmacy saw their own brand as diminished. The school was caught in a bind. It could not afford to operate on its own, but LIU was a problematic partner. The full merger, which seemed so promising during Conolly's last days, now locked Pharmacy in to its old and inadequate building. When the saga was over, the Trustees were not sure any building on the Brooklyn campus was in Pharmacy's best interest.

Edward Neimuth was both an LIU Trustee and Chair of the Pharmacy Board of Trustees. His was the key voice linking the two. A well-respected owner of a specialty pharmaceutical manufacturer, he concluded that Pharmacy's interests would be better served if the Brooklyn College of Pharmacy moved to the bucolic C.W. Post campus rather than stay in Brooklyn. In that way the legal agreement would stay in place but the College would not be ensnared in Brooklyn's problems. Pharmacy needed a new home, up-dated labs and more room. All three objectives could be found at Post.

The issue had been high on Hoxie's agenda, but it was not until the Board meeting of January 13, 1969, that Neimuth, having discussed the option privately beforehand, raised the idea with his fellow LIU Trustees. The College would build its long-sought health sciences building with its own funds; would take a ninety-nine year lease in Brookville or in Old Westbury (depending where it was sited at Post), and would move its entire operation out of Brooklyn. The City University, which had talked about a Health Sciences campus over the LIRR train yards in Brooklyn and had shown some interest in buying the old facility, could move some portion of the CUNY's operation into that facility on a long term or interim basis. This seemed to be a solution that could be accomplished swiftly and without legal challenge.

The LIU Board understood Pharmacy's frustration, dating back to when Conolly was still alive. The University Board had hired an architectural firm, (the same one which designed the Southampton gym) with the understanding that the schematic would be a key document in an application to various Federal funding bodies. As the Trustee Minutes indicated, "The total cost of this program will be borne by the College of Pharmacy." (The scheme was abandoned several years later when the National Institutes of Health (NIH) agreed to fund partially a new building, on the condition that it be built in the inner city on the Brooklyn campus. Several years later, Bush-Brown, as mentioned earlier, secured a naming gift from Arnold and Marie Schwartz, the brother and sister-in-law of B. Davis Schwartz, in whose memory the Brookdale Foundation had named the library at C.W. Post.)

Baiardi also reported to Stoddard that the State Education Department planned an on site review of the University in the spring of 1969. The turmoil at Long Island University had not gone unnoticed there. Baiardi corresponded with Charles Minert at the Department. "He indicates that we can expect a two or three day visit in the latter part of April at the Southampton campus and a three to four day visit in early May inspecting and evaluating the Brooklyn Center, the Merriweather Campus, and the Administration Centre. The inspection committee will consist of approximately twenty representatives with four of them assigned to each of the three campuses (Pharmacy excluded) and the balance as a sort of coordinating over-all committee." Minert expressed his serious concerns about the reorganization of the University and the published faculty handbooks, "I wish you both a very happy and pleasant stay in the serene jungle of Africa." Baiardi closed, "and hope you will occasionally give a thought to your colleague, the undersigned, in the not too serene jungle of LIU."

There was one other piece of business at that Board meeting that still deserves attention a half century later. It had to do with the funding of the new chapel at C.W. Post, one of Hoxie's pet projects. The University was struggling to fund this building, which reflected in an ecumenical way Hoxie's belief in the role of religion to train men and women to become thoughtful leaders in America. It was a 19th century conceit, one which harked back to church-sponsored universities in a secular era of student unrest and revolt, but the building and its funding were both partially completed. There was little opportunity to turn back.

Marjorie Post had previously advised Gordon Hoxie of her contribution of 200 shares of International Business Machines Corporation (IBM) common stock. On April 8, 1968, Hoxie had acknowledged this gift and advised her that the value was $117,500. She had made the gift at Hoxie's request for the then proposed law school. When Hofstra had moved forward on its own, Stoddard wrote to Mrs. Post, "there is little or no expectation that the State Department of Education will authorize the establishment of a second law school in Nassau County in the foreseeable future. Therefore, the prospect of establishing a Long Island University law school on the Merriweather Campus is indeed remote." The costs for building the Chapel at that time was $883,750 and the University had only received in pledges or in cash some $540,000. The real cost was likely to be above $1.1 million "after providing for architects fees, site development, landscaping, furniture, etc." Upon Mary Lai's recommendation, Stoddard's letter asked Mrs. Post to transfer her pledge for the law school to the Chapel campaign.

As usual, Marjorie Post had made her gift to C.W. Post College, not to Long Island University, as Frank McGrath pointed out in a cover letter to Baiardi. Under any circumstance, she had to give specific approval authorizing this transfer. But once Hoxie was fired, she said in no uncertain terms that she had no intention of providing any further support to Long Island University. As the English sports phrase would put it, "it was a sticky wicket." General of the Army James Van Fleet wrote to Bill Zeckendorf on January 24, 1969, "My immediate thoughts are, 'To hell with Mrs. Post.' But upon reflection, I think we might wait a reasonable amount of time for her to change her mind, with an apology included. Somehow I feel she will live to regret her hasty action." In February, she wrote to C.W. Post College, Merriweather Campus, "in view of the fact that the establishment of a law school is not now in immediate view and prospect, I do hereby authorize that said stock or the proceeds of sale, be applied to the construction funds of the chapel on the Merriweather Campus." This gift had already been made, the tax deduction taken. She thus grudgingly permitted the fund to be transferred internally.

Even though Stoddard was able to restore some normality to the University, the concept of an uneventful academic year in an era of such national turbulence was, in itself, a contradiction of terms. Students marched, traveled to protest, issued non-negotiable demands and held teach-ins all across the country. On virtually every college campus, student protests were partially linked to local issues or grievances, and partially to student movements across the country, such as civil rights, the war, and the draft.

```
FINANCIAL SUPPORT OF THE BOARD OF TRUSTEES  (9/1/69)
"GET" reflects known gifts that were solicited on behalf of the University

                        GIVE      GET        COMMENTS
JOHN P MC GRATH         13,300   23,850
ARTHUR T ROTH          120,452    1,500
VINCENT J MACRI            200              possibly other through alumni CWP
DR. GEORGE STODDARD      1,450    1,000
DAVID G. BAIRD           1,100              +100,000 note in re stock deal
ADM. JOHN J. BERGEN '61  6,000      700
CLINTON W BLUME          3,000      200
EMILIO G COLLADO         2,637    2,000
EUGENIE M DAVIE '65      1,000
DR. IRVING INNERFIELD   10,000              per BC alumni office-alumni gifts
JOSEPH S LINDEMANN      22,043              +100,000 pledge 50/BCP-50/LIU (?)
EDWARD NEIMETH           2,800
JOHN H G PELL              660
HON. OGDEN R REID '62      200
FRANZ SCHNEIDER         17,143
SPYROS S. SKOURAS       17,500    6,700
SIDNEY L. SOLOMON       13,735   39,231
GEN. JAMES A VAN FLEET   1,400
WM. ZECKENDORF, JR. '56    100
WM. ZECKENDORF, SR.     618,075   2,600  (2600 '69 only..undoubtedly he has
                          880             influenced gifts totalling thou-
Dates given indicate date of last        sands of dollars during his years
gift recorded.                           as board chairman...most likely
                                         has given in excess of the gift
                                         figure recorded).
```

Facsimile of internal report to George Stoddard about Trustee giving, dated September 1, 1969. The Report mixes cumulative gifts with those of the prior year.

To cite one LIU example, there was a near student strike and confrontation in Brooklyn - "a major campus crisis" as *Seawanhaka* called it - until Sam Aldrich and other administrators backed away from expelling several student leaders of color, because of poor academic performance. At that moment in history, it was an old fashioned notion to insist that students be in "good standing" to attend college. The University, instead, established a credit-bearing tutorial program, to permit some eighty students, mainly of color, including SOBU's Harold Charles and Tony Farrell, to stay in the University, even though their GPA did not qualify them. *The Seawanhaka* issue of February 7, 1969, quoted Tony Farrell as threatening "trouble if he and Charles were not reinstated. Charles is going back to school and so am I." The Black Power advocate from Jamaica, declared, "the community is behind us." Grading was deemed racist and discriminatory; not only at LIU, but at colleges large and small, ancient Ivy League institutions and vast public-sector multi-versities. The threats of violence intimidated faculty, and some of them were delighted to mock existing academic norms by willfully joining in this attack on tradition. One Professor of sociology at Brandeis reputedly had a volleyball game in which the winning team all got "A"s while the losers got "A-"s.

There was an editorial in *The Pioneer* demanding student engagement so that a particular senior administrator would be chosen as the next President of C.W Post. The editorial appeared on March 21, 1969, noting that Stoddard was firm with his plans to retire in two months. Brooklyn had a President - Alexander Aldrich - and Post wanted one also. The students wanted Dean Andrew Spiegel and lobbied hard for him.

Edward Glanz wrote to Stoddard on March 3rd lobbying him to formalize student power in the new Bylaws. He noted, *"No adequate provision has been made to include students in the governance of the University."* He argued, "The participation of students in the selection of the new Chancellor and permanently in a new structure… must be provided for if we are to retain our new found University status."

Then, on May 1st, the C.W. Post students issued fifteen demands on the Administration, threatening to strike if they were not met. Among those demands were a tuition freeze; expectations of "substantial" Trustee donations; a student co-op bookstore; student management of all food services; abolition of dormitory curfews and a total open house policy; abolition of classes over forty students and so forth. The popular Dean Andrew Spiegel, whom *The Pioneer* had proposed as President at Post but a few months before, tried to answer these demands only to have the students express "their disapproval by calling for a student strike" and establishing a group called The Concerned Students and Faculty. The strike call was also triggered because the Nassau County police had raided five of seven dormitories on a drug bust, arresting twenty-three students initially and approximately twenty more in off-campus raids.

The demands were a mix of adolescent innocence and a student wish list. What happened at Post was surprising because the Post students were the least militant within the University community. But something similar was happening at hundreds of campuses elsewhere across the country. Underlying the fifteen demands was a rejection of adult authority and a denial, indirectly, that the University had any contemporary role *in loco parentis*. Perhaps the most interesting issue historically, was that the Brooklyn Center Student Council chose not to endorse the fifteen Post demands or the protest action taken by the students thereafter. "'We've demanded things and they didn't support us,' an angry President Steve Fischbein [of the Brooklyn Student Council] said. 'Now they're demanding things and we aren't supporting them.'" The *Seawanhaka* coverage quoted another student, Joe Failowitz, as saying "Let's worry about this campus." He became entangled in an angry verbal clash with members of Council when he refused to quit the floor.

There was no longer much solidarity between the Brooklyn and Post students, and very little willingness to repair the relations.

This fragmentation was the bitter legacy of the years of turmoil and distress. Against this tableau, the revised Statutes were written. The long-standing arrogation of power by the Board and its Chancellor was defined as a thing of the past; a new era of participatory democracy was being proclaimed. But so too was lost the political will to define Long Island University as a single institution. In its place, a new structure was being codified that fractured centralized authority, planning, athletics and all the other elements which typically combine to create what is often described as school spirit and a sense of pride. This notion is enshrined at most universities by the lusty singing of The Alma Mater. The Brooklyn anthem was pedestrian and never heard except at Commencement. The harmonic complexity of the Post anthem was written in twelve tones, by a famous European composer who had fled Hitler and never fully understood what American "school spirit" was. It lacked a single melodic line depending instead on four-part harmony to create a tune. It was impossible for regular students or faculty to sing, even when a choir or chorus led the performance. Neither set of lyrics made any reference to another campus. Southampton didn't have an anthem at all.

Preface to the Future prophesized the emergence within a decade of a great institution which would stretch from one end of Long Island to the other. It would have professional and graduate schools, a cluster of undergraduate learning centers and a national footprint. By 1969, institutional loyalty had shrunk to the campus level. Each campus had its own colors, its own Commencement, its own traditions, and a distinctive identity. Brooklyn teams played in a NCAA Division I conference. Post and Southampton played in Division II. When asked, a student would respond that she or he was a graduate of Southampton College or a student at C. W. Post rather than a student or graduate from Long Island University. In contrast, students at Fordham University would self-identify as a Fordham student, whether he or she went to class on Rose Hill or at Lincoln Center. Such was not the case at Long Island University. It was probably easier to transfer from any college in the world to either Brooklyn or Post than to transfer from one LIU campus to another.

One of the historiographical questions about the evolution of Long Island University was whether these endless Bylaw revisions were an historical continuity or discontinuity, as the University struggled time and again to define itself. Was there ever a shared Mission into which all stakeholders could buy? Did sufficient intellectual and conceptual glue ever exist to hold the place together? If not, why not? Most faculty at the campuses had degrees from Teachers College, NYU or Columbia. Most students came from similar socio-economic households; many were first generation collegians. Later on there were racial and ethnic divides, but up through 1972, all three campuses were still overwhelmingly white. To be sure, the Post and Southampton students usually came from families that had an additional generation in America. In Nassau or Suffolk, it was likely that only the grandparents still spoke Italian at home, while at Brooklyn more students spoke Spanish, or Yiddish or Polish or Hindi to parents and grandparents. If all of this was accurate, what created such campus-based anger and rivalry?

When Henry Mills left suddenly to take the Academic Affairs Vice Presidency at St. John's, he left Stoddard a note, dated August 25, 1967. "Here is one of the stickiest problems that I think you are going to face this year. After you read the file, which is quite voluminous, I think you might be wise to talk to Dean Arden, who is on the committee which did the initial spadework in preparation for possible revision of the Statutes and who is thoroughly familiar with everything that went on. I think something should be done to get the statues revised because, in addition to certain substantive changes that I think desirable, there are minor inconsistencies.... But watch your step. Rather strong feelings were aroused last year, and we decided ultimately to 'leave it lay.'"

Four days later, he followed up with a second memo to Stoddard. "You will find in the file in your new desk a folder entitled, 'Thoughts on Administrative Relationships.' I have a feeling that this is now out of date, particularly if my hunches with respect to the nature of the Heald - Hobson report are correct, but you might find it profitable to go through the file simply for the background it will afford you on some of the senior administrative staff. Birenbaum, of course, if [is] gone, but Ewald and Glanz are still here. The picture has been changed somewhat also by the fact that there are two new graduate Deans - Scott and VanderWerf- but the hassle of the three years I have been in this Chair still comes through the material in the file."

In Stoddard's first days as Acting Chancellor, he wrote McGrath "to clarify and regularize the plan of administration in the University.... That office of *President,* as now applied to the four Campuses, be abolished; [and] That, pending a determination of the titles and functions of the chief executive officers of the Colleges and the Campuses, the vacant positions of provost of the Brooklyn Center and provost of the Merriweather Campus be not filled."

In the October 31, 1968 issue of *Seawanhaka*, there was an article dealing with the search for a new chief executive officer at Brooklyn. "Originally formed last June, the Provost Selection Committee's name has since become outdated. A recommendation of the Heald-Hobson Report suggested the creation the post of President of Conolly College, which would do away with the positions of provost of the Brooklyn Center and Dean of Conolly College. The Provost Selection Committee has retained its original name because it is not definitively known what the new position would be called."

An adjacent story began, "If anything can be accomplished by the Committee on

Reorganization, it will be obtained with Emilio Collado," quoting alumnus Dr. Alan A. Livingston. Livingston was the alumnus serving on the Board who brought suit against his colleagues, and in this story he waxed enthusiastic about Collado's foresight. "Many constituents of the University," he said, "wanted him to be Chair of the Board of Trustees." Collado did have an excellent curriculum vitae. He was fifty-eight, the Executive Vice President of Standard Oil Company of New Jersey, and with degrees from MIT and Harvard earned during the Depression; he was a member of the Academy of Arts and Sciences, the American Economics Association and the Council on Foreign Relations. Collado was "a most brilliant man," as Professor Nathan Resnick noted.

At the opening meeting of the Organization Committee on November 5th, Collado noted, "A very broad or across-the-board issue is the relation of the individual campus and its divisions to the central organization. The University's position needs to be defined - somewhere between a strong centralized operation and a confederation." Both Collado and Stoddard wanted the process to be swift, so by December 3rd, the five sub-committees were to report out their work to the Committee of the Whole. Collado drove the process forward: there was active engagement by the project stakeholders similar to that generated by Hoxie during the preparation of the *Preface to the Future*. These participants brought to the project a shared enthusiasm rarely displayed at the University.

The Minutes of the November 18th Board meeting report that, "Prior to consideration or the regular agenda, Chairman McGrath opened the meeting with the discussion of the leadership of the Brooklyn Center. He referred to Dr. Stoddard's recommendation (by letter November 12, 1968) of Mr. Alexander Aldrich as President of the Brooklyn Center, commencing January 1, 1969. Dr. Stoddard referred to a proposed revision in draft of the Statutes, which would accommodate the establishment of the chief executive officer entitled President, for the Brooklyn Center. The proposed draft envisions that the President would have total internal administrative responsibility...." Then followed an enumeration of the scope of that new position. In general, it was proposed that, "the Deans of the various schools in operation at the Center would have direct access to the Vice Chancellor for Academic Affairs." Of course, opaque sentences like that failed to define exactly what was meant by "direct access." Any structure must of necessity depend on good will; at LIU that remained elusive.

"Dr. Collado discussed the theory behind organizational structures of universities, indicating that these were not typically straight line arrangements." Whether an Executive Vice President of a large oil company could truly grasp the theory behind organizational structures of universities was problematic. There was very little discussion in the Minutes about how the five subcommittees planned to reorganize the institution to address the fragmentation and isolation that had become an increasing reality. Collado felt optimistic that this time the University could get it right. The files contain long documents detailing how the University would achieve those objectives. Southampton College, for example, boasted that its report "is a most unusual document. It was adopted unanimously by our College Policy Council."

The most important subcommittee was Structure and Organization, chaired by Professor Rosalie Levine. The notes of its November 25th meeting quoted Stoddard as "pursuing a middle ground with regard to University control. Although centralized decision-making is not desirable neither is autonomy for the units." He stressed "the many administrative economies which would be available if the units are federated." The Minutes further indicate that most agreed with his view. Those notes continued, "Since each college has differing needs, each campus needs different campus leadership. Two subsequent sentences summarized the collective view of 1969. The first: "In the absence of specific restrictions, maximum leeway should be allowed the local campuses," and the second: "In general terms, it was agreed that the 'role of the central administration is to see that energies are liberated at the local level.'" When the discussion turned to the question of to whom graduate Deans would report, Rosalie Levine suggested that a dual structure "might increase the 'area of combat.' Where you have strong campus executives, perhaps the graduate Deans should report only to them."

These discursive notes were edited into a more structured document, which observed that while "the role of University officers vis-à-vis campus executives, seemed to be implicit in the preceding discussion, it was not precisely spelled out." It seems likely that the earlier set of rough notes was prepared by Professor Levine; the second edited version, by Stoddard himself.

Stoddard devoted a great deal of energy to this process. He received reports from the various subcommittees and sent detailed comments back to the working groups on a sentence-by-sentence or paragraph-by-paragraph basis. At the plenary meetings, Collado, both Zeckendorfs, McGrath, Spector and others participated actively.

At the meeting of December 3rd, for example, "The question arose as to the University Senate Bylaws - how they were set up and what authority they had?" Dr. Lettis (a Post faculty member who served as Chair of the Faculty Senate) and Dr. Baiardi, advised that the Bylaws had been prepared in Mr. Pell's administration, had been drafted in large part by Dean Eugene Arden, and had been approved by the Senate and the Trustees. There followed detailed discussion. The specifics are no longer relevant, but the tone of the meetings was collegial and cooperative. The key representatives of the various stakeholder groups worked comfortably with each other, with the shared consensus that a laissez-faire approach would allow each of the campuses to find its own destiny and mission.

"As to the relations between the campus and the central administration, Dr. Lettis suggested that the campus should retain all those prerogatives or rights or operations not specifically reserved to the central administration. (As States are supposed to possess all rights other than those specified as Federal)." The Minutes of that meeting continued, "Mr. Collado and others expressed the thought that in University organization, there seem to be agreement on the central principles. It is when we get down to details that there is difference of opinion. The suggestion was made, and approved, that a somewhat philosophical educational statement on the relations between the campuses and the central administration of the University should be drawn up, and used in connection with or as part of the Statutes."

A week later the Structure of the University Subcommittee met alone. "It was agreed that Long Island University should be neither completely centralized nor made up of completely autonomous units. Rather, there was consensus that the University should be a federation of semi-autonomous campuses." Moreover, an executive for each campus should have the responsibility for running that campus, including "academic programs, housekeeping affairs, athletic, student affairs, etc., and to some extent should also assume some responsibility for development for his campus. It was again affirmed that all powers not specifically delegated to the University Center should be reserved for the campuses."

Dr. Baiardi "suggested that if we move in the direction of strong campus executives, then campus officers should be directly responsible to their respective President rather than to the University officer (which is now the practice). The consensus seemed to be that while there should be flows of communication between the campus and the University Center, there should not be direct lines of authority to the Center (except through the President)." When the endless question of the graduate schools and "the lines of responsibility for the graduate Deans arose, it was suggested that Chancellor Stoddard be asked to form a separate subcommittee to deal with this matter alone."

Mirabile dictu, "after much discussion, there seemed to be general agreement on most matters. It was recognized by all at this meeting that a campus executive would probably be named. Graduate Deans would then be responsible to the President. Budgets for graduate schools would be determined by the President in consultation with the Deans."

Two areas remained unresolved, according to the Report of the Meeting of December 9th. "Chancellor Stoddard suggested that the Graduate Deans themselves meet with their faculties to consider the relative desirability of having a single Graduate School on two campuses or separate schools at each center." And the second issue "centered on the question of whether the Deans should be directly responsible to their Presidents alone, or whether they should concurrently report to the Chancellor." One view was that "by giving the Graduate Deans an alternative to the President's final authority (permitting them to have a 'Supreme Court' in the Chancellor), problems would never be finally settled at the campus level." The document indicated that the Graduate Deans took the opposite view. They felt that "their option of reporting to the Chancellor is a safety valve. They feel strongly that a President will 'want to keep us weak,' and in order to safeguard themselves, they must be able to report to the Chancellor."

The document then noted that this was "a very difficult issue and one the full Committee should discuss at length. The basic issue is that of the reporting of the Graduate Deans - but there is also a larger issue - what should be the relative positions of the Graduate and Undergraduate Schools. Is the Undergraduate College the heart of the Campus (as the Post memo suggests), or are the Graduate Schools and Graduate Deans all equal to the Undergraduate College and the Undergraduate Dean?"

The document then cited Stoddard's comments. To the question should the University be broken into its constituent parts, Stoddard answered "no." Should the University move towards a monolithic administrative structure, emphasizing centralization? "Again, the answer is no, with the proviso that some functions should be retained centrally in order to present a solid LIU front on such matters as accreditation, budgets and other financial operations, exchanges of students and staff members, purchasing, development campaigns, and general academic policy." Stoddard further felt "The centralization factors would reside in a small all-University administrative staff and in a single Board of Trustees. The Campuses or Centers would be expected to vary in their academic designs and programs; in fact, they would be encouraged to do so."

And finally, "There has been some discussion of the possibility of eliminating the office of Vice Chancellor for Academic Affairs. Experience over the country, however, strongly supports its retention. The alternative is to assign numerous duties to one or more assistants to the Chancellor, no one of whom is to be a person of academic stature." In sum, the University was redefining itself so that each campus was a tub on its own bottom with the challenge to pursue its own destiny in its own way in virtual autonomy from its sister campuses. There was little discussion about money or what would happen if one campus had substantial revenue while the others did not or what would happen if two campuses wanted to establish comparable programs. Would there be a common financial aid policy across the system, or would each campus determine its own net tuition revenue figures, based on student numbers or the wealth of their families?

In a memo to Drs. Collado and Lettis, Rosalie Levine wrote, "It is assumed that once an overall campus budget has been determined by the President and the Chancellor, the President will be free to implement it as he sees fit. For example, if the President requests a specific purchase (to be made by the University Purchasing

352

Office) the University office may advise against it, but may not refuse to make it, providing there is money available in the campus budget." George Stoddard had been President of the University of Illinois and understood that the great Mid-western universities all had a "flagship" campus and satellites. These Bylaws moved LIU in that direction, with the C.W. Post campus arrogating to itself the flagship role.

By Saturday, December 21st, the full committee met and, in effect, sealed the deal. Rosalie Levine, representing C.W. Post, "emphasized that a consensus [sic] to date indicated that full powers should reside in the campuses, with delegated powers to the central administration." John McGrath directed the group's attention to a Stoddard memorandum "which refers to the centralization versus autonomous issue." A general discussion followed without resolution. In like fashion, during the afternoon session of that same meeting, there was disagreement about whether the second officer of the University should be called an Executive Vice President. The faculty representatives in particular were concerned that the Presidents of the Campuses report only to the Chancellor not to a Vice Chancellor for Academic Affairs.

None of these issues were new. All had been argued again and again and left unresolved for further study or another process never articulated. Once again, the University was swinging back towards a confederation and away from becoming an integrated single entity. To drive that point home, Former Chancellor Gordon Hoxie intrusively wrote to the Board on December 27, 1968, a letter with the salutation, "Dear Former Colleague." Reentering the discussion as if he had been an active participant who had taken sick leave and just returned, he talked about his recommendation for University reorganization as he had in the days before he was terminated in September.

He used as a pretext, the suggestion made by Princeton President, Robert Goheen, in which he called for "*both* a President and a Chancellor for major universities, the one essentially in charge of external affairs and fundraising and the other internal affairs and education. Since Chairman McGrath and Dr. Collado advised me that you are currently studying the Long Island University organization, I hope the recommendation of President Goheen, reinforcing my own, might be helpful." This letter was sent while Stoddard was in Africa. One might still faintly hear Bill Zeckendorf's teeth grinding as Hoxie reasserted himself into such sensitive University matters. Many college CEOs lost their jobs in the late 1960s, but few stayed as obsessed as Gordon Hoxie with their prior institutions. Even fewer refused to go away. Hoxie's letter gave as his return address, 925 Hempstead Turnpike, Franklin Square, NY - the executive headquarters of Franklin National Bank.

On January 30th, the Committee on Reorganization met with the Faculty-Student-

Alumni Committee to broaden the stakeholder discussion on the proposed Bylaws. At that meeting, Lester VanderWerf, the Dean of the Graduate School of Education, again raised questions about the relationship between the Graduate Deans and the Vice Chancellor for Academic Affairs. The Minutes of the meeting indicate "Considerable discussion followed on just what could be the roles and powers of the Vice Chancellor for Academic Affairs, the Vice Chancellor for Development, and the proposed Vice Chancellor for Business, and whether they would be essentially assistants to the Chancellor or executives with considerable powers on their own." Dr. Collado suggested that "they derive their powers from the Chancellor and they would have what powers he assigned to them. Theirs was," he felt, "essentially a staff rather than a line function."

This issue, discussed consistently for a decade, was always explosive, and so it remained. Collado responded to Vander-Werf, an obvious loser in the new scheme, by citing his central, structural premise: "the individual campuses would have all powers not specifically reserved to the central LIU administration." "Dr. Levine said the Graduate Deans would have to 'work with' the campus Presidents under the organizational plan she had proposed." Jo Chamberlin, who took those Minutes, noted. "The discussion of the relation of the Roth School and the Graduate School of Education to the undergraduate divisions continued, but as this subject has been treated extensively elsewhere, I will not go into the details here." The Committee, at this meeting, "agreed that the title of Chancellor for the chief executive officer of the University should be retained. Other titles were ruled out for various reasons." The group discussed the renaming of the C.W. Post campus. "A discussion of names for the various campuses followed. The 'Brookville Center of LIU' [was] suggested." The group approved "phasing out 'Merriweather' as a campus name."

By February 1969, the devolution process had continued to the point "there are two separate Schools of Education, one at the Brooklyn Center and one at the Merriweather Campus, each Dean of the school reporting directly to the President of the Center. Similarly for Business, there would be two separate Schools of Business Administration, one at the Brooklyn Center and one at the Merriweather Campus, each Dean of the school reporting directly to the President of the Center."

On February 22nd, Stoddard prepared a "Statement of The Chancellor" and an annotated draft of the Statutes, warning the Committee that the devolution of authority from the Center to the campuses may have gone too far. "In the present organization chart of Subcommittee #2 [Rosalie Levine's subcommittee] it will be seen that six line officers report to the Chancellor, ten line officers report to the President of a Center, and a substantial high-level staff is implied for the office of Vice Chancellor for Business Affairs. Apparently, no high officer is to report to the Vice Chancellor for Academic Affairs; in the chart he has no staff and in the descriptive text no assigned duty except that of 'coordination.' It is designed as a weak office; no one need ever turn to it. Would a first-class man want it or be happy in it if he gave it a try?"

Too belatedly, Stoddard warned of the dangers of tipping the scale so heavily toward campus self-governance. All the parties eagerly sought to break free of what they argued was the oppressive centralization of the Hoxie years. All three campuses wanted its President to have decision-making control and a full measure of autonomy. Stoddard himself was planning to leave by the end of that academic term, so he was shouting into the wind when he sought "to restore a measure of influence and authority to the office of [Vice Chancellor of Academic Affairs].... I am proposing that the Presidents of the Centers report directly to the Vice Chancellor of Academic Affairs. It is the only place above the office of the Dean where one can be reasonably assured of academic expertise."

This eleventh hour less radical restructuring plan collided directly with what both Collado and Levine sought: an emasculated Academic Vice Chancellorship. Their interests lay in eliminating as much centralized control as possible, certainly in the academic management of each campus. Admiral Conolly would have been stunned. Stoddard was too accidental a Chancellor to be willing to resist the tide. He spoke his piece, but had little invested in the outcome. He did mail a thirty-page document to key faculty, Trustees and administrators outlining his views. A few agreed with him, although most, especially those at Post, fervently wanted a weak or non-existent Vice Chancellorship of Academic Affairs.

Florence Miller, (the Brooklyn faculty member earlier deposed as head of its AAUP chapter), was one of the few who agreed with Stoddard. On February 27, 1969, she wrote to the Committee on Reorganization actively expressing her opposition. She was against a "decentralized administrative structure, consisting of semi-autonomous campuses in the loose federation, with central administrators acting as resource people." She reminded her colleagues in the University community that LIU was ignoring "entirely the fact that both Middle States and the New York State Board of Education have cautioned Long Island University against developing such 'a loose federation.'" Speaking as a Brooklyn faculty member who taught Business Administration, she noted, "the Brooklyn Center faculty of the Arthur T. Roth Graduate School of Business Administration has not been called into meeting by the associate Dean for more than two years. (The only meetings had been those held jointly under the leadership of the all-University Deans.) Under the present leadership, the Brooklyn Center faculty does not function as a faculty. Why? Because the C.W. Post faculty has little interest in working with colleagues in Brooklyn."

Ed Glanz, the Provost at Southampton also agreed. He wrote Stoddard on February 28th, "A strong Vice Chancellor for Academic Affairs is highly desirable. The Center or Campus Presidents may always seek the Chancellor's approval in an appeal situation if they disagree with the Vice Chancellor for Academic Affairs."

PART III - THE AFTERMATH

Jo Chamberlin wrote his "one hundred percent "support of Stoddard's recommendation that the Vice Chancellor for Academic Affairs constitute a 'strong post,' with clearly defined functions and powers and what Mayor Daley of Chicago called 'clout'…. It was most unfortunate for the University that Dr. Hoxie did not delegate responsibilities to the office of Vice Chancellor of Academic Affairs." But popular opinion remained overwhelmingly negative; Stoddard had shared his views and was, in effect, finished.

When Stoddard met next with the Committee on Reorganization and the Faculty-Student-Alumni Committee on Revision of the Statutes on February 25th, he still remained uncertain. He was committed to get those Bylaws to the Board for approval. But based on his extensive experience at the University of Illinois, NYU, and the Board of Regents, he was ambivalent at "having one professional Dean to cover more than one campus," noting that one Center or another was really assigned to an associate Dean. Chamberlin's Minutes indicated Stoddard conceding that, "if the President of a Center is to have full authority, he should have supervision over graduate and professional instruction, as well as undergraduate."

At the same time, his insistence that the Academic Vice Chancellorship be a real job forced Rosalie Levine to back off from the maximalist position she took some weeks earlier. As Chamberlin recorded it "A discussion followed on the role of the Vice Chancellor of Academic Affairs. Dr. Levine noted that at the last reorganization group meeting, she believed it had been decided that the language of the Statutes relating to the (Campus) President's relations with Chancellor had to be rephrased. It was agreed that there should be strength in the office of Vice Chancellor of Academic Affairs." In the end, the 1969 Statute revisions were slightly amended in the final search for consensus. There was no mention of the past debates on the same topic.

In mid-March, Mary Lai sent Stoddard a memo she had first written in 1963 about the "Total Image of the University." Much had happened over the six years between that first memo (which had been shared with the Middle States site visitors) and this revision of the Statutes. Yet her prior observation that "relatively few people who know about Post College are aware that it is a part of Long Island University. Nor does its name suggest just where it may be located" remained accurate. Mary Lai continued to believe that "the C.W. Post name needed to be replaced by Long Island University in Brookville." She argued to Stoddard that it would be easy to re-assign the name, "C. W. Post College" to the undergraduate College of Arts and Sciences, letting geography define each of the campuses. Since Mrs. Post had now made it clear she would not make a transformational gift, Mrs. Lai argued there was no reason to reward the Post family with immortality. Her proposal got nowhere.

On April 18th, at a special meeting of the Board of Trustees to vote on Statute revision, Frank McGrath drafted a resolution to approve the new Statutes based on the recommendations of Heald, Hobson and Associates. That resolution noted the multiple stakeholders who participated in the re-drafting effort, and celebrated the consensus that was formed with faculty, alumni, and students. It asked the Trustees to approve the Report of the Committee on Reorganization so that it would come into effect on July 1, 1969. When Emilio Collado was asked to speak, he "indicated that the Committee Report represents a unified University embracing a federation of semi-autonomous colleges."

On June 27th, George Stoddard wrote to John McGrath, copy to Glenn W. Ferguson, by then Chancellor-elect of the University. He thanked McGrath for granting him a terminal leave of absence from the post of Vice Chancellor of Academic Affairs starting July 1st. He wrote, "This will give me a chance to get my personal and professional affairs in order in advance of my new assignment in September. This will involve an arts curriculum project and nineteen high schools under the joint auspices of the U.S. Office of Education, the National Endowment for the Arts, and the JDR 3rd Fund. My office will be at the JDR 3rd Fund...." He observed that there had been "well-documented turbulence of Long Island University and elsewhere," but he spoke about how "the past two years have supplied a colorful climax to 44 years in teaching, research and administration."

With a gentle, self-deprecating humor, he wrote McGrath "Your most generous comments on my work at L.I.U. are indeed welcome; I shall see that they come to the attention of my family who more than once have wondered what I have been up to in Brooklyn and other parts east! Especially I have enjoyed your absolute support on every occasion and I treasure your friendship." Stoddard clearly saw himself as an interim Chancellor; his job was to hold the fort until a permanent replacement to Hoxie was found.

Clearly, he did more than that. By acknowledging the reality of what faculty, students and Trustees fervently wanted, the redrafting of the Bylaws seemed a route to peace. The various stakeholders, who met so passionately to redraft, made common cause. Collectively they pushed to decentralize the University and devolve power. In a year when many other American universities were imploding, Stoddard calmed the waters and achieved consensus. The April 18th issue of *Seawanhaka* published a long interview with Stoddard, celebrating his beneficial impact on the University.

"Despite his age, and his reluctance to assume the many responsibilities Fate seems to have unwillingly thrust upon him," Stan Gelman of *Seawanhaka* wrote, "the man who replaced the excoriated R. Gordon Hoxie has rapidly moved in stamping his own imprimatur on the 22,000 student University he has governed since last fall. With a progressive outlook of a man half his age, the elderly Stoddard has revamped the Chancellor's Cabinet, played a leading role in reorganizing the

Statutes and, in general, sought to obliterate the image of the dictator...." Gelman spoke with respect of someone who had been defined as Hoxie's henchman when he arrived. The students were angry because Stoddard had supported Hoxie when he was Vice Chancellor of Academic Affairs and because he had been delegated to negotiate with the City University. Moreover, the students were peeved that the Board had appointed Stoddard without any consultation with them, despite the centrality of that issue. "In sponsoring all these liberalized programs, however, Stoddard managed to confound his critics...."

Stoddard's greatest achievement was to get through that first year with the University still intact. He brought normality back. The 1968-1969 academic year, had a clear beginning, middle and end. If he was somewhat stolid in both appearance and in manner, he produced a soothing and much needed uniform tone to the place. Sometimes stolid is good.

In the decades that followed, his role at LIU has been virtually forgotten. His name does not grace any building and few remember him or his contributions. By allowing the faculty, especially at Post, to get its long-coveted autonomy, he permitted what the University community seemed so desperately to crave-separation. The new structure and Stoddard himself won wide initial approval, as the hypercritical *Seawanhaka* acknowledged. There was a new optimism and a real chance that the University could regroup. The community was granted a year to heal. It needed it.

It turned out that the new Bylaws did not solve the university's structural tensions as hoped. In fact, things got worse. But that was not clear in the spring of 1969. By 1973, there would be a new set of Bylaws drafted. The University was lucky at that particular time to have found such an experienced professional. Given what would happen during the next few years, this interregnum was a crucial respite.

George Stoddard died in Manhattan on December 29, 1981 at eighty-four. *The New York Times* celebrated his long and distinguished career in an elegant obituary. Just prior to his death, his own autobiography, *The Pursuit of Education: An Autobiography*, was published, including a mini-chapter entitled, "Long Island Interlude."

In it he chronicled how Hoxie had invited him in October, 1966 to become a part-time consultant to help with the drafting of *Preface to the Future*. He observed that few Manhattanites had even a "general familiarity with the sociological and cultural problems of Brooklyn,..." He assumed that Hoxie had got his own contact information from his good friend, Henry Heald, but his name might also have been referred by Jim Hester or others at NYU. Stoddard wrote: "No more need be said about the 165-page report, *Preface to the Future*; I had practically nothing to do with it, and it in turn had very little to do with the course of events at the

University."

A few pages on, he noted: "The issuance of the Heald report did not quell the turbulence over the chancellor's fitness to stay in office; the split involved not only faculty and student body, but also the Board of Trustees. Happily, at the climax, I was busy and far away... [in] East Africa.... Asked if I was in the running as a candidate for the permanent chancellorship, I replied that 'I'm not in the running; I'm not even in the walking'"

He spoke of himself rather as folding his tent and silently stealing away. "Mr. John P. McGrath... gave me a farewell blessing which I unblushingly reproduce here- I have had so few of them...." After celebrating Stoddard's "assistance, support and wise judgement," McGrath mused: "the academic year 1968-1969 has been in all probability the most turbulent single year in academic life anywhere. It is no accident that life at Long Island University has been relatively calm. I attribute this to your leadership, your personal stature and the respect in which you are held by all the elements of the University."

Long Island University must create a rationale for its existence as a corporate entity. At the present time, there is no meaningful faculty, student, or curricular enrichment resulting from the affiliation of the three Centers. There are deep feelings and factions, a high degree of subjective opinion, and a lack of good will for the holding corporation called Long Island University. If it does not have meaning, let us not perpetuate a façade.

Glenn W. Ferguson

The Chancellor was not engaged to restructure the University or to preside over its dissolution....it is no news to our Board members that the theoreticians of the academic world have looked upon Long Island University as a series of achievements that could not happen, have not happened, and cannot continue to happen. Our University has its weaknesses but it also has its strengths.... We have faith.

John McGrath

Chapter Ten

Glenn Walker Ferguson: A Shooting Star

If Hoxie could not separate and would not go away, Stoddard was not willing to stay a day longer than he had to. He had seen his first assignment as revising the Statutes and gaining critical buy-in from the three campuses and faculty, students, and administrative leadership on each. In the process, he created an era of good will, because the process of drafting those Bylaws generated the shared governance desperately sought during the Hoxie era. The collective wisdom of the time was that the University needed to be as fragmented as possible while somehow maintaining the structure of a single corporation. Stoddard was not unaware of the risks to the University, but went with the flow, and the flow craved the fragmentation that the Stoddard Statutes reflected.

The second critical assignment that he had to fulfill was the successful recruitment of the next Chancellor. He felt hostage to Long Island University until a new Chancellor could be identified and elected. The University needed leadership. It needed a dynamic young visionary who understood the 1960s, could relate to students effectively, and could chart a corrected course that would permit the University once again to thrive. Virtually everyone within the University craved a charismatic leader and Stoddard believed he had found the ideal candidate in Glenn Walker Ferguson. A forty-year-old United States Ambassador to Kenya, Ferguson had it all: youth, charm, high intelligence, prior experience and the capacity to carry the University well past its troubles toward Conolly's dream or a new one.

Chancellors George Stoddard and Glenn Ferguson.

He was born in Syracuse, New York and got his Bachelor's and Master of Arts Degrees from Cornell University. At Cornell, he majored in economics, won a national scholarship and was selected as class orator at Commencement. An undergraduate leader, he was elected President of the Inter-fraternity Council. He played baseball, football, and track on the varsity teams. He served in the armed forces during the Korean War and was stationed in Korea, Japan and the Philippines as a psychological warfare officer in the Air Force. He earned a law degree from the University of Pittsburgh, working there as a teacher and then an administrator from 1956 to 1960. He served in the central administration as an Assistant to the Chancellor, became an Assistant Dean in the Graduate School of Public and International Affairs, and was recruited as a rising star by the Kennedy Administration. He was the first Peace Corps director in Thailand, Associate Director in Washington for recruitment of Peace Corps volunteers and, in 1964, was appointed Special Assistant to Sargent Shriver, John F. Kennedy's brother-in-law and the first Director of the Peace Corps. He became the first Director of VISTA (Volunteers in Service to America), the domestic counterpart to the Peace Corps. Prior to government service, he had worked as a management consultant at McKinsey & Company, one of the world's foremost consultancies.

Lyndon Johnson appointed him United States Ambassador to Kenya in 1966, and when he arrived, he conducted his introductory press conference in Swahili. Stoddard, who had met him in East Africa during his visits there, regarded Ferguson "as one of the outstanding young men in the United States. When I visited East Africa on a consulting assignment, I found him to be not only a highly admired member of the diplomatic corps, but also a person who deeply appealed to the leaders of the ten million blacks in Kenya." The American government concurred in that assessment: he was awarded the Arthur S. Fleming Award as one of the ten outstanding young men in the federal government. Ferguson was married with three teenage kids and, in 1968 needed a job, since Richard Nixon had little interest in a young democratic idealist recruited by Kennedy. It is a long established practice that politically-appointed Ambassadors and other senior officials tender their resignations so that a newly-elected President may appoint his/her own choices to Ambassadorial positions worldwide.

The match between Ferguson and LIU, which seemed made in heaven, almost faltered at the marriage ceremony. The Board of Trustees failed to consult with faculty and students, choosing instead to appoint Ferguson as it had prior Chancellors: solely by its own will. Perhaps the Board felt Ferguson's extraordinary curriculum vitae would give him a pass. Perhaps they simply forgot what the new Bylaws now demanded. Perhaps they were so insensitive to the cultural changes around them that they just didn't get it. In any case, they mindlessly damaged their own golden choice. The Faculty Senate, Chaired by Professor Robert Spector, voted to reject Ferguson's appointment. It called for the resignation of the entire Board.

The sequence of events defies comprehension decades later. The July 3, 1969 issue of *Seawanhaka*, chronicled a classic case of mishandling instead of what should have been a triumphant moment. Right after Hoxie had been fired, McGrath met with a new all-University Committee to discuss both Statute revision and the selection of a new Chancellor. The students were angry that Stoddard had become Acting Chancellor, then Chancellor. The faculty grudgingly accepted the idiosyncratic, almost random, way Stoddard got to the Chancellorship. But it was clear going forward that the faculty would expect a say in the hiring of his successor.

Emilio Collado had been approached to see whether he was interested in the position. He declined, later commenting, "I don't want to be Chancellor." John H.G. Pell's experience might have influenced his decision, or as a successful corporate officer, he did not want to interrupt his career at Standard Oil. Or, having discovered the depth of anger within the University, he did not want to become the focal point for this rage.

On May 8th, Jo Chamberlin commented that, "there is not one chance in fifty million" that a successor to Stoddard could be named before June 30th" He went on, "We are by no means ready to move on the selection of a Chancellor. There has been no discussion of the matter." But he was either outside the loop or willing to shade the truth. On May 24th, "a high University administrator told a *Seawanhaka* reporter: "The die's been cast. Next Chancellor: Glenn Walker Ferguson." On May 26th, Ferguson attended a meeting of the Brooklyn Center Reorganization Committee, where he was greeted with open hostility. No questions were allowed. Richard Lettis, President of the All-University Senate, said, "The faculty feels it would be worth it to lose a good man in order to establish a precedent for future selections." One of the student representatives, Richard Shapiro, commented: "You can never be optimistic when dealing with the Board."

McGrath was quoted as saying, "we have not advanced anyone else for the job." This prompted *Seawanhaka* to editorialize, "It would appear that the officials waited until the school year had closed...and then sought to take action before the new Regulations [the 1969 Statutes] became effective." The newspaper also quoted John McGrath as saying, "I don't understand if they approve of his qualifications, then why don't they endorse him? It seems they want to be informed of things before the fact. It takes a great deal of time to find the right man for the job and there are very few men who qualify as college administrators." Names had, in fact, been sent to McGrath by the Advisory Committee to Select a Chancellor, including Robert McCambridge.

The Board was obviously not interested in a truly open search. They had found whom they thought to be an ideal candidate. This man seemed so perfect that they were willing to ride roughshod over the structure they earlier had so laboriously worked out. It was too bad that Ferguson became the sacrificial lamb caught between the Board's insistence that it had the sole right to select the next Chancellor and the pent-up demand by both faculty and students that they collectively be given a voice. The Brooklyn Student Government President, Ronald Berman, the Chair of the Council's legal committee, Peter Walter, and the students' attorney, rushed to seek a Temporary Restraining Order (TRO) in Brooklyn Supreme Court from Judge Frank Pino to delay the formal Board vote.

What followed was a bad slapstick comedy. The students sped from downtown Brooklyn to The Century Association in mid-town Manhattan where the Board was meeting. Carrying Pino's newly issued Restraining Order, they arrived at 4:10 in the afternoon. The club manager refused them entry, accusing them of trespassing. He even denied that the Board was meeting upstairs, even though it was. The police stood by, but did not force the Club to allow the writ to be served. The writ, therefore, was not served until after the Board had voted 16-0 to elect Ferguson Chancellor. The students and their attorney vainly called Judge Pino, asking him to enforce the court order on the Board of Trustees. But by the time the chaotic process played itself out and the students entered the Club, Ferguson had been elected. Once the vote had taken place, the TRO effectively became null and void. One of *Seawanhaka*'s banner headlines in a summer special dated July 3, 1969, read, "The Chancellor Who Walked into the Cold."

Eventually, the students' suit was withdrawn, a promise was made that henceforth the Board would engage both students and faculty in discussion, and Ferguson expressed his relief that his appointment was not blocked by a Temporary Restraining Order. The Board was excoriated for its tactics, but many faculty and students were genuinely impressed by Ferguson's background. He did seem very qualified, dynamic and ideally suited to become Chancellor. And it was summertime. The students were away, and the faculty was happy to wait until September to focus on the University and her problems.

The frenzy of the appointment doomed any honeymoon by demonstrating that Long Island University had not emerged from the post-Hoxie chaos. Ferguson, partially to mollify the furious stakeholders on each of the campuses and partially to telegraph his intentions, said "he would exert less power over the university's three campuses than his predecessor had," according to a *Newsday* article on July 10th. He went on to indicate that "he would consider dividing the University into completely autonomous colleges." As he put it, "in other words, I would be doing myself out of my job." Ferguson acknowledged that intercampus "interaction is minimal where students on one campus hav[e] virtually no relationship to the other University campuses."

While it was crystal clear that Ferguson was potentially a highly talented young Chancellor, he was undiplomatically blunt during his first weeks on the job. With clinical detachment he lamented that the University had lost its way over the prior decade. He articulated this valid but probably damning conclusion when few were on campus and his Chancellorship was in its infancy. He shared his views long before he had talked through his assessment with faculty and administrators, the men and women who won combat medals for surviving the Hoxie years. He spoke so definitively, he sounded arrogant. *Newsday's* headline summarized his view, "LIU's Three Campuses May Be Given Autonomy."

Politically, he should have taken advantage of the summer hiatus. In those first weeks William Zeckendorf Sr. had written with enthusiasm on August 14th, "Again my congratulations on the extraordinarily well conducted meeting yesterday. It was one of the best meetings of the Executive Committee that I have ever attended, in fact, it was not one of the best, it was *the best*."

But Ferguson chose instead to vent, addressing the faculty rather than the Board. It was almost as if he decided from the start that he wanted to leave. He sounded, in fact, like the Prophet Jeremiah. Asserting that those three summer months were enough time to ensure that he fully understood LIU's core problems, he challenged the several faculties in the opening days of the new academic year to tell him what collectively they wanted. If they could not articulate their goals, he indicated he would soon be gone. He spoke with a dismissiveness that was breathtaking, with words that were liberating for some, outrageous to others. Even though much of what he said was on-point, his was a distancing voice. Perhaps he saw the task as hopeless. Perhaps he regretted taking the job. Perhaps his temperament did not allow him to try to articulate a solution and lead the institution toward it. In any case, the LIU he saw was like Humpty - Dumpty. It seemed shattered beyond repair.

There were, of course, very complicated and elusive questions to follow, if he was correct in his initial judgment. What should be done next? Were there other options or variations? Was a three-campus divorce financially or legally possible? What were the risks of starting down such a path? Ferguson, unlike several prior consultants brought in to define what was needed to be done, had effectively only one solution: to make each campus an independent institution. For Ferguson, the 1969 Bylaws needed to be carried to their logical conclusion.

After he spoke to the Brooklyn Center faculty on September 15th, the Minutes quoted Ferguson as saying, "Long Island University must create a rationale for its existence as a corporate entity. At the present time, there is no meaningful faculty, student, or curricular enrichment resulting from the affiliation of the three Centers. There are deep feelings and factions, a high degree of subjective opinion, and a lack of good will for the holding corporation called Long Island University. If it does not have meaning, let us not perpetuate a façade."

Ferguson went on to point out that the University was solvent but had serious financial problems. "For income, we are approximately 97% dependent upon tuition. As a general rule, if tuition dependency exceeds 50%, a university lacks the requisite financial flexibility. In the fundraising area, I am not aware of many private donors who have expressed any interest in supporting Long Island University as an institution. On the other hand, several possible donors have expressed interest in Post or Southampton, and to a lesser extent, the Brooklyn Center."

Declaring that it had to be the faculty which articulated its own long-term objectives, Ferguson said that he had "yet to hear 'cogent arguments or sound reasons, at the Brooklyn Center, which point to the continuation of the present organizational structure.'" Ferguson went on, "What is needed now at LIU is a rational dialogue between and among the University's constituent elements. Realistically, we must discuss the options available to us. If a separate Brooklyn Center is what is clearly indicated, I will support it and recommend that proposal to the Board of Trustees." Ferguson urged the Brooklyn faculty "to ignore the errors and attitudes of the past and to stop looking for scapegoats for present difficulties and frustrations." He invited the Brooklyn faculty to consider "both a unified institution and the separation of units, but in the context of the question what are the cogent reasons for either system?"

Those Minutes had been taken by Jo Chamberlin and had been reviewed by Dean VanderWerf and Mrs. Lai. Chamberlin commented, "At the Faculty Reception which followed the Chancellor's informal remarks, I made a special effort to listen to faculty reaction to his talk. I heard such remarks as: 'what a change from the past,' 'he laid it on the line,' 'he said to fish or cut bait,' he didn't fool around,' 'he told us to stop sniping and to make up our minds where we wanted Long Island University to go.'"

Three days later, speaking to the Southampton faculty, he observed "Long Island University is a holding corporation, in the legal sense of the word. As a result of the revised Statutes which were enacted by the Board of Trustees, we have decentralized the central authority to the Centers and those Centers today, enjoy semi-autonomy and certainly greater autonomy than existed on the June 30th of this year." Drawing a contrast to "many consortia, state universities, universities including more than one center or division or college, Long Island University is composed of three disparate entities...."

Ferguson then analyzed the tension between Brooklyn and Post, noting among other things that, "there is little, if any, sensitivity manifested on the part of Post specifically, toward the future aspirations and the unique role, currently, of the Brooklyn Center." He spoke of the anger, much of it explosive if incorrect, in Brooklyn. "Brooklyn was Long Island University, and as a result of mistakes, including a potential sale of the Brooklyn Center, the people of Brooklyn feel, somewhat justifiably, that their assets, generated from tuition, provided by young people coming from less than affluent homes, have been used to create a campus of Long Island called Post." At Post, he noted that, "there is a feeling that this [C.W. Post] *is* the University, C.W. Post University, and that the awareness of the existence of Brooklyn is lost in terms of any entity called Long Island University. Ferguson had "searched in vain for the existence of programs" which would permit the two communities "to nurture common interests, to develop a meaningful rationale for the existence of a university." He observed that one did not need a legal structure to build a consortium.

With a dismissive mix of candor and pessimism, he saw "inept leadership, disinterest of individual members of the Board of Trustees, lack of geographical proximity, lack of common curricular interests that would sustain the very real deterrent of geographical [isolation] in separating the Centers." He spoke of the failure of the faculty to engage in a common enterprise and the failure of the faculty to be sufficiently interested in the larger University to have meetings with a quorum present.

"While Columbia is searching for community involvement, and starting belatedly to obtain that involvement, we at Brooklyn have it, by osmosis, because we are here. Sixteen percent of our student body is minority; not exclusively black but a large segment Puerto Rican, in contrast to you, Post, less than one percent total, less than fifty students, half of whom are Martin Luther King scholars and half of whom are on athletic scholarships."

He asked the Southampton faculty, "Where does Southampton fit into the equation? Fourteen hundred, approximately, day time students," and he answered himself: "You have two tremendous assets, in my opinion: your location which points to marine science and your location which points to the fine arts." In contrast to Brooklyn, Southampton had a reasonable chance to find external funds from private sources.

He noted that he originally thought, it would take a year or two to discover if a rationale could be created to justify Long Island University as an entity. "In my opinion it would not take a year or two. The facts are clear-cut. They are available...." Ferguson, after scant weeks on the job, was ready to leave. "I have no vested interest in whether Long Island University proceeds as a single entity, as three separate legal entities, or as two. I have no vested interest in whether Southampton as an entity wants to continue a relationship with Post for a number of years until the requisite financial security is assured. I have no vested interest in the continuation of a Chancellor who at this moment must create a job, but I will only attempt to create that job, if from your point of view, as the people who determine the future of this institution, you are convinced that it is not counter-productive to continue trying to develop something that may be, as I said, anachronistic." In sum, Ferguson did not see his function to be a Chancellor who would lead others to answer those questions collectively.

The *Seawanhaka* September 19th issue devoted pages to analyze what Ferguson was telling the University. In its lead story, the student news editor, Ed Weintrob, described how most faculty members were surprised by Ferguson and very cautious. Whereas, William Zeckendorf Sr. seemingly backed everything that Ferguson said "And so too do most of the Trustees..." Zeckendorf told *Seawanhaka*, "If we can't get the appreciation of the beneficiaries on whose behalf the university is run, we don't belong in the business and the hell with it. If we get any more backtalk and ingratitude, we should just get out. The university doesn't have to apologize to anyone.'"

The faculty Executive Committee, nonetheless, passed a resolution: "Perplexed by the content and intention of the Chancellor's initial address to the faculty at the Brooklyn Center, we seek clarification of his statement about the dissolution of the University. We have no doubt about the educational and fiscal viability of the Brooklyn Center. However, the Chancellor's statements about 'the near criminal" operation of the University raises serious questions about the moral and fiscal fitness of the board to make decisions about the future of the University." *Seawanhaka* ran an editorial that began, "Chancellor Glenn Ferguson's music to the Brooklyn Center's ears has suddenly become a sour note; poor paranoids that we are, it has to. After years of being lied to, cheated and made fools of by the Board of Trustees, the first good news we hear is treated with a fanatical mistrust."

On September 29, 1969, Glenn Ferguson addressed a letter to John McGrath as Chairman, which began, "At our meeting on September 16th, I submitted notice of my decision to resign as Chancellor of Long Island University. This letter constitutes formal communication of that decision."

He went on to explain that after three months of extensive exposure "to all elements of the University, I am convinced that Long Island University, with three disparate Centers, should not continue in its present form…. If the Board of Trustees," Ferguson went on, "endorses the proposal to re-structure the University, I would be pleased to serve as Chancellor until August 31, 1970. During the intervening period, my responsibility would be to implement the re-structuring plan incorporating a request for new charters, the distribution of assets and liabilities, the relocation of University Center personnel, the securing of public and private funds to insure reasonable financial flexibility for the independent educational units and all other critical transitional issues pertaining to a decision of this magnitude…."

"If, after due consideration, the Board of Trustees decides not to support the restructuring proposal, you will undoubtedly wish to appoint a new Chancellor as soon as feasible. In that event, I pledge my personal support in insuring a smooth transition." Ferguson's last substantive point was his conviction that "a re-structuring of the University, reflecting the initiative of the Board of Trustees, is the only viable alternative," and he concluded,"I am tendering my resignation."

Accompanying that letter was an eighteen page single-spaced, confidential draft to the Board outlining how Ferguson came to his recommendation to divide the University and how he proposed to the Board to restructure the University. It was *the* critical document of Ferguson's brief Chancellorship, a document of historical importance in the life of the University.

Ferguson analyzed in detail the problems he saw facing each of the campuses. He started with the Brooklyn Center and the decision by Mayor Lindsay and the Trustees of the City University to move aggressively to "Open Enrollment" for the City University of New York. Since Brooklyn was dependent on tuition revenue, he argued, such competition would inevitably imperil Brooklyn's capacity to finance itself, especially since "the Brooklyn Center is not a distinguished academic institution. Freshman entrance scores are the equivalent or less than comparable scores at competitive colleges." Noting that, "historically private donors have not clamored to assist the Brooklyn Center," he saw the best chance for success was to depend on public financing for survival. "If the curriculum is unique, and if the Center reflects good management, and if a reasonable percentage of graduating seniors are willing to pay tuition in order to take Brooklyn Center offerings rather than attending a free-tuition University, the City of New York, the State of New York, and the Federal Government *may* be willing to sustain the Brooklyn Center (until private financing can be generated to sustain the academic program)." He further noted that, "With few exceptions, the present membership of the Board of Trustees of Long Island University does not reflect interest in the educational objectives and needs of the Brooklyn Center."

Post had the greatest chance to make it, in Ferguson's assessment. He noted that, "Rather than tapping the extensive private financial resources available in Nassau County, the University chose to rely, to an alarming extent, on borrowing from Government." Moreover, he observed that a "building should not reflect the name of a donor unless the donor contributes a significant percentage of the total cost of that building. In some cases, at the C.W. Post Center, the University has sold its goodwill cheaply, and all future potential donors will be cognizant of this fact."

"In recent years, the largest single private donor has been Mrs. Marjorie Merriweather Post. Since the departure of the previous permanent Chancellor, Mrs. Post has refused to contribute to Long Island University. Based on recent direct and third party contacts with Mrs. Post, she stated that as long as Long Island University retains it present composition [management], she will not contribute to the University. If C.W. Post were independent, it is quite possible, but not certain, that Mrs. Post's interest in the C.W. Post University could be rekindled."

Ferguson analyzed the Post student body savagely. "Predominately, the student body at C.W. Post College comes from middle- and upper-income families. On a per capita basis, it may well be that more cars are driven by Post students than in any other major university campus in the country." With clinical cruelty, Ferguson assessed "the students (and faculties) are basically conservative in the broadest sense, and with very few exceptions, the students entrance scores are lower than the average at many of the other universities and colleges on Long Island." Post students were there because they had been rejected at "their first, second, and even third choices." Ferguson observed, "there is no present curricular offering at C.W. Post Center which represents academic excellence. This is not a condemnation. It is only a personal judgment." But he concluded that, "The C.W. Post Center meets a community need, and if it is allowed to exist as a separate University, it will survive as a private institution."

He next assessed the Brooklyn School of Pharmacy and saw its move to the Post campus as a complex task of integration, but one which would strengthen the intellectual and professional standards at Post.

Finally, he assessed Southampton, his obvious favorite, as a place that was coming of age. He wrote "The campus is beautiful, the facilities adequate, and the prospects independent of financial realities are excellent." He celebrated the emergence of fine arts and marine science and commented "Southampton College can become a distinguished academic institution, but only with financial security."

He then turned his attention to the University Centre, arguing that it was "created in response to the demands of the Chancellor and the Board of Trustees to formulate a mechanism by which Long Island University [meaning the Brooklyn Center] and C.W. Post College could be an integral part of the same educational institution. Unfortunately, the creation of the Administrative Centre [University Center] did not reflect the express needs or institutional aspirations of the two Centers. The Administrative Centre was superimposed, and then, an effort was made to insure that the central authority would be able to provide essential services to each of the Centers." Arguing that each action at the Center "was suspect, each appointment to the staff was subject to critical scrutiny, and each physical development at the Post Center became psychologically a gain for Post and a loss for Brooklyn," Ferguson submitted that the Administrative Centre was located on a plot almost four times as large as the Brooklyn Center. (In fact, it just was slightly larger.) But the Finance Building, (now the Mary M. Lai Building), was constructed *before* a library for the Brooklyn Center. "The converted estate residence in which the Chancellor and his principal assistants were located represented 'opulence,' 'waste' and a 'lifestyle' which was anathema to many students and faculty at the Brooklyn Center, to a few at the Post Center....The trappings appeared to represent a false sense of wealth and security at an institution that was struggling for solvency."

Ferguson commented that, "Although the University Centre is only one hour from Brooklyn via automobile, it is a light year apart re the façade which it represents." Arguing that "location, style, and motivation for existence have never been communicated adequately to the Brooklyn Center," the result was that "remedial action, at this time, merely scratches the surface."

As a result of "The current revolution on the American campus," he argued "Clark Kerr's concept of the university conglomerate was now in disrepute. "University administrations must be 'relevant.'" "Relevance is difficult to define," Ferguson continued, "but it is clear that absentee management, inaccessibility, the holding corporation concept, and growth per se do not represent the wave of the future."

Ferguson then launched a broadside against the fundraising efforts, staffing and priorities he thought to be misguided. The working draft, located in the University files, was shared with others, perhaps one or more senior colleagues, who wrote marginal notes. There were comments disagreeing with what he said, but at this point it is impossible to know with whom he had shared the draft document. Ferguson's negativity was pervasive and he dismissed all possible hope that the situation could be altered. He cited unnamed experts at Princeton, Brandeis, Fordham, and Cornell all of whom "reacted negatively to the prospects of Long Island University, in its present form, obtaining private endowment funds at a sufficient level to meet projected commitments."

He next turned his rapier on University Centre personnel. "Under the Revised

Statutes, the substance of higher education has been delegated to the three Centers. The intent of the Revised Statutes was to decentralize, but in effect, for the reasons previously cited, a practical separation has already taken place. Academic policy is being, and must be, established at the Center level. The role of the Chancellor and his staff is advisory and informational rather than related to command." Condemning *Preface to the Future*, he wrote, "Since the Ten-Year Plan lacks reality, since the goals of the three Centers lack a common theme, and since the University Centre does not represent a felt need of the Centers, University Centre personnel operate in a vacuum."

Addressing the consequences of Stoddard's revised Statutes, Ferguson noted that, "Under the Revised Statutes the University Centre does not possess authority to formulate University-wide academic standards, to create new academic programs, to establish priorities in graduate and professional education, to control the employment of Center personnel, to establish admissions policies, or even to represent the Centers externally." He went on to observe that the "Center Presidents report directly to the Chancellor rather than through the Vice-Chancellor for Academic Affairs. The intent of this approach was to insure the Center Presidents direct access to the Chancellor and to place more authority in the Office of the President. In effect, this reporting arrangement makes the Vice Chancellor a staff rather than a line official and minimizes the advisory role of the Vice Chancellor."

Ferguson then excoriated the formula by which each of the Centers paid for the centralized functions of University Centre, noting that those funds could pay for instructional purposes were the business operations further decentralized. This assertion was passionately rejected by Mrs. Lai, who for decades had argued that through single management of the three campuses the University was able to generate great savings. "With $900,000, the Brooklyn Center would be able to supplement functions already duplicated by the University Center and still retain funds for instructional purposes."

And so the document continued, finding nothing but fault with the University he had agreed to serve. "In summary, the University Centre was superimposed on the structure of the College Centers. Subsequently, the Revised Statutes decentralized substantive functions to the College Centers. This accelerated the trend toward independence…. In the absence of these factors, the Chancellor has only one legitimate option - to recommend to the Board of Trustees that the present University be reconstituted into three separate educational institutions." There followed pages of detailed options to deal with personnel, division of endowment, liabilities, future staffing and other anticipated needs by which a single corporate structure could be disentangled into three free-standing institutions.

Obviously, this extraordinary analysis was a bombshell. Ferguson presented the Trustees a Hobbesian choice: fire him immediately or give him one year to dissolve the University. The story was leaked by Alexander Aldrich to *The New York Times,* which reported on October 1, 1969, "The board of trustees of Long Island University is considering giving greater autonomy, and perhaps even total independence to the University's Brooklyn Center." The following day, the *Daily News* had a longer story which began, "A crucial question for Long Island University's Brooklyn Center - should it cut its ties with the parent university and become independent - will be taken up for the first time tonight the executive committee of the LIU board of Trustees."

On October 6th, Jo Chamberlin took extensive and confidential notes for John Baiardi of a meeting at the Brooklyn Center with the faculty Executive Council and Ferguson. The President of the Alumni Association, the President of the Student Government, reporters from *Seawanhaka,* and a member of SDS were also there.

Chamberlin quoted Spector as indicating "that the Brooklyn Center wanted 'separation on our terms.'" According to Chamberlin, McGrath had held back Ferguson's eighteen-page document to the Board. Instead, he had decided to convene the Executive Committee on October 2nd and to recess the Board meeting until October 14th.

When Ferguson spoke to the faculty, he indicated, "There is no 'deal' affecting the future of the Brooklyn Center of LIU." McGrath was fearful that the faculty might assume Ferguson was in some way trying to resurrect the deal with the City University. Ferguson told faculty leadership that he was used to public-sector institutions with full disclosure and sunshine laws. But he observed, "I do not believe that the Board will make an independent decision splitting off Brooklyn Center from the University." There followed a fairly intense give and take during which Ferguson's reported views were challenged. Spector asked, for example, "I would like to know what kind of approach has been made to fundraising? 'You have been here seventy-seven days. Some of us have been here for years.'" Ferguson responded by declining "to go into this, saying that 'the Board had to authorize to him to present a specific proposal for discussion.'" But he observed that the three Centers had only been able to raise one million dollars total in endowment. Those "hard facts have to be faced."

Another professor, Hildreth Kritzer, asked "'How do you think that Post has an opportunity for fund-raising in the private sector, when in fourteen years, it has not raised any substantial amount of money?'" Ferguson responded that major private donors want to know how much money the LIU Board had given. He spoke publicly that "At C.W. Post, buildings have been named for some donors whose gifts have been far, far less than at other institutions." There followed an outspoken diatribe against the Board, including its reluctance to allow Alumni Representatives, faculty representatives, and students to participate.

PART III - THE AFTERMATH

Following this meeting with the faculty, Ferguson met with the *Seawanhaka* reporters, encouraging a very candid further discussion to take place. One of those reporters, David Medina, "announced that he was now a stringer for *The New York Times*." "David Medina asked if the Chancellor had been invited to the Executive Committee on October 2nd, and he [Ferguson] said he had not."

The students actively supported Ferguson's plan to break up of the University. A petition was sent to the Trustees dated October 1, 1969, indicating "the students of the Brooklyn Center favor the establishment of this Center as an independent University, providing such separation into a separate corporation is done in such a way as not to endanger the financial or educational stability of the institution." There was a wide range of opinions expressed. Colonel John Tyler, who was then Director of the Office of Research Administration, wrote a piece on October 13th called "Long Island University - Together or Separate?" asking the question "why will the "parts have a better opportunity to survive than the 'whole?'" It was his conclusion that separating the University back into its constituent parts would set back the pursuit of excellence substantially.

Some of what Ferguson had to say resonated, even though his assessment was bleak and his criticism was merciless. He showed little charity for an institution badly bruised over the years. Not only was this a classic case of my way or the highway, Ferguson limited even his commitment to oversee the break-up to one year. Becoming the Chancellor had solved his immediate problem of what to do after an Ambassadorship. But what would happen if a break-up took more than a year? What if the Department of Education said no? What would happen if the bondholders rejected in court a reissue of the Long Island University bonds? What if there were other types of lawsuits?

Once the shock of his condemnation had passed, the Board became both angry and unified. The fact that much of the criticism may have been on point only strengthened Trustee resolve. Ferguson's solution was dead on arrival, in part because the delivery was condescending in tone as well as brutal. Ferguson exhibited an intellectual arrogance clearly demonstrated in his meeting with the Brooklyn faculty after seventy-seven days in office, there was but one solution: his.

Ferguson made his recommendations on September 29th. McGrath recessed the Board until October 14th, requesting that the Executive Committee, in particular, study the report and make its recommendations. On the 14th, after a thorough discussion, the Board rejected Ferguson's proposal to reorganize the Corporation and to separate the three Centers functionally and legally. Their formal statement stated: "The Chancellor was not engaged to restructure the University or to preside over its dissolution. He assumed office with full knowledge that the University Statutes had just been re-written and he welcomed the opportunity to take charge of the administration of the University under these Statutes." Wounded and angry, the Board pushed back, "it is no news to our board members that the theoreticians of the academic world have looked upon Long Island University as a series of achievements that could not happen, have not happened, and cannot continue to happen." The Board regretted that the Chancellor "found it necessary to pursue a search for a hypothetical rationale instead of seizing the helm and providing the leadership necessary to assure a viable future for the University as a whole."

It further argued that Ferguson's reasoning confirmed the conclusions which Dr. Henry Heald had made, because he also thought that Brooklyn had "dim prospects of future success in competition with City University's tuition free facilities." At the time the Board endorsed Heald's conclusion and was met with "passionate resentment" from "certain elements of the public, and faculty, students and alumni at the Brooklyn Center...." "The Trustees" the statement continued, "were denounced for trying to perpetuate a 'real estate deal' and were subjected to unwarranted vilification." The Board at that time clearly stated that disposing of the Brooklyn Center was a closed issue. This statement reaffirmed that resolve. The Statutes, it continued, had given greater autonomy to Brooklyn.

The Board acknowledged the changing realities of higher education, especially in urban centers. It indicated its willingness "to consider or engage in a discussion of any constructive proposal that may be generated from some other source, whether within or outside the University." The Board believed it took a reasonable and open stance. It understood that "the whole concept of urban higher education is undergoing dynamic changes and saw the need for "co-existence of public and private education on the contemporary scene." It was amenable to change and looked forward to the dialogue. The Board filed a list of multiple University successes and an assertion that it had "not suddenly become oblivious to the needs of the seventies. Our University has its weaknesses but it also has its strengths. We have created a total plant valued at $75 million for the student body of over 25,000, one of the largest private enrollments in the nation." It ended this statement with a simple but powerful sentence, "We have faith."

The Minutes of the Board meeting on October 14th, included a Board Resolution that "the Chancellor's report and the Chairman's proposed response be placed on file in the archives with the Board as a confidential document not to be disclosed to the public. Further, that the Board will not initiate or sponsor any program for the restructuring of the University any of its Centers at this time."

The New York Times covered Ferguson's plan in a four-column article on October 14th. *Newsday* and the *Daily News* also gave the story substantial coverage. Since Ferguson was so open about sharing his views, there was much public discussion. *Newsday* wrote an editorial on November 15th, entitled, "LIU's Shrouded Future." Censuring the Trustees for keeping hidden under a shroud of secrecy the litany of problems faced by the University, the newspaper lamented that, "the Trustees have voted to sit on a comprehensive report by Glenn Ferguson, LIU's freshman Chancellor, in which Ferguson is reliably reported to have argued strongly for dismemberment of the University into three independent schools." The editorial celebrated Ferguson's candor: "Mr. Ferguson is one of the few people we've heard of anywhere who has taken the lead in trying to abolish his own job."

And then, most curiously, public and private discussion stopped. Ferguson was nominally Chancellor for the rest of that fiscal year. *De facto* power devolved to the offices of President Alexander Aldrich in Brooklyn, a new President at C.W. Post, Robert Payton, and Edward Glanz at Southampton. In a letter to Mrs. Post, Hugh Behymer, her friend and the first Post librarian, wrote on December 2nd, "I tell you quite frankly, that I am less and less impressed with the new Chancellor. I think he often goes off half-cocked, and I also think (but cannot prove) that he sulks when things don't suit him. I may be wrong."

Robert Spector became a Trustee under the new Bylaws in his capacity as President of the University Faculty Senate. The Board also elected three other community Trustees: Edward F. Cavanagh Jr., the former deputy mayor of the City of New York; Mrs. Martha L. Pate, the former President of Sweetbriar, and Mrs. Winthrop Palmer, poet and widow of Carleton Palmer. Sol Atlas, a developer of New York real estate and Great Neck resident, joined the Board at its next meeting. A few months later Arnold Schwartz, another brother of the Paragon Oil family, and Lord Robert David Lion Gardiner, an heir to Gardiner's Island from a seventeenth century Royal Charter, were also elected Trustees. Joseph Lindemann rejoined the Board, and Emilio Collado became Vice-Chairman. It was a different Board as the new decade dawned. As that year progressed, it seemed to be business as usual, almost as if Ferguson's Report and the Board's response were a sunspot, an explosive interruption that suddenly vanished, barely leaving a trace.

On December 24th, Charles Minert wrote a memo to Ferguson captioned, "General Observations on Long Island University." Minert, then the head of the Bureau of College Evaluation for the State Education Department, began his memo, "Since the University is a collection of its parts, most of the comments in the three center reports apply directly to the University. Ultimately, the University must assume responsibility for the operation of its several units." It is distantly possible Minert did not know of Ferguson's plans to divide the University into three and to leave at the end of the year. But if he did, it must have seemed bizarre to Ferguson to receive this missive from the State.

Quoting the Heald-Hobson Report, Minert wrote "the administration of the University is responsible for serious faults in planning and management. Centers have been allowed to drift for a year without even an Acting President, administrators with little experience in higher education have been appointed and communication between levels of management have been extremely poor. For example, the recent effort to reorganize the Brooklyn Center was going on simultaneously and independently of the plans to reorganize the total University." Much of this was a swipe at the Governor's cousin, Alexander Aldrich.

The dressing down continued. "There has been a tendency to treat faculty without professional respect and involvement. Committees are, therefore, weak and inoperative in many cases. Consequently, teachers have little sense of corporate identity as a faculty. Some have responded by retreating to their own narrow departmental interest; others have accepted the employee role and developed outside sources of income and self-expression." Minert asserted that there was a lack of academic leadership. "One center continues to ignore reality and speak of itself as a high-quality liberal arts college, while the others seem to have no focus at all."

Minert excoriated the University for its allocation of resources. "While the administrative headquarters and one center exists in relative luxury, the other centers operate in marginal facilities. A monumental library is constructed at one center while a library facility hardly worthy of the name exists at another."

The Board of Trustees was judged very harshly. "They are charged with an unwillingness to share power and decision-making with students and faculty. Their selection of administrators has been slow, and they have apparently not given clear direction and support to appointees." Minert saw "no clear or easy solution to the difficulties facing the University." He noted that there were countless areas of academic cooperation possible…but this does not seem to be the crux of the matter. Given the physical distance and the current state of suspicion and hostility existing between centers, it might be easier for each center to negotiate cooperative arrangements with educational groups outside of Long Island University."

He did suggest that he had seen the press clippings, if nothing else, asking "what configuration is most appropriate. More specifically, should the University continue as one legal entity or should it divide into separate institutions?... One Board for three colleges may be possible when strength and sound organization already exist. But it seems unwise when each college is so beset by difficulties that it needs the full attention of a sophisticated and hard-working Board. Whether such a tripart Board can be effectively developed within the context of one University is a question that only those with a more intimate knowledge of the personalities and factors involved can answer."

What a curious document! Was it written to assist Ferguson? Was it a specific issue that prompted such a non-bureaucratic, openly judgmental letter? It was addressed solely to Ferguson - it showed no cc's - and if there was a formal response, none exists in the University's files. The State clearly had little respect for the corporate entity, Long Island University. Would Minert have written such a letter without the approval of his superiors? At the January 13, 1970 Board meeting, there was a bland note that "the State Education Department evaluations of each of the Centers will be reported on by the President at the next meeting of the Board, February 19, 1970." Minert's confidential memo was linked to those documents, but since Ferguson had announced himself a lame duck, why was this scathing report seemingly sent solely to him?

At that same January 13th Board meeting, Sol Atlas asked whether development was organized on a Center-by-Center basis or led by a central University development office. There was further discussion on this point and then "Chancellor Ferguson, who continued to attend Board meetings as Chancellor, 'indicated that he had devoted approximately seven months of work on this matter and felt that development should be on a Center by Center approach'." At that point President Aldrich commented that the Brooklyn development office had "six persons [who] concentrated on annual giving."

On January 27th, John Baiardi, the Vice Chancellor for Development, submitted a detailed memo to Ferguson and McGrath describing the structure and function of the development effort at University Centre. He argued that, "there should be a strong coordinating administration, serving and supplementing the programs developed at the Centers." It was a given that Ferguson would disagree, but under the tacit truce established by Ferguson and McGrath, the document was forwarded to the Executive Committee and the Chairman with the Chancellor's permission.

Baiardi had written, "Since the Statutes became effective on July 1st, it appears that the administration of the Brooklyn Center, C.W. Post Center, and Southampton Center are seeking complete autonomy - academic, administrative, and fiscal. We believe that this would be unsound academically, administratively, and financially..., and would result in unrestrained competition among the Centers for students, faculty, and funds." *Plus ca change, plus c'est la meme chose.*

The May 22nd edition of *The New York Times* reported that Glenn Ferguson had accepted the Presidency at Clark University effective the following July 1st. He remained there for three years, then from 1973 to 1978 was President of the University of Connecticut. After a five-year term as the Chief Executive of Radio Free Europe he briefly was named President of Lincoln Center. Neither he nor Long Island University looked back on their association as a high point. It exacerbated tensions that were already raw. As John McGrath wrote, "the Chancellor was not engaged to restructure the University or to preside over its dissolution." By focusing on the central contradiction of the University's structure and identity, he raised an explosive issue at a particularly vulnerable time. His memory, like that of George Stoddard, was soon forgotten.

The key issue in years 1968-71 was not the integration of the whole, but rather that the center had collapsed almost completely. There were serious consequences for the management and identity of the University. Each campus President gained a long-sought unbridled freedom to direct that campus free from its sister campuses. The pendulum had swung as far as it could without the Board embracing Ferguson's dissolution of the University. For the next three years the University history was that of three quasi separated units each trying to find its way forward without the checks and balances that had seemed so inhibiting. Like the medieval duchies of England or France, each campus raised its own flag, declared its own agenda, and cut off as much communication as possible with the others. Everyone assumed that Ferguson would be replaced. Before that happened, each campus sought to create a survivable local bureaucracy, an autonomous identity and a viable Mission Statement. The University Centre had imposed mandatory and unfettered allegiance, a revenue sharing that was onerous, and multiple regulations governing what could be taught. The new freedom was suddenly liberating and more than a little scary.

On December 30, 1970, the CFO, Mary Lai, professionally and personally unhappy at the way the University was devolving, wrote "Recommendations for the Organization and Structure of Long Island University." This was one of the rare times she wrote a policy memo that extended beyond her own areas of responsibility. She took as a tag line, "Centralized in policy, Decentralized in administration" and had the memo professionally produced and bound. Her goal was to influence the Board. It was a 24-page document that started by quoting Benjamin Franklin's famed aphorism, "We had better all hang together or assuredly we shall all hang separately."

The core of her argument was the failure of leadership, focusing primarily on Ferguson's, but implicitly also criticizing the Trustees. She was adamant that the new Statutes drafted under Stoddard failed to reflect Heald - Hobson recommendations. "Instead of strengthening central administration, center administration was strengthened. The centers were now led by a President rather than a Provost."

After chronicling a brief history of the University's founding and growth, she made a ringing defense "for a strong unified Long Island University." For her, Presidents Metcalfe and Conolly had "courage, fortitude, and vision." She argued that, "When they were leading the University, everyone was on the same team. Everyone pulled together, working for the goals and objectives the President and the Board of Trustees set forth." She was firmly convinced that individuals shape institutions and that external dynamics such as the Vietnam War or changing social mores at universities played a relatively minor role.

She also made a financial argument that "the debts of the University bind the three centers together." Specifically, "individual bondholders would have to agree" before the University debt could be parceled out to the three campuses. Each of the campuses would have a portion of the debt if approval could be won. She challenged the notion that bondholders would willingly or quickly take ownership, especially when the Southampton Campus had such a weak balance sheet. At its core, her argument was that "University Centre functions as a consortium. Long Island University recognized the merits of centralized services years ago." Finally, she offered as a case study the dynamics at General Motors in which the holding corporation performed the main business functions for each of the units while allowing Chevrolet or Buick or Cadillac room to develop a unique product marketing and brand identity. In sum, she maintained that, "center administration [on the campuses] should support a Chancellor and get on the University team. With everyone working towards a better Long Island University, each center will flourish. The parts will grow as does the whole."

From her lonely perch in a substantially reduced University Center, she argued that, "Individual ambition, not the organization structure, is responsible for recent turmoil and conflict. With proper leadership and teamwork, the present organization can and will work."

A year later in a second broadside, she lamented that, "the Presidents have not had to answer to a Chancellor in two years." But few at the University were listening and each campus was on its own for better or for worse.

McGrath came to realize, however, that as Chairman of the Board, he had to do something to prevent further drift. There was still a single corporation and it had to be able to function. There had to be a certified audit. Bondholders needed to know who was liable, responsible, and in-charge. Employment and other contracts required a legal signature. Thus, on July 13, 1970, he sent out a memorandum, "Re The University Centre." Noting that, "the University Centre had been operating without the leadership of the Chancellor, the staff is without direction and many members do not have sufficient work to do. Accordingly, it would appear that certain interim arrangements would be in order pending the selection of a new Chancellor." He sought and got authority to act in place of the Chancellor himself so that there was someone who could sign applications or honorary degree citations or an audit report.

He encouraged John Baiardi, the Vice Chancellor for Development, to take a leave of absence for three years to direct the Oceanographic Institute at Montauk, then called for a meeting to help place those members of the University Centre staff who could be gainfully employed on one or another of the campuses. Most important, by September 2nd, he proposed to the Board hiring a special assistant to the Chair similar to when Bill Birenbaum was hired to assist John H.G. Pell some eight years before.

McGrath recommended and got approval to retain the former President of Channel 13, John Kiermaier, to serve as his eyes and ears. Kiermaier had sufficient *gravitas* to be effective on each of the three campuses. As McGrath wrote, "in these dynamic times, it is imperative that we have an authorized spokesman, sitting in and participating for us as decisions effecting our future are made."

Kiermaier had a strong curriculum vitae. He had been a consultant to the Sloan Foundation after he left the Educational Broadcasting Corporation-Channel 13, where he had served as its President. Prior to that he had served for five years at CBS News in its Public Affairs Programming Department. A Phi Beta Kappa graduate of Wesleyan University and a graduate of Yale Law School, he had been an alumni Trustee of Wesleyan. McGrath personally saw him as a possible candidate for the permanent position of Chancellor. He had the charm, prior experience and potential skill to be a strong candidate. Whether he could surmount faculty and student resistance, however, was another question entirely.

The Minutes of the September 22, 1970 Board meeting indicated, "Members of the Board inquired if the approval requested would entail any commitment by the Board to support Mr. Kiermaier as future Chancellor. The Chairman advised that it did not. The Chairman stated, however, that in his discussions with Mr. Kiermaier he committed himself individually to recommending Mr. Kiermaier for consideration as Chancellor to the advisory bodies…. Upon the understanding that the Board was making no present approval or recommendation for the Chancellorship, the Chairman was authorized to appoint a special assistant to the Chairman of the Board of his own choosing."

Southampton had been getting the best grades for its future prospects but was probably the most vulnerable of the three residential campuses. As the youngest and smallest unit, it needed the kind of protection that a Chancellor could provide. It was still very new, isolated and uncertain about its academic mission. Outsiders, including Ferguson, assumed (not incorrectly) that its physical proximity to the sea and easy access to the arts community of the East End would give it special panache. This was the decade when American contemporary artists achieved fame. The New York School of abstract art was burgeoning. Many of the most successful artists, men and women, either had houses on the East End for the summer or lived there year round because the light was so good. Adjunct teaching helped pay for food and liquor, and during those first years, extraordinary artists taught both interested and disinterested students.

Also during those years, marine science and its allied fields at the undergraduate level became the identifying core for the campus. But marine science everywhere has always been a boutique discipline, with relatively few undergraduate students declaring it their future life's work. Since Post had claimed graduate work in marine science, Southampton centered its efforts on undergraduates, even though most marine science programs nationally were at the graduate level. Stony Brook was already building a graduate program on the North Shore, a natural connection for both institutions. Southampton developed a much happier relationship with Stony Brook than with colleagues at Post.

At first Southampton had a virtual monopoly nationally on undergraduate marine science, but soon had to contend with other colleges and universities developing their own undergraduate majors as a way of growing their centers of excellence. Moreover, marine science programs were expensive to sustain. There was never adequate money for Southampton to build quality labs or buy research vessels. Thus, even though marine science was the focus of the campus's intellectual energy, it was not strong enough or profitable enough to define the campus pedagogically.

A goodly number of local students in the sixties came to avoid the draft. It was the most convenient local college for students from the North and South Forks of Long Island. These students, who studied accounting and business, prepared to be teachers or took other subjects, were taught with less rigor than those in the sciences. The student body became bi-modal: one division operated as a mini-graduate institution, placing students in internships literally around the globe; the other functioned as a residential junior college. When the State evaluators visited Southampton in the autumn of 1969, they found, for example, "that of the sixteen transfer students admitted into the business programs, no less than eleven had been dismissed or suspended for academic reasons by other institutions." The State found fault, as well, with Southampton's teacher education programs, complaining that the way in which student teaching was organized was "one of the most unusual and possibly least satisfactory that is in existence in New York."

Southampton was fragile financially. It needed the marine science students to define itself intellectually; it needed the local youngsters to help pay the bills. It ran a chronic deficit and never had adequate funds to build a campus infrastructure sufficient to create a happy environment when the winter made the beaches in hospitable. The town was cold and desolate. The summer playgrounds were all boarded up when school was in session.

The Southampton campus lacked a founding donor, religious order or sheltering patron. The College lacked the resources to mount a sustaining development and public relations campaign. The owners of the great estates were only in the Hamptons when school was out and viewed the college as a place to send the maid's or gardener's kids, not their own children. The College struggled to hire recruiters who could travel to landlocked States, seeking men and women who might be interested in art or studying one of the marine science disciplines.

There were other issues that challenged Southampton's potential success. The year round residents were connected to agriculture, such as growing potatoes or poultry, or were dependent on servicing the summer colony population. The population density on the East End of Long Island was relatively thin, especially on both Forks. Moreover, for year-round folks who did live on the North Fork, the commute could be difficult. A potential student had to drive west to Riverhead before heading south, and then back out onto the South Fork to the campus.

A large percentage of marine sciences students at Southampton came from families who lived far enough away to require their children to board in dormitories on campus or find off-campus housing. Room and board costs were the same at virtually every college in America, but were expensive. Living at home was always cheaper.

Southampton College, with no endowment and very little scholarship money, heavily discounted its tuition to compete with other colleges that were either wealthier or received a state subsidy. The dormitories and student life facilities at Southampton were spartan; despite the discounts, the students and their parents complained that they had to pay too much for what they got. The consequence was that students had to have a compelling academic reason to study at Southampton to justify paying top dollar for substandard accommodations and student life facilities. The campus was chronically under-enrolled. Campus administrators never had enough money for scholarships to compete with other colleges offering undergraduate marine science majors.

Many students who did come to Southampton for marine sciences chose to live off-campus, renting houses built for revenue in the summer months when the area was a vacation resort for the many urban men and women who chose to come for two week vacations to enjoy the beach. In the winter, those same houses were rented to Southampton College students at greatly reduced rates, especially since landlords would rather get some revenue than see their property stand empty. In an era when the drug culture came into its own, a group of students, living unsupervised in one of these houses, risked turning that house into a den of booze and pot. The local police saw these youngsters as proof that America's young had lost all moorings; the students, in turn, saw the local gendarmerie as "fascist pigs." The University administrators were caught between the two.

During the years of the Vietnam draft, students had external reasons to protect their student deferment and remain at college until graduation. In the years that followed, though, it became harder and harder to retain students until graduation. Almost from the first year, the challenge for Southampton faculty and administrators was to keep enough students from leaving to go somewhere cheaper, closer to home, with better facilities, or somewhere with more students and options. Every year, unsophisticated seventeen year olds came to Southampton thinking that they would swim with the dolphins only to discover that marine science demanded complex introductory courses and many hours at a scientific bench studying zoology. When they looked to transfer majors, the other class offerings were found marginal.

Notwithstanding the many structural issues and problems that threatened South-ampton's long-term viability, the campus clearly won the affection of external ex-aminers and outside observers. Because it was such a residential, beaucolic cam-pus, it attracted committed teaching faculty and staff who loved the intimacy and were committed to its future. People came and people went by subway to the City urban campus and there was no 24/7 sense of community. At C.W. Post, no faculty lived on campus, even though students in large numbers did. Because adjoining real estate was so expensive, faculty and staff commuted to Brookville, educating their own children in towns across Nassau and Suffolk or in one of the City bor-oughs.

Moreover, a great many of the Southampton and Post residential students chose to go home on Thursday evenings for long weekends. Suburban automobiles were a reality for suburban college students. At Adelphi, Hofstra, and C.W. Post, Thurs-day night was devoted to bar-hopping. On weekends the campuses were thinly populated and without the dynamism that students inevitably more residential campus, for example, Colgate or Ann Arbor or Bates. In the sixties, many Post students would drive from home back to campus for a Saturday football game, leaving soon after for the rest of the weekend.

Southampton had a more vibrant student culture and undergraduate camaraderie that the other two campuses lacked. Allan Kuusisto, chairing the site visit for the Board of Regents, wrote Edward Glanz, the Southampton Provost, on January 27, 1967, just as Southampton was completing its obligatory self-assessment report after one full cycle of students had graduated. Kuusisto noted, "I was very much impressed by the comprehensiveness and wealth of information of your previous progress reports…. I am sure that your progress reports and the registration team's report will give us an excellent perspective of what has taken place on the South-ampton campus."

In Hoxie's fourth annual report - the one presented after he was fired - he wrote "I believe history will record in retrospect that the founding of this College was one of the most significant events in the more than three centuries of recorded history of eastern Long Island." A four-year report to the State self-described the campus as "A Liberal Arts College Within a Multi Campus University." The report Kuu-sisto and his colleagues issued detailed all the constraints and risks of this new venture and accurately identified the lack of resources, the inadequate numbers of faculty to properly teach so many programs, under enrollment et cetera. But, in summary, the visitors wrote, "If deficiencies appear to be stressed rather than the fine qualities of the school, it is because improvement is essential for the continued registration of your curricula. Our general impression is that Southampton College is capable of achieving distinction as a liberal arts college; so much has already

been accomplished in such a short a time through good planning and rational allocation of resources that we are convinced that the remaining obstacles to be overcome will not prove to be overwhelming."

Discrete objectives were laid out and Glanz responded, quoting a series of specific
college challenges and objectives, and creating five study panels with students,
faculty and administrator participation. To be sure, events at University Center
and in Brooklyn had echoed as far east as Southampton. If Brooklyn was sold to
CUNY, how many of Brooklyn's tenured faculty could Southampton absorb, especially since Southampton only had nine of its own. By seniority, would Brooklyn
faculty bump their Southampton counterparts? Distance did help to protect that
campus, giving it an opportunity to worry about itself without becoming entrapped
in the struggle over Hoxie, the Brooklyn sale or the Stoddard Bylaws.

However, the campus was never insulated from student protests about tuition increases, Vietnam, civil rights or campus specific issues-no campus in the nation
was. Students and faculty were well aware of what was happening in Nassau and
Brooklyn, even though both seemed light years away. During the year of Hoxie's
termination, the explosive issue at Southampton was whether the students could
and should be taxed twenty-five dollars a semester to help fund the construction of
a new gymnasium.

Southampton's chronic penury, made it dependent on the rest of the University. For
decades it was a frail third sibling. In the fall of 1967, for example, Glanz wrote
an internal memo with a copy to both Hoxie and Mary Lai: "it appears to me as
provost that unless we are able to provide new funds through a tuition rise, development funds, or other means of support from the University it will be necessary
to cut into the specific budgets of the College to a point which appears to be dangerous and inconsistent with our express goals of developing a quality college."

Moreover, faculty protested when University Graduate Dean Eugene Arden proposed that graduate students from Post teach courses at Southampton. Southampton envisioned itself as "a small liberal arts college that hopes to provide for the
student, intimate contact and intellectual intercourse with his instructor....The
suggestion that we use graduate students from the Merriweather campus to teach
courses at Southampton is also totally unacceptable," wrote the Chair of the Curriculum Committee, Arnold Weinstein. To use cheap labor through untested graduate students was an anathema to the faculty, even if it would lower the cost of
instruction.

Southampton was, in sum, a chronic mendicant, always in need of capital and operating funds, almost always at the expense of the needs of the other campuses. And
yet, Southampton College was also, from the beginning, an intimate community
that embraced a shared governance structure. The Faculty-Student-Administration

Council was always a forum for vetting important issues and seeking consensus, unlike the other two campuses.

A memorandum from Charles Minert, then in charge of the Bureau of College Evaluation for the State, dated October 18, 1969, noted, "To evaluate Southampton College today without considering carefully what it was two years ago and what it was only six years ago, would be to overlook its remarkable achievements. The college now has some fourteen hundred plus students and a series of new functional buildings in which to house them. Only by carefully considering what the college was at the time of the last evaluation visit, do the signs of progress become clearly evident."

There is no question, however, that Southampton College still has problems. Minert "still sense[d] a serious discrepancy between theory and fact." He cited as an example, "the stated goal of the institution, to be a small liberal arts college of high quality, implies a considerably above average student body. The test data indicates, however, that the majority of students admitted still come from the lower half of the graduating class and score below five hundred in the quantitative and verbal scholastic aptitude tests." Southampton had to admit students who were marginal or simply not prepared to handle college-level work.

Ferguson's resignation, therefore, left Southampton particularly vulnerable. There was no one at University Center prepared or able to defend the campus and give it room to grow while in chronic deficit. No one in authority would set a policy willing to accept the hard realities of its newness and allow it to position itself as that high quality small college. No one off the campus focused on its problems or opportunities; no one cared enough, especially because Southampton was far away and its deficit was relatively small. Southampton was simply left to muddle through as best it could.

This was in sharp contrast to Brooklyn, which was by this time in need of triage. It required, support and stability to regroup. It had to find new friends and generous supporters. It needed loyalty from its alumni and a vote of confidence from the Brooklyn business community. Only a few years earlier William Birenbaum had engaged the leadership at A&S to fund new initiatives. That support was no longer available; the Borough was in free-fall. White flight was accelerating. The downtown Brooklyn property market was sagging. As predicted, those socio-economic realities, coupled with the overly rapid growth of CUNY, presented monumental problems for the Brooklyn campus. The tuition shortfall, which was anticipated but had not yet become a reality during the Hoxie years, finally became a chronic challenge. Sam Aldrich, a very likeable and well-meaning administrator, was overwhelmed, especially since he knew so little about providing effective higher education to disadvantaged men and women from the inner city.

Brooklyn President Alexander (Sam) Aldrich and Mrs. Lucy McGrath.

Born in New York City on March 14, 1928 to one of the wealthiest families in New York, Aldrich began college at MIT, then earned his Bachelor's and Law degrees at Harvard. In 1960 he also earned a Master's in Public Administration from NYU. The year before, he was chosen, "Young Man of the Year" by the Brooklyn Chamber of Commerce. Aldrich practiced law for three years at Milbank, Tweed, then became actively involved with the New York City Police Department, first as Secretary to the Department and then as a Deputy Police Commissioner in charge of its youth programs. In 1960, his first cousin, Nelson Rockefeller, appointed him director of the Division of Youth in the Executive Department of the State of New York. He focused on juvenile delinquency, remained active in the Police Athletic League and attempted to formulate a response to drug addiction. He was particularly interested in getting inner city teenagers out of the City into forestry camps and other outdoor settings. In 1966, he resigned his position to run in the Republican primary for Congress in the 28th Congressional District. When he lost, the Governor brought him back to his Executive Office where he had a range of projects, including the building of the State Office Building in Harlem.

Aldrich became very involved in the movement to preserve the Hudson River and was actively planning a second run for Congress in 1968 when "Fate intervened again, though, in the form of a spectacular New York City real estate entrepreneur, William L. Zeckendorf Sr.... [who] was then in his sixties, intent on rebuilding his real estate empire, and had decided to risk all on the development of the Newburgh waterfront on the Hudson River just north of Storm King Mountain." In his autobiography, *Dancing with the Queen, Marching with King*, Aldrich described how one afternoon he was given a lift back to the City by Zeckendorf in his limousine. After sharing that Zeckendorf had bought the Essex House on Central Park South by using his new-fangled car phone while on the drive, Aldrich remembered, "He then offered me the presidency of Long Island University in Brooklyn."

Son of the former head of Chase National Bank and Ambassador to England's Court of St. James, Alexander Aldrich was a charismatic charmer. By wealth and position, he was at the apex of New York Society. Whether Zeckendorf had identified him to be Hoxie's successor as Chancellor is unclear. Hoxie claimed this was what Zeckendorf planned as a weapon to protect his own position. The announcement of Aldrich's appointment as President of the Brooklyn campus was reported by *The New York Times* on page one, November 20, 1968.

A week before, on November 12th, Stoddard wrote to McGrath that he was "pleased to recommend that Mr. Aldrich be appointed President of the Brooklyn Center of the University beginning January 1, 1969. On November 18th, the Board ratified this recommendation without either faculty or student consultation.

Jackie Robinson meeting with William (Buck) Lai and President Aldrich, January, 1970. Courtesy of Mary M. Lai.

The November 22nd issue of *Seawanhaka* reported that Aldrich was confident he had the contacts to bring in substantial resources for Brooklyn. He also had the charm to create a new mood in Brooklyn. He seemed so perfect for the position that the Student Council President, Steve Fischbein, furious to have had no voice in the decision, still said, "I accept his appointment with reservations." His early admission that he did not know the story of the savage struggles at Brooklyn over the previous several years indicated how much of a novice he was. The December 5th, *Seawanhaka* ran a headline which read, "Students express mixed emotions but are peaceful towards Aldrich." At that meeting, SDS members and others took a "wait and see" attitude. The paper quoted one female student as saying, "I don't know anything about him, but anything must be an improvement." He gained student approval when Mary Lai agreed to roll back a tuition increase for the following academic year to help keep the Brooklyn students calm. Aldrich commented, "we can raise a lot more money than that." Foregone tuition was the launch of his charm offensive; by mid-December, Aldrich received a standing ovation when he met with five hundred staff and faculty. He never was able to raise any money as he promised.

Aldrich was welcomed as someone who cared about the Brooklyn campus. It helped that he knew Brooklyn and had lived there. It helped that he knew how to work with adolescents and understood the temptation of students to experiment with drugs. He had personal wealth. He was smart. His friends had money. His wife was charming and gracious. He had contact with the New York power elite. He had many of the skills needed to give the Brooklyn campus hope. As part of his institutional dowry, Mary Lai then identified a million and a half dollars in federal grant monies which could be used toward the cost of the long delayed campus library, an essential bedrock for any good university and a marker of the future for Brooklyn.

In May 1969, Charles Minert sent a team of ten to assess the quality of Brooklyn's teaching and course offerings and determine if the Board of Regents should re-register those educational programs. After all the *sturm und drang* of the previous several years, the Department of Education wanted to test how badly the educational mission had been damaged at the Brooklyn campus. Minert wrote a damning report to Aldrich on October 31st, "In the case of the Brooklyn Center, the vague and general statement of goals and priorities make evaluation on this basis most difficult." While Brooklyn claimed to offer small classes, the evidence did not corroborate. Of the thirteen hundred courses offered in the fall of 1968, for example, less than one fourth had five to nineteen students, while a third of all courses had thirty or more per section. Admissions practices were faulted and there seemed to be "very little commitment to the 'experimental, the innovative, the new,' described … in the catalog." Departmental meetings took place only once or twice a term, and the Journalism program, for example, was staffed "by only one full-time faculty member."

"The degree of research and scholarly activity taking place in the Chemistry Department was disappointing in view of the fact that it does offer graduate work at the Master's level. The department is, furthermore, proposing the offering of a Ph.D at an early date. This expansion is totally unwarranted at this time." Moreover, there was a "lack of overall coordination of the science efforts. There was very little in the way of significant communication between the faculty members in the various departments, and almost as little at the level of the department Chairmen." And so for pages upon pages the site visitors found fault. "The quality of the faculty teaching graduate programs is called into question by the fact that well over 75 teachers listed in the 1968-69 Graduate Bulletin do not have doctoral degrees." The graduate library was deemed clearly deficient in the "size of its collections and research space." The campus library was "inadequate to support the instructional program of the college with its current enrollment. This inadequacy extends to the physical aspects of the library, resource materials, services, and staff. The space was inadequate in size and internal space relations.... In effect, there is no single, unified library," although the site visitors did praise "The existence of co-operative agreements with neighboring institutions," finding it "commendable and desirable."

"The faculty did not appear to be vitally involved in the governance of the institution, and they manifested little evidence of initiative or independence of action. A clumsy senate structure militates not only against efficient operation, but even against the gathering of a quorum for routine meetings. The committees of Brooklyn are, for the most part, inoperative or ineffective.... The Director of Admissions indicated that he had never met with an Admissions Committee and operated on the basis of 'finding a class to meet the budget.'"

The site visitors recommended that State registration be extended only to September 1, 1971, with the requirement that five key issues be addressed before future registration would be granted. The review was so negative that the *Daily News*, in a story of December 28, 1969, had as a headline, "In Dog House, LIU Gets Kicks and a Bone."

Building an appropriate campus library by a date certain was *sine qua non*. Identifying the funding for that library had been a challenge dating back into the Conolly administration. The campus head Librarian, Nat Resnick, had long been frustrated at the University's failure to build this structure. He looked jealously at the grand facility built and opened at Post, while the Trustees dithered about Brooklyn. The Brooklyn building had been planned and re-planned; each time, the project increased dramatically in cost, as the nation was gripped by inflation.

On February 24, 1969, Aldrich wrote Mrs. Lai "the decision to proceed on the construction of the library will make it necessary to revive the planning steps which were apparently begun last August 9th, according to the enclosed memorandum from Gordon Hoxie to Nat Resnick. I would like to press ahead with the planning again and await your recommendation." But funding this building had become a monumental challenge. The most likely corporate donor was Abraham & Straus, an old-fashioned, 19th century, inner-city department store headquartered within walking distance of the Brooklyn campus. Already owned by Federated Department Stores in Cincinnati, whose flagship in New York was Bloomingdales, A&S was loosing market share rapidly as the Borough of Brooklyn was hemorrhaging what was left of its wealth and power.

On March 28th, Sidney Solomon, the Board Chair, wrote John McGrath, resigning his seat. McGrath, in accepting his resignation, responded," I have naturally been aware that you are having problems in connection with your continuing service on the Board and I realize that we must accept your decision to retire." He indicated that new Statutes were about to be amended and "within the next sixty days we will probably select a new Chancellor, a new Vice Chancellor for Academic Affairs, and a new President for C.W. Post." He asked if Solomon would support Walter Rothschild Jr., an executive at A&S and the son of the former A&S Chair, to take his place. The elder Walter Rothschild had been an LIU Trustee who died in 1960. A&S was no longer able to make major capital gifts to any Brooklyn institution, especially one that had a $7.5 million price tag. A gift of $100,000 was made to name the reading room in that new library. It was a tiny fraction of what was necessary.

In a memo of May 7th, Mrs. Lai outlined how the library could be financed using public and private debt. There was a federal grant of $1.5 million available. The University hoped "to obtain a $2.5 million federal loan. This national loan is questionable at this point as a result of a lack of federal funds." Mrs. Lai commented, "we can always borrow the money from private sources at the going interest rate." She went on, "long term debt in Brooklyn is quite modest, particularly on the academic facilities."

Albany was pushing Stoddard to confirm that, "the construction of the library at Brooklyn will proceed, if necessary, without the federal grant...." A few days earlier Stoddard had received a letter from the Department of Health, Education and Welfare regional office in Manhattan that "Title III direct loan funds previously appropriated and made available for the fiscal year 1969 had been withdrawn." The letter went on to "advise you at the possibility of obtaining direct Title III loan funds is quite remote."

At a Board meeting on January 13, 1970, a Development Report indicated that Brooklyn needed $10 million for the construction. The Board approved a campaign seeking $5.5 million, of which $2.5 was identified as coming from the Trustees. The Minutes recorded "it was pointed out that the status of the commitment for the federal loan and grant might be jeopardized in the absence of some expression by the Board with respect to raising $2.5 million." It was followed by yet another Resolution committing the Board members to contribute at a level that no one on the Board seemed willing or able to do. Debt, which was a deferred burden on future students, was constantly a substitute for philanthropy.

Throughout this period, a passionate Nathan Resnick, waged a one man campaign to force the construction of the library, drafting an open letter to the University community on "Why the Library Learning Center MUST Be Built Now!" Resnick wrote, "A University without a library is a blind institution. Its students live in an intellectual cave. There are no vistas to the future. Long Island University has been advised, cajoled, and threatened by State Education Department officials, by Middle States, by the American Chemical Society, as well as by psychology and business accrediting agencies. They have asked that the students of the Brooklyn

Center be provided with a proper library. Are students at the Brooklyn Center less deserving than students at the C.W. Post Center? The Board of Trustees voted to build such a library even after Chancellor Hoxie did everything in his power to kill the project which was begun in 1965."

"When President Aldrich arrived here, he permitted progress on the plans to continue but chose to bring in the Academy for Educational Development" (a competitor to Heald-Hobson and Associates). Once again, others were being asked whether they thought that LIU could get from its Trustees and other supporters enough money to rebuild the University. Resnick was more than unhappy that the Academy of Educational Development (A.E.D.) concluded that the Trustees would not collectively give or get enough to pay for a new library for Brooklyn.

Professor Nathan Resnick

In effect, building that new library had become the litmus paper test to explore if the Brooklyn campus had the capacity to remain a competitive institution. At the very least, Resnick wanted to ensure that the $1.5 million of existing grant funds would not be diverted for any purpose other than for this building. Resnick argued that if the assumptions of the A.E.D. Report were true: "we ought to close our doors now and give up the idea of running this campus altogether." He lamented that there had been four major designs for the library over a fifteen-year period without any construction getting underway.

On November 18, 1970, Aldrich met with the Brooklyn Development Council. Jo Chamberlin wrote that the University should take the lead in a Brooklyn based, not-for-profit consortium to erect jointly a very large inter-university library. Participants would include Brooklyn Poly, Pratt and other local institutions. This idea had been floated some years earlier by William Zeckendorf Sr. with Governor Nelson Rockefeller and had surfaced periodically throughout the preceding decade.

This became the alternate option against which Resnick raged. In his mind, a consortium-sponsored library would not get built for a decade or more. Administratively, he saw the idea as impractical. "It was out of the question to think that Pratt or any other institution would send its students by bus to use a consortium library. I could add that it might be hazardous to walk." Chamberlin, a seasoned political veteran, warned, "I believe that a flat turn down of the Library Learning Center at this time could fire BC [the Brooklyn Campus] up and result in a large scale faculty and student strike."

Resnick maintained that a Library Learning Center could not be paid for using operating funds; that the $5 million of debt would stretch for three or four decades and "that the rate of interest on these loans are ridiculously low and probably such liberal terms will never again be available." Moreover, there would be a grace period so that LIU would not have to start paying down the debt for three or four years. Plus, there was already on the books several million dollars of University capital funds set aside for this project.

On July 13, 1970, Aldrich reported to the Board several potentially negative factors that would inform a decision on the Library Learning Center. He told them that senior A.E.D. consultant, Sidney Tickton had recommended the consortial alternative, since Brooklyn and its sister institutions were each inadequately funded but had a common need. Brooklyn faced a serious admissions crisis because of "Open Enrollment" competition from the City University. Using a date-to-date comparison with the previous year, Aldrich pointed out that there had been 1,515 deposits for freshman and transfer students in the previous year, but in the current year there were only 751 deposits. He further warned, "open-enrollment at the State University will begin to develop soon and will probably become a reality within a few years." There would likely be a $2 million LIU deficit in Brooklyn in 1970-71. Brooklyn needed 1,800 students to break even; it looked to end that current enrollment season with only about 1,000.

Zeckendorf actively resurrected the idea of a consortial sharing of educational infrastructure by writing to Richard Furlaud, President of E. R. Squibb, on July 23, 1969, asking that Squibb donate rather than sell its downtown Brooklyn factory - located close to the campus in what later became Dumbo, - and take a charitable deduction, making its donation more valuable than any sale in such a weak real estate market. He argued that the company would "receive a tremendous public relations lift": that the image of E. R. Squibb would be greatly enhanced everywhere if the deed to this property were to be given to Long Island University. He sought out Carleton Palmer, Furlaud's predecessor, asking his help in brokering this deal.

Furlaud, in turn, suggested to Zeckendorf that he write to Alger Chapman, the Chairman of Squibb Beech-Nut, since Squibb was now a division of this merged pharmaceutical corporation. In that second letter, dated July 31, 1969, Zeckendorf proposed that the abandoned factory become "Squibb Center," a space in which Brooklyn Poly, Pratt, Brooklyn Law School, and other Brooklyn colleges and universities could establish a joint library and other shared facilities. Zeckendorf acknowledged that Aldrich had helped shape the proposal. It was an intriguing idea that never happened, but it did prompt Ferguson, two weeks after he had been interviewed by *Newsday,* to pen a handwritten note to Aldrich on his copy of Zeckendorf's letter which read, "As you know, I am attempting to make 'decentralization' work; however, this presents an issue in which the University has a legitimate interest. When convenient, would you please brief me, Glenn."

Universities are complicated institutions. They work in mysterious ways, even for those who spend their entire lives within the hallowed halls. For someone like Alexander Aldrich, the Brooklyn campus proved to be far more opaque than he obviously thought it would be when he took the job. He was a smart man, but clearly unprepared for the tensions and cross currents that swirled about the campus and the University.

Brooklyn was in trouble. The community was downwardly mobile and both the City and State were establishing tuition-free institutions that put public sector colleges and universities in direct competition with working class, independent institutions such as LIU. The staggering costs to CUNY and SUNY were still only dimly understood. LIU's future looked bleak. A new library would cost many millions of dollars; the A&S Foundation had only $100,000 to contribute, and other donors were few and far between. Any consortium library serving multiple institutions would of necessity be located, off-site. The Brooklyn faculty and students would be inconvenienced, so Resnick continued to lobby against any variation of a major library on campus.

It is not surprising that Aldrich had wanted external, professional advice. At the Board of Trustees meeting on September 22, 1970, he reported that both the Carnegie Foundation and the Esso Foundation had each contributed $15,000 so that he had raised one half of the $60,000 he had needed to hire the Academy for Educational Development (A.E.D.). Middle States, specialized accrediting bodies and the Department of Education in Albany existed to assess the quality of an institution and to judge whether it was fulfilling its mission or deserved to award credits and degrees. Heald, Hobson, and now the Academy of Educational Development, consulted for a hefty fee, often wisely, but also often without authority to effect change.

The Board Minutes of September 22, 1970, reported that the new Trustee, Sol Atlas, asked the obvious question: "what the report might accomplish?" The answer he received was "the question of the relation of the Brooklyn Center to other universities, especially in light of the "Open Enrollment" policy, would be studied." In selecting the A.E.D., the University had picked one of the most skilled and competent organization of its kind. The company was led by Alvin C. Eurich, who had been an Executive Director at Ford and was the first President of the State University of New York. But most important, the staff members assigned to this project were Sidney Tickton and John R. Everett, the former President of the New School for Social Research, the Senior Vice President of the Encyclopedia Britannica and a former Chancellor of the City University of New York. Tickton was the point person. He was technically savvy, experienced and very smart.

On November 20, 1970, Tickton sent Aldrich a preliminary letter outlining A.E.D.'s likely findings, even though "the final report would not be completed until the end of February 1971...." The interim document was thirty-three pages long with an attached series of critical questions that still needed to be resolved. While the Report and interim letter focused on library issues: need, feasibility and other options, it was clear to Tickton and Aldrich that library construction on the Brooklyn campus was subordinate to a much more significant assessment: the continued viability of the campus itself.

The interim document addressed why two separate documents would be generated: "You felt you needed this earlier report because a decision must be made before the end of the year on whether or not to go ahead with the construction of the new library building. The letter went on to indicate that A.E.D. agreed to focus its attention on: (1) What the Center has to do "in order to survive as a viable University during the next five years both educationally and financially;" and (2) "How what has to be done can be done; what options exist; and what avenues are already closed and why."

The firm interviewed more than one hundred members of the faculty, administrative staff, library staff, students, and Trustees. It spent substantial time with Resnick, Aldrich and Mary Lai, among others. By the time the library plans were complete, inflation had raised its cost to $8.9 million.

Tickton examined enrollment patterns and projected an operating deficit of $600 thousand for 1970-71 and $1.075 million for 1971-72, "with the possibility of even a higher deficit in the following year, obviously, if the existing trends continue." Additional library costs over the campus operating budget were estimated to be $640,000 thousand dollars. Tickton's conclusion was that the new library was "clearly beyond the University's financial capacity."

The dilemma was clear. For pedagogical reasons, campus pride and hope of future recovery, the Brooklyn campus had to build the library, as Resnick argued so doggedly. But the economic reality and diminished enrollment prospects made that decision extraordinarily difficult to justify, as Tickton so logically explained.

Soon after A.E.D.'s letter was received, Resnick wrote a detailed, scathing rejoinder to Aldrich, recapitulating what he said orally when he met with Tickton, Mary Lai, Gene Arden and Aldrich. His arguments were based on the premise that LIU-Brooklyn has long-range viability. He rejected outright the notion of a "MAMMOTH CONSORTIUM" as "a new pie in the sky". Better, he argued, would be "to postpone a decision on the Library as long as is humanly possible," in order to study "enrollment potentials, recruitment possibilities, additional state funding, the possibility of providing contract education to CUNY students, and the hope that the national economy would turn around if the war in Southeast Asia ended soon." Resnick took his appeal to Kiermaier and John McGrath himself.

John Tyler whose title at that point was Director of Research Administration, also rejected Tickton's conclusions, making the point, that "it seems obvious that failure to proceed with the Library Project will be interpreted as abandonment of the Center as a quality unit of the University. Furthermore, delay of the project can also be interpreted as tantamount to abandonment, for construction costs are increasing at the rate of at least one percent per month and if this trend continues, the cost of comparable facilities in 1975 will be prohibitive, at least sixty percent more than the present costs."

Following the December 5, 1970, Trustees meeting, the Board authorized Aldrich "to complete the plans and working drawings for the Brooklyn Center Library; to press ahead with fundraising and development plans; and to re-affirm the Board's commitment to the students and faculty of the Brooklyn Center to provide them with adequate, modern library facilities. The Board's action indicates its reluctance to accept the interim recommendations of the consultant organization, the Academy for Educational Development, that Long Island University shelve its library plans because of currently lower enrollment at the Brooklyn Center."

The University Board, trapped between hard financial realities and the politics of the previous five years, gambled that there was greater risk in further postponement than in forward movement. An elated Nate Resnick wrote a memo to faculty and student leadership, on December 7, 1970, laying out five ways that the debt could be minimized, even while construction was going forward. He speculated, for example, that "We might find that many CUNY students disaffected by 'open enrollment' might look for our kind of private university." Indeed, over the years there was annually a flow of such students, although nowhere nearly enough to make a substantial difference in the budget deficit. As the World War II popular song put it, the University was coming in on "a wing and a prayer."

On March 1, 1971, as contractually promised A.E.D., submitted a detailed report to Aldrich. The document was entitled "Change for Survival." It was a potent description of the damage done to the Brooklyn campus during the post-Conolly years, as the University's flagship campus was reduced to a shell of its former vital self. Not all the wounds were self-inflicted. Not all the blame could be leveled against University leadership. But only through austerity, conservation of assets, cutting expenses, working harder and longer, recruiting students and raising money, could the Brooklyn campus remain a "viable private University for at least five years until, hopefully, state and federal money becomes available for all." A.E.D.'s introductory remarks continued, "these may be hard ideas for a University Center to buy, particularly a Center with $24 million in net assets and 7,600 students enrolled. But we believe the Brooklyn Center has to buy these ideas. There is no other choice." The report was 181 pages of tough reading. In many ways, it was substantially more candid and detailed than Aldrich wanted to read.

"The plain fact is that Long Island University in Brooklyn and nearly all the other private colleges and universities in downtown Brooklyn, in New York City, and in New York State are in financial trouble as they face the future." The report corroborated Mrs. Lai's assessment that the University was truly a single corporate entity that could not be broken apart by campuses. "The intertwining of the legal commitments of the various campuses makes it clear that these campuses are bound together tightly by their liabilities, and that the prospect of creating three completely separate institutions, as has been discussed time and again, is remote. What happens at the Brooklyn Center is a direct and immediate concern to Post, what happens at Post affects Southampton, and so on."

The A.E.D. Report also addressed one misperception that continued to thrive in the University's folk mythology. "Contrary to widespread belief, no significant amount of Brooklyn Center funds was diverted over the twenty years, 1950 to 1970, to build C.W. Post and Southampton College. Like the Center, these campuses were built out of their own operating surpluses and borrowed money, although, in borrowing money, they did draw upon the credit of the Brooklyn Center.... the use of operating surpluses and borrowed money for construction has for a number of years put Long Island University as a whole in the position of being 'long' on real estate assets and over committed on ready cash." In sum, the Brooklyn Center had built its valuable plant through operating surpluses over the previous two decades. Repayment became possible because inflation reduced the cost of debt.

The report singled out the paucity of funds from private gifts for the plant and other purposes. It noted that the last sizable gift to Brooklyn was made by William Zeckendorf Sr. in 1954. Moreover, "In 1970, only 8.6 percent of all alumni solicited, donated money to the Center; their contributions amounted to $23,513, an average of $15 per contributor, but only $1.30 per alumnus."

Credits sold at the Brooklyn campus were down 13.6 percent from 1967 to 1970. Liberal Arts credits were down 17.7 percent. Perhaps most threatening, freshman credit hours declined 39.8 percent from 1967 to 1970.

In those same three years, Brooklyn faculty grew to 348, an increase of 6.7 percent, even though full time equivalent (FTE) enrollment had dropped by 12.3 percent. The student-faculty ratio had declined from 19.4:1 for each faculty member to 16:1. Tenure had increased to 46 percent of the full time faculty, whereas it had been only 31 percent three years before. "This rapid rise, the Academy staff was told, occurred because tenure had been granted fairly automatically in recent years, and more on the basis of longevity, at times, than on scholarly output or academic contribution to the Center." A.E.D. candidly noted, "Less than one half of all faculty members have a doctorate,... and about 20 percent of those who do not have a doctorate have tenure."

The A.E.D. surveyed the entire faculty and interviewed over 50 members, including all Department Chairs. Most were optimistic, thinking the enrollment decline was a temporary phenomenon. The general view was that "students will soon become disenchanted with the City University and will return to private institutions such as the Brooklyn Center."

In 1970, 80 percent of the students came from the New York area. There were 300 foreign students from 60 countries. "A large proportion of the student body is Jewish; about five to eight percent of the undergraduate day students is estimated to be Black or Puerto Rican." Many of the students were the first in their families to attend college and financial aid of some sort went to 22 percent of all full time undergraduates. The Brooklyn campus granted approximately $1.3 million in student aid, about nine percent of its total operating expenses.

The average freshman who entered Brooklyn directly from high school in 1969 had a high school average of 79.6 percent, a mean SAT math score of 471 and a verbal score of 458. That average freshman ranked in the third fifth of his or her graduating class. Less than ten percent of the incoming freshman had high school averages of 90 or better, ranked in the top fifth of their graduating classes, or scored 600 or better on the verbal or math part of the SATs. The Report also noted that despite these mediocre high school records, graduates gained admissions to some of the nation's top graduate and professional schools. Many did well in business. "This reflects on the motivation of the students while in college as well as on the quality of their preparation. In the same positive vein, 'Student leaders told the Academy staff that most students are comfortable at the Center and see it as an institution where classes are smaller, attention more personal, and opportunities for personal growth greater than they would be at City University or at a unit of the State University.'"

In 1969-70, the Brooklyn campus granted 93 associates' degrees, 1,276 bachelors' degrees and 207 masters' degrees. The first doctorate was awarded in Clinical Psychology in 1972. But as A.E.D. noted, "Taken as a whole, the educational program at the Center does not have a clear rationale and focus....the lack of overall goals and objectives is regarded by many people on campus as a major problem."

Political turmoil had led to a rapid turnover in academic leadership. With this lack of stability, clarity of program offerings had became blurred. Course and degree offerings were no longer "as the [Brooklyn] catalogue would have the students believe, 'committed to the experimental, the innovative, the new and the untried'."

A.E.D. reviewed curricular offerings carefully. It concluded, "the existence of so many required courses [set by departmental faculty] has served to bolster artificially the enrollment and, as a consequence, the number of faculty in some departments. The Department of Philosophy, for example, had a total of nine full time faculty members, although only ten students had graduated in philosophy in 1969-70." The report also put a spotlight on what it described as "section" creep. There were 420 undergraduate courses and 999 sections. Statistics was offered simultaneously by economics, psychology and business administration. The schedule of classes at Brooklyn, as at Post and most other universities, was sharply tilted towards midday sections. 991 hours a week the classrooms were vacant.

The Board of Trustees was not spared critical review "Compared with members of other Boards with which the panel is familiar, the Board Members of Long Island University spend a minimal time on University matters." It censured the Board for its abdication of a primary responsibility - that of raising funds. "Key members of the Board told the Academy staff they should not be expected to engage in private fundraising in as much as this function is now and should continue to be the responsibility primarily of the President of each individual campus. No Board Member has raised or given any substantial amount of money for the Brooklyn Center; nor has any member expressed the intention of spending any time in the immediate future on fundraising."

"The Board's rejection of any major fundraising responsibility runs counter to views expressed by College and University Board Members all over the country at institutions large and small, in urban suburban or rural locations and with greater or less prestige." Making the case that private fundraising would be critical to the future of independent sector higher education in America, the A.E.D. staff was startled by the passivity of the LIU Board of Trustees. "In commenting on the functions of Trustees in financing Private Colleges, one government policy maker in Albany said: 'if the Board of a Private College or University in New York State doesn't think enough of its own institution to raise money to help sustain it, why should the State be expected to provide financial help?'"

The report further took the Board to task because "the shift in the Chancellorship over the past few years from Dr. Hoxie to Dr. Stoddard to Dr. Ferguson to Mr. Mc-

Grath (with the assistance of Mr. Kiermaier), with a hiatus in command between changes, has made the development of a continuous cohesive policy outlook at the top level absolutely impossible."

By the time the A.E.D. report reached its conclusions, the narrative observed, "If the Brooklyn Center continues its present policies, programs and procedures, it faces imminent ruin....The only way the Brooklyn Center can survive and prosper is through a hard, concerted, immediate, all out effort to change the status quo with respect to all operations." Without such a change "it can expect to enroll substantially fewer students in the next few years."

A.E.D. proposed a ten-point plan, because "nothing less will do. There is no lead-time. Since the crisis is here now, the Center must act during the next month - quickly, decisively and purposefully. Delay could cause a fatal loss of time." Tickton and his colleagues, warned "at this moment in its history, the Center cannot afford to upgrade its admissions standards. Almost totally dependent on student tuition, it must be prepared, as a general rule, to accept all students who can pay the cost of higher education, providing them with a variety of educational services, including pre-college remedial work if necessary." It urged the campus to recruit foreign, graduate, evening, part time and transfer students aggressively. And it repeated "that the initial responsibility at the Center for finding funds rests squarely with the Board and with the leadership of the President." The report buttressed its arguments by referring to a position paper of the Middle States Association.

A.E.D. drew sharp comparisons with the recent turnarounds at Northeastern in Boston and Pace College in New York City. Tickton, wrote, "Long Island University as a whole, and the Brooklyn Center in particular, needs the active efforts of Trustees on a day-to-day, week-to-week basis, not just once every few months." Tickton quoted Beardsley Ruml, his mentor and the Chair of Macy's: "since the liberal college is a body corporate in the public interest, the power, privileges, and immunities of its Trustees are in fact duties and obligations."

An equal opportunity critic of current practices, Tickton argued, "faculty members will have to work longer and harder than in the past. They will have to agree to accept uniform measures of productivity if the Center is to eliminate the wide disparities between departments. Teaching workloads will have to be increased." He observed: "From the very beginning of his term of office the President [Aldrich] seems to have been bogged down in detail work involving day to day work operational matters." Other senior administrators were critiqued with each office found to be underperforming in one way or another, often because the presiding administrators lacked the skills necessary. "The Office of Admissions and the Office of Development, in particular have suffered from instability and poor leadership...the main problem seems to have been that they were amateurs, relatively, in fields that have become highly professionalized in recent years."

Meticulously, the report listed in order the panel's multiple recommendations, ranging from generalized austerity to moving the student faculty ratio from 16:1 to 25:1 in two years with a reduction of release time for faculty. A.E.D. recommended that all classes with fewer than 15 students be eliminated or, at least, be scheduled for alternate years. It urged the freezing of tenure. In its own way, the report was a tour de force. No group was spared; no savings overlooked. Eeyore in the gloomy part of the forest would have felt right at home in the A.E.D. study.

What the Academy for Educational Development did was to drill deep down into the actual realities of how the Brooklyn Center functioned. Whether the dry rot was as pervasive as the report claimed or not, Tickton and his colleagues excoriated virtually everyone. "Unbelievable as it may seem today, the Brooklyn Center has never been heavily involved in recruiting students. It didn't have to be....The center has for years been the recipient of all the applications it needed without doing much more than being a busy application-receiving office."

The campus was enjoined to focus on urban studies because of its location, while urged to drop music since Brooklyn Academy of Music was nearby, and art, since Pratt was nearby. It noted that physics had nine faculty members and nine majors, but argued that biology, with 80 degrees awarded in 1970, was a core major. It recommended Brooklyn explore cooperative education by attempting to provide its students "as many work study arrangements as possible." In that context, it noted that the Chair of the Department of Political Science had proposed that undergraduates receive "credit for work experience in governmental offices, community organizations, political parties, and public administration."

Cooperative education, in which the campus, employer and working students informed theoretical learning was a natural option for LIU to promote, especially since accounting, teaching and the health sciences were so ideally suited for that kind of practicum. The students would mature and gain valuable experience from the workplace. They would gain sophistication from interacting with professionals and older employees. And they would get a paycheck to help pay for tuition or rent or both. The notion of "earning while learning" was an ideal option for disadvantaged students seeking to enter the workforce. Co-op built Northeastern into one of America's largest universities. Yet the Brooklyn faculty rejected it as transforming LIU into a trade school. This was not the only time Co-op Education was rejected by the Post and Brooklyn faculty, even though the Southampton faculty enthusiastically embraced it, awarding credit for each succesful co-op placement.

The report urged the establishment of a Vice President for Academic Affairs. "Without one, the Center's academic program has drifted for a number of years.... and there is no control on faculty productivity or cost per hour taught." There were, in all, forty-six detailed recommendations and eight options not recommended for action. Those included closing down the Brooklyn Center and selling the property, raising tuition, cutting salaries, merging with other private institutions in Brooklyn to create an extended Brooklyn university, and to eliminate first and second year programs so that the Brooklyn campus would be solely a senior college and graduate school. A.E.D. rejected the possibility of the Brooklyn campus becoming a state or city supported institution or a technical or vocational center.

Tickton's Report was remarkable for its detailed hectoring. Aldrich had asked what A.E.D. thought LIU should do, and Tickton told him, in chapter and verse. In effect, the University was taken out behind the woodshed for a transforming scold. What Tickton failed to do, however, was to appreciate the exhaustion, anger and loss of energy suffered by Brooklyn in the years following Conolly's death. The Academy's prescription demanded the University self-administer a colonic, without factoring in how to manage the residual tensions of so much animosity. There was no manual detailing which small step should came first and which second. If everything could not be done in one fell swoop, how could Aldrich or Ferguson's successor begin to salvage Brooklyn?

The Tickton Report was universally excoriated by various Brooklyn stakeholders. The campus community had been badly battered and bruised for five years. It had been told what was wrong and how to fix it one time too many. The nascent faculty union, in a March 1971 issue of *Union Facts, Comments, Talk…*, argued that, *"Change for Survival*, [the Report] ought perhaps not be dignified by a response from the UFCT. AED, selected and charged by the President [Aldrich], inevitably reflects an administration bias." For the next six pages, the faculty union offered an unrelenting rebuttal. At an open meeting called on April 21st, the UFCT formally voted no. "This assemblage of faculty rejects the report-that is, the philosophy behind its implementation, the procedures involved, and much of its content."

What was expected of Aldrich was infinitely more than he had bargained for when he accepted Zeckendorf's invitation to become President. Aldrich taught Public Administration while he was at Brooklyn. He wrote many years later that "the course was a delightful relief from the contentious struggles between the two wings of the faculty (deeply conservative, Catholic-educated science faculty on the right, versus radically leftist, public college graduates on the left), compounded by a totally clueless group of Trustees." He might well have embraced any number of recommendations and observations made by A.E.D., but he had neither the interest nor the desire to devote so much time to such a monumental challenge.

He was no Conolly nor did he wish to be. In his memoir Aldrich wrote, "The issue came to a head in the spring of 1971 when the Brooklyn Center librarian demanded a new library. I flatly opposed him; we didn't need it and the board knew it." Aldrich went on, "I am certain I could have survived such an event, but I saved myself from embarrassment by calling the meeting to order and announcing that Governor Rockefeller had asked me to return to state service as Commissioner of

Parks and Recreation."

John McGrath and Alexander Aldrich presiding over the Brooklyn Commencement.

With that, Aldrich, walked away. His memoir, *Dancing With the Queen, Marching With King,* makes no reference to Sidney Tickton or the Academy for Educational Development. To rebuild Brooklyn would have required passion, time and luck. The campus students, faculty and other stakeholders needed far more from him than he wished to give.

Alexander "Sam" Aldrich was rapidly forgotten. A.E.D.'s recommendations were buried. The Board of Trustees remained distant and philanthropically ungenerous. For the next fifteen years, the campus deteriorated, and the library was built on debt. The entrance to the Admissions Office was painted black, with a small window covered with thick wire mesh. One out of every three light bulbs was removed to save money. Enrollment declined to a low of approximately 3,500 students. Brooklyn and Southampton both borrowed from Post's surpluses to stay alive. Post's distain was palpable. Brooklyn hated living in dependency. Cash transfers kept the campus alive, but barely enough money was transferred to Brooklyn to keep the doors open.

C.W. Post continued to expand, constantly dreaming of emancipation from Brooklyn and Southampton. The new Bylaws had given Post a great deal of autonomy by dramatically diminishing the power emanating from University Centre, situated just two traffic lights away. In the early 1970s, funding remained tight because inflation was rampant and the other campuses were desperate for transfer funds.

403

But it was easy for Post to coast because students seemed to come, no matter what. Nassau and Suffolk Counties were growing rapidly.

One pressing question, when Ferguson was briefly Chancellor, was who would become the new President of C.W. Post College. The right person could possibly transform that campus into C.W. Post University. The students and the alumni clearly wanted an inside candidate, Dr. Andrew Spiegel. He had served as Dean of the College and had been its chief administrator in the absence of a President. The Overseers, known as the Council of C.W. Post College, petitioned the Board of Trustees of the University to name that individual as quickly as possible. The candidate that Glenn Ferguson wanted was Robert L. Payton, the former Ambassador of the United States to the Federal Republic of Cameroon.

Payton had a CV very similar to Ferguson's. From the Midwest, he was educated at the University of Illinois and received a Master's degree from the University of Chicago. He first became an editor of a small weekly newspaper in Iowa and then, between 1957 and 1966, served under the Chancellor at Washington University in St. Louis. He was the editor of the Washington University magazine then promoted through University Relations and Development to became Vice Chancellor for Planning in 1966. He moved to Washington, DC as a Special Assistant to the Undersecretary of State and was named by President Lyndon Johnson as Ambassador to Federal Republic of the Cameroon. Like so many other University leaders in that era, he was from the Midwest. Born in South Bend, Indiana on August 23, 1926, like Ferguson, he was appointed by President Lyndon Johnson. Thus, he had to find a job out of government service as the Republican administration of Richard M. Nixon took over.

In a hand typed letter to Ferguson dated August 24, 1969, Payton laid out what he understood would be the terms of his contract should be become President of C.W. Post. He planned to begin to work on September 8th initially for a period of only one year. He defined that contract as an "interim agreement... to protect both of us. It means I can't accept another position in less than a year, if you don't have someone else, and that I'm assured some leeway should you find someone you want to have move in before the year is up." The letter discussed salary, clubs, and travel to St. Louis, until he could get his family moved to Long Island. It also talked about his son, Matt, struggling with adolescent cancer and ongoing treatments.

Payton, who was a charmer, noted "There are many questions that involve both of us: for example, how are we going to present ourselves to the faculty and students. Have you planned something along these lines? .... Any reason to expect an early confrontation with students, in view of the challenge you faced last month?"

Payton indicated that he had enjoyed meeting with a faculty committee Ferguson had appointed. He observed to Ferguson that "they asked a number of difficult questions, but I detected no closed-mindedness to what I had to say in reply…. The fact you and I hit it off so well made the big difference, however, and I'm looking forward to working with you. Consider this official, informal, confidential."

On September 8th, Ferguson wrote a four page single-spaced and printed letter to the faculty, students, and alumni of Post. In this memo, Ferguson told the community that the Board would also meet on the 8th of September to select an interim President for the campus. Ferguson stressed how important a decision it was. "When I assumed the Chancellorship on July 1st, it became readily apparent that one of the most urgent problems of the University was the imminent crisis in leadership at the C.W. Post Center." He went on to indicate that the Dean of the College had resigned a few days before; that under the revised Statutes, three graduate professional schools had become an integral part of Post, and that to date, no mechanism existed to select senior officers, even though the former Dean had appointed an ad hoc faculty committee to consult on the search. That committee had never met.

C.W. Post Provost Robert L. Payton

Ferguson asked the faculty to appoint a Presidential Screening Committee which would represent all stakeholders. "It was patently clear that Center communications were inadequate, that subjective personality clashes made good faith a scarce commodity, and that factional disputes vitiated the atmosphere. With few exceptions, the Center representatives whom I met were more concerned with promoting the cause of a candidate with whom they personally identified than with insuring that the future leadership of the Center would have the judgment, perspective, and experience to lead a complex academic institution."

The newly reconstituted Search Committee, announced in this memo by Ferguson, was chaired by Arthur Zupko, the Dean of the Brooklyn College of Pharmacy. It included faculty, student leaders, active members of the C.W. Post Council and alumni. It had 24 members. Of the twenty-seven candidates on a winnowed list, six (four external and two internal) candidates were interviewed. Only one candidate was endorsed: Robert L. Payton.

Payton was then forty-three years old. "As a part of the talent search, the Director of Alumni Relations at Cornell University presented the name of Robert Payton," Ferguson wrote publically. A copy of his resume was requested and his experience appeared relevant for many of the previously delineated positions. An appointment was requested, and I met Mr. Payton for the first time on August 19th at University Center." Ferguson asserted that he did not know him in Africa, even though both had served as Ambassadors in Africa at the same time. Payton would come only for an interim year as President, declining "to be considered for the C.W. Post presidency on a permanent basis."

The blunt four-page letter spoke of the ill-will and conflict that riddled all prior Post deliberations. "In the past, stereotypes replaced content, and good faith was not assumed." Factionalism seemed so rife that Ferguson decided the University had to go outside the Post community to find a leader. The initial appointment would be interim, and Payton was presented as keeping his suitcase packed.

The Board Minutes of its meeting on that same day, illuminate this somewhat opaque document. "The Chancellor reviewed the recent history of C.W. Post Center, covering generally the events of the last six months and including by reference a description of some of the internal struggles." The Board Nominating Committee, which included McGrath, Bergen, Franz Schneider, and William Zeckendorf Sr., reported that it had met Payton and approved him.

According to those Minutes, "Further discussion developed the following points: The Post Center has in its short history suffered of a great deal of internal strife and politicking which is said to have an unpleasant effect, and to have created an unpleasant atmosphere and further, in actuality, to have impeded, educational progress - the Post Center was facing a critical time and, in effect, was dealing with a crisis in leadership, as well as a vacuum in leadership - composition of the Screening Committee which had nominated Mr. Payton as a candidate was explored - the question of length of service for a President and a reasonable period for a term of office was covered - Mr. Payton's availability for an interim period only was mentioned - supporting the Chancellor in a team effort was fully discussed."

Seawanhaka reported on September 19th "the Post faculty voted 86 to 71 to vote censure against the University Board, for the manner in which they appointed" Payton interim President. The censure also included "the twenty four member screening committee that approved of Payton," They called it "a board group not representative of the school." The Post faculty termed Payton's election 'a gratuitous insult to the faculty.'" It also moved to censure Ferguson who had nominated Payton and had dissolved the original committee. That vote was defeated. The following day Glenn Ferguson confirmed his appointment with a salary of $30,000 per annum, a University house, car and benefits.

Robert Payton was charismatic. He was young, savvy and dynamic. He had prior experience in university administration and saw great possibilities for himself personally and for the Post campus, especially if Post could go it alone, free of Brooklyn and Southampton. By December, a thirteen-member committee of faculty and students had recommended that he be offered a permanent appointment. Vincent Macri, a Post alumnus, a trustee and Secretary of the Board of Trustees, was asked by McGrath to assess his response to Payton's election. In response, he wrote, "I cannot over-emphasize my pleasure with having received a uniformly positive response with regard to electing Bob Payton President." After talking to a great many people, he concluded that there was "an overwhelming endorsement of Robert Payton as President of C.W. Post Center."

In early January 1970, Payton moved to consolidate his position with several promotions and new hires. Most important, he moved Edward J. Cook, who had been serving as Acting Dean of the College, to Vice President and Controller of Post. Cook, who was a Professor of Economics, had spent twelve years at Fordham and had a *gravitas* that instilled confidence both with the faculty and students. He, in turn, brought in Denton Beal from Carnegie Mellon "to the newly-created position of Vice President for Development at C.W. Post Center." He did this without either consulting or introducing Beal to John Baiardi who was still Vice Chancellor of Development a quarter of a mile away at the University Centre.

Anticipating that the College of Pharmacy would move from Brooklyn to the Post campus, Payton tried to assure the Brooklyn College of Pharmacy community that it would have freedom and respect in the faculty handbook that was being drafted by a task force chaired by Rosalie Levine.

By the beginning of the academic year 1970-71, the reorganization of the Post campus was near complete. On August 25th, Payton wrote the faculty, "The reorganization has met with near-unanimous support. It will enable us to enter the 1970-71 academic year with a stronger administration, and a stable one, for the first time in several years." Among his central points was that decentralization of the entire University required the integration of academic programs at each Center. Key senior administrators were charged with the task of merging various schools and programs, including, for example, creation of the Schools of Business and Education, as well as the position of an Executive Dean for Post College.

This was a further step in developing cohesive, academic, administrative structure to make C.W. Post an autonomous, self-regulating college. The draft C.W. Post Faculty Handbook was seen as a final step in the emancipation process to "reflect the professional standards and traditions of the faculties involved." Although never ratified by the Board of Trustees, it was considered by the Post faculty to be a binding compact defining their rights and responsibilities with regard to the academic operations of the campus. Emended by the faculty over the years, it has remained in force to this day.

It seemed that Post was gaining academic strength. Then, the Department of Education choose to visit the campus on May 13-14, 1969, to decide whether it was meeting the rules and regulations established by the Regents. Re-registration of the curricula has always been the basis on which the State claimed authority. Eleven site visitors came during this period.

Charles Meinert wrote to Robert Payton on November 26, 1969 to report out their findings. He noted that the registration team visit, "took place at a sensitive and difficult period in the institution's history. The Chancellor's resignation had been announced and the Merriweather Center was operating without a permanent or even an Acting President. It acknowledged these problems and gave latitude, indicating this "administrative state of flux would negatively influence the academic operations of the college...."

Having made allowances, the Report was very hard on what it discovered at C.W. Post. It found the practice of allowing classes smaller than twelve to run only on a per capita basis or by imposing a salary cut was "completely unacceptable from both a qualitative and legal point of view; if such a practice does exist, it must terminate at once." Similarly, it took to task the advisement system and, in particular, saw the "employment of full-time academic advisors an "abdication of the crucial relationship between students and faculty...." It warned, "This new system is a questionable experiment," and it wanted it carefully evaluated at the end of the 1969-1970 academic year.

It called for greater imagination in instruction and curricular design. "The Science area at C.W. Post poses organizational and academic problems. The Division of Science has a director with apparently very little actual responsibility. He has little or no control over department budgets and only meets with the Dean in the presence of his department Chairmen." It noted that a Marine Biology Program was created without his knowledge, much less approval. "The Engineering Science Program is in extremely serious difficulty. This program is an orphan; the Department of Physics has tried to eliminate it, and has successfully removed it from the daytime program." The litany continued around most of the other undergraduate programs.

At the graduate level, the site visitors were even more negative. " We are seriously concerned about the quality of graduate programs at Long Island University." Many of the faculty either lacked a terminal degree or were themselves not doing research. The organizational structure of University Deans had failed to create an effective structure. The facilities were below par. Equipment was antiquated or non-existent. "Certainly there is no evidence to support any further extension of graduate work, and one questions the advisability of retaining all existing programs."

Both C.W. Post and the University at large were faulted for organizational-admin-
istrative shortcomings. "The most obvious and recent example of this has been
the impossible position of the Dean at the Merriweather Center. He has not had a
President to report to and has not been designated as Acting President. Yet he has
been expected to assume responsibility without authority." And the site team recommended that both undergraduate and graduate programs be re-registered only
until September 1, 1971 - less than two years hence. This was the shortest of short
leashes. It was a clear warning that the State was unhappy about how the educational product was being delivered. It was, as well, a tangible sign of the pedagogical decay that had hobbled enrollment, eroded retention and damaged reputation.
Despite claims of excellence and ambition to break free from the other campuses,
C.W. Post, nominally now the strongest unit within the University, was taken behind the woodshed for a solid dressing down.

In addition, the financial and budgetary impact of the Vietnam War, which had
escalated dramatically in the early 1970s, complicated Payton's tasks. All universities, especially those with little endowment, were caught in a complex financial
squeeze, since inflation rose more rapidly than tuition could keep pace. The cost
of borrowing skyrocketed and construction expenses reflected the increased prices
of goods and services that inflation imposed on institutions and families. Post was
building a new Student Union; the bids to build it were twice the estimates provided by the architect in the period just before the construction bids were sent out.
It was to be named "Hillwood Commons" (the name of the estate owned by Mrs.
Post in Washington, D.C.), almost for certain because Payton still held out distant
hope that he could charm a gift from Marjorie Merriweather Post to finance the
College's secession from LIU.

On December 3rd, Payton wrote to Mrs. Post in Florida explaining that the costs
of completing the Interfaith Chapel had shot up. He wrote that he was not seeking funds from her, but rather wanted to "request your permission to re-designate
two earlier gifts which you made through the college." He sought to transfer the
gift she had made for the Law School as well as a second, unrestricted gift, which
Hoxie had parked in the Endowment. He asked to see her in Florida and Washington; her Archive at the University of Michigan indicates how eager Payton was for
that next appointment.

Hoxie was also soliciting her for his new venture and complaining to her about
Long Island University during these same months. On April 21, 1970, Payton
wrote Mrs. Post: "I have been troubled since my visit with you in Palm Beach.
As a new arrival on the scene, I am still only partially aware of the details of the
history of C.W. Post College - it appears that the present Constitution of C.W. Post
College as part of Long Island University, effectively prevents your involvement in

an institution that should bear your mark more clearly than any other."

Payton, who marked this letter personal and confidential, continued, "The continuation of this is clearly intolerable. Your absence from the college, and the drift of the college towards an uncertain future, require more than platitudes on my part. Payton then noted that, "there is widespread dissatisfaction with the present arrangement. The students and faculty at Brooklyn and at Post are receptive to some reorganization that will bring real independence for each of the constituent parts. As I told you in Palm Beach, there is no doubt in my mind that Post should and will become independent in the near future."

He continued boldly to make the case for complete secession. "[The] fiction of membership in Long Island University has simply lost whatever validity it may once have had. The question to be faced is not *whether* Post will become independent, *but when* and *how*." He then went on to suggest," The creation of a Post Endowment modeled on the lines of the Duke Endowment that was created at the same time as Trinity College became Duke University." His goal was explicit: "to guarantee that monies made available at Post were not used elsewhere at Long Island University. In fact, it is my own conviction that even the fiction of Long Island University will by that time [have] begun to disappear."

Under Payton's scheme there would be three Trustees, two chosen by Mrs. Post and himself. It "would function as an entirely independent foundation" and there would be a new board that "after would entirely be a new body, or one on which the endowment was substantially represented, or one with membership identical to the endowment." Payton wanted this new institution to be known as Post University in order to have a future "which you would be proud to associate your name and presence." Payton was explicit that, "the problems of the past must be eliminated once and for all." And he urged her to make it happen.

On May 6, 1970, she responded to tell him that she was "very sorry to have to tell you but I cannot accede to your suggestion. Post College must stand on its own feet." She went on to indicate that she was in no position to provide an endowment or, "certainly for the present, to be of any financial assistance whatsoever. As I am sure I have told you, my hands are completely tied with a gift of Hillwood [her Washington estate] to the Smithsonian Institution." She noted that she did not have adequate funds for a Foundation sufficiently large to care for various "other affairs." She was as clear as Payton was direct. She wrote, "unfortunately, with my situation as explained above and with the added burden of the present economic condition of the country, I am absolutely prohibited from assisting you at this time."

Her biography made it clear that she was no longer the stupendously wealthy woman she once had been. Whether she was as poor as her biographer presented was another matter. It was probably a bit of both. She also remained angry at what had happened. A shrewd businesswoman, she had the name recognition without having to make the gift, unlike the Duke family. Whatever her mix of motives, she was no longer the agency of change that so many people dreamed she could be. The Post cereal empire had became tied to the vagaries of other companies and other managements.

It has always been wise never to count someone else's money. However many estate homes there may be around the world, circumstances change. Stuff happens. Zeckendorf over-reached at a bad time and twice became bankrupt. Mrs. Post lacked the philanthropic gene, or was not interested in higher education, or truly was outraged by Hoxie being fired, or, as C.W. Post's only child, never felt the need for the immortality conferred by naming an institution. Many people, within the University community and outside it, saw the continued involvement of William Zeckendorf Sr. and Marjorie Merriweather Post and concluded that LIU had access to all the money it would ever need. Thus, it was a cruel reality that Brooklyn, C.W. Post and Southampton were all fated to remain tuition-driven, under-endowed institutions for a long, long time.

Early in Payton's presidency he met with John Baiardi who took minutes of their meeting on October 20, 1969. Baiardi wrote, "He is interested in establishing an image for Post, perhaps as a separate University. He would like to get a different identification - C.W. Post College, Post University, or Post campus." Baiardi reported that Payton was not interested in revising the *Preface to the Future* plans for Post, choosing instead to abandon it completely. "He does not feel that Post was sufficiently involved in the preparation of the present Ten Year Plan." He wanted to focus on a few things already started - the Chapel, the Student Union building and Auditorium - and he wanted to do it with his own people. He wanted to review all printed material generated on behalf of the University, feeling that Post should have "complete autonomy here and each campus should be free to pursue its needs independently, including catalogues, format and design for the catalogues."

College Management, a trade magazine, ran in its October 1971 issue three inter-related articles chronicling how C.W. Post was struggling in adverse economic times. Payton was quoted as saying "we are actually in the process of creating a campus and paying for it at the same time all out of current operating income...." In the second of the trilogy, there was an extended Q&A with Payton. The third piece addressed the effort through private fundraising to reposition C.W. Post College. Alumni support was "feeble;" the mid-year number was only approximately $5,000. Alumni, whatever their campus, always grossly under-performed, both in numbers who contributed and in the amounts donated.

Local problems in 1972 were exacerbated by national and international tensions. Thousands of students, faculty and staff engaged in the spasm of national anger when the United States invaded Cambodia on April 29th and the Ohio National Guard killed four Kent State students at on May 4th. On May 8th, several hundred construction workers attacked high school and college students protesting the Vietnam War: the "hard hat riot" rallied construction workers and other blue collar workers to support Nixon. The country was spinning perilously toward wide-scale domestic violence. Watergate was looming as the Presidential election approached.

Virtually every college in the country grappled with a crisis as the nation came perilously close to Armageddon. Students and faculty marched. Student-led protests in Washington drew hundreds of thousands, including busloads of Long Island University students and faculty. The Humanities Building in Brooklyn was firebombed. Only half of the Brooklyn students who normally would graduate attended that ceremony. Payton, like virtually every other college President in the country, was challenged by the faculty and students to clarify his own views on a host of subjects including Cambodia, the Vietnam War, the role of students and the outrage of faculty, many of whom pontificated in endless teach-ins. Would classes, finals and grades be suspended?

C.W. Post students protesting the Vietnam war.

In a long and thoughtful memo to the community, Payton tried to navigate that dangerous landscape. He articulated his personal position to the community by stating," I consider the decision to invade Cambodia reckless, ill-advised, and an arbitrary extension of Presidential powers .... Were I twenty again, I would be participating on the protest against the present-and previous-Administration policies in Viet Nam." Indicating that he respected "the students-most of them-and the faculty-most of them-" he refused to "apologize for working at C.W. Post, and for trying to make it the best university on Long Island." With elegant prose, he discussed both the "rights and responsibilities of dissent and protest." He rejected sacrificing the campus for a "higher cause," arguing that such a move would be pointless and destructive. He concluded his memo, "the campus is a delicate mechanism, easily unsprung. Perhaps it isn't strong enough to survive. I think it is."

And two days later he wrote again to the University community, "The Faculty Council has met almost without interruption since this morning (Friday, May 8th)." It recommended unanimously its support of a national strike with classes suspended, but with classroom education continuing on a voluntary basis." Normal grades, exams, and satisfactory completion of work were suspended. In respect for the many students who chose to go on strike, he implemented the faculty resolution, approved 21-0, and gave both his personal and official support for it. There is no indication he consulted anyone at University Center or on the Board. He ended that second memo, "It has been in my judgment, the best expression of our respect for the memory of the students who died at Kent State."

Virtually every college and university in America was caught in tumult that spring. Local issues receded in importance as LIU became but one of many universities forced to suspend the essential task of judging the performance of students with exams, term papers and grades. The friction between the national polity and the higher education network of colleges and universities, became combustible. Back in August 1969, Dean Andrew Spiegel wrote parents and students outlining the policy at C.W. Post "concerning protest and dissent." He affirmed "our belief in the right of students to engage in peaceful dissent, but at the same time we hold it as our obligation to protect the rights of all students and other members of the college community." But what would it mean if the dissent escalated so dramatically that by spring 1972 the tension was between the higher education community at large and the general society? In dealing with Vietnam Moratorium Day on October 15, 1969, Payton wrote the community: "Decisions to participate in activities related to the Vietnam Day Moratorium are left to individual conscience." By Kent State and Cambodia, however, "individual conscience" had been replaced with a suspension of all traditional rules and regulations measuring the learning process. This was a very tough time for higher education.

... any assumption that all merit now stands with C. W. Post or that Brooklyn drags and drains her suburban sister will not survive measurement in any arena whether financial or educational.

Albert Bush-Brown

Chapter Eleven

Albert Bush-Brown's Early Years: Stasis

The decentralized University did not function to anyone's satisfaction. Faculty and administrators raged against perceived impediments that they claimed existed everywhere. Secessionists grumbled about the legal realities of a comingled bond debt, a single Charter, and a salary and benefit package that tied all employees into an enforced alliance. Mrs. Lai staunchly maintained that a University Center performing service tasks for everyone was cheaper than three discrete administrative structures That assertion was disputed by those who sought to untie the last remaining administrative knots that bound the campuses together.

Mary M. Lai explaining a budgetary fine point to Chancellor Albert Bush-Brown.

415

PART III - THE AFTERMATH

After Glenn Ferguson's proposal to untie those knots was bluntly rejected by the Board, he assumed the most passive of passive roles. While looking for a job, he signed what he had to, attended what was required, received and answered mail and went to conferences to represent the corporate entity, Long Island University.

Mary Lai's staff met the weekly, bi-monthly and monthly payrolls. It managed the books, prepared the audit; negotiated with TIAA/CREF, health insurance companies, or bought life insurance for employees. Innumerable contracts with vendors were negotiated. In fact, the Treasurer's office performed all the chores required to run a multi-million dollar business cost effectively and lubricate the delivery of educational services. Collecting tuitions was a common task wherever the students were scattered: each had to be billed; many had scholarships or other discounted rates that had to processed correctly. On the one hand, these services were routinized, often mechanical and increasingly digitally automated; on the other, none of the campuses could operate for more than a few days without them.

The Trustees quickly realized that as soon as Ferguson's year was up, the University would need a new Chancellor who would function proactively in that elusive grey zone between a highly centralized administration and the unstructured autonomy emergent since Hoxie. The Board was far less clear about what authority to grant the corporate University in the years ahead. That would be a task for the new CEO. All the Trustees knew was that it was crucial that he-it was still in 1970 a job limited to men-find a sweet spot that would bring some peace to the internal struggles that plagued LIU. The internecine battles had fatigued everyone, leaving the University diminished in its ambition and weakened in its reputation. Three teams of site visitors from the State had made that abundantly clear, and the University was to be visited by another Middle States team for its decennial review in 1972.

This time the search process involved faculty, alumni and students from the beginning. Chaired by a faculty member at the Brooklyn College of Pharmacy, Chester Riess, the Search and Screening Committee delivered three candidates to the Board for final selection. Reiss's letter to McGrath of January 25, 1971 began, "The Chancellor's Search and Screening Committee is happy to report that after many hours of interviews, discussion, frustrations and politicking, it is now prepared to present candidates for the Board's evaluation and final judgment. They were selected from a field of some thirteen individuals who offered themselves as candidates, eight of whom were asked to appear before the Committee." The fact that only thirteen people applied for this job was an unequivocal warning that few across the country saw the Chancellorship of Long Island University as a wise career move.

The committee's three top candidates were: Albert Bush-Brown, Glenn A. Olds, and Francis H. Horn. "Dr. Bush-Brown was clearly the first choice of the Committee with Dr. Olds and Dr. Horn equally acceptable as second choices." Reiss suggested the Board meet with his full committee, or, if they preferred, a subset of five which would include himself, the Chairman of each Senate Council, and one student.

Reiss concluded his letter, "permit me to add that the members of the Committee have asked me to extend to you and to the Board our appreciation for delegating to us so important and sensitive a task. We are also aware of the fact that the Board has conducted no search of its own, and for this additional evidence of respect for our judgment we are also appreciative. This is the first time in the history of the University, I believe, that so much power and so great a responsibility have been given to faculty, alumni, and students. Whoever is elected Chancellor should therefore receive the full support of all constituents of the University."

Glenn Olds was the United States representative to the Economic and Social Council of the United Nations. He had graduated from Willamette University in Oregon, magna cum laude; he had then gone to Divinity School to earn a Bachelor's of Theology degree; he had an MA in Philosophy from Northwestern and a Ph.D in Philosophy from Yale. He had worked in the Nixon administration, served as Dean of International Studies for the SUNY system, and President of Springfield College. He had been University Chaplain and Professor at the University of Denver

Chancellor Albert Bush-Brown

Francis Horn was born in Toledo, Ohio, educated at Dartmouth and Yale. Had served as President of Pratt Institute in Brooklyn, President of the University of Rhode Island, and since 1967, had been President of the Commission of Independent Colleges and Universities (cIcu) in the State, serving as the lobbyist for the not-for-profit, private sector universities of which LIU was one. He had nineteen honorary degrees and many awards over a very long career.

Albert Bush-Brown was born in Connecticut in 1926. He held three degrees from Princeton where he was awarded Phi Beta Kappa as an undergraduate. He was a Junior Fellow at Harvard, a very prestigious program for a few select graduate and post-doctoral students, which enabled them to study without regard to disciplinary requirements. McGeorge Bundy had also been a member of that Society of Fellows. Bush-Brown taught at MIT from 1954 to 1962 before he became the President of the Rhode Island School of Design. His last position was Vice President for Planning at SUNY Buffalo. His presidency at the Rhode Island School of Design had been problematic.

On March 29, 1971, McGrath invited Bush-Brown to serve as Long Island University's Chancellor. He accepted the offer and assumed the position on July 1, 1971. John McGrath's statement said, "The Board of Trustees is most enthusiastic about the future of LIU under Dr. Bush-Brown's leadership. He brings not only the youth and energy necessary to cover the many facets of this multi-facet position, but he possesses a unique combination of academic and administrative talents."

The *Post Pioneer* quoted Robert Payton on April 22, 1971. "It would be presumptuous of me to speak specifically of Dr. Bush-Brown or how he should approach his new position. It would seem to be a matter of the new Chancellor and the three center Presidents sitting down to talk about the situations existing at the three centers. Anybody who can help us raise money from public or private sources and deal the with serious financial problems of the University is bound to be a valuable asset." The University was still struggling to manage its budget. Even at C.W. Post, the most affluent of the three campuses, the Board mandated that forty percent of the expenditure budget be released in January and then in May, with twenty percent reserved for the summer. The Board also insisted that a reserve be created at Post of $1.1 million, which could only be released after enrollment data had been reviewed by its Finance Committee for the fall, spring, and summer terms. Payton's Vice President for Business Affairs sent a memo to the campus indicating that the money could only be released by President Payton. There followed on July 19th a memo from Bush-Brown to Payton, informing him that it would be the Finance Committee of the Board that exercised this authority.

At Bush-Brown's first Board meeting on July 20, 1971, he spoke to the Trustees about militancy within the faculty seeking to establish a union that would provide them with job security. Given past institutional chaos, this was hardly surprising. He observed, "The Brooklyn Center appears to present the most urgent problems. Unionization reflects insecurities regarding employment, continuation of the Center, and a strong plea for regularized process. While the Union negotiators have submitted a long, scattered list of potentially ruinous demands, there is evidence of less than overwhelming support among the faculty and the Union is anxious to gain nation-wide attention through a negotiation that will demonstrate gains without fundamental penalties."

There were, in fact, two distinct sets of Board Minutes created, the first more bland;

418

the second, addressing more candidly several of the complex problems awaiting Albert Bush-Brown's arrival. It is not clear whether the new Chancellor chose to revise the Minutes in order to make them a more honest reportage, or if this was done at John McGrath's behest. In any case, there was an additional item entitled, "Progress Report For Labor Negotiations." Frank McGrath, reported that his negotiating committee had met with the Union several times; the Union now had twenty-two demands before the University negotiators.

McGrath commented that this had been the first time that "the NLRB has conducted negotiations on behalf of a faculty of a [private] University, and many questions have arisen." In remarks by Robert Payton, omitted in the first edition, he "reported that everyone at C.W. Post Center has been aware of changing circumstances, particularly with relation to the NLRB election, and they're watching with interest the progress of negotiations at the Brooklyn Center." There was also a sheet on cash flow prepared by Mrs. Lai's office. The optimistic forecast was a $1 million deficit in 1971-1972 with the following year at break even. The pessimistic cash flow option showed a $2.5 million deficit over those same two years. She noted that the cumulative operating deficit of approximately $4.4 million "is largely attributable to Southampton ($2.4 million) and C.W. Post ($1.3 million). On a cumulative basis Brooklyn, with a $.7 million deficit, has a lesser adverse effect on our cash flow. However, its future outlook could change the picture." She noted the obvious, "Credit from banks is not only dependent on [the University's] fiscal position at that time, but upon future prospects."

Money was tight. There was little external support for underwriting the Brooklyn library and other construction projects at Post, Brooklyn and Southampton. LIU needed fiscal control to a far greater extent than had previously been the case. Albert Bush-Brown would have to moniter each campus, especially since each was slipping into debt.

As part of a national lobbying push, the Student Government Associations at the three campuses proposed that students be allowed to participate as voting members of the Board of Trustees. The Southampton Faculty-Student Assembly sought membership for three students and three faculty members, one from each Center. In a November 23rd document, Bush-Brown commented that these proposals had been reviewed with Trustees. He indicated that he had examined those proposals with the Bylaws and, on the 23rd of November, wrote that there were already "manifold avenues for representation of constituent bodies" which offered students, faculty, and administration "functional means for effecting governance of the University through the existing Statutory provisions for organization and membership on the Board." Bush-Brown was against placing constituency (i.e. student and faculty) votes on a Board. He understood that the Presidents and Executive Deans stood "demonstrably in favor of student and faculty participation in their

Center's operations," but he disagreed. Thus, one of the central demands of the previous five years - to secure voting membership at the Board table - was blocked successfully by the new Chancellor.

The students also sought via legal action (Gary Thatcher, et al. vs. Long Island University, et al.) to block the University from appointing two academic Vice Presidents for Academic Affairs without first vetting those individuals through a search committee process which included students. The Presidents of the Brooklyn and Post Student Government Associations were the lead plaintiffs. They offered as evidence the Agreement made in 1969 after the Board had rushed Ferguson's election. Consultation would not do. Only formal membership on a duly consti-tuted "Search Committee" would satisfy the student leaders. The Court decided against them. "Under the fact pattern of this case," the Court ruled, "the court will not interfere with the reasonable processes of the administration of Long Island University."

At a special meeting of the Board on June 27th, John Kiermaier was elected as Vice Chancellor of Long Island University. Bush-Brown had consulted with faculty, who did not object to Kiermaier, and separately, had isolated the Post and Brook-lyn Student Government Presidents so that other potential groups did not join in their Court case. Bush-Brown was clearly asserting that he was the *de facto* as well as the *de jure* Chancellor.

Another important early Bush-Brown initiative was his aggressive effort to recruit a new cadre of Trustees who would bring Board membership to its statutory limit. By the annual meeting of September 19, 1973, he had a new slate to be voted. The slate included Donald H. Elliott, who was head of Lindsay's City Planning Com-mission before joining the Manhattan-based law firm of Webster, Sheffield. Elliott lived in Brooklyn Heights and was part of a new generation of Brooklyn leader-ship. Also nominated was Jerry Finkelstein, the publisher of the *New York Law Journal*, with homes in Manhattan and Southampton. Bernard Gifford, a talented scientist, alumnus and non-radical member of the emerging Black elite, was also selected. (Years later Gifford became Chancellor of the New York City School System.) The President of Bloomingdale properties, Jack Lyons, was recruited, as was David Minkin, a major property owner and developer in Brooklyn. George Patterson, the former Chairman of Buckeye Pipe, and a Southampton resident, and Paul Pennoyer Jr., a Manhattan lawyer, Locust Valley resident, and the son-in-law of J.P. Morgan, also joined. The President of the University Faculty Senate, Eric Kruh, a gentle humanist on the Southampton faculty, was elected *ex officio*, bring-ing the Board to its full complement of twenty five Trustees.

Bush-Brown was, simultaneously reining in the autonomy of the three campus Presidents. Faculty unionization became a game changer, requiring "a permanent, professional labor relations person on our staff," Bush-Brown informed Aldrich in Brooklyn. But when Aldrich appealed for "a principal academic officer here to assist me in the supervision and coordination of the work done by the Deans, the admissions officer, the registrar, and the director of libraries," Bush-Brown penned the marginal notes across the letter: "defer," and "wait," because he wanted Kiermaier established in control. Aldrich indicated that the A.E.D. Report recommended four Vice Presidencies, but "the last time I spoke with the Chairman of the Board about this matter, he preferred to wait until the new Chancellor was appointed."

A month later, Aldrich again wrote to Bush-Brown: "this letter refers back to the part of my letter of May 21st, concerning the organizational problems at the Brooklyn Center. Specifically, I urge again the creation of the office of Vice President for Academic Affairs." He indicated that he would appoint Gene Arden as Acting Vice President and "convened a search committee consisting of the Executive Committee of the Faculty Senate and the Student Council."

On July 9th, Aldrich wrote Bush-Brown yet again. "The Brooklyn Center plans at this time the elimination of thirty-seven faculty positions, effective September 1, 1972 or sooner. Thirty-two of these positions are in the Conolly College and five are in the School of Business." He indicated that the termination letters would be sent on July 16th. Of the total, twenty-nine were "faculty being terminated for budgetary or other reasons." Aldrich was not an academic. The faculty was talking about petitioning to form a union. The Brooklyn campus was facing a deficit. Aldrich wanted his own Academic Vice President to help in this very painful exercise. Bush-Brown simply stalled. The confluence of these several issues hastened Aldrich's decision to leave the University and join his cousin Nelson's Cabinet as Commissioner of Parks. Aldrich was an able and witty man, who grossly underestimated the complexity of University life and unique problems of the Brooklyn campus. It would be a fair assessment to assume that the A.E.D. Report prompted him to start looking for another job; the reality of firing so many faculty accelerated his decision, and working under a new Chancellor sealed the deal.

Earlier, on May 25th, Aldrich sent Bush-Brown a draft letter from Bill Zeckendorf Jr., the Chair of Buildings and Grounds, addressed to John McGrath. In his cover note, he wrote the letter was intended to achieve several goals: (1) "a strong recommendation not to build the Library Learning Center, as presently designed." (2) "to develop an academic, physical, and fundraising development plan for Brooklyn;" (3) "an effort to bring the Board of Trustees strongly behind these efforts;" and (4) "an approach which will place you, as Chancellor, in direct charge of this entire matter, with me, Bill Jr., and Martha Pate as your 'blue ribbon committee.'" He concluded, "I hope this package discharges my responsibility to you, which I took on a couple of weeks ago at Martha Pate's apartment."

The letter is fascinating. Which part was drafted by the younger Zeckendorf and which by Aldrich is not clear, but in Zeckendorf's voice the letter stated, "I feel the time is come now for a thorough restatement of the situation at The Brooklyn Center for the Board of Trustees." Zeckendorf noted, "a year before the Board had voted to proceed with the plans for the Library Learning Center." He then itemized what had changed over the subsequent period, including the negative recommendation from the Tickton study in November, further enrollment decline which "would tend to support the AED conclusion, and a vote of the Faculty Senate Executive Committee in Brooklyn against building the library at that time and a vote by the Student Council Executive Committee in March 1971, also voting against building a new library. Student opinion apparently was sharply divided, but the Davis Brody architectural designs and the escalating cost of construction suggested to many students this was too grand, and therefore expensive, a library, when it was the students themselves who would have to fund the costs. Everything seemed so convoluted. The City has recently demonstrated its concern about building the Library Learning Center on the only open space in the center of the Campus. Aldrich had created a special blue ribbon committee of faculty to respond to the Academy for Educational Development report. This faculty group "recommended strongly that Library Learning Center not be built in the center of the Campus, but that library facilities be explored elsewhere."

The Zeckendorf draft observed, "It is clear that we not only need new library space. Some of our laboratory facilities are forty years old, and must be renovated or replaced in the very near future. Our gymnasium, theater, student activities and faculty and administrative office space are all obsolete and cry out for rebuilding or replacement." The draft then linked the construction of any new facilities to a new academic plan at the Brooklyn Center, which, "in turn, requires intelligent and far-reaching faculty input into the general equation." Zeckendorf argued that the academic plan had to be decided upon first, followed by a physical development plan and, simultaneously, a fundraising plan that would succeed.

Zeckendorf recommended "that the newly appointed Chancellor, Dr. Bush-Brown, should be invited to review this decision and recommendation, and that his conclusions should be presented to the Board so we can make a final decision on the present plan prior to July 15th...." The goal was to set a target date of September 1, 1971, for Board adoption of an integrated plan. His draft letter concluded, "In my judgment, the Brooklyn Center has a great future. It is our job to make sure that it is ready to discharge that future, academically, physically and financially."

By December 8, 1971, Bush-Brown reached out to Sidney Tickton, both to discuss his Report and to tell him that it would be Albert Bush-Brown not Sidney Tickton who defined in what ways the University needed to go forward. It was all very amicable, but Tickton got the message. In his letter to Bush-Brown he wrote, "what you need is a plan which describes how to make Long Island University as a whole strong enough financially to afford a new learning library center in Brooklyn." He indicated it would take several months for his group to come up with proposals. "We would have to develop some new ideas like increased productivity and apply some new approaches such as performance contracting. Obviously we would like to work on such a plan, but I am not sure you that could (sic) ask us to. But it would be fun!" Bush-Brown responded, "The plan you described is indeed what is needed but I suspect that your further doubt about your participation at this time is probably equally wise." The Chancellor listed many things that demanded the University's focus, including reaccreditation, budget preparation, union negotiations, while developing faculty appointment schedules and searching for Presidents and Trustees. Further studies by outside professionals were not on the list.

Rejecting the consortium approach recommended by the Academy for Educational Development, Bush-Brown committed to build the new library using New York State Dormitory Authority debt, a $5.3 million borrowing, plus the existing $1.5 million already set aside for this project. The plans developed by Davis, Brody & Associates were accepted. He ignored faculty and student ambivalence and Zeckendorf's letter to McGrath, if it was actually sent. In the press release announcing his decision, Bush-Brown stated, "It is difficult to exaggerate the importance of this project to the Brooklyn Center and to the educational resources of the region." The total cost was eventually $12 million.

In a letter to all Brooklyn alumni, he characterized the Dormitory Authority loan and interest rate reduction granted by the Department of Health, Education and Welfare as "expressions of faith and confidence in the future of private higher education, and specifically in the Brooklyn Center." The Library-Learning Center was the tangible sign that the Brooklyn campus had a viable future as a unit of Long Island University. It also was Bush-Brown's unequivocal declaration to faculty, administrators and students that he, the new Chancellor, was in charge.

On June 7th, Bush-Brown announced that Lester I. Brookner would be the next President of the Brooklyn Center. Brookner had served as a faculty member and administrator at New York University for almost twenty-five years, with a responsibility for planning, institutional research, and space allocation. He was recommended by a search committee chaired by Leslie S. Jacobson, a professor of biology at Brooklyn, and populated by faculty, students, administrators and alumni. During this period, Bush-Brown also appointed Eugene Arden as Executive Dean, charging him with negotiating a contract with the United Federation of College Teachers, gaining State Dormitory Authority approval for the new Library-Learning Center and making "major advances in education of nurses, handicapped persons, and teachers."

PART III - THE AFTERMATH

The Brooklyn campus was searching for and finding new curricular niches to sustain enrollment and to meet the specialized needs of students with physical challenges or learning disabilities or seeking professional and certifiable skills available at the undergraduate or Master's levels. The "Open Enrollment" policy of CUNY compelled institutions like LIU to identify students with special needs or markets in which a lower ratio of students to faculty would favor independent-sector colleges and universities. Nursing, pharmacy, teaching, allied health fields like sports medicine, physical therapy, and accounting were attractive to students, both because there were decent paying jobs after graduation and also because the quality of professional instruction was better in small classes than in the over-crowded campuses of CUNY. While arts and sciences majors continued to attract some students, enrollment growth, when it happened at all, was in those professional or pre-professional disciplines. Since the State mandated sixty credit hours in general education for all students, even those in the professional programs, much of the liberal arts instruction that survived became service oriented. Many on the faculty, especially those in the Conolly College of Arts and Sciences, lamented the shift in the balance of power within the faculty. But it was a condition to survival of the Brooklyn campus.

Bush-Brown, grasping that the Brooklyn College of Pharmacy had to be a linchpin of this trend, wrote to the LIU Board that the "Trustees of the Brooklyn College of Pharmacy endorsed a resolution authorizing the relocation of the Brooklyn College of Pharmacy to the Brooklyn Center, the consolidation of the college with Long Island University, a fee for new architectural studies, and the preparation of an application to NIH for funding." It became obvious that if the Brooklyn campus was going to succeed, the College of Pharmacy had to stay in Brooklyn, not transfer to the C.W. Post campus.

During discussions with the National Institutes of Health, that resolve was confirmed. NIH did not want to place professional education in pharmacy beyond the reach of inner city applicants. St John's, the only other College of Pharmacy in the greater New York area, was already in a suburban part of the Borough of Queens. To allow the Brooklyn College of Pharmacy to migrate to the suburbs would further drain the City of professionally trained pharmacists who were either first generation Americans or men and women of color. Keeping Pharmacy in Brooklyn was also a not-to-subtle signal to Robert Payton that the educational jewel of the College of Pharmacy would remain in Brooklyn, as Admiral Conolly had sought a decade earlier.

On June 6th, Bush-Brown reported to the Board, "Eight months of negotiations with representatives of the United Federation of College Teachers, representing the faculty of the Brooklyn Center, produced a contract, and in accordance with the resolution adopted by the Board on May 16, the agreement with UFCT was signed at a luncheon at the Brooklyn Center."

The emergence of faculty collective bargaining at private institutions like Long Island University was of such consequence in the decades to follow that it bears close examination. Faculty collectively for generations had claimed to be the heart and soul and of every university, wherever located. Tracing this claim back to Oxford, Cambridge and the other ancient universities of Europe, faculty resisted any assertion that today's university was a special type of modern corporation. In modern companies, the Board of Directors or the CEO hires and fires, imposes benefits and conditions of employment and determines corporate direction. Almost always, corporate law mandates the existence of a self-perpetuating Board of Directors. A modern corporation has salaried management which pays to hire labor, a point not lost on Karl Marx or College faculty with lifetime tenure, who fit poorly into that model.

Instead, faculty everywhere assume the right to choose colleagues, determine curriculum, establish standards of grading and fix graduation requirements. The Senior Combination Room where Dons met, dined and drank port at Oxford was where the critical decisions in the life and development of that College were made. To be sure, there was a Master, but the Dons or Fellows usually chose that individual, and certainly had a powerful voice in vetoing anyone the faculty did not want. C.P. Snow, the famed English writer, chronicled powerfully this ancient form of governance in his novel, *The Masters.*

So, what was an American faculty? Was it "management" or was it "labor?" At public colleges and universities, teachers were state employees or public civil servants paid by the public through taxes to educate the young, expand practical knowledge like agronomy or forestry and theoretical knowledge like political thought or astrophysics. After regular state employees were granted the right to bargain collectively as part of the social revolution that started during the Progressive Era and reached fruition during the New Deal, teachers at public-sector universities, colleges, normal schools and junior colleges were included in the collective bargaining process-to be sure, with very different conditions of employment and wages. But would unionization apply, as well, to those who taught at private sector institutions?

This was a thorny issue before the National Labor Relations Board for several decades, because there were two competing realities in conflict with each other: credits were sold and degrees conferred because the faculty labored in a classroom and a faculty member alone determined what happened in his or her classroom. Faculty were the heirs to the self - governing monks and friars who taught the craft of letters - how to read and write - at the ancient universities of Oxford, Cambridge, the Sorbonne or Trinity, Dublin. To be a master of arts from one of those institutions was analogous to being a master plumber or a master joiner in medieval Europe - a certification of proficiency and skill. In the contemporary classroom and lab, these professors are truly sovereign individuals of authority. One the other hand, individual faculty were often ignored, illtreated, underpaid or powerless - certainly the experience for many at LIU.

Twentieth century faculty retained that traditional authority to manage the delivery of learning to students, controlling the central teaching function of all modern universities. Moreover, the national professorate had also won a twentieth century contractual right to a lifetime appointment, a unique tenure, granted as an institutional guarantee and assuring each professor the safety to teach freely his or her academic subject without the risk of censorship.

In 1981, the United States Supreme Court finally ruled in the *Yeshiva* case that faculty at private universities needed to be classified as management, not labor, and thus were denied the legal right to bargain collectively. Since faculty, both as individuals and collectively, managed an institution's pedagogy and since the transmission of knowledge was at the core of every college and university's mission, the Court determined that faculty could not be covered by the National Labor Relations Act. That decision came late, a decade after many New York area faculty at private institutions had already won approval from the NRLB to unionize. Those unions existed and actively negotiated for their memberships. It was a done deal at many area institutions, including Adelphi, Hofstra, St. John's, Pace and the three residential campuses of LIU along with the College of Pharmacy.

Once unionized, faculty demands were simultaneously both matters of salary, benefits, conditions of employment and job security as well as a concerted effort to redistribute power by challenging the paramountcy of trustees and administration. Adlai Stevenson, paraphrasing Karl Marx, once quipped, "Eggheads of the world unite; you have nothing to lose but your yokes." The condemnation and distain for faculty by the general public during the war in Vietnam further exacerbated the political need for self-protection and security.

Given the tensions between campuses and LIU's precarious financial situation, faculty members had good and sufficient reason to worry about job security and pay benefits. Could an individual faculty member be transferred to Southampton if Brooklyn was sold? How ironclad was the award of tenure? In the chaos of the previous decade, what was a faculty member's protection from arbitrary dismissal or a pay cut? Faculty got paid more at CUNY, for example. Many LIU faculty members were keen to negotiate rights, establish common benefits, and receive larger salary increases. The power to strike or take some other legally protected action assuredly would improve wages and fringe benefits. It could also guarantee class schedules, conditions of employment and other, less tangible, benefits long

426

sought by individual faculty to provide better teaching and research opportunities.

Moreover, by the end of the sixties, campus unrest had reached such a fever pitch that traditional modes of conflict resolution and decision-making had broken down. The faculty itself was divided not only by tensions between professional schools and the liberal arts but also by generational issues: older faculty versus younger colleagues, both tenured and non-tenured. The most prominent institution in the nation, Harvard, was convulsed with its own collapse of comity and respect for traditional modes of communication in 1968. Such governance issues were very different from salary and benefits questions, and the more a faculty demanded the right to shape policy, the murkier the question became as to whether that faculty, and, by extension, all faculty, should be classified as management or labor.

At many of the underfunded private colleges and universities, especially in the greater New York area, threatened faculty felt the collective need to use unionization to reassert hegemony in the academic sphere. In June 1970, the NLRB issued a ruling ironically involving non-academic employees at Cornell University, which opened the door to faculty at private institutions seeking legal protections defined by the 1935 Wagner Act.

Long Island University and Adelphi University were among the first independent sector universities to be ruled eligible to bargain collectively. The Brooklyn and C.W. Post campuses became, in 1972, the first two faculty collectivities granted formal status to negotiate contracts with management. Many universities, including LIU, had argued vigorously that faculty, as a class of employees, was not eligible to bargain. These fights-and the many strikes that followed-were very expensive for a poor university, but both sides thought that the soul of the institution was at risk. In the decades that followed there were more than twenty strikes at one campus or another at LIU. Some lasted a few hours or days; others went on for weeks, occasionally threatening the academic term or year.

This is neither the time nor the place for learned argument about the legality and wisdom of the NLRB ruling or its reversal by the United States Supreme Court in the Yeshiva case. Virtually all universities were under extraordinary stress during the late 1960s, and that dynamic, especially for tuition driven institutions, helped to create the environment in which collective bargaining changed the power relationships.

As early as 1963 John Pell had circulated to the Trustees, including the Brooklyn College of Pharmacy Board, the C.W. Post Executive Council, and the Brooklyn Board of Governors a memo entitled, "Exemption from Collective Bargaining" which was circulating to all the private-sector institutions. The document noted, "Since its enactment in 1937, the New York State Labor Relations Act has exempted nonprofit educational institutions from its collective bargaining provisions." (This was a state law modeled on the federal one.) The document warned of "a further heightening of the already burdensome cost of operations and the constant threat of disruptions in the educational program because of strikes." Each college and university was urged to organize a Trustee-led letter campaign to Governor Rockefeller.

To make matters more confused, there were two different organizations seeking to mobilize faculties at LIU and elsewhere. The older and more genteel was the American Association of University Professors (AAUP), which dated back many decades and was originally conceived as a national membership organization to protect faculty rights and serve as a counterbalance against trustee or administrative abuse of power. It was the AAUP, which drafted the seminal document that justifyed the importance of academic tenure as a bulwark to protect the centrality of free speech in the classroom. This oft-cited 1940 document defined tenure at virtually every American college or university, certainly at Long Island University.

The Brooklyn Chapter of the AAUP was an active voice in arguing for or against particular policies or conditions of employment. As such, it was moving increasingly to function as a union, even though it was not then so recognized. For example, the AAUP Chapter President, Professor Thomas Stirton, wrote to Pell on September 4, 1963 commending the administration on establishing a sabbatical leave policy "which should do much to improve the morale and the scholarly productivity of the members of the faculty." The AAUP was also very active in the issue of salary increases and the fairness of how increases were distributed. On November 18, 1963, the C.W. Post College Chapter sent Hoxie a sixteen-page document, arguing vigorously for salary increases as well as an across the board equity pool rather than merit increases. The document went to both Hoxie and Pell with a visible copy to Admiral Wood.

A year later, a faculty committee established by Hoxie reported back to the full Faculty: "at the beginning of its second decade of existence, C.W. Post College has reached a size and stage of maturity which calls for a continued, but more formalized sharing of the growing burdens and purposes of the college." That 1964 Report asserted, "the faculty should have primary responsibility in shaping of academic policies and an advisory role on administrative and fiscal matters." Many of the items in that Report eventually found their way into the Faculty Handbook, a governance document that the faculty approved (but not the Board) in 1972. Separating governance issues from issues related to the terms and conditions of employment, was from the beginning the crux of every negotiation.

The files contain protests at the way individuals were terminated, teaching loads set, and courses scheduled. Personal grievances and departmental organizational matters were argued and sometimes adjudicated. At one point Vice Chancellor Mills took exception to the fact that the AAUP had presented to the full faculty a motion for action. Mills wrote Provost Ewald on July 15, 1965, "May I point out that the A.A.U.P. is a body of faculty. *It is not a faculty body.* Consequently, it has no rights or privileges as such at a faculty meeting and cannot present motions as coming officially from the Chapter. Only faculty committees who are bodies may present motions or bring up matters for action."

For many years, the AAUP published national salary data by State, by university, and by unit within that university. Individual faculty members almost immediately turned to the relevant sections to see how they individually were doing and how one campus, one division or another of LIU ranked against other institutions and other campuses of the University. It was an academic handicapper's favorite crib-sheet, but the AAUP generally publicized rather than organized, at least through the 1960s.

For example, on January 17, 1966, Eugene Arden wrote Mills and Hoxie, "on November 10th, the Brooklyn Center Chapter of the AAUP requested that the administration adopt three of its statements on academic principles and practices as official university policy." One dealt with notification of non-reappointment, the second concerned termination of tenure, and the third and most vexing focused on "Faculty Participation in College and University Government." The questions, obviously, turned on who was vested with the authority to make decisions and what was the structural means to adjudicate, when consensus did not exist between a faculty and a Dean, or a tenure review committee and the University Center or a campus and the Board of Trustees.

Mills prepared a draft for Hoxie on the AAUP's request. Hoxie signed his name and forwarded it to Florence Miller, the President of the Brooklyn Center Chapter of the AAUP, who had been a dissenting voice in the long struggle in Brooklyn over the Birenbaum affair. The draft document spoke of the "many complexities and issues." It challenged the AAUP statements "which need rigorous definition and do not have it. Who holds, for example, 'primary responsibility' for determining education policies? Is there a secondary responsibility? What does 'participate in decisions mean?' A veto power? And if so, what is the role of the Board of Trustees, which is, after all, the corporation and where all power ultimately lies."

That was the nub of the issue. Negotiations, at least at LIU, were almost always adversarial. Long Island University had been convulsed in the 1960s with spasms of conflict and ill will that made consensus in the 1970s and beyond almost impossible. The movement to establish collective bargaining meant that there would be "winners and losers" on every point. Finding amicable consensus might not have been possible at any university and was, certainly in this era, almost impossible at Long Island University. The AAUP, as a membership organization, lacked the power to bargain. When Florence Miller responded to Hoxie, she enclosed her Memo to Robert Spector, then Chair of the University Senate, because that body could claim statutory authority to speak collectively on behalf of the faculty.

On May 2nd, Miller sent Hoxie "a memorandum concerning the AAUP *Statement on Government Colleges and Universities*, which I am sending to all members of the Board of Trustees. As I have indicated in the memorandum, this is a most significant document which, because of its adoption by the AAUP, as well as the commendation of the Board of Directors of ACE (American Council on Education) becomes, in effect, the set of principles, which should guide an institution in developing governmental procedures. It will undoubtedly take a place alongside *The 1940 Statement of Principles on Academic Freedom and Tenure* as criteria for the evaluation at any institution of higher learning."

To cite an additional example, there was an exchange between Leo Pfeffer, then the Brooklyn Chapter President of the AAUP and George Stoddard when he was Vice Chancellor for Academic Affairs. Pfeffer wrote Stoddard that the AAUP had "instructed me to convey to you its concern regarding a report of a change in requirements for tenure." Stoddard replied, "that the Statutes required an 'earned doctor's degree' or other post graduate training or experience which the University finds acceptable." He noted that there were twenty-five assistant professors already tenured of whom nineteen had neither received a doctoral degree or its equivalence at the time of tenure. Of new requests for tenure that year, fourteen out of twenty-one lacked the doctoral degree or its equivalent. Several were also short of completion of "at least three years in service in the professorial rank." Stoddard asked "why it is that forty-six assistant professors should be on tenure without having had a single promotion at the professorial rank. Why should we promise permanent employment to faculty members who are, for the most part, young, inexperienced, and devoid of terminal degrees. Away from the University, many of them are graduate students."

There had long been a concern that personal friendships, collegial relations or an erosion of standards might let some members of the faculty receive a lifetime appointment without proof of their seriousness of purpose, their teaching skills, their publications of work or evidence of service to the institution - the standards universally held out as essential for promotion to tenure. The issue was not whether Pfeffer or Stoddard was right or wrong. Pfeffer, on behalf of the faculty, started with the individuals, and Stoddard with the rules. Probably some of those individuals deserved tenure; others were probably not worthy. The AAUP chapter could raise an issue but not resolve it, whereas a recognized union had the opportunity to redress the balance of power.

And thus under the initial leadership of Professor Hildreth Kritzer, a Professor of English at Brooklyn, a local Chapter of the United Federation of College Teachers (UFCT) was founded. This would be unequivocally a labor union defining its legitimacy under the Wagner Act of 1935. The United Federation of College Teachers first began to organize faculty in 1970. A constituent member of the AFL/CIO, the UFCT originally built its base with K-12 teachers in public schools, almost all of whom were deemed public sector employees. Whereas the AAUP's starting point was the rights and privileges of a professor, the United Federation of Teachers started with a professor's conditions of employment, salary and benefits. The UFCT was eager to increase its footprint and prestige by signing up college faculty. The two organizations became competitors, and, in the process, made the AAUP a more militant, activist organization.

The faculty was deeply divided over which organization it should select to represent it. Professor Elliott Schuman, then Chairman of the UFCT Chapter, wrote an undated polemic, claiming the AAUP "appeals to elitism, to a desire to be viewed as above other professional workers. It fosters a foolish pride that hides the economic and political realities of our lives…. The AAUP stands for the genteel adequacy of yesterday which is the poverty of today." In a subsequent memo to the faculty, again undated, Schuman wrote, "The C.W. Post faculty is almost certain to certify the UFCT as its collective bargaining agent. If the Brooklyn Center faculty does likewise, we can present a truly united front to the administration. If our faculty does not, the C.W. Post faculty might extract benefits from the Trustees which may not be accorded our faculty."

The AAUP leadership in Brooklyn, after much debate, voted by the closest margin, to approve the formation of a union for the Brooklyn faculty. Hildreth Kritzer, had, according to *Seawanhaka*, "denounced the element of 'snobbery' inherent in the views of those who feel collective bargaining is 'inconsistent with true professionalism.'" At that same meeting, Leo Pfeffer asked the group which organization should be chosen as the bargaining agent.

The University files hold a letter from the President of Cornell, Dale Carson, dated May 8, 1972. "There is a growing concern," he wrote, "as to the role of the American Association of University Professors, the AAUP, as a union. It is my understanding that this is one of the principal issues to be discussed by delegates to the AAUP's annual meeting. Because the AAUP has been recognized as a union by the National Labor Relations Boards on several campuses, my advisors, who are our labor counsel, raise many questions, including our cooperation with the AAUP salary schedule, permitting the AAUP to use university mailing systems etc."

Professor John Turner, a professor of history at C.W. Post and later President of UFCT the local, wrote to his colleagues on March 20, 1970, "A recent State law has made it possible for the faculty at private educational institutions to engage in collective bargaining. Because of widespread dissatisfaction with salaries, tenure, promotion, and other matters, a number of us have approached both the United Federation of College Teachers and the AAUP to investigate the possibility of their representing us in negotiating a contract with the administration. We concluded the UFCT alone was a viable bargaining agent for us. The recent AAUP Chapter [meeting] on this campus unanimously supported our decision to begin collective bargaining."

Turner noted that, "We were surprised to learn that Post College is just about the last institution on the Island to organize. St. John's, Hofstra, Adelphi, Nassau Community, Suffolk Community, Kings Point, and New York Tech. have done so already." He continued, "the faculty at these institutions have achieved impressive salary raises well beyond what they would have obtained if they hadn't organized." He pointed out that Hofstra "which has many of our problems, has agreed to give its faculty a *16% increase.*"

The fragmentation of LIU and the antipathy to Brooklyn prompted Turner to write: *"All policies and decisions on contract terms are made exclusively by the C.W. Post Chapter.* We are a professional organization representing professionals, seeking a professional standard of living and acting in a professional way. We have the resources behind us - legal, advisory and monetary of the UFCT, its parent organization, the American Federation of Teachers and, should it be necessary the AFL-CIO." The University was sufficiently fractured so that each campus defined itself as a sole bargaining unit negotiating its own contract, and seeking from a single LIU administration a separate set of terms and conditions. Had the three faculty unions chosen to make common alliance, the way the contract is negotiated in the auto industry, the faculty would have gained additional leverage, since a "strike vote" would then have shut the entire University, not a single campus. But the Post faculty had no real interest in a united front with Brooklyn, Pharmacy or Southampton.

Several months earlier, Turner had written the faculty, "It is time that the faculty genuinely control its own committees and that our faculty representatives truly represent all of us, not just one point of view or one department. If this faculty acts resolutely, the old political ways of doing things that have been so much part of our academic life can be permanently changed." Unionization represented two diverse faculty ambitions. The first was to improve conditions of employment-days off, time commitments to the students contractually set, wages, fringe benefits for each member of the full time faculty, going out on strike if necessary. The second was to change the balance of power within the institution; to give the faculty voice, as already mentioned, on management structures and power sharing. The challenge from the beginning was whether all existing faculty institutions would of necessity be changed, and, if so, how. What role, for example, would a union have in the tenure process? Could faculty members individually and collectively don and doff their union caps, depending on the particular issue under discussion at any particular time? What was the relationship between collegiality and hard bargaining?

In a letter from John McGrath to Robert Spector of August 25, 1970, McGrath wrote, "As you know, I have had misgivings about *ex officio* positions on the Board. The reason is that such members have been known to regard their service merely as a means of reporting the proceedings instead of becoming a loyal participating and functioning member of the Board itself. I have always felt that the duty of any Board member is primarily to the Board and its functions." Could a union President also become, for example, a faculty representative to the Board of Trustees?

To address another uncertainty, what was the role of merit in awarding salary increases? What should happen if one member of the faculty published six books while another published nothing? Could the productivity of one be rewarded or was it necessary for all faculty to receive the same annual increase, irrespective of scholarship or teaching ability? Yet another thorny question was whether librarians were professionals entitled to union membership in the same way that individual faculty were: Did they get the summers off? What was their workweek? In sum, how did the new system adjudicate between a professor's professional career and her or his membership in a trade union?

Another unresolved question was what role, if any, did an AAUP Chapter have on campus, if that faculty had voted for UFCT to represent it? On March 10, 1969, Professor Thomas Haresign, then President of the Southampton Chapter of the AAUP, wrote to Stoddard and Emilio Collado to complain that LIU had violated the 1940 statement of the AAUP. The question he raised focused on whether there was a finite term limit for instructors and assistant professors. Did Stoddard's new Statutes define what a probationary period might be? Haresign argued that "Faculty who were retained beyond their probationary period must receive tenure, *de jure*." In a related way, Haresign argued that, "The burning issue on this campus is the restriction of tenure to Associate and full Professors." Did the AAUP's norms for tenure still apply? Was this properly a union matter? Or, should the Board through its officers have the power to make those decisions after consulting, for example, with the Faculty Senate?

On June 19, 1970, the United Federation of College Teachers, Local 1460 and the Administration participated in a series of hearings in front of the NLRB. On April 20, 1971, separately but on the same day, both Brooklyn and C.W. Post were granted official recognition to engage in collective bargaining. In the Post ruling, the NLRB wrote, "Mindful that we are to some extent entering into an unchartered area, we are of the view that the policy making and quasi-supervisory authority which adheres to full-time faculty status, but is exercised by them only as a group does not make them supervisors within the meaning of Section two (eleven) of the Act or managerial employees who must be separately represented." It was that very issue which ultimately was challenged by the Trustees of Yeshiva University in the United States Supreme Court. The NLRB was overruled. Existing unions could continue to represent their faculties, unless the college or university moved formally to decertify that bargaining unit. Bush-Brown and the LIU Board did launch a formal decertification application in the early eighties, but the new Chairman of the Board decided to withdraw the petition a few weeks before it was granted.

As a routine part of the organizing process, on April 29, 1971, the National Labor Relations Board conducted an election at Post "to determine whether or not the faculty wished to be represented for the purposes of collective bargaining by the C.W. Post Chapter of the United Federation of College Teachers, Local Union 1460, American Federation of Teachers, AFL-CIO." The faculty voted "yes," but there were so many challenged ballots that the outcome was initially clouded.

On May 3ʳᵈ, a few days later, the Executive Board of the Post Chapter wrote a memo to the faculty: "This year the Administration has been more active than usual in *vetoing departmental tenure and promotion decisions,* [sic]. Moreover, by using the quota system on ranks, it has drastically reduced the possibility of promotion. Finally, the Administration is attempting to *increase the workload* of full professors in the graduate program to twelve hours." From the very beginning of the new era, the union leadership was insisting that every management change had to be bargained before it was implemented. Professor Arthur Kruger, according to the Post *Pioneer* of May 6ᵗʰ, was quoted as saying "The union will make the faculty strong, not scared." There was to be an industrial model, with every comma of the contract becoming a battleground. Labor disputes were often adjudicated in federal court or through arbitration. Unionization enhanced the already litigious environment. Collegiality, already in short supply at Long Island University, became a casualty. At the same time, collective bargaining was a boon to the individual faculty member whose benefits and salary increased even while his or her teaching load and advisement requirements went down.

Complicated issues abounded from the very first days. On May 7, 1971, the Chair of the new Post Chapter UFCT, Professor Arthur Coleman, wrote a very angry memo to Robert Payton. "We were *never consulted about the reorganization of the Center* and the appointment of the many new Deans and Vice Presidents which occurred over the summer." Coleman concluded his memo by commenting, "the cooperation between the UFCT, Faculty Council, and AAUP has served the faculty well this last year. Representatives of the Faculty Council and the AAUP are members of the UFCT Executive Board." This interpenetration of roles and com-mingling of different groups originally established for discrete tasks in managing how the University ran its academic business blurred the distinction between what was unequivocally a labor union matter and what properly belonged before a fac-ulty Senate or Council.

There is a "Dear Colleague" letter of June 24, 1971,which was a five page litany of things the administration was doing wrong. Payton certainly had his flaws, but he was not evil incarnate. It is the tone of the letter that is most striking, perhaps because the angriest and most politically active of the faculty assumed the leader-ship roles, after a decade of turmoil. Both sides then took up combative, ritualistic stands. It was Kabuki like. Other universities have had comity even with collec-tive bargaining; somehow this was always an alien concept to administration and faculty at Brooklyn and Post. Interestingly, the union relationships at the College of Pharmacy and at Southampton never displayed the anger, the ill will that so permeated discussions at the two major campuses.

On March 14, 1972, the Executive Board of the C.W. Post Chapter wrote to the Post faculty about the certification election. At that point, the final outcome still remained clouded by a dispute over who was entitled to be in the bargaining unit and, therefore, to vote. "As you know, the union led 214 to 208 in the collective bargaining election held last spring. The union victory remained in doubt, how-ever, because of forty-seven uncounted contested ballots." There were hearings held to adjudicate this matter, and "as a result of the hearings held by the Local NLRB, the hearing officer recommended that only eleven ballots be counted." This was not an overwhelming mandate, but was sufficient to change the trajectory of the University from that day on.

The Brooklyn labor contract was formally ratified by the Board of Trustees on May 16, 1972, after an eight-month negotiation. Bush-Brown hosted a luncheon to celebrate. It was perhaps the last time there was an era of good feelings connected to labor negotiations!

The full history of unionization at Long Island University is for another book at another time by another author. It is a story of litigiousness, mistrust and multiple strikes. The discontinuity of unionization transformed the University, even as the multiple traumas an earlier ages contributed to creating the morass of anger, much legitimately felt, that fueled the years that followed. Unionization introduced a new dynamic in how the institution was run and how it defined its mission. It de-serves its own complex narrative.

As a matter of transition, it is worth noting that Brooklyn and Post faculty unions were both openly hostile to the Statute revisions that Bush-Brown drafted to address that elusive search for equilibrium between the Center and the three campuses. One salvo read, "The proposed Statute revisions result in the increased centralization of power in the hands of the Chancellor. The Center's prerogatives are reduced. Faculty rights are likewise eroded. For example, tenure will not be granted before the beginning of the seventh year. The Chancellor will also assume the power to decide both 'availability' and 'eligibility' for tenure."

The Post union was unhappy at the new restrictions on the powers of the campus Presidents. At one point there is a complaint that "there is no mention of the President's budgetary powers. There is no mention of his right to attend Board meetings. The only knowledge the Board might have of C.W. Post affairs is through the Chancellor." The union conveniently listed the Stoddard Statutes, as if they had been issued at Mt Sinai, on one side of the page and Bush-Brown's proposed revisions on the other. The faculty unions were to be his most vociferous foes in his effort to rebalance, or, at least, address the relative influence of the campuses and University Center.

Aldrich had already taken himself out of the contest. Bush-Brown concluded he needed someone stronger at Southampton, both because Southampton was failing to recruit an adequate number of students to balance its books and because Glanz was not successful in interesting the wealthy summer residents to support the college. At the Board meeting July 20, 1971, when Bush-Brown was made a member of the Board, "Dr. Glanz reported that the serious Southampton deficit" resulted "from a sharp decline in enrollment." While he was bullish about the upcoming year (he always was), enrollment did not allow the campus to function in the black. Glanz further reported, "Attitudes of the staff, faculty, and students have improved tremendously with this up-turn at Southampton after the disheartening downward trend of the past year or two." But finding money in the community to help underwrite the construction of a modest gymnasium was proving very difficult.

Glanz felt that Bush-Brown condescended to him. His ebullience and optimism, so manifest in those first pioneering years, had all but vanished after crises over student drug use, the Vietnam war, deficits and unionization efforts. Bush-Brown, in an effort to drive expenditures down, imposed additional cuts that Glanz opposed. Glanz and Bush-Brown eventually agreed to a face saving agreement, one in which Glanz would serve an additional year and then return to faculty.

Conolly's and Admiral Wood's dream for Southampton, so hyped by Hoxie in *Preface to the Future*, dissipated into a far more mundane reality. Southampton became a chronically underfunded, bipolar institution with Marine Science attracting a very solid level of students while the rest, admitted to help pay the bills, were several cuts below.

To end the era of autonomous campus Presidents, Bush-Brown had to reshape the role played by Robert Payton, regaining for himself paramount authority as Chancellor. On December 14, 1971, Payton wrote Bush-Brown a confidential memo which began, "In a variety of conversations, formal and informal, over the past month or two, it has become increasingly clear that there are elementary matters affecting Long Island University and C.W. Post Center that should be clarified. Most of these matters reflect differences of opinion about the degree of autonomy that is appropriate to C.W. Post Center, and the degree of centralized administration that is appropriate to Long Island University."

With more than a touch of arrogance, Payton went on, "We accept, as I have said, the continued existence of Long Island University with C.W. Post Center as a central element. Although some of us feel that Post might develop more rapidly as a completely independent institution, we accept the Board's implicit decision to continue as a single University." What Payton did not mention, but perhaps Bush-Brown knew, was the rejection by Mrs. Post of additional philanthropy. Was it the royal "we" that Payton was using? Was he arrogating to himself the right to speak on behalf of the campus?

This three-page, single-spaced document clearly challenged Bush-Brown. For example, one of the points enumerated was: "we take our budgetary responsibilities very seriously. We are quite ready to be held accountable, within any reasonable guidelines, for all expenditures. We are, however, greatly concerned that even routine budgetary decisions are being removed from campus jurisdiction." This document was sent to the Executive Committee that Payton created and ended with an invitation for Bush-Brown "to meet with me and the Executive Committee of Post to discuss this, and other matters you may wish to raise."

On June 1st, Payton sent a hand-typed letter to Bush-Brown seeking to separate two items "so as not to be ungracious. The first is the set of alternatives you offered as the basis of my compensation next year.... The second matter, that of term appointments...." There followed an obscure paragraph, which Bush-Brown had marked by hand with a question mark. Payton had written, "As for as my separatist activities and inclinations, it is probably better that I remain on an annual appointment if people are fearful of the harm I might do. As Long Island University proves itself, its wholly-owned subsidiaries will become persuaded and I can be persuaded, too. I will try not to lose my sense of humor in our discussion of the matter (although my temper is sometimes less reliable). Speaking of my sense of humor, I gather it was yours that prompted you to include the maid as part of my compensation. Is she deductible?" And he ended this letter with "Peace. Bob."

These two men clearly enjoyed each other's company - the verbal jousting, the puns, the jokes and intellectual banter. But beneath the droll and witty exchanges was a deep tension over their professional relationship. Nothing in the file indicates whether Payton ever told Bush-Brown about his efforts to get a transformative gift from Marjorie Post. On August 4th, Payton received an unequivocal letter from one of Mrs. Post's attorneys, Henry A. Dudley, of the Washington firm McNutt, Dudley. It read, "Your letter of July 19, 1972 to Mrs. Marjorie M. Post has been handed to me for reply. Unfortunately, Mrs. Post, at the age of eighty-five, will no longer able to participate on Boards or any other activity of social organizations that in the past she has enjoyed so much.... while Mrs. Post is physically well, the doctor's feel that any activities outside of her normal everyday routine would not be in her best interests." There would be no philanthropic angel altering the discussions between Payton and Bush-Brown about the relationship of C.W. Post to the larger University at large.

On November 30 1972, Payton wrote to Professor George Small, with a copy to Bush-Brown, asking him as Chairman of the Statute Revision Committee, "to recommend that your committee give the most serious consideration to the possibility of each campus identifying itself in a way that best reflects its present status, as well as its affiliation with Long Island University." He wanted the Statutes to "permit the Post Campus to be known as 'C.W. Post University, a campus of Long Island University.'" That proposal "would have the overwhelming support of the C.W. Post campus, and would put to rest present sensitivities on the part of graduate and professional schools that they are a part of a 'college' when in fact that they are constituents members of a university 'campus' by every accepted usage."

Just before Christmas on December 21st, Payton wrote another of his hand-typed letters to Bush-Brown, who had been laboring to redraft the statutes. Payton responded, "I don't envy you the task of imposing order on the structure that is so deeply lacking in order or purpose; from the macrocosmic level of the University, the ordinary work of campuses must seem unreal as well as unrelated." He went on, "From my vantage point, of course, the real work of the University is the daily work of the campuses, the teaching and learning by faculty and students." Bush-Brown's effort to create a more cohesive structure prompted Payton to observe that finding "some coherent, purposeful set of goals and objectives is interesting in its way but empty of blood, sweat, and tears. I do sense in your paper some of the problems of making the Board's involvement effective, and the familiar problems of bringing discordant views together in some plausible summary of Presidents' meetings, and budgets, and planning processes."

Payton then turned to the very core of the issue. "There remain the familiar arguments about structure and identity that are, I think, essentially avoided here. Perhaps that is wise; there is entirely too much of that in Post's Middle States visit. But then Post, as I said the other day, does not feel that the autonomy was tried and found wanting; it wasn't really tried, but even the degree of autonomy that was achieved is thought to have been preferable to anything else that has been tried before or since."

"The new concept that the President is a member of the Chancellor's staff - or member of the Chancellor's office, which may mean something different - is a new concept, at least for me. It is certainly a change in fact and practice from my earlier days here, if not a newly inspired and presented interpretation of the 1969 Statutes. In any case, I am not yet able to grasp it other than to think of it as effectively changing my title from President to Vice Chancellor. Am I mistaken in my inferences?"

Payton felt sure that Post had thrived during the period of autonomy, unlike Brooklyn and Southampton, and that its success was directly related to its being uncoupled from the burden of any association. The assertion was that the University was a millstone holding Post back in ways that were deleterious. For Payton "Post turned around from its threatened and unresponsive condition of 1969 and became what it is now: a creative and energetic institution that has demonstrated leadership in various and useful ways." On January 10, 1973, Payton wrote to John McGrath, "Our Middle States report, as you will notice, does make reference to the relationship of the Center [C.W. Post] to the University. The Middle States committee found widespread confusion and misunderstanding about that relationship during its visit to the Post campus; the committee seemed to believe that the Trustees should review the matter with the intention of reducing the frequency of these misunderstandings."

Payton indicated that he personally would welcome such clarification, "and for that reason I suggested that I attempt to put on paper a statement of my own position. It is a position sometimes identified as 'separatist,' in ways that may be prejudicial to the best interests of C.W. Post Center. My comments will limit themselves to the structural and functional questions that I think appropriate to the Board's consideration." Payton was hopeful that the Board would actively attend to this issue to improve "the morale of the C.W. Post community." Once again, Payton not only sent a copy of this letter to Bush-Brown, but also copied all the members of The Executive Committee of the Board of Trustees. This was a fight he wanted to have in public.

On January 22, 1973, Payton wrote to Bush-Brown with a copy to McGrath, informing the Chancellor that one of his sons, who had been suffering from adolescent leukemia before the Payton's came east to LIU, was dying. "It appears that there is no longer the possibility of curative treatment and that he has entered the terminal phase." It was a terrible time in Payton's life and the tension with Bush-Brown was becoming ever more strained.

PART III - THE AFTERMATH

On March 16th, there is a two-page recollection by Bush-Brown of the dialogue from a meeting with Payton. The two started by discussing the number of tenure slots and salary increases that would take place during the 1973-74 year. It is, of course, impossible to know whether Bush-Brown altered the exchange as he reconstructed it. But also present was Theodore C. Streibert, a Laurel Hollow resident on Long Island and Eisenhower's first director of the United States Information Agency. The files are unclear whether it was Payton or Bush-Brown who brought Streibert into this meeting. Bush-Brown probably invited him to have witness.

Payton was quoted by Bush-Brown as saying, "no one knows on my campus where the buck stops, in my office, or where? It is unclear." Bush-Brown responded that, "the buck stops with the Board we serve, and even they are subject to law." Payton is described as saying "many people on my campus believe that salaries and budgets should be decided on campus, not by the University or Board. And, faculty and tenure appointments, too, they're campus, not University or Board matters, and I agree with them." Then Streibert interjected, "Yes, and that's the problem right there."

In a personal and confidential letter to John McGrath dated March 23rd, Payton wrote, "the present campus situation is strained, as you know. Student and faculty concern over matters of tenure and compensation policies require that there be no ambiguity in the decision-making process. For that reason, I believe that I must make known at this time my decision not to continue as President of C.W. Post Center after the expiration of my current contract (August 31, 1973). The reasons for my resignation are well known to you. It is not appropriate for me to make known my future plans, but [my] decision to leave Post is final."

The University and Post College Public Relations offices issued conflicting press releases about Payton's decision to resign. The University Center document referenced "differences of opinion about the structure of Long Island University and the appropriate degree of autonomy at C.W. Post. These are not matters of opinion. They are arranged by statute and history. C.W. Post is Long Island University at Brookville. During the earlier part of his service as President, we were searching for a new Chancellor, and Mr. Payton ran things with a relatively free hand. We now have an able Chancellor. He is the chief executive officer of all the University.... Although this is the structure, Mr. Payton has never been hospitable to it."

In the campus-generated press statement, Payton's decision resulted "from differences of opinion about the structure of Long Island University and the appropriate degree of autonomy for C.W. Post as a campus of the University." The release then quoted Payton as saying, "I no longer feel I have the authority to perform my duties as I see them, and it is necessary to make this decision if we are to avoid further misunderstandings." The document continued with a page celebrating Payton's

440

achievements. While he declined at the time to indicate what his next career step would be, he subsequently became President of Hofstra University.

In covering Payton's resignation, *The New York Times* indicated that there had been a three-hour "suspension of classes by the faculty on March 14th, "because there had been disagreements both about the number of tenure lines that would be filled in the next year and the percentage increases awarded to faculty. Approximately 250 faculty attended the protest meeting; the faculty then had about 350 full time professors. The faculty originally asked for a six percent increase, but after the meeting said it would have to be more than ten percent." *Newsday* in its coverage wrote "Behind Payton's resignation is a problem that has beset Long Island University for a decade: how much power should the central University Board of Trustees give to the three semi-autonomous campuses?"

Martin Buskin, the education editor at *Newsday*, wrote an op-ed on April 4th, that like many of his other news reports, was sympathetic to Payton. He was swayed by Payton's charisma. Focusing on the structural ambiguities of LIU, Buskin wrote, "In the end, [Payton] helped change the image of Post from the blundering, badly administrated bad boy of higher education on Long Island to the point where students and faculty have nothing to be ashamed of in comparison with Hofstra, Adelphi, or the New York Institute of Technology." Acknowledging that Payton was "no superman" and recognizing his share of troubles with tenure, the unionization of faculty members and drugs on campus, Buskin acknowledged that Payton did not wind up his career "universally beloved by faculty and students at Brookville." Buskin concluded his op-ed by raising what he viewed to be "the larger issue that LIU has yet to face": that the institution needed to search "not only for a new President, but for new policies and structure to prevent a loss like this from happening again."

An historical footnote: on June 18, 1976, Payton resigned as President of Hofstra after three years of service. The Chair of the Board of Trustees, George Dempster, noted that Hofstra had a nearly balanced budget in 1973 but "last year the deficit was $1,980,000." That contretemps did not seem to hurt Payton's career. He went on to become the President of the Exxon Foundation.

Toward the end of Bush-Brown's tenure, he sent a handwritten letter to Payton, seeking the Exxon Foundation's support to study the possibility of offering bonus incentives for University Deans based on enrollment increases. Because his LIU stint had been many years earlier, Payton answered Bush-Brown, "You pique my curiosity, but you challenge my memory." Bush-Brown remembered "John McGrath then saying he did not want to hear of it." Payton responded, "I gather that one of the efforts we made to keep Post from sinking under the weight of the University's problems (share that line with Mary Lai; it fairly rings of historic struggles) was to propose that each campus be measured by its ability to be a profitable cost center."

Such discussions move chronologically well beyond the scope of this book. But one major issue must still be addressed: preparations for the Middle State Commission's visit of 1972. Each of the campuses had been instructed by now to work closely with its Visiting Committee of trustees, overseers, and alumni to conduct its own intensive self-study. Stakeholders on each campus were asked to draft detailed introspective documents dealing with a wide range of topics, including a historical summary; an assessment of the plant; the dynamics and details of the faculty and student bodies; fundraising, academic priorities and a host of other similar concerns.

At Southampton, the Committee, chaired by three Trustees - Winthrop Palmer, Sol G. Atlas and Vincent Macri - completed its work in May 1971. These Trustees met with the stakeholders and included in their Report a set of recommendations designed to strengthen the planning process at Southampton and simultaneously signal to Middle States the priorities that the Visiting Committee saw as important. The Committee acknowledged the pressing need to reorganize administrative responsibility for academic programs and improve extracurricular residential life. Some of these recommendations were non-starters, presented with the caveat that there first be enough money in hand to undertake the improvement. Many others were serious efforts to drill down into actual reality as it existed on each campus.

On May 22, 1972, Payton wrote Bush-Brown that Post continued to be handicapped because of limited Board participation on its Visiting Committee. George Pidot, an attorney at Shearman and Sterling, and a member of the Post Center Council, and Sol Atlas, again were Co-Chairs of the Post Committee. A central cause of the delay was political; many on the Visiting Committee team, especially the alumni members, were strong Payton supporters, while Pidot listened closely to Bush-Brown. That Report was not submitted until 1973.

In a confidential letter to Pidot dated August 15, 1972, Bush-Brown wrote that many at Post, "propose expansionist assumptions that do not square with current experience in applications and enrollments, much less the predictions for a decade that would bring increasing capacity within public institutions. Related to that unjustified optimism about admissions is the problem of retention of students and how to improve the educational effectiveness of the first two years of study. Thirdly, the Center narrowly missed unionization of the faculty in 1971 in an election still contested, and it is essential to revise past personnel policies and practices so as to achieve programs for developing faculty resources justly and consistent with our financial means and goals. Fundamental to the relations between Center and University is the faculty tenure and contract system." Pidot was a relative

442

newcomer to the University, someone who lived off Piping Rock Road, as did Bush-Brown (one of the grand addresses of the North Shore).

Bush-Brown wrote this letter to counter-balance the flights of fancy, as he perceived them, from the alumni members of that team. There was some question about whether individual members were looking to benefit personally from doing business with the campus. His letter noted, "The theme in several sections of the report is 'autonomy.' No question about it: that word appears often in the discussions and actions at C.W. Post, and it is sometimes combined with 'how can we be accountable for something we are not responsible for?'" He went on to comment to Pidot that this "theme is unexamined, unanalyzed, used casually, even by academic men who pride themselves upon dispassionate analysis. It is hardly sufficient to let it stand that way. Autonomy from what? Autonomy to do what?"

Writing candidly, Bush-Brown noted, "Some Centers entertain reservations against other Centers and against those University obligations arising from being one center among several. It is a natural, if immature, consequence of pride in the nascent, but any assumption that all merit now stands with C.W. Post, or that Brooklyn drags and drains her suburban sister will not survive measurement in any arena whether financial or educational."

Bush-Brown went on to indicate that the Brooklyn Center had negligible debt and no cumulative operating deficit. "Indeed its assets, with high equity, are the credit structure underlying the building development of C.W. Post and Southampton. There is even reason for speculating that the Brooklyn Center may achieve a stronger position than other Centers by 1975." Bush-Brown was well aware that "there may come a time when C.W. Post, having eliminated its cumulative operating deficit, as we continuously urge, will achieve budgets that protect the University's credit rating at a time when both Southampton and Brooklyn cast deficits; all University policies and the set of the new Presidents at Brooklyn and Southampton are aimed at balanced budgets so that any surplus budget at C.W. Post will serve to reduce the total debt structure." Bush-Brown went on to chronicle additional problems including, "with unions, with libraries, with athletics, with campus planning, with income." And he called Pidot's attention to the fact that several of the alumni serving on the Visiting Committee were seeking contracts for University business, in clear conflict with standard business practices.

Despite Bush-Brown's fairly blunt observations, some months later Pidot in a memo to the other members of the Visiting Committee wrote to his colleagues "With reference to the identity of Post College, as discussed on page four of the memo, it has been strongly urged that steps be taken to change the designation to C.W. Post University, because of the graduate and professional divisions or schools. Offhand, I see no objection to that designation, assuming that is does not produce any technical complications or burdens such as the procedural and substantive requirements for chartering."

Over the summer of 1972, Pidot became substantially more engaged in this process. He chaired the Community Relations Subcommittee, and that part of the larger document reflected the worldview and attitudes of the Post community. "The people interviewed at Post, without exception, do not consider that any real relationship exists between the various centers. They view the Post faculty and students as being significantly different than those at the other centers without thereby creating any implications as to quality or otherwise.... Accordingly, any movement in the direction of imposing some continuing functional relationship between these centers would appear to be at variance with the situation as viewed at Post." Noting that the students, on the other hand, had allied with their counterparts at Southampton and Brooklyn to gain a seat on the Board of Trustees, "the faculty favor greater local autonomy and a minimum of administration tie-in with the University Center."

While a lot of time and effort was put into these Visiting Committee reports, they exacerbated the friction between the three campuses, as biases and even prejudices were incorporated. Virginia Clarkson, an adult Post student who lived on the North Shore and was both witty and very smart, wrote a one-page "General Comments About the C.W. Post Visiting Committee," in which she observed, "There was general discontent among the various subcommittees." Attitudes stiffened rather than softened. The effort generated vast amounts of paper, but hardened the arteries of the University in unfortunate ways.

The decennial Middle States process of self-study, site visit and reaccreditation by the Commissioners are like mile markers in a marathon race - they identify what has changed and what has not; what is new and what is long standing in everything from the Mission Statement to the delivery of educational services. The routinized annual cycle of every college and university from its opening day of school to commencement falls away to a much more intensive period of self-reflection and judgment from both the site visitors and the stakeholders at the institution itself. For Long Island University, the decade from 1962 to 1972 had been truly tumultuous. The Stoddard Statutes raised interesting questions about how the Middle States Report ought best be organized and subsequently assessed by the Middle States Commission. The decision was to file four distinct "Reports."

In October 1971, Middle States sent members of its professional staff to each of the campuses to meet with various groups involved in the reaccreditation process. On October 25, 1971, Payton briefed Bush-Brown on the visit. There were universal questions "directed at the 'seriousness' of the accreditation process. How much of the process is superficial and pro forma recording of detail, and how much goes to the substance of the organization, function and performance of the institution?" Such questions for the staff are the standard fare for every campus going through this process.

Of greater specificity was the "matter of unit accreditation," as Post faculty, students, administrators and others worried that one or another part of Long Island University might not win full reaccreditation. Middle States staff member Martha Church "repeated the view that each unit would be considered separately as would the administration center at some later date." Students in two meetings and alumni had raised this question for fear that other unnamed units of Long Island University would pull Post down if one or both failed. Dr. Church made it clear that "all issues of the University and the Centers would be reviewed, whether they were explicitly included in written reports or revealed in campus visits." She urged that there be "serious output evaluation" and that the report satisfy the Steering Committee of each campus; in effect, each campus "should try to be judged on what we consider to be our merits" based on a clearly expressed set of goals that were suffused into a mission statement. This visit, which was duplicated on the other campuses, contained both a universal message that would apply to any college during any decennial visit and the unique reality of Long Island University in 1972.

Each campus generated a massive amount of information both in its Self-study report and in the appendices. Much of that material had first been gathered in response to the internal Visiting Committee efforts. Each self-study was quite different, although all dealt with student profiles, curricula matters, facilities and the budget. From a historical point of view, however, the more interesting documents are the four assessments drafted by the site visitors in response. The Middle States Commission staff was itself uncertain about how to organize their task. There were eight members on the site team (plus a representative of the State from Albany) just to visit Southampton. There were nine plus an Albany staff member for Brooklyn, and ten administrators, faculty and librarians plus two others who visited Post. Five very senior administrators made up the team visiting the University Center, including the Executive Vice President from Tulane, a Dean from Rutgers and the Presidents of Fairleigh Dickenson, Hartwick College, and Hobart and William Smith Colleges.

Allan A. Kuusisto, who was involved with LIU while working at the Department of Education in Albany and now a college President, served as overall Chair. This must have been one of the largest teams ever mobilized by Middle States. It was not lost on the visitors that there were three new Presidents on the three campuses and a new Chancellor at University Center. For the University, that very newness meant that there was no one to blame, no one to hold responsible for historical missteps.

Southampton College continued to capture the fancy of the visitors, celebrating "its nucleus of strong faculty. The members of this nucleus hold excellent credentials, are gifted academicians and superior teachers. Moreover, the faculty as a whole is well prepared and quite competent to mount and sustain outstanding academic programs. Also, most of the faculty members are very positive about their attitudes toward the college and its highest leadership. [Dr. Harry Marmion had just become President.] They are deeply concerned about some of the problems facing the college, but believe they can be satisfactorily resolved and want to help resolve them."

The visitors were made aware of all the problems: poor facilities, counter-culture tendencies of the student body, difficulty in recruiting students, deficits that were already chronic at Southampton by 1972. But these were issues that needed to be addressed, rather than flaws so threatening that the campus was at risk. Moreover, "generally speaking, the faculty and administrative staff at Southampton believe that their relationship with the University and its central office is decidedly advantageous to them; they think that the central office carefully considers their requests and that the office has been strongly supportive of the college's efforts." The site visitors concluded, "the top leadership is quite competent and that strong leadership will be forthcoming. However, we continue to stress the eleventh-hour solutions to some very fundamental problems."

Not surprisingly, the formal response to Middle States from the campus was "the evaluation from the Middle States Team is perceptive and reflects accurately the conditions present last December at Southampton." The site visitors had called for certain issues to be addressed further and, with delight, Marmion promised "to make a thoughtful response to the team's report by May 1, 1973." The last sentence of the campus response was, "The ten-year-old infant faces adolescence with increased confidence."

The site visiting team to the Brooklyn Center also clearly understood that "the recent adoption of an open admissions policy in the City University of New York" required the campus to adjust itself "to the changing conditions under which it must operate." The visitors commented that enrollment had fallen from 6,605 in 1968 to 4,308 in 1972 - partially offset by an increase in graduate enrollment in that same four-year period from 1,208 in 1968 to 2,941 in 1972. "The Center has been shifting the faculty assignments from standard undergraduate programs (where the load has fallen) to graduate work and to special programs. A commitment is being made to meet many special educational needs of the community." It understood the reality and had little additional advice to give.

The team also already knew about the "new faculty union contract and the revised Statutes of Long Island University. The union contract has not been in existence long enough to have had effect on operations. The revised Statutes have not yet been adopted." And thus, the site visitors informed their colleagues on the Commission as well at the campus that, "Both developments must be watched very carefully in the near future...."

In their introduction, the Middle States visitors observed, "The fact that there have been recent changes in the top management of the Center and of the University is part of a long pattern at Brooklyn. The churning effects of administrative changes have always been countered to some extent by the presence of a stable core of faculty and staff members." Brooklyn was changing so rapidly because of external and internal dynamics. It followed that it was difficult to use usual yardsticks of measurement.

The narrative was like a TV soap opera. It was legitimate to feel sorry for this buffeted campus in a transformed Brooklyn. The site visitors had been aware that "its emergence as a self-contained unit," was a result of the 1969 Statutes. Events since the 1962 visit had been "marked by years of turmoil, assaulted by problems of identification, financial crisis, political power plays, faculty dislocations, and the traumatic impact of CUNY's 'open door' admissions policy." As the visitors looked at what had happened over the decade, they commented, "The fact that the Brooklyn Center exists at all today is a tribute to the administrators, faculty, and other concerned individuals of Long Island University."

It was clear that "the Brooklyn Center is not an autonomous unit of Long Island University in the complete sense of the word. The Board of Trustees through the Chancellor's office holds control over the budget, ultimate faculty matters, and the academic missions of its Centers and their several colleges." Middle States observed that all of the campus Presidents met periodically with the central administration, noting "The Chancellor makes it a point to appear at the Brooklyn Center frequently enough to give visual evidence that central administration does indeed exist." That was exactly what was said about Hoxie in the past. "There appears to be an intentional effort in the revised Statutes of February 1973, currently under consideration, to modify the autonomous designation of the Centers into one of a federated organization, allowing each to arrange itself into appropriate academic ventures and yet be accountable to the whole. Under the present set of circumstances this appears to be a healthy move."

Brooklyn had a brand new President, "one who entered into office after several years of interrupted leadership...." It was no secret to anyone that he had "an enormous task to repair communication links and to develop an effective organization." The site visitors noted that, "Progress is being made, but the total picture is still somewhat fuzzy." What did fuzzy mean? Probably that Middle States had decided to postpone any negative action, choosing instead to kick the can down the road until a decade hence. Like a wounded but plucky prizefighter, reeling at the end of a brutal round, these visiting faculty, administrators and librarians simply could not bring themselves to call for a technical knockout. The men and women who worked and taught there were trying so hard to be ready for the next round that they deserved the chance. And they got it.

They did observe that only $15,246 had been raised in unrestricted private giving. It was a dreadfully small sum, but also revealed a transparent on-going problem: "the Brooklyn Center will continue to have serious financial problems." The site visitors had become an amalgam of cheering section and Greek chorus, saying "the administration is clearly cognizant of the situation and has instituted controls which should prevent serious deficits, at least for the time being."

"Open admissions at the City University has forced the Brooklyn Center to follow suit. Many students are now being admitted who could not meet earlier the criteria." The site visitors understood that remediation was an essential task and flagged the serious contradiction that degree credit was being awarded for courses that were not taught at the college level. In the section dealing with conditions and responsibilities of employment, the Middle States team commented, "only thirty percent of the Brooklyn faculty are members of the union" at the time the site visitors were on campus in March of 1973. The visitors were surprised that there was "evidently some faculty dissatisfaction with the forbidding of 'merit' salary increments in the union contract." They found it worthy of comment, "that new contract mechanisms have not always replaced already existing mechanisms. Even Union members prefer recourse to the Faculty Grievance Committee instead of the Union grievance procedure and arbitration."

Non-tenured faculty members had to be dropped in numbers because of enrollment contraction such "that by 1973-74 seventy-seven percent of the faculty will be tenured." The group opined, "One would hope in view of declining enrollment and the corresponding effect on financial resources, that the institution would be especially mindful not to permit such concerns to erode its sense of mission."

The new library was due to open by the start of school in September, 1974. The Middle States team visited the "exciting, new, versatile, and imaginative library building...now under construction." It saw this as a commitment to keep the Brooklyn campus alive and growing, and closed its report: "with the new President in office and new University Statutes being prepared, the time is right for a comprehensive study of the plans for the future of Brooklyn Center." Ideally, "the Center may be able to exercise some control over its destiny rather than react, after the fact, to rapidly changing conditions." Brooklyn had been given a free pass, escaping the censoring scrutiny that normally defines such a Middle States decennial visit. There was too much flux, too much bad news, too much historical baggage to do anything other than that. The Middle States visitors understood that Brooklyn was at risk of spiraling toward a vortex. All the site visitors could do, at least during that visit, was wish it well.

Post received the greatest scrutiny from its visitors. The Chair of this visiting team was the President of Hartwick College, Adolph G. Anderson. He wrote that Post was "in significant transition, striving to meet new conditions, with new educational answers. In fact, C.W. Post, throughout its relatively short life, has been an institution in flux, with all of the concomitant stresses and tensions." This very large team "without intending to point any accusing finger," felt "a profound need for improved communication within the [Post] Center community, both in breadth and depth and throughout all segments of the Center." He noted, "Inevitably and relentlessly, however, we have been forced to consider a larger aspect, the relationship that exists between the Center and its parent, Long Island University. We therefore feel obligated to speak to this issue in this report."

It was no surprise that the visitors heard University Center blamed for C.W. Post's woes. Anderson quoted a senior member of the Post faculty who said, "There is general agreement that University Center is a major sources of difficulties.... We feel no sense of identity with something called Long Island University.... encumbrances to be borne, road blocks in the path to education." Anderson concluded that the tension over the budget was but "the tip of the iceberg of uncertainty, confusion, and potential rebellion." He went on, "there seems to be, then, signs of illness. Whether the causes are malignant remains for others to decide. Whatever the causes, until they are removed the corporate body cannot enjoy full health." No doubt the visitors were fully exposed to the distain and deep antipathy felt by the Post community toward University Centre, still located two stop-lights away.

Given the love affair Hoxie had with Post, what happened? How did such animus develop so quickly? Was it because Post was not allowed to escape fiscal entanglement with Southampton and Brooklyn? From its opening days, when it was still the Brookville campus, it rejected the offers of support from Brooklyn. Was it insecurity? Arrogance? None of the above? During the several years of Stoddard, Ferguson and the first days of Bush-Brown's fourteen year Chancellorship, Post was never asked to absorb Brooklyn's faculty or what were widely believed to be Brooklyn's debts. No young faculty member was "bumped" so that a senior Brooklyn member might retain his or her job. Brooklyn's balance sheet was much stronger than Post's. During those years of Nassau's rapid growth, Post seemed to have everything going for it, yet it never developed any sense of charity or obligation or empathy. Was it embarrassment or a sense of superiority? Many Post faculty and staff were themselves émigrés from Brooklyn or Queens, born and bred in the outer Boroughs, who moved to the burbs to escape.

449

Or was it that University Center was viewed as the defender of Brooklyn, the weakened older sibling, and Southampton, the sickly third sibling? Could Post only be triumphant if it could jettison its shared past with these other campuses?

In an unsigned and undated campus response to the visiting team report, the Post, "faculty, student body and administration are buoyed by the evaluation team's comment that: 'yours is an institution of which can all be proud...'" The visitors had expressed confidence that "a bright and well deserved future lies ahead." Whoever drafted the response, probably Acting President Edward J. Cook, acknowledged: "this communication difficulty is seen to manifest itself in a search for institutional identity, disagreement on the goals of the Center, confusion and frustration within the faculty about areas of responsibility and authority, and disagreement about the roles of the Center and the University."

What did that mean? Brooklyn had reason to be angry about what had happened, but did Post? Robert Payton certainly was vocal in trying to free Post from its entanglement with the rest of the University, as Hoxie had been. Did their attitudes direct the anger or merely reflect it? Albert Bush-Brown's name was never mentioned in the campus response.

On April 15th through April 17th, 1973, the final site visit from the Middle States Commission visited LIU specifically to review University Center. Allan Kuusisto who had become President of Hobart and William Smith Colleges, served as both chair of the overall three teams and of the senior administrators asked to assess Bush-Brown's new administration. Also participating were: President Anderson of Hartwick, President Fuller of Fairleigh Dickinson, Clarence Scheps, the Executive Vise President of Tulane and Elmer Easton, Dean at Rutgers. LIU was clearly getting a top-tier review to explore how seaworthy the LIU ship still was after such a stormy decade.

Albert Bush-Brown himself wrote the obligatory self-study report, a 73-page document entitled "An Introduction to Long Island University." His was a rejoinder to the negative assertions which came from the campuses. What Bush-Brown told the visiting team was that he had come from SUNY Buffalo to deliver triage, to nurse LIU back to health. His document was elegantly drafted. He was a consummate stylist. As a newly appointed Chancellor, moreover, he did not have to own the decisions made by his predecessors. His document was rich in platitudes and sweeping generalities instead of proposed action steps.

He started in the right place. "One of the remarkable examples of private agencies built for public service, Long Island University today affects the learning of 20,000 persons.... Lacking significant private benefaction or public subsidy, it was molded less by intent to become comprehensive than by attention to serving local needs

450

for general and practical education." He stressed the University's commitment to "broad, populist need." With mannered prose, he described the core elements of LIU's institutional mission: "By standing close to conventional, native ambition, which celebrates commerce and practical education, and by embracing the nurtured American faith in liberal education, the University built basic resources." What did that mean? A page or two further, Bush-Brown wrote, "A Jewish physician recently testified to that mission when he remarked at a meeting of Brooklyn Center alumni, 'Long Island University, for us, was the first step out of the ghetto,' and the Black judge sitting next to him agreed."

Acknowledging that the sharp economic downturn of recent years and the dramatic inroads of both CUNY and SUNY had a crippling effect on all of the campuses, he wrote, "retraction and austerity have resulted in an unwelcome but necessary reduction of resources: the loss of excellent, young, untenured faculty who are the university's short-term investments toward long-term assets; reductions in library acquisitions; fewer repairs and less maintenance of buildings; the shelving of special educational programs that promised quality." These were clearly the consequences for a University that had ambitiously borrowed against future tuition to pay for capital construction.

Bush-Brown sounded more like a removed but judgmental consultant than a Chancellor, especially one charged with reconstructing a viable university from three warring camps. "In an earlier year, debates within the University reflected preoccupations with territorialities, separations, autonomies, structure, authority, and government, and those preoccupations linger still." Elegant but opaque phrases flowed easily. "The Centers today reveal serious problems resulting from earlier optimism and indifference to planning the financial and educational consequences of growth by expansion…. Plans for several buildings are defective in size and location. Lacking endowments, burdened by mortgages, all Centers strain tuition revenues to cover costs."

Consider this Germanic sentence: "The decade when subdivisions within this University acted independently, with near autonomy in curricular revision and rapid expansion of full time faculty appointments, has been a decade of experiment in method, sub-division of subject matter, innovation of program, extension of purpose, creation of opportunities for study toward new careers: perhaps to the point of proliferation; but it has also been a decade when these same generative forces divested themselves of the sense of need to husband long-term commitments in relation to their ability to draw the students who would sustain them financially." Bush-Brown was intentionally spinning his Report to lay out in the most abstruse terms a political dynamic that could be summarized in simple declarative sentences, had he so chosen.

To cite another example: "A suggestion to build a new Library at Brooklyn provoked jealousies, opposition, and deferral. Prospects for the Brooklyn Center's fiscal decline, in the outlook for 'open admissions' at City University, raised question of closing or sale.... In the midst of rigidities, often mere transience of people and themes was mistaken for change and innovation. Officer succeeded officer, but leadership could not summon students, faculty, and Trustees to concerted action.... Two Presidents stood close to censure in 1970-71; a Chancellor resigned in 1970; a budget with enormous deficits for 1971-72 gained approval in the Spring, 1971, without much justification or opposition; faculty governance was in disarray; and a mandate came for collective bargaining through an external agency."

As the visitors read all of this they must have wondered why Bush-Brown had accepted the job of Chancellor, especially as he himself wrote, "One can become intrigued to inquire into the slope of despair in 1968-1971." Bush-Brown saw his recent revision of the Statutes as critically important. "During the brief administrations of three Chancellors in three years, the University went from virtual centralization to near autonomies, borrowing finances, without even trying federation along the way." It is interesting to note that he made no mention of earlier consultancies, Heald, Hobson or AED or the innumerable administrative efforts to resolve the university's structural problems during the previous decade.

Bush-Brown chronicled complex strains created by new arrivals at the top, tensions over unionization, competition with the public sector institutions and the consequences of inflation as a result of Vietnam. He focused on the chaos of "unauthorized contracts with vendors, non-reviewed drawings and budgets for a building, desirable departures in educational programs that required approval of new fee and salary schedules, and unapproved appointments of personnel; the most serious was the presence of fifty-eight untenured faculty members whom the Centers had reappointed past their sixth year, without review, and whose claim for statutory tenure had to be sustained by the Board as a class action." Like a comic book superhero, Bush-Brown was on the case, to do things confident that his formula would work. His document was self-referencing, perhaps arrogant, but it was written to buy him and the University time to turn around. It worked.

In a document shared with the University and sent to the Commission, he commented: "During these ten years administrators have come and gone, and crises have been the order of the day. With survival a very real question, the Board and staff have occasionally wandered into a sea of uncertainty over institutional directions. But the over-arching hard fact that transcends all these changes is that the institution has not only survived but has maintained a continuing will to live and a capacity to cope successfully with its successive difficulties." The visitors themselves then slipped into generalizations. No one at Long Island University, or probably even the Middle States Commission, needed to be told the "Brooklyn

Center, after years of growth, has been subjected to attrition and declining enrollments and potential deficits, faced with the aggressive open admissions policy of the City University of New York."

Allan Kuusisto took the lead in drafting this document. He acknowledged the obvious when he observed, "The decision-void that has existed in the Central Office from time to time in the past decade because of weak or no leadership has caused a whole set of conditions which have haunted the institution. The Team feels that the institution may be at a turning point now that there appears to be strong leadership at the Chancellor's level and Center leadership of his choosing at two of the Centers with a third to be selected." By narrowing his backward look to thirty-six months, rather than ten years, Bush-Brown had structured what he would hear back from Kuusisto. That worked too.

The Middle States document focused on important but lesser concerns - the lack of an adequate development effort, poor public relations, the need for internal audit. Kuusisto complained that he missed a coherent statement of the Mission-a first tier issue-but most of his Report was rich in bromides and platitudes, possibly drafted to glide over the bruises and internal injuries that the institution had endured.

Kuusisto expressed delight at Bush-Brown's leadership team. "The new Chancellor has in turn made good appointments to the unit presidencies that he has had the opportunity to fill, and he has begun a systematic effort of overhauling the relationships between the Central Office and the units. Further strength is evidenced in the slow but sure growth of the University Faculty Senate...." Unfortunately there is little evidence that much of this was accurate. Certainly in hindsight it proved to be wishful thinking.

After more than four decades of foundering, Kuusisto's assessment of the Board's successful role in the survival and growth of the University was overly generous. He wrote in his Conclusion that the University's "capacity for renewal has been engendered by the considerable resilience of a Board which has been willing to overhaul its own membership and organization to adapt to new circumstances." A few sentences later, Kuusisto urgently called for a new emphasis in fund-raising and development. It was a familiar appeal that once again fell on deaf ears, clogged either by the cacophony of the previous decade or by ear plugs inserted to block out sound.

The cumulative consequence of what might be called a lack of philanthropic generosity has been one of the central themes of this book. *The Preface to the Future* campaign failed for many reasons, but The Board had consistently refused to embrace its collective obligation to lead by philanthropic example and that painful truth could only bend downward the institution's trajectory.

PART III - THE AFTERMATH

The beginning of this book contains some comparative remarks about the founding of Brandeis University and Conolly's assumption of the LIU Chancellorship. There were many similarities between Larry Wien and William Zeckendorf, the two Chairs - both New York real estate moguls. Of course, one key difference was that Zeckendorf's empire collapsed while Wien's partnership with Harry Helmsley went from success to success to success. In the years that followed, however, the generations of Board members at the two institutions also differed markedly in their giving behavior, and the two Universities as a result have very different histories. The comparison offered is not flattering to the Trustees of Long Island University.

There was no evidence in 1973 that those circumstances would change under Bush-Brown's Chancellorship. The problem was never that the LIU Board members lacked status or wealth or influence in the New York City or Long Island communities. But it was an enigma that so few of them ever took their obligations as Trustees as seriously as their counterparts at other universities. Kuusisto wrote, "Perhaps the Board's chief achievement is the recruitment of strong new leadership as it attempts to develop forward looking progressive plans." But the Middle States visitors a decade thereafter found the University still in shambles and its fundraising, still marginal. The pious hopes expressed in 1972 glossed over a reality that remained self-evident a decade later.

Indeed, those Middle States visitors chose to give Bush-Brown and LIU a great deal of slack. A truly negative review could have closed Long Island University down. Neither the Middle States Commission nor the State of New York had much stomach for something so draconian. Despite all the noise and commotion on each campus, the University was fulfilling its central task of education, graduating thousand of students, men and women, trained to lead successful lives and contribute to society. It was doing that in multiple disciplines and doing it quite well. The visitors were thus more like consultants than judges. It was perhaps significant when Kuusisto wrote, "Although the original dream of a major private and prestigious institution on Long Island has never been realized, Long Island University is a good institution performing an important service on the Island."

The site visitors were only at Long Island University for three days. Their recommendations to the full Commission were structured to give Bush-Brown and his new team a decade, leaving to the 1982 Middle States site visitors the task of assessing whether meaningful progress had been made. In fact, that next team had the gravest of doubts on most of those issues and insisted on coming back after only few years. It concluded that the University required a radical reorganization yet again. This time the issue *was* about survival. But that also is a story to await a future book by a different author.

454

Throughout this volume, many historical questions have tumbled out one after the next, as they always do in history. The "what ifs" of history are always tantalizing. *Preface to the Future* projected that Long Island University would become a national powerhouse, a twentieth century multi-versity, combining the best elements of a flagship public-sector university with the autonomy and flexibility of an independent-sector institution.

What would have happened if the Post faculty had seen its affiliation with Brooklyn as a positive not a negative? Too many faculty at Post seemed to regret that their careers had tenured them to Long Island University. The other campuses and, University Center were typically defined as the enemy. Even Gordon Hoxie was viewed as a turncoat once he became Chancellor. Collegiality was begrudged rather than embraced.

The Brooklyn faculty and staff were proud but battered. The collapse of the Borough's economy, and the growing societal schisms such as Black Power and white flight, exacerbated racial, religious and cultural points of friction. New York City's infrastructure, and deterioration of the public school system, weakened the applicant pool and increased demands for remedial education. The transportation system was decrepit-equipment was ancient, dirty and prone to breakdown. There was a dramatic rise in street crime such that riding the subways to campus became a daily, scary challenge. The City itself was dirty and seemingly had lost its collective New York brashness, its mojo. Many were convinced that New York was over the hill and the outer boroughs were in a death loop. Thomas Wolfe's famed depression-era short story, *Only the Dead Know Brooklyn*, seemed to capture the mood perfectly.

NYU was itself been forced to retreat to the East Village, its inner city campus, because it could not meet its payroll and had to turn to the State for emergency aid. The institution got about $40 million, but had to sell its elite uptown campus, which became Bronx Community College; transfer its School of Engineering to the Polytechnic Institute, and move all of its operations into its shabby downtown buildings. Without those steps it would have had to declare itself bankrupt. *Mirabile dictu*, the East Village turned out to be New York's answer to Haight-Ashbury in San Francisco. It was full of hippies and tolerated a drug culture that had been created by students and dropouts from San Francisco to New York. Those brownstones, ancient five-story walk-ups, near "Alphabet City" were dreadful slum buildings, among the worst in the City, but they became a twentieth century equivalent to the Left Bank in Paris. The Broadway musical, *Rent*, captured the energy that helped transform NYU.

The East Village around NYU became the new bohemian enclave of New York, just as the West Village has been the hip place during the Roaring Twenties. It was filled with the zest of a student movement that thrived on a counter-culture created in the 1960s. The tacit deal between NYU parents and students was that the students could live in five-story walk-up brownstone firetraps, provided they went back to college, got their degrees and took jobs to rejoin society. It was a great deal for both generations and NYU seized the opportunity to transform itself into a high end, urban University. NYU and LIU had been Bobbsey twins in 1970. The Brooklyn campus, then still trapped by its eroding environment, would have to wait many more decades for a similar urban renaissance.

The modern history of those two universities is a story of "two roads diverged…." to cite the Robert Frost poem. NYU became an elite university, while Brooklyn had to struggle to survive with one out of every three bulbs removed to husband electricity. NYU forgot that it once had that twin in Brooklyn, setting its competitive sights on Columbia. Brooklyn, to its everlasting credit, accepted the transformation around it and recommitted itself to a different kind of teaching to meet the needs of its next generations of students.

The Brooklyn College of Pharmacy which became the Arnold and Marie Schwartz College of Pharmacy in 1975, remained a quasi-autonomous center of excellence even after it moved physically onto the Brooklyn campus at the insistence of the National Institutes of Health, which helped finance the new building. The Pharmacy degree was a hybrid undergraduate-graduate program. It was small, it had loyal alums and was not as battered as the rest of the Brooklyn campus. It became the most plural professional school of its kind in America.

Southampton found a partial identity in marine science and to a lesser extent in the visual and performing arts. But its specialty had limited enrollment appeal as other colleges and universities increasingly developed their own marine science programs. As the campus became run down, it slipped further into its bipolar existence. Marine science students did extraordinarily well and the record of Fulbright Scholarships over the years was legitimately a matter of great pride. But it needed more paying students than it was able to attract, and therefore, it admitted students who were marginal. Those other admittees needed remediation and access to year round jobs in an area that was truly rural at first and, even today, dependent on seasonal agriculture and tourism. Decades later, with a cumulative operating deficit in the tens of millions, Southampton was sold by the Board of Trustees to the State University of New York.

C.W. Post continued its quest for a coherent mission throughout the decade, something that would create a transcending identity and shared sense of unity among the entire learning community. Over the years there have been fabulous majors and great teaching. The several Brookville schools and colleges have taken great pride in the dedication of master teachers like Stanley Jarolem and Michael Soupios, each of whom did wonderful things with and for their students. Nevertheless, the culture of the campus, the *gestalt,* has continued to radiate anomie and detachment. To this day there remains a collective if unspoken belief that Post would soar if it were C.W. Post University.

The Post Collegial Federation, the (UFCT) Union Chapter, led for decades by Professor John Turner and then Professor Ralph Knopf, sought enemies and found them, irrespective of whether those perceived foes were actually blocking the way. The faculty went on strike frequently, almost always on the opening day of the fall semester, and won for its members generous contracts, because Administration and the Board dared not tolerate too much damage to the revenue stream that Post was accustomed to generate. But the culture of the community suffered. Too many faculty members came to campus as infrequently as possible and worked as little as possible, consistent with fulfilling the minimum set of obligations defined by the labor contract. Faculty meetings were ill-attended and the members were "no shows" at campus-wide sessions.

The exploration of such issues, indeed, even their validity, is beyond the scope of this volume. It is sufficient to note here that the dream of the University of Long Island captured the imagination of some remarkable people who struggled and succeeded in building an institution of higher learning, one that has served this unique 110 mile long island, this fish shaped "Paumanok." Long Island was and is a Manhattan bedroom. It was and partially still is an agrarian producer of ducks and potatoes and seafood and wine, even as it became a sophisticated community, that built the spacecraft which went to the moon and helped invent the very meaning of suburban living. On Long Island are America's fourth and fifth largest cities, Brooklyn and Queens. The total population of Long Island would make it the tenth largest State in the Union, if Long Island was, by itself, a freestanding State. Ralph Jonas, Tristram Walker Metcalfe, Richard Conolly, William Zeckendorf, father and son, and thousands more lived that dream and helped to make it happen, as did Long Island University itself.

Our student body is largely drawn from lower middle-class, self-employed, and wage-earning groups. They are first-generation college goers and often first-generation Americans. And increasingly they are coming from the poverty belt of downtown Brooklyn itself.

Robert Spector

The intertwining of the legal commitments of the various campuses makes it clear that these campuses are bound together tightly by their liabilities, and that the prospect of creating three completely separate institutions, as has been discussed time and again, is remote.... Contrary to widespread belief, no significant amount of Brooklyn Center funds was diverted over the twenty years, 1950-1970, to build C. W. Post and Southampton College.

Sidney Tickton, "Change for Survival," The Academy for Educational Development

Afterword

Early in the twentieth century, the great American historian Henry Adams wrote in his autobiography, *The Education of Henry Adams,* "Historians undertake to arrange sequences-called stories or histories-assuming in silence a relation of cause and effect. These assumptions, hidden in the depths of dusty libraries, have been astounding, but commonly unconscious and childlike; so much so, that if any captious critic were to drag them to light, historians would probably reply, with one voice, that they had never supposed themselves required to know what they were talking about." Adams wrote that he had "toiled in vain" to find out what he meant, publishing a dozen volumes of American history "for no other purpose than to satisfy himself whether, by the severest process of stating, with the least possible comment, such facts as seemed sure, in such order as seemed rigorously consequent, he could fix for a familiar moment a necessary sequence of human movement. Where he saw sequence, other men saw something quite different, and no one saw the same unit of measure."

Adams has been haunting me throughout the process of writing this history of Long Island University. As long-serving President (I turned down the title of Chancellor), I inherited the position of chief executive of a vast, complex institution from my predecessors, their key aides, the several faculties, thousands of students and tens of thousands of alumni and alumnae. It was never "my" university, but ours collectively, even though for more than a quarter century it was my privilege to help articulate its Mission, the underlying dream of an independent-sector institution committed to the education of all those who sought access of the democratic premise of the American dream. It was also, of course, my burden to deal with the realities of the deficits, the intra-campus legacy of distrust, the chronic anger amongst the stakeholders, and the reluctance of both Trustees and alumni to support generously their Alma Mater and, beyond it, its mission of "Access and Excellence."

My challenge throughout this four-year project has been to see if I could write about LIU in the third person, somehow a dispassionate historian looking at a complex story. Even now at the end of the project, I wonder if I have injected myself too directly- my inherited problems, my own priorities- onto my predecessors and into the institution's history. In other words, has it been possible to detail what happened analytically, when I have been so involved with the institution and its people, many of whom I either know or knew over the last decades? In a very personal sense, the research and writing of this book has allowed me to understand more profoundly key issues, people and angers that previously remained shrouded in hazy fog. On some level I already knew much of this from gossip, or observation, or my probing a given point. But there were also major lacunae, the historical equivalent to navigating in the Bermuda triangle which just never made sense to me. Motivated by a drive to understand my own years better, in one sense I wrote this book for myself. However, I also felt it essential to share the tale, because no one can really understand LIU today without a detailed grounding in that turbulent decade, 1962-1972.

I do worry that my irritation at individuals and clusters of stakeholders whom I consider to have acted selfishly, ungenerously, or in petty anger against what I would define as the institutional good, comes through in my text. For allowing my own frustrations as President to cloud my fairness as an historian, I feel compelled to make apology to those who struggled then in the trenches. It is easy to find fault, and much harder to empathize, to identify, or to forgive.

Again and again outsiders from Middle States site visits, from the State of New York, from foundations and consultancies, looked at Long Island University and found it severely lacking in money, in harmony, in structural integrity and in quality control. Time and time again, those who served her argued back that it was fulfilling its own Mission, it was doing its job and proving that by attracting large numbers of students. I understood that truth when I arrived on the scene in 1985, and I believe it even more now. Yet, the dozens and dozens of external critics were not wrong in exposing deep institutional flaws. My challenge as historian, therefore, was to capture the idiosyncrasies and the shortcomings, while celebrating the grit that kept the institution open and fulfilling, in its own unique way, its secular

460

commitment to the American Dream.

Was R. Gordon Hoxie simply a rotund, pompous, self-aggrandizing conservative who didn't understand the rapid flux of a society changing at warp speed? Certainly that is how many in Brooklyn then defined him, and those students and faculty saw in him traits they loathed. He also was like the Energizer Bunny, whose commitment and love of the place never ran down. The people who rallied to his defense saw in him something profound to admire, even after he had been fired. Many of them were folks of high intelligence and great success. Many of those who wrote to John McGrath spoke in apocalyptic terms: Hoxie was for them a bulwark against the chaos they sensed emerging in the society. Most were deeply conservative, to be sure, but there was and is much of that pre-sixties world to cherish and miss.

There was, alas, much in that sixties revolution that was lamentable. To cite but one higher educational category as example: the collapse of standards defining academic rigor. There was a blurring of respect for the knowledge and wisdom held by faculty to be transmitted to students. The sixties encouraged a mockery of grades as a measure of achievement. The college experience as a time for reflection and self-growth was replaced with a sense that college was a necessary if expensive hiatus in order to find a lucrative job. That transformation made a mockery of learning, debasing all higher education in America for the worse. Long Island University was profoundly damaged and so were Harvard, the University of Michigan, CUNY and Hofstra. To the degree this became true, and I fear it had, it was a stain on every university in the nation. In his own high Victorian way, Hoxie was a staunch defender of the preciousness of education as a vital part of a more humane world.

A key question, therefore, was whether Hoxie was a tragic figure out of some latter-day Greek tragedy or 'The Man From La Mancha,' a stoop shouldered colonel in the Air Force Reserve riding out to do battle against the collapse of traditional verities? Should he be compared to Sancho Panza, trying to preserve Admiral Conolly's dream against all odds? For Hoxie, the Admiral had articulated a final combat mission. For Hoxie, those objectives became a battle plan that had to be pursued despite the odds-an educational equivalent of the Charge of the Light Brigade. In much of his prose there is a sense that he sought to bring to his fallen Admiral the victory Conolly never lived to savor.

Dare one ask whether Conolly, had he lived, would have recognized by the mid-sixties the changing reality sweeping across American colleges and society at large? Was the imperious but charismatic Admiral somehow a hidden culprit, an unindicted co-conspirator, in this drama? Did he put to sea with a forecast of storm clouds and rough seas already on the radar? Or was his still a good weather transmission, one of calm seas and a prosperous voyage? On the other hand, if one concludes that that in 1962 his ten-year dream was achievable, when Glenn had started America toward the moon, Kennedy was yet alive and the glow of the Eisenhower era still existed, can blame still be placed on Conolly's shoulders?

Richard Lansing Conolly was looking for one more campaign in his life when he took the Presidency of LIU. He was not interested in Sunday golf and a comfortable retirement as the CEO of a steel company. "Close in" Conolly was a warrior - fearless, ambitious, successful, dynamic. He had a vision to build the "University of Long Island," and he sloughed off, or, at least, discounted the advice and, perhaps, wisdom of the bureaucrats who warned him of ill-conceived or overly ambitious plans. Like his mentor Douglas MacArthur, who had to defeat North Korea completely and reach the Yalu River, Conolly knew only one strategy, all-out, "close in" attack-a law school, a medical school, a school of science and technology, a full spectrum of graduate schools, professional schools et cetera, all within a decade.

But even he, the transformative President, could not unlock the safe deposit boxes of his Trustees and key donors. His passion was not rewarded by the philanthropy of others. Mary Lasker didn't give, but she did follow James Hester to NYU. She chose to give very generously elsewhere. Joshua Logan and so many others didn't attend meetings, and did not contribute. John H.G. Pell, recruited as a Trustee by Conolly and Zeckendorf, was himself the Chancellor for more than two years, but never became a donor who even began to fulfill his donor potential. Most of Zeckendorf's friends, partners and clients, didn't contribute except to buy an occasional table or come to an event. Conolly hung everything on government largesse but that well dried quickly over the decade, as subsequent Chancellors discovered.

For my twenty-eight years as President, I grappled with this truth, as it carried forward over time. As my colleagues can attest, I kept wondering how philanthropically to market LIU more successfully. Why couldn't I convince more trustees, donors or alumni to see the majesty of our mission? There were some wonderful successes on my watch, but too many more unsuccessful fundraising solicitations, appeals which could have enhanced the University and provided its students with the scholarships, labs and classrooms to enrich their educations. It has been comforting to me that Conolly did not succeed either. Not surprisingly, I have emphasized that hard reality in this book.

The decline of Brooklyn and the emigration of corporations, wealthy individuals and many hundreds of thousands of middle-class citizens had to play a potent role. Could *Preface To The Future* possibly have succeeded in a downwardly mobile Borough of 2.5 million souls? In addition, how many fund-raising campaigns can possibly succeed during a time when virtually every donor was hostile to almost every college or university, because the donor was sure each seemed to be harboring scruffy youngsters, anti-American war protesters and radicals? The national angst and the global unrest that marked this decade probably doomed any effort, even if Brooklyn had not lost both its panache and its wealth. History is indeed a tease, as Henry Adams so gloomily noted.

Certainly, by 1973, LIU was a battered, angry and fragmented place. Consensus and comity were long gone. Fratricide turned campus against campus and stakeholder against stakeholder. Like a finely crafted antique clock that is powered by springs, weights and a balance, a University is a complex, fragile mechanism. It depends on thousands of people working in relative harmony and with shared objectives to deliver education in the classroom, on the playing fields, and through all of the intangible other ways men and women, mainly post-adolescents, learn. Every effective college and university must be that proverbial village. Each is a complex community trying to deliver the most illusive of services, the transmission of knowledge from one generation to the next. Willing compliance (and, indeed, a certain degree of coercion) are both essential realities to make any organization of men and women function effectively.

In the years after Hoxie, LIU lost control of its capacity to regulate itself. The pendulum swung so erratically that the clock failed to function accurately. The gears and flywheels did not mesh. The historiographical question was whether this was because of those external factors across the society-student protest, loss of respect for authority and similar changes in the body fabric-or did LIU get trapped into its own perfect storm? The answer is, probably, some amalgam of both.

There are other key questions that fill my head. What was the role of luck, dumb luck, in this tale and in most other histories. What if Zeckendorf had not lost his authority and power in the mid-sixties because his business went bust? To be sure he was a gambler, leveraged to the hilt always. He pyramided his real estate empire and the boom-bust cycle was a constant risk factor. But what if it had not collapsed until the seventies? What if John F. Kennedy had not been shot, and as President, had avoided the lunacy of Vietnam? The dominoes fell quickly domestically, even if they never fell in far-off Southeast Asia, as the Johnson Administration so feared. At home, America was left with that endless, mournful, curved memorial wall in Washington and a myriad of diminished institutions, like LIU, which were collateral damage on the home front.

Even if America had gone to fight the same war but Johnson had raised taxes to pay for it, and thus inflation had not run riot, what would have been the impact on Zeckendorf, on Webb & Knapp, on LIU struggling to make it? What would have happened if Hoxie had not known Al Jacobs, if Conolly had not postponed his vacation by a day, if the TWA Super Constellation had not had engine trouble at Idlewild? What would have been the search process for Conolly's successor the following fall? What if Carleton Palmer had said yes to the Board's appeal that he become interim Chancellor? Or what might have been the consequence if Mrs. Post had been truly philanthropic rather than as she was-a beautiful, vain but ungenerous tycoon? Or what if Zeckendorf had read the tea leaves better and organized a real search rather than give the Chancellorship away to Hoxie? So many questions. So many alternate paths!

In a quarter of a million words, I have told the part of the story that most captured my curiosity. It is a story mainly of the elite leadership of each constituency-the Board, the Administration, the faculty, and students (in homage, and in passing, I would like to celebrate those extraordinary students who published *Seawanhaka* throughout those turbulent years). But I am, always have been, acutely aware that there were many other stories unfolding simultaneously.

As I wrote at the beginning of this saga, more than a thousand faculty taught tens of thousands of students during those same years. Men and women fell in love, fell out of love, and some married. Teams won and lost, occasionally ending up in a draw. Personalities were formed, suicides sadly occasionally happened. Buildings were built or not built, and fought over. Students learned to drink, smoke pot, became hooked on hard drugs, went "cold turkey." Many an hour, students slept in libraries, even while at the next table students were reading something that changed their lives, their careers or their souls.

I openly acknowledge that my book does not capture the totality of the experience of any one campus or the institution as a whole. Simply put, every university is a universe, a microcosm of life. Eating habits changed, a dress code disappeared, the notion of standing when a great professor entered the classroom vanished completely. The popular music that blared ever louder, filled dormitory rooms with a new sub-culture -Bob Dylan and the Weavers gave way to rock and roll, the Beatles and Elvis -and those songs reflected a changing society which started at places like Southampton and altered America for better and worse. Other books, many of them, capture this revolution, as do movies and other mass media. I urge the reader to explore further.

Is the tale of LIU a modern day morality play, posing questions such as how do groups within any society or institution resolve conflict, behavior or decision-making? What is the responsibility of an individual to lead, fail to lead, or simply waffle? Trustees in the mid sixties, for example, were tone deaf to the structural changes demanded by almost all student bodies, not just at LIU but nationally. This was generational, attitudinal and cultural. The sexual revolution, scruffy hair and dress, open rebellion at home, in class, and at demonstrations were all ways the young gave the finger to adult society. Adult society responded with other but equally clear signals: the draft, the Rockefeller drug laws, a corporate dress code at IBM.

A Brooklyn faculty job action.

Another quandary: was unionization a war of revenge for the sixties? Once faculty units were authorized to bargain collectively, the LIU unions at Brooklyn and C.W. Post (but not the small ones at Pharmacy and Southampton) became the angry voices of pent-up faculty discontent. Community, to the extent it existed, totally disappeared. Leadership transferred from institutionally committed individuals like Robert Spector to those who simply sought greater pay and benefits, who saw unionization as a vehicle to redress real or imaginary grievances, or who dreamed of a utopian commune where the workers, the faculty, would collectively make decisions. In sum, leadership shifted to those within the faculty who were frustrated with their lot, their tenure at LIU, and, perhaps their own career decisions. Even when the specifics of grievances were forgotten, the resentment has somehow survived. Anger, painfully equally present on both the administrative side and within the faculty, is a sad legacy of this decade. It has been periodically corrosive ever since.

The historian is not just the playwright. He or she almost always brings to the story the biases of his or her own generation. The historian happens also to be the stage director, the lighting engineer, the sound technician and the costume designer. Each and every historian gets to set the stage, to decide how the speech is to be delivered, whose microphone is live and so forth. And since this historian has had skin in the game, I freely acknowledge what the Marxists would describe as my 'contradictions'. I only hope they did not get too much in the way of this riveting story. By allowing in so many voices, I have tried to let those good folks speak for themselves.

It has been a long journey for you and was for me as well. In the text I have summoned up periodically the Icarus tale in Greek mythology. *Preface to the Future* was a fantasy, one discarded within months of publication. It smacked of hubris. It projected a utopian, elite institution, not the populist place LIU had been (and continues to be) on Whitman's beloved island, the "Isle of the salty shore and breeze and brine!" Other institutions have crossed through the membrane which Conolly sought to penetrate. But, increasingly, I have wondered whether the dream of bootstrapping LIU into becoming an elite research institution, should ever be defined as winning some brass ring.

LIU ambitiously tried to expand too rapidly, to become a private multi-versity, and it came up short. There was a high price that was paid. And yet, on each campus, albeit differently, the University somehow managed to return to its original commitment of access, of providing the skills for upward mobility. I am more convinced now than years ago that both Walt Whitman and Emma Lazarus would smile down, and perhaps even give a quick wink, upon Long Island University. It might just be that that the experiences suffered during the tumultuous decade of the sixties brought LIU back, older and wiser, to its true calling, which Professor Robert Spector so clearly understood to be educating men and women "drawn from lower middle-class, self employed, and wage earning groups. They are first-generation college goers and often first-generation Americans." America was until now an aspirational nation, welcoming immigrants and those who, born here, seek a better life. LIU, almost after a century, still exists as a private institution devoted to speeding them on their way. *Dayenu,* is this not enough?

There is an old Vietnamese proverb that reaches across the years and the cultures. Translated it states," If you know something speak, if not, lean against the pillar and listen." Wise advice for both you and me!

An Historical Concordance

Larger historical events are printed in normal type. The LIU chronology appears in **bold**. Germane higher education dates are in *italics*. This chronology interlineates LIU's history with events elsewhere in the higher education universe, setting both against the tableaux of national and international events.

1920s

1920- New York City's population reached 5.5 million. Brooklyn's population was just over 2 million. Meanwhile, the north shore of Long Island hit the peak of its Gold Coast opulence.

1926- Brooklyn banker Ralph Jonas and a group of the borough's civic and business leaders convened to form LIU after years of effort.

December 9, 1926- NYS Board of Regents approved a provisional charter for LIU.

September 21, 1927- 312 students began their first classes at LIU in rented space in downtown Brooklyn.

April 5, 1929- Brooklyn College of Pharmacy became formally affiliated with LIU to teach pharmacy students the arts and sciences courses required under its curriculum.

October 1929- Stock market crashed. Many fortunes were lost in the ensuing Depression, **including that of LIU founder Ralph Jonas. His personal wealth and the paltry LIU endowment were wiped out by the financial crisis.**

1930s

LIU was denied accreditation three times by the Middle States Association of Colleges and Secondary Schools during this decade.

February 19, 1931- Regents approved LIU's permanent charter.

March 4, 1933- FDR was sworn in as President and within days announced his plans for his first one hundred days in office.

July 5, 1935- FDR signed the Wagner Act, clearing the way for collective bargaining rights and for millions of Americans to join labor unions.

1936- LIU's men's basketball team, led by coach Clair Bee, was invited to represent the United States at the Berlin Olympics. Several players declined to participate in protest against Hitler's racism and anti-Semitism and the team collectively declined to compete.

1939- LIU's charter was expanded to allow the school to issue a doctorate in podiatry. This formalized a merger between the University and the Manhattan based College of Podiatry. It also brought LIU into contact with the most significant Trustee in its history, William Zeckendorf Sr.

1939-LIU's men's basketball team, The Blackbirds, went undefeated for the season yet again and won the national championship.

1940s

---TRISTAM WALKER METCALFE---

1941- Tristram Walker Metcalfe, a major part of the LIU administration since the early 1930s, first as Comptroller and later as Dean of Arts and Sciences, became the first President of Long Island University.

1943- The University struggled with drastically decreased enrollment due to the war and military draft. Prior to the war, LIU had enrolled over 1,000 students; this year it had 307. To prevent the University from closing, Metcalfe and the Board filed for court-protected bankruptcy, an arrangement that lasted until 1947.

1943- Ralph Jonas resigned as Trustee. The Board elected William Zeckendorf, Sr. in his place. Zeckendorf became Chairman of the Board in 1947, a title he held for twenty-five years.

April 5, 1944- New York Governor Thomas Dewey signed the bill creating the Dormitory Authority of the State of New York.

June 22, 1944- Roosevelt signed the Servicemen's Readjustment Act (G.I. Bill), allowing millions of veterans to attend colleges across the country, and causing college enrollments to skyrocket in years following World War II.

1945-1947- LIU experienced dramatic growth and recovery as enrollments quadruple in 1945, and again in 1946. By 1947, LIU had well over 6,000 students and a million dollar budget surplus.

April 15, 1947- Jackie Robinson played his first game in Major League Baseball, for the Brooklyn Dodgers. At the time, the Dodgers were one of the best teams in baseball, winning the pennant in 1941, 1947, 1949, 1952, and 1953 (though each time, much to the dismay of Dodgers fans, they lost the World Series to the New York Yankees).

May 1947- Metcalfe negotiated to buy Marjorie Merriweather Post's 123-acre Gold Coast estate to become the site of a future LIU campus in Nassau County.

468

July 15, 1949- Harry Truman signed the American Housing Act. Among other things, the Act provided federal funds for "urban renewal" and "slum clearance" under Title I. **Zeckendorf, having secured the active support of Robert Moses, had LIU use Title I to acquire the property on and around Flatbush Avenue that eventually became the Brooklyn campus.**

1950s

1950-1951- Point-shaving basketball scandal. Men's basketball players from colleges across the New York City area, including a number at LIU, were implicated in a far-reaching scheme to "shave" points for money and manipulate betting odds. Most notably, LIU's star player Sherman White, at the time the league's leading scorer and *Sporting News*'s 1951 Men's College Basketball Player of the Year, was imprisoned for eight months, the rest receiving suspended sentences. White and five other players were barred-for-life from entering the NBA. As a result of the scandal, coach Clair Bee resigned and LIU temporarily disbanded its athletics programs.

February 22, 1952- Metcalfe died of cancer. Chair of Economics William Marion Hudson was appointed Acting President in his stead.

---WILLIAM MARION HUDSON---

April 14, 1952- The Regents of The State of New York informed Hudson that LIU would be granted only a one-year provisional registration. Future approval was contingent upon progress and improvement in sixteen areas of institutional weakness.

October 1953- After a five-year legal dispute between a local Zoning Board and LIU, an appellate court ruled in favor of LIU's right to develop a college on the former Post estate, clearing the way for the opening of the Brookville Campus.

---ADMIRAL RICHARD LANSING CONOLLY---

January 1, 1954- Richard L. Conolly became President of the University.

May 17, 1954- In its Brown v. Board of Education decision, the U.S. Supreme Court declared state laws segregating public schools unconstitutional, overturning the 1896 Plessy v. Ferguson standard of "separate but equal."

June 1954- Board of Trustees formally named the Brookville campus the C.W. Post Campus of Long Island University, after Marjorie Post's late father.

1955- After five heartbreaking World Series losses between 1941 and 1953, the Brooklyn Dodgers finally won the World Series.

November 1955- LIU was granted limited accreditation from the Middle States Commission, after rejection the previous year. The Commission stipulated specific conditions and insisted on continued progress toward these objectives in the near future.

September 24, 1957- The Dodgers play their last game at Ebbets Field. The team moved to Los Angeles the following year. The LIU men's baseball team played the last game ever in that iconic stadium. The stadium was demolished in 1960.

1958- Although the G.I. Bill boom had slowed, the school sustained manageable enrollments, with 2,100 students at the Brooklyn campus and 950 at C.W. Post, primarily because women increasingly sought a college degree.

January 1, 1959- Nelson A. Rockefeller took office as Governor of New York.

December 1959- Rockefeller appointed Henry T. Heald to Chair a committee to examine the need for an expanded State University system.

1960

According to Conolly's Report to the Board, LIU had 6,500 students across its various campuses and extensions.

The population of New York City was around 7.8 million, 2.6 million of whom lived in Brooklyn.

Students for a Democratic Society (SDS) founded as an outgrowth of the socialist Student League for Industrial Democracy (SLID).

February 1- Four black college students, the Greensboro Four, "sat in" after being refused service at Woolworth's lunch counter.

April- Inspired by sit-ins, students launched the Student Nonviolent Coordinating Committee (SNCC) to fight for civil rights.

May 1- Gary Powers' U-2 spy plane was shot down by the Soviet Union.

May- President Eisenhower approved CIA plan to train Cuban exiles to overthrow Castro regime.

November- Heald Committee published its report outlining the need of dramatic growth in public sector enrollment, and articulating the "foundation for the State University's major expansion."

(1961) Stony Brook was designated a SUNY University Center, relocat-

470

ing to its current location in 1962.

1961

3,000 American military advisors, as well as American helicopters arrived in South Vietnam.

January - Eisenhower delivered his farewell address warning of the military-industrial complex.

January 20- John F. Kennedy was inaugurated President.

March 1- JFK announced the formation of the Peace Corps.

April -Yuri Gagarin became the first person to orbit the Earth.

April 11- Governor Rockefeller signed the New York State Education Law, granting university status to a unified system of City College, Hunter College, Queens College, and Baruch College, as well as three community colleges, thus, formally establishing the City University of New York.

April- Failed Bay of Pigs invasion of Cuba.

October 22-25- 1961 Middle States visit and Report.

December- James Davis became the first American soldier killed in Vietnam.

1962

January- United States launched Operation Chopper against the Vietcong, the first combat Vietnam combat mission.

The United States launched Operation Ranchland, spraying Agent Orange throughout the Vietnamese jungle, to impede the ability of the Vietcong to launch guerilla attacks.

February- The first United States helicopter was shot down in Vietnam.

February 20- John Glenn became the first American to orbit the Earth.

---JOHN HOWLAND GIBBS PELL---

March 1- Admiral Richard Connolly was killed as American Airlines Flight 1 crashed in Queens, NY shortly after take-off. John H.G. Pell took over as Interim Chancellor.

June- Kennedy denied that there were combat troops in Vietnam, insisting they were solely military advisors.

June 15- University of Michigan student and SDS Field Secretary at Michigan, Tom Hayden drafted the Port Huron Statement, which became the official manifesto of SDS.

September- With the assistance of U.S. Marshalls and the Justice Department, and over the strong objections of Governor Ross Barnett, James Meredith became the first black student to attend classes at the University of Mississippi.

October 14-28- Cuban Missile Crisis: *Approx. 1,500 students at Berkeley protested Kennedy's decision to blockade Cuba.*

(1962) The SUNY campus in Albany was designated a SUNY University Center.

1963

More than 15,000 United States troops were stationed in Vietnam.

January 2- Three Americans were killed in fighting against the Vietcong.

February- LIU administration contemplated creating a Vice Chancellor of Academic Affairs; William Birenbaum was considered for the position eventually filled by Henry Mills in 1964.

May 8- Beginning of the Buddhist Crisis; Nine Buddhists were killed in Hue protesting the ban on the Buddhist flag.

May- Around one thousand people were arrested in civil rights march/ protests in Birmingham, Alabama.

June 10- Kennedy delivered a speech at the American University, "A Strategy of Peace," in which he outlined a new diplomatic agenda and the beginning of negotiations toward a nuclear test ban treaty.

June 11- Ngo Quang Duc publicly self-immolated himself in an act of protest against the Diem government.

June 12- John F. Kennedy spoke to the nation in support of Civil Rights; hours later, NAACP field Secretary for Jackson, Mississippi, Medgar Evers, was murdered.

August- Diem's troops openly attacked Buddhists.

August 5- Partial Nuclear Test Ban Treaty signed by US and USSR (ratified by Congress- Sept. 24; signed by JFK Oct 7; became law Oct 10).

August 28- Approx. 200,000 people including SNCC President John Lewis attended the March for Jobs and Freedom in Washington, D.C., and heard Dr. King's "I Have a Dream" speech..

August 30- Secret diplomatic hotline opened between Moscow and the Washington, D.C.

Southampton Campus officially opened for students.

October 11- Kennedy signed the National Security Action Memo (NSAM) 263, ordering 1,000 American troops withdrawn from Vietnam by the end of 1963, with the remainder of troops scheduled to be removed by 1965.

October- Committee on the Future State of the College (C.W. Post) completed its report.

November 2- Diem assassinated in coup backed by the CIA and the United States.

November 22- Kennedy assassinated in Dallas, Texas. Lyndon Johnson sworn in as President.

November 26- Johnson signed NSAM 273, reversing Kennedy's Memo 263 and its plan to withdraw troops.

(1963) Based on Heald Committee recommendation, the Trustees of SUNY established a standardized low-cost tuition charge for all state-operated campuses. Undergraduate tuition was set at $400 per year.

1964

February- C.W. Post President Hoxie announced a $20 million building expansion plan for that campus, to supplement a $10 million building plan in place for the past five years. Hoxie's recommendations were based on the "Report on the Future State of the College."

February 9- Over 70 million people watched the Beatles' first appearance on *The Ed Sullivan Show*. The band's controversial haircuts were credited with the start of a popular trend of long hair throughout the country.

April- 1964 Middle States Report Released

Summer- Mississippi Freedom Summer. Around 900 white college students (including a number of the future leaders of the Free Speech Movement at Berkeley) went South to augment voter registration efforts.

July 2- Johnson signed the Civil Rights Act into law.

---RALPH GORDON HOXIE---

July 15- R. Gordon Hoxie became University Chancellor. Henry Mills was confirmed as Vice Chancellor for Academic Affairs; Chester Wood confirmed Vice Chancellor for Development and William Birenbaum became Provost of the Brooklyn Center.

August 4- Captain of the *U.S.S. Maddox* reported his ship was attacked by North Vietnamese. Despite the fact that within hours, the captain revised his previous report to say that his ship was never attacked, the United States retaliated by bombing North Vietnamese naval bases.

August 7- Congress passed the Gulf of Tonkin Resolution, granting Johnson broad powers to protect American forces in South Vietnam.

Mills began his revisions of the University Statutes (up to 1967).

1964-65 school year- Birenbaum abolished the dress code at the Brooklyn Center, noting that the "overwhelming majority [of students] have shown that they can take care of themselves."

September- Following Mississippi Freedom Summer, SNCC and CORE (Congress for Racial Equality) set up tables on Berkeley's campus in defiance of campus administration policies against political speech. Numerous students were suspended as a result; petitions and protests abounded.

October 1- Berkeley student Jack Weinberg was arrested at the CORE table. Students sat in, surrounding the police car for the entire night, preventing it from taking him away. Hundreds of other students occupied the administrative building (Sprout Hall) overnight.

October 2- Around 7,000 students were sitting in at Sprout Hall. 500 police officers arrived on scene by the evening, and students agreed to end that protest.

October 3 and 4- Free Speech Movement (FSM) founded; widespread protests began, largely against university policies. The movement was led by Mario Savio, Art Goldberg, and Jackie Goldberg.

(1964)- Start of six-year run in largest percentage increases in SUNY budget history; SUNY began expanding rapidly, hiring top faculty, establishing medical schools and colleges of education, opening campuses throughout the state (one in every county) and broadening community colleges.

Mid-1960s

New York City and other major urban centers across the country engaged in major urban renewal efforts to revive slum neighborhoods, stem the trend toward suburban flight and reduce crime.

1965

January-February- Fatalities of American servicemen spike after attacks by the Vietcong and North Vietnamese Army.

January- Chancellor Strong resigned as Chancellor at Berkeley. The new administration legitimized and recognized FSM, allowing it to hold legal rallies on campus.

February- Nearly 10,000 students and faculty at the University of Wis-

consin held an anti-war rally to protest the war in Vietnam.

February 13- Johnson ordered Operation Rolling Thunder, an aerial bombardment of North Vietnam, beginning in March.

February 21- Malcolm X was killed while giving a speech in Harlem, NY.

March 7-25- Civil rights activists conducted three major marches from Selma, to Montgomery, Alabama to advocate for voting rights and protest racial discrimination in the South, eventually prodding Congress to pass the Voting Rights Act later in the year.

March 22- LIU released its "Development Plan for the Brooklyn Center."

March- The first Filthy Speech Rally at Berkeley. Numerous students were disciplined for their actions.

March 24-25- SDS organized the first teach-in against the Vietnam War at the University of Michigan; this model was promptly emulated at other campuses across the country, including a large teach-in at CUNY's Queens College. At the Michigan event, nearly 3,000 attended a marathon of lectures, debates and films.

April 17- Around 15,000 protesters marched outside the White House to protest the War in Vietnam.

April 22- Art Goldberg and other activists were expelled for their role in the Filthy Speech Rally.

April 26- Mario Savio resigned as head of FSM.

April 28- FSM disbanded.

May 10- As the result of the financial collapse of his firm, Webb and Knapp, William Zeckendorf Sr. submitted his resignation as a Trustee of Long Island University. On June 14, the Board unanimously rejected his resignation, preserving his status as Chair of the Board of Trustees.

May 21-22- The Vietnam Day Committee at Berkeley, led by ex-graduate student Jerry Rubin, organized the largest teach-in up to that point, with 30,000 in attendance. The event concluded with a march to the Berkeley Draft Board, in which protesters burned their draft cards and hung Lyndon Johnson in effigy.

July 24- Vice Admiral Chester Wood, Vice Chancellor of the University and a passionate supporter of the Southampton Campus died of cancer, aged 62.

July 30- Johnson signed the Medicare Bill, as an expansion of the Social

Security Act, which went into effect in 1966.

August 6- Johnson signed the Voting Rights Act into law.

August 9- Around 350 anti-War protesters were arrested in Washington, D.C.

August 26- Johnson signed an executive order stating that married men would no longer be exempt from the draft. Students with less than 12 credits per semester were subject to the draft, and single, male students became eligible to receive draft notices 21 days after graduation.

September 30- NYC Mayoral candidate John Lindsay spoke at LIU, the first time a mayoral candidate had spoken at the University.

October- Birenbaum delivered a positive speech to the faculty, assessing the Brooklyn Center's future as bright and full of expansion possibilities. Hoxie was in South Korea, at a time of heightened awareness and controversy about South Korea's involvement in Vietnam.

October 15- Anti-war rallies erupted in Berkeley and NYC; the NYPD made its first arrests under the new draft card burning law.

November 2- Norman Morrison, a Quaker anti-war activist, self-immolated in front of the Pentagon.

November- SDS led and organized a March on Washington for Peace in Vietnam; around 20,000 attended the rally outside the White House.

November 20- Albert H. Bowker, Chancellor of CUNY resigned after proposing an extremely controversial $400 per year tuition plan for CUNY students. Bowker returned as Chancellor after a few months, and pursued a different approach to fund the struggling system.

December- Senator Robert Kennedy spoke at the Brooklyn Center packed with adoring students.

(1965)- SUNY Old Westbury was founded; Binghamton designated a SUNY University Center.

1966

January- John Lindsay succeeded Robert F. Wagner as Mayor of NYC.

January 4- St. John's University faculty began a strike to protest dismissals. The protests continued until July 1968, when the University agreed to arbitration. However, none of the dismissed faculty were reinstated.

March- Birenbaum committed the University to cooperate with Selective Service by only providing student information. He was against

476

instances in which students appear to have been drafted for political reasons. He offered free legal counseling to students and stated that he was willing to discuss liberalizing the University's flat-rate tuition structure.

March- Student-Faculty Committee to End the War in Vietnam was formed.

March 24- The Student-Faculty Committee to End the War hosted a 10-hour long teach in to protest the war, in which over 1,000 students participated. A related protest march to the NY draft board occurred the following morning.

March 30- Hoxie said that University would provide all "reasonably required" student information, and would cooperate fully with Selective Service. An editorial in the Seawanhaka called Hoxie's statement "a vast disappointment."

May- Stokely Carmichael became the new Chair of the SNCC; he soon excluded whites from the organization and emphasized Black Power instead of nonviolence and Christian charity.

May 11- A Student-Faculty Committee hosted a 36-hour peace festival to protest the war. Poet Allen Ginsburg conducted a poetry reading during the event.

May 12- University of Chicago students seized its administration building.

May 13- City College of New York students seized its administration building.

May 15- Approx. 8,000 anti-war protesters surrounded the White House for over two hours.

July- Race riots happened in Chicago, Cleveland, and NYC.

October- Huey Newton and Bobby Seale founded the Black Panther Party in California.

October 10- Campus protests against Dow Chemical erupted at Berkeley.

November- Over 500 students, led by Brooklyn Center student council President, Charles Isaacs, protested proposed tuition hikes at the Brooklyn Center. The tuition strike spread to the C.W. Post and Southampton campuses.

December- In New York, the City Board of Education was temporarily taken over by black and white militants known as the People's Ad Hoc Board of Education.

The Gallup poll indicated that 47 percent of all college-aged persons supported Lyndon Johnson's handling of the Vietnam War.

By end of year, there were approximately 385,000 U.S. ground troops in Vietnam, 60,000 stationed in the U.S. fleet, and around 33,000 in Thailand. More than 6,000 Americans were killed in Vietnam in 1966.

1967

January- *Time* magazine chose the "25 year- old- and- younger generation" as its Man of the Year.

February 13- Birenbaum was asked to submit his resignation at Hoxie's request. News of the event broke on March 15.

February 15- around 2,500 women protested at the Pentagon saying "Drop Rusk and McNamara, Not the Bomb."

February 16- After more than two years of preparation, Hoxie announced at the annual Charter Day Dinner speech, the completion and publication of the University's Ten Year Plan, *Preface to the Future,* proposing a $138 million dollar expansion over the decade.

February 28- Birenbaum submitted his resignation.

March- Rockefeller appointed a panel Chaired by McGeorge Bundy to study the future funding of private institutions of higher education.

March 16- Brooklyn students and faculty rallied in support of Birenbaum. 1,500 students attend the rally in the gymnasium led by Student Council President Charles Isaacs.

March 21- About 1,500 students attended another rally in support of Birenbaum, as student and faculty petitions circulated in support of Birenbaum's reinstatement.

March 27- Hoxie revealed that he had been seeking Birenbaum's removal as early as September 1965.

April 3- Over 1,000 students boycotted classes at the Brooklyn Center, demanding Birenbaum's reinstatement and Hoxie's resignation.

April 4- MLK gave the "Beyond Vietnam" speech in New York, opposing the war.

April 6- Full-time faculty at Brooklyn Center voted 168-32 to seek Hoxie's dismissal as Chancellor, as the student boycott of classes continued into its fourth day.

April 10- Charles Isaacs vowed to continue the student strike, threatening to begin holding classes at "a university in exile" in the streets.

April 11- Student leaders suspended their boycott, following the intervention and mediation proposal of William Zeckendorf; Birenbaum addressed a rally of 2,500 students, advising them to resume their studies.

April 15- 400,000 marched from Central Park to the United Nations in NY to protest the war; In San Francisco, 100,000 marched, including Dr. King.

April 28- Muhammad Ali refused to be drafted into the U.S. Army. He was stripped of his heavyweight title and eventually sentenced to 5 years in prison. His conviction was overturned by the Supreme Court in 1971; he did not spend any time in prison, as he was free on bond while appealing his case.

May- The Gallup poll indicated that 49 percent of students considered themselves hawks, and 35% doves, the remainder were undecided.

June- Six Vietnam veterans founded Vietnam Veterans Against the War (at its height it would have 40,000 members.)

June- Carmichael left the SNCC to join the Black Panther Party; his replacement was H. Rap Brown. The SNCC collapsed in the ensuing years. Brown spent five years in prison for robbery in the 1970s, before being sentenced to life imprisonment in 2002 for the murder of two police officers.

July 24- Henry Heald delivered an oral report to the LIU Board of Trustees, recommending that the Brooklyn Center be sold to City University.

July 26- William Zeckendorf Sr. announced he would step down as Chair of the Board of Trustees in October, remaining a Trustee.

July 28- Hoxie and CUNY Chancellor Bowker made the case for the sale of the campus to New York State education authorities.

September 23- Following rumors circulating throughout the summer and in contrast to previous denials, Hoxie announced that the University was negotiating with City University to sell the Brooklyn Center, with an effective date of June 1969.

October- Hoxie announced that Brooklyn Center would be phased out, regardless of sale to CUNY.

October and November- Various University officials appeared before the Joint Legislative Committee on Higher Education, including Hoxie, Bowker, Heald, and Mary Lai.

October 9- John P. McGrath named as Chair of the Board of Trustees.

October 19- All-day teach-in was held to discuss sale of Brooklyn Center.

October 23- Hoxie failed to show up for a second appearance before the Joint Legislative Committee on Higher Education. Assemblyman Bertram L. Podell spoke in opposition to the sale of the Brooklyn Center. Podell labeled *Preface to the Future* **"a very misleading book" and "nothing more than a big lie."**

October 24- Brooklyn Assemblyman Stanley Steingut announced the formation of a bipartisan group of 29 Brooklyn legislators opposing the sale of the Brooklyn Center to CUNY.

October 21-22- 70-100,000 protesters marched in Washington D.C. (**including approximately 100 LIU students**); around 600 were arrested as Abbie Hoffman attempted to exorcise and levitate the Pentagon.

November- The Brooklyn Student Council planned a sleep-in on Chancellor Hoxie's lawn to protest the sale of Brooklyn Center.

November 30- Draft of the Joint Legislative Committee on Higher Education's Findings (The Kottler Report) severely criticized the LIU and CUNY administrations, but tacitly accepted the prospect of a sale.

December- The sale of Brooklyn Center postponed by Board of Higher Education, pending Board of Regents report due in early 1968.

1968

January- A blue ribbon panel headed by McGeorge Bundy released its report, urging an innovative formula for direct state aid to all private colleges and universities in the state. The report (now known as Bundy aid) recommended delivery of $33 million to the state's 143 private institutions for the first year.

January 21- North Vietnamese Army captured Khe Sanh.

January 24- The Supreme Court upheld that laws against burning draft cards do not violate free speech (*U.S. v. O'Brien.*)

January 30- The Tet Offensive began.

February- A Gallup poll indicated that only 35% of Americans approved of Lyndon Johnson, 50% disapproved.

February 15- The Board of Regents met with students and faculty to discuss the sale of Brooklyn Center to CUNY.

480

February 23- The Board of Regents unanimously approved sale of Brooklyn Center to CUNY. Acting Provost William T. Lai called for a student meeting to explain the sale, while the Student Council called for a rally to occur at same time to protest the sale. Within days, the Student Council formally called on Board of Higher Education to block the sale.

February 27- CBS aired Walter Cronkite's critical assessment of the Vietnam War, Report from Vietnam: Who, What, When, Where, Why?

February 29- Approximately 700 students marched to City Hall in an attempt to get Mayor Lindsay or City government to block the sale.

February 29- McNamara left office as Secretary of Defense.

March 6- Mrs. Zeckendorf was killed alongside 62 others when their Air France plane crashed into a mountain in Lima, Peru.

March 16- 300-500 Vietnamese civilians were massacred by U.S. troops at My Lai. This would not become public until November 1969.

March 25- Approximately 100 LIU students participated in demonstrations outside the Board of Education's monthly meeting. Protesters also demonstrated on Wall Street, 42nd Street Library, Grand Central Station, Baruch College, and in Fort Greene as a part of Save LIU Day.

March 31- In a live television address, Johnson discussed limiting the war in Vietnam; he also announced that he would not run for a second term in office.

April 1- Muhammad Ali, at the height of his controversial status over the draft, spoke at the Conolly Gymnasium, sponsored by the Student Government Association.

April 4- Martin Luther King Jr. assassinated in Memphis; widespread riots ensued across the country.

April 11- Mayor John Lindsay, in a letter to Hoxie and the Board of Trustees, publicly announced his opposition to the sale of the Brooklyn Center to CUNY.

April 24- The Board of Trustees sent its official response to Mayor Lindsay's April 11th letter.

April 23-30- SDS Columbia leader Mark Rudd organized the takeover of buildings on the Columbia campus. For eight days, five buildings (including the office of President Grayson Kirk) were controlled by approximately 1,000 students. Black students occupied an additional build-

ing. Students protested the University's ties to the Institute for Defense Analysis, a Defense Department-affiliated organization, as well as the University's plans to build a gymnasium in Morningside Heights Park overlooking Harlem. On April 30, the NYPD ended the student occupation at the behest of the administration, resulting in widespread arrests and beatings of students. In response to the arrests, the students engaged in a month-long strike.

April 25- Ten to twenty black students, members of the Student Organization for Black Unity (SOBU) occupied the office of William Lai, protesting the sale of the Brooklyn Center, and civil rights issues.

May- The NYC Board of Higher Education under strong pressure from Mayor Lindsay, reversed itself, rejecting sale of Brooklyn Center to CUNY. On May 3, as Hoxie attempted to announce this news at a faculty meeting, he was interrupted by nearly 100 students, led by Student Council President Jay Dravich. Hoxie was unable to continue and promptly adjourned the meeting.

May 8- Hoxie and John McGrath met with Mayor Lindsay at City Hall.

May- William Lai resigned as Acting Provost of the Brooklyn Center despite being offered the permanent position by Hoxie. Hoxie served as Acting Provost until September.

May- NY State legislature approved the program to aid private schools (Bundy Aid). The bill provided institutions with $400 per completed bachelors and master's degrees, and $2,400 per completed doctorate, based on the previous academic year.

June- Gov. Rockefeller signed Bundy Aid bill into State law.

June 5- Robert Kennedy was shot in Los Angeles after winning the California Democratic Primary; he died the next day.

June- Hoxie booed and hissed by students at graduation, many of whom sported "Resign" buttons. In his speech, he mentioned that beginning in July 1969, the University would begin receiving State aid.

July- LIU Trustee Arthur T. Roth ousted as CEO of Franklin National Bank.

August- William Zeckendorf Sr. declared personal bankruptcy.

August 23-28- Prolonged and violent anti-war demonstrations occurred during the Democratic National Convention in Chicago. The Chicago Police were brutal in the crackdown on demonstrators. The main organizers of the protests (The Chicago Eight-including Tom Hayden, Bobby Seale, Dave Dellinger and Abbie Hoffman) were charged with conspiring to start a riot.

September 16- In an attempt to appeal to younger voters, Richard Nixon appeared on the popular television show *Laugh In.*

September 20- The Heald-Hobson report was released. It favored the centralization of University government and an abandonment of the plans detailed in *Preface to the Future.* **In response, Hoxie called the report "too pessimistic." Regarding widespread rumors of his impending dismissal, Hoxie declared, "I will stand or fall on the Ten Year Plan."**

September 30- Hoxie is forced to resign as Chancellor of the University at the insistence of the Board of Trustees. George Stoddard automatically took his place until Board selected a new Chancellor/ President.

---GEORGE STODDARD---

c. October 1968- c. April 1969- Stoddard led another revision of the University Statutes.

November 6- Students at San Francisco State University went on strike and shut down the campus for nearly six months.

November- Alexander "Sam" Aldrich became President of the Brooklyn Center. The local SDS Chapter formed an Ad Hoc Committee to protest Aldrich's appointment.

December- Aldrich canceled a proposed tuition increase, as Brooklyn Center had a financial surplus previously denied by the administration.

December- Mark Rudd spoke at Brooklyn Center.

Late 1960s-Early 1970s
NYC and NY State fiscal crises grew increasingly severe, as the Mayor and the Governor requested more assistance from the federal government.

1969

January- University approved per-credit tuition plan.

January 20- Richard Nixon inaugurated President.

February- Nixon authorized the secret bombing of Cambodia beginning in March (Operation Menu.)

March- Aldrich proposed $8 per credit tuition increase. Outraged students sought an audit of Center finances, and threatened to strike. The Board of Trustees voted to increase tuition from $47 to $55 a credit, while simultaneously agreeing to student demand for an audit.

April 10- 300 to 400 students took over the administration building at Harvard University for 17 hours before police were called to break up the strike. 400 policemen made widespread arrests and engaged in beatings as students fled.

April 15-17- Woodstock Festival held in upstate New York.

April 19-20- Over one hundred armed black students, with some support from SDS, occupied Willard Straight Hall at Cornell University demanding a black-run African Studies Center. Pictures of the students wearing ammunition, and carrying firearms appeared in newspapers, drawing further widespread attention to campus unrest.

April- Students and faculty struck at C.W. Post campus after over 40 students were arrested in narcotics raids on and around campus. The Concerned Students and Faculty issued a list of 15 demands. In a telling sign of inter-campus tension, the Brooklyn Student Council did not vote to support the strike in Brookville.

April-May- Protesters and California Governor Ronald Reagan engaged in a standoff over a People's Park in Berkeley. Reagan eventually called the National Guard to clear the park, using tear gas. Riots followed as the National Guard occupied Berkeley. On May 21, students boycotted classes in memory of the victims of violence.

May- Dean of Connolly College, Samuel Bieber, quit.

May 10-20- Battle of Hamburger Hill.

June- The Weathermen emerged as a radical offshoot of the fracturing SDS; the new group was led by Mark Rudd, Bill Ayers, and Bernadine Dohrn.

---GLENN FERGUSON---

July- Former U.S. ambassador to Kenya, Glenn Ferguson was elected Chancellor; his brief tenure was marked by his unsuccessful plan to split up the three campuses into separate colleges.

June 27- *Life* Magazine published photographs of the over 200 American servicemen killed in recent combat in Vietnam.

September 3- Ho Chi Minh died.

September 8- Robert L. Payton was unanimously elected President

of the C.W. Post Center by the Board of Trustees.

October 6-11- The Weathermen started a riot in Haymarket Square in Chicago, after destroying a monument to police. Over the next few days, widespread mob violence and property damage occured. Six Weathermen were shot, and around seventy were arrested in the chaos. A few months later, the Weathermen decided to go underground, changing their name to the Weather Underground Organization.

October- A Gallup poll revealed that 58% of Americans believed that entering into the war in Vietnam was a mistake.

November 3- Nixon appealed to the Silent Majority to continue to support military efforts in Vietnam.

November 15- Over 250,000 people protested the war at a rally in Washington D.C.

1970

A publication, A New Depression in Higher Education, highlighted the financial distress in colleges throughout the nation.

CUNY opened admissions to anyone with a NYC high school diploma.

February- October- The Weather Underground set off bombs across the country, including numerous bombs in San Francisco, Berkeley, Harvard, and the New York Police Department Headquarters.

March 17- Fourteen officers were charged in the My Lai massacre.

April 10- The Beatles announced that they were breaking up.

April 13-17- Apollo 13 narrowly avoided disaster, and managed to return to Earth safely after an accident in space.

April 29- The United States invaded Cambodia, resulting in widespread protests.

May 1- Students at Kent State University began a protest of the United States invasion of Cambodia; thousands rioted at Berkeley over the invasion.

May 4- 2-3,000 students resumed anti-war protests at Kent State. Ohio National Guard troops fired into the crowds, killing four students. These events triggered immense outrage across the country and caused the largest campus demonstrations over the course of the war. Millions of students protested across the country, shutting down campuses and canceling classes, final exams and the term.

May 8- The Hard Hat Riot. 200 construction workers attacked 1,000 high school and college students protesting the Vietnam War and the Kent State shootings. In the following days, Mayor Lindsay showed support for the protesters and was highly critical of the New York Police's response to the matter. Blue collar workers accused the Mayor of holding Communist sympathies, and held protests of their own for days, culminating in a peaceful demonstration of over 150,000 construction workers in a pro-Nixon rally in the streets of New York.

May 9- Hundreds of thousands again protested against the war across the country, most notably in Washington D.C.

May 9- The Humanities Building at LIU Brooklyn was firebombed, causing an estimated $100,000 in damage. The Fire Department concluded that the fire was caused by arson, and corresponded with a note sent by The Stop the War Coalition to Aldrich threatening additional fires and firebombs unless the Brooklyn Center remained closed.

May- Numerous colleges around the country remained closed for a week following the Kent State shootings, amidst widespread protests. **C.W. Post and Brooklyn Center faculty and staff separately voted to suspend the remainder of the semester's classes.**

May- Aldrich condemned violence in his Commencement address, a ceremony attended by only about half the graduating class.

May 14- Two black students at Jackson State University were killed by police while protesting Kent State and civil rights issues.

June 19- C.W. Post Center/American Federation of College Teachers filed a petition with the National Labor Relations Board (NLRB) to obtain union representation.

July 22- Brooklyn Center/American Federation of College Teachers filed its own petition with NLRB to obtain separate union representation.

September 22- Board of Trustees approved construction funding for the Brooklyn Center Library "at a cost not to exceed $7.6 million."

September 22- Aldrich gained approval from the Board to contract the Academy of Educational Development to conduct a broad study of the health and integrity of the Brooklyn Center. The AED report was released in March 1971.

December 30- University Treasurer Mary Lai's Report, Centralized in Policy, Decentralized in Administration urged inter-campus unity for the survival of the University, and strongly criticized those promoting a federated approach to governance.

The U.S. reduced its forces in Vietnam to under 200,000 (Vietnamization.)

March 1- C.W. Post President Robert Payton announced austerity plans to balance the school's upcoming budget for the next fiscal year.

March 1- Academy of Educational Development released a draft of its report to Aldrich, Change For Survival: A Report to the President of the Brooklyn Center of Long Island University.

March 3- Adelphi University President Charles Vevier, and two Vice Presidents, James B. Kelly and Daniel L. Bratton announced their resignations.

April 20- The NLRB issued two separate decisions, allowing faculty at the C.W. Post Center and Brooklyn Center to unionize.

April 22- John Kerry, decorated Vietnam veteran and a leader of Vietnam Veterans Against the War, testified before the United States Senate.

April 24- 200,000 marched on the National Mall in D.C. to protest the war; over 150,000 marched in San Francisco.

May 9-10- C.W. Post faculty voted approval of collective bargaining.

Spring term- Mary Lai wrote a second paper, Impact of Personalities on the Organization of Long Island University decrying the University's lack of centralized leadership since the tenure of Gordon Hoxie. Lai blamed Hoxie's actions as Chancellor for creating widespread animosity toward centralized administrative leadership in the University.

June- The Pentagon Papers published as leaked information in *The New York Times.*

---ALBERT BUSH-BROWN---

July 1- Albert Bush-Brown became University Chancellor (later President)

July 20- Aldrich announced his resignation as President of the Brooklyn Center, effective October 1971. He took a position as the Director of Parks and Recreation in the administration of his cousin, Governor Nelson Rockefeller. Eugene Arden became Acting President of the Brooklyn Center from October 1971 to August 1972.

October- Robert Payton addressed the Joint Legislative Committee on Higher Education to request additional state aid for C.W. Post.

November- Rockefeller appointed a task force led by T. Norman Hurd to study financial hardships in public and private institutions.

December- NYU President (and former LIU Brooklyn Provost) James Hester requested additional state aid, after revealing that NYU experienced a record deficit in the 1970-71 school year, with higher deficits projected in years to follow. The school had been experiencing multimillion dollar per year deficits since the mid-1960s.

1972

January 18- Rockefeller's State of the State address touched on the crisis facing NY institutions of higher education. He caused outrage by proposing that CUNY be incorporated into the State University system.

January 19-20- The Hurd task force recommended that in light of the fiscal crisis, CUNY should begin to charge tuition, and that SUNY should raise its tuition fees considerably, causing a considerable backlash. CUNY would eventually begin charging tuition in 1976.

February 16- Hester declared his public support for the sale of the elite Bronx campus of NYU, causing considerable student protest; NYU sold the Bronx campus in 1972 to the City University Construction Fund for $62 million. NYU departed from the campus in 1973, moving all units to the Village.

North Vietnam launched the Easter Offensive, an invasion of South Vietnam; the United States tried to fend off the invasion with an aerial campaign known as Operation Linebacker.

June 17- Watergate Break-In.

August 1- Lester Brookner took office as President of the Brooklyn Center.

August- Disabled Vietnam Veterans interrupted Nixon's acceptance speech at the Republican National Convention in Miami.

November- Nixon re-elected in landslide victory against George McGovern.

December 1- Chancellor Bush-Brown wrote a Self Study Report to Middle States, An Introduction to Long Island University. Middle States visited the Brookville and Southampton campuses on December 3-6; they visited the Brooklyn campus on March 4-7, 1973. Reports of their findings followed shortly thereafter.

December- Nixon ordered bombing of Hanoi (Operation Linebacker II) in order to get North Vietnamese to sign peace agreement.

488

1973

January 27- The Paris Peace Accords signed, ending the U.S. operations in Vietnam.

March- Robert L. Payton fired by Bush-Brown as President of the C.W. Post Center.

March 29- Final American troops leave Vietnam. More than 58,000 Americans were killed over the course of the war.

September 12- Marjorie Merriwether Post died, at age 86.

December 18- Nelson Rockefeller left office, having drastically increased the State's budget deficits during his time as Governor.

December 31- John Lindsay left office as Mayor of New York. Despite being at the height of his popularity during the mid to late 1960s, by the time he ended his term, the City was in deep fiscal crisis. Nearly two thirds of New Yorkers disapproved of his performance as Mayor.

Prepared by Alexander Gailing

Facsimile Board List 1954 - 1969

492

Name	Elected	Termination
Van Atten, William T.	October, 1952	September, 1957 Honorary Member until death, November, 1968
Van Fleet, General James A.	January, 1959	May, 1969 (resigned)
Voorhees, Tracy S.	1954	1955 (resigned)
Whalen, Grover A.	March, 1954	January, 1962 (resigned)
Winthrop, Robert	January, 1967	May, 1969 (resigned)
Zeckendorf, William, Jr.	May, 1959	
Zeckendorf, William, Sr.	October, 1942 1942 (Board Chairman) 67	1967

Index

497

Morelli, James V.
  undergraduate student at Brooklyn, 213
Moses, Robert
  obituary for Zeckendorf, 311
  Title I scandals, 67
  Zeckendorf Sr., William realtionship with, 66
Moyers, Bill, 324

N

National Labor Relations Act, 426
Neimuth, Edward, 262-263, 342-343
Nevins, Allan, 331
New Republic
  "behind the scenes at LIU" 1967 article, 221
  trustees borderline corruption, article accusing, 221
New York Institute of Technology
  management agreement, meeting for possible, 285, 291
  Schure, Alexander, 284-285
New York State Dormitory Authority, 74
New York University, 272
  contrast to LIU, 455-456
  similarity to LIU, 36-37
  Stoddard relationship to, 337-339
  tuition increase, student protest over, 202
Nicholson, Isidore, 207
Nyquist, Ewald B.
  approval of Brookville campus, 76
  Association Commissioner of Higher Education, as, 57
  deficiencies at LIU pointed out by, 57-60
  limited accreditation granted by, 81
NYU. *See* New York University

O

Ohio National Guard and Kent State University, 33
Olds, Glenn, 416-417
Open Enrollment, CUNY, 37
  establishment of, 29
Organizational structure
  changes proposed by Meder, 84-85
Ormandy, Eugene, 207

P

Palmer, Carleton H., 211, 464
  Acting-President, 98
  resignation of, 284
Palmer, Winthrop, 376, 442
Parietal rules, 31
Pate, Martha L., 376
Patterson, George, 420
Payton, Robert L., 404, 434, 439
  background of, 404-405, 407
  College Management article, 411
  de facto power, 376

508

Made in the USA
Columbia, SC
22 November 2017